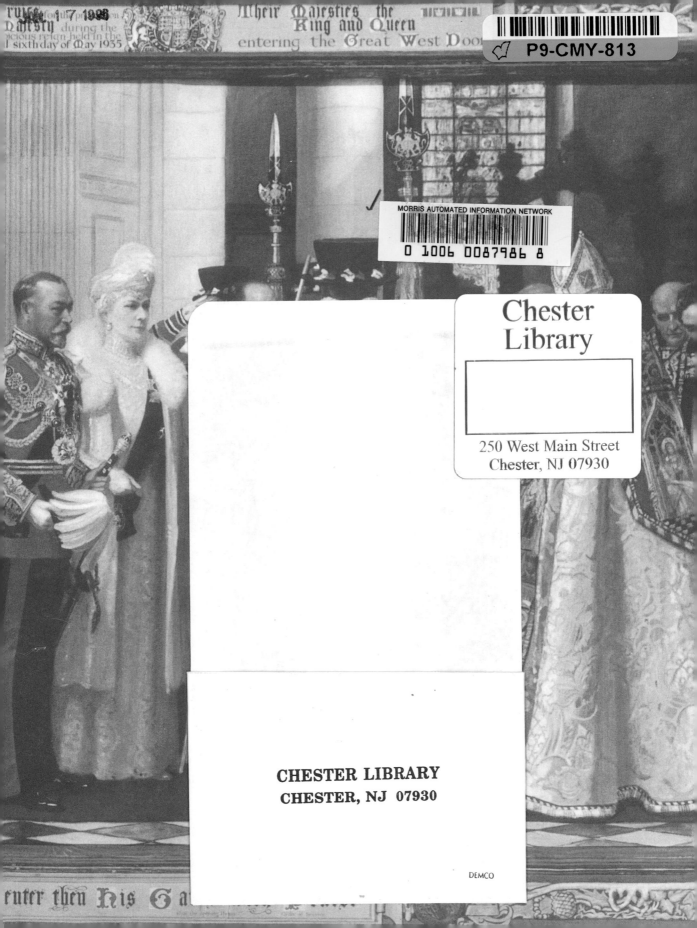

THE OXFORD
ILLUSTRATED HISTORY
OF THE
BRITISH MONARCHY

THE OXFORD
ILLUSTRATED
HISTORY
OF THE
BRITISH
MONARCHY

JOHN CANNON

AND

RALPH GRIFFITHS

Oxford   New York

OXFORD UNIVERSITY PRESS

Oxford University Press, Walton Street, Oxford OX2 6DP

Oxford New York Toronto
Delhi Bombay Calcutta Madras Karachi
Petaling Jaya Singapore Hong Kong Tokyo
Nairobi Dar es Salaam Cape Town
Melbourne Auckland
and associated companies in
Berlin Ibadan

Oxford is a trade mark of Oxford University Press

Published in the United States
by Oxford University Press, New York

British Library Cataloguing in Publication Data
Cannon, John, 1926–
The Oxford illustrated history of the British monarchy.
1. Great Britain. Monarchy, to 1987
I. Title   II. Griffiths, Ralph A.
(Ralph Alan), 1937–
354.4103'12'09
ISBN 0–19–822786–8

Library of Congress Cataloging in Publication Data
Cannon, John, 1926–
The Oxford illustrated history of the British monarchy.
Bibliography: p.
Includes index.
1. Great Britain—Politics and government.
2. Monarchy—Great Britain—History.
3. Great Britain—Kings and rulers—Biography.
4. Great Britain—Social conditions.
5. Great Britain—History.
I. Griffiths, Ralph Alan. II. Title.
DA40.C29 1988   941   88-5172
ISBN 0–19–822786–8

Printed in Hong Kong

Chapter headpieces by John Lawrence

The endpapers show a detail from 'Reception at the West Door
of St Paul's Cathedral before the Jubilee Service, 1935, for King
George V and Queen Mary' by Frank Salisbury. By kind permission
of Mrs M. Norris (photo Bridgeman Art Library).

FOREWORD

SINCE the departure of the Roman legions from Britain early in the fifth century, England's form of government has been monarchy. Apart from a mere eleven years from 1649 to 1660, its hierarchical society has been headed by monarchs. The same is true of Scotland, save for two even briefer periods at the turn of the thirteenth and fourteenth centuries, when dynastic dispute rather than republicanism disrupted its political life. In Wales and Ireland, too, monarchies thrived until the later Middle Ages, when English kings began to impose colonial rule upon the Welsh and Irish.

One must not be sentimental about monarchy as an institution. There have been inept, foolish, and oppressive monarchs and individual kings and queens have frequently been unpopular. In most centuries, the British monarchy has had fierce critics and in recent decades it has been accused of helping to perpetuate snobbery and inequality. Nevertheless, for most of the millennium and a half, monarchy has been the foundation for political and social life and the symbol of statehood and nation. Profiles of kings have graced coins since Anglo-Saxon times and stamps since Victoria's reign. For centuries, justice has been administered 'in the king's name' and roads have been 'the king's highway'. We use and abuse the King's English, take tricks with the King of Spades, and, if we are foolish, smoke King-sized cigarettes. Ships of war have been named after kings since before Henry VIII's reign and inns and taverns since at least the sixteenth century— 'the Crown', 'the King's Head', 'the King's Arms' and the ubiquitous 'the George'. Not for nothing is the longest-running of all television serials called 'Coronation Street'.

John of Salisbury, the humanist scholar who knew Henry II's court well, placed the monarch second to God's representatives in his vivid metaphor of the body politic as akin to the human body and soul:

The place of the head in the body of the Commonwealth is filled by the prince, who is subject only to God and to those who exercise His office and represent Him on earth, even as in the human body the head is quickened and governed by the soul. (*Policraticus*)

Thomas Starkey, a royal chaplain in Henry VIII's reign, thought that 'the ground of all felicity in civil life' was 'to have a good prince to govern and

A ROYAL MARRIAGE. Margaret of Anjou is presented with a book of romances on the occasion of her marriage to Henry VI.

rule' (*A dialogue between Cardinal Pole and Thomas Lupset*). By claiming for himself supreme authority in the Church, Henry VIII moved aside those spiritual intermediaries between the ruler and God, enabling James I to advance the claim that 'the state of monarchy is the supremest thing on earth; for kings are not only God's lieutenants upon earth, and sit upon God's throne, but even by God himself they are called Gods'. This was rather excessive, even by sixteenth-century standards, and the events of 1649 and 1688 helped to bring the theory of monarchy down to earth a little. Nevertheless, even the limited monarchy of George III seemed to Jean Louis de Lolme, a Swiss visitor, majestic and imposing:

In the language of the law, the king is Sovereign Lord, and the people are his subjects; he is universal proprietor of the whole kingdom; he bestows all the dignities and places; and he is not to be addressed but with the expressions and outward ceremony of almost oriental humility. Besides, his person is sacred and inviolable; and any attempt whatsoever against it is, in the eye of the law, a crime equal to that of an attack against the whole state. (*The Constitution of England*)

Though, in the course of the nineteenth century, the political power of the monarch decreased, the growth of an empire overseas gave the crown a new role, which Balfour described in 1901:

The King is no longer King of Great Britain and Ireland, and of a few dependencies. . . . He is now the great constitutional bond uniting together in a single Empire communities of freemen separated by half the circumference of the Globe. All the patriotic sentiment which makes such an Empire possible centres in him; and everything which emphasises his personality to our kinsmen across the sea must be a gain to the Monarchy and the Empire.

It is not always easy for the historian to recognize the realities of the situation when set against such lofty ideals and concepts, for the monarchies of the British Isles have, in truth, been buffeted from time to time by political, economic, social, and religious forces. To compare theory and practice is one of the aims of this book. Like most enterprises, it has its hazards. One must strike a balance between cynicism and sentimentality, knowing that no reader is likely to be wholly satisfied with the result. The monarchy is an unusual concept in that, unlike the Church, the aristocracy, or the trades unions, it is both an institution and a person. There is therefore a further balance to be struck between the study of institutional development and the commentary on individual kings and queens, bearing in mind that, particularly in the earlier period, strong-minded rulers put their stamp on the institution itself.

There are, of course, plenty of histories of England and of the Celtic countries, and Parliament, the Church, and the Law have had their development studied by distinguished writers. Some outstanding biographies of kings and queens have been published; the royal household in certain periods has been studied; and the court has attracted much attention. Today all aspects, trivial and significant, of the monarchy and the royal family command an interest that appears inexhaustible. Yet, strangely, no modern authoritative study of the overall development of monarchy in these islands has been attempted. The reasons for this neglect are not difficult to suggest. Professional historians are often reluctant to venture far from their chosen fields, and in British historiography it is still rare to find Wales, Scotland, and Ireland given their due treatment, even after the unification of those countries with England. The long survey necessary for such a subject means that the historian is peculiarly dependent upon the work of others. Furthermore

ROYAL EMBLEMS on the bronze gates of King Henry VII's chapel, Westminster Abbey.

the survival of documentary and other materials over so long a period is very uneven. Very little personal correspondence survives for George II but the printed correspondence of George III runs to several volumes. Before the fifteenth century, private letters to or from British monarchs hardly survive at all, if they were even written. King Alfred may have penned or dictated his thoughts about the duties of a king of Wessex, but journals, memoirs, or commentaries by kings did not become common until much later. Eulogies and hagiographies have blurred the image of many medieval kings, though they are a species of writing far from extinct today.

These and other considerations dictated the shape of this book. It seemed sensible to treat the first millennium of monarchy in the four countries in an analytical way, laying the foundations for subsequent discussion. The later treatment is more narrative in character, though pausing from time to time to take stock. We should make it clear that the illustrations are far from being icing on the cake but are an integral part of the whole volume, for two reasons. First, the impact of monarchy itself upon subjects has always depended greatly upon visual magnificence—the awe inspired by coronations, the sense of participation engendered by jubilees, the solemnity of great funeral ceremonies. Elizabeth I was by no means the only monarch to be greatly concerned with the public representation of her image. The visual remains of royal activity and taste, particularly in buildings and paintings, can convey the reality of kingship in striking fashion. Second, the integration of illustrations and text permits the more extensive treatment of certain themes, such as royal patronage, which run through many reigns and over several centuries.

ACKNOWLEDGEMENTS

The publishers are grateful to Susan le Roux for her great assistance with the selection and design of the illustrations; to Philippa Lewis, the picture researcher; and to Mary Worthington, who copy-edited the text.

CONTENTS

LIST OF MAPS

THE OXFORD
ILLUSTRATED
HISTORY
OF THE
BRITISH
MONARCHY

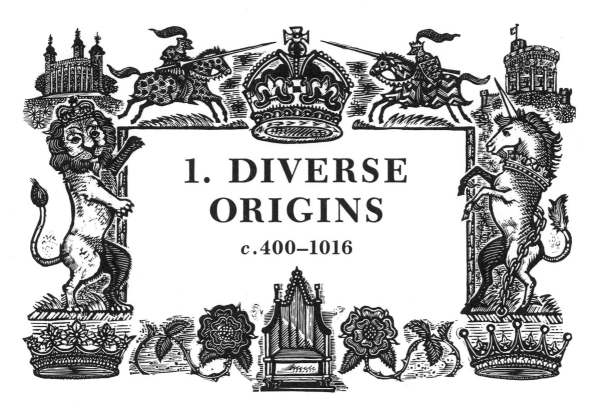

1. DIVERSE ORIGINS

c.400–1016

Kingdoms

IN the darkest of the Dark Ages, the fifth and sixth centuries, there were many kings in Britain but no kingdoms. Instead there were communities of peoples which we might describe as tribes if the language of condescension used by European conquerors in America, Africa, and south-east Asia had not altered the meaning of the word. They were organized and led by men—hardly ever by women—whom Latin writers came to call *reges* or kings. In an unevenly populated land, these communities inhabited homelands that were geographically distinct but probably did not have defined borders or frontiers; with that reservation in mind, we may call them kingdoms. Among such 'community-kingdoms' were the Hwicce, Anglo-Saxon settlers in the luscious lower Severn and Avon basin who remained an identifiable community even in the tenth century, long after their kingdom had been subdued by more powerful neighbours. The Cantii, by contrast, had lived in the south-east peninsula during Roman times; and although they were overrun or put to flight by invading Anglo-Saxons, they gave their name to the early English kingdom of Kent and to the shire that later replaced it. Relations between such communities as these and between their leaders were doubtless regulated by co-operation, agreements, and alliances, and on a personal level liaisons were formed and marriages celebrated. It is equally likely that their relations were marred by disputes and

KING EDGAR, the triumphantly Christian king of all England, pictured standing between the Virgin Mary and St Peter and offering to Christ the charter by which he confirmed the conversion of King Edward the Elder's New Minster at Winchester into a Benedictine monastery. The charter, in book form, is dated 966 and was witnessed by leading courtiers, including Queen Ælfthryth and Edward the Elder's widow, Queen Eadgifu.

violence, and it is not difficult to imagine how some communities were in time overwhelmed by aggressive neighbours and their kingdoms subjugated.

One of the most crucial factors which governed the emergence of such kingdoms in much of Dark Age Britain was the final withdrawal (AD 408) of the Roman legions from the provinces of Britannia, and the withering and eventual extinction of Roman imperial authority and administration during the course of the turbulent fifth century. The mass of British inhabitants were left to their own devices to preserve order and rule as best they could, and most immediately to repel the 'barbarian Picts' from beyond Hadrian's Wall, the Scotti (or Scots) from Ireland, and, more threatening still, the Angles, Saxons, and Jutes from the continent, all of whom assailed the tottering Roman Empire. They had no option but to rely on localized, morcellated, and fragmented authority where once there had been Roman unity. In short, Roman rule in Britannia disintegrated and left a host of small, ill-defined kingdoms which formed a polity not much different from that of Scotland and Ireland at the same time. King Arthur has often been portrayed as the larger-than-life leader of one or more of these kingdoms, wielding his sword in the far north against the Scots or in the south against the Anglo-Saxons or even, say some, in South Wales. His name is now more credibly quoted as a symbol of British resistance against the invaders, a resistance which was spectacularly, but only temporarily, successful around AD 500 at the battle of Mount Badon, which may (or may not) be located in Dorset.

A second major factor in the emergence and early development of kingdoms in Dark Age Britain was the irresistible waves of migrant peoples: from Ireland to West Wales and south-west Scotland from the fourth century (or perhaps even earlier); from the Old English-speaking plains of north-west Europe to eastern England somewhat later; whilst from Scandinavia and the Baltic, Viking hordes descended on all the British islands from the end of the eighth century onwards. Heroic tales and sagas of such peoples and their warrior leaders, ancient-sounding place-names, mysterious burial grounds and standing stones, these are the only keys we have left to unlock the story of the communities and kingdoms which the invaders disrupted or destroyed. And these keys are seriously defective.

Yet the immigrants gave a new dynamism to the relationships among communities and kingdoms in Britain. It is striking that the later kingdom of England took its name from the invading Anglo-Saxons, and the later kingdom of Scotland was called after the Scots from Ireland. Even in West Wales, where one of the first of the migrations occurred in the late fourth and fifth centuries, the Deisi from south-east Ireland seem to have seized control in a kingdom of Dyfed and to have settled as far east as the Gower peninsula. At about the same time, other Gaelic-speaking Scots, the Dalriada, sailed from north-east Ireland across the narrow channel which is only twelve miles wide at one point, to settle in what

DUNADD ROCK AND FORT, Argyll, citadel of the Scottish kingdom of Dalriada. It was captured by the Picts in 736. There are four lines of wall on the rock, dating from the Dark Ages. It has a well and carvings (including a footprint), some of which may be connected with king-making rituals.

is now Argyll in Scotland. Along the coast and in the Western Isles they established three distinct communities which, together with their Irish homeland, came to be known as the kingdom of Dalriada. The royal dynasty of Dalriada had itself migrated to Scotland by the sixth century; the link with its Irish homeland was effectively cut in AD 637; and a century later, the hill of Dunadd had become the major stronghold of the mainland kingdom of Dalriada.

The Dalriada and the Deisi came from an Ireland that was itself a polyarchy of communities and kingdoms (or *tuatha*), each with its own petty king. As elsewhere in the British Isles, in the sixth century there was a tendency for the larger and more powerful of these kingdoms to establish control over others, and most prominent was the dominion forged by the Uí Néill in the midlands and north of Ireland. The kings of the Uí Néill have long been associated with the heavily fortified and sacred hill of Tara. The land of the Picts which the Scots had invaded was probably settled in a similar fashion. In the sixth and seventh centuries great Pictish kings seem to have been able to impose a personal hegemony over the kingdoms of Pictland, even perhaps as far as the Northern Isles.

TAPRAIN LAW, Edinburgh. An almost impregnable fortress of great age, its summit is protected by pre-Roman ramparts. It may have been fortified as a post-Roman capital of the Picts.

NAVAN FORT, Ulster, a great circular bank and ditch enclosing eighteen acres. Inside is a large mound, possibly an ancient ritual structure and reputedly the burial-mound of Queen Macha. It is said to be the pre-Christian fortress of the kings of Ulster. Excavations suggest the large mound was deserted in the mid-second century AD, though an early Christian rath was placed inside the outer enclosure.

The most momentous of the migrations were those of the Angles, Saxons, and Jutes from what is now north Germany and the western shores of the Baltic Sea. Some of these peoples had drifted to Britain even before the Roman legions departed and others continued to come thereafter; they were recruited as mercenaries in the armies of Roman masters and British kings alike. Many of them stayed, realized their power and rebelled just when further waves of migrants reached the southern and eastern shores of Britain later in the fifth century and early in the sixth. With the clarity that comes with hindsight, the Venerable Bede, writing in the Anglo-Saxon monastery at Jarrow around AD 731, described this great movement thus:

From the stock of the Jutes are the people of Kent and the people of Wight, that is, the race which holds the Isle of Wight, and that which in the province of the West Saxons is to this day called the nation of the Jutes, situated opposite that same Isle of Wight (that is, Hampshire). From the Saxons . . . came the East Saxons. Further, from the Angles . . . are sprung the East Angles, the Middle Angles, the Mercians, the whole race of the Northumbrians, that is, of those peoples who dwell north of the river Humber, and the other peoples of the Angles. . . . (*Ecclesiastical History*, bk. I)

Bede forgot the Franks and the Frisians, who were also involved in this demographic upheaval, but in broad and simplified terms his account was sound enough. The invaders and their collaborators subdued or ejected the British communities and overwhelmed their kingdoms as they pushed gradually westward, seemingly making for the old Roman towns and following the network of straight Roman roads.

Beginning with Kent, each of the invading communities mentioned by Bede quickly created new kingdoms in place of the old, sometimes, as with Kent itself and its Roman centre at Canterbury, on the foundations of earlier political and urban structures. Other of their kingdoms—like those of the Hwicce and the Magonsæte in the west country, or Surrey in the east—may have lost their independence by Bede's day and become absorbed in larger organizations, though their peoples did not lose their identity until much later.

Elsewhere, some British kingdoms survived the onslaught, especially in the south-west peninsula, in Wales, and the north-west. Wedged between Pictland and Dalriada to the north and the new Anglo-Saxon kingdom of the Northumbrians to the south, were the enduring kingdoms of Rheged, Gododdin, and Strathclyde. By the later sixth century these were being hard pressed from both sides. Even the seventh-century Northumbrian palace at Yeavering in the Cheviots has been revealed by archaeologists to have been built within an earlier British complex which was expropriated by the newcomers from overseas. Strathclyde was the only one of these northern British kingdoms to survive for several more centuries. Gododdin had collapsed before the end of the sixth century and its stronghold at Dunbar had an Anglo-Saxon hall built on its site.

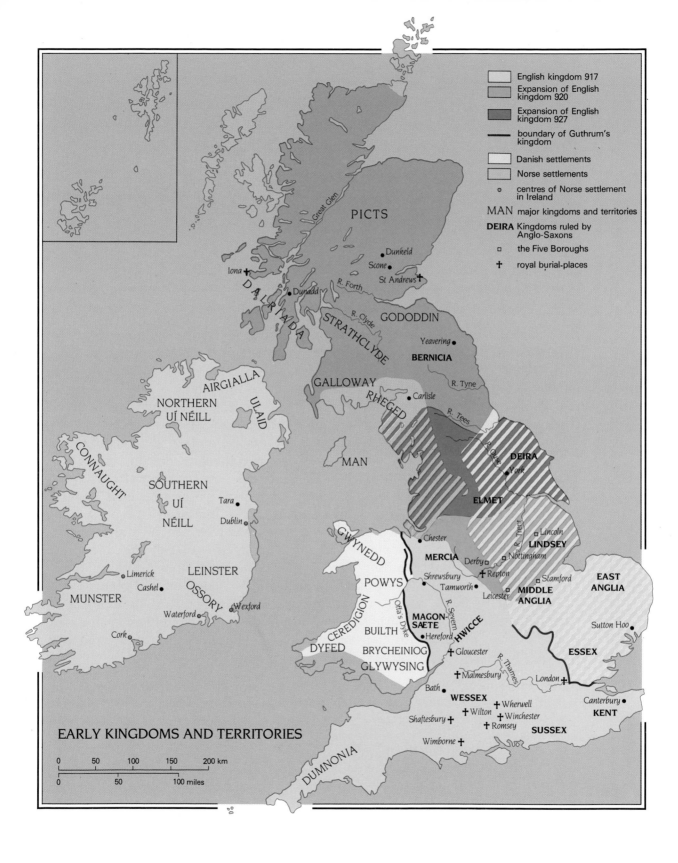

English kingdom 917
Expansion of English kingdom 920
Expansion of English kingdom 927
boundary of Guthrum's kingdom
Danish settlements
Norse settlements
○ centres of Norse settlement in Ireland
MAN major kingdoms and territories
DEIRA Kingdoms ruled by Anglo-Saxons
□ the Five Boroughs
✝ royal burial-places

PICTS

Great Glen

Dunkeld
Scone
St Andrews
Iona ✝
Dynadd ·
R. Forth

DALRIADA

STRATHCLYDE
GODODDIN
Yeavering ·
BERNICIA
R. Clyde

GALLOWAY
RHEGED
Carlisle ·
R. Tyne
R. Tees

AIRGIALLA
NORTHERN UÍ NÉILL
ULAID

CONNAUGHT

SOUTHERN UÍ NÉILL
Tara ·
Dublin ○

MAN

DEIRA
York ·
ELMET

LEINSTER
Limerick ·
Cashel ·
OSSORY
Wexford ·
Waterford ·

MUNSTER

Cork ·

GWYNEDD
Chester ·
MERCIA
Derby □
Nottingham □
Repton ✝
LINDSEY
Lincoln □
R. Trent

POWYS
Shrewsbury ·
Tamworth ·
Leicester □
Stamford □
MIDDLE ANGLIA
EAST ANGLIA

CEREDIGION
BUILTH
MAGON-SÆTE
Hereford ·
R. Severn
HWICCE
Olfa's Dyke

DYFED
BRYCHEINIOG
GLYWYSING
✝ Gloucester
Sutton Hoo ·
ESSEX
R. Thames
London ✝
✝ Malmesbury
Bath ·
WESSEX
✝ Wherwell
Canterbury ·
Shaftesbury ✝
✝ Wilton
✝ Winchester
KENT
✝ Romsey
Wimborne ✝
SUSSEX

EARLY KINGDOMS AND TERRITORIES

DUMNONIA

0   50   100   150   200 km
0   50   100 miles

THE GRAVESTONE OF KING CADFAN OF GWYNEDD, dating from as early as *c.* AD 625. It is now in Llangadwaladr Church, Anglesey. The inscription reads 'Cadfan, the wisest and most renowned of all kings'.

Rheged fell sometime later, and in the middle of the seventh century its stronghold at Carlisle was captured by Oswiu, king of the Northumbrians.

By about AD 650, then, the British Isles were a patchwork of innumerable kingdoms founded by many different communities, both native and immigrant, and they were organized by powerful warlords or kings. The differences between them were many: the kingdoms at the western extremities of England and in Wales could boast a tradition of Roman rule; others in Ireland and Scotland were Gaelic-speaking and scarcely touched by Rome; and the kingdoms in south-west Wales, western Scotland, and much of England were the creation of intruders. Yet they all strove to survive in a highly competitive, unstable, and violent epoch. From the cauldron of their incessant struggles for survival, control, and supremacy emerged a smallish number of kingdoms which in seventh-century England were the famous Heptarchy: Bernicia and Deira (which merged to form Northumbria in AD 651), Lindsey, East Anglia, Mercia, Wessex, and Kent. The process was little different in Ireland, Wales, and Scotland, or so it seems.

According to Bede, seven outstanding warrior-kings in turn established a personal sway over most—if not all—of the Anglo-Saxon kingdoms in the 200 years between the late fifth and the late seventh centuries. And this dominion supposedly passed from southern into northern hands.

Æthelberht, king of the people of Kent . . . was indeed the third of the kings in the nation of the English to hold dominion over all their southern provinces, which are divided from the northern by the river Humber . . . the first who had sovereignty of this kind was Ælle, king of the South Saxons; the second Cælin, king of the West Saxons, who in their language is called Cæwlin; the third, as we have said, Æthelberht, king of the people of Kent; the fourth, Rædwald, king of the East Angles, who, even while Æthelberht was alive, had been obtaining the leadership for his own race; the fifth, Edwin, king of the nation of the Northumbrians, that is, of that nation which dwells on the north side of the river Humber, ruled with greater power over all the peoples who inhabit Britain, English and Britons as well, except only the people of Kent . . . ; the sixth, Oswald, also a most Christian king of the Northumbrians, held a kingdom with these same bounds; the seventh, his brother Oswiu, governing for some time a kingdom of almost the same limits, also subdued for the most part and made tributary the nations of the Picts and Scots, who hold the northern parts of Britain. (*Ecclesiastical History*, bk. II)

The writer of the Anglo-Saxon Chronicle much later used the word *bretwalda*, meaning 'Britain-ruler' or, more probably, 'wide ruler', to describe the personal dominion of these kings within the Anglo-Saxon polity. This *bretwalda*-ship had no institutional dimension and did not represent the dominance of one particular kingdom over all the others. But it may articulate a vague ambition cherished by certain outstanding individuals to reconstitute the Britannia of the Romans, and all but the first two or three of the kings mentioned by Bede would have had the objective of a single Christian Church of the Anglo-Saxons formulated for them by popes and bishops. Such personal hegemonies, won by force, were likely to collapse as quickly as they were established, and their very existence reflects the perpetual animosities and feuds among neighbouring and rival kings rather than any coherent programme of state-building.

CRUX GURIAT, a ninth-century cross-slab from the Isle of Man, commemorating Gwriad, who married a daughter of the king of Gwynedd. Their son, Merfyn Frych ('the Speckled'), became king of Gwynedd (d. 844) and was the father of King Rhodri the Great. Gwynedd claimed pre-eminence among kingdoms in Wales—and even further afield prior to the Viking invasions.

ÆTHELBERHT

(*c*.560–616), king of Kent

... the third of the kings in the nation of the English to hold dominion over all their southern provinces, which are divided from the northern by the river Humber and the boundaries adjoining it; but the first of them all to ascend to the heavenly kingdom.

(Bede, *Ecclesiastical History*)

ACCORDING to Bede, Æthelberht became king of Kent *c*.560, though this may be too early. He cultivated contacts with the Franks of Gaul, encouraged the conversion of the English, and enjoyed personal authority over other Anglo-Saxon kings. After his marriage (before 589) to Bertha, the Christian daughter of the king of Paris, he allowed Christians to use the old Roman church of St Martin, Canterbury. His reign is imperishably associated with the mission of St Augustine from the pope (597), and Æthelberht was the first English king to be converted. At Christmas 597, 10,000 are said to have followed his example; existing churches were reopened and new ones built at Canterbury and Rochester. The spread of the faith beyond Kent was facilitated by his authority over other kings south of the Humber: his nephew became king of the East Saxons and King Rædwald of the East Angles was baptized in Kent. Bede called Æthelberht one of the English *bretwaldas*. His influence extended even beyond the Humber when his daughter married King Edwin of Northumbria. His law-code, the first to be written in any Germanic language and the product of a

THE 'MEDALET' OF BISHOP LIUDHARD, who came with the daughter of the king of Paris, Bertha, when she married King Æthelbert of Kent. The conversion of English kings and kingdoms followed (approx. × 2½).

literate administration, was modelled on 'the example of the Romans' and included ninety laws. Before his death, his primacy in southern England was challenged by King Rædwald, whilst his own son and heir, Eadbald, reverted to paganism. Æthelberht was buried in his new monastery at Canterbury dedicated to Sts Peter and Paul.

The eighth and ninth centuries witnessed many more instances of smaller kingdoms falling victim to, and being absorbed by, greater ones, not only in England but elsewhere in the British Isles. It was a political phenomenon common on the continent too, though paradoxically it was most marked in the kingdoms situated round the Irish Sea: Gwynedd and Dyfed in western Wales established temporary primacies, Dalriada did so in Scotland, Munster and Ulster in Ireland; above all, Mercia and then Wessex came to dominate in England. The explanation is not entirely obvious. The seaways were the best channels of communication, commerce and Christian missions in the Dark Ages, the Irish Sea pre-eminently so; and the kingdoms beside it appear to have had the space, resources, and energy to embark on campaigns of expansion, conquest, and settlement. Under its great king, Offa (d. 796), Mercia subdued all the other Anglo-Saxon kingdoms south of the Humber, with the exception of Wessex, and it

OFFA'S DYKE, a frontier work constructed by King Offa of Mercia (*facing page*). It is the most spectacular and largest protective frontier built in Anglo-Saxon England. Wat's Dyke, possibly constructed by King Æthelbald (d. 757), runs parallel to it in the north. Offa's earthwork between Mercia and Welsh kingdoms such as Powys is 149 miles long 'from sea to sea', with some gaps probably explained by natural features and forest.

did its best to acquire land that belonged to Welsh kings too. Offa's formidable frontier marker, known to posterity as Offa's Dyke, left substantial tracts that were probably part of the kingdom of Powys on the Mercian side of the great ditch and rampart.

The decline of Mercian power after the death of King Cenwulf in 821 demonstrates that such territorial supremacy was still fundamentally the achievement of individual great kings rather than of peoples or kingdoms. And when, according to the Anglo-Saxon Chronicle, the mantle of *bretwalda*-ship passed to King Egbert (d. 839) of Wessex, things seemed no different. It was the appearance on the shores of the British Isles of further and more fearsome waves of migrants, the Vikings from Scandinavia, which quickened the process of absorption and led to a degree of centralized state-building that transcended the talents of mere individuals.

Ever since the 'sea-kingdom' of Dalriada had broken apart in AD 637, the Scots in Argyll had concentrated their attention and pinned their prospects on the mainland and on relations with their Pictish neighbours to the east and with Strathclyde to the south. The appearance of Viking raiders in the northern and western seas from the 790s onwards confirmed this inclination and encouraged the Dalriadans to expand their horizons eastwards. When Kenneth mac Alpin, king of Dalriada, imposed his power on the Picts in the 840s, he was merely

placing the coping-stone on developments towards interpenetration and integration that had been under way for some considerable time. Thereafter, the chief Pictish kingdom ceased to exist. It is true that another Dalriadan advance north-eastwards through the Great Glen may have established a separate kingdom of the Scots in Moray, but the dominant kingdom, which the Scots called Alba and Latin writers Scotia, was in the more prosperous south and midlands under the control of Kenneth and his descendants.

In Wales, the aggression of Anglo-Saxon kings, especially those of Mercia in the eighth century and Wessex in the ninth, combined with the attacks of Viking marauders to create circumstances in which certain powerful kings were able to enforce their authority over weaker neighbours. By the ninth century, the rulers of two kingdoms in particular—Gwynedd in the north and Dyfed in the south-west—seemed capable of extending their power over most of the others. Rhodri Mawr (d. 878) of Gwynedd, the only Welsh king to bear the title 'the Great', and Hywel Dda (d. *c.*949) of Seisyllwg (modern Carmarthenshire and Cardiganshire) and Dyfed, the only one to be called 'the Good', became kings of several kingdoms; this was as much the consequence of their personal qualities and achievements as of the vagaries of marriage and inheritance. Across the Viking-infested water in Ireland, where the Norsemen settled in larger numbers and formed a kingdom on the east coast, no single king or kingdom was able to master the entire island or lend substance to a 'high kingship' that was anything more than transient and bitterly contested, and dependent on the military accomplishments of a figure such as Brian Boruma (d. 1014), king of Munster.

Had it not been for the Viking invasions of eastern England, and the subsequent defeat and conquest of every Anglo-Saxon kingdom apart from Wessex, there is no certainty that a single kingdom would have been created in England either, at least not in the tenth century. As it was, after the Viking onslaughts were renewed in the 860s, mac Alpin's kingdom in southern and central Scotland seemed in a class of its own, vigorous, independent, and a successful union of several kingdoms. A century later it did indeed have its counterpart in England—a southern kingdom that would soon outstrip in wealth and power the kingdom of the Scots. Under the weight of the Viking

A SILVER PENNY OF KING RAIENALT, the Viking king of York, *c.*920. Copied from Anglo-Saxon coins, the obverse shows a bearded figure; the reverse has a bow and arrow, reflecting the military nature of his kingship. (× 1¾)

attacks from 865 onwards, the Anglo-Saxon kingdoms of Northumbria, East Anglia, and Mercia quickly succumbed, leaving only Wessex to lead any resistance, though it too was badly mauled by the invaders. It was Alfred's success in halting the Viking advance and throwing back the Viking king, Guthrum, which ensured Wessex's survival. Alfred's son Edward, and especially Athelstan among his grandsons, so extended their power over the other Anglo-Saxon kingdoms as they recovered them from the Vikings that for the first time a single, permanent kingdom of England was in prospect.

The task was immense. The Vikings had themselves seized York (867) and established their own kingdom in the southern part of Northumbria (the old kingdom of Deira of centuries before). Two years later (869), they overran East Anglia and made it too a separate Viking realm. The fragmentation of the English polity seemed likely to be intensified rather than reduced by these events. In 874 the last independent king of Mercia surrendered and his kingdom was dismembered; the eastern part fell under Viking control. Of the independent Anglo-Saxon kingdoms, Wessex alone survived. It also would have fallen in 877–8 had its king, Alfred, not withdrawn to the Somerset marshes to regroup his forces and reassess his strategy; he emerged to inflict an unexpected defeat on Guthrum at Edington in May 878. This proved to be the turning-point in Wessex's struggle to preserve its independence: it is one of the decisive battles of English history. By 896 the Vikings had been forced to withdraw north of the Thames.

Although Alfred sought to bring parts of other southern Anglo-Saxon kingdoms—notably West Mercia and Kent—under his control, and even perhaps certain kingdoms in South Wales which dreaded the Viking attacks, this hardly amounted as yet to a major or purposeful enlargement of the West Saxon kingdom. Yet the first step in this direction had been taken by Alfred in a treaty with Guthrum (*c*.886–90) which demarcated a precise frontier between Anglo-Saxon and Viking England along Watling Street, placing areas under Alfred's control that had formerly lain beyond the borders of Wessex. Nevertheless, it was Alfred's son, Edward 'the Elder' (d. 924), who took the path of reconquest and began to roll back the frontiers of Viking England. The recovery and ultimate unification of Anglo-Saxon England took place exclusively under the leadership of Wessex, the only Anglo-Saxon kingdom not to be overwhelmed by these latest immigrant conquerors. When King Edward died, his eldest son and successor, Athelstan, was the first West Saxon king to be acclaimed king of Mercia too, and by the time of Athelstan's death (939) the two kingdoms were well on the way to becoming indissolubly linked.

Edward the Elder had gradually reconquered midland England almost as far north as the Humber and the frontier with the Viking kingdom of York. During the reigns of his sons, Athelstan, Edmund (d. 946), and Eadred (d. 955), the task was pursued relentlessly until the Vikings had been expelled even from York, and

RÆDWALD

(d. by 627), king of the East Angles

Rædwald had long before been admitted in Kent to the sacraments of the Christian faith, but in vain; for on his return home he was seduced by his wife and certain perverse teachers, and being turned from the sincerity of his faith, his later state was worse than the former; so that . . . he seemed to serve both Christ and the gods which he had served before . . .

(Bede, *Ecclesiastical History*)

MUCH of what we know about Rædwald is inferential. Excavations at Sutton Hoo, Suffolk, suggest that the site, the size of a cricket field, is the burial ground of East Anglian kings. It is four miles from their residence at Rendlesham. If the largest mound is indeed Rædwald's, then he was buried in a huge wooden row-boat, surrounded by fabulous treasure and war gear, 250 objects from the continent, the Mediterranean, Scandinavia, and the Celtic lands, signifying wealth and power reminiscent of descriptions in *Beowulf*. The treasure has associations with Rome and paganism as well as with Christianity. Rædwald was baptized at King Æthelberht's court, but he soon reverted to paganism. He challenged Kent's primacy among the southern Anglo-Saxon kingdoms and Bede regarded him as *bretwalda* after Æthelberht. His influence may have reached Northumbria, where he helped King Edwin to seize the throne (617). To Bede he was 'noble by birth, although ignoble in his actions'.

THE EXCAVATED SHIP-BURIAL AT SUTTON HOO, Suffolk, revealed treasure of a seventh-century king, probably Rædwald of East Anglia. Among the rich items unearthed was this 'ceremonial whetstone' which may have been a sceptre.

with that done Northumbria could be brought back into the Anglo-Saxon polity. The dynasty of Wessex could now justifiably claim to rule virtually all of England. By the end of the millennium, the word and concept of 'England' had appeared. It had all been a notable military achievement, the work of a line of southern kings who by a whisker had survived the Viking onslaught that had subdued every Anglo-Saxon kingdom but theirs. Only in Scotland had something comparable been achieved, and there it had been by the efforts of a western—ultimately Irish—kingship.

The reconquest of Viking England and the assertion of West Saxon claims to power throughout England were a prelude to the imposition of effective control by the house of Cerdic in the old kingdoms outside Mercia and the south. This was undertaken pre-eminently by King Edgar (d. 975). The imposing regal style which he used in his charters (*Albionis Imperator Augustus*) implied a superiority over all Englishmen, and there is no doubt that he was determined to exert his rule and apply his legislation in East Anglia and Northumbria just as much as in Mercia. He went further. He repeated more insistently and consistently the claims made by his predecessors as kings of Wessex to overlordship over the British kingdoms in Wales and Strathclyde, even over the Scottish kingdom further north and some of the Viking kingdoms established round the Irish Sea. Edgar's fourth law-code was avowedly intended to embrace 'all who inhabit these islands', English, Briton, and Viking; he tried to absorb his Danish subjects

KING ALFRED, portrayed as the heroic leader inciting the West Saxons to resist the Danes. This Victorian representation, painted by G. F. Watts (d. 1904) in 1847 for the reconstructed palace of Westminster, is part of the cult of Alfred, which reached its height in the Victorian era, exactly a millennium after the king's reign.

into the English polity and Church, and employed some of them in his personal service. In 973 he secured the submission of the Scottish king and in return granted him Lothian under Edgar's overlordship. Soon after his coronation in that year, Edgar sailed to Chester to receive the formal obeisance of the kings of Strathclyde, the Scots, and the Isles, and of five Welsh kings too; if, as tradition tells us, they rowed him from his palace to the minster on the Dee, in doing so they were publicly displaying their deference to him. All this was an imperial conception that would have been understood by contemporaries who read or heard about Charlemagne's empire and the Byzantine empire centred at Constantinople.

One word of caution is necessary. We should not take it for granted that the unification of England and the acceptance of English overlordship in the British Isles were inevitable or unchallenged, still less pre-ordained. Mercia, East Anglia, and Northumbria, let alone Lothian, Strathclyde, and the Welsh kingdoms, preserved strong identities; they continued to enjoy varying degrees of practical independence, and they could draw on powerful traditions and lengthy histories to bolster their sense of separateness. To weld all of them, or even merely the English kingdoms, into a single political entity under the house of Cerdic would be no easy task—indeed, it was not fully achieved until after 1707. Overlordship of the Scottish and Welsh kingdoms and of Strathclyde still depended on the personal power and abilities of individual English kings and on the relative strength of the rulers with whom they had to deal; it was very much as kings and kingdoms had stood in relation to one another ever since the fall

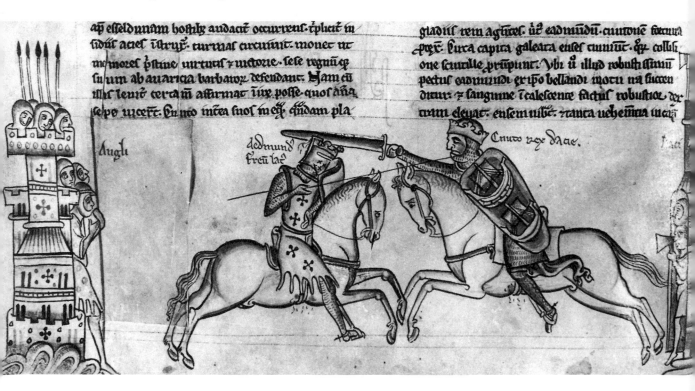

of Rome. Even within the English kingdoms unity was hard won. Northern Northumbria, north of the river Tees, was for long a reluctant province of the kingdom of the English, and when Domesday Book was compiled in 1086 it was omitted from the great survey as if it were scarcely part of the kingdom. Southern Northumbria, south of the Tees, which the Vikings previously had made into their own kingdom of York, was more securely held, though King Edgar and his successors were unrepentantly southern kings who hardly felt at home in this former kingdom.

That the independent traditions of the old kingdoms were still strong is well illustrated by events which took place after King Eadred's death in 955. By 957 Edgar managed to set himself up as ruler of Mercia, and he virtually seceded from the kingdom of his elder brother, Eadwig; only in 959, when Eadwig died, did Edgar become king in all the English kingdoms. Moreover, the very size of the enlarged realm made it vulnerable to centrifugal forces that had not yet been fully mastered. And renewed Viking invasions from 980 onwards, ultimately with territorial conquest as their aim, caused England's traditional divisions and regional separatism to surface once again. King Æthelred II may well have aggravated such divisions by his massacre of Danish immigrants predominantly in midland and eastern England:

... all the Danes who had sprung up in this island, sprouting like cockle amongst the wheat, were to be destroyed by a most just extermination, and this decree was to be put into effect even as far as death ... (Charter of Æthelred to St Frideswide's monastery, Oxford, 1004)

Towards the disastrous end of his reign (1016), his son Edmund deserted Æthelred and established himself in Northumbria and Mercia; when Æthelred died and Cnut defeated Edmund at Ashingdon (Essex), the treaty of peace between them (1016) allowed Edmund to rule in Wessex, his forebears' kingdom, and Cnut to take the rest. Even after Cnut's death (1035), following a reign during which unity had been restored ironically by a Viking dynasty, Harold Harefoot was accepted as king in Mercia and Northumbria, while his brother, Harthacnut, became king of Wessex. Only in 1040, when Harold Harefoot died, was the kingdom of England once more reassembled.

As to the claims to overlordship beyond the kingdom, English kings did not again come as close to implementing them as they did in the tenth century—not, that is, until Edward I three centuries later. During Athelstan's reign and for a time thereafter, Welsh kings regularly attended the royal court of Wessex, and they were used as distinguished witnesses of royal charters. In Edgar's reign the king of the Scots acknowledged English overlordship. Only Ireland stood beyond the reach of these claims and aspirations, and the establishment of the Viking

THE DUEL BETWEEN KING EDMUND IRONSIDE AND KING CNUT at Deerhurst, Glos., in 1016. It was supposedly fought to decide how the English kingdom would be divided between them after the death of King Æthelred II and Cnut's victory at Ashingdon. The illustration is in Matthew Paris's *Greater Chronicle*, c.1240–59; the kings therefore appear in thirteenth-century dress.

kingdom of Dublin and of Viking settlements along the east coast facing Britain placed a barrier against efforts to exert an effective overlordship there—though King Æthelred did venture into the Irish Sea in the year 1000 to neutralize a Viking threat. Elsewhere in Ireland, a modest number of provincial kingdoms had won a stable dominance over more petty kings, as had the Dál Cais dynasty of Munster by the late tenth century. But the 'high kingship' of all Ireland was a highly personal and ephemeral phenomenon, almost an illusion.

Even in Scotland, the achievement of mac Alpin's dynasty ran foul of Viking incursions in Caithness and Sutherland in the far north, as well as in the Isles, where Scandinavian kingdoms were established in the ninth century. In the south, too, the very success of the Scottish kingdom under Malcolm I in finally absorbing Lothian and Strathclyde in the eleventh century meant that new tensions arose between north and south; these have an echo in Shakespeare's *Macbeth*. Norse power enveloped the Hebrides and the Isle of Man until the mid-thirteenth century, and the Orkneys and Shetlands for two centuries more. But to have created a kingdom out of English, British, Scots, and Picts by the mid-eleventh century—with all its strains and stresses, to be sure, and with frontierlands in Norse hands—was as notable and permanent an achievement as that of the kings of Wessex.

Kingships

Although there was a multitude of kings in the British Isles in the fifth century and later, we have only the vaguest notion of the character of their kingships. Writing about the year 1000, Abbot Ælfric, the forthright Anglo-Saxon scholar, declared that

No man can make himself king, but the people has the choice to select as king whom they please; but after he is consecrated as king, he then has dominion over the people, and they cannot shake his yoke from their necks.

Yet this had not always been so. The instability and insecurity caused by the dissolution of Roman authority and the great migrations put a premium on warrior-kings capable of defending their communities and conquering their enemies. There was nothing peculiarly Baltic or Germanic about this quality of kingship: that of the good fighter, leading a victorious warband made loyal by the success and patronage that were implied by contemporary terms such as 'treasure-guards', 'king-givers', and 'gold-finds'. Tacitus' remarks about the noble warriors whom Germanic tribes chose to lead them are well known and have been applied to the leaders of the warbands that founded Anglo-Saxon kingdoms. But surely such martial qualities were needed—and were to be found—among the Scots who established the new Dalriada, among the British kings who fought for survival after the fall of Rome, and in the petty Irish kings who contended with one another in a violent world. For all the differences between the polities they inhabited, the Dark Age kings were expected to hold fast the territory of their own communities, to master or conquer their neighbours, and to protect their own people and enable them to live securely. The bellicosity of kingship retained significance wherever kings survived—even beyond the Middle Ages. Every adult medieval king of England, with the exception of the pallid Henry VI (1422–61), led his armies personally into battle at one time or another; and those who were defeated in battle ran grave risk that their kingship would be undermined, as Æthelred II and King John were made to realize.

We might expect that the long Roman experience in England and Wales would have left its mark on the outlook and habits of successor kings, but it is far from clear that the host of fifth-century kings took any particular qualities from Roman tradition. It is possible, as we shall see later, that certain administrative arrangements and practices were lodged in the memory, to be revived by ambitious kings of the English or the Welsh, and the developing role of Dark Age kings as law-givers may owe something to imperial Rome. The king as warrior, the king as governor—these were more likely ancient and fundamental qualities of kingship. They are characteristics whose outward trappings are today represented by the wardrobes of uniforms worn by British kings and the consorts of queens, and whose substance is recalled by the vague, residual authority of government that still reposes in the monarch.

A third and newer quality of kingship in Dark Age Britain was its Christian quality, with the king being regarded as somewhat akin to a priest. Old Testament stories in particular underscored the position of the king as governor, and gave to his role as warrior a religious aura that made his wars righteous and attributed their success to God's approving will. The conversion of vanquished heathen enemies to Christ was but one edge of a two-edged sword in battle, as Guthrum quickly learned when he was required to be baptized after his defeat at Edington in 878. More than that: Christianity transformed the very nature of kingship in England. It magnified the powers of kings and gave them more extensive rights, as well as emphasizing their obligations and duties in a Christian society. The emergence of Christian kingship was indubitably the most profound and revolutionary change that kingship underwent in the early medieval West.

Ancient Irish laws, which survive fossil-like from the seventh century, suggest that early Irish kings, who owed little or nothing to a Rome that never planted its civilization in Ireland, were made different from other men by primitive pre-Christian inauguration rites that imparted what contemporaries regarded as some sort of sacred or divine quality, well before the arrival of Christianity in the

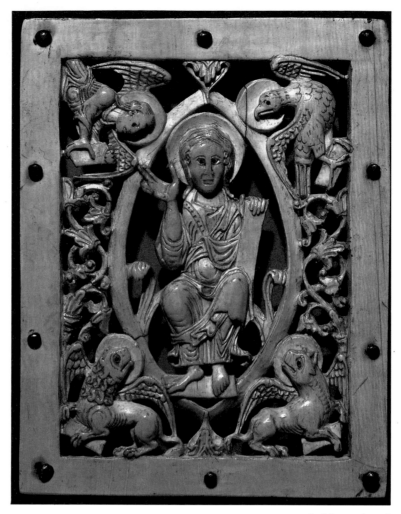

AN IVORY-PIERCED PANEL OF CHRIST IN MAJESTY, probably produced in England in the early tenth century and with close links with King Athelstan's court.

fifth century. The British kings who faced the Anglo-Saxon immigrants were possibly Christian, but it was the migration from Dalriada to western Scotland that first forged that strong link between Christianity and kingship in mainland Britain that is the unique achievement of the early Middle Ages. Columba, whose Gaelic name (meaning 'Dove of the Church' in English) helped to raise this Christian missionary above the violence of his age, was one of the royal Uí Néill kin from central Ireland. In 563 he founded his famous monastery on Iona, in the newly established kingdom of Dalriada. He consecrated King Ædan, grandson of the kingdom's founder, Fergus mac Erc, and this is the first consecration of a king known to have taken place in mainland Britain. Columba soon made contact with the high king of the Picts, Bridei or Bruide (d. 584), and converted him too. The British kingdoms further south, Strathclyde among them, were probably Christian already, for missionaries were fully aware that to convert kings was the best way of converting their peoples. From the kings' point of view, it meant more than shrugging off one loyalty and set of rituals and adopting others: it transformed their attitudes to themselves and to their role on earth. Henceforth, they could look forward to joining the company of other kings under the aegis of the Heavenly King of Kings; they had His protection and favour and, in war, every expectation that He would give them the victory over their enemies and assure them of prosperity and fame in peacetime.

Soon after Columba's missions, emissaries arrived in Britain quite independently from Rome to convert the kings of the new Anglo-Saxon kingdoms in the south. Augustine made for the court of Æthelberht of Kent in 597, and Paulinus, a tall, stooping, ascetic figure, was later sent to Edwin of Northumbria, who was converted to Christ in 627. Not that the conversion of the Anglo-Saxons was swift or unhindered. There was uncertainty initially that the newly Christianized kings would remain steadfast in their new faith; some, like Rædwald of the East Angles, continued to be ambivalent and were just as likely to worship at a pagan altar as at a Christian one if the occasion or politics demanded it. Even Æthelberht's kingdom of Kent reverted to paganism in 616, and Paulinus was forced to flee from Northumbria in 633 when Edwin died. Moreover, after missionaries from Iona reached Northumbria in the 630s, at the invitation of the new kings, Oswald and then Oswiu, the scene was set for an unedifying confrontation between the two traditions of Christianity that were battling for the souls of Anglo-Saxon kings and their peoples. Nevertheless, by the middle of the century, kingship everywhere in the British Isles very probably was Christian. In Bede's day, in the early eighth century, the Pictish King Nechtan was known to be a committed Christian

THE MONYMUSK RELIQUARY, made in Pictland in the eighth century to hold the relics of St Columba. It is a small shrine carved from wood and decorated with metal, with enamelled hinge-mounts for carrying. It was later carried into battle by the Scots to ensure victory.

ST COLUMBA PREACHING BEFORE BRIDEI, KING OF THE PICTS, at his fortress beside the river Ness. This Victorian fresco of W. B. Hole (d. 1917) represents a scene from Abbot Adomnán's seventh-century *Life of St Columba*. The painting was designed (1898) for the Scottish National Portrait Gallery, and the attendant's crozier and the Picts' weaponry were copied from surviving originals in the National Museum of Antiquities of Scotland. St Columba's tonsure is correctly portrayed in the Celtic, rather than the Roman, style. This is one of a number of nineteenth-century treatments of this inspiring episode in Scottish history.

who liked the company of learned priests. And a century and a half later, the newly united kingdom of the Scots had its ecclesiastical capital established at Dunkeld, where some of St Columba's relics were brought from hallowed Iona (849). Only with the incursions of Vikings at the end of the eighth century were pagan kings installed in Britain once more—and at least one of their kingdoms, Dublin, lasted until Christianity penetrated it in about 980.

Kings in the British Isles maintained a close connection with the Church: religious authority and secular authority were inextricably entwined and Church and State were the twin pillars of society. Offa, king of Mercia, presided in person over Church councils in 786–7. Bishops were frequently councillors of West Saxon kings, certainly by Athelstan's day: they helped to formulate secular as well as religious legislation and were involved in secular administration as well as monastic reform. Kings were central to the aspirations of Church leaders and vice versa. In Ireland, several 'over-kings' of the province of Munster were themselves clerics, a curious phenomenon hardly ever encountered elsewhere. The fruits of this fraternal collaboration are graphically exemplified in the careers of the brothers Egbert and Eadberht, the one archbishop of York and the other king of Northumbria; together they established a court school at York which has a good claim to be the first court school and the model which the great Alcuin used when establishing his school at the court of the Emperor Charlemagne. Politics, learning, and Christianity were hitched between the same shafts well before Alfred's day, to the mutual advantage of both Church and State, priest and king.

The Church's role in advancing political unity was fully appreciated in Northumbria in the mid-seventh century. King Oswiu, who had been brought up in the tradition of St Columba and his Irish brand of Christianity, decided at the synod of Whitby in 664 to adopt instead the practices of the Roman Church in order to strengthen his political control and his reputation as an English 'over-king' (or, in later parlance, *bretwalda*) of the kingdoms south of the Humber, whose ecclesiastical capital was Canterbury. Offa of Mercia had a realist's appreciation of the English Church's organization when, in 787, he persuaded the pope to create an archbishopric of Lichfield, which was within his kingdom of Mercia. A subservient archbishop close at hand was more likely to do his bidding

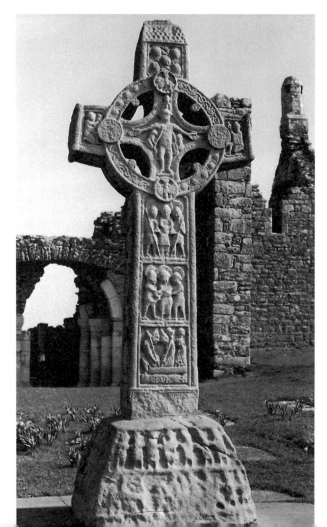

THE CROSS OF THE SCRIPTURES at Clonmacnoise. It was erected by a king called Flann early in the tenth century and symbolizes the Christian character of contemporary Irish kingship. The monks of Clonmacnoise compiled informative annals; whilst the monastery had a close connection with early Irish kings, and O'Connors were still being buried there in the middle of the twelfth century.

than the primate at Canterbury, for although Offa had made Kent a client kingdom some two decades earlier, it remained a troublesome dependency. The close identification of the political and ecclesiastical dominance of Mercia hardly lasted beyond Offa's death (in fact, only until 803); the tradition of St Augustine, which by then was two centuries old and vigorous, was too robust to be flouted.

From the Church's point of view, royal protection and patronage were the keys to Christian advance and consolidation. This is best illustrated by the impetus which Christian kingship gave in the tenth century to the movement for Christian rejuvenation and reform, spearheaded in England by a new rash of Benedictine monastic foundations. This reform movement was a regal movement, associated as much with King Alfred and his successors as with the great religious figures of Dunstan, Æthelwold, and Oswald. Alfred himself was the harbinger of a movement which gathered speed under his son Edward the Elder and reached full vigour, with whole-hearted royal support, under Athelstan and his brothers. Its greatest glories came under Edgar, whom Æthelwold likened to 'the Good Shepherd': new bishoprics were created; Benedictine monasteries were enthusiastically reformed; old monastic sites—often in former Viking-held territory—were refounded, reorganized, and re-endowed with royal grants, some of which were of land recovered from the Vikings. The synod which Edgar summoned to Winchester (c.970) produced the *Regularis concordia* (Monastic Agreement) in which the king was lauded as 'the glorious, by the grace of Christ illustrious king of the English and of the other peoples dwelling within the bounds of the island of Britain'. This tenth-century reform movement owed much to royal encouragement in its early stages and continuing royal support was crucial to its long-term success, ensuring endowments, protection, and a secure legal title to the resources, privileges, and property of individual religious houses. In return, the kings had monks and bishops at their side, and by Edgar's reign the king himself exuded something of the quality of a priest.

Christian kingship was conferred and publicized in new ceremonies of anointing and consecration which in the tenth century were central to the coronation and which have been the most solemn part of king-making ever since. From the time when kings in Britain began to sit on thrones—as early as the sixth century, it seems—the Church has been associated with the inauguration of kings, no matter how they might be chosen. The kings of Dalriada are the first kings known to have undergone a ceremony of hallowing. Columba laid his hands on Ædan when he became king, well before the conversion of Æthelberht, king of Kent. Much more elaborate was the coronation rite which King Edgar underwent amid the Roman buildings of Bath in 973. Edgar's coronation,

KING EDGAR, crowned and holding a palm, seated between Sts Æthelwold and Dunstan. The miniature is in an eleventh-century manuscript of the 'Monastic Agreement' (or *Regularis concordia*), c.970, whereby Edgar encouraged the revival of religious life in the English kingdom.

OFFA

(757–796), king of the Mercians

. . . the glory of Britain, the trumpet of proclamation, the sword against foes, the shield against enemies; [though later] you know very well how much blood [he] shed to secure the kingdom on his son. This was not a strengthening of his kingdom, but its ruin.

(Alcuin's Letters)

IMAGINATIVE, bold, and ruthless, Offa was descended from Penda (d. 654), king of the Mercians. He came to power after a civil war (757) and subjugated Kent, Sussex, and Essex (including London, where he may have resided). The East Anglian King Æthelberht had the last laugh since, after his execution at Offa's court (794), he was regarded as a martyr. Offa was also aggressive towards the Hwicce and in several expeditions (778–95) he seized parts of Powys from the Welsh. Regarding himself as king of the Mercians by God's dispensation, his pretensions were yet wider; only Wessex and Northumbria kept their independence, though Offa married his daughters to their kings. He enlisted Church and pope in support of his kingship, perhaps in imitation of Charlemagne, whom he called 'brother'; Charlemagne's letter to Offa (796) is the only letter to survive of correspondence between a continental king and an Anglo-Saxon ruler. Offa used the visit of two legates in 786–7, the first papal envoys to Britain since St Augustine, to issue religious and secular decrees and to urge an archbishopric for Mercia based at Lichfield. He organized his kingdom's defences by stressing the obligations of his subjects and

ONE OF THE NEW SILVER PENNIES STRUCK BY KING OFFA OF MERCIA (d. 796). The bust of the king, uncrowned, with a mop of hair and large ears, may be an attempt at portraiture. Offa made a number of lasting changes to the monetary system in England and its exploitation by kings. (× 2½)

also by building a great dyke against the Welsh. Offa's wealth and his exploitation of trade were underpinned by a new silver coinage. Although St Albans' monks claimed that he was buried near Bedford, his burial place is not certainly known. For all his greatness, his son Ecgfrith reigned only 141 days, Kent rebelled, and Mercian supremacy soon collapsed.

masterminded by the reformers, was the culmination of that alliance between Church and State, religious and secular, that had helped to transform the character of kingship during the previous four centuries.

Although it is likely that Columba's hallowing of Ædan was a ceremony repeated for his successors as kings of Dalriada and, later, of Scotland, we have very little precise knowledge of the Church's association with king-making in England before 900 and even less in Wales and Ireland. Nevertheless, an important step in the development of a formal Christian ritual at the inauguration of kings was taken in 787, when Offa of Mercia, anxious that his only son Ecgfrith should be assured of the succession to the Mercian throne, persuaded the papal legates visiting England to anoint Ecgfrith as king. This may or may not have been the first time that a king had been anointed in an Anglo-Saxon kingdom; it was certainly the first time that a king's son was anointed in the lifetime of his father. Significantly, Charlemagne, who had exchanged letters with Offa, had arranged that his son should be consecrated in similar circumstances not long before, in 781. Some sort of Christian sanction, comparable with that known in Scotland, may have been attributed to kings in England much earlier. Offa evidently believed that he had God's approval for his kingship ('I, Offa, by the divine controlling grace king of the Mercians', he proclaimed), though as far as we know, he himself was as unconsecrated as all his predecessors. By contrast, Offa's successors, Ecgfrith and Cenwulf, were publicly consecrated kings and regarded as 'the Lord's anointed'.

In Wessex, the evidence from the ninth century is more cloudy. Yet when King Æthelwulf returned from Rome in 856 and married Judith, princess of Francia, at Rheims, he allowed the archbishop of Rheims to consecrate her as his queen. It seems most unlikely that a West Saxon king who had not been anointed himself would have allowed his queen to be so; perhaps consecration had already become customary at the inauguration of West Saxon kings.

However that may be, the role of West Saxon kings in the rescue of Christian England from the Vikings, and the gradual spread of their repute and authority elsewhere in the British Isles were reflected by the tenth century in a truly elaborate inauguration ceremony. It seems probable that a coronation ritual (or *ordo*) had been formalized by 900 and that consecration and anointing were central features of it even before Edgar's remarkable coronation in 973. Moreover, all the West Saxon royal consecrations that have left a record took place at the royal township of Kingston-on-Thames, which significantly was sited close to the border between the old kingdoms of Wessex and Mercia, and actually on the recognized frontier between Alfred's kingdom and the domain of Guthrum the Dane. Athelstan (d. 939) is the first English king to be shown on his coins wearing a crown or circlet, and he appears similarly 'crowned' in the contemporary

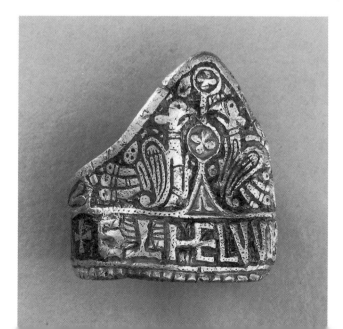

THE GOLD RING OF KING ÆTHELWULF, King Alfred's father. It is in the shape of a mitre. Inlaid with niello, the lower border has the inscription *Æthelwulf Rex*. (× 2)

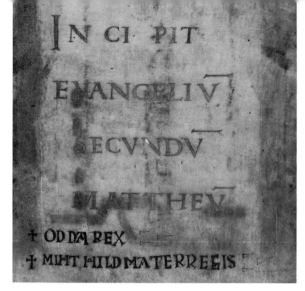

INCIPIT

EVANGELIV̄

SECVNDV̄

MATTHEV̄

✝ ODDA REX
✝ MIHT HILD MATER REGIS

picture of the king in the copy of the Life of St Cuthbert which he himself presented to the monks of St Cuthbert towards the end of his reign. The anonymous biography of St Dunstan, written about the year 1000, includes a description of King Eadwig's coronation day in the winter of 955–6. Eager to make Dunstan's character shine more brightly, it amounts to a slur on the king and a nasty slander of the women who would soon be closest to him as his wife and his mother-in-law. But its account of the court at Kingston on that great day is a vivid one:

. . . when at the time appointed by all the leading men of the English he was anointed and consecrated king by popular election, on that day after the kingly anointing at the holy ceremony, the lustful man suddenly jumped up and left the happy banquet and the fitting company of his nobles for the aforesaid caresses of loose women. When Archbishop Oda saw that the king's wilfulness, especially on the day of his coronation, displeased all the councillors sitting around, he said to his fellow-bishops and other leading men: 'Let some of you go, I pray, to bring back the king, so that he may, as is fitting, be a pleasant companion to his followers in the royal banquet.' But one by one, fearing to incur the king's annoyance or the women's complaint, they withdrew themselves and began to refuse. Finally they chose from them all two whom they knew to be most firm of spirit, namely Abbot Dunstan and Bishop Cynesige, Dunstan's kinsman, that they should in obedience to the command of all bring the king, willing or unwilling, back to his deserted seat. When in accordance with their superiors' orders they had entered, they found the royal crown, which was bound with wondrous metal, gold and silver gems, and shone with many-coloured lustre, carelessly thrown down on the floor, far from his head, and he himself repeatedly wallowing between the two of them in evil fashion, as if in a vile sty. They said: 'Our nobles sent us to ask you to come as quickly as possible to your proper seat, and not to scorn to be present at the joyful banquet of your chief men.' But when he did not wish to rise, Dunstan, after first rebuking the folly of the women, drew him by his hand from his licentious reclining by the women, replaced the crown, and brought him with him to the royal assembly, though dragged from the women by force. (*Life of St Dunstan*)

Edgar's coronation on Whit Sunday 973 at Bath—which had a famous monastery and, like Kingston-on-Thames, stood close to the Mercian–Wessex frontier—was an elaboration of these highly suggestive developments. The public ritual expressed not only Edgar's claim to extraordinarily wide authority in the British Isles (which the ancient stones and associations of Roman Bath doubtless enhanced), but also his priestly role as a Christian king who had waited for coronation until his thirty-first year, the age at which priesting took place in the Roman Church and the age when Christ himself began his public ministry. With Edgar bedecked with the roses of martyrdom and the lilies of chastity, this was Christian kingship at its most sublime. Archbishop Dunstan may have had a hand in devising and organizing this imaginative and deeply symbolic ceremony as a solemn expression of Christocentric kingship, which stressed the king's semi-religious quality, accorded him divine protection, and, at the same time, laid on his shoulders an array of moral duties. It was reminiscent of the crowning as German emperor (952) of his kinsman, Otto the Great, with whom Edgar had friendly relations. This *ordo* of 973 remained virtually unchanged until the Norman Conquest. And at Edgar's side, Ælfthryth was anointed as his queen: so far as is known, this was the first time that a double coronation like this had taken place in England, perhaps in the entire British Isles.

Raising the consecrated king above other men powerfully protected him. If the king were also a priest he could hardly be deposed by mere men. Not even Æthelred II, in his thirty-four-year-long reign, faced a challenge to remove him; he was still regarded as the rightful king even when he was in exile, though in the meantime his people were forced to accept and acknowledge Sweyn the Dane as ruler of England. This special shield of a consecrated king protected King John, and when, in a less spiritual age in the fourteenth and fifteenth centuries, deposition was contemplated and contrived, men resorted to it with heavy heart, desperate to escape the spiritual consequences of their act by publicly justifying the unjustifiable. As Ælfric had said, 'they cannot strike his [the king's] yoke from their necks'.

The consecrated king had large duties and obligations that were expected to dictate his actions. These duties and obligations came to be summarized for public consumption in the oath which he swore at his consecration. This oath was made formal in the tenth century and remained virtually unaltered until the twelfth century. And such an oath is a central part of the coronation ceremony of British monarchs today. Anglo-Saxon kings swore to defend and preserve the Church and Christian people, to ensure peace and order in their kingdom, and to assure justice and mercy in their judgements. These promises amounted to a manifesto of good Christian kingship which, in difficult circumstances or in the case of unsatisfactory kings, could be publicly reiterated with powerful effect; Æthelred II was induced to do just that when he returned from exile in 1014. By

ALFRED 'THE GREAT'

(871–899), king of the West Saxons

. . . we should also turn into the language which we can all understand some books, which may be most necessary for all men to know, and to bring it to pass, as we can very easily with God's help, if we have the peace, that all the youth now in England . . . may be devoted to learning as long as they cannot be of use in any other employment . . .

(Alfred's translation of Pope Gregory I's *Pastoral Care*)

BORN at Wantage, Alfred is the only English king called 'great'. His reputation rests on his defence of Wessex against the Danes and his embodiment of the ideals of Christian kingship. Asser's biography and the Anglo-Saxon Chronicle stress his decisive role in the creation of an English kingship. His early years established his priorities. As a boy he was taken to Rome, where he was honourably treated, and his father's second wife may have popularized Carolingian culture at the West Saxon court. From 865 Alfred's main preoccupation was the Danes, and when his elder brother was killed 'in the year of battles' (871), he succeeded to the West Saxon throne. Forced into the Athelney marshes (whence stories of how his preoccupation with strategic planning made him neglect his baking had emerged by the eleventh century), his determination gave him victory at Edington (878). Alfred spent the next decade consolidating his hold on Wessex; he recaptured London and concluded a treaty (886) with Guthrum the Dane which fixed the Anglo-Danish frontier between London and Watling Street. Alfred was now the acknowledged leader of Englishmen outside Danish-held territory. During this period he built a fleet of large ships, developed at least thirty burhs, and organized the army (*fyrd*) so that renewed Danish attacks were less effective. By the 890s his charters and coins could refer to him as 'king of the

SILVER PENNY OF KING ALFRED (d. 899), struck at London. The bust, with its diadem, appears on the obverse and is based on Roman models. The reverse records its origin in London, probably after Alfred occupied the city in 886. (× 2)

English', and Welsh kings sought his alliance. Even more significantly, his conception of regal authority, Christian morality, and religious devotion was stamped on Wessex and its dependent kingdoms by his law-codes, copies of which were sent to the dioceses he controlled; these were also the principles of his educational and religious reforms and his English translations. Alfred's intellectual curiosity and energy, his religious devotion, and sense of duty preserved Wessex's independence and so revitalized its kingship that it could rule all England in the next century.

the end of the tenth century, anointing and promising went hand in hand in England's theocratic kingship.

On a practical level, Christian kingship was expressed most obviously in royal patronage of the Church and, especially in the tenth century, in the sponsorship of Church reform. It also meant that from time to time the king was at the heart of literary renaissances which directly served the Christian cause. Throughout the Middle Ages, the place of kings as educators, literary patrons, and sponsors of learning and culture was as much spiritual and religious in inspiration as it was cultural and practical. Though Alfred gave it scant acknowledgement when he said that learning in the England of his day was in decay, the era of Mercian ascendancy in the eighth century had seen several examples of royal patronage of scholarship in the Church's interest. But it is Alfred who is accorded the finest accolade of all—and rightly so—as a royal patron of that intellectual triad, religion, education, and learning. He has retained this reputation over the centuries and in the fifteenth century his devotion in these fields was mirrored by Henry VI, who showed more interest in Alfred than in all other Anglo-Saxon kings and sought to have him canonized. Alfred was especially concerned that the youth of his kingdom should be able to read books of religious instruction, philosophy, and history, but there were 'some books which [he stated in his prologue to a translation into English of Gregory the Great's *Pastoral Care*] may be most necessary for all men'. His was a radical programme of education, in which he strove to raise the standard of learning in his kingdom and at the same time the standard of Christian observance. His campaign reflected both the secular and the spiritual sides of his conception of Christian kingship; small wonder that he saw himself as a latter-day David. Alfred was the only English king before Henry VIII to write a book. His own translations and those which he sponsored—of the works of Bede, Boethius, Orosius, St Augustine, and others—show how deep the Christian influence on kingship had penetrated: the king now served God's purposes as well as his own. And this was made into a tradition by the activities of his immediate successors, especially Athelstan.

Among the motives behind Alfred's campaign to improve education, standards of learning, and literacy was the need to ensure that his people could read and understand his pronouncements, orders, and legislation. To judge by the seventh-century Irish law-codes and what is known of Welsh kingship in the same era, kings whose main role was as warlord and defender of the community had little to do with law-making and judgement; their legal powers seem decidedly few and circumscribed when placed beside the community's self-regulation of behaviour. In more thoroughly Romanized regions, however, it is possible that Roman ideas and habits of legislating and judging were indeed adopted by kings who succeeded the imperial governors. The Christianizing of kingship, and the Bible's stories about great judges and Christian law, gradually emphasized the duty of the king as law-giver and judge at the expense of self-regulation by leading figures in the community. Welsh law, recorded in the twelfth century and made up of layers of earlier custom and regulations current during the previous two centuries, speaks of judges appointed by kings and fines imposed by kings. The concept of royal legislation was changing radically.

The Christian king made and proclaimed law and to do so became a mark of kingship. Though some of his 'laws' were redolent of pagan values and practices, Æthelberht of Kent, a pagan warrior recently turned Christian, is the first

TRANSLATION INTO ANGLO-SAXON OF POPE GREGORY THE GREAT'S *PASTORAL CARE*. The translation was probably the work of King Alfred himself *c*.890, and was intended for distribution in his kingdom in order to popularize the spiritual and intellectual qualities required of those in responsibility. This surviving contemporary copy was sent to the bishop of Worcester, who was enjoined (ch. xxiv) to admonish women more lightly than men, and (ch. xxv) the old more lightly than the young.

Anglo-Saxon king known to have issued laws in the vernacular but in a Latin, Christian tradition. Early Irish law-codes tell a similar story of pagan customs surviving in a Christian context. Thereafter, the publication of law-codes became common and they gradually attained a sophisticated character. The tradition of West Saxon kings as law-givers was well established from Ine (*c*.694) to Æthelred II (d. 1016), each king assembling the pronouncements, administrative regulations, and laws of his predecessors to form a body of Anglo-Saxon law. Alfred described how carefully and cautiously he went about it:

Then I . . . collected these together and ordered to be written many of them which our forefathers observed, those which I liked; and many of those which I did not like I rejected with the advice of my councillors . . . For I dared not presume to set in writing at all many of my own, because it was unknown to me what would please those who should come after us. But those which I found which seemed to me most just, either in the time of my kinsman, King Ine, or of Offa, king of the Mercians or of Æthelberht . . . I collected herein, and omitted the others. Then I . . . showed those to all my councillors, and they then said that they were all pleased to observe them. (Laws of Alfred, *c*.885–99)

The roots of this law were pagan, Roman imperial, and especially Christian. The law itself served, on the one hand, to develop the powers of kings and, on the other, to direct—even to limit—their actions. Law subjected a king's people more precisely to his authority. In Edgar's case in the 970s, when he issued laws that dealt for the first time with Mercia and Northumbria as well as with Wessex, it helped to fashion a more uniform and united kingdom based on a conception of royal justice and order. On all this, the Church and its bishops were a strong influence. Wulfstan, bishop of Worcester and also archbishop of York, seems to have been the genius behind the drafting of some of the law-codes of Æthelred II and Cnut. And the incorporation of the laws of royal predecessors actually strengthened a king's position and grafted the reputation of earlier kings on to his own. Alfred was conscious of this when he composed a prologue to his law-code that linked the tradition of royal law-making with the Bible as the best repository of moral law. On the other hand, legislative power imposed responsibilities on kings, especially the responsibility to ensure order and punish crime, and to modify the self-regulatory habits of an earlier age by limiting the feuds and violent self-help characteristic of community justice.

The fundamental question was: who was and who was not a king to exhibit these qualities of kingship? In Tacitus' day, Germanic peoples were led by noble men of great valour and it is reasonable to suppose that those who led the migrations within and to the British Isles were of a similar calibre. So too would have been the leaders who resisted such invaders. If some of these leaders or warlords established dynasties of kings in the territories they conquered and occupied, as later pedigrees and genealogies claim, this is more likely to have been the result of opportunities grasped, the resources available, and perhaps too a belief that military ability could run in families, rather than of any attachment to ideas of dynastic or hereditary succession. The Roman tradition of provincial government did not suggest such ideas either. Once again Christianity wrought a change, albeit slowly. When it came to choosing a king, old habits and traditions, and

KENNETH MAC ALPIN

(841–858), king of the Scots and Picts

THE most famous of the Scots of Dalriada, his dual monarchy of Dalriada (841) and Pictland (843) is regarded as the beginning of the kingdom of Scotland. He faced enemies on all sides—Picts, Britons, Anglians, and Norse—and shifted the headquarters of his rule to Scone in Perthshire and its ecclesiastical centre to Dunkeld (*c*.849). Kenneth pointed Scotland in new directions, though he chose to be buried in the traditional royal cemetery on Iona. His son, Constantine I, was slain by Norse raiders in 877.

DUNKELD, on the river Tay, Perthshire. The first monastery may have been founded before 700, when Adomnán, who wrote the *Life of St Columba*, settled here. The Pictish King Constantine built a bigger church *c*.815, and *c*.850 King Kenneth mac Alpin brought some of Columba's relics from Iona and made Dunkeld the ecclesiastical centre of his Scottish and Pictish kingdom. Only a carved cross-slab dates from this early period.

practical considerations died hard. At the end of the tenth century, Ælfric could still maintain that 'no man can make himself king, but the people have the power to choose as king whom they please'. But where did they look?

In the seventh century, the first century of Christian kingship in Anglo-Saxon England, men looked to the royal family or kin for their kings, and the act of choosing or 'electing' was made by a body of leading and influential figures, mainly nobles. Within the royal family or kin they scrutinized all adult male descendants of earlier kings. The importance of having an adult as king was publicly stressed, seemingly for the first time, as late as 858, when Æthelwulf of Wessex died; perhaps there was a possibility at that time that the custom might be ignored in favour of the legitimate first-born, regardless of his age. The same custom was observed in contemporary Ireland, if the laws are to be believed: males of a king's descent (known as the *æthelings* in Old English) provided new kings. This meant that a brother, a nephew or a cousin of a king might be chosen in preference to the son of a king. Even bastard youths were regarded as eligible,

THE KING AS JUDGE, from an Anglo-Saxon translation of parts of the Old Testament, written in the early eleventh century and illustrated in contemporary style. The first picture (*below*, and unfinished) shows two crowned kings standing in a roofed and arcaded royal hall of the period, one holding a long spear and ordering a prisoner to be taken into custody by an attendant. The scene is the captivity of Lot after a battle, as recorded in Genesis. The second picture (*facing*, and fully illuminated) shows a king, wearing an open crown, sword unsheathed and a staff in his hand, surrounded by his counsellors, doing justice and ordering an execution. The manuscript may have been written at St Augustine's, Canterbury.

though that had its own hazards, for if the late king's wife still lived she might reasonably resent such a choice. It was the Church which eventually stepped in to disqualify bastards. The legates who visited King Offa's court in 786 had decisive views on the subject:

... we decreed that in the ordination of kings no one shall permit the assent of evil men to prevail, but kings are to be lawfully chosen by the priests and elders of the people, and not to be those begotten in adultery or incest; for just as in our times ... a bastard cannot attain to the priesthood, so neither can he who was not born of a legitimate marriage be the Lord's anointed and king of the whole kingdom and inheritor of the land ... (The legates' report to Pope Hadrian I)

Hope springs eternal: Athelstan, who was made king of Wessex in 924, was Edward the Elder's eldest son and illegitimate. This 'open kingship' which existed in all the kingdoms long after the seventh century—even into the twelfth century in Scotland—meant that rule might occasionally be divided between two or more irresistible claimants (as happened in ninth- and tenth-century Wales); joint kings might be chosen in some instances; violence could accompany the act of choosing; and the crown might easily pass from one line to another within the royal family. Only Pictish kings may have adopted succession in a female line— matrilinear succession—which, in its turn, enabled neighbouring kings, especially those of Dalriada, to marry Pictish princesses and father sons who could succeed in Pictland. That may have given significant impetus to Kenneth mac Alpin's conquest of the Pictish kingdoms by the 840s.

When all is said and done, power and practicalities were the decisive factors. 'Open' choice often drove the losers into exile, there to plot against the new king in order to topple him from his throne. Witness the Wessex exiles in Francia between 789 and 792, and the Northumbrian exiles in Dalriada even earlier, in

the seventh century. Before the robust assertion of Christian kingship in the tenth century, assassination and civil war frequently followed a contested royal election and dynastic feuding was not uncommon among the royal brood in the seventh and eighth centuries—even in dominant Mercia, after the death of King Cenwulf (821). Disputes over the kingship surfaced regularly among the royal family of England in 956, 975, and 1035.

For a king to nominate his son as king during his own lifetime, as did Offa in 787, was one way of reducing the likelihood of such quarrels and disputes, and it is a strategy that seems to have been adopted by Dalriadan kings before the 840s. Indeed, the fewer the male relatives a king had, the more secure he may have felt himself to be and the less fraught the choice of his successor. Neither Æthelberht of Kent nor Offa of Mercia was the son of the previous king; in both cases their dynastic claims stretched back several generations, in Offa's as much as a century. With luck the purging of *æthelings* might bring security too, as Offa believed when he attempted to do just that in order to reduce the number of counter-claims to his throne.

In order to control what was an inherently unstable situation, towards the end of the ninth century the West Saxon kings sought to regulate the succession by a final will or by family agreement, which could be adjusted from time to time as circumstances altered, in the interests of the surviving adult kinsmen. The aim was to transmit the kingship intact to one claimant alone, but at the same time to provide property and satisfaction for his relatives. Even this did not eliminate all violence and counter all claims, as the situation in Wessex after 899 indicates. But it did express a feeling that joint kingship and shared kingship were things of the past: the kingdom of the English should be indivisible.

There remained, of course, scope for choice in the event of lack of agreement or the abandonment of agreement, and in 924 the Mercian witan chose Athelstan as their king. Choice remained an element in the Christian coronation ceremony, and acclamation by nobility and people is still heard at British coronations, though after the crowning, not before it.

The Church's teaching may have begun to influence the choice of a king in the tenth and eleventh centuries, for it was bound to emphasize the importance of the consecrated royal blood that flowed in the veins of the legitimate descendants of kings, especially those born legitimately after their father had become king. In 975 the notion that a son born after his father's consecration should be preferred—a Byzantine practice, be it noted—was actually canvassed. King Edgar's eldest son, Edward, was the first English king to succeed while still a boy (he was about thirteen in 975); and despite his murder three years later, his younger brother Æthelred then secured the throne at the age of only ten. Faction and disorder marked both minorities. Yet, if these ideas were to be accepted, then the field of choice would be limited and the rule of

SILVER PENNY OF KING EDWARD THE MARTYR (d. 978), from the Lincoln mint. Based on the designs of King Edgar, the obverse shows the king, who was murdered while still a young man, wearing a diadem; the legend reads *Eadward rex Anglorum*. (× 2½)

primogeniture—succession by the eldest son of the late king—would be established. Realities dictated that such a development would be gradual, and not until the early thirteenth century did England risk having a minor as king solely because he was the eldest son of the late king; the matter still caused trouble in the fifteenth century. The sword, resources, and the realities of power—these ultimately were the factors governing the choice of a king, even in the later Middle Ages. Valid title was of little account without the ability to induce election, command allegiance, and maintain authority. This was as true in the eleventh century as it had been in the fifth.

Kings

There were literally hundreds of kings in the British Isles between the fifth and the eleventh centuries, if we include the petty kings in Ireland. Even without these, the tally is a long one. And yet we know very little—if anything—about the vast majority of them. As for the remainder, until the ninth century our information is mostly confined to their campaigns and battles, their victories over other kings and their defeats, to judge by the Irish annals and the Chronicles of the Welsh Princes. King-lists, often even the Anglo-Saxon Chronicle, simply record the fact that they had once ruled, whilst genealogies frequently name fathers and sons but not always very accurately. If the dates of the deaths of kings are usually known, that is because they died suddenly and violently; if the dates of their accessions are recorded, it is often because kings won their crowns by killing other kings. If further details are sometimes known to us—churches patronized or monasteries founded by them, even rare character sketches—these most likely refer to Anglo-Saxon kings, for in England a literate class of clergy put pen to parchment on several occasions from the sixth century onwards and composed more rounded impressions of selected Anglo-Saxon kings. Where similar details are known of Scottish, Welsh, or Irish kings, they were written from an English point of view. Pictish kings lie almost completely in the shadows, since no literary memorials of the Picts survive at all.

What we can learn about individual kings and their kinsfolk in the Dark Ages does, however, help us to construct a more personalized picture of the development of monarchy in these islands. What such kings and their relatives looked like, we can hardly say. None has, I think, been disinterred as has Charlemagne, whose tomb in Aachen Cathedral revealed him to be a man over six feet tall. The art of portraiture barely survived the decay of Roman civilization and was not properly revived until the later Middle Ages. And yet, the famous silver pennies issued by King Offa and struck by highly skilled native artists and sculptors using late Classical models, carry distinctive representations of both Offa and Queen Cynethryth which just possibly may be portraits of the Mercian king and his consort. Of the spoken or written words of these early kings, nothing as impressive is certainly known. The closest we get to the authentic views of an Anglo-Saxon king is in King Alfred's prologues to translations of Bede's *Ecclesiastical History* and Pope Gregory the Great's *Pastoral Care* which he commissioned and inspired—and had a hand in composing. Alfred's assessment of the state of his kingdom, culturally and spiritually, has the air of a rare analysis by a king of his own times, the sort of analysis which few later kings have had the will or the intelligence to write.

As to the origin of Dark Age kings, after the age of the migrations, it is a fact that until Sweyn Forkbeard, the Dane, was acknowledged by some as king of the English in 1013, in place of the defeated and demoralized Æthelred II, the kings of the English kingdoms were born to the royal family of their own kingdom or else to that of another English kingdom. And the same was true of Irish, Welsh, and Scottish kings before the Vikings established their own kingdoms in the British Isles in the ninth century. Kings of Morgan and Gwent in south-east Wales might intrude themselves into the kingship of Deheubarth, but never into Wessex; the Mercian kings might overcome Kent or East Anglia, but never Gwynedd or Powys; and kings of Dalriada gradually penetrated the Pictish kingdom and Strathclyde, but never Irish kingdoms after the mid-seventh century. In the early eleventh century, however, an overseas Scandinavian dynasty intruded itself into the large alien kingdom of the English and seized its crown. That was unprecedented. It is true that Tolargan (d. 657), the son of the king of Bernicia, had been installed as king of the Picts in the mid-seventh century, but he was probably a puppet-king and certainly was not the first of a new, intrusive dynasty of Anglian origin.

Many royal kinsmen of Wessex were brought up in fosterage away from the West Saxon court, not least because this removed them from the infection of royal intrigue and rivalries. Even the great Edgar was reared in Mercia by Athelstan 'Half-King', rather than by his own father and mother. The fosterage of royal offspring was probably common elsewhere in the British Isles. But in the tenth

CAREW CROSS, Dyfed, one of the most impressive sculptured Celtic crosses in Britain. Standing over 13 ft. high it probably dates from the eleventh century. Its inscription is thought to commemorate Maredudd ab Edwin, king of Deheubarth and great-grandson of King Hywel Dda; he died in battle in 1035. The shaft is decorated with panels of carved interlacing ornament characteristic of Celtic art.

century, in the Anglo-Saxon royal house at least, queens and their households played an important part in the upbringing of potential royal heirs, and this gave queens, whose own significance was growing, opportunities for power and influence should their offspring succeed to the throne.

The rearing of kings was more active than cerebral, still less intellectual, and almost all Dark Age kings were illiterate. If those in East Anglia and Northumbria in the seventh century were able to read or write, that was because they had been educated in Francia or Ireland and were exceptional cases. Not until Alfred and his successors can English kings be placed among the literati, and Alfred himself probably did not learn to read until he was nearly forty, though he then mastered both English and Latin. As for Athelstan, a much underrated intelligence, he is the most famous book-collector among the Anglo-Saxon kings and surely would have been able to read the books he gave to the monasteries he founded or patronized.

The marriages of kings were as carefully and purposefully arranged then as now, though the relative ease with which unwanted wives could be discarded and replaced meant that early kings were able to look on marriage as an instrument of policy that could be adapted to changing circumstances. That being so, it is extraordinary that at a time when the West Saxon dynasty was becoming the focus for a kingship of all England, two of its kings did not marry at all and (so far as we know) fathered no children. They may have denied themselves intentionally in order to limit the claims and counter-claims to the throne that would very likely arise at their death, but for two such kings—Athelstan and Eadred, both sons of King Edward the Elder—to ignore the political value of marriage shows either great self-restraint or foolishness or an overwhelming personal disinclination for the married state. Others, on the other hand, caused trouble by their uxoriousness. Edward the Elder's three wives (and even more children) were to result in disputes and divisions once Edward was dead, and so did Edgar's three sons by his two wives: Edward 'the Martyr' and Æthelred became the focus of rival factions after their father's death in 975 and the consequence was Edward's murder three years later.

As far as we can tell—and there is much about queens and kings' consorts that we do not know, frequently even their names—most kings chose a wife from among their own nobility, or sometimes from the royal or noble families of neighbouring kingdoms. No Mercian, Northumbrian, or West Saxon king before the ninth century is known to have married other than the daughter of another Anglo-Saxon king—certainly not a Welsh, Irish, or Scottish woman. If Oswiu of Northumbria took as his first wife Fina, the daughter of the Irish 'high king' of the Uí Néill, it may simply have been because he was in exile during his brother Oswald's reign; he is known to have visited Iona and to have sought refuge in Dalriada, and he may have travelled to Ireland. Similarly, if the Leinster royal house married several times among the Scots of Dalriada in the sixth and seventh centuries, it was because Dalriada was as much an Irish kingdom as a Scottish one at that time, only a century or two after the migration from Antrim. Even the Kentish kings, who were in close touch with the continent, sought wives from across the Channel on only two occasions. In the late sixth and early seventh centuries, when contacts with the Franks were flourishing, Æthelberht the pagan married Bertha, daughter of Charibert, the Christian Merovingian king of Paris, and their son Eadbald married Emma, who was also the daughter of a Frankish king.

KING ATHELSTAN (d. 939) portrayed presenting Bede's *Lives of St Cuthbert* to the saint himself. The manuscript was given by Athelstan to St Cuthbert's shrine on a visit in 934. This frontispiece is the earliest surviving presentation picture produced in England.

In Ireland, too, neighbouring kings, even long-standing enemies, took brides from across borders that were usually hostile and stained with blood. The aim on both sides may have been to extend influence, seal treaties, or forge alliances, though such queens were just as likely to be ineffective as effective in preventing further violence. When the Viking kingdoms were established round the Irish Sea, their kings generally married Norse women. But several in Ireland did marry into Irish dynasties in the late ninth and early tenth centuries. Olaf, king of Dublin, put away his queen, the daughter of the Norse king of the Hebrides, when an opportunity arose for him to marry a daughter of Kenneth mac Alpin, king of Scots; whatever political gain he may have made by this second match must be balanced by the likely hostility he invited by ending the first. Kenneth mac Alpin's father may earlier have married a Norse queen in an effort to come to terms with the fierce naval and military power on his western flank. This, incidentally, is the earliest evidence we have of an alliance between a native dynasty in the British Isles and the marauding Vikings.

There were exceptions to the common practice of kings marrying within a comparatively narrow geographical compass, especially when there were important political, diplomatic, military, or dynastic prospects. Before and after the extinction of all but the West Saxon dynasty, the English kings carefully considered the possibility of foreign alliances on several occasions. When Charlemagne proposed to Offa, king of Mercia, that his eldest son should marry Offa's daughter, the Mercian responded with a suggestion that at the same time Charlemagne's daughter should marry his eldest son and heir, Ecgfrith; Charlemagne took offence and broke off the negotiations. Yet such foreign matches became more frequent in the ninth and tenth centuries. On his way back from Rome in 856, King Æthelwulf took as his queen Judith, the daughter of Charles the Bald, king of the Franks. Just as Offa's plan had been to enhance the reputation of his Mercian kingship in European halls, so Æthelwulf may consciously have regarded his marriage as one means of securing an alliance with the most powerful monarchy in Christendom in order to withstand the Viking menace. His son by an earlier marriage, Æthelbald, took care not to lose this advantage by himself marrying his stepmother once his father was dead. Similar considerations moved Æthelred II in 1002, when he took as his second wife Emma, the sister of Richard II, duke of Normandy; partly because of its Scandinavian origins, Normandy was a haven for Viking fleets attacking England. Whatever his faults, Æthelred saw clearly that by this marriage he might neutralize the Viking menace in at least this one significant sector. His successor in England, Cnut the Dane, was astute enough to realize the value of Emma, a widow since 1016: by marrying her he could bind his Norman cousins to him and, at the same time, signal to his English subjects that the new dynasty need not involve too radical a change in England. There may be an echo of the desire of

KING CNUT AND HIS QUEEN, EMMA OF NORMANDY, the widow of King Æthelred II. In this picture from Winchester's New Minster register, or Book of Life, they are shown presenting a gold altar cross to the New Minster. The book was written *c.*1031, and a few years later (1035) Cnut was buried at Winchester.

RHODRI MAWR ('THE GREAT')

(844–878), king of Gwynedd, Powys, and Deheubarth

His achievement in uniting for the first time the three largest kingdoms of early Wales inspired others to attempt the same, and later dynasties in Gwynedd and Deheubarth emphasized their descent from him. He acquired Gwynedd (844) from his father, Powys (855) from his mother, and Deheubarth (872) through his wife; by his own abilities he defeated the Vikings (856). Rhodri was forced into exile (876) by the Vikings and after his return he was slain by the Mercians.

Æthelwulf and Æthelred to keep the Vikings at bay in the marriage which Kenneth II of the Scots contracted in the tenth century with a Leinster queen; the kingdoms of both were trying to cope with bands of Viking settlers, and they may have identified the best possibility of effective resistance in alliance with each other.

In Wales marriage was one of the means—sheer naked force was another—whereby larger kingdoms and more powerful kings were able to subdue others and create 'over-kingships', albeit of a highly personal and temporary sort. Rhodri Mawr ('the Great'), who inherited dominion over Gwynedd and Powys by 855, by his marriage to Angharad, daughter of the king of Ceredigion and Carmarthenshire, was able to create (872) a kingship whose sway extended to every corner of Wales except the south-east and the far south-west. His grandson, Hywel Dda ('the Good'), married Elen, daughter of the last king of Dyfed, so that by the time that Hywel died (c.949) only the kingdoms in Glamorgan and Gwent lay beyond his control.

In the north, marriage had played a part in forging relations between the Anglo-Saxon kingdom of Northumbria and the surviving British kingdoms on its northern flank. King Oswiu's marriage to a princess of Rheged may have been the decisive step in bringing that ancient kingdom under Anglian control. Further north and later still, cultural interpenetration took place between the intrusive Scots of Dalriada and the indigenous Picts, and the marriage between Fergus, king of Dalriada (d. 781), and the daughter of a Pictish king may have been the first of several royal marriages that ultimately enabled Fergus's descendant, Kenneth mac Alpin, to rule in both kingdoms three-quarters of a century later. Duncan I, king of Scots (d. 1040), married a cousin of Siward, earl of Northumbria, no doubt to strengthen his hand through a southern alliance with the most independent of the nobles in the new English kingdom. His aim was to counter the power of his kinsman and enemy, Macbeth, who dominated northern Scotland; but the alliance could not prevent Macbeth from killing Duncan and deepening the cultural rift between the northern ways of Macbeth and influences from south of the English border.

AN ENTHRONED KING, crowned and with an unsheathed sword, depicted with his queen and son passively seated to one side, and his armed nobles listening to his exhortation. These figures are inserted in an Anglo-Saxon narrative (*c.* AD 1000) of *Genesis*, and are intended to illustrate the story of Cain (the enthroned figure).

In the first centuries of Christian kingship in England, spiritual 'conquest' as much as political alliances or territorial absorption was likely to be the motive in the search for a royal bride. Although the circumstances in which Queen Bertha, of the Merovingian royal house, met and married King Æthelberht of Kent are now beyond recall, she was accompanied to England by the bishop of Senlis; later, in 597, Pope Gregory the Great sent Augustine and his band of monks to conduct a mission to the pagan English. The plan worked, despite Æthelberht's death and his son's reversion to paganism. Although King Rædwald's aggressively pagan queen may have made Rædwald and his East Anglian kingdom ambivalent towards the new faith, despite his conversion at the Kentish court, King Edwin of Northumbria's marriage to the Christian Æthelburg of Kent, performed by Paulinus, the Christian bishop sent to York in about 625, established the Cross of Christ at Northumbria's court. In the atmosphere of Church reform in the tenth century, West Saxon queens could still play a vital role: King Edgar's first wife was instrumental in revitalizing the ideal of a regular life for nuns and was responsible for founding nunneries in her husband's kingdom.

The greater stress placed by the Church on the sanctity of marriage and the rights of legitimate children underscored the growing importance attached to the wives and consorts of kings in several parts of the British Isles by the ninth century, and gave heavier emphasis to the status and position of queens. This was reflected in their more public profile and, in England, their own coronation ceremony. King Offa had associated his queen, Cynethryth, with him on his new coinage. Æthelwulf of Wessex had attended (and presumably approved) the

SILVER PENNY STRUCK BY KING OFFA
FOR HIS QUEEN, CYNETHRYTH. The
bust on the obverse seems to be an
image of the queen, with flowing locks.
The inscription *Eoba* is that of the
moneyer. (x 8)

public consecration of his Frankish bride Judith in Rheims in 856, though a
Frankish chronicler noted that this was 'something hitherto unusual for him or his
people', and the ceremony is the first known instance of the anointing of an
English king's queen. Bishop Asser, in his book of reminiscences about Alfred,
could still maintain that 'the people of the West Saxons do not suffer a queen to sit
next to a king, nor do they even permit her to be called a queen but only wife of a
king'. Queens had had a significant role in the age of the conversion of the
English, but the more formal elevation of queenship seems to be a novel feature
of a later period. When Edgar arranged his special coronation at Bath in 973,
Queen Ælfthryth was anointed at his side.

The consequence was that English queens assumed a prominent political
role—even a mischievous one—in the tenth century. With the rules of royal
succession still uncertain, and with some English kings taking more than one wife
and siring more than one royal brood, a queen who survived her husband could
be crucial in advancing the fortunes of her sons. Eadgifu, the wife of Edward the
Elder, was openly acknowledged to be queen and she proved a key figure when
her sons, Edmund and Eadred, succeeded in turn to the throne left vacant by the
death of the illegitimate, unmarried, and childless Athelstan. She played an
important role, too, in securing the accession of her youngest son, Edgar, in 959.
Then, when Edgar himself died in 975, his queen Ælfthryth, who had worked
hard for the designation of her son Æthelred as his father's successor during
Edgar's lifetime, took care of Æthelred when her stepson Edward succeeded to
the throne; she may even have had a hand three years later in Edward's murder,
which paved the way for Æthelred's accession. Until her death round about 1000,
long after Æthelred had become king, Queen Ælfthryth dominated the court,
brought up Æthelred's own sons, and so completely eclipsed his first wife that we
are not even sure of her name. Nor is it too fanciful to suggest that Ælfthryth
murdered her first husband so that she could marry King Edgar!

EDWARD THE ELDER

(899–924), king of the West Saxons

... many people who had been under the rule of the Danes both in East Anglia and in Essex submitted to him; and all the army in East Anglia swore agreement with him, that they would [agree to] all that he would, and would keep peace with all with whom the king wishes to keep peace, both at sea and on land.

(Anglo-Saxon Chronicle, 917)

THOUGH overshadowed by his father Alfred and upstaged by his son Athelstan, it was Edward who reconquered much of England from the Danes (909–19), permanently united Mercia with Wessex (918–19), established an administration for the kingdom of England, and secured the allegiance of Danes, Scots, Britons, and English. Well educated and well trained by Alfred, he nevertheless had to overcome a rival for the throne (899–903). Using Alfred's methods and in alliance with Mercia, he spread English influence and control. The Danes of Northumbria were defeated (910) at Tettenhall (Staffs.), the Viking kingdom of York acknowledged his power (918), and most Welsh kings submitted to him. In 921 the submission not only of Viking York and Northumbria but also of the kings of Strathclyde and the Scots gave his kingdom primacy in the British Isles. Edward was a patient planner and systematic organizer as well as a bold soldier. By the time he died, he had completed the New Minster at Winchester where

SILVER PENNY OF KING EDWARD THE ELDER (d. 924). On the reverse is a building which, though based on Roman models, probably represents the newly fortified burhs established by Edward and his sister, Æthelflæd, in Mercia. The moneyer's name, Eadmund, appears in two lines of lettering. (× 3)

he himself was buried. Though twice married, his eldest son and successor, Athelstan, was the son of a mistress.

The reform movement in the tenth-century Church, which helped to raise the status of the king's legitimate wife, benefited from the patronage of these queens. Edgar's first wife was an eager advocate of the regular life for women and a founder of nunneries. Emma of Normandy, the queen of two kings who survived to be queen mother under a third, was among the most powerful figures in England in the first half of the eleventh century. She may even have taken the initiative in proposing marriage to her second husband, Cnut, in order to perpetuate a position which her sons by Æthelred II were as yet too young to ensure; and it was she who seized the royal treasure at Winchester in a bid to influence the succession when Cnut died.

Moreover, queens in tenth-century England needed a personal endowment to give them a certain degree of independence and some scope for patronage. The queen's household, though inevitably an offshoot of the king's, emerged for the first time as an organized entourage which enabled a queen to act independently and even politically, especially if her sons were at her side.

A king's children could be both a danger and an asset. In kingdoms where all the adult males among the royal kin—the *æthelings*, as they were known in England—had a claim to the throne, the upbringing, control, and marriage of the royal youngsters were matters of cardinal importance. A wayward son, such as Edmund Ironside, the son of Æthelred II who married in defiance of his father and established his own rule in Northumbria and Mercia in 1015, was a threat to the kingship itself. Æthelwulf of Wessex in the mid-ninth century seems to have tried to settle his sons' future relations by agreement and his last will 'so that his sons should not dispute *unduly* among themselves after their father's death' (reported Asser of St David's, in his contemporary biography of Æthelwulf's youngest son, King Alfred); and despite some strains he seems to have been successful. But at other times such arrangements soon collapsed. Events in mid-eleventh-century England illustrate the fact that stable relationships depended on restraint, forbearance, and ambition rather than on agreement and a dead man's last will and testament. As the status and power of queens grew, their intervention could destroy such agreements if their own offspring were faced with rival claimants to the throne. Later in the Middle Ages, cadet branches of the royal kin often supported their royal kinsmen. But in Anglo-Saxon England this was exceptional; the temptations were too strong so long as the rules of succession remained imprecise. The line of Athelstan 'Half-King', a West Saxon thegn whose father was of royal descent, placed itself loyally at the disposal of the house of Cerdic in tenth-century East Anglia and Mercia; but this was a relatively rare instance of royal kinsfolk being diverted into thegnhood in the service of the royal house.

As for the king's daughters, care was shown in arranging their marriages because they would transmit the royal blood to their husbands' families; the problem was solved at one extreme by shunting several Anglo-Saxon royal girls into nunneries. Furthermore, social conditions in the Anglo-Saxon and other kingdoms allowed kings to take concubines, whose offspring frequently were acknowledged by their fathers and accorded a special place. The Church might frown on such behaviour—especially in the reformist atmosphere of the tenth century—but injunctions like those of the papal legates at King Offa's court in 786 were not observed. The illegitimate Athelstan succeeded to Wessex's throne even though he had legitimate, though younger, brothers living.

More frequently, the marriages of royal offspring had political, dynastic, diplomatic, or territorial advantages to commend them. As the West Saxon dynasty gradually asserted its primacy in England in the ninth century and then, when standing virtually alone, defeated its enemies in the British Isles, it showed itself adept at securing foreign recognition and foreign allies by utilizing the sons and daughters of its kings. In the 890s Alfred married one of his daughters to Baldwin II, count of Flanders, a naval power of strategic importance at a time when the Vikings were raiding and settling in eastern England. Edward the Elder and Athelstan, who later were bent on expanding their kingdom at the expense of the Vikings, were anxious that the invaders should not receive aid on the continent. Several of Edward's daughters were therefore dispatched to key rulers of western Europe: Eadgifu to Charles the Simple, king of the Franks (*c*.916–19), Eadhild to Hugh the Great, duke of the Franks (926), Eadgyth to Otto, later emperor of the Germans (930), and Ælfgifu probably to Conrad, king of Burgundy—and yet another daughter married Louis, prince of Aquitaine. This was an impressive and far from fortuitous series of links, largely designed for political and territorial ends. Of all the kings of the British Isles, it was Athelstan who showed greatest imagination in harnessing these female relatives of his— and yet he fathered no children of his own! Later on, Æthelred II and Emma married their daughter to Drew, count of Mantes. Æthelred needed allies wherever he could find them against the Vikings and his wife's French connections provided some.

Vikings had to be combated at home with even greater urgency. As it turned out, Alfred's decision to marry his eldest daughter, the courageous Æthelflæd, to the ealdorman of Mercia, Æthelred, was a stroke of genius: she proved a notable ruler in her own right after her husband's death and a worthy counterpart to her brother, Edward the Elder, when he was forcing back the Viking conquerors. In 926 King Athelstan even arranged the marriage of his sister to the Viking king of York, Sihtric, as part of a far-sighted policy of extending West Saxon power throughout England, whether it be in English-held territory or not.

Similar considerations underpinned the efforts of Malcolm II of Scotland to extend his royal authority into the Viking-dominated Northern Isles of his kingdom. He married his daughter to Sigurd, earl of Orkney, and established good relations with him and with their son Thorfinn when he succeeded in 1014. Even earlier, Kenneth mac Alpin had used his daughter in a not dissimilar way in the context of the pressure which Scottish kings of the ninth and tenth centuries exerted on the British kingdom of Strathclyde: Kenneth's daughter married Rhun, the Strathclyde king. Their son proved to be the last effective king of his line, so that the marriage was a significant step on the road to the absorption of the old kingdom by the newer Scottish kingdom a century later. On other occasions, the daughters of Scottish kings were sent across the sea to marry Norse kings of Dublin: Olaf of Dublin married Kenneth mac Alpin's daughter in the mid-ninth century and Constantine II's married Olaf III Guthfrithsson in the 930s. The intention was to contain the Viking menace and establish a more stable relationship with the Norsemen of Ireland through royal marriage—and perhaps too, in the latter case, to check the advance of Wessex in northern England.

Personal links between kings and clergy were strong in the British Isles, and
perhaps strongest where the Irish brand of Christianity was dominant, with its
emphasis on the penitential and ascetic life. In the earliest centuries of Christian
kingship, the sixth and seventh centuries, a number of kings even abandoned
kingship and embraced the religious life. Several in Anglo-Saxon England
entered monasteries, and so did Maelgwn Gwynedd, king of Gwynedd, as well as
a number of Irish kings in the late eighth century (as many as five became monks
within twelve years). Clerics were even chosen as kings in Ireland in the ninth
century, perhaps under the strain of the Viking assaults when every source of
resistance had to be mustered. Pilgrimages attracted some early kings, especially
the pilgrimage to Rome, though Irish kings had less ambitious destinations.
Æthelwulf of Wessex travelled to Rome as king in 856 and so did Macbeth in
1050. But such demonstrations of Christian kingship were less common in later
centuries, despite the renewed enthusiasm for Church reform. It may be that to
discharge the responsibilities of kingship properly was demonstration enough of
devotion to the faith.

In death, Christian kingship was elevated by sacred rituals during the Dark
Ages. Among the all-too-frequent instances of violent death among kings in the
British Isles, more so in the kingdoms of Ireland than elsewhere and in the earlier
centuries than in the later, are to be found occasional cases of royal sanctification
and martyrdom that were exploited to serve political and dynastic purposes. The
burial of kings, too, acquired its own elaborate ritual, marking the Christian king
off from other men even in death. To judge by recent excavations, Mercian kings
seem to have regarded Repton Church and its large crypt as their royal
mausoleum. Winchester assuredly became the mausoleum of the West Saxon
royal family. The Old Minster, adjacent to the royal palace, was built by King
Cenwahl in 648, and he and his successors were buried there—some were even

crowned there—until a much grander New Minster was built nearby in the tenth century. The kings of Northumbria may not have had a single mausoleum of this kind, but it is significant that King Oswald placed the relics of the first Christian king of Northumbria, Edwin, in the New Minster at York when it was finished in the mid-seventh century. And even the Danish king of York, Guthfrith, a convert to Christ, was buried in the Minster in 895, perhaps

THE CRYPT OF THE ANGLO-SAXON MONASTERY AT REPTON, Derbyshire. It apparently became a mausoleum of Mercian kings in the eighth and ninth centuries. Kings Æthelbald, Wiglaf, and Wystan were buried here and apparently venerated.

ATHELSTAN

(924–939), king of the West Saxons and Mercians, and king of the English

... I, Athelstan, king of the English, elevated by the right hand of the Almighty, which is Christ, to the throne of the whole kingdom of Britain ...

(Charter to the church of York, 934)

THE eldest, but illegitimate, son of Edward the Elder, he was admired during the Middle Ages almost as much as Alfred; what a pity the contemporary *Life* is lost! Unique among West Saxon kings in having been brought up in Mercia, this gave him an advantage in imposing his rule beyond Wessex. Overcoming opposition to his accession (924–5), he gained recognition from other kings in the British Isles and on the Continent, partly by astute royal marriages. He was cultivated by foreign monarchs, with whom he had fruitful cultural and religious contacts. As a result of his military conquests in the British Isles, his overlordship was recognized by Vikings, Scots, English, and Welsh, and was greater than that of any previous English king. Only in his last years was his hegemony challenged by Scots and Vikings (934), though it is the measure of his stature that on his expedition to Scotland he was joined by three Welsh kings, two archbishops, fourteen bishops, and Scandinavian and English nobles. A Joshua among his enemies, he never lost a battle, and when his foes again invaded northern England (937), he routed them at Brunanburh, one of the decisive battles of English history long celebrated in song and verse. He seems an eccentric figure, neither marrying nor fathering children, and preferring burial at Malmesbury where no royal predecessor was buried. His councils were attended by underkings, bishops, and Scandinavian and English nobles,

SILVER PENNY OF KING ATHELSTAN (d. 939), from the Norwich mint, depicting a crowned king. The crown is not dissimilar to that in the picture of the king in the *Lives of St Cuthbert*, but here the king is shown beardless after the Roman habit. (× 3¼)

and his travels took him throughout England. In his charters he advanced pretensions that would have been understood in Carolingian and Byzantine Europe. His expressions of piety were prodigious, for he collected relics by the cartload and patronized many churches. A man of decision, fearless energy, and vision, he built on the achievements of others: he also shaped his own times and yet stood out from them.

resuming a practice favoured by the Northumbrian kings. Iona, queen among Christian shrines in Dark Age Britain, home of the Columban mission to the Scots and northern English, continued to be the burial place of Scottish kings even after St Columba's relics were translated, some to Ireland and some to Dunkeld, by Kenneth mac Alpin in the mid-ninth century. A long line of Dalriadan and Scottish kings, from the sons of mac Alpin to Macbeth (d. 1050) and Donald Bane (d. 1097), were buried there in a tradition which associated Scotland's holiest shrine with Scotland's kings and which weathered the Viking storms of the ninth and tenth centuries.

Monarchy

In an important sense, 'Monarchy' may be regarded as the governmental, institutional, and administrative framework of kingship, the means by which kings ordered the lives of their subjects. If such a framework is exceedingly intricate and complex in the modern British monarchy, in the early Middle Ages it was spare and sketchy, and the evidence for its existence is quite scanty. In the centuries when kings were primarily warlords, their responsibilities and range of activities in their communities and kingdoms were limited. Moreover, most kingdoms were then so small that complex and sophisticated institutions were unnecessary when the king could achieve all that passed for government and administration face to face with both his greater and lesser subjects. And these petty monarchies served well enough and for a very long time in Ireland, which never experienced conquest or drastic political and social transformation in the Dark Ages. When Viking raiders and settlers arrived on its eastern seaboard, the intense patriotism and particularism of centuries stood the test; the collapse of 'high kingships' that were ephemeral, even nominal, were mere ripples on the sea of monarchies that survived beneath the surface.

A kingship with few governmental powers required few administrative structures. Small kingdoms could be managed, controlled, and dominated by messengers and by word of mouth; they required few administrative procedures or techniques, still less institutions. Monarchies were simplistic, limited in their powers and their responsibilities.

By the year 1000, the picture in Ireland seems not to have changed a great deal in its essentials, and perhaps not greatly in Wales either. Even in Scotland the stability and authority achieved by kings of the Scots do not appear to have involved any significant growth of monarchical institutions that might fundamentally alter the powers and actions of kings in relation to their subjects. But in England, particularly as its kings struggled to avoid complete defeat by the Vikings, a monarchical system evolved which enhanced the powers of English kings and produced a range of institutions and new methods of government, some of which were to characterize the British monarchy down to the twentieth century.

Because monarchy seems to have changed so slowly in Ireland, Wales, and, until it was overtaken by the Scots of Dalriada, in Pictland, it is easier to observe early monarchy at work in these sparse Celtic lands. What royal organization there was revolved around the royal estates, be they fortresses as in Ireland and Scotland or 'vills' as in the Anglo-Saxon kingdoms. The kings, with their powers to exploit land and people, were supported by the dues and services demanded of neighbouring settlements, which were organized in a direct and simple fashion to support the king and his companions. This seems to have been the pattern, too, in the monarchies of Kent and Northumbria, and doubtless in others besides. By

HYWEL DDA ('THE GOOD')

(*c*.904–949/50), king of the West Welsh

. . . the head and glory of all the Britons . . .

(*Brut y Tywysogyon*: *Chronicle of the Princes*)

CALLED 'good' by the early twelfth century, he was the grandson of Rhodri Mawr, king of Gwynedd. He and his brother inherited Seisyllwg (modern Carmarthenshire and Cardiganshire) from their father, but in 920 his brother died and Hywel became sole ruler. He controlled Dyfed from *c*.904 following his marriage to Elen, probably the daughter of its last king. In 942 he became ruler of Gwynedd and Powys too. Yet faced with Viking attacks, he acknowledged Edward the Elder (918) and Athelstan (927) as overlord, frequented their courts and learned much from them: like Alfred he travelled to Rome (928), he called his son Edwin, and, perhaps, he minted silver pennies—if so, the only Welsh ruler to do so. There is a strong tradition that he was also a legislator. The earliest surviving text of 'The Laws of Hywel Dda' dates from the early thirteenth century, but parts seem older and may well have been first codified by Hywel. His reputation has never been undermined, though his kingdom disintegrated after his death.

THE SO-CALLED SILVER PENNY OF KING HYWEL DDA with its legend *Rex Houel*. If this, the only coin thought to have been minted for a Welsh king, is indeed his coin, then it was minted at English Chester, not in Wales. (× 3)

the end of the seventh century, this pattern may have involved a crude means of assessment—by the geographical division of the hide, for example—in order to make the burdens imposed by kings tolerable, but if this was monarchy it was indeed simplistic. It is far from clear to us today that there was any remnant of Roman systems underlying such arrangements. The government of these earliest monarchies rested more squarely on the practices and customs of the communities themselves than on authority associated with kingship and imposed by kings. This was so in early Welsh kingdoms, even those with a veneer of Romanization and easy communication with Anglo-Saxon kingdoms from the seventh century onwards. There is no clear sign that their kings had substantial powers of government or law-making, or that it was their regal authority that maintained law and order and gave justice. The obligations of kings and the functions of monarchies were decidedly limited and confined mainly to soldiering. If Gildas, writing like an asp about the sixth-century Welsh kingdoms, expected his kings to judge and keep domestic peace, he placed greater emphasis on their duty to defend and protect the Church. Christian and other peoples stressed the military capabilities of their rulers and their efficiency as leaders and conquerors.

Monarchy was, in truth, a military phenomenon. Kings had their responsibilities, but they were mainly those of protector and victorious warrior.

In Ireland, even the most powerful of 'high kings' had no rights or direct authority outside their own petty kingdom (or *tuath*); if they enjoyed a dominance, it was personal, not institutional. Lesser kings might acknowledge personal overlordship; they might attend an overlord's assembly or court; they might even pay tribute in cattle and kind and contribute men to his host. But not even the great 'over-kings' of Munster had other than a personal sway over the kingdoms subject to them. Still less had the 'high kings' of all Ireland when they began to appear in the ninth century. 'High kingship' was a personal prize. At no stage did it imply an Irish monarchy, with governmental authority over the entire island. 'High kings' reigned but hardly ruled.

The same may well have been true of the 'over-kings' of the Picts before their extinction in the ninth century. The kings of Atholl and Fortrui (between the rivers Forth and Tay) owed personal allegiance to the 'over-kings' of the Picts, and there may have been petty kingdoms beneath them on the Irish pattern. But

THE CROSS OF CONG, made, according to its inscription, in 1122–36 to house a piece of the True Cross. It commemorates Turlough O'Connor (d. 1156), king of Connacht (1106) and high king of Ireland (1121), who had obtained the relic.

their own powers were meagre, the governmental organization of their superiors non-existent. It was a world of warrior kingship, exploiting kingdoms directly and personally, the kings face to face with their communities.

It is no accident that down to the eleventh century (and sometimes beyond) regal titles preserved the notion that kings were kings of their communities rather than of kingdoms: *rex Merciorum* and *rex Anglorum*, rather than *rex Angliae*, expressed the close personal relationship which they had with their communities and peoples, in whom for long resided the effective authority of monarchy.

This picture changed gradually and at different speeds in different kingdoms under the influence of sometimes different factors and in response to different geographical and anthropological circumstances. For example, the Anglo-Saxon kings were much more open to continental influences, especially from the vast creative empire of Charlemagne in the late eighth and ninth centuries, influences that eased monarchy in England along paths familiar in western Europe—even, in a few respects, in far-off Byzantium. On the other hand, the Vikings conquered more than half of England, including some of the prosperous and best organized parts, but they did no more than establish peripheral kingdoms in the north and west of Scotland, leaving the kingdom of Kenneth mac Alpin to develop largely unhindered. This meant that the strain of reconquest was not present in Scotland to foster institutions of royal authority as quickly as it did in Alfred's England. Moreover, the wealth of Anglo-Saxon kingdoms in the seventh century, as reflected in the dazzling artefacts and war equipment unearthed in the burial mounds at Sutton Hoo, underpinned monarchical institutions in ways which could not be copied in poorer lands. In Ireland the tribalism of its communities made it impossible for kingdoms to submerge their differences and loyalties to a degree sufficient to allow provincial monarchies to evolve easily.

Itinerant kings of small kingdoms had no need of elaborate structures of government and administration, except possibly to assess, collect, and store the dues which their peoples were obliged to provide for them and their warband. Early Welsh kings, their shadows reflected in the more antique portions of their laws, toured their estates and were sustained by the community. Royal itineraries were planned according to the siting of royal estates (or vills), where the routines of royalty were played out. Kings in much later ages continued to travel for a host of reasons—politics, religion, sport, and leisure. If royal assemblies seemed periodically advisable, they could be held *en route*, sometimes at royal hunting lodges. Even where monarchical structures were more sophisticated, West Saxon kings of the tenth century, whose authority was gradually fanning out to the northernmost parts of England, generally travelled from estate to estate in southern England, and issued most of their charters in Wessex, the royal homeland. Not until Edgar's day did they found monasteries of the reformed sort in the midlands and north on the model of Glastonbury, Malmesbury, or

Winchester. Even Canterbury was not a regular destination of English kings before the martyrdom of Thomas Becket (1170) provided the cathedral town with a notable shrine.

This is not to deny that these early kings had certain favourite or much frequented residences, and particular fortresses to which they could retire in emergencies. The revealing excavations at Yeavering in the Cheviots have unearthed a seventh-century palace of the Northumbrian kings, built inside an earlier British complex doubtless overrun at the time of the Anglian migration northwards; it seems to have been more than a temporary hunting box or summer residence. London was the early capital of the Middlesex kingdom, developing alongside Roman fortifications that still stand in part today. Gregory the Great intended it as the seat of an archbishop for the English, so much better was its geographical position than that of any other royal capital. Canterbury, too, had been the centre of a kingdom, Kent, in which Kentish kings had a number of other estates and residences (like Reculver) between which they constantly travelled. At the time of the extinction of the Kentish kingdom in the ninth century, Canterbury had a street plan that was the basis of the later medieval borough, and it too grew inside Roman walls. That Rendlesham was a favoured seat of the East Anglian kings in the seventh century is suggested by what seems to be a royal and community burial ground only four miles away at Sutton Hoo. Provided a kingdom was compact, a main fortress-residence could be

THE BURIAL GROUND AT SUTTON HOO, Suffolk. Aside from the much earlier burials roundabout, there are seventeen burial mounds of Dark Age date, of which the largest has been excavated. Its treasures were probably associated with King Rædwald. The burial ground is only four miles from the royal centre of the East Angles at Rendlesham.

associated with outlying estates to ease the burden of supporting whatever monarchical structures early kings needed. It is easy to imagine that something very similar existed in the petty kingdoms of Ireland, with Tara, Armagh, and Cashel as substantial fortified residences; and in western Scotland by the eighth century, Dunadd was the pre-eminent stronghold of Dalriada.

The expansion of kingdoms, and the subjugation of weaker kings by the more powerful, need not have created governmental structures even if the itinerant king were unable to meet the various parts of his subject community regularly. This is the lesson of Ireland and Wales, and of the relationship between Strathclyde and the kingdom of Scotland in the ninth and tenth centuries; it is, too, the lesson of those great conquerors among the Anglo-Saxon kings who were later called *bretwaldas*. Even Offa, master of the kingdoms south of the Humber (apart from Wessex), controlled lesser English kings by force or marriage, allowing them to remain in their kingdoms provided they acknowledged his power and will; he did not attempt to erect administrative and governmental structures that would absorb their kingdoms in Mercia.

THE HILL OF TARA, CO. Meath. The site dates to as early as the second millennium BC. The larger circles are ring-forts enclosed within a hill long known as 'the royal enclosure', which dates from the early Iron Age. The left-hand circle is traditionally the coronation place of pre-Christian Irish kings. The continued sanctity of the site is indicated by later burials in the mound.

The remarkable expansion of Wessex in the tenth century and the ambition of its kings to release all the old Anglo-Saxon kingdoms from Viking thraldom, inevitably posed questions of organization and administration that were beyond an itinerant monarch's capacity to resolve. Instead, the augmented resources of Wessex's monarchy enabled the creation of a more permanent monarchical system based on the existing royal estates and on newer fortress-burhs or -towns which in any case had precedents in planned Mercian towns such as Hereford and Tamworth. These became centres of administrative units, the hundreds and the wapentakes, with royal agents (or reeves) supervising not only the dues and payments of earlier days, but also the newer institutions of a more sophisticated government that ultimately became the English monarchy. No other kingdom in the British Isles had the opportunity to show such resilience or the capacity for such creativity in the early Middle Ages. Alfred began the process by combining Offa's legal pronouncements with those of himself and his predecessors in Wessex, in an attempt to blend Wessex and Mercian custom. He had such success that by the tenth century community custom and royal law were common to both kingdoms, with only minimal differences between them. In religion, he sought to extend his educational and ecclesiastical reforms throughout Wessex and Mercia, and copies of his translation of Pope Gregory's *Pastoral Care* were produced for distribution to the bishops in both kingdoms. If literacy and education in English could be effectively spread, his peoples would not only be able to read his laws and instructions but would also feel themselves part of a governmental order that bestrode Wessex and Mercia. We should not exaggerate his success, but at least his agents were able to communicate directly with local communities on a common basis in both kingdoms.

In his son's reign, the process went further. Certain details of the West Saxon administration that had served Alfred well were applied beyond West Mercia and the south to reconquered areas in the midlands and East Anglia: the system of raising taxation (or geld), of organizing military service, of employing ealdormen to preside over assemblies, alongside the king's reeves and local bishops. A skeleton structure for more ample and more uniform government was in the making. King Edgar in the 970s even legislated for Northumbria. Before the end of the tenth century there was in existence throughout England a governmental system under royal control, albeit with varying degrees of effectiveness: there were shires in the south and midlands which lasted until 1974; there were hundreds within each shire; the burghal system and planned towns were widespread from the Welsh border to the Humber; geld was assessed and levied throughout the country; and a currency had been developed that was to last until 1971. All this amounted to an extraordinary degree of creativity in government, administrative sophistication, and extended royal control. As a monarchical system it was unique in the British Isles.

EDGAR 'THE PEACEABLE'

(959–975), king of the English

[He] obtained by God's grace the whole dominion of England, and brought back to unity the divisions of the kingdom, and ruled everything so prosperously that those who had lived in former times and remembered his ancestors and knew their deeds of old, wondered very greatly . . .

(Æthelwold's translation of the *Rule of St Benedict*)

HANDSOME and charming, short, slim, and strong, Edgar was the younger son of King Edmund I (939–46) and Queen Ælfgifu, and was probably brought up at the court of his uncle, King Eadred (946–55), and his brother, King Eadwig (955–9). Chosen king in Mercia and the Danelaw in 957, it was only when Eadwig died that he was proclaimed king of all the English. His reputation among European rulers and in the Middle Ages rested partly on his association with Archbishop Dunstan, and his patronage of Bishops Æthelwold and Oswald and the monastic reform movement. The *Regularis concordia* (Monastic Agreement *c*.970) praised him as 'the glorious, by the grace of Christ illustrious king of the English and of the other peoples dwelling within the bounds of the island of Britain'. He was spared Viking attacks and so was able to treat the south and 'the Danelaw' as integral parts of his kingdom. He led an expedition against the king of Gwynedd (*c*.968) and established friendly relations with Kenneth II by ceding Lothian; he conciliated his Danish subjects by employing some in his service. Edgar's dominion was signalled by a series of self-conscious acts *c*.973: his coronation at Bath which was reminiscent of the crowning of his kinsman, Otto the Great, as German emperor (952), and the formal submission of British, Scottish, and Welsh kings at Chester, where they

SILVER PENNY OF KING EDGAR the product of his reform of the coinage. It shows a diademed bust with a legend, *Eadgar rex Anglorum*. After 973 the king was shown facing left rather than right. (× 3¼)

supposedly rowed him on the Dee. He raised new fleets (*shipfyrd*) and was remembered as having sailed round his kingdom every winter and spring! His coinage (*c*.973) was uniform throughout the realm and used as a model during the next two centuries. A stern and uncompromising judge, he instilled order in the realm and promoted effective government. Yet when he died, a succession dispute arose on behalf of his two sons, one of whom, Edward 'the Martyr', was murdered (978).

Some of its elements may have been present in other kingdoms. The military role of kings was as old as kingship itself. Each petty king in the British Isles had his host, though in many cases it may be anachronistic to regard it as anything more than a military entourage, a warband. Some kingdoms had ships organized in fleets, among them the kingdom of Dalriada, for which sea communication between Scotland and Ireland was an early necessity. When Columba visited King Bridei of the Picts in about 565, he discovered, according to his later biographer, Adomnán, that the king had both a host and a navy. And when the masters of the seas, the Vikings, sailed into English waters, the English developed

A LATE-ANGLO-SAXON SHIP OR 'ARK' (*above*), which accompanies an English scriptural poem, *Genesis*, of *c*.1000. The ship appears as built of horizontal planks running from stem to stern; it was propelled by rows of oars, steered by a rear rudder and entered by a lateral ladder. The prow was carved into a ferocious animal design, and the ship presumably had a single sail. The ninth-century cargo boat (*left*) discovered (1970) in the Kent marshes at Graveney is not so very different in construction.

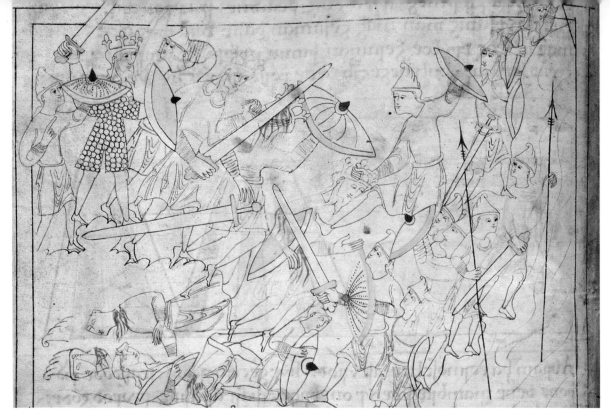

A BLOODY BATTLE SCENE, recorded in an early eleventh-century Anglo-Saxon translation of the early books of the Old Testament. It shows kings, crowned and armed with great swords typical of the Anglo-Saxon period, contending with helmeted soldiers clutching long spears and round shields. The scene is the battle of kings recorded in Genesis; the book seems likely to have been produced at St Augustine's, Canterbury.

a fleet of ships in response. We know most about how the kings of Wessex rose to the Viking challenge: Alfred maintained a protective fleet from 875, and by 893 he was co-ordinating resistance to the nimble enemy by organizing mobile armies which probably depended on levies from the shires. Similar arrangements were very likely used to raise men and crews for his ships. Not for nothing has Alfred been known ever since as the founder of the English navy—a considerable exaggeration, to be sure, but a comment none the less on his initiative in organizing a royal system of defence at sea as well as on land. It was a system that was extended country-wide by his successors.

Even in Welsh kingdoms by the late eleventh century, there was a common obligation to serve in the king's host for the protection of the king and the community. It was probably an ancient obligation, but the practical implications for royal power had only recently been realized as kingdoms grew larger and their kings' commitments grew correspondingly greater.

The defence and control of an early kingdom required few administrative structures. But communications were vital, and among the earliest services to which Dark Age English kings were apparently entitled by the eighth century was the obligation of their peoples to repair bridges (and perhaps roads too in the Irish kingdoms) and construct walls. These activities were crucial to defence, and they reflect a community's fundamental duty in an itinerant kingship to help its king personally. Whether this required much administrative organization is doubtful, at least before the kingdom of Wessex grew larger and operated on a broader front. Then, the massive effort required to roll back the Vikings and to construct burhs and fortified centres meant that this customary obligation was developed in ways that needed precise assessment and careful recording in what became known as 'the Burghal Hidage'. This gave details of the building, manning, and garrisoning of Wessex and Mercian burhs according to their size, the length of their ramparts, and the number of men needed to garrison them. If 'the Burghal Hidage' approximates at all to reality—and there is a striking correlation between the length of the ramparts and the numbers required for garrison duty, 24,000 at Winchester, one of the largest of burhs—a remarkably high proportion of the male able-bodied population was enlisted, most probably by an orderly system of assessment. Such a system for organizing labour, assembling materials, and constructing fortifications for the king is reminiscent in its scale of Edward I's formidable castle-works in North Wales four hundred years later—and hardly less impressive as an achievement of the English monarchy. Yet it is worth remembering that a century earlier, King Offa's Dyke, which extended from the mouth of the Wye to Basingwerk-on-Dee, had required similar organization and effort by a veritable army of workers. Crises of this kind utilized, formalized, and developed an obligation that had evidently existed long before.

Along with armed service (or *fyrd*), which replaced the ancient warband with a king's army, these two services of bridge repair and the maintenance of fortifications came to be known as *trinoda necessitas*, the common burdens or necessities; they were obligations owed by peoples to their kings. Military service doubtless arose out of the aggressive and defensive needs and instincts of early kings, although the more ambitious of them, like the Mercian kings of the eighth

THE ABINGDON SWORD, an iron sword with silver mounts inlaid with niello. It dates from the late ninth or early tenth century, and belonged to an elaborate Anglo-Saxon weapon. Its affinities with King Æthelwulf's ring and the Alfred jewel, its discovery near Abingdon, and its Christian decoration, all suggest an association with King Alfred's entourage.

century, may equally well have been responsible for devising *fyrd* service as a specific obligation on all freemen. And that required organization and assessment which the strain of the Viking wars converted into permanent administrative arrangements. The 'ship sokes' of Edgar's time and Æthelred II's reign, when the hundreds in groups of three were required to raise ships and crews, were a logical extension of the reliance placed by Alfred and his successors on a royal fleet. This organization was paralleled on land by even earlier arrangements based on the hides, so that by the tenth and eleventh centuries one man came from every five hides to do army service. The resources, organization, and powers of settled kingship were rooted in the soil, and Alfred and his successors appreciated that the campaign against the Vikings depended on the continuing prosperity of England's countryside: victory and reconquest would be achieved by good harvests as well as by successful battles. The Anglo-Saxon Chronicle noted this reality when (under the year 893) it described how Alfred 'divided his army in two, so that always half of its men were at home and half out on service, except for those who were to garrison the towns'. In intention, it was a society of beautiful symmetry geared for war under regal direction.

These were the most important of the obligations of kings and peoples, as organized and recorded by monarchical institutions that were developing a notable degree of sophistication. To enforce such obligations was an act of royal authority.

As legislators, too, kings were in frequent communication with their peoples in late Anglo-Saxon England. It had not always been so, for in earlier centuries—and still to some extent in Ireland in the eleventh century—the king's role in law-making and law enforcement was minimal. But in the Welsh kingdoms it seems likely that by the end of our period kings were not only preserving ancient custom but also playing a part in augmenting it, and 150 or 200 years later it seemed quite credible to ascribe the origin of the Welsh law-codes to the early tenth-century king, Hywel Dda. Likewise in England, the king's initiative in law-making had gradually extended beyond codifying custom and ancient law; by the tenth century law-codes were being drawn up from time to time and their content was wide-ranging in both the secular and ecclesiastical fields. In Alfred's reign (probably as a result of his own intellectual and cultural vigour), law-making received new impetus, with the king adding his own glosses to what he reiterated and codified. Legislation and its enforcement came to be a central feature of monarchy, binding peoples to respect and obey their kings' authority. By this stage law-codes were stressing royal rights, royal justice, and royal control in a monarchy where the balance between the king and the community as the fount of law and the dispenser of justice was being perceptibly altered in favour of the king.

The financial organization of kings had its origins in the dues with which

ERIC BLOODAXE

(947–954), king of York

Eric had so great an army [in 954] that five kings followed him because he was a valiant man and a battle-winner. He trusted in himself and his strength so much that he went far up country, and everywhere he went with warfare.

(Fagrskinna Saga)

A VIOLENT, pagan freebooter of a king, Eric is commemorated in later sagas and Scandinavian epic verse. He was the son of Harold Fairhair, king of Norway, and married a daughter of the Danish king. Forced into exile (*c*.935) after he tried to secure his father's kingdom, he was eventually (947) invited to be king of Northumbria, based at the prosperous, cosmopolitan Anglo-Scandinavian city of Jorvik (York). With the support of Archbishop Wulfstan, he led Northumbrian resistance to southern English claims to dominance. Although he was soon expelled by King Eadred (948)—adventuring perhaps as far as Spain—he returned to raise the standard of Northumbrian independence (952–4). As king he may have embraced Christianity; he certainly minted coins at York. But along with his brother and son, he was slain by Eadred's army at Stainmore (954). This ended the Scandinavian regal tradition at York and removed a major obstacle to West Saxon supremacy in England.

SILVER PENNY OF KING ERIC BLOODAXE, Viking king of York. The unsheathed sword between his monogram reflects the heathen, military basis of his rule in England, though at the same time in imitation of Christian rulers in England and elsewhere. (× 3½)

communities supported them and their warband, and in the tribute which more minor or defeated kings, whether in Ireland, Wales, or elsewhere, were required to pay, usually in kind. To regularize such demands, and impose them efficiently without exhausting the source, was one of the arts of government which in larger kingdoms required methods of assessment and collection, and systems for storage and use.

In Welsh kingdoms by the eleventh century, payment of taxation was among the normal expectations of the king's subjects and the taxes were presumably assessed and collected by his agents. The 'high king' of Ireland dared to levy a tax even on the Dublin property of Viking settlers in 1002. But it was, once again, in England that the systematization of taxation, by monarchs with extensive regal powers, can be seen at its most impressive, mainly because the reconquest of Viking England forced West Saxon kings to capitalize on their rich resources as effectively as possible in order to implement their military strategy. Moreover, even in the eighth century, English kings (and Irish ones too) seem to have been capable of exploiting trade, both by imposing tolls at ports like London, and by regulating and milking markets and fairs in the countryside. Traders, particularly foreigners, needed special protection when plying their trade, and it was the king who was the giver of best protection and, therefore, the regulator of the movements and activities of foreigners and merchants. One of Charlemagne's letters to King Offa assumed that the Mercian king had such powers as these over the production and export of textiles, which were so popular on the continent.

The minting of coins was certainly under royal control. After an interval of 200 years, coins were once again struck in Britain in the seventh century. By 800 they regularly bore the names of the kings for whom they were struck; and by the end of the tenth century the English monarchy had the most sophisticated coinage system in western Europe—and the only one in the British Isles. It was a system that enabled the king to exploit the wealth of a much enlarged kingdom. It made possible the great crusade against the Vikings, and it enabled English kings to raise very substantial sums of money indeed with which to bribe the Vikings at the end of the tenth century. Æthelred II raised sums that seemed to grow larger with almost every demand: £22,000 in 991, £16,000 in 993, £24,000 in 1001, £36,000 in 1005, and as much as £48,000 in 1012. Vast quantities of silver coins were in circulation; a fraction of them—amounting nevertheless to tens of thousands—have been unearthed in Scandinavian countries where they were taken as booty or tribute. The so-called danegeld (and the later heregeld for the hiring of mercenaries) was a notable system of taxation capable of exploiting the wealth and organizational potential of the Anglo-Saxon monarchy. Its assessment was based on the old hidage system, which had served so many other purposes and was the basic framework of governmental control in the localities of England. 'The Anglo-Saxon financial system, which collected the Danegeld, was not run from a box under the bed' (V. H. Galbraith).

In large part, Anglo-Saxon government was urban government, focused on the burhs which Mercian and West Saxon kings developed as an instrument of defence and reconquest. They became centres for minting, trade, and government, and they were frequently organizational centres for the shires in which they stood. The very success of this system may have caused some of the resentment against Æthelred II's regime at the beginning of the eleventh century: it was a system that worked only too well, but when it did not produce military successes against the enemy, it could lead to disillusion and revolt. The central planning and local organization for defence and territorial expansion, for urbanization and commercial exploitation, revealed the power of the late Anglo-Saxon monarchy, certainly jn southern and midland England—and to some degree beyond the Humber too, at least as far as legislation and justice are concerned. This monarchy's practical achievements were without parallel in the British Isles.

So long as kingdoms were small—as they remained in Ireland—kings could

THE ANGLO-SAXON BURH OF WAREHAM ('town by the weir') in Dorset, from the north. It was built as a defended settlement on Roman foundations by King Alfred. The ninth-century defences are visible in the foreground, the Saxon church in the distance, and the rivers Piddle and Frome gave added protection to a town that was in the front line of resistance against the Vikings.

order their relations with their peoples directly, with help and advice from their immediate entourage and their nobles. The pattern of succession throughout these centuries ensured that most kings were adults, generally chosen for their suitability from among the royal kinsfolk. Impersonal central organs of government were hardly needed. Yet even petty kings had their courts. 'Over-kings' certainly did, and when Columba visited King Bridei of the Picts, he found him at an impressive court with a rudimentary council, a treasury, priests, slaves, and messengers, as well as an army and a fleet. Although this description by Adomnán was penned at the end of the seventh century, it is unlikely to be overly anachronistic as a depiction of a Pictish court 150 years before. Adomnán also allows us several glimpses of Irish and Scottish kings in his writings, which picture them accompanied by their nobles, lay and clerical; these were something more than the mere warband of a chieftain. In Wales, too, there are signs that notables and advisers were at the courts of kings in the seventh and eighth centuries, discussing, advising, and arbitrating; by the tenth century we can see a royal household, whose members by the twelfth century included a hierarchy of officers and royal clerks, a steward, chief huntsman, hawker and groom, chamber servants, and household troops. Such a household was the heart of the court, and so it remained for centuries thereafter. Yet this picture, drawn from the evidence of the Welsh law-books, cannot be assigned to any precise period between the mid-tenth and the mid-twelfth centuries, when Anglo-Saxon and even Anglo-Norman habits may have begun to modify what had been a more primitive organization a century or so earlier. Out of this personal entourage or court, rudimentary administrative organs of government were sprouting even in Wales.

In the course of translating St Augustine's *Soliloquies*, King Alfred introduced a simile which amounts to an acute observation of his own court:

Consider now whether many men ever come to the king's estate when he is in residence there, or to his assembly, or to his army, and whether it seems to you that they all come thither by the same road. I think, however, that they come by very many different roads: some come from a great distance and have a very long, very bad, and very difficult road; some have a very long and very straight and very good road; some have a very short, yet crooked, narrow and miry road; some have a short and smooth and straight one; and yet they all come to one and the same lord, some more easily; some with greater difficulty; they neither all come thither with equal ease, nor are they all equally at ease there. Some are in greater honour and greater comfort than others, some in less, some almost without any, except only what has the lord's approval. So it is also with wisdom. Each of those who desire it and pray zealously for it can come thither and dwell in its court and live by it, though some may be nearer it, some farther off. Just so all kings' residences: some men are in his chamber, some in the hall, some on the threshing-floor, some in prison; and yet they all live by the mercy of one and the same lord . . . (*Soliloquies*, bk. 1)

From Alfred's entourage of clerics, craftsmen, and scholars came much of the inspiration for his educational and religious reforms and for his plans to defeat and throw back the Vikings. He and his successors, with the witan, the noble advisers of their kingdom, gave coherence and continuity to royal government in a range of spheres—military, judicial, police, law-making, financial—in an expanding kingdom, and they developed ideas of centralization and bureaucratic administration which the hidage system and the corps of royal agents reflect. Athelstan's staff of clerics is well known, some of them foreigners, and they accompanied him on his progresses and possibly undertook missions for him at home and abroad. Many of them were recruited in the great monastic and episcopal churches of his kingdom, especially at Winchester in Wessex and Worcester in Mercia, serving him temporarily before returning to their houses. The instrument of royal communication in an enlarged kingdom was the charter, which may have been introduced to England first by St Augustine as early as the end of the sixth century. It conveyed the king's will, and became such an indispensable link between the king and his court, on the one hand, and his people, on the other, that some historians believe that by the end of the tenth

† Ego Aethilbalt dno donante rex nonsolum marcersium sedetomnium
prouinciarum quae generale nomine sutangli dicuntur proremedio
animae meae et relaxatione piaculorum meorum aliquam terrae par
ticulam idest .x. cassatorum uenerando comitemeo cyniberhte
adconstruendum coenubium inprouincia cui abantiquis nomen in
ditum est huic uuerae iuxta fluuium uocabulo stur, cumomnibus ne
cessariis adeam pertinentib, cumcampis siluisq, campiscariis pratisq
inpossessionem ecclesiasticam benigne largiendo trado. Itautqui
diu uixerit potestatem habeat tenendi acpossidendi cuicumq uoluerit
uelco uiuo uelcerte postobitum suum relinquendi. Est autem supra
dictus ager incircuitu exutraq parte supranominati fluminis
habens exaquilone plaça siluam quam nominant cynibre exocci
dentale uero aliam cuinomen est moerheb. quarum pars maxima
adpraefatum pertinet agrum, siquis autem hancdonationem uio
lare temptauerit sciat se intremendo examine tyrannidis ac
praesumptionis suae dorationem terribiliter redditurum
scripta est haec cartula anno abincarnatione dni nri hu xpi septin
gentissimo tricessimo ui indictione quarta

† Ego Aetdilbalt rex Britanniae propriam ... subscripsi ... confir
† Ego uuor episcopus consensi etsubscripsi
† Ego uuilfrious episc iubente aethilbaldo rege subscripsi
† Ego aethilric subregulus atq comes gloriosissimi principis ethilbal
        huic donatione consensi etsubscripsi
† Ego ibeacsi indignus abbas consensi etsubscripsi
† Ego beamdberht frater atq dux prae patri regis consensi etsubscripsi
† Ego ebbella consensum meum accomodans subscripsi
† Ego onoc comes subscripsi
† Ego oba consensi etsubscripsi
† Ego sigibed consensi etsubscripsi
† Ego bercol consensi etsubscripsi
† Ego ealduulf consensi etsubscripsi
† Ego cusa consensi etsubscripsi
† Ego bede consensi etsubscripsi

A CHARTER OF KING ÆTHELBALD (d. 757) of Mercia to Ealdorman Cyneberht concerning land in Worcestershire in 736. Æthelbald is described as 'king of Britain' (*rex Britanniae*), and as 'king not only of the Mercians but also of all provinces which are called by the general name "South English"' His power, therefore, was akin to that ascribed to earlier *bretwaldas* by Bede—south of the Humber.

century the clerics at court formed a kind of writing office (or chancery) that was the secretariat of monarchy.

Royal assemblies reflected the breadth of kingly control and gave a semblance of unity to a kingdom that had provinces as far-flung as Northumbria. Edgar expected Northumbrian officials and nobles to attend his assemblies after 970, and even before that Athelstan had included nobles from Mercia and Northumbria among the witnesses of his charters, which presumably means that they were present at his witan's discussions. Such people acted increasingly as the king's agents in the provinces, regarding the king as the ultimate source of their authority and the fountain-head of a patronage that was much more extensive after the recovery of the Viking 'Danelaw'

Kings found their nobility mostly among the ranks of the royal families of the kingdoms that had disappeared. The kingdom of Lindsey, for example, had been absorbed in Mercia by the middle of the eighth century, and its kings and their kin were taken into the Mercian nobility. In Pictish Scotland, smaller kingdoms that survived the Scots' migration and the Viking wars lost their independence and their royal kin became Scottish nobility: the former king of Atholl was described as 'governor' by 966; in Angus there were earls or counts where previously there had been kings; whilst in Moray the great rulers (or mormaers) retained such a degree of hereditary independence that they could lay claim to the Scottish crown itself in the early eleventh century. In Wales, too, nobles were not created by kings, though they were close to kings, who could enhance their power and their wealth; they did not owe their position to kings, but were the royal companions.

In an advanced kingdom like tenth-century England, the nobility was gradually subjected more and more to the king's control and the creation of a nobleman was a royal act. As the kingdom expanded, so kings needed nobles to aid them in provincial government and it seemed appropriate to use native noble families in the subordinate kingdoms, just as in Mercia Alfred relied on Æthelred of Mercia, though the king was artful enough to marry his strong-willed daughter, Æthelflæd, to him. Edgar relied on Ælfhere as ealdorman of Mercia (956–83). But at other times, there was much to be said for importing ealdormen from Wessex or Mercia into the newly acquired provinces, and these men had more the air of powerful royal agents about them, rather than of hereditary nobility. The well-named Athelstan 'Half-king', of noble Wessex birth, was sent by Edward the Elder to East Anglia, after its reconquest from the Danes, in order to introduce the administrative system of southern England and make the region loyal and quiescent. He was then transferred to Mercia, to supervise the old Mercian nobility after the death (918) of Edward's sister, Æthelflæd. Edward's brothers saw similar service, if not as distinguished or spectacularly successful, in other provinces of the kingdom such as Wessex and Kent. This was provincial rule by powerful royal agents of exalted birth, a philosophy of government that was to recur many times in the medieval English monarchy. Edgar went a step further and created new regional spheres under trusted lieutenants. These were larger than the ealdordoms based on earlier kingdoms, and he created among his nobility an élite who were often drawn from families of West Saxon origin or associations and who were given wide-ranging powers in these regions. This design had the virtue of severing the link between provincial rulers and the local hereditary nobility. But it had its dangers, too: it might create powerful nobles-turned-kingmakers, as seems to have happened after Edgar's death in 975. Equally dangerous was the possibility that provincial patriotism might be revived by dominant and self-important local rulers, as happened in Mercia where, in the final catastrophe of Æthelred II's reign, his son contemplated seceding from his father's kingdom.

A centrally directed monarchy in England—and probably in Scotland too—acquired what may reasonably be described as a governmental capital. The early development of Christian kingship encouraged a close geographical association between the spiritual and secular headquarters of British kingdoms. Kent was unique in having its royal capital and the pre-eminent seat of the Roman Church in the British Isles in the same town. By contrast, the mission of Columba to the Pictish mainland in the sixth century, and his foundation of the religious community on Iona, meant that the foremost Christian shrine was some distance from the probable focus of the Scottish kingdom of Dalriada on the fortress-rock of Dunadd. The development of Christian kingship in the centuries that followed tended to bring the ecclesiastical and secular centres into a closer relationship. King Offa of Mercia, though he dominated Kent for much of his reign, found it

ÆTHELRED II 'THE UNREADY'

(978–1016), king of the English

. . . the king ordered the whole nation from Wessex and Mercia to be called out . . . yet it availed no whit more than it had often done before; for in spite of it all, the Danish army went about as it pleased, and the English levy caused the people of the country every sort of harm, so that they profited neither from the native army nor the foreign army.

(Anglo-Saxon Chronicle, 1006)

ÆTHELRED was unlucky in his problems, and the Anglo-Saxon Chronicle judges his reign in the light of its disastrous end. Mounting the throne after the murder of his elder brother Edward, his kingdom was eventually dismembered by his son, Edmund Ironside, and Cnut the Dane. If Æthelred was not of the calibre of his forebears, neither was he a complete disaster and he reigned longer than any of his predecessors. His derogatory nickname, current from the twelfth century, is merely a pun on his name, meaning 'noble counsel'. The early years (973–83) were dominated by his mother and the legacy of Edward's death. His early personal rule (983–93) was oppressive, especially after the death of Dunstan (988) and Bishop Æthelwold. Maturity unfortunately coincided with Viking assaults (from 988) of a ferocity unmatched since Alfred's day. He could do little but negotiate temporary respites and massive tribute which encouraged further attacks. He tried to combat the Vikings by diplomacy, notably by marrying Emma, daughter of the duke of Normandy (1002), and he raised a fleet and large armies. He even led an expedition to Strathclyde (1000) to disrupt Viking settlements round the Irish Sea. But his energetic measures were not always well organized. Sweyn, the Danish king's son, began conquering territory (1003), and his blitzkrieg in southern and midland England destroyed the morale of king and country and so

SILVER PENNY OF KING ÆTHELRED II, depicting the bare-headed king as *Æthelred rex Anglorum*. Based on Roman models, many of these coins have been found in Scandinavia, whence they were taken as danegeld payments during Æthelred's reign. (× 3¼)

disillusioned the nobility that Æthelred could no longer trust them. Sweyn was chosen king (1013) and Æthelred fled. After he returned (1014), promising better rule, he failed to reassert control and his son Edmund made himself independent ruler in the Danelaw. The collapse of Æthelred's kingdom was not sudden—its strength and resources and Æthelred's efforts ensured that. Yet if the kingship and kingdom were sounder than the king, they also had structural weaknesses which the Vikings exploited.

far from easy to control the archbishop of Canterbury. For this reason, he sought leave from the pope's legates to appoint his own Mercian archbishop of Lichfield, close to what may have been his main residence at Tamworth. In Wessex, it was Winchester, a religious centre since at least the seventh century, which became the capital of the kingdom. By the year 1000, Winchester was the principal seat of English kings, the greatest single complex of royal and ecclesiastical buildings in the entire British Isles, and a centre of government with administrative offices, including the king's treasury.

The Scottish kingdom of Kenneth mac Alpin and his successors had nothing comparable, though the ecclesiastical and secular pivots of their kingdom were fairly close together in Perthshire. The English kingdom was always a southern kingdom with a southern capital. By contrast, the Dalriadan kings, when they expanded eastwards and overcame the Picts, moved the administrative heart of their kingdom eastwards too. Although the traditions of Iona were tenacious and Scottish kings continued to be buried on the holy island until the late eleventh century, the religious centre of the kingdom from the ninth century onwards was Dunkeld, and then it was St Andrews after King Constantine II abdicated to become abbot there in 943. The move to Dunkeld, at the very heart of the new kingdom, was accompanied in 849 by the translation of some of Columba's relics. Not too far away in Perthshire was Scone, which was soon to be the secular and ceremonial centre of Scotland, the place of assembly of its kings and the inauguration site of Scottish kings from Kenneth mac Alpin's time onwards. The Stone of Scone, said by ancient tradition to have been brought by Scots from Ireland to Iona, and then to Scone following the union of Dalriada and Pictland, was the hallowed stone on which Scottish kings were inaugurated. The determination of Scottish nationalists in the 1950s to retrieve it from beneath the coronation chair in Westminster Abbey had deep roots in the independent identity of the early Scottish monarchy. Scone and Dunkeld were only some twelve miles apart: their relationship was similar to that planned for Tamworth and Lichfield.

SARCOPHAGUS SAID TO BE THAT OF KING CONSTANTINE II, who is the only early Scottish king known to have been buried elsewhere than at Iona—at St Andrews. A Dark Age masterpiece of ninth- or tenth-century date, it is now in the site museum of St Andrews Cathedral.

The Irish and Welsh kings, ruling smaller kingdoms with less developed kingships, never possessed such capitals, though the 'high kingship' of the Uí Néill was based at Armagh, which was one of Ireland's main ecclesiastical centres and the mausoleum of the 'high kings' of the north in the tenth and eleventh centuries. If 'high kingship' had been able to develop beyond personal hegemony and spawn institutions of government, then Armagh too might have become the capital of a truly Irish kingship.

The institution of monarchy was popularized in all kingdoms of the British Isles by what may be termed royal propaganda. It was at its most imaginative and persuasive in the English monarchy, utilizing the arts and techniques of English culture to portray a monarchy that was far more than an organization for waging war. Origin-myths, ceremonial, and magnificence were highly effective in projecting a monarchy headed by Christian kings who commanded the loyalty of their peoples. King Alfred was a past master of these arts, though some of his successors were able to build effectively on his work.

The magnificence of a king conveyed the wealth and power of his monarchy. The precious objects placed in the Sutton Hoo burial ship in the seventh century reflect something of the opulence of the royal house of East Anglia, whose kings were presumably surrounded by such riches when they were alive. Bede, in

THE ATHELSTAN PSALTER (*facing*), probably produced in the Liège area. King Athelstan is said to have given this ninth-century manuscript to the Old Minster at Winchester. There additions were made in the tenth century, including the picture of the enthroned Christ surrounded by heavenly choirs.

THE ALFRED JEWEL (*below*), inscribed *Ælfred mec heht gewyrcan* ('Alfred had me made'). It was found near Athelney marshes, where King Alfred sought refuge from the Danes in 878. The enamel figure is covered by a rock crystal and the jewel may have been one of the elaborate bookmarkers known to have been circulated by Alfred with his translation of Pope Gregory's *Pastoral Care*. (approx. × 2)

writing of King Edwin of Northumbria (d. 632), was more explicit in describing the symbolism of power:

Truly he kept such great state in his kingdom, that not only were his banners borne before him in war, but even in time of peace his standard-bearer always went before him as he rode between his cities, his residences and provinces with his thegns. Also, when he walked anywhere along the streets, that sort of banner which the Romans call 'tufa' and the English 'thuuf' was usually borne before him. (*Ecclesiastical History*, bk. II)

The Alfred jewel, though it displays Carolingian enamelling techniques, expresses the wealth of the Wessex monarchy in the late ninth century. And if Athelstan received the fabulous gifts of Carolingian regalia sent by the duke of the Franks in 926, we can be sure that he impressed his continental allies with gifts of similar value and artistry to those he gave to the shrine of St Cuthbert (some of which can still be seen at the saint's shrine now in Durham Cathedral). Magnificence was the imposing outer face of monarchy.

King-lists, royal genealogies, and origin-myths told a different, though related, story, one that stressed the ancient foundations and glorious development of the monarchical tradition. In England, the earliest lists can be dated no earlier than the eighth or early ninth century, but they trace the descent of kings to a dim Germanic past made heroic by invaders and conquerors of the calibre of Hengist and Horsa in Kent, and Cerdic and Cynric in Wessex. Beyond that, they link the kingly lines with heathen gods, in most cases the predictable Woden, God of War, from whom all warrior kings were believed to be descended. This was myth-making for practical purposes in the interest of stability, status, and reputation. These myths reflect a desire for order, continuity, and antiquity, and they imply an expectation that good leadership was to be found in royal families. The sanction of antiquity was of immense value to monarchies which, like Mercia in the eighth century, were bent on expansion, and to others, like Northumbria, which needed confidence to resist ambitious kingdoms further south.

More minor monarchies, too, sought reassurance and legitimacy in pedigrees and myths. In ninth- and tenth-century Wales, genealogies were compiled which placed the British-born Emperor Magnus Maximus (d. 388) at the head of a number of Welsh royal lines, notably those of Dyfed and Powys; in Gwynedd, sub-kings claimed descent from Cunedda, who came to power in the year of Magnus's death. No Scottish king-list can be dated earlier than the thirteenth century and it is therefore difficult to draw any comparable conclusions from the surviving evidence; but the British kingdom of Strathclyde looked back to a fifth-century figure, Ceretic of Dumbarton, as father of the kingdom which eventually succumbed to mac Alpin's dynasty.

Christianity played an important part in the search for venerable ancestors, not least because the Bible provided good examples of the significance of king-lists

The illustration contains several Latin genealogical inscriptions surrounding the central figure:

Upper left: Woden genuit vectam qi gẽ witram qi g witgelsum qi genuit beslam cebengelst.

Upper right: Woden geñ beldeiū qi geñ brond qi g freođegarum ni g freawinum qi geñ witcam qi g goenlsse qi g eslam qi g eltam qi g beroic.

Middle left: Woden g feodulgeat qi g waga qi g witdeleg qi g wermundum qi g offa qi g ongeltheou qi geo merum qi g ichel qi g cnibbam qi g kineswaldū qi g cryda qui g bibbam qui genuit pendam.

Middle right: Woden g beldei qi g brond qui g benoc qi g aloc qi angenwita qi g inguui qi g eslam qi g eopam qi gj oam a qj regesl nordanhymbroʒ ceperunt oeigineam.

Bottom center: Woden genuit wegdam qi genuit sigegarum qui g swaebdegum qui g sigegeat qi g scabadum qi g seafugel qi g westerfalene qi g wegilf qui g wesctren qi g yffe qi g ella.

WODEN, THE GERMANIC GOD OF WAR, from whom Anglo-Saxon kings proudly claimed descent. Their genealogies, as recorded from the ninth century, sprang from him, and in this late twelfth-century version of the history of England attributed to Symeon of Durham the frightful Woden is shown crowned and surrounded by (*left to right*) six of his mythical sons: Vectan (Kent), Beldei (or, correctly, Bealdeah, Wessex), Feothulgeat (Mercia), Beldei (Northumbria), Casere (East Anglia), and Wegdam (Sussex).

and dynastic histories. King Alfred was most adept at exploiting the Christian and literary arts in the service of his monarchy. His patronage of the Anglo-Saxon Chronicle is well known and the result is a masterly history of the English in these islands, seen from Wessex's point of view. It is a story that has prompted generations of historians to see the creation of a united English kingdom as the inevitable and inspiring outcome of the struggles of Wessex and of Alfred in particular. His court entered into the spirit of his patriotic propaganda. The picture of Alfred painted by the emigré Welsh bishop, Asser of St David's, in his biography of the king (893–4) is at once heroic and realistic: of a man who overcame his own physical disabilities to become England's greatest royal warrior, committed to the advance of Christianity, a protector of the Church and clergy, and the inspiration of educational, moral, and religious reform. This is a biography which Alfred, who saw himself as a latter-day David, would have

ħ. DCCCLXXI. Hҽr cōm rehere corea
ðingum on peſeſeaxe. ⁊þær ymbe .III. niht rioon
cþegen eorlaſ up. þaſe mecce æþelþulſ ealdor
man hic on engla felda. ⁊him þær þið geſeaht.
⁊rigenám ⁊hcorra peard oþær þæn oſſlagen
þær nama þæſ Sidrac. Ðā ymb .IIII. niht æþered
cyning. ⁊ælſred hir broþen þær mýcle þyrð
corcadingum geleddon. ⁊þið þone here ge
ſuhcon. ⁊þær þær mýcel þæl geſlagen on ſeþþone
hánð. ⁊eaðelþulſ ealdor man þeard oſſlagen.
⁊þa ðenmrcan ahton þealſcope geþealo. ⁊þær
ymb .IIII. nyht geſeaht æþered cyning ⁊ælſred
hir broþon þið ealne þone here on æreſ dune.
⁊hi þæron on cþám geſylcum on oðrum þær
baſ ſecſ. ⁊healſ dene þahæðenan cyningaſ. ⁊on
oþrum þæron þa eorlaſ. ⁊þa ſeahc ſe cyning
æþered þið þara cyninga geþuman. ⁊þær
þeard ſe cyning baſ ſecſ oſſlagen. ⁊ælſred
hir broþon þið þara eorla geþuman. ⁊þær

A PAGE FROM THE ANGLO-SAXON
CHRONICLE (*above*), which was
originally sponsored at King Alfred's
court. Its aim was to celebrate the
history of Wessex, but the chronicle,
written in Anglo-Saxon, was widely
copied in several monasteries and
supplemented up to 1154. This page,
from the version written at Abingdon
Abbey in the 1040s, recounts the Viking
thrust into Wessex in 871, 'the Year of
Battles', and the resistance mounted by
King Æthelred and his brother Alfred
before Alfred's accession later in the
year.

EMBROIDERED STOLE PRESENTED BY
KING ATHELSTAN (d. 939) to the shrine
of St Cuthbert at Chester-le-Street in
934 (*right*). When the shrine was moved
to Durham, the stole went too. It
portrays Peter, Pope Gregory's deacon.

savoured and endorsed. It may not have been much read in later centuries, but at the time it helped to glorify the king and his monarchy; if it was written first and foremost for a Welsh audience, then it is certain to have inspired among Welsh kings an admiration for, and a trust in, their distinguished West Saxon overlord. Like all propaganda, the intention of the Chronicle and Asser's biography (and they may not have been independent in composition) was to encourage, exhort, inspire, and celebrate Alfred and his monarchy, and the Chronicle especially succeeded marvellously.

The new English coinage had the same purpose and the more often the coins passed through men's hands, and the further afield they were taken by plunder or trade, the more famous their royal sponsors became. A regular coinage seems to have reappeared in England in the seventh century, imitating Roman models. But the recoinage of King Offa was a radical departure which has won admiration ever since—as was its purpose. Alfred reformed the coinage once again and extended its minting to the burhs he had founded. The English royal coinage attained its finest development under Edgar: its intrinsic quality, its use of the royal image, the regular reissues, and its wide use at home and abroad, popularized his monarchy and committed to it all who acquired, exchanged, or stored his coins. Curiously, the English monarchy was the only monarchy in the British Isles to introduce a coinage for practical and propaganda purposes in the early Middle Ages. Hywel Dda is alone among Welsh kings in having minted a coin, though it may not have been produced in Wales itself. The Scottish kingdom did not enjoy the resources of the English at the end of the tenth century, nor did it have such a well-developed tradition of written government, though in evolving a stable and united monarchy incorporating Picts, Scots, British, and even Anglians, in some respects it had advanced further than the English.

2. THE AGE OF 'EMPIRES'
1016–1216

'Imperial' Kingdoms

JUST as the emergence and disappearance of Dark Age kingdoms had been caused, above all other factors, by the migrations of peoples and their warrior leaders, so between the eleventh century and the thirteenth the kingdoms of the British Isles were transformed by newer waves of immigrants. These migrants were very probably far fewer in number but, because of their greater cohesion and resources, their influence was no less fundamental. They changed the territorial configuration of kingdoms in these islands, and linked them more closely to the monarchical system of northern Europe. After a relatively brief return of Scandinavian kingship to Britain in the early eleventh century, French influences became paramount and left an indelible mark on all British kingdoms.

The language and imagery of 'empire' had been current in tenth-century England, and were not unknown in contemporary Ireland. They reflected the extraordinary territorial conquests of individual kings and the amplitude of West Saxon achievement. The first English empire was, therefore, West Saxon and Edgar was its first undoubted emperor, *Albionis Imperator Augustus*. After 1016, England was one part of far larger continental dominions, whose sheer extent merits the epithet 'empire' with equal justice. William of Newburgh certainly thought so: witness his *History of England*, written in about 1196:

Moreover in all parts of his realm the king [Henry II] won the renown of a monarch who ruled over a wider empire than all who had hitherto reigned in England, for it extended from the far border of Scotland to the Pyrenees.

Cnut's inauguration as king of all the English (1016) marked an extraordinary extension of Scandinavian power in the British Isles, and it was the most important step—far more important than the earlier foundation of Viking kingdoms in Dublin, York, and the Western Isles—in creating a Viking dominion or 'empire' around the northern seas. By 1020, when his elder brother Harold died, Cnut was undisputed king of Denmark, and his authority was no longer contested in Norway once the forces of King Olaf (d. 1030) had been defeated. He seems also to have won other, though smaller, lands on the southern shore of the Baltic Sea. To this day, he is known in the Scandinavian world as 'Cnut the Great'.

If these kingdoms and territories are to be regarded as an 'empire', it is pre-eminently because they were held together by Cnut himself. It is true that there were commercial, personal, and cultural links between them, but in no substantial way did they form a political or governmental unity. Danes settled on English estates, as their forebears had done in midland and eastern England a century and more before; and the Danish title of 'earl' ousted the traditional English 'ealdorman' at about this time. Englishmen became bishops in Denmark, and Cnut's English wife, Ælfgifu of Northampton, ruled as regent for their son in Norway in the 1030s. His three kingdoms were interdependent: Cnut's control of Denmark and Norway removed the spectre of further Viking attacks on England, whilst his English resources helped to sustain the entire 'empire'. But the most significant element of unity was Cnut himself, and it would be unreal to expect much common institutional development. This being so, it is not surprising that the personal maritime dominion of this great king should disintegrate soon after his death.

Olaf's son, Magnus, led a long struggle against Cnut's son, Harthacnut, who was so preoccupied in Denmark that he temporarily lost his chance of obtaining the English crown (1035) as his father had intended. Instead, Cnut's elder son, Harold Harefoot, was chosen king of the English and at a stroke that shattered his father's 'empire'. It is true that when Harthacnut eventually set sail for England (1039), arriving only to find his brother dead and he himself chosen king at last, the Danish and English kingdoms at least were once again united under one ruler; but this was a much more fragile edifice than Cnut's and did not survive Harthacnut's death in 1042. The unabashed ambition and aggressiveness that had created Cnut's northern sea-empire were fortified by tradition and a refusal to surrender earlier conquests, so that his Scandinavian successors periodically laid claim to the English kingdom during the next half-century and launched expeditions to recover it not only in the 1040s but also in 1066 and 1085. These were unsuccessful. In England in 1042 the new king, Edward the Confessor, was

THE LEWIS CHESSMEN, found (1831) on the west coast of Lewis in the Outer Hebrides. They appear to be Anglo-Scandinavian in origin, dating from the late twelfth century. These selected pieces (from a cache of seventy-eight) are made of walrus ivory and represent (from *left* to *right*) a knight, king, queen and bishop in the dress of the period. The king is crowned and clutches a sword on his lap.

no Scandinavian, even though his mother was also the mother of Harthacnut; he was her elder son by Æthelred II. Nor did Edward have any northern ambitions: he disbanded the great fleet which had held Cnut's various dominions together, and in 1051 he abolished the tax (heregeld) which had largely financed it. By the mid-eleventh century, the Scandinavian phase in the history of the English kingdom was drawing to a close. It faded unlamented by most Englishmen. The Anglo-Saxon chronicler noted, when civil war loomed in 1052, that Englishmen 'did not wish the country to be laid the more open to foreigners through their destroying each other'. But if these were their wishes, they were to be roughly ignored a decade and a half later.

William the Bastard was, first and foremost, duke of Normandy and count of Maine; from 1066 he was also king of England. He thereafter ruled a cross-Channel dominion which may be compared with Cnut's (and it is worth recalling that the Normans were part-Scandinavian). But unlike Cnut's sea-empire, William's was geographically compact and even developed a certain institutional coherence beyond the person of the king-duke himself. For one thing, William 'the Conqueror' and his sons, William Rufus and Henry I, spent a greater proportion of their time as king in their continental domain than in England, and the Normans who settled in England were probably more numerous than the Danish settlers of Cnut's day. The result was that many nobles and churchmen had relatives, lands, and interests on both sides of the narrow Channel, across which communication was easier, speedier, and therefore more frequent than

CNUT 'THE GREAT'

(1016–1035), king of the English, Danes, and Norwegians

... I have humbly vowed to Almighty God to amend my life from now on in all things, and to rule justly and faithfully the kingdoms and peoples subject to me and to maintain equal justice in all things ...

(Cnut's letter to the English, 1027)

SILVER PENNY OF KING CNUT, from the London mint. The obverse has a representation of the king, wearing a traditional diadem of Roman Style. Although based on Anglo-Saxon coin design, this Danish king's coin seems a crude imitation. (× 3)

Possibly the younger son of Sweyn Forkbeard of Denmark and Sigrid, widow of Eric, king of Sweden, Cnut was a self-consciously Christian ruler of a northern sea-empire of Denmark and Norway (1014–15) and England (1016). Before invading England with his father (1013), he was baptized in Germany. Despite set-backs after Sweyn's death (1014), he returned and swept through England with such energy that he could claim Æthelred II's crown by conquest and be chosen by the witan. The death of Æthelred's son, Edmund (1016), left the field to Cnut: Edmund's sons fled to Hungary, Æthelred's to Normandy. Cnut was a cruel, ruthless but capable king, a legend in his lifetime and the most commanding figure in the northern world; yet according to oral tradition in the twelfth century, it was Christian humility that made him rebuke the flattery of his nobles by showing that not even he could halt the waves. To retain the Normans' alliance, he set aside Ælfgifu of Northampton, the mother of his sons Harold and Sweyn, and married (1020) Æthelred's widow Emma; his pact with William V, duke of Aquitaine counterbalanced Norman power. Cnut spent four periods in Scandinavia (1019–28), whilst in England his powerful English and Danish earls were the mainstay. Despite the Scots' victory at Carham (1018), he forced their king to submit, and his coins were minted in the Norse kingdom of Dublin. Cnut's Christianity was a matter of faith and politics. His pilgrimage to Rome (1027–8) strengthened links with pope and emperor, and his daughter Gunhild was betrothed to the emperor's son Henry (c.1035). Cnut's 'empire' was preserved largely by himself: English methods and personnel of government were hardly altered. This personalized rule was undermined towards the end of his life: in Scandinavia his Christianity offended some, and by 1035 his grip on Norway was broken and relations with Normandy deteriorated. He died at Shaftesbury and was buried at Winchester, a final identification with the English monarchy he had superseded.

had been possible between eastern England and Scandinavia earlier in the eleventh century. For these reasons, it ultimately proved more practicable to attempt to keep the entire Anglo-Norman dominion united under one ruler, despite the fact that French kings and French nobles were all too ready to gnaw at the Norman frontiers and promote rebellion in the duchy. This Anglo-Norman 'empire' was more likely to last than Cnut's, provided its ruling dynasty survived and remained united. The hazards that it faced were apparent as soon as the Conqueror died (1087). It was William's will that the Norman and English parts

Within the illustration, the following labels appear:

Willimus. II.

Henricus primus

Stephanus Rex

PANEL MINIATURES OF THE FOUR NORMAN KINGS OF ENGLAND, William I, William II, Henry I, and Stephen. They appear in Matthew Paris's thirteenth-century *Greater Chronicle* and are unlikely to be realistic portraits. Though stylistically cruder than those in other copies of Matthew's chronicle, these panels have an unusual iconographical significance. Each king is shown enthroned and crowned, and each holds an emblem reflecting some aspect of his rule: William I's sword and eleventh-century ship suggest his expedition in 1066; William II's arrow is a reminder of his death; the book in Henry I's left hand indicates his scholarly reputation, the church in his right his ecclesiastical patronage; while Stephen's sword and church reflect two aspects of his disturbed reign.

of his dominion should be ruled separately by his two eldest sons, Robert in Normandy and William in England, and so they were until William Rufus succeeded in reassembling his father's dominion in 1096. When Rufus died (1100), the links were once again sundered and remained so for another six years until Henry I reforged them. These first three Norman kings of England laid great store by their continental possessions and sought to make them secure, even to extend them. Military campaigns enabled them to overrun adjacent territories so that the inflated Anglo-Norman 'empire' came to include the counties of Boulogne and Maine and even the duchy of Brittany.

This obsession with secure frontiers and territorial conquest led these kings to clarify their relationships with Welsh and Scottish rulers, who had periodically acknowledged their own dependence on English rulers and recognized the overlordship of Anglo-Saxon and Scandinavian kings in England. The Norman monarchs sought to make these relationships more concrete and the claim to overlordship more precise. In doing so, they ensured that all the kingdoms in the British Isles would experience French influences.

As was the case after the death of Cnut, it was the personal weakness of the ruling dynasty that threatened the existence of this Anglo-Norman cross-Channel 'empire'. The bitter rivalry between King Stephen and his cousin Matilda, only daughter of Henry I and the wife of Geoffrey 'Plantagenet' (so-called from the broom sprig he wore), count of Anjou, caused its dismemberment. Angevin forces, aided by the mischievous French king, stripped Stephen of his Norman and continental dominions and once more (as in 1087–96 and 1100–6) made of the kingdom of England a sea-bound realm.

Even in England itself, regional identities and provincial loyalties were exploited by Matilda's invading forces so that the political unity of the kingdom was temporarily threatened. By 1142 the Angevins controlled those outer parts of the kingdom—Norfolk, the north of England beyond the Tees, and the far south-west—whose independent spirit had posed problems for England's kings since the tenth century. Dejected and disillusioned by the time of his death (1154), Stephen's effective control had been so reduced as to raise the possibility that the kingdom might even disintegrate. This was prevented by the death of Stephen's eldest son and heir (1153); thereafter, the demoralized monarch was reconciled to accepting Matilda's son, Henry Plantagenet, as his successor. Not only did Henry's accession restore the Anglo-Norman dominion (for six years after Count Geoffrey overran Normandy in 1144, he handed it to his son to rule); in the event, it also paved the way for the creation of a yet larger maritime empire—an Atlantic 'empire' this time—of which the English kingdom was to be an important, though not necessarily the most important, part.

By the time he mounted the English throne, Henry Plantagenet had been ruler of Normandy since 1150, count of Anjou since 1151 (when his father died), and

MALCOLM II

(*c*.1005–1034), king of Scots

The son of Kenneth II (d. 995), who may have designated him as his heir, Malcolm became king after killing Kenneth III (1005). His reputation rests on his extension of his kingdom's frontiers south to the Tweed–Solway line. Though repulsed at Durham (1006), he defeated a Northumbrian army at Carham (1018) and asserted his claim to Lothian. In the west, he had the alliance of Strathclyde and when its last king died, Malcolm secured the succession of his grandson, Duncan. These conquests were recognized by English kings, though in return for Malcolm's submission to Cnut when the latter marched as far as the Tay (1031). The marriage of his daughter to Sigurd the Stout, Norse earl of Orkney, took his influence even to the far north.

duke of Aquitaine by right of his wife, the beautiful heiress Eleanor whom he married in 1152. As king, he embarked on a venture in Ireland which—and probably for the first time—extended English lordship across St George's Channel. The clutch of dominions over which he ultimately ruled may fairly be called an 'Atlantic empire', which passed in turn to two of his sons, Richard and John, before it fell victim to internal and external forces similar to those that had destroyed the Anglo-Norman dominion of William the Conqueror. If the Anglo-Norman 'empire' had been able to forge some kind of governmental unity by virtue of the proximity of its parts and the willingness of its rulers to cross and recross the Channel time and again, the sheer size of the expansive Angevin 'empire', stretching from the Pyrenees to the Scottish border and from the Auvergne to the bogs of Ireland, put even rudimentary developments in that direction out of the question. The unity of this 'empire' lay in its ruler and his family; any institutional coherence that existed was quite limited. Moreover, England was not obviously the core of the Angevin dominion nor closest to its creator's heart, for Henry II had been born in Anjou; and when he died at Chinon, his body was taken for burial to the abbey of Fontevrault, where his tomb-effigy and the tomb-effigies of his wife Eleanor and his son Richard can still be seen. Richard's body was indeed interred at Fontevrault, but his heart was buried in Rouen Cathedral, and he intended no disrespect—quite the contrary—when he bequeathed his entrails to Charroux in Poitou. In short, no corporeal part of Richard was left to England. King John was buried in Worcester Cathedral, but that was some years after he had lost most of the French territories of the Angevin 'empire'. Yet so long as it lasted, this was the largest and wealthiest dominion under one ruler in Europe: England was part of it and so, in one way or another, were Wales, Scotland, and Ireland.

For the thirty-five years that Henry Plantagenet ruled his 'empire', he strove to preserve its territorial integrity and even managed to extend its frontiers and power. He refused to cede Anjou to his younger brother, Geoffrey, not least because it was part of his personal, inherited dominion, but also because Anjou was a vital link between his grandfather's inheritance of England and Normandy, and his wife's great duchy to the south. Without control of the Loire valley and its river system the practical difficulties of holding his inheritance together would have been immeasurably greater.

Ambition, jealousy, and a zest for conquest led Henry to covet other territories in France which would also protect his large possessions and eliminate rivals along the Atlantic seaboard. His brother Geoffrey was installed as a dependent count in Nantes in 1156; Henry exerted his overlordship over Toulouse (1159) and Brittany (1166), whose heiress was married to his third son Geoffrey. Within the British Isles similar encroachments were made in Wales, and as a result of military expeditions in 1157 and 1165 Welsh kings once more acknowledged the overlordship of their powerful neighbour. The king of Scots, Malcolm IV, was induced to go further, for Henry restored the northern boundary of his kingdom by recovering (1157) Cumberland, Westmorland, and Northumbria, which had been overrun in Stephen's turbulent reign. The Angevin 'empire' was expanded, the kingdom of England restored. Finally, Henry II's aggressiveness and his passion for security led him to assert his overlordship over those Anglo-Norman nobles from South Wales who had begun to conquer lands in Ireland in 1169. Two years later he began that fateful quest of English kings to subjugate Ireland which would never be completed and which has left the bitterest legacy of any of the territorial dependencies of medieval English kings.

Unlike his Anglo-Norman predecessors, Henry II appears to have decided (1166) to use his brood of sons to help him maintain his vast 'empire'. His son Geoffrey was betrothed to the heiress of Brittany as one means of extending the control of 'the family firm' westward. To his older sons, Henry and Richard, he gave titles and some powers of government in the territories to which they were assigned; only the youngest, John 'Lackland', at first received nothing. This device of personal delegation might help Henry in the task of ruling his disparate dominions, but it was unlikely to promote governmental or institutional unity or to forge a single massive kingdom where a variety of traditions and habits held sway. Such delegation also promoted jealousies and rivalries among the brothers and their father, while the queen-duchess, Eleanor, retained strong interests in her own duchy of Aquitaine. Mutual distrust within the king's family, the changes Henry made in the arrangements following the death of his sons Henry and Geoffrey, and the growing uncertainty as to what would happen to the kingship of England and the 'empire' when he himself should die—all these factors contributed to the several revolts which were initiated by his sons and their mother and were eagerly encouraged by the French king and French nobles. In the event, the entire dominion remained undivided when Henry died in 1189, though there was no agreement about its future disposition. That Henry

KING HENRY II, AS COUNT OF ANJOU, MARRYING ELEANOR OF AQUITAINE. This window in Poitiers Cathedral, which commemorates their marriage there in 1152, was donated by them in celebration of the alliance between two great territorial lordships, at whose crossroads Poitiers stood.

had contemplated a dynastic dismemberment of his 'empire' underlines the basic fact that it was his creation and that ideas of perpetual 'imperial' unity took second place in his mind to a determination to preserve the family's possessions in the family's hands. It would not, and was not expected to, survive as a single political, territorial, or governmental entity. And within a generation of 1189, Henry's dominion had indeed partly collapsed and the Plantagenet rulers found themselves confined to the British Isles and Aquitaine.

Although the astute French king, Philip Augustus, seized the opportunity of King Richard I's imprisonment in Germany (1193–4) to intensify his assaults on Normandy and along the Angevin border, by sheer military skill Richard was soon able to assert his authority and effectively protect his inheritance. But when he died (1199), further French pressure and exploitation of Angevin family differences seriously undermined the position of his younger brother and successor, John, during the first five years or so of the new king's reign (1199–1205). England, Normandy, and Aquitaine had accepted John as their ruler, but Anjou, Maine, and Touraine, the very heartland of the dynasty and a wedge between its other territories, gave their allegiance to John's nephew, Geoffrey's young son, Arthur. This wedge was driven hard into the Angevin 'empire' by the French, who eventually conquered Normandy and Poitou (1203–4); John's ineffectual expeditions of 1206 and 1214 failed to recover the lost territories. 'Lackland' now became 'Softsword'. About the same time (1204–6), the king of Castile tried to seize Gascony in southern Aquitaine, claiming that Henry II had promised it to him when he married Henry's daughter Eleanor.

By the end of John's reign (1216), the dynasty had lost its homeland and one of its greatest territorial acquisitions, Normandy. From then onwards, the kingdom

Hen: secundus

Johēs Rex

Henricus III

PANEL MINIATURES OF THE CROWNED KINGS HENRY II, RICHARD I, JOHN, AND HENRY III, taken from a version of Matthew Paris's thirteenth-century *Greater Chronicle*. They are somewhat crudely executed and are unlikely to be realistic portraits, but each has an iconographical interest. Each king is shown enthroned and crowned. Henry II, the persecutor of Becket, looks askance from the church he is holding. Richard the Lion-heart holds a sword and the shield of arms he is said to have popularized. John, the excommunicate who almost lost his throne, is shown with a church obscured by his frame and with a precarious crown on his head. And Henry III, who venerated Edward the Confessor and built a new shrine for his body, is shown with a shrine on his lap.

of England and its relations with its neighbours in the British Isles became, by dint of circumstance, the prime preoccupation of English monarchs for the first time since 1066—or 1016, if the Confessor's reign be ignored. Nor did the threat of disruption stop at the Channel. John's oppressive regime produced widespread discontent in England, particularly among the nobility, for many of whom the dismemberment of Henry II's 'empire' was a humiliating disaster. This disenchantment came to be focused on the French king's son, Louis, who was invited by some to take the throne of England. His invasion (1216) bade fair to undermine the integrity of the kingdom of England itself, perhaps even to hitch England to another French 'empire' in which it would doubtless have taken an even less central part. As it was, when John died later in 1216, few felt justified in continuing the civil war against his nine-year-old son, Henry III, and support for Louis soon evaporated. Henceforward, the kings of England gave at least as much of their attention to England and its place in the British Isles as to the continent and their ambitions there.

The French influences that transformed the English kingdom and its monarchy had a profound impact on all the other kingdoms in these islands, one way or another, at one time or another. In the eleventh century the English king's overlordship in Wales was not precisely defined nor was it enforced by military

CHÂTEAU GAILLARD, the 'Saucy Castle', built under Richard I's personal supervision in the 1190s to protect Rouen, dominate the river Seine, and facilitate the recovery of Normandy from the French. It is a fortress of concentric walls built around a massive keep; its novel design had great influence on castle-building in England in the following century. Philip II of France seized it from King John in 1204.

GRUFFYDD AP LLYWELYN

(1039–1063), king of Gwynedd and Powys

. . . King Griffith was killed on 5 August by his own men because of the fight he fought against Earl Harold. He was king over all the Welsh, and his head was brought to Earl Harold, and Harold brought it to the king, and the figurehead of his ship and the ornaments with it.

(Anglo-Saxon Chronicle, 1063)

THE 'head and shield and defender of the Britons', Gruffydd was little more than a warlord who was conspicuously successful in creating a personal hegemony in Wales and combating the English. The son of Llywelyn ap Seisyll, king of Gwynedd, and Angharad, the king of Deheubarth's daughter, he was slow and listless as a youth but grew into a courageous and ambitious leader who won Gwynedd and Powys in battle (1039) and defeated the Mercians. His conquest of Deheubarth took longer (1055). His alliance with Earl Ælfgar of Mercia, whose daughter he married, sustained a long struggle with Harold Godwinson, but Harold's attack on his court at Rhuddlan (1062) led to Gruffydd's death at the hands of his own men and the destruction of his territorial dominion.

might. Indeed, the boundaries between individual Welsh kingdoms and between them and the English kingdom were still fluid, and so were relations among Welsh kings and between them and their great neighbour. Although the kings of Gwynedd and Powys, and even the mighty Gruffydd ap Llywelyn (d. 1063) who imposed his rule on much of Wales in the 1050s, recognized Edward the Confessor as their overlord, this did not imply any practical sovereignty or involve any governmental interference. But from the second half of the eleventh century onwards, the ambition, aggressiveness, and desire for security that motivated the king-dukes of the Anglo-Norman dominion and their nobles produced a more robust attitude to the territories adjacent to the English kingdom in the British Isles. These factors explain the vigorous thrusts into the Welsh borderland within a year (1067) of William I's conquest of England. This Anglo-Norman advance was prolonged, and to begin with it was confined to the lowlands of the east, south-east, and south-west. Far from being unopposed or unimpeded, it took more than two centuries to complete. The most rapid advances were made (1067–75) during the Conqueror's own reign, not by the king himself but by some of his powerful Norman nobles established in the key strategic centres of Gloucester, Hereford, Worcester, and Chester. However, William himself traversed the country of South Wales as far as St David's in 1081, the first time an English king is known to have ventured so far; and he demanded tribute like an Anglo-Saxon monarch from at least one Welsh king. Later, William Rufus and especially King Henry I themselves took a hand in the conquest, adopting a conscious feudal policy of subjecting not only their Anglo-Norman 'marcher lords' but also the Welsh kings to their suzerainty, and taking personal possession—a novelty this—of territories such as western Dyfed, which became the royal county of Pembroke. In Henry's time the Welsh kings had little option but to

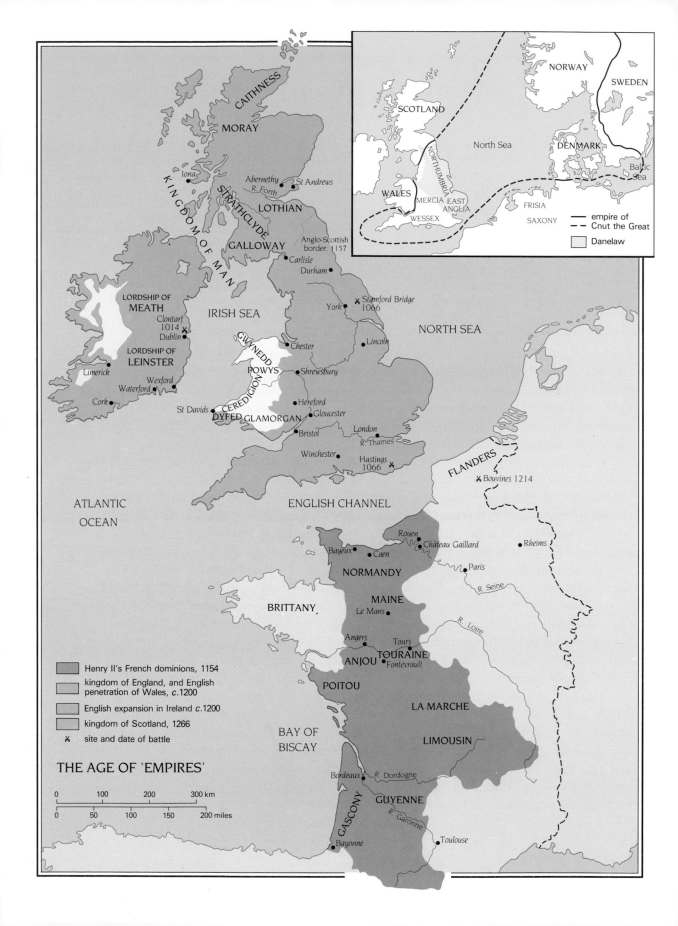

Inset map (top right)

NORWAY
SWEDEN
SCOTLAND
North Sea
DENMARK
NORTHUMBRIA
Baltic Sea
WALES
MERCIA EAST ANGLIA
FRISIA
WESSEX
SAXONY

—— empire of
- - - Cnut the Great
Danelaw

Main map

CAITHNESS
MORAY
Iona
KINGDOM OF MAN
Abernethy
St Andrews
R. Forth
STRATHCLYDE
LOTHIAN
GALLOWAY
Anglo-Scottish border, 1157
Carlisle
Durham
Stamford Bridge 1066
York
LORDSHIP OF MEATH
Clontarf 1014
Dublin
IRISH SEA
NORTH SEA
Lincoln
Chester
GWYNEDD
LORDSHIP OF LEINSTER
Limerick
POWYS
Shrewsbury
Wexford
Waterford
CEREDIGION
Hereford
Cork
St Davids
DYFED GLAMORGAN
Gloucester
London
Bristol
R. Thames
Winchester
Hastings 1066
FLANDERS
Bouvines 1214
ATLANTIC OCEAN
ENGLISH CHANNEL
Rouen
Château Gaillard
Rheims
Bayeux
Caen
NORMANDY
Paris
R. Seine
BRITTANY
MAINE
Le Mans
Angers
Tours
R. Loire
ANJOU
TOURAINE
Fontevrault
POITOU
LA MARCHE
LIMOUSIN
BAY OF BISCAY
Bordeaux
R. Dordogne
GUYENNE
GASCONY
R. Garonne
Bayonne
Toulouse

Henry II's French dominions, 1154
kingdom of England, and English penetration of Wales, c.1200
English expansion in Ireland c.1200
kingdom of Scotland, 1266
✕ site and date of battle

THE AGE OF 'EMPIRES'

0   100   200   300 km
0   50 100 150 200 miles

acknowledge their subordination to the king's power, visiting his court and paying him tribute as their predecessors had done before them. One enthusiastic writer in England felt that by 1135 'it might easily have been thought that parts of Wales were a second England', so forcefully had the king and his nobles advanced into the country. Yet in practice the new marcher lordships established by Anglo-Norman nobles were little different in their relationship to the king from the Welsh kingdoms they replaced, though their lords were indisputably more dependent personally on him. One certain consequence of the creation of such lordships in eastern Wales was that boundaries were more precisely defined, and by 1200 it was reasonably clear which lands lay in the English shires and which lay in the march of Wales. Apart from periodic retaliation by Welsh kings who recovered lost territory (especially in 1094–1100 and in Stephen's reign), three of the largest Welsh kingdoms stoutly resisted the conquerors at various times during the twelfth century and with varying degrees of success: Deheubarth (to 1197), Powys (to 1210), and Gwynedd (to 1282). Confronted by their opposition, Henry II and his Angevin successors pursued no coherent policy for the subjection of Wales, except maybe in one particular. They demanded acknowledgement of their overlordship, and it is possible that Henry II actively discouraged Welsh rulers from bearing the title of king (or *brenin*). King John went further: he insisted on committing to parchment not only his rights and powers in Wales, but also the obligations of Welsh rulers to him.

HAROLD GODWINSON, later King Harold II, shown on the Bayeux Tapestry swearing an oath to William, duke of Normandy, later William the Conqueror, during a visit to William's court before 1066. The oath signifies that Harold has become William's liegeman; he may even have accepted him as Edward the Confessor's heir on this occasion. A similar oath of allegiance may have been sworn by Welsh and Scottish kings to the Conqueror and his successors.

MACBETH

(1040–1057), king of Scots

Few details of Shakespeare's play come close to reality, except the central theme of bitter conflict between Macbeth and Duncan I. Possibly the son of Malcolm II's daughter by Finlay, mormaer of Moray, Macbeth's marriage to a royal kinswoman strengthened his claim to the throne. His struggle with Duncan was also a campaign against growing English influence at court; he was champion of the Scottish north. When Duncan was slain near Elgin (1040), Macbeth mounted his throne. For the next seventeen years, he defended his position against Duncan's son, Malcolm Canmore, and his allies in Orkney and Northumbria, who occupied part of southern Scotland. Macbeth felt secure enough to make a pilgrimage to Rome (1050), but he was killed by Malcolm and the Northumbrians at Lumphanan. With the overthrow of his stepson and heir (1058), his line's regal pretensions ended. Apart from Duncan II (1094) and Donald Bane (1097), Macbeth was the last Scottish king to be buried on Iona.

If similar factors were at work in Anglo-Scottish relations, they were not exploited by the kings of England with the same ruthlessness and military determination. Although the Scots won a victory over the Northumbrians at Carham in 1018, when Cnut was still consolidating his position as king of England, and despite Malcolm II's success in extending his power in Lothian and Strathclyde, no further Scottish offensives were launched. One explanation for this is that Galloway, in the south-west, seems to have been ruled by an independent dynasty. So too was Moray, even though Kenneth mac Alpin's successors had striven to impose their overlordship there. The use of military force to make regal authority effective was shown to have its dangers in Scotland: when King Duncan I attempted to use force, he was killed by Macbeth (1040), who fastened his own Moray grip on the kingdom of the Scots until he was slain by Duncan's son (1057). Even then Moray separatism could not be snuffed out and a native dynasty that continued to flourish there was only forced to accept royal rule in 1130. The annexation and reorganization of Moray by David I and his successors were truly significant developments in the evolution of the medieval Scottish kingdom. Relations with the rulers of Galloway remained tense during the twelfth century, and Henry II capitalized on this to intervene across the border when he visited Carlisle (1185). But by the time King William the Lion died in 1214, the Scottish king's authority had been well established in Galloway and accepted by its dominant family. Royal control was much feebler in the Western Isles and Man, where Scandinavian earls of Orkney and kings of Dublin and Norway vied with one another to assert their power. Man was ruled by a Norse dynasty until 1205 and only in 1266 did the treaty of Perth cede the Isles to Scotland.

When Cnut visited Scotland in 1031, he received the submission of Malcolm II. It was a traditional expression of personal homage and had no unusual significance. In any case, the divisions in England during the Confessor's reign, and then the upheaval of the Norman Conquest, meant that Scottish raids and attacks continued in the borderland. By 1072, however, William the Conqueror was secure enough in his new kingdom to retaliate and invade the northern realm; at Abernethy, Malcolm III, king of Scots, was forced to do homage just like his predecessors. The defeat and death of Malcolm at Alnwick (1093) brought this series of hostilities to a temporary end and the frontier between the two kingdoms was carefully defined for the first time. After William Rufus helped Malcolm's sons to become, each in his turn, king of Scotland (1095–7), their sense of indebtedness and allegiance to the Anglo-Norman king seemed likely to lay the foundations for much closer relations between the two kingdoms. But during the following century, turbulence and civil war in England gave the Scots new opportunities to overrun Northumberland and the Carlisle region on more than one occasion; David I also acquired the earldom of Huntingdon through his wife. Eventually, William the Lion was captured in 1174: he was stripped of all his gains in England, forced to surrender key Scottish castles such as Edinburgh and Stirling, and was required to swear unconditional homage to Henry II. These were the most precise and extensive concessions to English overlordship yet made, and although William secured release from his oaths in return for helping to finance Richard the Lion-heart's crusade (1189), the memory of formal declarations of Scottish subjection lingered long in English minds. For the moment, the Scottish king's control over the region between the Clyde and the Solway was preserved and his acknowledgement of the English king's overlord-ship was confined (albeit with difficulty) to the personal level. Moreover, the frontier between the two kingdoms was now fixed. The Solway in the west and the Tweed in the east were linked by the Cheviot Hills, which were themselves a considerable barrier to communication and settlement. By river, burn, and weir, the Anglo-Scottish border was marked, and in 1237 both sides acknowledged it. The expansion of the Anglo-Norman and Angevin dominions northwards had been successfully contained, though French influences continued to seep across the frontier.

Ireland, which had been spared large-scale immigration for a millennium, at last began to have its political development and territorial configuration modified by immigrants from overseas. By the eleventh century, the Norse settlements along the eastern seaboard were being integrated into the polity of native kingdoms (or *tuatha*), even to the extent of sharing some of their characteristics. The long tradition of political separatism and independence was too pervasive and deep-seated to allow the growth of any centralized administration—even under temporary 'high kings'—that could mobilize resistance to even more powerful immigrants. When French nobles arrived in the later twelfth century, the opposition they encountered was ill-coordinated. Ironically, it was this

BROUGH CASTLE, CUMBRIA (*above*). It was built at a crossroads on the Anglo-Scottish frontier by King William II when he conquered Cumbria in 1092. It used Roman defences but was partly demolished by King William the Lion (1174), after which a rectangular keep and even later buildings were constructed. Eighteen miles away is Brougham Castle (*below*), which was built by King Henry II *c*.1175 at the time of the English occupation of Westmorland. This and the rebuilt Brough Castle mark Henry's consolidation of the Anglo-Scottish frontier.

pattern of political and territorial morcellation which made it impossible for the newcomers to complete their conquests. Although there was no single Irish ruler with resources sufficient to mastermind resistance, equally there was no single outstanding king whose defeat would have meant the conquest of the entire island.

The slaying of Brian Boruma at Clontarf (1014) brought to a dramatic end the most promising attempt to create an effective 'high kingship' in Ireland; yet the great Irish victory in the battle also dashed Norsemen's hopes that they could lord it over Ireland. The attractions of 'high kingship' continued to make it a prize to be fought over by the strongest provincial dynasties in Ireland, which in the eleventh and twelfth centuries sought power, territory, and resources just as dukes of Normandy and counts of Anjou did in France and England. Three such kingdoms in particular dominated Ireland and overawed their weaker neighbours in the century and a half following Brian's death: those of the O'Briens in Munster (Brian's descendants, who publicized their ambitions by calling themselves 'the French kings of Ireland'!), the O'Connors in Connacht, and the Mac Lochlainns of Ulster. Brian's grandson was even called 'magnificent king of Ireland' by Archbishop Lanfranc of Canterbury, and the saintly Anselm soared even higher when he referred to Brian's great-grandson as 'by the grace of God most glorious king of Ireland'. It was the O'Connors' ruthless attempts to depose lesser kings and divide their kingdoms which provoked such resistance that Dermot MacMurrough of Leinster ('Dermot of the foreigners') took the extraordinary step of appealing to Henry II for aid. As far as Henry was concerned, the request may not in fact have been a bolt from the blue. Always the voracious and aggressive dynast, an Irish venture had already occurred to him (1155) as a way of providing territory for his young son, William; and the pope, who needed an effective instrument with which to reform the Irish Church, had granted Henry the overlordship of Ireland in 1154. But these ideas did not leave the drawing-board until Dermot's appeal in 1166–7. Thereafter, Anglo-Norman nobles from West Wales were licensed by the king to go a-conquering in Ireland, and soon the king himself resolved to intervene (1170) in order to retain personal control of what his nobles were doing. The outcome was a mass submission to Henry by Irish kings and Anglo-Norman nobles alike. Henry II's lordship over Ireland became a legal reality when he concluded the treaty of Windsor (1175) with the 'high king' of Ireland, Rory O'Connor, through whom a feudal relationship was established for the first time with all the other kings of Ireland. Ten years later (and perhaps as early as 1177), Henry announced that his youngest son, John, was to be king of Ireland. In practice, of course, the situation was far less clear-cut, for some Irish kings did not recognize the supremacy of a 'high king'; still less were they prepared to submit to a new foreign overlord. In any case, Henry II persisted in encouraging more of his nobles to conquer the

CORMAC'S CHAPEL ON THE ROCK OF CASHEL, Ireland. It was built by King Cormac mac Carthy, *c.*1127–35. He encouraged Church reform and designed his new chapel for a small community of Benedictine monks. English, French, Irish, and continental features have been detected in the architecture, and it is therefore the earliest datable Irish church to display elaborate sculptures of international inspiration.

DROMORE CASTLE, co. Down (*below*), a classic motte-and-bailey structure. It was built in the later twelfth century by Anglo-Norman settlers in Ulster.

unsubdued parts of Ireland and to create new lordships there. Thus if, by the end of the twelfth century, the Angevin 'empire' had been extended yet further, it had been done partly by proxy, partly by direct conquest, partly by receiving acknowledgement of overlordship, and partly, even, by papal fiat. A permanent dominance could be achieved in Wales, Scotland, and Ireland, as in England and the French territories, only by military power, good luck, and a coherent plan.

Authoritarian Kingship

During the two centuries when England was part—but rarely the dominant part—of a far wider dominion or 'empire', the character of its kingship underwent fundamental change. The basic elements of kingship in the British Isles during the previous half-millennium still lay at its heart in the eleventh and twelfth centuries: its military and Christian qualities and its governmental function. But events inaugurated by Cnut's conquest of England set in motion changes which in time modified the nature of kingship throughout the British Isles, now emphasizing the powers, authority, and status of kings, now stressing their limitations and their need to co-operate with the communities over whom they ruled.

This was an age when the trend towards larger and more cohesive kingdoms was marked, even in Ireland and Wales. It was an age, too, when the emphasis in kingship shifted noticeably from consensus and co-operation in ruling towards more pronounced regal authority. This was made possible by the size, resources, and sophistication of kingdoms; royal administration became more pervasive, more centralized, and more effective. In achieving this, the acts of military conquest so characteristic of England's history in this period, and undertaken by foreigners for whom expansion and migration were a compulsion and a livelihood, were crucial: the conquests of Cnut, William I, and Henry II. The fact that almost all English kings in the two centuries after 1016 were either Danish or French, established in England by victory in the field, strengthened the authoritarian element in their kingship. They were, too, more than merely kings of England and they regarded their English realm as part of far greater agglomerations of territories, each with traditions and practices of ruling that were bound to influence their attitudes to their kingship in England, most likely in the direction of personal authority. Moreover, as conquerors or the sons of conquerors, most of these English kings were men who brooked no contradiction or correction: William I and his sons, William Rufus and Henry I, seem to have been hewn from a rough, tough stock that is easily associated with bloody ruthlessness. To judge by the violent relations between Henry II, his wife, and their sons, including Richard I and John, these were no less the characteristics of Angevin rulers.

With rather less conviction, it can be said that in Scotland, too, the struggles that took place in the eleventh century between rival claimants to the Scottish crown, and the more fundamental confrontation between the Anglicized south and the Scottish north which these dynastic struggles partly reflect, shaped a kingship that stressed the powers and authority of the Scottish kings. Even in Ireland and Wales, the successful campaigns of one or two great dynasties to impose an (albeit temporary) hegemony over the others seem to have edged the concept of 'high kingship' towards a broader overall regal authority.

Paradoxically, the strains of military conquest and the growing influence of the English kingdom on other kingdoms in the British Isles could have a contrary effect. Moreover, a more precise definition of kingly powers made some people aware of the limitations of these powers, whether such limitations were imposed by the kings' own subjects or by external authorities such as the pope and neighbouring monarchs. And the nobility, whom conquering kings enlisted in their victorious enterprises—whether it be Cnut or William I in England, or Anglicized kings in Scotland, or noble conquerors of the Welsh and Irish marches—were a feudal class that had a role in war, society, and government which kings could hardly ignore, no matter how powerful they felt themselves to be. It is unhelpful to designate this period as 'the age of feudal kingship', but this dependence of kings on their nobility is a large and important factor that modified the authoritarianism of kingship in these centuries.

The role of kings as military leaders and defenders of their kingdoms was bound to be one of the most prominent characteristics of kingship in an age when Scandinavian and, then, French kings subdued the Anglo-Saxon kingdom in quite lightning fashion. Henry I may have relished the role of a strategic commander more than that of a general in the field, but all kings of England could be found at the head of their armies, in England itself or in the transmarine dominions which they strove to hold together around the Baltic Sea or in France. William Rufus campaigned as vigorously against the Scots as did Henry II in Ireland, and—the greatest warrior of all—Richard the Lion-heart was a famous crusader in the Holy Land. Nor could the Scottish kings afford to leave the saddle for long, and ambitious Welsh and Irish kings campaigned long and hard, and wherever it was necessary, in order to crush the resistance of their rivals. An early thirteenth-century Welsh poet relished, next only to godliness, 'mead and the feastings of a victorious ruler, a long bright summer, a well-fed horse in April, the play of spears and the waving of banners'. As Stephen and King John could unhappily testify, the king who failed in battle, or whose military capabilities remained unproven, was likely to fail as a king.

Yet the time was long past when kings could rely solely on their prowess and success in arms in order to maintain and justify their kingship. Kings in the British Isles were Christian kings, and whilst this quality consolidated and enhanced

EDWARD THE CONFESSOR

(1042–1066), king of the English

> . . . it is our duty courageously to oppose the wicked and take good men as models, by enriching the churches of God, relieving those oppressed by wicked judges, and by judging equitably the powerful and the humble.
>
> (Charter of Edward, 1063)

EDWARD is a shadowy figure. The elder son of Æthelred II and Queen Emma, he and his brother Alfred (d. 1036) lived in Normandy from 1013. The childless Harthacnut brought him to England (1041) perhaps to be his heir, despite a lack of military ability and reputation. When Edward was chosen king, he was acknowledged by Duke William of Normandy and by Germany and France. Apart from a kingly bearing and bushy beard, little is known of his appearance; the gentle saint of the *Life* (*c.*1066) conceals his poor judgement and childlike nature. At first, he sought to remove the threat from Denmark and Norway, though England remained in the grip of Cnut's earls, including Godwin of Wessex, whose daughter Edward reluctantly married (1045). Obsessively religious, he made contact with the reforming papacy and his finest monument is Westminster Abbey. But in favouring mostly Norman companions, Edward created a court of intrigue which produced the pivotal crisis of the reign (1050–2). The king fell out with Godwin, whose family was exiled (1051) while Queen Edith entered a nunnery. Godwin's return (1052) raised the succession question; failure to solve it led to a war (1066) between Harold Godwinson and William of Normandy, with the Norwegian king in the background. When Duke William, Emma's great-nephew, visited England, he may have been designated Edward's heir. But in 1054, with Godwin's sons in control, Edward decided to make Edmund Ironside's son his heir. Edward the *ætheling*'s death (1057) may have encouraged Harold to think of himself as a claimant; his influence was certainly paramount in the last decade of the king's life. Faced with the Northumbrian revolt (1065), when Harold visited Normandy he acknowledged William to be Edward's successor. As the king lay dying, he may have compounded uncertainty by naming Harold, who ignored his promise to William and precipitated the Norman invasion. Edward was buried in his new abbey at Westminster, and his tomb was venerated from the early twelfth century. He was canonized (1161) and his body translated three times (1163, 1269, 1557). The *Life* and posthumous cult bestowed on Edward the reputation of a saintly and beneficent king, the last of his line.

THE CROWNED EDWARD THE CONFESSOR ON HIS DEATH-BED, in the presence of a cleric, two liegemen, and two ladies (one perhaps Queen Edith). In this double scene from the Bayeux Tapestry, the shrouded corpse beneath is laid out, with the attendant cleric.

A MEDIEVAL KING AND HIS COUNSELLORS. This drawing is taken from a thirteenth-century manuscript of the 'Romance of Alexander', but since the book was probably written and illustrated at St Alban's Abbey, the scene is likely to be based on contemporary English practice. Here King Darius, bearded, crowned, and seated, is shown in animated conversation with his barons, who are also seated.

their kingship, it also laid on them religious and moral responsibilities of which they were increasingly made aware—and of which they were sometimes reminded by popes and their agents (or legates). Cnut, whose father Sweyn was a recent and uncertain Christian, had a perception of the Church and its faith that was unusually sharp when he acquired the English crown in 1016; he himself had been baptized only three years before. The Normans had the same viewpoint. The Christian faith and the support of the Church's clergy were an essential accompaniment to their conquest of England and to the stability of their rule in the decades following 1066. The king's customary role in the appointment of English bishops and abbots placed in the new dynasty's hands a means whereby congenial Norman and other continental monks and clergy could be brought to England and installed in bishoprics and monasteries, so that by the end of the Conqueror's reign few of England's bishops and abbots were English. By embracing the fashionable cause of Church reform, these Norman kings were able to extend their practical authority over the English Church and thereby fasten their rule on English society more generally. Stimulated by this reforming impulse, they transferred the headquarters of several ancient English sees to what had become more populous and strategic urban centres. This facilitated royal control of the kingdom by a Christian king, and at the same time it met the spiritual needs of these newer centres.

The wonder is that the unique contribution made by the Church to the development of English kingship survived the bitter conflicts between Church and State during the reform movement in the Church Universal from the mid-eleventh century onwards. But it did—and more successfully than in most kingdoms of the medieval West. The popes of the eleventh and twelfth centuries, taking their cue from the high-principled Gregory VII, advanced explicit and uncompromising claims to sweeping powers over Christian society; most particularly, they reacted against the idea that kings and other rulers should invest bishops and abbots with the symbols of their spiritual and temporal authority and require acts of homage from them before consecration. This was the unvarnished practice of the Norman kings, enhancing their royal power over the Church and its clergy; but the possibility of conflict with the pope and the reformers on this issue was stark once Pope Gregory's battle-cry was heard in his struggle with the greatest lay ruler of all, the emperor. A similar struggle threatened to break out in England. That it did not do so is a tribute to the personal skills of Archbishop Lanfranc, an Italian whom William I brought from the Norman abbey of Bec (where he had been abbot since 1063) to be archbishop of Canterbury in 1070. Rather did a period of practical accommodation and co-operation follow, under Lanfranc's wise direction, between the claims of pope and king in England; like Dunstan and his colleagues in the tenth century, the archbishop gave central direction to the English Church in ways that supported the king in his new realm. Privately, Pope Gregory was not unhappy with this compromise, as he confided to two French bishops in 1081:

The king of the English, although in certain matters he does not behave as devoutly as we might hope, nevertheless in that he has neither destroyed nor sold the churches of God; that he has taken pains to govern his subjects in peace and justice; that he has refused his assent to anything detrimental to the apostolic see . . . in all these respects he has shown himself more worthy of approbation and honour than other kings . . .

But it ultimately proved impossible to prevent the 'investiture contest' from spawning disputes even in England. Under the exceptionally high-minded Archbishop Anselm (called ironically from the same Italo-Norman stable as his predecessor), and confronted by the more brutal and assertive William Rufus and Henry I, Church and State fell to quarrelling in England as bitterly as anywhere else. The uncompromising Thomas Becket, archbishop of Canterbury from 1162 until his martyrdom eight years later at the hands of Henry II's hot-headed knights, shattered the all too delicate compromise that had been constructed earlier in the century and formalized by Henry I (1107). This serious rupture was bound to undermine the authority of a Christian king, even though Henry II, in his constitutions (or legislation) proclaimed at the royal manor house at Clarendon in 1167, had tried to defend his control over the clergy of his kingdom and to supervise their links with Rome and the pope. A king who, like Henry in 1170, was declared an excommunicate came perilously close to having a crucial prop knocked from beneath his throne. There were compelling reasons why Henry moved swiftly to be reconciled with the Church (1172).

The added difficulties which King John encountered from his subjects, including the clergy, made the king's relations with the Church and its leaders yet more precarious. His authority as a sovereign ruler in his kingdom was further undermined by an interdict that was placed on his realm in 1208 and which forced him to accept an archbishop, Stephen Langton, whom he had earlier rejected; in 1209 John too was declared excommunicated. By strong implication, a Christian king had been declared unworthy of kingship, and he and his realm found themselves denied the sacraments of their faith. This was potentially the most serious blow that the kingship of England had sustained since its beginnings in the mid-tenth century. Fortunately for the English monarchy, for John and his dynasty, this spiritual onslaught did not last long. John realized that his own and his kingship's future was at stake and in 1213 he made the greatest concession of all to an imperious papacy. The kingdom of England became a papal fief, and its king acknowledged what no previous king of England had ever acknowledged; he and his predecessors might have had a special relationship with the Almighty, but John now conceded that he and his successors would be subordinate to God's earthly representative, the Holy Father in Rome. This placed a formal constraint on English kingship which no Christian king of England had hitherto been prepared to acknowledge so explicitly or so publicly. When John's son, Henry III, showed himself ready to espouse the pope's terrestrial ambitions and policies in Italy and Germany, the tensions between Church and State in England were heightened and they helped to pitchfork the monarchy into a major political and constitutional crisis by 1258. Papal influence on Henry and his kingdom was intensified by the energetic missions of the friars, whose authority came directly from the pope, by more insistent papal demands for taxation to finance enterprises like the crusades and an elaborate Church government in Rome, and by the greater number of papal appointments to bishoprics and lesser livings in England. It is true that English kings learned how to divert much of the taxation

THOMAS BECKET, ARCHBISHOP OF CANTERBURY (*top*), standing, mitred and holding his archiepiscopal staff, arguing with King Henry II, who is shown crowned and seated on a cushioned bench. This argument symbolizes the clash between Church and State which was made more bitter in England by the hitherto close relationship between Becket and the king. Behind Becket lurk several knights in chain-mail, one ominously clutching a sword.

THE CASKET WHICH CONTAINED RELICS OF ST THOMAS BECKET (*below*). Made of wood at Limoges *c.*1190, it is overlaid with engraved and gilded copper plaques. The scene tells the story of the saint's murder by Henry II's knights before the high altar in Canterbury Cathedral in 1170, in the presence of shocked monks. In 1173 Becket was canonized by Pope Alexander III and the upper scene shows the dead archbishop with a halo.

of the clergy into their own coffers, and they were able to exploit papal appointments (or provisions) for their own purposes and to reward royal clerks, servants, or relatives. Nevertheless, the reform movement in the Church bade fair to modify the character of English kingship by restraining the scope of the king's authority itself. It took the rebellion against Henry III, and the firmness of Edward I and Edward III in their relations with Church and popes, to prevent this modification and restraint from becoming permanent.

It was, indeed, the English monarchy which spearheaded Church reform in the British Isles, though outside England the impact of reform does not seem to have been sufficiently pervasive or powerful as to threaten the authority of kings— rather, the contrary. Close co-operation between Church and State in the decades immediately following the Norman Conquest enabled the kings of England and their clerical agents to reassert English dominance beyond the borders of the realm. The Church in Scotland was brought under the authority of the archbishop of York and in the 1120s the pope supported this arrangement, no doubt seeing it as the best way of introducing reform and extending papal power in the northern kingdom. For the Scottish kings, many of whom were receptive to English ideas and practices without conceding complete domination, the development of a diocesan system by the twelfth century was a considerable support to their dynasty's claims to rule all of Scotland. Eventually, in 1192, the pope granted a bull to William the Lion that recognized the separate identity of the Scottish Church, with its nine dioceses, and its independence of all ecclesiastical authorities apart from Rome. This was an enormous boost to the authority and standing of the monarchy, whose kings responded by taking the Scottish Church under their guardianship, founding new monasteries that looked directly to the king for protection.

In Wales, the hold of the English Church remained strong, and a separate Welsh Church was not established, despite the efforts of a few ambitious bishops

KING DAVID I (d. 1153) AND HIS GRANDSON, KING MALCOLM IV (d. 1165), framed in a large initial M of a charter granted by Malcolm to Kelso Abbey in 1159. David is portrayed crowned, brandishing a sword, and holding an orb; the young, crowned Malcolm (who was about seventeen at the time) is shown more pacifically, a sword on his lap and holding a sceptre.

of St David's—Anglo-Normans to boot—who were seduced by the tradition of St David and claimed a special primacy independent of Canterbury. The four bishoprics that became a fixture in Wales during the first century of Anglo-Norman rule, each under mainly Anglo-Norman bishops, were of considerable assistance to the Anglo-Norman conquerors of Wales and for that reason did not consistently provide Welsh kings with the sort of aid that rulers in Scotland and England could expect. Furthermore, Welsh kings took to patronizing monasteries established by the spate of new religious orders that entered Wales in the wake of the conquerors, often at the expense of venerable Welsh foundations. Even in Ireland, sponsorship of reform gave to the Anglo-Norman archbishops of Canterbury a degree of influence over the Irish Church which they had never previously enjoyed. They were encouraged by both king and pope to believe that their ecclesiastical powers extended to the entire British Isles. Despite the creation of four archbishoprics in Ireland in 1152, and the appointment almost exclusively of Irish men to Irish sees before the thirteenth century, Henry II's invasion enabled Canterbury to reassert its primacy.

The most memorable involvement of an English king in the affairs of the Universal Church in the twelfth century gave Christian kingship a new meaning, but at the same time it also endangered England's monarchy. The Angevin monarchs, in particular, were conscious of their dominant place in western Europe and this may have made them more responsive to the appeals of the pope and their own crusader-kinsmen on behalf of the Christian colonies in the Holy Land—especially the kingdom of Jerusalem—which were threatened by the forces of Islam. The idea of the crusade had been harnessed by no less a king than William I in 1066, when he had invaded England under a papal banner, preaching the cause of Church reform in a kingdom untouched by the current religious enthusiasms in Italy; after Hastings he could pose as the righteous warrior on whom God had smiled. But whatever deference later kings showed towards crusading, whatever vows they may have sworn to prove their Christian commitment as soldier-kings, none of them actually went on pilgrimage to Rome in the twelfth century, let alone led an expedition to Jerusalem—until the famous exploits of Richard the Lion-heart in Palestine in the 1190s.

It is not without significance that in the later twelfth century, the kingdom of Jerusalem was ruled by kinsmen of King Henry II, and he accordingly gave a measure of financial support to his relatives settled on the eastern Mediterranean seaboard. His son Richard, however, not only vowed to go crusading himself, but he actually fulfilled his vow with a distinction and panache that has captured the western imagination through its writers, novelists, and film-makers. He commanded a fleet that traversed the Mediterranean (1190–1) and subjugated Cyprus, and he generalled a huge army that included Philip Augustus of France (the Emperor Frederick Barbarossa died on the way) and achieved an initial success

PICTORIAL TILES DEPICTING KING RICHARD I, mounted for combat, and his adversary during the Third Crusade, Saladin the Saracen. The decorated tiles are from Chertsey Abbey, which has since been demolished.

that was spectacular, though its long-term results would have disappointed Richard himself had he lived long enough to see them. His enterprise was an example of Christian kingship at its most pretentious, with an English monarch posing as the guardian of the faith and the Holy Places against the heathen aggressor. When Richard left Palestine in 1192, his renown as a warrior and his reputation as a Christian king were much enhanced. Yet within ten years of his death (1199), his successor had been excommunicated and his kingdom laid under interdict.

The king's duty to maintain peace and order in his kingdom and provide justice for his subjects underwent a major transformation in the twelfth century which emphasized the king's authority throughout England and made more explicit his obligations and the parameters within which he ruled. It is not simply that the twelfth century witnessed an explosion in the amount of official writing that was produced or that more records of government survive from that century compared with earlier periods. The king's role as judge and law-maker was revolutionized. The same kind of development seems to have touched the Scottish kings and certain Welsh and Irish rulers, too, though for Wales and Ireland the surviving evidence is too sparse and enigmatic, and the local annals too sketchy, to reveal much of substance about the morcellated kingship of those two countries in the eleventh and twelfth centuries.

The Scandinavian monarchy of Cnut was probably too short-lived for significant changes of this kind to have taken place early in eleventh-century England.

Cnut himself was at pains to embrace the customs and practices of his Anglo-Saxon predecessors and to add pronouncements of his own in law-codes devised by himself and Archbishop Wulfstan, who had been Æthelred II's adviser, though we know all too little of the methods the king used to convey his judgements and implement his laws. Indeed, it is noteworthy that all his successors in the eleventh century, be they Danish, English, or Norman, consciously preserved, adapted, and modified the body of English custom which time and acceptance by the community had hallowed and past kings had published. There were good political reasons for doing so, as William the Conqueror recognized when he promulgated what were regarded as the customs of England operating in the Confessor's time; and so did his youngest son, Henry I, who issued a tradition-laden 'charter of liberties' after he seized power in 1100.

Once the Norman dynasty was well established in the kingdom, major changes got under way to emphasize the king's role as law-maker and especially his obligation to ensure that whatever law was current in his realm should be made available to all his subjects and be effectively enforced. Availability and effectiveness were the keys to this transformation, rather than the creation of new law by royal fiat, though in due time that too became more common and underlined the authority of the king. The reigns of William Rufus and, especially, of Henry I saw a widening of the scope of royal justice, by means of new royal officials: local justices in each shire and roving (or itinerant) justices in groups of

A WELSH KING DISPENSING JUSTICE, from a thirteenth-century Latin version of the Laws of Hywel Dda. The king is seated on a cushioned seat, holding a sceptre and wearing a circlet, though it is far from certain that Welsh princes even in the thirteenth century had such paraphernalia of kingship.

shires. Their numbers multiplied as the twelfth century wore on; the geographical bounds within which they travelled broadened and so did the sort of cases with which they dealt. They took with them the king's authority and the royal conception of kingly power.

Once the civil war of Stephen's reign (1135–54) was over, the process continued. It was made more urgent by the disorder of the times and the onset of a serious confrontation between the king and the Church. In Henry II's day, the royal courts, presided over by his justices, gradually became the nerve-centre of justice in both civil and criminal cases. But it was more than a question of better enforcement and organization—which in themselves meant that the royal power had greater impact locally and regionally than ever before. Under Henry II the law itself developed significantly, largely as a result of royal decisions: the criminal code was made more severe by several of his assizes (or law-codes); case-law supplemented what was customary with increasing frequency; and in cases relating to property and landholding new procedures were devised which amounted to novel law. At the centre stood the king, himself taking an active part in his own court (or *curia regis*), with justices at his side forming a central tribunal at Westminster which, by the end of John's reign, co-ordinated and supervised the giving of justice throughout the realm. People could have recourse to a court of professional justices who translated the king's obligation as judge and law-

THE GREAT SEAL OF KING JOHN, depicting on the obverse the crowned king enthroned. He is holding an orb and sceptre in his left hand and a sword in his right, representing the king as ruler and judge, and as protector of the faith. The legend reads 'John by the grace of God king of England and lord of Ireland'. On the reverse, the king is mounted, holding a shield in his left hand and a sword in his right, representing the king as warrior. The legend reads 'John, duke of Normandy . . .'.

giver into reality. In these two spheres, the king's authority came to touch all his free subjects equally, and helped to tilt the balance of the content of English law from traditional custom towards the law of its kings. 'The king's peace' was now the most awesome peace in England.

The obligations and duties of English kings were publicly proclaimed in general terms at their coronation. By the tenth century the inauguration of a king at his coronation ceremony was the first and most significant act of his reign. The order of service which had been devised for King Edgar's coronation in 973 was probably still in use, little changed, in the eleventh century. Norman and later kings deliberately used this hallowed rite to emphasize their rightful possession of all the powers and prerogatives of Anglo-Saxon kings.

At the core of the ceremony was the deeply religious act of anointing the king with sanctified 'holy oil', symbolizing the part which God and his Church played in king-making in medieval England. Despite the endeavours of Church reformers to lessen the religious significance of this sacrament of unction in the coronation of kings, and to remind a new monarch that popes had deposed kings in recent times, their campaign seems to have had little effect in Norman England, where the idea of the priestly king was repeatedly endorsed. In the twelfth century, the political theorist, John of Salisbury, noted that ordinary people still believed that crowned kings enjoyed the spiritual authority of a priest. Even Stephen's submission of his election as king to Pope Innocent II for confirmation (1136) was not used as a precedent, nor was it exploited by a pope who had his own preoccupations.

Although we know very little about the coronation of some medieval English kings, the symbolism of its various stages is generally well understood. The primitive act of electing, proclaiming, and acclaiming kings preceded the coronation ceremony itself. In Edward the Confessor's case, the proclamation took place in London before even his predecessor, Harthacnut, had been buried; speed was presumably of the essence when a change of dynasty was taking place. For the same reason, and with at least two other pretenders to Edward's throne in the offing in January 1066, Harold Godwinson was acclaimed in London on the morrow of the old king's death. And when Richard I's death became known in England, and some thought of his nephew Arthur as a possible successor, certain nobles swore an oath of fealty to John before ever he set foot in England to receive his coronation.

Some coronations took place many months after the proclamation and acclamation of a new king: the Confessor was crowned almost ten months later at the great Church festival of Easter in 1043. At times of political uncertainty, it was wise to stage the coronation more swiftly—as in January 1066, when Harold was crowned the day following the Confessor's death and only hours after his acclamation. Regardless of when it took place, the king was not fully or lawfully

THE CORONATION OF EDWARD THE CONFESSOR on Easter Day 1043. This picture, from a mid-thirteenth-century history of Edward as a saint, shows the enthroned king being crowned at the Anglo-Saxon capital of Winchester by Archbishop Eadsige of Canterbury and Archbishop Ælfric of York, who had both been appointed by Cnut the Dane. Eadsige concludes the investment of the king with the royal regalia by handing him the rod of equity and virtue.

king until he was crowned. Indeed, the uncrowned Matilda used the style 'lady of the English', and Richard I and John, in the weeks between their election and their coronation, were usually designated 'lord' rather than king. And until Edward I's accession in 1272 (when the king was abroad on crusade, where he remained until 1274), a reign was considered to begin only at the solemn and formal crowning. Not that in the interval government in practice ceased and people did not know who their king was; but only with the crowning was God's endorsement unmistakeable and royal acts given cast-iron authority.

HAROLD II

(1066), king of the English

[He] met little quiet as long as he ruled the realm.

(Anglo-Saxon Chronicle, 1066)

THE eldest son of Godwin, earl of Wessex, there was no royal blood in Harold's veins. Opportunity, designation by Edward the Confessor, and the absence of a suitable candidate from the royal house justified his seizure of the throne when Edward died (5 January 1066). His earlier career was that of a great nobleman and successful warrior, an indispensable adjunct to the political and territorial mastery of his father. He was earl of East Anglia (c.1044) and led the army that forced Edward to reinstate his family (1052). He succeeded his father as earl of Wessex (1053) and his brothers were earls by 1057. Their only rival was the family of Leofric of Mercia, supported by the Welsh; both were defeated by Harold and his brother Tostig, earl of Northumbria (1063). His failure to support Tostig when Northumbria revolted (1065) turned his brother into a bitter enemy. When the succession problem became immediate, Harold had himself hastily crowned (6 January). It is doubtful if he had time in his short reign to think of anything but his own security. He was opposed by William of Nor-

mandy, whose accession he had sworn to accept, and by Harold Hardrada, king of Norway, and Tostig. Harold swiftly mobilized an army and fleet against William, but instead had to deal with Tostig's raids. The invasion of Tostig and Hardrada forced him to divert his army to defeat them at Stamford Bridge (25 September). Some men had been dismissed through lack of supplies, and William landed unopposed at Pevensey (28 September). After a 250-mile march from the north, Harold's army was depleted, weary, and bloodied, William's fresh and intact. Victory at Hastings (14 October) went to heavily armed cavalry supported by infantry and archers, who overcame the dismounted English unsupported by archers, who were induced by a feigned flight to desert their defensive position. Harold, struck in the eye and battered by Norman knights, according to the Bayeux Tapestry, and two of his brothers lay dead at the end of the day's fighting.

THE ENTHRONED, CROWNED, AND MOUSTACHED KING HAROLD II, holding a palm (or sceptre) and an orb. An attendant offers him the sword, and Stigand, the schismatic archbishop of Canterbury, stands to one side. The scene is from the Bayeux Tapestry.

After Edward the Confessor, who was crowned at the Anglo-Saxon capital of Winchester, all English kings for the next 200 years (except Stephen) were crowned in Edward's new abbey church at Westminster. Ignoring Harold's brief rule, Edward was regarded as the last king of the Old English dynasty, and an association with the saintly monarch was important to usurping Normans; indeed, the Conqueror's coronation is reported to have been 'by the tomb of Edward the Confessor' on Christmas Day 1066:

And he promised Aldred [archbishop of York] on Christ's book and swore moreover (before Aldred would place the crown on his head) that he would rule all this people as well as the best of the kings before him, if they would be loyal to him. (Anglo-Saxon Chronicle, 1066)

This, after all, was a novel experience for a Norman ruler, for no Norman duke had ever been anointed at his accession: girding with a sword (as was King Richard as duke of Normandy in 1189) or crowning with a circlet (which was provided for John's use by his mother ten years later) had been usual in the duchy.

On coronation day in the late eleventh century, the king, perhaps already wearing his crown, was led by a procession of clergy to the high altar. In the abbey acclamation by clergy and people preceded the taking of the triple oath, an oath which expressed the fundamental qualities and duties of kingship in

THE OLDEST ITEMS OF THE ENGLISH ROYAL REGALIA: the anointing spoon (of late twelfth-century date) and the ampulla in the form of a golden eagle (dating from the late fourteenth century), which presumably contained the holy oil alleged to have been revealed to Thomas Becket by the Virgin Mary. Both pieces were renovated in 1661 after the Restoration of Charles II.

WILLIAM THE CONQUEROR

(1066–1087), king of England

He was a very stern and violent man, so that no one dared do anything contrary to his will . . . Amongst other things the good security he made in this country is not to be forgotten.

(Anglo-Saxon Chronicle, 1087)

THE son of Robert I 'the Magnificent', duke of Normandy, and Herlève, a tanner's daughter of Falaise, he was a shrewd, crude, and vigorous man who inspired both fear and respect. His main aim before 1066 was to assert his authority as duke of Normandy against disloyal nobles and his overlord, Henry I of France. After a turbulent minority (1035–42), William mastered his duchy by determination and skill, defeating rebels at Val-ès-Dunes, near Caen (1047). He sought external security by subduing neighbours or, as with his marriage to the count of Flanders's daughter Matilda (c.1052), winning their alliance. His English ambitions stemmed from personal and political links between the two countries, and Edward the Confessor seems to have promised him the succession (c.1051). He obtained papal approval for his invasion and held a papal banner at Hastings where, 'near the hoar-apple tree', he defeated Harold II. The submission of the rest of England, by ruthless harrying, castle-building, and confiscations, took three years; William suppressed risings in several areas and marched as far as Hexham and Chester (1068–9). He invaded Scotland (1072) and forced Malcolm III to do homage at Abernethy; in 1081 he visited St David's, receiving Welsh submissions on the way. William was no less concerned to maintain his authority in Normandy, where he spent long periods especially dealing with rebellion and French invasions. In England his rule was firm, disciplined, and equitable, and owed much to Archbishop Lanfranc, on whom he had relied in Church and State since 1063. The 'Domesday' survey (1086) recorded the resources of his kingdom,

KING WILLIAM I, bearded, crowned, holding a sceptre and seated on a cushioned bench. He is pictured receiving a copy of *The Deeds of the Norman Dukes* from its author, the monk William of Jumièges. This is from the chronicler Orderic Vitalis's autograph copy of his edition of the work.

and the oath of fealty at Salisbury (1086) from all important landholders stressed their obligations to him. Anglo-Norman writers were excellent publicists for him; William of Poitiers called him another Caesar, and even contemporary English writers gave him respect. William died in Normandy and was buried in his abbey foundation at Caen. Huguenots (1662) and Revolutionaries (1793) destroyed his tomb and scattered his bones.

England: to protect the Church and people, to offer justice to all, and to act with mercy. With people, clergy, and king as one, there then followed the most solemn act of the ceremony, the unction or anointing on head, chest, and hands. (Propriety, incidentally, demanded that the anointing should be confined to head and hands at Victoria's coronation in 1837!) This was usually performed by the archbishop of Canterbury, though in 1042 both archbishops officiated at Winchester, whilst at Harold's coronation (1066) it is uncertain which of them did

THE CORONATION

THE coronation service may stand as a symbol of the monarchy, since it is a mixture of ancient ritual and ceremonies, some of them dating back to before the Norman Conquest, with modern modifications and innovations to suit changing circumstances. It matches the political evolution of the monarchy, also marked by change within continuity. At the coronation of Elizabeth II in 1953, the origins of the act of anointing went back at least as far as 787, when Ecgfrith, son of Offa of Mercia, was consecrated, while the coronation oath contained references to the new Commonwealth countries of Pakistan and Ceylon, which had been in existence but a few years.

The service has been held in Westminster Abbey since the Conquest. The most important features are the recognition, when the monarch is presented by the archbishop of Canterbury; the oath, the part of the ceremony which has most reflected political and religious change; the anointing with holy oil, which is the central act; the crowning and presentation of the regalia; and the homage by the peers of the realm. The banquet and the challenge by the royal champion, one of the more colourful parts of the ceremony, were discontinued by William IV in 1831, partly as an economy measure and partly because the gargantuan banquet given by George IV in 1821 had been marred by unseemly behaviour.

At the coronation of Edgar in 973, a ring, sword, and sceptre were delivered. Most of the regalia was destroyed or sold during the Commonwealth, though the anointing spoon and the ampulla in the form of a golden eagle survived from medieval times. Replicas were made for the coronation of Charles II at the Restoration. The Bible made its appearance in 1689 at the coronation of William and Mary. The coronation chair was made for Edward I and includes the Stone of Scone, brought back from Scotland in 1296. The crown of England is a seventeenth-century replica of that supposedly worn by the Confessor: a lighter imperial crown was made for Victoria in 1838. The anthem 'Zadok the Priest and Nathan the Prophet' was sung at Edgar's coronation: Handel's setting dates from George II's coronation in 1727. The invocation 'Vivat' by the boys of Westminster School was introduced into the ceremony at the coronation of Charles I in 1625.

---

the crowning. By the time Henry II came to be crowned in 1154, Canterbury was the acknowledged transmitter of the spiritual quality of kingship. Even in 1100, Henry I had been quick to apologize to Archbishop Anselm for allowing himself to be crowned by the bishop of London:

> ... with God's approval, I have been elected by the clergy and people of England and, albeit unwillingly, already crowned king in your absence ... I beg you not to be displeased that I have accepted the royal title without your blessing; for, had it been possible, I would sooner have received it from you than from any other. But the need was urgent because enemies would have risen up against me and the people I have to govern, and in consequence my barons and people were unwilling to delay the ceremony longer. (Letter from Henry I)

And when Henry III was crowned by a mere bishop (of Winchester), the exiled Archbishop Langton was assured that this was in no way intended as a slight.

With the spiritual part of the ceremony complete, the king was then invested with regalia that symbolized the more secular, human qualities of kingship: the ring as 'the seal of holy faith'; the sword, implying protection of his kingdom and people; and the crown, sceptre, and rod representing the glory, virtue, equity, and justice reposing in an anointed king. According to the detailed record that survives of Richard I's coronation, he took the heavy gold crown himself from the

THE CORONATION OF AN ENGLISH KING, possibly Edward III, from an Order of Service of *c.*1330–9. The crowned king, holding sceptre and orb, is seated on a throne similar to the coronation chair still in Westminster Abbey. He is surrounded by courtiers and priests, including (*rear, left to right*) a lawyer, the bishop of Rochester, the archbishop of Canterbury, the abbot of Westminster, the archbishop of York, and a lay officer holding a gold piece; and (*front, left to right*) a layman with the king's white gloves, two priests, and a bearded lawyer. The populace peer through a grille as a backdrop.

WILLIAM II RUFUS

(1087–1100), king of England

He was very strong and fierce to his country and his men and
to all his neighbours, and very terrible. And because of the
counsels of wicked men, which were always agreeable to him,
and because of his avarice, he was always harassing this
nation with military service and excessive taxes, for in his days
all justice was in abeyance.

(Anglo-Saxon Chronicle, 1100)

WILLIAM's bad press is mainly due to hostile
monastic writers and denigration by his
younger brother, Henry I. He was his
father's favourite son, strong, thickset, and ruddy. But
his character is a puzzle: he seems ebullient, self-
confident, intelligent, and outspoken—even blasphemous—but in extending the Conqueror's policies
and methods he appeared to many oppressive and
brutal. William was the Conqueror's choice to inherit
England (1087), but his elder brother Robert inherited
Normandy. He proved single-minded in securing his
grip not only on the kingdom but also on the duchy,
which became his when Robert went on crusade
(1096). Despite friction with Archbishop Anselm (from
1093), he did not surrender control of the Church.
William made greater headway than his father in
securing his realm's frontiers: three Scottish kings
swore homage to him and William took royal power to
the far north of England. He helped make Westminster
the administrative centre of the kingdom and added a
great hall to the Confessor's palace. With wide support
from nobles, bishops, and talented agents, he died a
well-established king, though unmarried and childless.
In 1100 he was shot, probably accidentally, while
hunting in the New Forest and was buried in Winchester Cathedral.

WILLIAM RUFUS, as represented on a stone capital, now
lost but originally probably in an arcade in the cloister of
Westminster Abbey which was built during his reign. In
this engraving of the 1830s, the king is shown seated but
uncrowned, holding a parchment roll and flanked by the
abbot of Westminster and one of the monks. He can
hardly have been as repugnant to the Church as is often
suggested.

high altar and handed it to the archbishop of Canterbury for the actual crowning.
It is not known whether this was novel or caused any eyebrows to be raised, but if
he (like his predecessors) had proceeded crowned to the abbey, it would seem not
unnatural that an anointed king should deliver his own crown to the Church's
representative for the actual crowning.

Following the blessing on the day's proceedings and on the crowned king,
those present—often including foreign envoys—as appropriate either greeted
the new king or swore homage to him as a mark of feudal subordination.
Thereafter, kings could describe themselves in their charters as (to use the

Confessor's words) 'king of the English by the gift of God' or (as on William Rufus's great seal) more simply as 'by the grace of God', a sublime phrase still used by Queen Elizabeth II. The swearing of homage by his tenants-in-chief and of fealty by other subjects acknowledged that, since the Norman Conquest, an English king was the feudal suzerain of all England and had its land ultimately at his disposal. He was now different from all other men: in the words of the twelfth-century law-book associated with the name of the great justice Ranulf Glanville, 'the lord king can have no equal, much less a superior'.

If the regular crown-wearings that William the Conqueror introduced— usually at the religious festivities of Christmas, Easter, and Pentecost, and frequently at Gloucester, Winchester, and Westminster—were designed to remind as many of his conquered people as could see or hear him that he was their duly crowned and anointed king, they also served to re-emphasize the importance of the coronation and, by their pageantry and ritual, popularized its spiritual and secular symbolism. In the middle of the civil war, in 1147, Stephen held an extraordinary, solemn crown-wearing at Lincoln which amounted to a political declaration, for Lincoln Castle had been held until recently in Matilda's interest:

. . . King Stephen wore his crown during Christmas at Lincoln, which no King, because of some superstition, had ever ventured to do before. This showed his great resolution and how little importance he attached to such superstitions. (Henry of Huntingdon, *History of the English*)

Crown-wearings were held until at least the fifteenth century, even if the movements of kings and their growing responsibilities made them rather less regular.

The coronation oath offers but a brief and simple insight into the tasks of kingship, and we must recognize that it represents a formal, ideal, and, most probably, a clerical view of the king's obligations and duties. Yet the speed with which new kings sought their crowning and anointing, especially at times of dynastic uncertainty, suggests that the accompanying oath and its promises were of awesome significance as the consummation of a king's accession and the moral guidelines of his rule. Many coronations—though perhaps not all—were associated with much more elaborate promises couched in charter form from Henry I's reign onwards. These largely reiterated how earlier kings had approached their duties, with an assurance that the newly crowned king would do likewise. Edward the Confessor, in a charter of 1063, revealed his conception of his obligations, descanting on the triple oath he had sworn all of twenty years before:

I, Edward, through the contribution of divine providence, by which all things are governed, appointed king and defender of the English bounds, invoke God with unsleeping mind not only that I may be famed for my royal protection, but also that, invested with God's aid, I may prevail in thought and deed against God's enemies and earn the right to advance my kingdom in the quietness of peace . . . it is our duty courageously to oppose the wicked and take good men as models, by enriching the churches of God, relieving those oppressed by wicked judges, and by judging equitably between the powerful and the humble: all things which are pleasing to God.

Henry I was prompted to distribute a fuller declaration of his intentions in 1100 by his eagerness to commend himself to his new subjects and marshal them against his elder brother and rival, Robert Curthose. He did so in a 'coronation charter' which disavowed the evil rule of his predecessor and, following Rufus's sudden death by an arrow-shot in the New Forest, guaranteed that orderly government and good justice would be restored, along with the customs of England as they had stood in Edward the Confessor's reign. Stephen, who found himself in an even more parlous situation when he succeeded in 1135, took his cue from Henry, and a 'charter of liberties' issued at Easter 1136 promised the good laws and ancient customs of Henry I's reign. After the civil war, it seemed necessary to lay stress less on the king's duties than on the rights and authority of the crown itself which had been undermined since Henry I's death. Thus, at the outset of Henry II's reign (1154), a royal proclamation did duty as a manifesto of future rule, embracing (as it did) both the obligations that earlier kings had shouldered and the belief that the traditional qualities of English kingship needed to be restored.

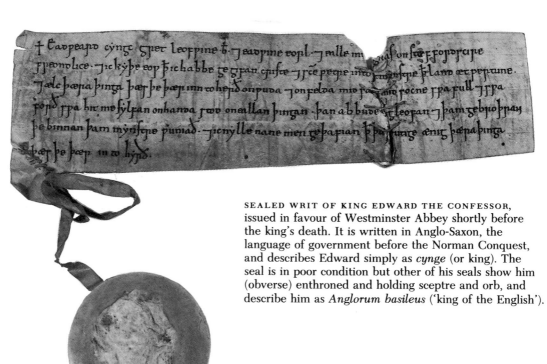

SEALED WRIT OF KING EDWARD THE CONFESSOR, issued in favour of Westminster Abbey shortly before the king's death. It is written in Anglo-Saxon, the language of government before the Norman Conquest, and describes Edward simply as *cynge* (or king). The seal is in poor condition but other of his seals show him (obverse) enthroned and holding sceptre and orb, and describe him as *Anglorum basileus* ('king of the English').

MALCOLM III CANMORE

(1058–1093), king of Scots

[Margaret] was destined to increase the glory of God in the land, and set the king right from the path of error, and turn him to the better way, and his people as well, and put down the evil customs that this nation had practised, just as she afterwards did.

(Anglo-Saxon Chronicle, 1067)

THE eldest son of Duncan I, Malcolm is best known for his role in Shakespeare's *Macbeth* and in the hagiography of his wife, Margaret of England, granddaughter of Edmund Ironside. English influence grew as a result of his exile in England (from 1040) and his marriage (*c.*1069) to Margaret, a severe, pious, and domineering woman. He may have married his first wife, Ingibjorg (d. *c.*1069), probably the earl of Orkney's daughter, to gain help against Macbeth, though Malcolm did not secure the throne until Macbeth (1057) and his stepson (1058) were killed. He sought to extend his rule southwards, though not with conspicuous success, and if he encouraged Hardrada's invasion (1066), he miscalculated for it enabled William of Normandy to land unopposed. The Conqueror forced Malcolm to become 'his man' (1070), and in the last of his invasions of England (1093) Malcolm and his eldest son by Margaret were killed; his widow died three days later on hearing the news. Malcolm was a benefactor of churches, including Durham; his wife became a saint (1249), her reputation enhanced by her confessor's eulogy. The internal stability and English character of Malcolm's reign are indicated by the succession of his three sons Edgar (1097) and Alexander (1107) (both of whom married daughters of Henry I of England) and David I (1124), after a brief struggle between Malcolm's eldest son, Duncan II (1094), and his younger brother Donald III Bane (1093–7). In Edgar's time, these southern ways were resented by some, and *c.*1098 Magnus Barelegs, king of Norway, reasserted Norwegian sovereignty in the Western Isles (including Iona).

Know that for the honour of God and Holy Church, and for the common restoration of my whole realm, I have granted and restored and by this present charter confirmed, to God and to Holy Church, and to all my earls, barons, and vassals, all concessions, gifts, liberties, and free customs which King Henry my grandfather granted and conceded to them. Likewise all evil customs which he abolished and relaxed, I also grant to be relaxed and abolished in my name and that of my heirs.

Though King Richard did not follow his father's example in considered detail— he left England to go on crusade within four months of his arrival in England in August 1189 for his coronation—his actions demonstrate that similar thoughts were in his mind to those that had been in Henry I's in 1100. Before even landing in England, he ordered the release of those who had been arbitrarily or unjustly imprisoned in English gaols by Henry II, and when he disembarked he dragged in chains behind him one of Henry's most unpopular ministers—as eloquent an announcement as could be made that the good times would be restored and the bad disowned.

An ideology of kingship was clearly developing in England in the late eleventh and twelfth centuries. It was expressed in the secular and religious symbolism of the coronation and in the prospectus of kingship which the coronation oath and formal royal charters publicized. It enhanced the status and dignity of the crown, it formulated the prerogatives of kingship, and it struck a bargain between the

THE MARRIAGE OF AN IRISH KING TO HIS COUNTRY in northern Ulster, as recorded by Gerald of Wales in his *Topography of Ireland*, *c*.1187, and illustrated in the margin of an early copy of the work (mid-thirteenth century). A horse was boiled in a bath, in which the king then sat, surrounded by his people; they all ate the horse-meat and quaffed the water, symbolizing the unity of king and people. This ceremony, in its essentials, was revived in the later Middle Ages.

king and his subjects. In all this, English kingship appeared to move far away from the character of kingship elsewhere in the British Isles. To judge by the delightful drawings in Gerald of Wales's *Topography of Ireland*, primitive pre-Christian rituals at hallowed sites seem to have continued in use at the inauguration of kings in Ireland. These rituals symbolized the marriage of a king to his kingdom and people, and as proof of his title poets recited his genealogy before assembled nobles and clergy. Things were not so very different in Scotland, where royal rituals (along with the Stone of Scone itself) may have owed much to early Irish custom. There was no religious ceremony of coronation, no vital role accorded to unction, until the fourteenth century, despite petitions to the pope by some Scottish kings, notably Alexander II (1214–49), that they should be both crowned and anointed. Rather was the new king inaugurated on the sacred Stone of Scone in the presence of his nobles who heard his genealogy intoned. In both Ireland and Scotland, the inauguration rite was predominantly secular in character, though leading clerics had a role to play. Less is known of the creation of Welsh kings, but there is no reason to suppose that they underwent anything more sophisticated or solemn than the kind of girding and acclamation of Norman dukes. In England, by contrast, kingship was moving rapidly to a new level of sanctity and formality, where kings as well as subjects found themselves morally and spiritually bound to discharge duties and obligations to one another.

What if a crowned king broke his coronation oath and violated his own charter of liberties? This was a practical dilemma of Christian kingship which contemporary theorists were reluctant to face. The true Christian king observed his oath and met his obligations; the tyrannical king and royal oath-breaker could not be removed or killed because he had no superior on earth. The constraints on a tyrant were moral and religious, and they were wielded by the Almighty. The ideology of English kingship could hardly admit otherwise. Matilda's cause was immeasurably weakened after Stephen's coronation in 1136, and when she captured the anointed king in 1141 her failure to eliminate him there and then, and his eventual release, were a confession of her reluctance to wrest the crown from him to whom God had given it. Only in 1215–16 did the king's subjects come close to undermining the foundation of Christian kingship itself. The leaders of the rebellion took the precaution of making it clear that they, rather than their anointed king, were on the side of the angels:

Those who therefore gathered together in a strong force accused the king of many things, and, when he had been accused, condemned him saying that they should no longer have him for king, and their voices gathered strength, and a powerful conspiracy arose against him. Leaders of the army were appointed, called marshals of the army of God . . . (The Barnwell Chronicle)

Almost every previous rising against an English king had championed a claimant from the royal family who maintained that he had been wrongfully deprived of the crown. Rarely had such risings aimed to correct an oppressive or unsuitable monarch, still less impose an elaborate programme of reform on him. Magna Carta, as a treaty between King John and his greater subjects couched in language that involved the whole community, was mainly an attempt to define anew the king's powers and his duties towards his subjects, and it took its cue from Henry I's coronation charter of 1100. Later kings who swore to uphold Magna Carta were issuing their own charter of liberties, swearing to protect the Church, uphold the law, and remove abuses—rather as Henry I and Henry II had done decades before. The supervisory committee established in 1215 to enforce John's observance of Magna Carta was removed from these later confirmations, and that was an acknowledgement that the good faith of the king alone bound him to perform his sworn duty. But in 1215–16, when John denounced the committee and abandoned his undertakings, it was the feudal remedy to which his greater subjects resorted to bring him to heel, renouncing their homage and fealty to him. A few went so far as to try to replace him with Louis, the son of the French king and the husband of Henry II's granddaughter. But he was an unconvincing alternative beside John's own son and heir, Henry, of the line of anointed Anglo-Norman-Angevin kings. Ironically, the accession of England's first minor king since the tenth century—Henry III was only nine in 1216—took place in the afterglow of the most threatening uprising an anointed king of England had had to face, and within weeks the new king's advisers had adopted the essentials of the rebel programme by reissuing Magna Carta on his behalf.

Of course, Magna Carta had a life of its own after 1215. It came to be regarded

HENRY I'S NIGHTMARES, as illustrated in John of Worcester's *Chronicle*, written *c*.1140, soon after the king's death. The sleeping king is shown dreaming of the various problems of kingship, represented by complaining peasants, violent barons, and petitioning churchmen, both secular and religious.

as a safeguard of the rights of the subject in relation to the crown's power, and its repeated confirmations and reissues in the thirteenth century gave it a status, in Englishmen's eyes, as inalienable custom and fundamental law, comparable with the so-called customs of Edward the Confessor.

Here is another paradox. The heavy stress laid on feudal obligation after the Norman Conquest strengthened the position of the king. The homage of his tenants-in-chief bound them in faith to serve him and he to protect and defend them; the fealty of his free subjects expressed their subjection to his authority as their suzerain. The famous 'oath of Salisbury', sworn to William the Conqueror in the year before his death, was a formal witness of the king's feudal power.

Then he travelled about so as to come to Salisbury at Lammas [1 August]; and there his councillors came to him, and all the people occupying land who were of any account over all England, no matter whose vassals they might be; and they all submitted to him and became his vassals, and swore oaths of allegiance to him, that they would be loyal to him against all other men. (Anglo-Saxon Chronicle, 1086)

It was a personal demonstration of the territorial lordship of an English king which Domesday Book recorded for posterity. Moreover, the gradual spread of the king's control, either directly or indirectly, over all the land of England, the very nexus of the feudal relationship, enabled kings to enhance their practical powers and to prevent noble lordship from usurping some of the king's powers in the kingdom (as happened in France).

Yet it is worth remembering that English kings after 1066 did not refuse to acknowledge that they themselves owed homage to the kings of France for the duchies and counties they held there. They may not have performed it before Matilda's husband, Geoffrey of Anjou, overran Normandy in 1144, but to deny

SILVER PENNY OF KING WILLIAM I, *c.*1077–80. The obverse shows the crowned king holding a sword in his right hand. The sheer power of the Norman monarchy stares out from the image, even if the coin itself is well within the tradition of the Anglo-Saxon coinage. ($\times 3\frac{1}{2}$)

MAGNA CARTA. This exemplification (or authorized copy) of the 1225 version was sent to the sheriff of Wiltshire and given to Lacock Abbey for safe-keeping (it remained there until 1945). It is authenticated by Henry III's great seal, whose obverse represents the young king enthroned and holding the symbols of kingship. This was the third reissue, with amendments, of Magna Carta, and others followed in the thirteenth century, expressing good royal intentions usually in return for some tangible benefit to the crown, such as taxation.

that it was due would run the risk of undermining their claims to their nobles' homage in England. Thus, kings of England in the later twelfth century were prepared to do homage to French monarchs, though they resisted French attempts to intervene in any practical way in their French 'empire'. William I was duke of Normandy and count of Maine, as well as king of England, and although it was his regal title that he often used (and no doubt proudly) no matter where in his cross-Channel dominion he happened to be, he never denied his formal subjection, as a French noble, to the king of France. William was conscious of his regal position and enjoyed flaunting it, but at the same time he was keenly aware of the nature and value of feudal lordship. His successors, William Rufus and Henry I, behaved no differently for most of the time when they too ruled dominions astride the Channel. Henry II, when he sought to conquer Toulouse in 1159, declined to make war on his French suzerain in person, and at various times he did homage to Louis VII and his son, Philip Augustus, for his vast French dominions. Only towards the end of the twelfth century did this delicate relationship show signs of rupturing: King John, who was to lose the allegiance of his own nobles in 1215–16, refused to attend the court of Philip Augustus and forfeited his Norman inheritance as a consequence. As the price of retaining Gascony, in 1259 Henry III formally acknowledged in the treaty of Paris that he was a vassal of the French king—but he had lost the northern territories for good.

It was even more sobering for Englishmen at the end of John's reign to realize that their most recent kings had recognized the overlordship of both the German emperor and the pope in Rome. Richard the Lion-heart became a vassal of the Emperor Henry VI in 1194 as the price of his freedom from captivity, and in the 1230s some still feared that the realm would be subjected to Henry's son, the Emperor Frederick II. On the other hand, when King John had needed allies against his own subjects, in 1213 he placed himself and his kingdom under the protection of the pope and acknowledged His Holiness's overlordship, agreeing to pay an annual tribute of 1,000 marks (£666·67). It was a curious constitutional conundrum: the English king was a vassal of the most majestic overlords in Christendom. But it was no more than that: English kings were spared future confusion and embarrassment by the rapid decline of imperial power and pretensions, and by the more gradual decay of the papacy's moral and political authority.

England's incorporation in three sea-empires in turn in the eleventh and twelfth centuries significantly affected its kingship. It is true that in Normandy by 1066, even more certainly than in England, the idea that an inheritance, including the ducal inheritance, should pass intact to an inheritor had taken firm root, and the custom that the first-born male child had first right of succession was hardening.

This was rather less true in England where, as far as the kingship was concerned, an heir's suitability and adulthood entered into the discussion. It was still accepted that all male members of the royal family (the *æthelings*) had a claim to the patrimony which it would be wise for a new king to satisfy. Moreover, when Danish, Norman, and Angevin kings had several inheritances in the eleventh and twelfth centuries, the temptation to endow each surviving son with one or more of them made jealousies and disputes more likely. The Anglo-Norman and Angevin dominions presented peculiar problems, because of the determination of almost all kings of England to preserve the unity of their disparate inheritances. Thus, when a king died or became incapacitated, there was an expectation—even stronger than in tenth-century England—that conflicting interests would come to the surface and disrupt the peace, as rivals competed for inheritances or tried to exclude their kinsmen from power. The result was a series of partitions and a number of succession wars that occupied much of the eleventh and twelfth centuries.

Cnut had thought to partition his dominions at his death in 1035, but his plan for Harthacnut to rule in England and Harold in Denmark and Norway went awry immediately for personal and fortuitous reasons. In 1066 the throne was challenged by an English earl, Harold Godwinson, who had no royal blood to speak of in his veins, and then by a foreign duke who was scarcely better endowed. In the prevailing uncertainty, each saw the main chance and seized it, claiming the Confessor's blessing. Such *coups* were never to happen again in English history. William of Poitiers, writing in about 1071, gave the Conqueror's genealogical tree a vigorous shake in order to produce a sound hereditary claim for him; but his tortuous prose betrays a basic uncertainty:

This land he has gained as the legal heir with the confirmation of the oaths of the English. He took possession of his inheritance by battle, and he was crowned at last with the consent of the English or at least at the desire of their magnates. And if it be asked what was his hereditary title, let it be answered that a close kinship existed between King Edward and the son of Duke Robert whose paternal aunt, Emma, was the sister of Duke Richard II, the daughter of Duke Richard I and the mother of King Edward himself . . .
(*The Deeds of William, duke of the Normans and King of the English*)

The quarrels between William the Conqueror's three sons, Robert Curthose, William Rufus, and Henry, were mirrored later by the ugly disputes between Henry II's sons, Henry, Richard, Geoffrey, and John; while in between, civil war blighted England because Henry I's only legitimate son was drowned (1120) before his father died, and Henry's daughter Matilda and his nephew Stephen struggled for a crown that had never previously been worn by a woman. This war was ended by a treaty that could not conceal the fact that Stephen accepted Matilda's son Henry as his successor only by virtue of brute force and cruel luck.

HENRY I

(1100–1135), King of England

... to him the kingdom seemed to pertain as of right since he was the only one of William's sons who was born when his father was a king. He was early instructed in the liberal arts, and so throughout imbibed the sweets of learning that no warlike disturbance and no pressure of business could erase them from his noble mind ... his learning ... though obtained by snatches, assisted him much in the science of government ... (William of Malmesbury, *The Deeds of the Kings of the English*)

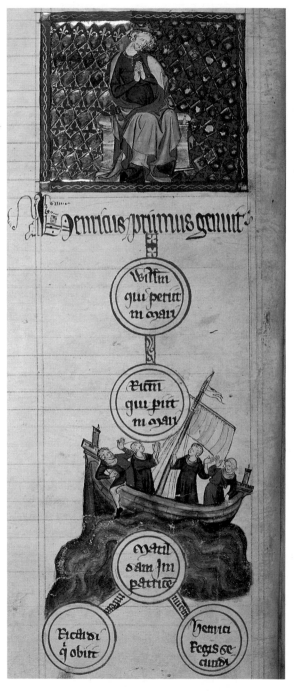

THOUGH brought up in England, like his father, William I, and his brother, Henry regarded Normandy as equally important. Strong and stocky, later tending to fat, with black hair and a cheerful disposition, he was cruel, lustful, avaricious, and a stern judge. Well educated, even studious, by the thirteenth century he was known as 'clerk'. Largely landless in his youth, when Rufus was killed (1100), he made straight for Winchester and after a difficult moment was declared rightful king by the witan. Henry shrewdly disowned the harsher aspects of his brother's rule, and his 'coronation charter' offered reconciliation, as did the return of the exiled Archbishop Anselm. But this was mostly propaganda, for he continued his brother's policies and methods, extending them to the point of administrative innovation. A restless monarch, he spent much time in Normandy, which he eventually (1106) seized from his brother Robert, whom he imprisoned for life. He was a decisive and energetic ruler, and determined to ensure security for both his dominions: he established peaceful relations with Scotland (partly by his marriage to Matilda, daughter of Malcolm Canmore), and in Wales asserted his power over Welsh kings on a broad front. He set great store by marriage diplomacy. Henry's imagination is apparent in government: he centralized the administration of England and Normandy in the royal court and patronized officials and families who owed all to him. Henry had one legitimate son, William, whose drowning in the White Ship (1120) posed a succession problem. Henry sent (1126) for his only legitimate daughter, Matilda, widow of the German emperor who was widely accepted as his successor; she married Geoffrey, son of the count of Anjou (1128). When Henry died, after eating too many lampreys, civil war broke out between Matilda and his nephew Stephen. Henry's achievements stood squarely on those of William I and William Rufus, taking their policies to a new level. The fatal flaw was his family.

KING HENRY I, crowned and seated on a cushioned bench, is shown in this fifteenth-century pedigree-chronicle lamenting the wreck of the White Ship, in which his only legitimate son William perished, along with one of his bastard children, Richard. This left Henry's only daughter Matilda, 'the Empress', as the king's heir.

These succession wars not only disrupted the vast 'empires' of which England was a part, but they also denied to the English monarchy a stable principle of hereditary succession which might have underpinned its growing powers. Henry II's plan to provide just that by arranging the coronation of his eldest surviving son, Henry, 'the king, the king's son', in 1170 foundered when the young man died in 1183. Only in 1199 did the last war of succession come to an end, when John inherited all his brother's (and father's) dominions, in preference to his nephew Arthur. It may be that John's subsequent loss of most of his French dominions prevented further succession disputes in the future. As it was, in 1216 a nine-year-old boy, John's eldest son Henry, was able to succeed to all his father's inheritances in England, Ireland, and Aquitaine, and to his claims of overlordship in Scotland and Wales, as well as to forlorn claims to the lost territories in northern and western France. Louis of France, at the head of a rebel army in England in 1216–17, presumably claimed the throne as a more suitable candidate through his wife Blanche, a granddaughter of Henry II; but this was no serious threat to Henry III's accession as the eldest male legitimate child of the last anointed king of England. That a king could succeed so young and in the midst of foreign and civil war is testimony to the acceptance at last in England of impartible hereditary succession in the male line. Not even the civil war later in Henry III's reign questioned the dynasty's right of succession.

THE CORONATION OF HENRY, 'THE YOUNG KING', 1170, during the lifetime of his father, Henry II. The picture depicts Henry's crowning (and his investiture with the sceptre but not with the orb of power) by the archbishop of York, which was deeply resented by the archbishop of Canterbury, Thomas Becket. On the right, Henry II delivers a closed cup to the 'Young King' at the coronation banquet. This unusual ceremony did not secure the succession or deter the 'Young King' (d. 1183) from rebelling against his father.

Parallel developments were taking place in Scotland, though rather more straightforwardly. When Kenneth II died in 995, it took his son, Malcolm II, ten years to establish himself as king in the face of resistance from several of his kinsmen, who presumably felt that they had as good a claim to the throne as his. And later on, Macbeth was prepared to challenge his cousin, Duncan I, when circumstances allowed. But the internal stability won by Malcolm III and his English-born queen ensured the succession of three of their sons in turn between 1097 and 1124, despite some initial squabbling. If 'twice makes a custom', this effectively established hereditary succession in the male line a century earlier than in England. David I sought to reinforce the practice by formally designating (*c.*1144–5) his only son Henry as his successor and associating the young man with him in the task of ruling. In doing so, he may have been copying French royal example, whereby the heir was designated king in the lifetime of his father and the succession made less problematic. Neither David I nor Henry II of England (who adopted this device a generation later, in 1170) achieved his particular objective since on each occasion the heir died before designation could be turned into reality.

The Royal Kin

The three conquering dynasties in England between 1016 and 1216 produced a line of conquering kings. Although contemporary writers and annalists were either clerics or cloistered monks, and therefore more sensitive to (and critical of) the harsher instincts and actions of their rulers, there can be little doubt that the kings from Cnut to John, with perhaps two exceptions, Edward the Confessor and Stephen, were rough, crude men, fully capable of physical cruelty and the harsh oppression of lesser folk. If the Confessor and Stephen appear different, it may yet be because monkish chroniclers were all too ready to exaggerate their gentler and more spiritual qualities.

One thing all these kings (except Harold Godwinson) had in common was their non-English blood. Beginning with Cnut, the first non-English-born king of the English, they were of predominantly Danish or French ancestry; indeed, between King Harold and Richard I only one of them—Henry I—is certainly known to have been born in England and not in France. Moreover, four of the seven Norman and Angevin kings of England died in France. In this, they stand in marked contrast to the earlier kings of Wessex and of all England. Even when the Old English dynasty reasserted itself in the person of the Confessor in 1042, it was stamped with Norman blood, for Edward was a Norman by birth, sentiment, and upbringing—and hardly less so than William the Conqueror and his sons. Apart from Harold Godwinson, it may be doubted whether any of the kings

KING EDWARD THE CONFESSOR accusing Earl Godwin (*right*) of murdering his brother, Alfred the *ætheling*. Alfred and Edward were sons of King Æthelred II and Queen Emma. They invaded England after Cnut's death; Alfred fell into Godwin's hands, and was probably put to death on King Harold I's orders. This thirteenth-century Anglo-Norman miniature blames Godwin, who is ordered by Edward to prove his innocence by the ordeal.

between Cnut and William Rufus could speak or even understand English. The Conqueror

> struggled to learn some of the English language, so that he could understand the pleas of the conquered people without an interpreter, and benevolently pronounce fair judgements for each one as justice required. But advancing age prevented him from acquiring such learning, and the distractions of his many duties forced him to give his attention to other things (Orderic Vitalis, *Ecclesiastical History*)

The well-educated Henry I probably did learn the language and may have been the first king in a century (again excepting Harold) to be at home speaking it.

In contrast to the kings stretching back from Æthelred II to the seventh century, Cnut was barely Christian; his father had probably been born a pagan in Scandinavia and Cnut himself was received into the Church on the very eve of his father's invasion of England (1013). William the Conqueror's ancestors in the comparatively new duchy 'of the Northmen' had become Christian scarcely a century-and-a-half before Hastings. Conquerors, colonists, and recent converts are likely to have retained some of their rough edges and tough habits. The Danish kings, Cnut and his two sons, Harold Harefoot and Harthacnut, were barely twenty when each acquired the kingdom of the English, and to a man they were short-lived and yet died naturally (as far as we know). The lives of Viking conquerors seem inevitably brief. The Normans and Angevins were a tougher breed and more experienced when they came to the throne. Before 1216, all of them succeeded as mature men schooled in the turbulent realities of English and French politics—apart from Henry II, who was only twenty-one in 1154 but quickly and triumphantly learned the arts and guiles of kingship. Of those English monarchs who died in their beds, rather than by the hand of an assassin or struck down in war, all reached their mid-fifties and several were in their sixties; the longest-lived of all, Henry I, was sixty-seven when he died and was England's longest reigning king before Henry III.

In a monarchy that had no precise rule of succession, the idea that kings could be specifically and specially trained for kingship was bound to be impracticable. On the other hand, certain pragmatic skills appropriate in a future king could be acquired by any competent male kinsman of a present or former king, through an upbringing within the royal family and involvement in its military and political activities. The situation was different later in the Middle Ages, when more explicit rules of succession made it reasonably plain who the future king was likely to be. Not until Richard I (1199) did a king of England succeed uncontestedly, though even he had not grown up in the certain knowledge that the crown would be his. In the Danish era there were English *æthelings* alive— the sons of Æthelred II—who had as good a claim as any Dane; and in 1066 William the Bastard's claims were no stronger—except in arms—than those of

EMMA OF NORMANDY, QUEEN OF BOTH KING ÆTHELRED II (d. 1016) AND KING CNUT (d. 1035), is shown here receiving an account of her life, *Encomium Emmae Reginae*, which she commissioned from a monk of St Omer *c.*1040 while she was in exile in Flanders. The author is presenting the book to her. Watching intently are her two sons, later Kings Harthacnut and Edward the Confessor.

several others, English and Dane. William himself never regarded his eldest son, Robert Curthose, as his successor in England, and to judge by what happened in 1087 and 1100 there was no certainty as to who should succeed or in what order. This uncertainty had not lessened by the time Henry I died (1135), leaving only a daughter as his heir; nor was the situation much different under Henry II, with his covin of sons. Without certainty of succession, a formal scheme of training for kingship was impossible to devise. Ultimately, it was the character and personal qualities of those who seized the crown that formed their attitudes to kingship.

And yet, the biographical eulogy (or *Encomium*) of the twice-queened Emma states that Cnut's father, Sweyn the former pagan, discussed the arts of government and the Christian religion with his younger son; but then, as a military conqueror and a recently Christianized ruler, these things may have had greater immediacy for Sweyn, who may have had a clearer idea than William the Conqueror as to how he wished his several dominions to be ruled after his death. When that occurred in 1016, Cnut was only twenty-one and doubtless valued any instruction for the task ahead of him in a foreign land.

A more general scheme of education was available to prospective kings of England in the twelfth century, the age of humanism, the schools, and universities; and among English kings, Henry I, soon to be called *Beauclerc*, stands pre-eminent for the depth of his learning. He was set to study by his parents, William I and Queen Matilda, perhaps in the expectation that, as the youngest of their sons, he would become a bishop. We must not allow his publicists to create for him a unique reputation for learning, for it seems likely that all English kings thereafter (with the possible exception of Stephen) could read; yet the famous maxim, 'an illiterate king is a crowned ass', was mentioned by the chronicler, William of Malmesbury, as early as about 1125, during Henry's reign. His grandson, Henry II, was brought up for part of his youth at the cultured French court of Anjou, where he was given a formal education; this was continued when he stayed in Bristol with his step-uncle, Robert, earl of Gloucester, during Stephen's reign. Henry was later described as 'very well up in letters' and Walter Map, the court watcher from Herefordshire who knew the king well, claimed that he had a knowledge of 'all tongues spoken from the coasts of France to the river Jordan, but making use only of Latin and French'. Walter also heard that Henry's mother, the Empress Matilda, gave him some practical, if less appealing, lessons in the wiles of rulership:

that he should spin out all the affairs of everyone, hold long in his own hand all posts that fell in, take the revenues of them, and keep the aspirants to them hanging on in hope . . . He ought also to be much in his chamber and little in public: he should never confer anything on anyone at the recommendation of any person, unless he had seen and learnt about it: with much more of the worst kind. (*The Courtiers' Trifles*)

Henry made sure that his sons (no mention, of course, is made of his daughters in this chauvinistic age) received tuition too. The eldest of them, young Henry, spent some time in Thomas Becket's household in the 1160s, while Richard I was confident (or arrogant) enough to correct the Latin grammar of his archbishop of Canterbury. Such training and education were bound to be a valuable preparation for a kingship that was gradually demanding talents other than those of the soldier and the politician.

Whether arranged for reasons of emotion, lust, or politics, whether suggested by an accidental meeting or dictated by the limited choice available, marriage was a crucial step for any king to take. Not every king of England married—not even some of those who survived to middle age. Harold Harefoot and Harthacnut may not have had the time, because both died at the age of twenty-four; and in

STEPHEN

(1135–1154), king of England, and

MATILDA

(d. 1167), lady of the English

... a man of less judgement than energy, an active soldier, of remarkable spirit in difficult undertakings, lenient to his enemies and easily placated, courteous to all. Though you admired his kindness in making promises, you doubted the truth of his words and the reliability of what he promised.

(William of Malmesbury, *New History*)

She, with a grim look, her forehead wrinkled into a frown, every trace of a woman's gentleness removed from her face, blazed into unbearable fury, saying that many times the people of London had made very large contributions to the king ...

(*The Deeds of Stephen*)

KING STEPHEN THE HUNTSMAN, crowned and seated on an elaborate bench. He wears a falconer's gloves and is holding a falcon. The king was a convivial and chivalric man who enjoyed hunting.

THIRD son of Stephen, count of Blois and Chartres, and Adela, the Conqueror's daughter, Stephen was charming and attractive, but did not inspire trust and to many he seemed sly. Henry I married him (1125) to his queen's niece, heiress of Boulogne. Matilda was already married (1110) to Henry V, emperor of Germany, where she remained until his death (1125). In 1126 Stephen led the nobles in acknowledging her as King Henry's successor. Her marriage to Geoffrey of Anjou (1128) was troubled and she returned to England in 1131. Yet in 1135 Stephen was widely preferred in England and Normandy to Matilda as Henry I's successor. A destructive civil war followed which neither was able to win. Stephen lacked ruthlessness and failed to inspire loyalty. Matilda, though supported by David I of Scotland and Robert, earl of Gloucester, was not decisive, and her regime in the areas she controlled (from 1139) was harsh. Stephen was captured at Lincoln (1141) and declared deposed, but soon after Earl Robert was taken and exchanged for the king, who was recrowned at Canterbury. Matilda eventually (1148) retired to Normandy which her husband had won (1144), and her eldest son Henry upheld her cause in England. Time ran out for Stephen: he became sick, his valiant wife died (1151) and so did his son and heir Eustace (1153). Henry forced him to a treaty (1153), whereby Stephen would remain king for life and accept Henry as his heir. Stephen died at Dover and was buried with his wife and son at Faversham Abbey, which he founded. Matilda died at Rouen (1167) and was buried at Bec Abbey; her coffin, rediscovered in 1846, was reinterred in Rouen Cathedral. She had some influence on her son as king of England, and her tomb inscription is said to have run: 'Here lies Henry's daughter, wife and mother; great by birth—greater by marriage—but greatest by motherhood.'

any case, the unsettled life of a marauding soldier may not have been particularly conducive to early matrimony. It is generally agreed that Edward the Confessor was not uxorious by nature (he produced no children, legitimate or illegitimate, and packed his wife off to a nunnery when opportunity allowed), whilst William

Rufus, who lived until he was forty-four, was a dissolute (and possibly bisexual) bachelor. But in general, the choice of a wife and queen was of cardinal importance both personally and publicly to almost every king.

It had not been unknown in the past for English kings to marry foreigners, but after 1016 it inevitably became a habit. This, in turn, accentuated the differences of birth, speech, and sentiment between especially the Norman and Angevin kings and their subjects. Cnut married Æthelred II's queen, Emma of Normandy, presumably for political reasons connected with his desire to forge an alliance with the Normans and to consolidate his hold on England. After Hastings, no reigning king of England married an Englishwoman until the mid-fifteenth century, and only King John succeeded to the throne with an English-born wife already in his bed—Isabella of Gloucester, whom he had wedded long before. (Henry Bolingbroke's English wife died several years before he seized the crown in 1399.) Setting aside more personal considerations which, in the case of kings, may not often have been allowed to intrude in the planning of royal marriages, the need for territorial security and alliances with other rulers, or, at other times, dynastic and territorial ambitions—these were the commoner motives for matrimony. It is in this context that Cnut's marriage with Emma should be placed, the Confessor's unenthusiastic marriage with Edith Godwinson, King John's with his second wife, Isabella of Angoulême, and Henry III's with Eleanor of Provence. Henry I's marriage to Matilda of Scotland in 1100 was later regarded as being of unusual significance for, as the daughter of Malcolm III's queen, Margaret of England, she was a direct descendant of West Saxon kings. Although this particular link may not have meant a great deal to Henry at the time of his wedding, it was emphasized by Ailred of Rievaulx when he came to

THE TOMB-EFFIGY OF ELEANOR OF AQUITAINE (d. 1204), queen of Henry II, at Fontevrault Abbey, which Eleanor patronized. It is a rare effigy that depicts its subject living, in Eleanor's case reading a book, which reflects her cultured interests.

write a new Life of Edward the Confessor in about 1163. Henry's and Matilda's grandson, King Henry II, had meanwhile come to symbolize the reconciliation of French and English at a time when the reputation of the sainted Edward was being cultivated at court:

He [Henry II], rising as the light of morning, is like a cornerstone joining the two peoples. Now certainly England has a king of the English race.

Not surprisingly, the importance of these ladies was muted once they had become queen. The *Encomium* of Emma of Normandy and the *Life* of Edward the Confessor, which was commissioned by his wife Edith, are the only books known to have been dedicated to English queens during their lifetime. Each, in part at least, amounts to a queenly biography; but not one of their successors attracted comparable attention. Cnut regarded his first wife, Ælfgifu of Northampton (who may not even have been canonically married to him), as sufficiently capable and dependable to be entrusted with ruling Norway during his absence in England. But no later queen was given such responsibilities and Henry II experienced so much trouble with his strong-willed consort, Eleanor of Aquitaine, that he imprisoned her for sixteen years. And yet queens shed lustre on the Norman and Angevin kings, and by their coronation they were set apart from all other ladies of the court and thereby contributed to the mystique of kingship.

It was probably the custom in England after 856, when Æthelwulf of Wessex witnessed the crowning of his new queen at Rheims, that queens should be formally crowned, and the description of Edgar's celebrated coronation in 973 includes an order of service for the consecration of a queen. This need not take place at the same time as the king's coronation, and it did not follow exactly the details of his crowning. After the Confessor married Edith Godwinson in 1045, she was solemnly anointed and crowned, and it is likely that between 1002 and 1035 Emma of Normandy was crowned twice, beside Æthelred II and Cnut. To judge by what is known of these and later queens' coronations, there was no suggestion that powers of government were conferred on a king's consort or that she should share the burden of ruling with her husband. Indeed, Matilda, the Conqueror's queen, was not crowned until 1068, by which time he had made himself reasonably secure on his throne. When Henry I married his second wife in 1121, her coronation was arranged for the next day, when the archbishop of Canterbury claimed his right to crown the king again; this implied that henceforth Henry and Adela shared in the drama and ritual of royal dominion, but not in the practicalities of government. And John, when he took his child-bride in 1200, endured a second coronation at which his wife was anointed and crowned at Westminster in a particularly solemn ceremony that emphasized the quality of regal dominion; but with Isabella aged only about twelve, this could hardly imply any right to rule. Like the coronations of kings, these ceremonies usually took place at Westminster and were presided over by the archbishop of Canterbury. The arrangements depended, ultimately, on the will of the king himself, as is reflected in Richard I's decision in 1191, when he was *en route* to the Holy Land, to marry Berengaria of Navarre and to have her crowned at the small Cypriot town of Limassol, with the Norman bishop of Evreux officiating. Two decades earlier (1170), the imperious Henry II had dismissed the idea that when young Henry was crowned his wife, Margaret of France, should be crowned with him, though both were crowned side by side at a later date (1172) by the archbishop of Rouen. The coronation of queens enhanced the dignity of kingship and gave kings an opportunity to flaunt their own God-given authority; but they did not impart rulership in any other than a formal way. Queens were to be seen, sure enough, but not often heard. The vociferous queen was likely to be unpopular with king or subjects—or both.

The marriage of a king's offspring, especially his legitimate offspring, was only a whit less significant than his own, and for the same reasons. Such marriages expressed the attitudes, and helped to promote the policies, of English kings towards their friends and enemies, neighbours and allies, both within the British Isles and in the wider 'empires' of which England was a part. As it happens, the Danish kings were neither fecund nor long-lived. And neither the Confessor nor William Rufus produced any children, either legitimate or illegitimate; Richard the Lion-heart seems to have fathered only one, a bastard named Philip. But Henry I, with a tally of more than twenty bastards, certainly made up for the relatively modest total produced by the other monarchs of his line.

The planning of such marriages often took place at an extraordinarily early age, even though the Church frowned on matches arranged for very young children. Henry II betrothed his second-born, Henry (the first, William, died at the age of three), to Margaret of France when he was three and the contract was ratified two years later. John, too, was proposed for marriage at the ripe age of four and the contract was sealed in the following year; when that arrangement collapsed, he was again betrothed—though still only nine—to Isabella of Gloucester, whom he later married. These kings of wide dominions developed a sharper awareness of the value of their kin, their royal family, and treated their offspring, legitimate and illegitimate alike, as instruments of policy. This, in turn, helped to define their role and status as royal children, and to create a sense of royalty that was to emerge more clearly and precisely in the following centuries.

In the three greater Welsh kingdoms of Gwynedd, Deheubarth, and Powys, weddings frequently symbolized an extension of power over more minor kingdoms and their rulers in the eleventh and twelfth centuries. The kings of Deheubarth were especially keen to marry northern girls from Gwynedd or Powys, while lesser members of their blood married into the families of more minor rulers nearer home; by this means, the grip of the Lord Rhys (d. 1197), who

OWAIN GWYNEDD

(1137–70), king of Gwynedd

SECOND son of Gruffydd ap Cynan (d. 1137), king of Gwynedd, Owain helped his father extend Gwynedd's power. As king (1137), he consolidated his hold on Church and State in North Wales and exploited English dissensions to advance into Ceredigion; he even had authority later as far east as the Dee (1165). His only major reverse was at Henry II's hands (1157), after which Owain acknowledged English overlordship over Gwynedd. Ambitious, far-sighted yet prudent, Owain was much lauded by contemporary poets as the pre-eminent ruler in Wales. After his death (and burial in Bangor Cathedral), his sons quarrelled over the inheritance; David (d. 1203) had dominion in Gwynedd in the 1170s and married Henry II's half-sister.

> Owain named the king,
> How wise in everything!
> With strength of eight his arm
> Keepeth our land from harm.
> Among the fierce, a valiant lion of gore,
> In screaming battle, cool, yet burning war;
> A man (if one draws breath)
> Strong in the face of death;
> An anchor against fear
> For all who bear the spear.
>
> (Gwalchmai ap Meilyr, court poet, *fl.*1130–80)

was well blessed with children, was extended throughout South Wales. Rhys himself had married Gwenllian of Powys. He even arranged 'mixed marriages' with some of the newly established Normans in the southern marchland of Wales. A precedent for this had been set before even the Normans arrived in the Welsh borderland: Gruffydd ap Llywelyn, fleetingly the ruler of much of Wales in the mid-eleventh century, married Ealdgyth, daughter of Ælfgar, earl of Mercia, with whom Gruffydd enjoyed an alliance against the sons of Earl Godwin of Wessex. In the first generation of the Anglo-Norman conquest, intermarriages served the purposes of both sides, the native and the invader: Nest, daughter of Rhys ap Tewdwr of Deheubarth, married Gerald of Windsor, the new constable of Pembroke Castle, in about 1100; it was the most inspired of matches for their grandson was one of the greatest of medieval writers, Gerald of Wales. The kings of Gwynedd in the twelfth century used marriage to extend their power in similar fashion in North Wales, and towards the end of the century they too began to forge links with Anglo-Norman families: David, the son of Owain Gwynedd, even aspired to marry Emma, the half-sister of no less a figure than Henry II himself. According to an English contemporary, David 'wanted to give the pride of descent from a royal house to his descendants, if he should have some, and to strike terror into the other Welsh because of his new relations'. All of Llywelyn I's daughters married into the English nobility of the marches, signalling Llywelyn's search for political and dynastic security in a predominantly English world. Indeed, each of the princes of thirteenth-century Gwynedd had an English bride. Nevertheless, this proved to be an effective way of spreading Anglo-Norman and English influence in Wales, underscoring those claims to overlordship which English kings had been asserting since the tenth century.

The Scottish kingdom, too, was the object of concerted Anglo-Norman influence from the eleventh century onwards, and royal marriages proved a direct way of promoting it. Duncan I had inaugurated a fateful trend when he married, for reasons of security, a cousin of Siward, earl of Northumbria. But it was the marriage (*c*.1069) of Malcolm III and Margaret, granddaughter of

Æthelred II's son, Edmund Ironside, that is most noteworthy. Their sons all sought English brides at the court of Henry I; their youngest, David I, wedded a daughter of the earl of Huntingdon (she was also Henry's kinswoman) who conveyed to the Scottish kings those territorial interests in England that would create a feudal embarrassment for Scotland thereafter. Henry I himself married Matilda, the daughter of Malcolm and Margaret, thereby reconciling the Norman and Old English royal houses. At the same time, Anglo-Scottish ties grew closer. Not only did Scottish kings tend to adopt English and French names for their children, but their queens were usually found in England, occasionally even by the English king, as William the Lion could testify after Henry II decided that he should marry one of Henry's French kinswomen, Ermengarde de Beaumont.

In the Irish kingdoms, royal inter-marriage was the norm, and it was

THE STONE COFFIN OF JOAN, BASTARD DAUGHTER OF KING JOHN and the wife of Llywelyn the Great, prince of Gwynedd. It probably dates from the fourteenth century and so was not her burial coffin. It is now in Beaumaris Church, Anglesey, whence it was taken after the Dissolution of the Monasteries from Aberconwy Abbey, where she was buried. A companion coffin of Llywelyn himself is in the Gwydir Chapel at Llanrwst Church, Gwynedd.

DAVID I

(1124–1153), king of Scots

Who can estimate the good done to the world by this gentle, just, chaste and humble ruler, loved for his gentleness, feared for his justice, admired for his purity and approachable by everyone through his humility . . .

(Ailred of Rievaulx, *Report of the Standard*)

Youngest son of Malcolm III and Queen Margaret, his upbringing in England (from 1093) made him Anglophile. He married (1114) Maud, the earl of Huntingdon's heiress, from whom he acquired English estates; and his sister married Henry I. As a youth he styled himself 'brother of the queen of the English' and an English writer thought him 'polished from his boyhood by his intercourse and friendship with us'. English and southern Scots saw this generous, pious, and chaste man as a paragon of kingship. The 'laws of King David' acquired a status like the Confessor's in England. Church and State were powerfully influenced by his Anglo-Norman sympathies: he patronized the Scottish Church and founded new monasteries; he reorganized the Scottish polity along feudal lines, establishing castles, burghs, and sheriffdoms, and encouraging Anglo-French immigration. A southerner by temperament, he countered resistance in Moray and the north (1130s). A supporter of his kinswoman Matilda against King Stephen, he occupied (from 1141) northern England (and he died at Carlisle), despite an early defeat at the battle of the Standard (1138). His surviving son Henry,

SILVER PENNY OF KING DAVID I (d. 1153), the first Scottish king to issue a coinage. This penny is similar in design to contemporary English coins and carries a stylized portrait-bust of the king. (× 3)

named after Henry I, was designated his successor (1144); when Henry died in 1152, David's grandson Malcolm was designated and succeeded peacefully.

no less an instrument of policy, ambition, and the quest for security than elsewhere. By the later twelfth century, however, several invading English lords were marrying the daughters of Irish rulers as a means of acquiring a territorial foothold and then turning themselves into independent rulers. Not only did the most adventurous of them, Richard Strongbow, earl of Pembroke, marry Eva, daughter and heiress of Dermot, king of Leinster, whose kingdom later fell to Strongbow; but Hugh de Lacy married a daughter of Rory O'Connor, the last of the 'high kings' of Ireland before English kings felt it necessary to intervene. These momentous marriages had been prefigured three-quarters of a century earlier (1101–2), when Arnulf of Montgomery, newly made earl of Pembroke under William Rufus, married an Irish girl, the daughter of Muircertach O'Brien, king of Dublin. The political and territorial possibilities of this match were never realized, but for anyone with eyes to see, it was a signpost for the future. As an instrument of English conquest, marriage was conspicuously successful and cost no legions.

MALCOLM IV 'THE MAIDEN'

(1153–1165), king of Scots

Even in his tender years he was a youth of singular gravity, and afterwards, amid the pride and luxury of empire, a man of transcendent and unexampled piety . . . For some years before his death he fell into a state of weakness and, in addition to his other troubles, suffered from such excruciating pains in his extremities, that is, in his head and feet . . .

(William of Newburgh, *The History of England*)

Whatever his personal qualities (and they were scarcely those admired in a king), his reign highlights the dangers of a minority and the resentment of the Anglo-Norman ways of his grandfather, David I. Designated David's heir (1152), he succeeded in 1153. But he immediately faced rebels in the north and west who won advantageous terms (1160). Meanwhile, he surrendered David's English conquests (1157) and did homage to Henry II in 1163. This subservience fomented further rebellions by 'native earls' (1161, 1164). A patron of the Church, he failed to secure metropolitan status for St Andrews. Malcolm died at Jedburgh and was buried in the royal mausoleum at Dunfermline.

So it proved in the continental dominions of English kings. In 1036 Cnut's daughter Gunhild married Henry, the son of the Emperor Conrad II; had the couple lived, their marriage might have been a bulwark of the Baltic 'empire' which Cnut left to his sons. To support his regime in England, Cnut's own marriage to Emma of Normandy served well enough, and it was reinforced in 1027 when his sister Estrith married Robert, duke of Normandy. It was a blow to Cnut's policy when Estrith was later discarded by Robert, but no political design can bargain for the vagaries of personal relationships.

The Anglo-Norman kings had the defence of both Normandy and England in mind whenever the marriages of their kin were arranged. William I intended that his eldest son, Robert Curthose, should marry the heiress of the county of Maine, which bordered Normandy and might one day be joined to it; but she died before the ceremony could take place. In similar mood, his daughter Constance was married to Alan, count of Brittany, and another, Adela, to Stephen, count of Blois and Chartres, two neighbouring rulers whom it was politic to cultivate.

Following his recovery of Normandy in 1106, Henry I showed the same concerns, which are as clearly reflected in the marriage plans devised for his children. This was apparent to at least one contemporary chronicler, William of Malmesbury, who commented drily that Henry produced his score of bastards in political, not pleasurable, circumstances. His daughters were accordingly hitched to rulers whose lands lay on the periphery of his dominions, in Normandy as well as in England, and his wife's sister reinforced the alliance on Normandy's northern border by marrying Eustace of Boulogne. Henry was thereby able to strengthen existing Norman alliances with his neighbours and he was careful not to squander his female relatives on less worthwhile English or Norman husbands. Above all, Henry's son and heir William was betrothed in 1113 to the daughter of

THE ENAMELLED EFFIGY OF GEOFFREY, COUNT OF ANJOU and father of King Henry II, on the lid of his tomb. It was made c.1150–60 and is still in Le Mans, where he was buried. Geoffrey's marriage to Matilda, daughter of Henry I, and his conquest of Normandy were two essential foundations of Henry II's accession to the English throne in 1154. A fulsome chivalric biography of Geoffrey was written c.1170 by John of Marmoutier. His nickname, 'Plantagenet', derives from the sprig of broom (*Fr.* genêt-broom) which he wore in his hat.

Fulk V of Anjou, in order to establish closer relations with the powerful state to the south and to detach it from its alliance with the predatory French king. The arrangement he made to marry his only surviving legitimate daughter Matilda to Geoffrey, son of Fulk V, in the winter of 1127–8 had the same end in view; Matilda was twenty-six, but Geoffrey was only fifteen. One day (if Henry's plans matured) Matilda would be ruler of both England and Normandy, and Geoffrey's Anjou would provide a stout buttress to Anglo-Norman power—and the marriage would also provide the English royal house with sons. It was not Henry's fault—more likely it was the irascible Matilda's—that these schemes went awry after Henry's death in 1135. Yet it was the army of Anjou which eventually reclaimed Normandy for Matilda (1144) and her young son Henry, who inherited Anjou itself when his father Geoffrey died (1151); and it was the Angevin forces which helped Henry to win the kingdom of England at last in 1154. Two years earlier, he gained control of Aquitaine by yet another notable match, with Eleanor, Louis VII's recently divorced wife who was the heiress of the vast duchy. Thus, under Henry II, both Anjou and the Anglo-Norman state had their frontiers protected and buttressed by new territories which helped to form an even greater dominion constructed by dynastic matrimony.

Henry's subsequent marriage policy had as its main aim the preservation of this huge 'empire'. In 1156, when he did homage to Louis VII for his French lands and, incidentally, secured recognition of his dominion, he also betrothed his surviving son, Henry, to Louis's daughter, Margaret. It was of a pattern with the objectives of earlier kings. Later on, another son Geoffrey was married to Constance of Brittany; Henry's daughter Eleanor married Alfonso VIII of Castile; and his daughter Matilda was married to Henry the Lion, duke of Saxony, a useful ally in Germany and on France's eastern frontier.

It was the disruption of this great 'empire' and the loss of many of its French lands that turned the marriage policy of English kings inward, towards partners who were predominantly powerful English nobles. It is true that one of Henry II's bastards had married an Englishwoman, and John 'Lackland' married the earl of Gloucester's daughter in 1189, the first time that a legitimate son of an English king had married a woman of English birth since before Cnut's conquest. Although King John's daughters married, after their father's death, Alexander II of Scotland and the Emperor Frederick II of Germany, another became the wife of William Marshal, earl of Pembroke, in 1224. John's son Richard also took an English wife during Henry III's reign. The change of pattern was neither sudden nor sweeping, and the marriage of Henry III's daughter to Alexander III of Scotland reflected the traditional English desire for security and influence on the northern border, as well as the customary insistence on English overlordship. Another daughter, Beatrice, married Jean de Dreux, whose aid as duke of Brittany might be valuable, not least in supporting King Henry's forlorn ambition to recover Poitou. But the gradual reorientation of English interests after John's reign, and his son's concern to win noble support once his minority had ended, led to a series of English noble marriages for members of the royal family, rather than weddings arranged on an international stage.

The king's offspring were not simply grist to the royal marriage mill; they had other uses too. In the second half of the twelfth century, honorific titles were given to royal sons to emphasize, not so much their status and birth, but rather their role as representatives and agents of the king. Henry II planned to crown his eldest surviving son Henry in 1162 when he was only seven, and although the ceremony was delayed, it was eventually staged in 1170, the first time that such a crowning had taken place in the king's lifetime in England since the tenth

THE TOMB-EFFIGY OF HENRY, THE
'YOUNG KING', eldest son of King
Henry II, in Rouen Cathedral. Crowned
king in the lifetime of his father, he died
in 1183 before he could succeed to the
throne. Henry was buried at Rouen, but
not before the citizens of Le Mans tried
to appropriate his body as it passed
through their city in order to bury it
there.

century. Young Henry was evidently not as other men and would, barring accidents, be the next king. Of Henry II's other sons, Geoffrey became duke of Brittany in 1169 at the age of eleven, Richard duke of Aquitaine in 1172 at the age of fourteen, and John may have been proclaimed king of Ireland in 1177 at the age of ten. These were titles conferred on legitimate sons by their father, who delegated to them at least formal authority in the various dominions subject to him. His imaginative design was an important stage in the emergence of a uniquely royal kin, engaged as a family group in regal business.

The English Monarchy at Large

What kind of monarchy developed in an England that was part of a larger aggregation of territories and whose king was not English? These two features of the history of monarchy in the British Isles were quite new after 1016, and they radically affected the character of monarchy not only in England but also in Wales, Scotland, and Ireland. Moreover, as the English monarchy grew more authoritarian in the eleventh and twelfth centuries, flaws and weaknesses were exposed which ultimately produced major changes in the course of the thirteenth.

In the 200 years when English kings were also rulers beyond the seas, a major problem arose as to how their disparate territories should be governed.

Traditional itinerant kingship had tried to adapt to the expansion of the West Saxon kingdom into the Viking-held lands of northern and eastern England, though its efforts were cut short by renewed Viking assaults which overwhelmed Æthelred II and incorporated his kingdom in the Scandinavian 'empire' of Cnut. Thereafter, kings—whether they were Danish, Norman, or Angevin—were bound to be itinerant, and most of them spent more of their time outside than inside England. Whereas the late Anglo-Saxon kings had been southerners who visited the midlands and north from time to time to assert their kingship, Cnut was king of Denmark, Sweden, and Norway, and paid four lengthy visits to his Baltic kingdoms (1019–24). William the Conqueror and his two sons were also dukes of Normandy and counts of Maine, and Norman affairs were at least as prominent in their minds as those of England; all in all, they spent at least half their time on the French side of the Channel. Henry II, whose dominions were augmented to include Anjou, Poitou, and Aquitaine, spent even more of his time out of England. Walter Map recalled that 'he was ever on his travels, moving by intolerable stages like a courier, and in this respect he showed little mercy to his household which accompanied him'. To Herbert of Bosham he seemed like a human chariot, dragging everybody else behind him. And Louis VII of France, who was often cast into despair on receiving news of Henry's lightning movements, was heard to say on one occasion, 'At one moment the king of England is in Ireland, the next in England, the next in Normandy—he must fly rather than travel by horse or ship' (Ralph of Diceto, *Images of History*).

One important consequence was that the English monarchy ceased to be a West Saxon monarchy writ large, though the old capital at Winchester continued to be its administrative centre well into the twelfth century. Instead, it became a transmarine monarchy whose main arteries of royal communication and travel were the Thames Estuary and the south-east ports. Kings from Cnut onwards were seen even less often in the midlands and north of England, and their

KING WILLIAM I'S CHARTER, in Anglo-Saxon, to the bishop, portreeve, and citizens of London, guaranteeing that their rights after the Conquest should be as ample as they had been in Edward the Confessor's day, 'and I will not allow any man to do you any wrong'. The charter and the undertaking reflect William's caution, conciliation, and determination to show himself as King Edward's true successor.

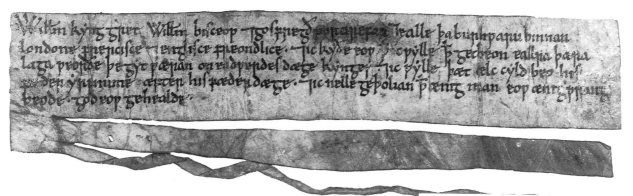

overseas commitments made it essential that an alternative method of asserting the royal authority in the provinces of the realm should be devised. Cnut resorted to government by viceroy, by great earls who between them had responsibility for four new earldoms, one of which was Wessex itself; in the social and administrative vocabulary of England, the Scandinavian 'earl' soon replaced the Anglo-Saxon 'thegn'. These largely autonomous earldoms survived through Edward the Confessor's reign into that of the Conqueror. There were, of course, dangers in devolving royal powers in the absence of the king to dominant earls such as Godwin of Wessex who, as events showed in the Confessor's reign, might act as if they were kings themselves; they quarrelled with other earls and undermined the royal authority which they were charged to uphold. It was one of William the Conqueror's achievements to break the hegemony of these regional viceroys and begin to reassert regal authority throughout the realm. Of course, the Normans were themselves forced to delegate authority to some degree, but they did so in a different way.

The rulers of Normandy before 1066 were itinerant, sure enough, and they and the ducal court were thereby able to organize and supervise the duchy's government, even though some of the duke's kinsmen ruled the frontierland as counts. They followed the same habits of government in England, though adapted to suit the greater distances involved. The sheer determination of the conquerors, who had more limited territorial responsibilities than Cnut, enabled William I and his sons to achieve what some historians see as a surprising degree of integration of their two dominions, England and Normandy. It is possible to visualize an Anglo-Norman monarchy, with the itinerant king at its head and practical authority delegated to governmental structures that allowed provincial administration to evolve without sacrificing central control, and all this despite turmoil in England and Normandy, and persistent threats from outside. A single chancellor for the Anglo-Norman 'realm' dealt with business relating to both territories, and historians admire the strength of this monarchy. After Henry I had permanently recovered Normandy (1106), a scheme of 'viceroys' was devised so that the duchy could be effectively ruled even when the king was in England. It may have been prefigured towards the end of William Rufus's reign when (1096) he obtained Normandy in pawn from his elder brother Robert; but it was Henry's design that gave Normandy an itinerant vice-regal court which acted on the king's behalf. When Henry himself travelled to Normandy, as he regularly did, this court was simply absorbed into his entourage, whilst he left in England a group of advisers who could wield power alongside his queen or his young son William. These vice-regal courts *in absentia* had no formal title: they were simply the itinerant king's *alter ego*, devised to meet the practical problem of how a cross-Channel dominion could be ruled by a personal monarchy.

Most historians see the Angevin dominions as far less tightly organized,

HENRY II

(1153–1189), king of England

. . . a man of reddish, freckled complexion with a large round head, grey eyes which glowed fiercely and grew blood-shot in anger, a fiery countenance and a harsh, cracked voice. His neck was somewhat thrust forward from his shoulders, his chest broad and square, his arms strong and powerful. His frame was stocky with a pronounced tendency to corpulence . . . he was a prince of great eloquence and, what is remarkable in these days, polished in letters.

(Gerald of Wales, *The Conquest of Ireland*)

ELDEST son of Matilda and Geoffrey of Anjou, he ruled the largest territorial dominion of his age. Imaginative, energetic, and commanding, with an alert and capacious mind trained in Normandy, Anjou, and England, he determined never to relax his grip on Church or State. He was designated Henry I's ultimate successor (1133) and took part in the civil war alongside David I, who knighted him (1149); he was invested with Normandy by his father (1150) and inherited the Angevin lands when Geoffrey died (1151). He married the vivacious and talented Eleanor, whose inheritance of Aquitaine made him the greatest French noble; they had nine children in thirteen years. King Stephen adopted Henry as his son and heir (1153) and in 1154 he succeeded to the English throne. Henry issued a charter of liberties and set about restoring royal authority, skilfully renovating the financial, military, and judicial machinery of government. He safeguarded his French fiefs by diplomatic marriages and by dominating neighbouring provinces, though he recoiled from confronting his overlord, Louis VII. He forced Malcolm IV to return the northern counties, and claimed homage from Malcolm, Welsh kings (1157), and native kings and English conquerors in Ireland (1171). His chief adviser was Thomas Becket, but when Becket became archbishop of Canterbury (1162), his views on Church and State led to a collision that damaged Henry at home and abroad; the dispute culminated in Becket's murder (1170) and a papal interdict on England. Henry's greatest problem later was his quarrelsome wife and sons and their territorial ambitions (from 1173), though his autocratic rule also caused unrest. The death of his sons Henry (1183) and

THE TOMB-EFFIGY OF KING HENRY II at Fontevrault Abbey. It dates from the end of the twelfth century and may have an element of portraiture about it. The king is shown robed and crowned as he was carried to his burial.

Geoffrey (1186) did not resolve matters, for Richard and John were still in revolt when Henry died at Chinon; he was buried at Fontevrault. An unattractive figure, he had a genius for government, developed the royal bureaucracy, and established the supremacy of common law under royal control.

perhaps like a confederation, with each dominion evolving its own pattern of government though under the ever-watchful eye of Henry II. His father Geoffrey, when he was dying, had counselled him never to rule one province according to the customs of another, and Henry mostly heeded this advice. His sons were later given a vice-regal role, subject to their father's supervision and supplemented by a system of homage and fealty that bound all his peoples to the king-duke-count. Each territory developed its own institutions and legal system, although the king and his court provided a key element of administrative unity. To expect the Angevin 'empire' to become an integrated monarchy is to forget the highly personalized nature of twelfth-century kingship and to underestimate the influence of geography and the difficulties of communication.

The transmarine 'empires' after 1016 saw significant changes in the methods by which these 'empires' were defended. Fleets of ships had been assembled intermittently by Anglo-Saxon kings in order to counter the Viking menace. Cnut relied heavily on mastery of the seas, using ships as his main line of defence and communication within his 'empire'; from 1018 a permanent fleet was available to him. Like earlier kings, he also relied on his household and entourage, whose 'housecarls' were a professional body of warriors. His sea and land forces were underpinned by a system of military taxation (or heregeld) which was first developed by Æthelred II. Perhaps in his enthusiasm to abandon the methods of a Scandinavian usurper, perhaps also to win the loyalty of his people, Edward the Confessor disbanded the royal fleet and discontinued this tax in 1051. Nevertheless, even this pacific king needed military resources, and the obligation to provide ships and crews was instead laid on certain ports in the south-east that were later known as the Cinque Ports.

The Norman kings altered still further the military establishment of the English monarchy, basing their ideas on their experience in northern France. Castles, which to begin with were built mostly of earth with wooden superstructures (as at Hastings itself) and then, in the twelfth century, often rebuilt in stone, became a key element in their conquest and settlement of the country, and in the assertion of their authority. An armed entourage, based squarely on the royal household, was maintained and much expanded by the revolution in landholding which accompanied the settlement of Normans and other Frenchmen, lay and clerical, throughout the country; each held his lands in return for military service in person or by delegation. This largely new system created a feudal army that ensured the permanence of the conquest and the extension of Anglo-Norman power elsewhere in the British Isles. It may have taken a good while to organize—perhaps not until after the compilation of the great source-book of English landholding, Domesday Book (1086). Meanwhile, William the Conqueror could draw on Norman resources to sustain his new monarchy in England. For instance, in 1085, when he was threatened by Danes and Flemings, he brought from Normandy what one chronicler believed to be the largest body of cavalry and infantry ever to set foot in England. By these means, his monarchy was made secure, at least from external attack and native English resentment. It was seriously threatened in Stephen's reign by internecine quarrels among the conquerors themselves.

The mixture of continuity and change which inevitably characterizes new, foreign dynasties is also apparent in the spheres of law and law-making, and in the machinery of government. Cnut was an admirer of Anglo-Saxon law, especially King Edgar's codes, which he adopted as the classic statement of the law to be enforced in his England. He adopted and adapted them as his own manifesto, which is judged to be a skilful attempt at conciliation and the model followed by Norman rulers when they found themselves in a not dissimilar situation. Cnut's methods of government were inevitably those of his Anglo-Saxon predecessors, if only because they were more sophisticated than those used in his Scandinavian kingdoms; in any case, the extent of his knowledge and the brevity of his rule made major changes unlikely in the first half of the eleventh century.

The administrative structures to which William the Conqueror had been accustomed in Normandy before 1066 may have been (though historians are sharply divided on this point) generally more primitive than those operating in the Confessor's England, but they were incontestably under the firm control of the duke. He dispensed justice at his court, where he also issued charters, and he supervised the minting of coins and the collection of revenue from Norman towns and the *vicomtés* (or districts) of the Norman countryside. English administration had emerged from the tenth century more elaborate though not necessarily any more effective: the itinerant king and his entourage worked through sheriffs in a system of shires, each with its own shire court and lesser hundred courts; the king's chancellor proclaimed the royal will by means of writs that were authenticated by the royal seal; the Treasury lay at Winchester, overseeing the

A SILVER PENNY OF WILLIAM II, minted at Wallingford early in his reign. For five centuries, until 1280, silver pennies were the only royal coins in circulation. Although the representation of the crowned king, with a sceptre, on the obverse of this issue is unusual in facing right—most of William's and the Conqueror's coins used a front-facing bust— there was no marked departure in fiscal or other government matters from the Conqueror's reign to Rufus's. (× 3)

financial exploitation of the shires, the mints, and, by means of the geld, the landowners of England. Practically all Englishmen were within the king's reach had he but the will to stretch forth his hand. The Norman kings brought with them no new technical knowledge to improve this system, but their ruthless pursuit of their interests meant that they exploited it more thoroughly and, perhaps, more oppressively, employing a growing number of officials to capitalize on their new resources and to provide royal justice throughout the realm. This was Henry I's message to the prominent men of Worcestershire in about 1110:

Know that I grant and order that henceforth my shire courts and hundred courts shall meet in the same places and at the same terms as they were wont to do in the time of King Edward [the Confessor], and not otherwise. And I do not wish that my sheriff should make them assemble in different fashion because of his own needs or interests. For I myself, if ever I shall wish it, will cause them to be summoned at my own pleasure, if it be necessary for my royal interests.

These 'royal interests' were articulated in French speech and Latin writing, though Henry I still regarded it as an advantage to learn English, the language of government before 1066.

The Anglo-Norman monarchy was riveted on the English countryside, and the crown's resources were vastly increased, by the very act of conquest and the subsequent redistribution of land to the king and his loyal (mostly French) subjects. The pages of Domesday Book reflect this harsh fiscal exploitation, but it was the sophisticated administrative organization and techniques of the Anglo-Saxon monarchy that made it all possible. The 'Domesday' inquiry was speedy (though incomplete) and the survey, which seemed like 'the Day of Judgement' to English observers, may have been presented to the king at Salisbury on 1 August 1086, barely seven months after it had been initiated by 'deep speech' at Gloucester.

After this, the king had much thought and very deep discussion with his council about this country—how it was occupied or with what sort of people. Then he sent his men over all England into every shire and had them find out how many hundred hides there were in the shire, or what land and cattle the king himself had in the country, or what dues he ought to have in twelve months from the shire. Also he had a record made of how much land his archbishop had, and his bishops and his abbots and his earls and . . . what or how much everybody had who was occupying land in England, in land or cattle, and how much money it was worth. So very narrowly did he have it investigated, that there was no single hide nor virgate of land, nor indeed (it is a shame to relate but it seemed no shame to him to do) one ox nor one cow nor one pig which was there left out, and not put down in his record; and all these records were brought to him afterwards. (Anglo-Saxon Chronicle, 1085)

A large step had been taken by William I and William Rufus, but it seems very likely that it was not until Henry I's reign (and then under the direction of his dedicated minister, Ranulf Flambard, 'the darting flame') that the monarchy effectively spread its tentacles throughout English society and the English countryside, and into more areas of English life than hitherto. By 1110 an Exchequer had been installed over and above the Treasury at Winchester in order to improve the procedures by which revenue was collected, audited, and recorded. Normandy, too, was given an Exchequer, as part of that delegated vice-regal arrangement that operated when the king was in England. Winchester may have become a more general repository for the records of an increasingly bureaucratic and literate monarchy, hastening the day when most organs of government would have a permanent headquarters; in the twelfth century, it became clear that this headquarters would be at Westminster, no longer at Winchester. Over all stood the king and his household and court. From them came the impetus for the due administration of justice and the efficient fiscal exploitation of the realm.

Exploitation and recreation went hand in hand when the Norman kings extended the royal forests (to cover a fifth of England by the end of the twelfth century) and regulated them more strictly. The Conqueror himself loved to hunt

KING JOHN, CROWNED AND ACCOMPANIED BY HIS DOGS, evidently taking pleasure in hunting deer in the forest. Rabbits look on apprehensively. This picture dates from the thirteenth century. John had a passion for the hunt (including falconry) which he pursued even at times of political crisis.

and Rufus met his death while hunting in the 'New Forest'. Later in the twelfth century the king's forests were described as

the sanctuaries of kings and their chief delight. Thither they repair to hunt, their cares laid aside the while, in order to refresh themselves by a short respite. There renouncing the arduous, but natural turmoil of the court, they breathe the pure air of freedom for a little space; whence it is that they who transgress the laws of the forest are subject solely to the royal jurisdiction.

This description is to be found, significantly, in 'The Dialogue of the Exchequer' (c.1177–9), for the large royal forestlands (which included fields and pasture as well as woods) were designated as much for security and the financial exploitation of fines, rents, and privileges as for the chase. The survival of Kincardine's deer park near the east coast of Scotland reminds us that the concept of the royal forest and of forest law also commended itself to those Scottish kings of the twelfth century who were much influenced by their Anglo-Norman kinsmen.

In the most disturbed years of Stephen's reign, especially the early 1140s when the country's allegiance was split in two and rival armies roamed the shires, it is likely that royal justice, co-ordinated at the centre, faltered or even collapsed temporarily; but the machinery itself did not decay and was there to be re-oiled and improved by Henry II and his Angevin successors.

It may be that Henry II's reign seems of great significance to us today because of the explosion of record-keeping that took place in his time and the chance survival of many of his records—and perhaps, too, because later generations regarded the year of his death (1189) as the limit of legal memory and the starting-point of chronicles. Nevertheless, it cannot be denied that it was Henry who gave Westminster its central role in English history as the focus of the monarchy and its administration. The establishment of the several government offices permanently in the royal palace at Westminster can be dated from the later years of his reign. Then, too, it was Henry who extended the system of royal justice, with itinerant justices dispatched from his court to the localities.

The bishops, earls and magnates of the realm assembled at Windsor, the king by their common counsel and in the presence of the king, his son, divided England into four parts. For each part he appointed wise men from his kingdom and later sent them through the regions of the kingdom assigned to them to execute justice among the people . . .

This he did in order that the coming of public officials of authority throughout the shires might strike terror into the hearts of wrongdoers, and those who cheated him of the taxes and thus affronted the king's majesty might incur the royal displeasure. (Ralph of Diceto, *Epitome of Chronicles*, 1179)

He scrutinized closely the sheriffs, ensuring that they were, first and foremost, reliable agents of his will, often with legal training rather than merely military

A PAGE FROM THE GREAT DOMESDAY BOOK, the largest and most comprehensive of the surviving volumes known collectively as Domesday Book. This page (vol. ii, fo. 132) relates to Hertfordshire and describes the borough of Hertford, the chief landowners of the county, and the royal lands. Land or tax surveys may have been made before 1086, but this Anglo-Norman survey is the most wide-ranging and detailed and its later use has given it a unique and authoritative reputation down the ages.

BVRGV HEREFORDE p̃ .x. hidis

se defend̃ .T.R.E. 7 modo n̄ facit.
Ibi ħnt .c.xl.vi. burgenses n̄
loca reg̃ .E. Eduuardi.

Debit ħt in comes Alan .iii. domos. que t̃
7 modo redd̃ consuetudinẽ.
Eudo dapifer ħt .ii. domos que fuer̃ Algari
cochenac.
7 t̃ 7 m reddeb̃ c̃suetud̃. 7 t̃cia domũ
tone
ħ ide Eudo que fuit Vlmari. non redd̃ c̃suetud̃.
Goisfrid de bech .iii. domos. c̃suetud̃ reddent̃.
Hunfrid de Ansleuile ten̄ sub Eudone .ii.
domos cũ uno horto. har̃ una acc̃modata
fuit cuidã p̃fecto reg̃. 7 altera cũ horto fuit
cuidã burgensi. 7 in reclamatio ip̃i bur
genses sibi iniuste ablatas.
Alios .xxiii. burgenses ħt rex .W. qui fuer̃
comes
hões Heraldi 7 Leuuini. om̃s c̃suetud̃ redd̃.
Petrus de ualonges ħt .ii. ecc̃las cũ una domo.
quas emit de Vluui de harfelde. redd̃ om̃s
eu
c̃suetudines. Ip̃e Vluui 7 dare 7 uende poterat.
Goisfrid de magneuile ħt occupatũ qdã.
qui fuit Wigari stalri. 7 vii. domos que
que
null̃
c̃suetudinẽ reddides. nisi geldũ reg̃ qdo
colligebatur.　　c̃suetud̃ redd̃
Radulfs bainard ħt .ii. domos. 7 t̃ 7 modo
Harduin de Scaleis ħt .xiii. domos. qs
habuit Achil .T.R.E. nulla c̃suetud̃ dabant
nisi geldũ reg̃. de qb; aduocat harduin
regẽ ad p̃tectorem. Adhuc una domũ ħt
harduin de dono reg̃. que fuit cuidã burgensis.
redd̃ om̃em consuetudinem.

Hoc suburbiũ redd̃ .xx. lib̃ ars̃as 7 pensatas.
7 iii. molini redd̃ .x. lib̃ ad numerũ.
Qdo petrus uicecomes recep̃ .xv. lib̃ ad numer̃.
redd̃ebat .T.R.E. vii. lib̃ 7 x. sol̃ ad numerũ.

.I. REX WILLELMVS.

.ii. Archieps̃ cantuariensis .xx. Willelm̃ de o̅.
.iii. Eps̃ Wintoniensis. .xxiii. Willelm̃ de odburuuile.
.iiii. Eps̃ Londoniensis. .xxix. Walterius flandrensis.
.V. Eps̃ Baiocensis. .xxx. Eudo dapifer.
.VI. Eps̃ Lisiacensis. .xxxi. Eduuard saresberiensis.
.VII. Eps̃ Cestrensis. .xxxii. Goisfrid de manneuile.
.VIII. Abbas de Ely. .xxxiii. Goisfrid de bech.
.IX. Abb̃ de Westmonast̃. .xxxiii. Gisbertus de beluaco.
.X. Abb̃ de s̃ Albano. .xxxv. Petrus de ualonges.
.xi. Abbatissa de cetriz. .xxxvi. Hugo arduin̄ de Escalers.
.XII. Canonica de Lundonia. .xxxvii. Edgar.
.xiii. Canonica de Wltham. .xxxviii. Algar̃ brito.
.XIII. Comes moritoniensis. .xxx. Gislebtus filius salomonis.
.xV. Comes Alanus. .xl. Sigar de Cioches.
.xvi. Comes Eustachius. .xli. Beringar̃ Salu anglici reg̃.
.xvii. Comes Rogerius. .xlii. Rohais uxor Ricardi.
.xviii. Rotbtus de olgi. .xliii. Adeliz uxor hugonis.
.xix. Rotbtus gernon. .xlii. filia Radulfi tailgebosch.
.xx. Rotbtus de Todeni.
.xxi. Radulf̃ de Todeni.
.xxii. Radulf̃ de limesi.
.xxiii. Radulf̃ bainard.
.xxii. Radulf̃ annullatus sc̃i Algeri.
.xxv. Hugo de Grentemaisnil.
.xxvi. Hugo de belcamp.

TERRA REGIS. In Bradeuuatre hund.

Willelm̃s Rex ten̄ Wiuuedeslai .viii. ħ se def̃.
t̃ra ē .xviii. car̃. In d̃nio .ii. hide 7 dim̃
7 ibi sunt .iii. car̃. 7 xxiii. uilli 7 xi
sochi 7 v. bord̃. v. cot̃. ħt .xv. car̃. Ibi vi. serui.
7 i. molin de xx. sol̃. p̃ti .i. car̃. 7 ii. bob̃ pasta ad
pecun̄ uille. Item ad sepes. hoc m̃ fuit in d̃nio ecc̃e
s̃ marie de cetris. sed H e q̃ald comes abstulit inde
ut tota s̃yra testat̃. 7 apposuit in his manerio suo
tribz annis ante morte reg̃ Eduuardi.

Rex .W. ten̄ Meulesdene. p̃ .iiii. ħ se def̃. t̃ra ē
viii. car̃. In d̃nio .ii. ħ 7 u. iiii. 7 dim̃. 7 ibi sun̄ .iii. car̃.
p̃br̃ cũ .iiii. uillis .ii. cot̃. ħt .iii. car̃. 7 adhuc .ii. possun̄
fieri. Ibi .vi. serui. p̃ti .i. car̃. pasta ad pecun̄ uille.
Silue .xxx. porc̃. Hoc m̃ iacuit 7 iacet in his. Herald
comit̃
tenuit.

experience. By the end of the twelfth century, England had the most sophisticated and effective monarchy in Europe. It was served by a body of
professional servants who moved easily between shire, court, and Westminster
at the king's command: they may pardonably be described as a royal
bureaucracy.

THE GREAT SEAL OF KING STEPHEN, adopted after 1139 and used for the rest of the reign. The obverse
shows the king enthroned, with a long sword in his right hand, an orb in his left; the legend reads
'Stephen by the grace of God king of the English'. The reverse shows the king mounted, wearing a
pointed helmet and carrying a lance; the legend reads 'Stephen by the grace of God duke of the
Normans'.

Such a transformation would not have been possible without the substantial
resources at the disposal of the English monarchy. The preface to the monu-
mental description of the workings of the king's Exchequer, which was written in
the late 1170s in the form of a dialogue between two Exchequer officials, puts it
well:

. . . the abundance of resources, or the lack of them, exalts or humbles the power of
princes. For those who are lacking in them become a prey to their enemies, while those
who are well supplied with them despoil their foes . . . The glory of princes consists in
mighty deeds both in peace and war, but it excels in those where, in return for an earthly
outlay, there follows an eternal and blessed reward.

Cnut had inherited a system of taxation (the geld) which was assessed locally on
property; in addition, the heregeld was designed specifically to meet the king's
military needs. He soon realized his good fortune, and in 1018 raised £72,000
(and £10,500 more from London) to pay off his invasion army and fleet. Cnut

RICHARD I 'THE LION-HEART'

(1189–1199), king of England

At about this time [1194] the king of England, imposing certain measures to improve the royal finances, announced that knights should come together from all over England to try out their strength in tournaments, thinking perhaps that if he should declare war on the Saracens or his neighbours, or if outsiders presumptuously invaded the kingdom, he would find them more vigorous, better trained and readier for warfare.

(Ralph of Diceto, *Images of History*)

THIRD son of Henry II and Queen Eleanor, Richard spent less time in England than any of his predecessors (1189–90, 1194) and over a year in captivity in Germany (1193–4). A brave, cultivated but cruel and tempestuous man, dogged by ill health, few English kings have been the subject of so many heroic legends. He was regarded as Eleanor's heir, schooled in the affairs of Aquitaine of which he was made duke (1168); his military skills were developed in struggles with his father and brothers (1173–89). Henry II acknowledged him (1189) as his heir and agreed to his marriage with Alice, sister of Philip II of France. Soon after his crowning, Richard resolved to fulfil his crusading vow and went to great lengths to raise resources. He bound his brother John not to enter England while he was away and declared his nephew Arthur his heir (1190); John later revolted (1193). Richard and Philip agreed on the mutual defence of their dominions and left for the Holy Land. On the way, Richard made conquests in Sicily and Cyprus, where he married Berengaria, the king of Navarre's daughter, instead of Alice. After his victory over Saladin, the capture of Acre, and the treaty of Jaffa (1192), Richard returned to Europe. He fell into the clutches of the German emperor who forced him to do homage for England and pay a large ransom. Richard eventually reached England to find that John had sworn homage to Philip for Richard's French lands and that Philip had invaded Normandy. Recrowned at Westminster (1194), he forcefully waged war on Philip,

THE TOMB-EFFIGY OF KING RICHARD I at Fontevrault Abbey. It may date from soon after the king's death (1199) and the thin, bearded face and formal dress may represent his appearance at his burial.

but was killed at Chalus-Chabrol, near Limoges; he was buried at Fontevrault, his heart at Rouen. England occupied a minor part of his mind and he left its rule to others.

inherited, too, a tradition of controlling and manipulating the coinage. Although Edward the Confessor abolished the heregeld (1051), the growing wealth of England in the eleventh century meant that the king was not significantly impoverished. The Treasury at Winchester continued to collect and store the royal revenues under the Normans. And Henry I used his control of the coinage to standardize the coins issued during his reign. The arrival of the Normans also brought a fundamental change in the way the land of England was exploited for the benefit of the crown.

The redistribution of land, including the king's estates, resulted in an enormous increase in the resources of the monarchy, both for direct exploitation and through tenants-in-chief who henceforward held their lands from the king in return for services. Moreover, whereas the royal estates had previously been concentrated in Wessex and the west midlands, the homeland of the West Saxon dynasty, William I's grand reorganization enabled the monarchy to acquire lands in the far south-west, in East Anglia, the counties round London, and even in the

SILVER PENNY OF KING HENRY II from the London mint, *c.*1180–9. It shows a bust of the king, crowned and bearded, perhaps to indicate his age, and with a sceptre in his right hand. (× 3)

north. By the time of Domesday Book, the king's own demesne lands had so expanded in size as to double his revenue. More impressive still was the relentless and ruthless way in which twelfth-century kings wrung revenue from the various rights, powers, and jurisdictions that made up their resources as feudal overlords of England. This lay at the root of the greater effectiveness of the English monarchy, its greater practical authority under Henry I and Henry II, and its capacity to create administrative structures that have survived in their essentials to this day. Walter Map, in his sharp but amusing 'Courtiers' Trifles' (*De nugis curialium*), recorded a remark made to him by King Louis VII which highlighted the disparity of wealth between the French monarch and Henry II: 'Your lord the king of England has men, horses, gold, silk, jewels, fruits, game and everything else. We in France have nothing but bread and wine and joy.' And observers in both England and France, and in the Holy Land too, were well aware that Richard I had richer lands and greater cash reserves than Philip of France. Nevertheless, to realize these resources meant harsh and heavy burdens for people to bear; when they were supplemented by new forms of personal

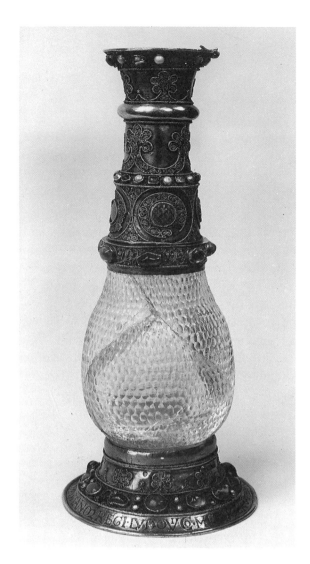

THIS BEAUTIFUL VASE, made of rock crystal and decorated with gold filigree and gems, was given by Eleanor of Aquitaine to her first husband, Louis VII of France, on their marriage (1137). Eleanor (1122–1204) was born into a richly cultured society; she embraced its chivalric ideals, and as Henry II's queen (from 1152) patronized art and architecture, literature, and song. She held her own court where, among her sons, Richard the Lion-heart was raised and came to share her chivalric tastes.

taxation towards the end of the century, especially under King John, the complaints were not confined to the formal clauses of Magna Carta. Nor ought it to be forgotten that although Normandy's wealth is unlikely to have been channelled to England after 1066, the Anglo-Norman kings—and, later, the Angevins—had more income after 1096 (even more after 1106 and 1154) than any of their predecessors, and at a time of economic upsurge in production and trade in western Europe as a whole.

England's foreign kings attached no less importance than their predecessors to assemblies of advisers—or witan—whether they be administrators, clergy, nobles, or soldiers. After all, Cnut and William I especially needed the aid of Englishmen as well as the advice and support of their own compatriots. It was at lengthy meetings of the royal council at Gloucester around Christmas 1085 that plans for the Domesday survey were thrashed out. Once again we have Walter

Map to thank for reminding us that Henry I's court was far from being unrelievedly solemn:

Those who were ripe in age or wisdom were always in the court with the king before dinner, and the herald's voice cited them to meet those who desired an audience for their business; after noon and the siesta, those were admitted who devoted themselves to sports; and this king's court was in the forenoon a school of virtues and of wisdom, and in the afternoon one of hilarity and decent mirth.

Prominent among the king's advisers were the nobles, the stoutest prop of medieval English kingship. The Danish and Norman dynasties brought their own nobles with them and although they did not displace the native nobility entirely, within a generation of the Norman Conquest most English nobles had been deprived of their estates, their power, and their status. Some nobles could be overmighty, especially under weaker kings. Edward the Confessor encountered severe difficulties with nobles whom he could not dismiss or replace, and who, if they were earls, enjoyed formidable regional power and wealth which they sought to make hereditary. The kind of problem that faced Edward, with Mercia and Northumbria pitted against Wessex, was to re-emerge on many occasions during the Middle Ages. And who does not know of the early Tudor adage, 'The north knows no king but a Percy'? In a predominantly southern-based monarchy, noble dissidence that exploited the deep-seated societal divisions of England— which were of far greater antiquity than the eleventh century—was particularly dangerous.

The Norman revolution created in brief time a new nobility bound to the crown in a feudal relationship of mutual dependence that proved of enormous support to the new kings—so long as this nobility could be controlled. Royal patronage of privileges, offices, wardships, marriages, and especially land kept the nobility loyal for much of the time; as they established hereditary possession of their estates, and even of certain offices, after the first generation or two, the possibility of serious tension between crown and nobility became greater. On the other hand, the unprecedentedly large fund of patronage available to Norman kings meant that dependable men could always be recruited to the king's household and administration; 'new men' were a phenomenon, long observed by historians of Henry I's reign but far from absent in others, that frequently aroused the suspicion and hostility of longer-established nobility. In Walter Map's opinion, they lent a vitality that was chameleon-like, perhaps even confused, to the royal court:

The Court is the same, its members are changed . . . We courtiers are assuredly a number, and an infinite one, and all striving to please one individual. But today we are one number, tomorrow we shall be a different one: yet the Court is not changed: it

THE EAST ANGLIAN KING EDMUND, depicted in Henry I's reign (*c.*1125–30) as a martyr. He was murdered by the Danes in 869, and Cnut venerated him as an act of reconciliation. There was renewed interest in the Anglo-Saxon past in Henry I's reign, and this representation of the martyred king crowned by angels was painted at St Albans. The symbols of regal authority—crown, staff, and the palm of martyrdom—are conferred by angels from heaven.

remains always the same ... [Henry I] had a register of all the earls and barons of his land, and appointed for them at his coming or during the stay of his Court certain presents with which he honoured them, of candles, bread, and wine. Every youth on this side the Alps whom he heard of as desiring the renown of a good start in life, he enrolled in his household ...

Nor was he blind to the self-seeking and sycophancy of the courtiers, though it was wit and observation, rather than experience, that enabled the cleric Walter to say that 'the king in his Court is like a husband who is the last to learn of the unfaithfulness of his wife'.

The Church and the higher clergy were staunch and eloquent allies of the new dynasties. Cnut relied on distinguished Anglo-Saxon clergy, who were not replaced wholesale by Danish prelates; indeed, he employed Archbishop Ælfheah in Scandinavia. And he supported the campaign to canonize the East Anglian king, Edmund the Martyr, who was murdered by the Danes (869); he was wise to do so because only hours after refusing to exempt Edmund's last resting-place at Bury St Edmunds from tribute, Cnut's father, Sweyn Forkbeard, fell into agony and died crying that Edmund had pierced him with a spear. At Cnut's elbow when he drew up his law-codes was Archbishop Wulfstan, Æthelred II's confidant. William the Norman was far less indulgent towards the native ecclesiastical establishment; after all, among the publicized aims of his 'crusade' in 1066 were the removal of the blatantly schismatic archbishop of Canterbury, Stigand, and the encouragement of Church reform in England. William had his own plans for enlisting clerical support for his monarchy. His close relationship with Archbishop Lanfranc led to the rapid Normanization of the higher echelons of the English Church by 1087; it also deprived the pope of a pretext for interfering directly in English Church affairs. If the example of William and Lanfranc could not be followed by William Rufus, Henry I, or Henry II, it was partly because the reform movement had so gripped the consciences of Archbishop Anselm and Thomas Becket, in particular, that English kings no longer had subservient prelates (or impotent popes) to deal with. Nevertheless, although relations between Church and monarchy might sometimes be turbulent, generally speaking the staunchest allies of English kings in the Middle Ages were the clergy.

The Church was an unrivalled source of propaganda for Christian kingship. But the French kings of England became their own propagandists in ways hitherto undreamt of. If Cnut had good cause but little time to utilize the arts of popular persuasion, by Henry I's time the Normans had set about projecting their monarchy in England and overseas. Harthacnut is said to have loved display and royal ceremonial. And the most famous piece of royal propaganda in English history, the Bayeux Tapestry, was woven soon after the battle of Hastings to publicize and celebrate the heroic Norman victory. This magnificent embroidery, an art-form peculiarly associated with the English, is all of 230 feet long, in colours that seem almost as fresh today as they must have been when it was finished. It relates the background of King William's claim and conquest and may have been intended for display in a hall or church, perhaps one owned by the Conqueror's half-brother, Odo, bishop of Bayeux and earl of Kent. The court of the Conqueror provided the environment of celebration (and justification) in which the saga was told.

Not until Henry I's reign was such propaganda consciously devised by the monarchy itself. More so than his predecessors, Henry saw himself as king of a united realm in which his French and English subjects would be treated alike. This vision was publicized from the 1130s: Henry and his successors took a sustained interest in the image of their monarchy and its projection. The cult of Edward the Confessor as England's last legitimate Anglo-Saxon king was widely promoted. The Conqueror had been crowned in Edward's new church at Westminster, and in the following century Edward's palace nearby became the headquarters of English government. In Henry I's reign curiosity about, and veneration of, the old king grew: in 1102 his tomb was opened, and in the 1130s the Life that had been written about him was revised. The Normans' desire for reconciliation with their English subjects explains this interest, which revived after the civil war. In 1161 Henry II promoted Edward's canonization; two years later his body was translated from its original resting place at Westminster—and Henry III moved it again to a new shrine in 1269. Strong links with a venerated king of a venerable dynasty had spiritual and practical advantages which the foreign kings of the twelfth century readily appreciated. Nor did royal interest in the Anglo-Saxons stop there. Henry II was fascinated by the genealogies of Anglo-Saxon kings which gained in popularity during his reign, and his son John arranged his own burial in Worcester Cathedral, between the hallowed remains of St Oswald and St Wulfstan. This Plantagenet trait was doubtless fortified by the cultured tradition in which Henry II and Queen Eleanor had been brought up, for at the Angevin and Aquitainian courts the cult of ancestors and their heroic deeds was prominent.

If kings could not control the place and manner of their birth, they at least had a say in where and how they were buried. In any case, the departure from this world of an anointed king was of far greater significance and public interest than the arrival in it of a mewling infant who might not even be destined for the purple (let alone attain it). The development of royal mausolea, associated with the symbolism of ceremonial burials, did much to enhance the uniqueness of monarchy. Winchester had long been the shrine of Anglo-Saxon kings, and it is solemn testimony to Cnut's earnest desire to plant his Danish dynasty firmly in English soil that he directed that he, too, should be buried there. The Norman

THE SHRINE OF KING EDWARD THE CONFESSOR (d. 1066), behind the high altar of Westminster Abbey, which Edward rebuilt. He was buried before the high altar in his new church. William I built a stone tomb on the spot for his remains; Henry II transferred the body to a new shrine (1163), and Henry III constructed the marble and mosaic base of the present exotic shrine for the body's second translation (1269). The wooden superstructure dates from Mary Tudor's reign (1557), following desecration at the dissolution of the abbey.

and Angevin kings were much attached to their French dominions, and they all viewed the choice of a burial site as an individual act of penance. In this age of reform, most kings were buried in religious houses which they themselves had founded or had come to regard as being under their special protection. The Confessor's choice of Westminster was in this vein, and so was the Conqueror's burial in St Stephen's, Caen, Harold's at Waltham, Stephen's at Faversham, Henry I's at Reading, and King John's at Worcester. It is very possible that Henry II looked on Reading as the pre-eminent mausoleum of his family: he interred the body of his first son William there in 1156, at Henry I's feet, and both Henry II and John gave relics to Reading. But it was to Fontevrault, in his father's province of Anjou, that the body of Henry II was taken in 1189; there, too, the bodies of his son and successor, Richard, and of his wife Eleanor were buried and placed beneath fine recumbent stone effigies—the first to be carved of English kings—early in the thirteenth century. Henry's interest in the mortal remains of his predecessors is said to have prompted the search for King Arthur's tomb at Glastonbury, where the monks claimed to have found it in 1191. The stories of Britain's antique past written by Geoffrey of Monmouth in the 1130s stimulated the popular imagination along similar lines. All this was an attempt to enhance the antiquity, distinction, and dignity of the English monarchy and to place the new dynasties in a line that was unbroken from the Dark Ages.

Even the manner of royal burials was more dignified, formal, and public in the second half of the twelfth century. The Conqueror's burial at Caen impressed all who were present—though not by its dignity. The owner of the burial plot complained that he had not been compensated, while the corpse, as attendants tried to stuff it into the coffin, ruptured and brought the service to a hasty and pungent end. Rufus's departure was no less shabby. His body was carried, still profusely bleeding, from the New Forest to Winchester, where it was buried in a simple, sullen ceremony. In marked contrast was the fate of Henry II and his two successors. They were borne to the grave in solemn ceremonies reserved for no other man: the face was uncovered, the head crowned. Anointed kings ought not to meet their maker unworthily or leave their earthly kingdom surreptitiously. An observer of Henry's last days reported on his funeral:

The day after his death, when he was borne to burial, he lay in state robed in royal splendour, wearing a gold crown on his head, gauntlets on his hand and a gold ring on his finger, holding the sceptre in his hand, with gold-braided shoes and spurs on his feet, girded with his sword, and his face uncovered. When this had been reported to Earl Richard, his son, he came post-haste to meet the cortège. At his coming blood at once began to flow from the dead king's nostrils as if his spirit was moved with indignation. (Ralph of Diceto, *Epitome of Chronicles*, 1189)

This mystical elevation of monarchy was in the spiritual field what the enhancement of its governmental authority was in the practical field.

The foreign phase in England's history accentuated the differences between the English monarchy and monarchies elsewhere in the British Isles; but it also intensified English influences in these indigenous kingdoms to the point where the large lowland kingdom almost overwhelmed the kingdoms of the north and west.

Let us first take Scotland, whose monarchy had greatest affinity with that of England, even though it lacked the resources of wealth and population of its southern neighbour. In Scotland, literate government was slower to take root. The Scottish kings were slower to create a Chancery, or professional writing office. During the twelfth century they employed clerks to write their charters, but these did not form a professional corps of clerks at court, but rather were members of the religious houses where the charters were produced. And yet, during the twelfth century, Anglo-Norman practices gained currency in Scotland, whose kings forged strong personal links with the royal house of England. King David I had his own chancellor by the late 1130s, his charters were like those of English kings in style and character, several of the clerks used by Scottish kings had English connections or English training, and letters sealed with a royal seal became customary about that time.

These developments were but one aspect of the growing centralized and feudalized authority of Scottish monarchs in the provinces of their kingdom. The more sophisticated English system was apparent to any Scottish observer, but not until the twelfth century, when Anglo-Norman influences were more acceptable at the Scottish court and among the Anglo-Scottish nobility, were some of its detailed features adopted by the Scottish monarchy. Sheriffs were introduced as royal agents, particularly in southern and eastern Scotland; castle-building, copied from the south, became a symbol of regal power, again mainly in the south and east. Indeed, the introduction of feudal institutions in the middle of the twelfth century was partly responsible for providing the Scottish monarchy with a machinery of government which in part closely resembled England's. The reign of William the Lion seems to have been crucial in confirming this process. He also sought to control the Scottish Church by vigorous royal patronage; he established royal burhs in eastern Scotland as far north as the Moray Firth; and he extended the use of the sheriff in the same general region. Places such as Perth and Stirling became major centres of royal administration—even of residence—instead of towns and castles nearer the English border. Anglo-Norman monarchical institutions were being superimposed on a monarchy whose past development had not been too different from that of England, and the rising prosperity and trade of contemporary Scotland helped to make it possible.

One result of this extension of kingly power was that Scottish kings set store by the public display of monarchy, as a means of enhancing its dignity. Margaret of England, offspring of the Anglo-Saxon royal house, is said by her contemporary

EILEAN DONAN CASTLE, built by King Alexander II *c*.1220 to replace earlier fortifications. It announced the king's presence in the north-west Highlands at a strategic spot opposite the Isle of Skye and at the entrance to several lochs (*above*). It was dismantled in 1719, after the '15 rebellion, but was rebuilt (detail *left*) in the twentieth century.

biographer to have brought a new magnificence to the Scottish court, making the royal palaces resplendent. He may have exaggerated, but the thrust of his remarks indicates that he considered her efforts to be significant in a Scottish context, at a time when rising prosperity was allowing similar developments to take place in Danish and Norman England. Margaret's fame and canonization (1249), and the Anglophile attitudes of the sons whom she and Malcolm III

WILLIAM I 'THE LION'

(1165–1214), king of Scots

. . . a man of outstanding sanctity . . . much preferring to have peace than the sword and to provide for his people by wisdom rather than iron . . .

(Gervase of Canterbury, *Deeds of Kings*)

THE younger brother of Malcolm IV, he was a vigorous champion of Scotland's interests. At the outset of his reign (1165), he felt close to Henry II, but in 1174 he supported the English rebels and invaded England; he was captured and in the treaty of Falaise acknowledged Henry as feudal overlord of Scotland. Relations later improved, and Richard I, in preparation for his crusade (1189), sold his feudal superiority to William for 10,000 marks. He coped with rebellions in the north and west (from 1174) with some success and established his sovereignty in Caithness (1196–7). William also obtained the long sought-after papal declaration that the Scottish Church was independent of any foreign archbishop (1192); indeed, he received signal marks of papal favour, notably gifts of the Golden Rose and, probably, the Blessed Sword and Hat. Why he is called 'the Lion' is unclear (but see below).

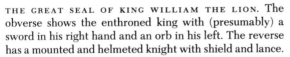

THE GREAT SEAL OF KING WILLIAM THE LION. The obverse shows the enthroned king with (presumably) a sword in his right hand and an orb in his left. The reverse has a mounted and helmeted knight with shield and lance.

William is credited with adopting the lion rampant as the royal arms of Scotland. The seal is modelled on the royal seals of England.

produced, not only encouraged the spread of ideas from the south, but led her most distinguished offspring, David I, to create a shrine to Scottish kingship at Dunfermline, where his parents had been married (*c.*1069). This provided a new focus for the ancient Scottish monarchy. The reading of the genealogy of kings at royal inaugurations was a public reminder of an antiquity even more venerable than that claimed for Anglo-Saxon kings and their French-speaking successors.

THE NAVE OF DUNFERMLINE ABBEY, built by King David I to commemorate his parents, Margaret of England and Malcolm III Canmore, who had been married at Dunfermline. Margaret had built an earlier church (*c*.1070s) on the site for a group of Benedictine monks; this was extended by David *c*.1128. Viewed here looking into the north aisle, the elaborate and varied piers have affinities with those of Durham Cathedral.

RHYS AP GRUFFYDD 'THE LORD RHYS'

(1155–1197), king of Deheubarth

*... Rhys ap Gruffudd, prince of Deheubarth and the uncon-
quered head of all Wales. And his dire fate [death] ...
should be narrated with tears and recorded with grief worthy
of an elegy, for it was fraught with loss for everyone.*

(*Brut y Tywysogyon: Chronicle of the Princes*, 1197)

THE younger son of Gruffydd ap Rhys (d. 1137),
king of Deheubarth, and Gwenllian, daughter
of Gruffydd ap Cynan (d. 1137), king of Gwynedd, he spent his youth (from 1146) helping his elder
brother Maredudd eject the Anglo-Normans from
West Wales; when Maredudd died (1155), he became
king. He acknowledged the overlordship of Henry II
(1158), but proved an unreliable vassal, prone to revolt
and taking advantage of the diversion of Anglo-
Norman lords from Wales to Ireland (from 1169). He
reconstructed Dinefwr and Cardigan castles, extended
his power into Dyfed, and married Gwenllian, daughter of the last king of Powys. He exploited his
kingdom's resources in new ways, welcomed new
religious orders to south-west Wales, and even held
an eisteddfod at Cardigan (1176); Rhys may have
inspired codification of Welsh law. After Owain
Gwynedd's death (1170) he had no peer in Wales — as
even Henry II recognized. At his death, his dominion
collapsed amid the quarrels of his unruly sons.

THE ALLEGED TOMB-EFFIGY OF THE LORD RHYS AP
GRUFFYDD (d. 1197) in St David's Cathedral. Although
Rhys was certainly buried in the cathedral, at the time
when it was being rebuilt, this effigy is a century and more
later in date but is identified as his by the raven, his
emblem, on his chest-armour. It may have been placed on
his tomb later to commemorate the most distinguished
member of a family that was all but extinguished by
Edward I.

Contrariwise, the Anglo-Norman invaders who were pressing against the Welsh within a year of Hastings (the Danish kings seem to have made no special efforts in this direction) paved the way for the ultimate destruction of every independent Welsh kingdom. The process was slow and, to contemporaries, by no means inevitable. In the meantime, in the twelfth century, a number of the administrative practices of Anglo-Norman monarchs were adopted by Welsh rulers. The financial and military resources of their lands were exploited more effectively and systematically as the years passed. Like the kings of Scotland, the greater Welsh kings took to issuing charters, though (as in Scotland) these were written in the monasteries that were the grantees, rather than in a royal secretarial office or Chancery. The books of Welsh law that are known to us today were most likely first produced with their encouragement (the oldest surviving text dates from the early thirteenth century). The pride of the dynasties of Deheubarth and Gwynedd was doubtless reinforced a mite by their association with the great churches of St David's and Bangor, though as a burial church St David's was tarnished by the fact that it was usually in the hands of Anglo-Norman bishops. As far as we know, the kings of these small and poor kingdoms were denied great displays of magnificence; after all, much of the prosperous seaboard of South Wales lay quite firmly in Anglo-Norman hands. Yet their court poets lauded them and perpetuated the memory of their virtues and deeds, not least at the festival of poetry and music (an early eisteddfod) supposedly held in 1176 under the patronage of Rhys ap Gruffydd, the last king of Deheubarth. But even the title of king was abandoned by all who wrote about these rulers after 1200, so that apart from the resurgent principality of Gwynedd during the thirteenth century, it is no longer appropriate to think of Welsh kings and monarchies by the end of the twelfth century.

As far as Ireland is concerned, its monarchies were still geared for war in the eleventh and twelfth centuries. It is true that certain kingly powers reflected an organizing capacity, even rudimentary administrative structures: the O'Briens and O'Connors could build bridges and fortifications, put fleets on rivers, loughs, and seas; they could campaign with armies right across the island, and even tried to install their own agents in defeated or divided kingdoms. But this was the monarchy of the warrior, with a household organized primarily for war; it is difficult to visualize such kings, whose dominance was bound to be ephemeral, being capable of developing more stable monarchical structures. Aspiring 'over-kings' and 'high kings' might have a strong sense of dynasty, and the O'Briens in the twelfth century showed deep interest in St Flannan, whom they put in their pedigree and of whom several Lives were then written, no doubt partly as propaganda for an ambitious dynasty. In the case of the O'Connors, the burial of Rory O'Connor at Clonmacnoise, near the spot beside the high altar where his father Turlough had been interred in 1156, may represent the hallowing of the

JOHN

(1199–1216), king of England

He was indeed a great prince but less than successful; like Marius he met with both kinds of luck. He was generous and liberal to outsiders but a despoiler of the inhabitants. Since he trusted more in foreigners than in them, he had been abandoned before the end by his people, and in his own end he was little mourned.

(The Barnwell Chronicle)

Notoriously cruel, suspicious, untrustworthy, and violent, John's reputation is not salvaged by an alleged constructive interest in administration or by assertions that contemporary writers were monks who resented his treatment of the Church. The youngest son of Henry II and Queen Eleanor, he 'lacked land' until made king of Ireland (1177), but his Irish expedition (1185–6) failed. Henry's plan (1183) to give him Aquitaine led to war with his brother Richard, and when Henry died (1189) John was also at war with the king. Richard treated him generously, but he intrigued in Richard's absence on crusade; he was reconciled when Richard returned and on his death-bed Richard made him his heir (1199). As king he was calculating and insensitive, and he made a number of enemies, English as well as French and papal. Nobles and clergy resisted his demands for resources to protect his French lands; allies were offended by his marriage to Isabella of Angoulême and his murder of his nephew, Arthur of Brittany; and by 1204 all were angry at his military ineffectiveness in losing Normandy and Anjou (hence the name 'Softsword'). He quarrelled with the new archbishop of Canterbury, Stephen Langton (from 1206), and so alienated the pope that England was laid under interdict (1208–13) and John excommunicated (1209). His success in forcing the submission of William the Lion, Welsh princes, and English colonists in Ireland cost money, which John raised by exploitation of clergy, nobles, and Jews, and caused resentment. His submission of the kingdom to the pope (1213) was a stroke of genius by a desperate man faced with growing opposition. He promised justice and Henry I's customs, while plotting revenge on his enemies. When expeditions to Poitou and in aid of the German emperor against Philip II (1214) proved disastrous, John's determination to defy his critics led to civil war (1215); at Runnymede he was forced to seal Magna Carta, guaranteeing justice and good government. His plans to exact further revenge drove some nobles to renounce their allegiance and choose Philip II's son, Louis, as king (1216). During a harsh campaign against his rebels, he died at Newark after consuming peaches and beer; he was buried, as requested, in Worcester Cathedral.

THE TOMB-EFFIGY OF KING JOHN in Worcester Cathedral. The king is flanked by smaller figures of St Oswald and St Wulfstan, whom John admired. The king asked to be buried at Worcester, and is the only English king to be so.

burial place of a successful dynasty that had vied with others for the 'high kingship' of Ireland.

If the administrative and governmental structures of the Anglo-Norman monarchy influenced Ireland, they did so not through the Irish monarchies, but as a result of the establishment of a foreign colony at the beginning of the thirteenth century. During King John's reign, several features of English government were exported to Ireland in a limited context. John introduced English law and custom, but only for English settlers and those Irish who were specifically granted English law by charter. The jury system was introduced, sheriffs were appointed, and a coinage for English Ireland was minted. Such developments, which had been welcomed in Scotland, at least by some, were associated with foreign invasion and oppression in Ireland; the psychology of 'two nations' was taking root and has had a long history. This was Irishmen's first taste of settled, permanent, centralized administration, based in Dublin Castle which John built, not as an Irish monarch but as a colonial governor. Under such pressures, even the title of king (or *rí*) in Ireland eventually fell into disuse—as had happened in Wales already. There is an irony here, for Henry II had the ambitious design of making his youngest son king of Ireland, to laud it over Irish kings and English nobles alike. But by the time papal sanction and a crown of peacock feathers and gold had arrived from Rome (1185), English armies had been defeated in Ireland and fourteen years later John became king of England and henceforth let the matter rest.

By the thirteenth century, then, monarchical developments had made rapid and far-reaching strides in England, and to some extent they were being emulated in Scotland. But they touched but lightly the ailing monarchies of Wales and Ireland. There monarchy died: English political and governmental structures were imposed piecemeal by conquerors and colonists, yet with insufficient strength to create a vigorous new monarchy in place of the indigenous old.

3. MONARCH AND NATION
1216–1509

Realms and Dominions

Not much has been written about the geographical bounds and territorial limits of the realm of England and the several dominions over which kings claimed lordship from the thirteenth century onwards. It is sometimes said—especially by historians of the Renaissance—that, after the fall of the Roman Empire, it was not until the sixteenth century that people defined the frontiers of lordships and kingdoms with precision, as traceable or measurable lines. It is admittedly true that there was still some dispute in the later Middle Ages about the exact extent of the borderlands (or marches) between England, on the one hand, and Scotland and Wales, on the other. And yet, Scottish land grants show that by about 1200 the notion of a geographical kingdom of Scotland, a precise territory ruled by the Scottish king, was firmly lodged in contemporaries' minds, at least as far as the frontier with England was concerned. The only area of the Anglo-Scottish borderland still being disputed in the fifteenth century was a comparatively small area specifically designated 'the Debatable Land', to distinguish it from the rest of the frontier which presumably was not debatable. Likewise, before the end of the thirteenth century, people were well aware of where the western shires of England ended and the largely autonomous marcher lordships of Wales began, and they knew what was 'within the county' and what was without it—and they often said so. Claims to territorial jurisdiction and

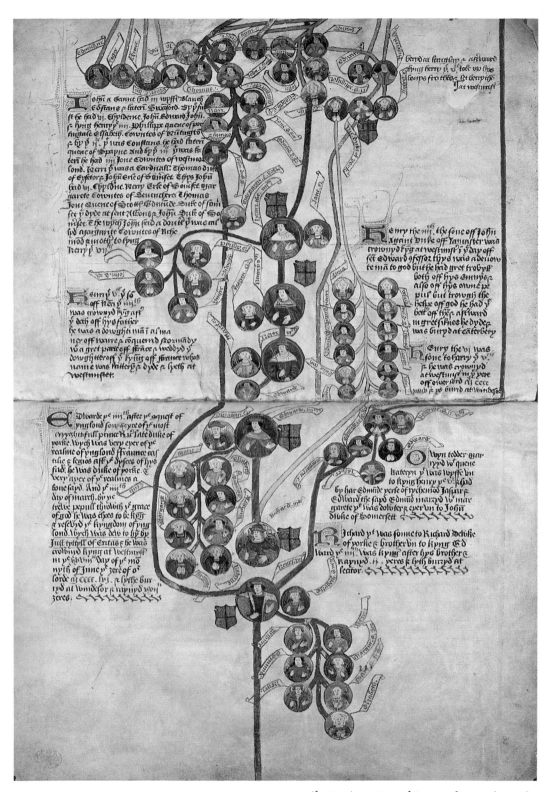

THE DESCENT OF KING HENRY VII AND HIS CHILDREN (*bottom*), portrayed in a pedigree-chronicle. Henry's relationship with the three Lancastrian kings is stressed (*centre*) as is his Welsh descent through Owen Tudor (*right*). Both connections were exploited by Henry for propaganda purposes.

rights led to the delineation of 'metes' and 'bounds' in contemporary English records, even to the 'beating' of bounds, a practice which traditionally minded or eccentric clergy follow even today.

This awareness of the geographical bounds of kingdoms in the British Isles did not mean that local patriotism and regional antagonisms had disappeared. They often shot to the surface, occasionally violently as in 1461, when southern Englishmen learned that a northern force was sweeping south 'like a whirlwind', 'like so many locusts', committing the 'unutterable crimes' for which those living north of the river Trent were notorious—and which a terrified southern chronicler could not resist uttering. The differences between northern England and the south, not to speak of those between Englishmen, Welshmen, Scots, and Irish, were so marked even among university students that halls at Oxford and Cambridge were organized according to the geographical origins of their members. The boisterous outcome was inevitable:

At this time also [1259], there arose a serious quarrel between the scholars of Oxford, who were of various nations, there being amongst them Scotchmen, Welshmen, and even from the north as well as the south of England; and the quarrel rose to such a pitch that (sad prognostic as it was) they displayed hostile banners, and the different parties attacked each other, with deaths and injuries on both sides. (Matthew Paris, *Greater Chronicle*, 1259)

An Italian visitor to England in 1506 noted that Cornwall, which had its own language and peculiar character, was still treated by many as a separate division of the kingdom, 'like Wales'; there 'no human being ever comes, save the few boors who inhabit it'. And he was echoing the reaction of a newly appointed bishop of Exeter, who lamented 150 years earlier, 'Here I am not only at the end of the world but even (if I may say so) at the ends of the very end, for this diocese . . . is divided from the rest of England.'

Since the eleventh century, English kings had ruled dominions beyond the frontiers of England. This was still so in the later Middle Ages, though the king's relationship with almost all of these dominions underwent significant changes. The centre of gravity of English kingship was, without question, England itself following the territorial losses of John's reign; the interests of subsequent monarchs shifted decisively away from France towards the British Isles. However, on two occasions, in the mid-fourteenth century and early in the fifteenth, some Englishmen became aware of the possibility—even if their collective memory did not remind them—that England might once again become part of a far wider French 'empire', and not necessarily the more important part. When Edward III and, later, Henry V publicized their claims to the French crown and embarked on campaigns of conquest in the heart of France, a genuine fear arose that the English realm would be subordinated to a conquered French realm. Edward and Henry reassured Parliament and the country that such fears were groundless in the later Middle Ages:

... whereas some people do think that by reason that the realm of France has devolved to us [Edward III] as rightful heir of the same, and for as much as we are King of France, our realm of England should be put in subjection to the king and to the realm of France in time to come, we, having regard to the estate of our realm of England and namely that it never was or ought to be in ... the obedience of the kings of France ... will and grant and establish for us and for our heirs and successors ... that our realm of England and the people of the same, of what estate or condition they be, shall not in any time to come be put in subjection or obedience to us, nor our heirs or successors as kings of France ... (Statute of Edward III, 1340, repeated by Henry V, 1420)

With minor exceptions, none of the English king's dominions in the later Middle Ages was actually incorporated in the kingdom of England, though that would happen to some of them later on. Instead of being part of the realm, they were described as 'parcels' of the English crown, a quaint, vague phrase which masks the subtly different relationships of these dominions with the king. Usually they were annexed and united to the English kingdom (as contemporaries put it), though the king was not formally acknowledged to be their king. In 1254, when Henry III granted his lands in Wales (the lordships of Carmarthen and Cardigan) to his fifteen-year-old eldest son Edward, he specifically stated that Edward and his heirs as kings of England should continue to hold them, and so they seemed to be linked inseparably to the crown. This grant was overturned in 1265, when Edward's younger brother Edmund was given these same lands, but it was reinstated in 1301 in favour

KING EDWARD I, crowned and seated on a cushioned bench, creating his son Edward Prince of Wales (1301). The prince wears a circlet and holds his hands in sign of fealty. The scene symbolizes the English acquisition of the principality of Llywelyn ap Gruffydd, Prince of Wales, extended to include other lands in Wales already in King Edward's hands. His son was created prince when he was seventeen.

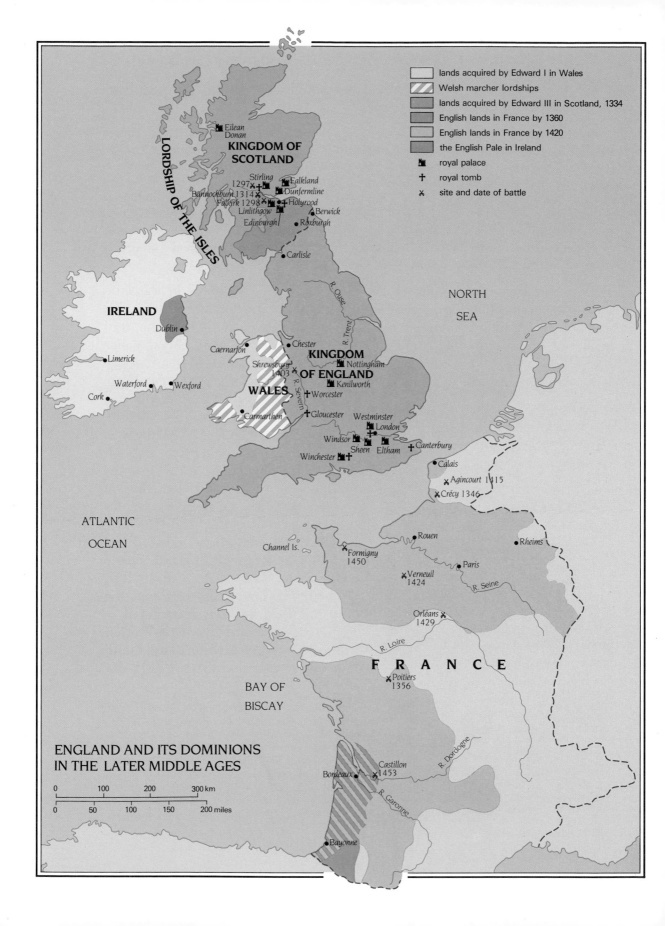

	lands acquired by Edward I in Wales
	Welsh marcher lordships
	lands acquired by Edward III in Scotland, 1334
	English lands in France by 1360
	English lands in France by 1420
	the English Pale in Ireland
	royal palace
	royal tomb
	site and date of battle

LORDSHIP OF THE ISLES

KINGDOM OF SCOTLAND

Eilean Donan

Stirling
Falkland
1297
Dunfermline
Bannockburn 1314
Holyrood
Falkirk 1298
Linlithgow
Berwick
Edinburgh
Roxburgh

Carlisle

NORTH SEA

IRELAND

Dublin

Limerick

Caernarfon
Chester
KINGDOM OF ENGLAND

Shrewsbury
1403
Nottingham
Kenilworth

Waterford
Wexford
WALES
Worcester

Cork
Gloucester
Westminster
Carmarthen
London

Windsor
Canterbury
Sheen
Eltham
Winchester
Calais

Agincourt 1415
Crécy 1346

ATLANTIC OCEAN

Channel Is.
Rouen
Rheims

Formigny
1450
Paris

Verneuil
1424
R. Seine

R. Ouse

R. Trent

R. Severn

R. Loire

Orléans
1429

FRANCE

BAY OF BISCAY

Poitiers
1356

Castillon
Bordeaux
1453
R. Dordogne

R. Garonne

Bayonne

ENGLAND AND ITS DOMINIONS IN THE LATER MIDDLE AGES

0   100   200   300 km
0   50   100   150   200 miles

of Edward I's own son and heir, later King Edward II, and his heirs as kings of England. Henceforward, the royal lands in Wales (and by 1301 they also included Gwynedd) were indissolubly linked to the crown, two and a half centuries before the union of England and all Wales in 1536. But prior to Henry VIII's momentous act, kings of England were not kings of Wales—or indeed of any other of their dominions outside England.

What were these dominions? By the thirteenth century, the duchy of Normandy was no longer one of them. King John had lost that in 1204. His son, Henry III, recovered neither Normandy nor the counties of Poitou and Anjou after they were overrun by the French king. When Henry sealed the treaty of Paris with King Louis IX (1259), he recognized that these dominions of his predecessors were lost for good. Off the coast of northern France lay the Channel Islands, Jersey and Guernsey the largest of them. Remnant of the duchy of Normandy within sight of Normandy, and with a general affinity with the Norman coast, they continued to be ruled by the English king as 'duke of Normandy'—as curiously they still are. But their relationship with the king-duke was anomalous. The ambivalent psychology of the islanders, who were English by allegiance but French by tradition and culture, emerges in two expressions of sentiment in the mid-sixteenth century: the Jersey men then declared that they would 'rather die English than live French', while Guernsey's cannier inhabitants said that they 'wish to be friends of all rather than subjects of any'. Yet all of them could justifiably claim (as they did in the fifteenth century) that

The Isles were anciently part of the Duchy of Normandy and the Islanders still hold of the king as their duke, and . . . in the Islands, they hold and observe, and have always observed, the customs of Normandy . . . with certain other customs used in the Islands time out of mind.

Even today, the Channel Islanders are not represented in the British Parliament and Queen Elizabeth II sports in the islands the title of duke of Normandy—and neither islanders nor queen seem at all perturbed by this state of affairs.

The largest English dominion in France in the later Middle Ages was Gascony, with which was associated the title of duke of Aquitaine. It was an extensive territory, whose frontiers expanded and contracted according to the persistence of French encroachment and the vigour shown by English king-dukes and their southern French allies in resisting them. In Gascony, the English king was lord and duke, sure enough, and by the treaty of Paris (1259) King Louis IX acknowledged that Henry III was duke of Aquitaine. For his part, Henry was forced to concede that he owed homage for Gascony and therefore was King Louis's vassal. The treaty gave French kings some right to intervene in Gascon affairs, and this lay at the heart of the long Anglo-French conflict from Edward I's reign onwards which culminated in the Hundred Years War (1337–1453).

And for that he [Louis IX] shall give us and our heirs in fief and in domain, we [Henry III] and our heirs will do him and his heirs, kings of France, liege homage, and also for Bordeaux, for Bayonne and for Gascony, and for all the land that we hold beyond the English Channel in fief and in domain, and for the islands, if there are any, that we hold that are of the kingdom of France, and we will hold of him as a peer of France and as duke of Aquitaine . . . And in making this peace we and our two sons have renounced and do renounce completely all claim upon the king of France and his ancestors and his heirs and successors if we or our ancestors have or ever had any right in things which the king of France holds or ever held, or his ancestors or his brothers held or hold, namely in the duchy and whole land of Normandy, in the county and the whole land of Anjou, of Touraine and of Maine, and in the county and the whole land of Poitiers, or elsewhere in any part of the kingdom of France or in the islands . . . (The treaty of Paris, 1259)

English kings steadfastly refused to acknowledge the implications of the homage they were required to swear to each new French king. In 1337 the issue erupted in war (the Hundred Years War). The English cut the gordian knot: they severed the tie of vassalage and claimed that their monarch was himself the rightful king of France, by inheritance through Edward III's mother, Isabella of France. The draft treaty of Brétigny, which they negotiated with the exhausted French in 1360, would have given Gascony to the English king free of any homage, but the treaty was never ratified or implemented, and full English sovereignty over Gascony was therefore never formally conceded to Edward III or to any of his successors. Indeed, the position seems to have been unclear to many Englishmen from that date until the final expulsion of the English by the armies of King Charles VII in 1453. That conquest brought to an end three

KING EDWARD I FACING KING PHILIP IV OF FRANCE in 1297. Each has his device above his crown, a lion rampant in Edward's case, the fleur-de-lis in Philip's. Crude though it is, this doodle in the margin of an Exchequer roll reflects the confrontation over Gascony which erupted in war in 1294–8.

centuries (almost to the year) of close association between Gascony and the monarchy of England.

The unimplemented treaty of Brétigny also affected an English enclave in France that had been acquired much more recently: Calais and its march surrendered to Edward III in 1347 after a year-long siege whose pathetic conclusion inspired, centuries later, one of Auguste Rodin's most moving sculptures, *The Burghers of Calais*:

[The garrison's captain], a knight who had much experience in military affairs, called Jean de Vienne, opened the gates and, seated on a little nag, for gout prevented him from walking, with a rope round his neck, came to the king's presence. Other knights and burgesses followed on foot, bare-headed and bare-footed; also having ropes round their necks. The captain offered to the king a warrior's sword, as to the chief prince of arms amongst all Christians. . . . Secondly, he offered the keys of the town. Thirdly, he asked of the king mercy and pardon, and brought him the sword of peace. . . . (Geoffrey le Baker, *Chronicle*)

After the surrender, Calais and its march were colonized by English merchants and their families. If the treaty of Brétigny had been put into effect, Calais would have been ceded to England in full sovereignty, and a vital bridgehead in northern France would have been annexed. As it was, the English king was its lord, and for ecclesiastical purposes it was transferred in 1379 to the archdiocese of Canterbury. After Henry VI became (in the eyes of Englishmen and Anglophile Frenchmen) King Henry II of France in 1422, following the triumphant conquests of his father, Henry V, it could logically be argued that Calais and its march were now part of his French realm and their inhabitants subject to French institutions, not those at Westminster.

Within the British Isles, thirteenth-century English kings claimed overlordship over the surviving Welsh rulers, most notably the formidable princes of Gwynedd, as well as over Anglo-Norman nobles whose families had been established in parts of Wales for almost 200 years and had created the marcher lordships of the east and south. Moreover, from the early twelfth century, kings acquired lands of their own in Wales, which were ruled by them directly. The plucky efforts of the princes of Gwynedd during the thirteenth century to establish and extend their own fledgling principality in North Wales, acknowledging a distant English overlordship but no more, were eventually defeated by Edward I (1282–3). This Welsh dynasty had taken advantage of the disturbances of Henry III's reign, and had adopted the style and title of 'prince', which contemporaries associated with exceptionally independent rule, only a mite short of kingship. But these princes could not match the resources and determination of a monarch like Edward. In 1282, Prince Llywelyn the Last was slain and his principality quickly conquered: 'And then all Wales was cast to the

KING CHARLES VII, mounted and brandishing a sword, chasing King Henry VI out of France, in a copy of 'The Chronicles of the Kings of France', *c*.1483. Henry's horse is trapped with the arms of England and beside him lies the broken English banner. The French royal banner, a sun in splendour on a red background, is held triumphantly aloft behind King Charles. The main instrument of French success in 1449–53, cannon, is represented by two cannons in the background.

LLYWELYN AB IORWERTH 'THE GREAT'

(1195–1240), prince of Gwynedd

. . . [1201] a young man graced with generosity and worthiness . . . [1240] a second Achilles . . .

(*Brut y Tywysogyon: Chronicle of the Princes*)

THE son of Iorwerth 'Flat nose' and a princess of Powys, and grandson of Owain Gwynedd, by vision and resourcefulness and by exploiting Welsh tradition and adapting feudal habits, Llywelyn sought to create a powerful and permanent principality based on Gwynedd. After a long struggle (from 1188), by 1203 he had mastered Gwynedd. He cultivated England's friendship and married King John's bastard daughter Joan (1205). But his aggression in Powys made John retaliate (1210–11) and Llywelyn allied with the French (1212). Taking advantage of civil war in England, Llywelyn supported the rebels and extended his dominion into Carmarthenshire and Cardiganshire, arbitrating the claims of the Lord Rhys's quarrelsome heirs, and made himself lord of Powys (1216). The English government acknowledged all this at Worcester (1218). Despite hostilities with some marcher lords in the 1220s, no significant inroads were made into Llywelyn's power; several marcher families were linked with him through marriage, though this did not prevent him from hanging his son David's father-in-law, William de Braose, for having an affair with Llywelyn's wife (1230). He wanted to perpetuate his principality by securing wide recognition (1229) of David as his sole heir, thereby breaching Welsh custom and snubbing his elder bastard son Gruffydd, a headstrong man who was deeply resentful. Llywelyn also took (1230) the unique title of prince of Aberffraw and lord of Snowdon which, it was claimed, traditionally implied a superiority over other Welsh rulers which Llywelyn already enjoyed. His homage to Henry III and his suzerainty in Wales made his principality somewhat akin to Scotland's kingdom. Llywelyn probably had a stroke in 1237 and David may have taken the reins of government; he died in 1240 and was buried at his favourite monastery, Aberconwy, where Joan already lay (1237). The hostility of Gruffydd

THE DEATH OF LLYWELYN AB IORWERTH (1240), with his sons, Gruffydd (a bastard) and David, looking sorrowfully on – as well they might, for after the short reign of David, it took Llywelwyn's grandson, Llywelyn ap Gruffydd, almost a decade to reassert undivided princely rule in Gwynedd. The sketch appears in Matthew Paris's thirteenth-century *Greater Chronicle*.

and Henry III threatened to undermine Llywelyn's achievement. Although David took the title of Prince of Wales (1244) and received papal approval, and Gruffydd died trying to escape from the Tower of London (1244), David's sudden death (1246) without children threw the new principality into confusion.

ground,' lamented a patriotic chronicler. Remaining Welsh lords were minor figures who were very quickly absorbed into the polity of the Welsh march or into the royal lands in the north and west of Wales. In 1284 Edward I could declare Wales to be 'annexed and united to the crown'. He created a new English principality out of the royal estates and gave it to his young son and heir in 1301;

it still survives as a concept focused on the heir to the throne, though now it encompasses the whole of Wales.

The situation in Ireland had some similarities with that in Wales. Since Henry II's day, English overlordship had been continuously proclaimed, though Anglo-Norman nobles had created lordships that were largely independent of the king for all practical purposes. Unlike Wales, the king's authority in Ireland was much more tenuous. This was partly because of the distance from Westminster, and partly because of the formidable obstacles to exerting royal control over the Anglo-Norman nobles, and still more over the unconquered Irish lords (or chieftains) in the north and west who continued to style themselves as kings for some time after Henry II's day. Since John's reign, the king of England had borne the title of lord of Ireland; but royal control of the areas around Dublin and the south-east ports waxed and waned according to Irish hostility and English resources.

In 1385 Richard II ceded his lordship of Ireland to his favourite courtier, Robert de Vere, earl of Oxford, retaining only the position of superior overlord, even in the Anglicized east. For a brief period (until de Vere's disgrace in 1388), the role of the English monarchy in Ireland was technically akin to its role in the march of Wales. After 1388, English kings waged a losing battle to reassert their authority even in what became known as 'the Pale' around Dublin, let alone in the bogs and hills of Ireland further west.

As to Scotland, English kings may have voiced high-sounding claims to overlordship that had been repeated since Anglo-Saxon days; but in reality this was an independent kingdom, recognized as such internationally and with well-defined frontiers that even English kings now accepted. In Edward I's reign, these claims to overlordship were trumpeted with renewed vigour. The Scots themselves implicitly acknowledged them when the young heiress to the Scottish throne was drowned on her way from Norway to Scotland in 1290. Edward was invited to arbitrate in a dispute ('the Great Cause') as to who should have the Scottish throne. In the Wars of Independence that followed the installation and then abandonment of Edward's favoured candidate, John Balliol, the English invaded Scotland and seized the enthronement Stone of Scone (which has remained in Westminster Abbey ever since, apart from its brief recovery by audacious Scottish nationalists in 1952). But stones are not kingdoms, and English kings from Edward onwards discovered that it was an illusion to believe that Scotland could be cowed, let alone conquered and ruled. Although in 1363 Edward III offered to renounce his claim to superior lordship, this was only on condition (which was unfulfilled) that he himself be acknowledged as heir to the Scottish crown. That would certainly have transformed the relationship between the two monarchies and produced that union of the kingdoms which in the event had to wait another two and a half centuries (until 1603). In the mean time, there

ALEXANDER II

(1214–1249), king of Scots

A RED-HEAD, whom King John allegedly called 'the little red fox', Alexander was instrumental in establishing the territorial configuration of later medieval Scotland. The nobles swore fealty to him when he was three; John knighted him when he was fourteen. Succeeding his father, William the Lion, in 1214, his early interventions in English politics on the side of King John's opponents did not regain Carlisle and Northumberland, which he claimed. He did homage to Henry III and married the king's sister Joan (1221). By the treaty of York (1237), he settled the long dispute over the Anglo-Scottish border: Alexander surrendered his claims in northern England in return for Tynedale and Penrith. There is some sign of concern to enforce and modernize justice in his kingdom. He also tackled vigorously (from 1215) the perennial disturbances in northern and western Scotland, imposing his authority in Caithness (from 1222) and Galloway (from 1235), and subjugating Argyll; but while preparing to wrest the Hebrides from Norway he died suddenly on Kerrera Island. Founder of Pluscarden Priory (1236) and patron of the friars, he was buried at Melrose Abbey, to which he and his immediate predecessors were deeply attached.

THE GREAT SEAL OF KING ALEXANDER II. It depicts, on the obverse, the king, crowned and seated on a cushioned bench, with a sword in his right hand and an orb in his left.

The reverse has an equestrian, if rather languid, figure with helmet and shield and bearing a sword aloft.

were echoes of an English overlordship which in England was dated to the legendary days of Brutus. The Scots responded with their own venerable tradition, which swept aside Brutus's claims and substituted even more antique claims to independence based on ancient Greek and Egyptian founders. When James IV invaded England in 1496, in one of those cross-border forays that pockmarked relations between the two countries in the later Middle Ages, he was

THE PRINCESS SCOTA, daughter of Pharaoh of Egypt, landing on the shores of Scotland, to which she allegedly gave her name. This is one of the patriotic legends of the beginnings of Scotland which claim greater antiquity for Scotland and its monarchy than the English claimed for the English monarchy. Such legends were popular in the later Middle Ages and this picture is from a version (*c.*1425) of the history of Scotland known as *Scotichronicon*, from Inchcolm Abbey.

severely chided in the English Parliament, 'for as much as he ought of duty to be homager; and hold of you, sovereign lord, his said realm, as his progenitours have done before'.

Finally, the Isle of Man, where English rule was unequivocally established only in 1333, after centuries of Norwegian and then, from 1266, Scottish overlordship, had its own peculiar relationship with the English crown. It was an acknowledged 'kingdom'. Though a possession of Edward III and his successors as kings of England, in 1406 the island was granted in perpetuity to the wealthy Cheshire and Lancashire landowner, Sir John Stanley, and his heirs. On several occasions thereafter, legal opinion had it that Man was 'no part of the Realm of England', 'though in homage and subjection to it'; and as late as 1505, the earl of Derby, who was a Stanley and an English peer to his coronet, prided himself on being 'King of Man and the Iles' like his predecessors (he said). The almost mystical relationship which Man had with the English crown persists even today.

Complex, complicated, even confused, was the English king's relationship with his various dominions in the later Middle Ages, though he could readily and justifiably claim that all their inhabitants were his subjects and—even the Scots—owed allegiance to him. These claims were not identical nor everywhere enforceable, though some of them have survived to our own time.

The way in which English monarchs regarded the realm and its dominions in

HENRY III

(1216–1272), king of England

... he acted imprudently and without advice of his nobles, alike rejecting all deliberation and prudence, which generally consider the results of actions beforehand ... he ought really to have learned wisdom, and taken pattern by his brother Richard ...

(Matthew Paris, *Greater Chronicle*, 1258–9)

HENRY's minority (1216–27) accentuated the problems bequeathed by his father, King John. As self-willed as any Plantagenet, he was well educated and cultured, and could be affectionate and generous; but his naïve, foolish, even deceitful actions, combined with a poor military showing, created disrespect and contempt. He was hastily crowned at Gloucester (1216), and William Marshal (d. 1219) took charge of both king and kingdom. After the treaty of Kingston (1217), Louis of France departed, public order was restored, and Henry widely acknowledged as king. He was recrowned at Westminster (1220) and the Scottish king did homage and married his sister (1221). Hubert de Burgh's regime outlasted Henry's minority (1227) and provided sound government based on Magna Carta. But when Henry took the reins of government (1232), he made disastrous interventions in France (1230, 1242, and 1253), where the French nobility opposed the restoration of his lands; in England his tax demands were resented. Henry was lucky to negotiate the treaty of Paris with Louis IX (1259), thereby preserving his Gascon lands. At home there was rising criticism of taxation, subservience to the pope, and abuses in government. His favourites were unpopular, especially those from Poitou and the relatives of his wife, Eleanor of Provence, whom he married in 1236. His bizarre plan (1254) to accept the crown of Sicily for his son Edmund, and help the pope against the emperor, united opposition in Church and State. Henry's and Edmund's appearance in Parliament in Apulian dress aggravated matters. In 1258 the nobles insisted on reform, including a permanent council, control of appointments, and regular Parliaments (Provisions of Oxford, 1258, and Westminster, 1259). Despite illness, Henry schemed to defeat them: he induced the pope (1261) to absolve him from his oaths to accept reform, and Louis IX's arbitration (1264) of the dispute was in Henry's favour.

THE GILT-BRONZE EFFIGY OF KING HENRY III in Westminster Abbey. Commissioned from William Torel in 1291, the care-worn face may bear some resemblance to the crowned king at the time of his death.

When war broke out (1264), Simon de Montfort, Henry's brother-in-law, led the noble opposition. At Lewes (1264) Henry and his sons were captured, leaving de Montfort in charge of king and government, widening his support through Parliament. After Simon was killed at Evesham (1265), where Henry was wounded in the shoulder, the civil war ended. Henry was restored to full authority (1266) and the statute of Marlborough (1267) affirmed the customs of the realm, Magna Carta, and some Provisions of Westminster. In poor health (from 1270), Henry turned increasingly to Winchester, his birthplace. He also rebuilt Westminster Abbey, the greatest of the religious houses he patronized; there the remains of Edward the Confessor were solemnly translated (1269), whilst Henry, when he died, was buried in the old tomb—until Edward I reinterred him in 1292.

the later Middle Ages rested on a large contradiction. In one breath, their publicists maintained (for example, before the great council of the Church at Constance in 1414) that the English monarchy was an ancient one and had divine sanction. In another breath, they insisted that this monarchy incorporated Ireland, Wales, and Scotland in an English 'nation'. How could Englishmen claim sovereign independence and uniqueness whilst ruling half-a-dozen dominions, all of whose inhabitants could be said to be the king's subjects, part of the English 'nation', and even English by nationality? How did English kings resolve this contradiction?

It could not be done by riveting English common law on all the peoples living in the dominions of the English crown. Though they may have disliked doing so, English kings acknowledged that their lordship encompassed a diversity of laws that were applicable in their various dominions, and in these formative centuries of the common law it was conceded that customary and provincial laws could coexist and intertwine with English law in several parts of the realm and dominions. Even Edward I, the most persistent law-giver, who was advised that Welsh law breached several of the Ten Commandments, did not expunge it completely after he conquered Wales. He had even greater distaste for Irish customs, which he regarded as 'detestable to God and so contrary to all law that they ought not to be deemed laws'. But abolition was not practical for him or his successors. Thus, in 1406 the laws and customs of Ireland and Wales, and Calais and Gascony too, were assured to their inhabitants by King Henry IV, and no amount of advocacy could induce English kings to eradicate them.

The consequences of English conquest and colonization in the Celtic lands also created problems and embarrassment for English kings. The ancient contrast between the civilized and barbarian worlds had been redefined in later centuries to suit medieval Europe. As far as the British Isles were concerned, it was a common conviction in England that the civilized English had a duty to subdue the more brutal and unpredictable—not to say immoral—Celtic peoples. The long hair of the 'wild' Irish and Welsh seemed a graphic sign of their barbarity, and to be called 'wild Irish' in fourteenth-century England was sufficient grounds for an action of slander in the courts. Sketches made by government clerks in Edward I's reign pictured the Irishman with a savage axe, and the coarse Welshman with a rustic bow and one shoe. By the sixteenth century, such stereotypes were the stuff of popular satire, and early Tudor collections of 'merry jests' include the gross Irishman and the dim-witted Welshman. The Scots, it need hardly be said, seemed no less 'wild' to Englishmen, and poems from the early fourteenth century harp on their guile. These prejudices went deep and inevitably muddied the relationship between the English monarchy and its dominions.

Political and social changes made matters worse. Popular movements in Ireland and Wales periodically forced the question of the ambivalent relationship

'WILD IRISHMEN', a mid-thirteenth-century depiction in a copy of Gerald of Wales's observations on the *Topography of Ireland*, *c.*1187. An Irishman, with long hair and a beard, is shown standing on the back of another and hacking at his forehead with an axe, the symbol of unrestrained violence.

between the dominions and the crown on the attention of English kings and their ministers. The Gaelic resurgence in the fourteenth century (or 'degeneracy', as critics viewed it) made Ireland, according to one excitable writer, like 'a woman who has risen again from the horrors of reproach'. The colonial area round Dublin contracted and the loyalty of the Anglicized lordships beyond was eroded. In the unsubdued Gaelic countryside further west and north, the population did not acknowledge the king as their lord and he did not treat them as anything more than 'mere' Irish. By 1341 it seemed as if 'the land of Ireland was on the point of separation from the lands of the king'.

The Welsh revolt of 1400 and the attempt by the self-styled Prince of Wales, Owain Glyndŵr, to establish a Welsh principality independent of the English monarchy and a Welsh Church separate from the see of Canterbury, were an equally potent factor in focusing attention on the relationship between England and its dominions, if only because for a century Wales had seemed fully conquered, and most of its inhabitants had been treated as the king's subjects, even outside Wales.

The Hundred Years War (1337–1453) also raised difficulties. Many Englishmen campaigned and settled on the continent, taking their wives with them or marrying in France; the birth of their children there posed the question of their status and their relationship with the English king. Parliament was forced to deal with the matter in 1343 and 1351 because of the birth of the king's own sons abroad, as well as the children of certain English nobles. The war also created severe financial problems for English kings; when they proceeded to tax their non-English-born subjects—the Gascons, and even the Channel Islanders—as if they were aliens, the protests were loud. And what about migrants to England from the king's other dominions: those Irish, Welsh, and Scots who for long had drifted into English towns and universities, their numbers swollen by Normans and Gascons after the English lands in France were finally lost between 1450 and 1453? How were they to be treated?

Moreover, when the Great Schism in the Church occurred in 1378, with two and sometimes three popes claiming the loyalty of Christendom, it was embarrassing and an affront to the king to learn that Gaelic Ireland gave its allegiance to the French pope at Avignon, rather than to the pope in Rome whom the English championed. The Channel Islands were even part of a French diocese, whose bishop supported the French pontiff. Owain Glyndŵr's Welsh rebels also declared for Avignon, so that for several decades Christendom's divisions were projected in the English king's dominions and threatened to fracture his monarchy.

All these circumstances highlighted the varying degrees of control which the English king had over his different dominions and the damage that could be done to his monarchy if the situation were allowed to continue. The ways in which English kings reacted lacked consistency, but they were in general accord with Englishmen's attitudes towards themselves and other peoples, especially those in the British Isles. These reactions included the cultural isolation of some peoples, the subjection of troublesome communities, and even the assimilation and incorporation of certain dominions in what was considered to be the superior English monarchy. Thus, only Englishmen born in England or in Ireland were regarded as the king's true subjects in Ireland, and efforts were made by language, marriage, dress, and hair-style to isolate them from the 'mere' Irish. In short, most Irishmen were treated as second-class subjects and frequently forced to leave England. This was eloquent testimony to the fact that much of Ireland was not fully under the control of the English monarchy. Likewise, after the Welsh rebelled under Glyndŵr, harsh restrictions were imposed on them both inside and outside Wales (1402–3). These disabilities reflected a revived fear of Wales which Englishmen keenly felt at this time. A political pamphlet of the day, the 'Libel of English Policy', communicated these fears to the government in 1436–7:

> Beware of Wales, Christ Jesus must us keep,
> That it make not our child's child to weep,
> Nor us also, if so it go this way
> By unwariness; since that many a day
> Men have been afraid of there rebellion
> By great tokens and ostentation.

More fundamental was the belief that the British Isles and the lands in France were England's, that the English king was their lord, that they owed allegiance to

KING EDWARD I PRESIDING OVER A PARLIAMENTARY SESSION, *c.*1278, as portrayed in the Garter Book, written and illuminated (*c.*1524) for Sir Thomas Wriothesley, Garter King of Arms. Alexander III (d. 1286) of Scotland and Llywelyn the Last (d. 1282), Prince of Wales, are shown flanking Edward, their overlord, though they probably did not attend a parliament. The closed crown worn by Edward is also an anachronism. Below the dais the justices and law officers sit in the centre on woolsacks; two clerks note the proceedings; the temporal lords are mostly on the king's left, the bishops and abbots on his right. No commons are present on this occasion.

him, and that therefore those of their inhabitants who were loyal should receive the benefits of closer association with England—ultimately incorporation in its monarchy. As early as 1331, Edward III offered English law to the colonists in Ireland and to the loyal Irish, but to go further proved impractical at that time. In Wales, English law had been gradually advancing since before Edward I's conquest, and it continued to do so until Henry VII gave charters confirming English law and rights to a number of Welsh communities (1506–8).

Irishmen were encouraged to adopt English names and some did so in order to conceal their birth. The Welsh patronymic was superseded by English-style surnames with growing frequency in the later fifteenth century. Official discrimination against indigenous languages and suppression of their bardic guardians took place in Ireland, Wales, and Calais. But the finest accolade that English kings could confer on their dominions was to regard their inhabitants as English. Welshmen who lived inside the walls of colonial towns in Wales—some of them even marrying English women—were adopted as privileged 'English' townsmen. Channel Islanders, after protesting at being regarded as aliens, were recognized as 'reputed citizens' of England, and so were the offspring of English settlers or soldiers in France. If anyone had doubts about his or her status, a grant of denizenship was available from the king and, more secure still, its enrolment in a parliamentary act which made its recipient 'naturally' English. Many cautious folk from the English king's dominions bought these privileges in the later Middle Ages, especially after about 1380. Their very number pointed the way towards a more systematic solution to the delicate problems of status and Englishness that arose from the relationship between the English monarchy and its dominions.

The first two Tudor kings, Henry VII and Henry VIII, displayed a passion for uniformity and a will to impose it. They added the coping-stone to later medieval developments in this field. Their task was made easier by the loss of all the French lands (except Calais) to the armies of King Charles VII (1450–3). Henry VII transferred the Channel islands to an English diocese instead of Coutances. Henry VIII, who was also worried about the imposition of his Reformation changes, 'incorporated' as well as 'united and annexed' Wales with England and created shires throughout the land (1536–43). And he incorporated Calais in the realm too. In distant Ireland his solution was slightly different but with the same effect: he exchanged the title of lord of Ireland for that of king in 1541, at the same time affirming the Irish to be 'true subjects, obedient to his laws, forsaking their Irish laws, habits and customs'. He summoned MPs from Wales and Calais to Parliament at Westminster, and he insisted that in Ireland, Wales, and Calais, English law and the English language should replace local laws, customs and usages.

Justification for these decisive steps existed in the constitutional and administrative practices of the medieval English monarchy. The unity of the king's dominions was implicit in his right to the allegiance of all born within them and it was made explicit in the institutions to which they all had access. Parliament (even though representation was confined to England) had long discussed the dominions, and its legislation was normally applicable throughout them. Occasionally MPs had been summoned from the dominions: from Scotland by Edward I, from Wales twice by Edward II, from Ireland by Edward III (though that summons proved abortive), and from Calais by Henry VIII. There was admittedly some uncertainty even at Westminister as to whether legal cases from Ireland, Wales, and the Channel Islands should be heard by the common law courts, but things were different as far as the king's prerogative courts were concerned: to Edward I's council came appeals from Ireland, and the chancellor of England later judged suits from Wales, Ireland, the Channel Islands, and Calais. The authority of the English king was evidently regarded as embracing his dominions too, foreshadowing a territorial and governmental unity that was the foundation of a monarchy that one day would extend much further beyond the borders of England itself.

To observe the evolution of the Scottish kingdom is to view the same scene through a different window. For much of the thirteenth century, Scottish kings followed a policy of territorial consolidation and definition, whereby their overlordship was effectively extended to the western flank of their kingdom and the Western Isles. Although strong feelings of independence persisted in Galloway, a partition of this old kingdom among heiresses in 1235 enabled royal Scottish influence to grow. The Isles remained a battleground between Norwegian and Scottish claims until 1266, when Scottish overlordship was acknowledged. By the end of the fifteenth century, the semi-independent lordship of the Isles had been replaced by effective royal control—though not as much could be said of the great earldoms of the Highlands. Beyond lay the Orkneys and Shetlands, which were transferred to Scotland when James III married Margaret of Denmark in 1469.

THE SILVER GROAT OF KING JAMES III, *c*.1485. It bears one of the earliest Renaissance coin portraits outside Italy: the king is wearing a closed crown surmounted by a cross, and an attempt has been made to give a realistic portrait of the king. (× 2½)

ALEXANDER III

(1249–1286), king of Scots

BUFFETED by noble factions and subject to English pressure in his youth, Alexander nevertheless became a strong-willed, sensible king, with some sense of rectitude, who preserved the unity and integrity of his kingdom. The son of Alexander II and his second wife, Mary de Couci, his minority (1249–62) opened with a hasty inauguration. He was soon betrothed to Henry III's daughter Margaret, whom he married in 1251 when Henry knighted him. Until he came of age, he and his government were fought over by Scottish nobles and the English king and his agents; he visited the English court on several occasions. He later resumed his father's efforts to establish Scottish mastery of the Isles: the king of Man did homage to him (1264), and by the treaty of Perth Magnus of Norway sold Man and the Hebrides to Alexander (1266). He steadfastly declined to swear homage for his kingdom, and he championed the independence of the Scottish Church against English claims; yet he supported Henry III against his nobles and attended Edward I's coronation in great state (1274). The greatest tragedies of his reign were the deaths of his wife (1275) and two sons. His daughter Margaret, who married Eric, king of Norway, died in 1283 but not before giving birth to a daughter who was acknowledged at Scone (1284) as Alexander's heir, should he have no other sons. His second marriage (1285) to a daughter of the count of Dreux produced none. Alexander was killed when his horse fell over a cliff in the dark (1286). When the young 'Maid of Norway' also drowned on her way to Scotland (1290), a succession dispute arose which posed a major crisis for the Scottish monarchy.

These successes in rounding out the geographical kingdom of Scotland and giving greater substance to the sovereignty of its kings were interrupted by the succession crisis which followed the deaths of King Alexander III (1286) and his granddaughter, Margaret (1290). Thereafter, much time and energy were spent in resisting English attempts to subdue Scotland and impose military rule in the borderland and southern shires between 1296 and the 1340s. Most Scots viewed these campaigns to implement long-standing English claims to sovereignty with deep suspicion, and they were prepared to counter them with force. Peace proposals that might ultimately have led to the two kingdoms being ruled by the same monarch were disowned. The alternative possibility that Scotland and the 'high kingship' of Ireland might be united in the person of Edward Bruce (1315–18), the heir presumptive of his brother, King Robert I, to form thereby a counterweight to England in the British Isles, came to nothing. As it was, England and Scotland became locked in an inconclusive and debilitating struggle—the one insisting on sovereignty, the other determined on independence—that lasted for two and a half centuries. Berwick, the 'Alexandria of the North', remained in English hands, and Roxburgh was only recovered by the Scots in 1460.

The Paradoxes of Kingship

English kingship in the later Middle Ages seems a mass—nay, a morass—of contradictions. These have their roots in the traditional character of English kingship and the traditional qualities of English kings as they developed from the Dark Ages onwards, as well as in the circumstances in which the monarchy found itself in the thirteenth, fourteenth, and fifteenth centuries. After 200 years during which it was one part of successive transmarine 'empires', in the course of the thirteenth century English kings came to look on their English realm and its affairs as their first priority. At the same time, their ambitions within the British Isles were pursued with renewed vigour, most notably by the domineering Edward I. And yet, the French preoccupation was not completely ended. Under Edward III, the English monarchy was enticed back into the French arena, armed with far larger claims—to the crown of France itself—that were reiterated by Henry V and of which a memory survived until 1802, when King George III finally surrendered the title of king of France which he and his predecessors had formally borne since 1340.

During these centuries, when warfare was the main weapon of politics, kings were still the defenders of their people, just as they had been in earlier times, and they were expected to lead their subjects in battle—and achieve victory. With hardly any exceptions, all later medieval kings of England campaigned at the head of their armies at one time or another in defence of what they regarded as their rights: in France attempting, as did Henry III, to recover what had been lost, or seeking under Edward III and Henry V to conquer what had never been in English hands; in Wales, where Henry III tried, and Edward I succeeded, in subduing the last independent rulers and Henry IV suppressed a widespread rebellion against English dominance; in Scotland, where Edward I tried hard, and failed, to assert his claims to overlordship, and Edward II, Edward III, and Richard II personally took revenge for hostile military or diplomatic acts; and even in Ireland, though after King John's expedition Richard II was the only English king to cross St George's Channel, where he had some success in re-establishing his overlordship in 1394–5 and 1398–9. Only Edward V, the boy-king who lost his throne (and most probably his life) within months of his accession in April 1483, and Henry VI, whose reign was the third longest in post-conquest history and one of the most disastrous, never led their armies into battle against a foreign foe. Indeed, Henry's poor reputation as a warrior in France and the British Isles had much to do with the growing disillusion with his rule in England. Certainly, Edward II's decisive defeat by the Scots at Bannockburn (1314) badly tarnished his reputation and helped to promote noble opposition to his regime. Conversely, Robert Bruce's skilful victory at Bannockburn against the much larger army of King Edward was a turning-point in the re-establishment of an

LLYWELYN AP GRUFFYDD, 'THE LAST'

(1246–1282), Prince of Wales

And the king granted that the prince should receive the homage of the barons of Wales, and that the barons should maintain themselves and their followers wholly under the prince, and that there should be princes of Wales from that time forth, and that they should be so named.

(Brut y Tywysogyon: Chronicle of the Princes, 1267)

INSPIRED by his grandfather's achievements, he was defeated by Edward I and the tensions created by his own ruthless methods. The second son of Gruffydd ap Llywelyn, and grandson of Llywelyn 'the Great', he seems to have become close to his uncle David, Prince of Wales, who may have regarded him as his heir. He matured in the humiliating atmosphere after David's death (1246) and the treaty of Woodstock (1247), by which Henry III confined Llywelyn and his elder brother Owain to 'Lesser' Gwynedd, west of the Conwy. But by 1255 Llywelyn had defeated his brothers and re-created Llywelyn 'the Great's' dominion. In 1256 he extended his rule to 'Greater' Gwynedd, east of the Conwy, and he exploited (from 1257) English disunity and marcher rivalries to overrun other lordships and raid as far as Gwent, Glamorgan, and Dyfed. Most Welsh lords submitted to him and recognized him as their overlord (1258); Llywelyn took the title of Prince of Wales and concluded an alliance with the Scottish nobles. Rebell-

ion in England enabled him to consolidate his gains, and at Pipton (1265) Simon de Montfort acknowledged his new status and suzerainty over Welsh lords and agreed to Llywelyn marrying his daughter (which did not take place until 1278). Henry III conceded the same recognition at Montgomery (1267). Aside from enemies in England and the march, Llywelyn's actions aroused serious misgivings in the Welsh Church and among his brother David's friends. David deserted Llywelyn (1274), against whom there was an assassination plot in Powys. Moreover, Llywelyn misjudged the new king, Edward I, refusing to fulfil his obligations as a vassal. The war of 1276–7 was a disaster: the peace of Aberconwy left Llywelyn with only 'Lesser' Gwynedd and overlordship of only five Welsh lords, even though he kept the title of Prince of Wales. Thereafter, he was more circumspect, though disputes did arise with Edward I, notably about the use of English or Welsh law in the prince's lands. But it was David's impulsive attack on Hawarden (1282) that precipitated the débâcle. Llywelyn was slain in Builth and taken for burial to Cwm Hir, one of the Cistercian houses he had favoured. His heir was his daughter Gwenllian, who was shunted into a nunnery. David was captured and executed (1283). Thus ended the most ambitious attempt to achieve political independence in Wales on a permanent basis.

independent Scottish monarchy and central to the place which King Robert has come to occupy in Scottish myth and history. Similarly, the extraordinary run of successes achieved by Edward III against the French in the first two decades of the Hundred Years War, culminating in his siege of Rheims (1359), where French kings were traditionally crowned, goes far to explain his magnetic hold on his subjects' loyalties for much of his reign and the glowing reputation he enjoyed abroad. Henry V's standing was, if anything, even higher after snatching a remarkable victory at Agincourt against all the odds (1415) and conducting a rapid blitzkrieg in Normandy in 1417–19. Victory in war, perhaps the most basic requirement in a king, was still seen as a vindication of good kingship in the later Middle Ages; and defeat was exceedingly difficult to live down.

This was because defeat in war discredited a monarch and encouraged his enemies, rather than because defeat signalled God's disfavour and prompted the faithful to desert their king. That had never been entirely so, though to claim God's judgement was valuable propaganda on behalf of William the Conqueror in 1066 and for Henry Tudor's cause in 1485. In some ways in the later Middle Ages, it seems that the Christian quality of kingship had rather less practical importance, and the alliance between Church and State, between kings, popes, and bishops, was of less consequence, than hitherto. There was no question but that English kings were still the stalwart defenders of the faith and of the Church in England and its dominions; the coronation oath continued to stress that. And when the Church needed help to combat the Lollard heresy in the late fourteenth and early fifteenth centuries, the crown provided it with the statute *De heretico*

HAND-TO-HAND FIGHTING AT THE BATTLE OF POITIERS, 1356, from a miniature in a French chronicle. The English forces (*left*) are led by Edward, the Black Prince, whose crowned helmet is surmounted by his emblem of feathers; the English banner is held aloft by his side. The French king, John II, wearing a surcoat of French fleur-de-lis and a crowned helmet surmounted by a fleur-de-lis emblem, is shown immediately before his capture by the prince, who led the reserve in a charge after the English archers had caused confusion among the French.

comburendo ('On the burning of heretics') in 1401. But the hold which the Church had on men's loyalties was weaker in an age when popular heresy flourished in large parts of England and the Welsh borderland, and the reputation of the Church and clergy was besmirched by decadence and scandal in Rome. English kings rarely faltered in their efforts to control the Church and dictate appointments to its bishoprics. Despite the reform movement of the eleventh and twelfth centuries, and the subservience of King John and Henry III to papal wishes, English kings had a well-oiled machinery for managing the election of bishops in the royal interest, and for exploiting the financial and administrative resources of the English Church (though often with less success in the dominions). This control was effective and permanent because it enlisted the support of the king's subjects, through Parliament. Statutes of the reigns of Edward III and Richard II in particular rejected the pope's temporal authority in England, thereby taking to a logical conclusion royal efforts to dominate the English Church that went back beyond the Norman conquest. It was left to Henry VIII to appropriate the pope's spiritual authority as well. And yet, the Church continued to be a valuable adjunct to the monarchy, and not simply as a source of wealth and skilled officials. Kings saw it increasingly as a practical means of supporting, vindicating, and popularizing their monarchy, in sermon, ceremony, processions, and, for intellectuals, in written argument; in return, kings patronized the Church lavishly, continued to found religious houses, even in the decades immediately before the Reformation, and sponsored church-building in the latest styles.

KING HENRY VI AT THE ABBEY OF BURY ST EDMUNDS, 1434. The twelve-year-old king is shown crowned, robed in ermine and seated on a canopied chair in the chapter house of the abbey while being admitted to the fraternity of monks. Several courtiers, including his uncle, the duke of Gloucester, and his guardian, the earl of Warwick (possibly holding the sword of state), were also admitted and are shown standing about the king. The illumination is from John Lydgate's *Lives of Sts Edmund and Fremund*, which was given to Henry during the visit.

THE CORONATION OF A KING AND A QUEEN in the later fourteenth century. The manuscript, which is associated with Westminster Abbey, the coronation church of English kings, is known as 'The Royal Book' and describes the coronation ceremony. It may have been written for the coronation of Richard II's queen, Anne of Bohemia, in January 1382, and both Richard and Anne may be represented here. Each is seated, crowned, on a throne, the queen's slightly lower than the king's; four prelates are grouped behind, with two laymen holding ceremonial rods and two others bearing the crowns.

The religious and mystical quality of English kingship was emphasized by a deepening reverence for Edward the Confessor, who was venerated as the last true Anglo-Saxon king of England. In 1269 Henry III had his body placed ceremonially in a new coffin which he shouldered himself when it was carried to its new exotic shrine in Westminster Abbey. Edward's name was inserted in the coronation oath thereafter, and it appears that the saintly king's personal robes, crown, and other ornaments, recently rediscovered in the tomb, were used at future crownings, as if his hallowed qualities could be passed to his successors. This tradition was reinforced by the newer myth of the holy oil or chrism, which had supposedly been given to Thomas Becket by the Virgin Mary. When Richard II rediscovered it in the Tower of London, he was apparently anxious to stage a second coronation, using this special oil at his anointing in order to enhance the mystical aura of his kingship. The archbishop of Canterbury is said to have refused his request, but the oil was indeed used in 1399 at the coronation of the usurper, Henry IV, who needed all means available to strengthen his nervous hold on the crown. The ampulla of oil and the golden eagle which contained it were carefully preserved, to be used at the coronation of each of Henry's Lancastrian and Yorkist successors. The spiritual, mystical quality of kingship seemed to have been proved since Henry II's day by the allegedly curative (or thaumaturgical) powers of 'the royal touch', an astonishing attribute to which some were still giving credence in Queen Anne's day. This was proof, if proof were needed, that an anointed king was indeed God's emissary on earth, with demonstrable powers that no one else could boast. In Shakespeare's noble words, put into the mouth of the defiant Richard II, newly returned from Ireland in 1399 to hear of Henry Bolingbroke's challenge to his throne:

> Not all the water in the rough rude sea
> Can wash the balm off from an anointed king;
> The breath of worldly men cannot depose
> The deputy elected by the Lord;
> For every man that Bolingbroke hath press'd
> To lift shrewd steel against our golden crown,
> God for his Richard hath in heavenly pay
> A glorious angel; then, if angels fight,
> Weak men must fall, for heaven still guards the right.
>
> (*King Richard II*, III. ii)

It was in this spirit that the captive Richard, when bullied by Bolingbroke to abdicate in 1399, declared that he could not divest himself of his spiritual quality as a king. The popular, mystical formulae of Christian kingship were being elaborated just at the time when the Church's authority was being firmly, not to say roughly, subjected to secular, regal authority.

Connected with the special relationship which English kings claimed to have with God was the belief in the later Middle Ages that England was an independent sovereign monarchy answerable only to God. It was, in medieval parlance, an empire, self-contained and sovereign; the focusing of its fortunes pre-eminently on the realm of England after 1216 encouraged such thinking. English publicists insisted that this imperial quality was historic. According to Sir John Fortescue, a distinguished lawyer and councillor of Lancastrian and Yorkist kings, 'from of old English kings have reigned independently, and acknowledged no superior on earth in things temporal'. The conviction that this was so was a fundamental feature of the English monarchy by the fifteenth century. It should be added that there was no question, until Henry VIII's marital adventures in the 1530s, of English kings exercising sovereign authority in spiritual matters too, since the pope was still universally regarded as Christ's vicar on earth and the supreme interpreter of God's will even to Englishmen and their kings.

These imperial claims had a mixed ancestry. Based on the precepts of Roman law, they rejected a Holy Roman Empire that had been narrowly German for several centuries. The homage which Richard the Lion-heart had been forced to swear to the Emperor Henry VI, as the price of Richard's release from captivity in 1194, was ignored. Rejected, too, was the temporal authority of popes, who were usually identified with French interests in the later Middle Ages and therefore kept at arm's length. And English claims were underpinned by a burning jealousy of the assertions being made by French monarchs by 1200 that they were emperors in their kingdom. A graphic demonstration of English imperial pretension was staged in 1416, when the Emperor Sigismund arrived in England. A ritual is said to have been played out at Dover, where Henry V's youngest brother Humphrey, duke of Gloucester, rode into the surf to bring the emperor ashore, thereby making it clear publicly that Sigismund entered the kingdom not by imperial right but with the permission of the king-emperor, Henry V. Six weeks earlier, Sigismund had raised a number of eyebrows in Paris. There, he had been invited to attend the king's court; he promptly sat in the king's chair and ennobled a French litigant, as if he were as much emperor in France as he was in Germany. Bad news travelled fast, and at the water's edge Henry V averted a similar display of imperial pretension. It may have been the first time that an emperor had come to England, but there may also have been a suspicion in the mind of some in 1416 that the surrender of the kingdom by Richard I was not forgotten at Sigismund's court.

As to the imperial notions of the French, their king might also claim to be an emperor, but since 1340 the rightful king of France was none other than the king of England—at least in English eyes. Ultimately, French claims hardly came to matter to Englishmen, since by 1453 their kings had lost all their possessions on the continent (save Calais) and never seriously sought to recover them. It was

Henry V pre-eminently who popularized the vision of the English king as an emperor in his kingdom; his son, Henry VI, was occasionally called 'Most Imperial Majesty'. For popular consumption, poems and songs made the point explicit and helped to persuade English subjects to accept the ideology of their king. When Henry V took Rouen from the French in 1419, the celebrations in England were ecstatic, if expressed in execrable verse:

> And he is king excellent
> And unto none other obedient
> That liveth here in earth—by right
> But only unto God almight
> Within his own, Emperor
> And also king and conqueror.

This was undiluted temporal sovereignty of a Christian English king acclaimed by a jubilant nation. It appears to have been Henry, too, who was the first English monarch to wear a new imperial crown of state: a closed or arched crown, with four curved hoops meeting in the centre above the diadem itself, and surmounted by a cross. It symbolized the self-contained sovereignty of a Christian king. Its

A SILVER GROAT OF KING HENRY VII (d. 1509), from the last decade of his reign. It represents a new tradition in the English coinage, the first major change since Edward III's reign. The obverse carries a profile bust which is a realistic portrait of the king wearing a closed crown (instead of the usual open one). The king here resembles Torrigiano's famous bust and the figure of Henry VII on his tomb. ($\times 2\frac{1}{4}$)

design may have been prompted by the visit of Sigismund in 1416, establishing, along with Duke Humphrey's wet feet, that Henry V's powers in England were no less than those of the emperor in his empire. This imperial crown appeared on the great seal of England after 1471, and Henry VII had it engraved on his new coinage in 1489. Cuthbert Tunstall, one of Henry VIII's advisers, explained its theory to the young king in 1517:

One of the chief points in the element of the emperor is that he which shall be elected must be of Germany; whereas your Grace is not, nor since the Christian faith the kings of

England were subject to the empire. But the Crown of England is an Empire of itself, much better than now the Empire of Rome; for which cause your Grace weareth a closed crown.

It was a short, but momentous, step for Henry VIII, when he could not have his way with Anne Boleyn, to develop this ideology further and extend his empire into the spiritual field by appropriating the pope's authority also.

The actual powers of an English king were not as awesome or unfettered as these grand claims suggest. Although it was argued that an anointed king of England acknowledged no superior under God and was answerable for his decisions and actions to no one other than God, it is also true that kings had obligations, including a solemn obligation to rule well. These obligations were formally accepted at the coronation ceremony and were expressed in the coronation oath, by which kings had long promised to provide justice, protect their subjects, and shield the Church. There was admittedly no recognized earthly means by which a king could be corrected or removed if he failed to discharge his obligations at least passably well. But practical pressures could be exerted on him, as happened on scores of occasions in the three centuries following the sealing of Magna Carta; at great risk to the perpetrators (in Heaven and on earth), extreme violence could be offered against him, as happened on at least six occasions between 1327 and 1485.

By such means, limitations were imposed on the king's exercise of his powers. The constraints that were formal and permanent were relatively few in number and, as the Tudor monarchs showed, could be circumvented or even ignored. These limitations were devised following two centuries during which the king's personal authority in law-making, decision-taking, and administration had been magnified; and the apparatus of royal government had developed greatly in the twelfth century. The tensions created by the growing authoritarianism and developing bureaucracy of the Norman and Angevin monarchies became acute in John's reign, especially when he failed to observe the safeguards inserted by his nobles in Magna Carta. These safeguards were the beginning of a lengthy search for a method by which wayward kings could be guided and controlled in the exercise of their regal powers.

The accession (1216) of the nine-year-old Henry III, the first minor to mount the English throne since Æthelred II, was a sign of the underlying strength and continuity of the Angevin monarchy. But acceptance of the principle of hereditary kingship in the male line increased the chances of a very young or an incompetent king succeeding, and that in turn would increase the likelihood of tension between the crown and its critics. In 1232 Henry III took the powers of kingship into his own hands after sixteen years when he had been of little account and certain nobles had wielded these powers for him. A similar sequence of events occurred during later minorities, notably those of Richard II (who was ten at his accession in 1377) and Henry VI (who was only nine months old when he became king in 1422). During these periods—and during the rare, serious illnesses of kings, such as the senility of Edward III in the 1370s and the mental collapse of Henry VI in the 1450s—nobles were usually in charge of decision-making and administration. They were often prone to political rivalries and personal jealousies, whilst the return to personal rule by the king himself was hazardous: it created its own tensions, often poisoned personal relationships, and led to criticism and opposition from those who had formerly enjoyed power and resented losing it. Personal kingship, the very essence of monarchy, could scarcely cope with the incapacity of the king.

The loss of English territories in France early in the thirteenth century meant that kings spent more time in England than had been common since 1016. They were henceforward able to give closer and more continuous personal attention to its government, whose administrative apparatus had become so much more sophisticated that it touched the king's subjects more often and in a larger number of ways than ever before. This, too, could cause tension. Criticism of the crown, especially by the nobles, became frequent in the decades after Henry III's personal rule began (1232). When this opposition was at its height by 1258, it found a focus in Parliament, where it received support from representatives of lesser landowners, merchants, and clergy. Such criticism, which was repeated on other occasions in the fourteenth and fifteenth centuries, never envisaged the abolition of the monarchy itself and rarely did the critics advocate depriving the king of his fundamental powers. The usual aim was to modify the way in which the king managed his government and to alter some of the policies he pursued. The personalities, policies, and habits of ruling of individual kings were most often the causes of friction—and determined the means by which criticism was countered. Edward I was not a man to brook much criticism, and his personality and qualities as a ruler effectively staved off opposition until the last ten years of his reign. By contrast, his father's policies and attitudes—particularly his indulgence towards his foreign relatives and his attachment to the papacy—were at the root of dangerous attacks levelled against Henry III in the 1240s and 1250s.

. . . he did not keep his promises, having little regard for the keys of the church and for the tenor of his Great Charter so many times paid for. Also he exalted his uterine brothers in a most intolerable manner, contrary to the law of the kingdom as though they had been born in this country . . .

In addition the king was reproached with advancing and enriching all aliens, and with despising and pillaging his own natural subjects, to the ruin of the whole kingdom. And he was so needy, whilst others possessed money in abundance, that he could not, for want of money, recover the rights of the kingdom . . . (Matthew Paris, *Greater Chronicle*, 1258)

EDWARD I

(1272–1307), king of England

In build he was handsome and of great stature, towering head and shoulders above the average ... His brow was broad, and the rest of his face regular, though a drooping of the left eyelid recalled his father's expression. He spoke with a stammer (or lisp), but did not lack a ready power of persuasion in argument.

(Nicholas Trevet, *Annals of Six Kings of England*)

An autocratic, short-tempered man who was intolerant of criticism, he could be cruel and violent even towards his children. Yet there is no denying his talent for leadership, his fearlessness and energy, and his vision. He raised the crown's authority to new heights, undertook daunting enterprises in Wales, Scotland, and France, reformed royal government, and developed the common law. In his last decade commitments outstripped resources, and opposition to his obstinacy mounted. Given large estates in England, Wales, and Gascony at an early age (1254), as well as a wife, Eleanor of Castile (d. 1290), he gained military experience in the Barons' Wars. He led the royalist reaction after 1264 and the reconciliation between Henry III and the rebels owed much to his good sense. Like Louis IX a devotee of the crusade, he went to Egypt and Syria (1270) and returned in 1274 after his father's death (1272). He resumed the task of elevating the royal authority, rooting out abuses, defining royal and noble rights, restoring order, and improv-ing justice by using Parliament and statutes (1275–90). He became known as 'the English Justinian'. He sought to implement English kings' claims to primacy in the British Isles. His wars against Llywelyn the Last (1276–7 and 1282–3) ended with the conquest of Llywelyn's principality and the reordering, by the statute of Wales (1284), of the royal lands in Wales, which were assigned to his son and heir (1301). In Scotland after the Maid of Norway's death (1290), he declared in favour of John Balliol as king and demanded recognition of his own suzerainty (1292). His determination to exercise this overlordship led to resistance and war, which was still being waged when Edward died at Burgh by Sands (1307). In the sixteenth century, 'Hammer of the Scots' was inscribed on his plain marble tomb in Westminster Abbey. In France, the feudal bond between the French king and Edward as duke of Aquitaine ruptured in war (1293). These conflicts were expensive and in 1294–7 the burden alienated clergy, merchants, and English landowners. Edward resented the nobles' 'Remonstrances' (1297) and was loath to make concessions or change his policies. When he died, his commitments were partly unfulfilled, his problems unsolved, and his high-handedness rankled. Yet his methods had emphasized the common law and the role of Parliament, and he set precedents which his successors must have regretted.

THE STONE HEADS, CROWNED, OF KING EDWARD I AND HIS SECOND WIFE, MARGARET OF FRANCE, in the form of corbels on the canopy above the Alard tomb in St Thomas's Church, Winchelsea, Sussex. Gervase Alard was appointed by Edward as admiral.

Later, the successful wars of Edward III's reign and the disastrous defeats of Henry VI's were crucial in determining the levels of opposition to their regimes. One way of accommodating criticism of an anointed king even in a personal monarchy was to deflect it against his 'evil ministers' rather than direct it at the king himself: this had a certain justice at the time of the Peasants' Revolt in 1381 (when Richard II was barely fourteen), but in 1450 it was unfair to the king's favourite minister, the duke of Suffolk, for Henry VI had been on the throne for all of twenty-eight years and had been fully responsible for his government for almost half that time.

The first attempt to wrest actual control of the direction of affairs from the king himself—the framers of Magna Carta never quite attempted that—took place in 1258. The nobles were under no illusion as to the treacherous waters into which they waded up to their necks:

The king, on reflection, acknowledged the truth of the accusations, although late, and humbled himself, declaring that he had been too often beguiled by evil counsel, and he promised and made solemn oath at the altar and shrine of St. Edward, that he would fully and properly amend his old errors, and show favour and kindness to his natural subjects. But his frequent earlier transgressions rendered him entirely unworthy of belief, and as the nobles had not yet learned what knot to bind their Proteus with (for it was an arduous and difficult matter), the parliament was prorogued . . . (Matthew Paris, *Greater Chronicle*, 1258)

The eventual outcome, the Provisions of Oxford, sought to place the king's powers in the hands of a council, as if Henry III were incapable of ruling himself. This had been acceptable during his minority and it might have been acceptable now if he were incapacitated by illness; but it could not last long when the king was an adult, master of his wits, and determined to be king in deed as well as in name. This radical attempt to put Henry in tutelage lasted no more than eighteen months. But the reformers had edged closer to a resolution of the problem of how a recalcitrant king could be corrected who broke his oaths, rejected advice, and scorned restraint.

In 1311, when nobles reacted against the incompetence and inexperience of Edward II in the early years of his reign and, to take a longer perspective, sought to prevent a recurrence of Edward I's authoritarianism, an attempt was made to force the king to alter his attitudes and behaviour. But with a vigorous and wilful young monarch on the throne, a reform programme could not be sustained and England fell into a civil war that ended in Edward II's dethronement in 1327, the first deposition of an anointed king of England. Revolutionary though this was, there was no question of destroying the monarchy; rather did Edward's opponents, eventually led by his queen, Isabella, aim to wield the regal powers themselves. In 1386–8 Richard II was on the threshhold of personal rule after a minority during which certain nobles had ruled for him, but he was already revealing traits of character of a sort that had upset the nobles under Edward II. Richard was faced with similar demands that would have curbed his personal direction of the government. As in 1311, there was no assault on the monarchy itself (though some may have threatened to depose him at one point), and the proposed limitations on the king may not have been intended to be permanent, only corrective.

THE WILTON DIPTYCH, possibly painted for King Richard II *c*.1394–6 (though some would date it to the time of Henry V's translation of Richard's remains to his tomb in Westminster Abbey in 1413). Richard kneeling, richly attired and crowned, is shown being introduced to the company of Heaven by St John the Baptist and two Anglo-Saxon saint-kings, Edmund and Edward the Confessor. His hands are raised to accept the banner of St George from the Christ Child. Angels wear Richard's emblem of the white hart, and the broom-cod emblem (possibly that of the Plantagenets) is round their and Richard's necks. If this diptych was Richard's, it would have suited well his cultured court and his own taste for regal display.

Indeed, it is remarkable that even when the most extreme of steps were taken—the deposition and murder of a king—his supplanter was desperately anxious that he should assume powers that were as full as those of his unfortunate predecessor. Dynastic revolution was not accompanied by constitutional revolution in later medieval England. In 1327 the fiction was maintained that Edward II had abdicated and there was no doubt that Edward's successor would be his eldest son and heir, who was crowned on 1 February 1327 whilst his father was alive. Some might have thought it a ticklish question as to whether God's anointed could abandon his crown, though kings had done so elsewhere in Dark Age Britain. Henry II was the most recent English king to have witnessed the crowning of his eldest son in his own lifetime (1170), but that had been in happier circumstances and the king himself had made the arrangements. If people could be persuaded to believe that Edward II did not die by a murderer's hand in Berkeley Castle (and care was apparently taken that there should be no external mark on his body), then his demise might, with a great deal of luck, be accepted as natural; his eldest son could be considered to have succeeded him, and the monarchy remain inviolate. On the next occasion when a king of England was deposed, Richard II in 1399, it was not at all clear that Henry Bolingbroke, who replaced the childless Richard, was next in line by hereditary right. Henry's anxiety to escape responsibility for dynastic overturn led him not only to assert that the defiant king had abdicated 'with a cheerful countenance', but also to make the ludicrous claim that instead of Edward I being the eldest son of Henry III, it was his own forebear, Edmund Crouchback, Henry's second son, passed over because of his deformity, who was the eldest. Bolingbroke insisted, too, that the regal powers he assumed in 1399 were every whit as great as those enjoyed by other English kings. Edward IV was just as conservatively minded when he seized Henry VI's crown in 1461. Henry Tudor had excellent

KING EDWARD II, seated on a cushioned bench and holding a sceptre in his left hand, is apparently shown in the act of surrendering his crown to his elder son and heir, Edward (henceforward King Edward III), at the time of the deposition of 1327. The faces are not portraits, but we may be forgiven for sensing a certain wariness in the eyes of the younger Edward.

reasons for not talking in precise terms about his weak hereditary claim to the crown he picked up at Bosworth Field in 1485, and the declaration of his accession took it for granted that his powers henceforward would be the powers of his predecessors and hardly required detailed description. With but slender justification, Henry VII claimed all, in phrases of resounding emptiness:

To the pleasure of Almighty God, the wealth, prosperity and surety of this realm of England, to the singular comfort of all the king's subjects of the same, and in avoiding of all ambiguities and questions, be it ordained, established and enacted, by authority of this present parliament that the inheritance of the crowns of the realms of England and France, with all the preeminence and dignity royal to the same pertaining, and all other lordships to the king belonging beyond the sea, with the appurtenances thereto in any wise due or pertaining, be, rest, remain, and abide in the most royal person of our now sovereign lord King Harry the VIIth, and in the heirs of his body lawfully come, perpetually with the grace of God so to endure and in none other.

Yet several significant limitations were imposed on English kings in the later Middle Ages which modified the character of their monarchy. If the opposition to kings such as Henry III, Edward II, and Richard II did not succeed in stripping the monarchy of any of its powers, the deep-seated problems created by the unprecedented number of wars in which England was engaged from Edward I's reign onwards had lasting consequences. The long absences on campaign of Edward III and Henry V, the difficulties of running a sophisticated administration during wartime and, above all, the unprecedented financial and manpower demands of a long series of wars, had a profound effect. After an initial period of uncertainty and administrative confusion (to 1341), Edward III was statesman enough to devise a workable relationship with his subjects, especially the most prominent of them in Parliament. He accepted that kings should not unilaterally tamper with parliamentary statutes; and he confirmed what Edward I had conceded in similar circumstances, namely, that extraordinary taxation should not be imposed without the consent of the taxpayers.

And we have likewise granted for us and our heirs to the archbishops, bishops, abbots, priors and other folk of holy church, and to the earls and barons and all the community of the land that for no need will we take such manner of aids, mises and prises from our realm henceforth except with the common assent of all the realm and for the common profit of the same realm, saving the ancient aids and prises due and accustomed. (Confirmation of the Charters, 1297)

These were important adjustments to the English monarchy which had practical merits in the short term for kings who needed their subjects' co-operation in war. The forum in which these adjustments were made was Parliament, a body that in its origins and purpose was an enlarged meeting of the king's council, but which became a public assembly in which townsmen and merchants, knights, esquires

HENRY VI, CROWNED AND KNEELING BEFORE THE VIRGIN MARY, at the beginning of the foundation charter of King's College, Cambridge, 1441. The king is overshadowed by his arms and the closed imperial crown of England. He is accompanied by the lay and ecclesiastical lords of Parliament and, below, the speaker and members of the Commons.

and gentlemen, nobles and bishops, as well as royal servants and officials, could exert their influence. And in the throes of war, Parliament became a regular feature of royal rule and a regular participant in decision-making.

The expansion and intensification of English government, the extension of the responsibilities of English kings within the British Isles and overseas, and, after 1337, the quest for the crown of France brought other changes in England's personal monarchy. Kings gradually came to rely more and more for the direction of affairs on their councillors. These naturally were chosen and dismissed by the king himself, but as a body they gradually developed a corporate existence and an executive function that from time to time made the exercise of royal authority less personal to the monarch himself. Some kings assiduously presided over their council, as did Edward I and Edward IV, but others, notably Henry VI, were less inclined to do so. Yet other kings (Edward III and Henry V among them) spent long periods in France and, regardless of their preference for keeping the reins of power in their own hands, found that they had to give a wide brief to their advisers left behind in England. As the importance of the king's council grew, so the question of who should be a councillor and to whom should he be answerable was sometimes posed by a king's opponents (as Henry IV discovered immediately after his usurpation in 1399). Not only did the royal council tend to become an institution with increasingly a routine role of its own, but the place of the nobility in it became more significant. This development represented some dilution of the king's personal role; but (as Edward IV and Tudor monarchs demonstrated) it need not mean a permanent loss of control over the powers and structures of monarchy.

The English monarchy was a hereditary monarchy in the male line from the accession of Henry III in 1216. But in 1399 and on several later occasions it seemed to depart from this convention. The explanation is to be found in high politics, personal ambition, and the consequences of kingly failure. Although the convention was publicly asserted each time a usurping dynasty captured the crown, the events of 1399 made room for arguments in the century that followed as to who had the soundest claim to England's throne: the descendants in the male line of John of Gaunt, duke of Lancaster, King Edward III's third son, or the descendants in the female line of Lionel of Antwerp, duke of Clarence, King Edward's second son. And was Henry Tudor, the descendant in the female and illegitimate line of John of Gaunt, the next best heir of Richard III, whom he slew in battle in 1485? How important was the uncertainty regarded by contemporaries? Those who seized the crown in the fifteenth century made strenuous, not to say ingenious, efforts to stress their hereditary claims and to cloak with dynastic respectability the naked force they had used. In 1399 Henry IV commissioned his publicists to popularize the story that Edmund Crouchback was the elder son of Henry III. In 1461 Edward IV published his legitimist claim to the English throne and denounced his predecessors, the three Lancastrian monarchs, as kings in fact (*de facto*) but not in law (*de jure*); after all, it was by no means established that a female—and Edward was descended from Lionel of Clarence's daughter—could not transmit a hereditary claim to the crown. Richard III went outrageously further and blatantly justified the removal of his nephew, Edward V, by insisting that the boy-king was a bastard born of an illicit marriage between Edward IV and his queen; he even suggested that Edward IV himself, Richard's own brother, was not legitimate—and while their mother was still alive.

The trouble was that there was no generally acknowledged rule that descent from a female of a senior line took precedence over descent from a male of a more junior line. Such a convention had not been needed before 1399, since English kings from Henry III to Edward III had produced strapping sons; and even though the Black Prince died before his father in 1376, he had sired a boy, Richard, whom the lords and commons were ready to honour as 'true heir apparent to the realm'. The deposition and murder of the childless Richard II, and the usurpation of his crown by Henry Bolingbroke, posed the problem for the first time. Contemporaries were reluctant to legislate on the matter: after all, kingship, the crown, and its descent were matters too high for earthly law to determine—as the king's justices stated when the question of the succession was put to them in 1460, after Richard, duke of York, the descendant of Lionel of Clarence, challenged the third Lancastrian king, Henry VI.

The convention of hereditary succession—it seems unwise to call it a principle in view of events in the fifteenth century—was put to the test on occasions other than those of 1399, 1461, and 1485, and it was generally upheld. King Richard II, the first minor to become king since Henry III, succeeded his grandfather Edward III in 1377 at the age of ten. King Henry VI, when he succeeded his

RICHARD, DUKE OF YORK (d. 1460), portrayed in armour in a fifteenth-century stained-glass window in the hall of Trinity College, Cambridge. It may reflect disillusion on the part of King's Hall (Trinity's predecessor) with the Lancastrian dynasty as the fifteenth century progressed. Richard was driven by a sense of personal victimization, and outrage at the deterioration of Henry VI's rule, to claim the throne, and in 1460 he secured recognition as the king's heir, despite the birth (1453) of Henry's son Edward. But Richard was slain in battle before he could succeed; his eldest son Edward became king instead in March 1461.

father Henry V in 1422, was only nine months old: a king could hardly have been younger and more vulnerable. Yet the dangers which a minority posed to a personal monarchy, and the temptations it offered to breach the convention, were not completely dispelled, for in 1483, when Edward V succeeded his father Edward IV at the age of twelve, he survived for less than three months. Ambition, apprehension, and examples of political ruthlessness and illegality since 1461 combined to set aside the convention on that occasion.

Even periods of royal illness had not previously undermined it. Henry VI was seriously ill or incapacitated on two occasions (1453–4 and 1455–6), and bitter quarrels ensued as to whether England should have a regency or not. It was decided to rule by an aristocratic council as if Henry were a minor, but there was never any question of replacing the king himself or abandoning the public fiction that he stood at the heart of the monarchy and that the government was his. Although this was the first lengthy incapacity of an English king since before 1066, when Edward III drifted in and out of senility in the 1370s a similar provision for conciliar government was made, with predictable noble quarrels to follow; but no one proposed that the old man abdicate. It was widely acknowledged in 1376 that his grandson Richard should succeed him and Edward secured formal acceptance of this. He was wise to do so since no minor had succeeded to the throne since 1216, and the turbulence of Henry III's reign did not inspire confidence in those who knew their history.

Poor rule was rarely portrayed as sufficient justification for dethronement in the later Middle Ages. Who was to say what poor rule was, or when it occurred, or how far it was safe to go in correcting it? There was some sort of precedent in the deposition of Edward II in 1327, and this was in men's minds in 1399 as they grappled with the implications of Henry Bolingbroke's challenge. In 1327 the public justification for Edward's deposition had been his own (enforced) abdication in favour of his eldest son and heir Edward. In 1399 Bolingbroke's ambition and determination, combined with Richard's insupportable rule and the precedent of 1327, risked breaching the convention of heredity and the sanctity of kingship—though Henry IV, for one, may have been overwhelmed with guilt for what he did. Each time a new dynasty seized power thereafter, disastrous rule was central to the justification: in 1461 it was Henry VI's, in 1485 it was the odious rule of Richard III, and even in the case of the young Edward V, his uncle Richard desperately sought to argue that the expectation of misrule by his mother and her grasping relatives was part-reason for the usurpation. The convention of hereditary succession ordinarily dictated the descent of the English crown in the later Middle Ages. But it was not deep-rooted enough to resist every political and personal pressure: perhaps it never could be so long as kings had vast powers that could be abused, and so long as ambitious and ruthless men felt they could get away with challenging even God's anointed.

EDWARD II

(1307–1327), king of England

. . . a handsome man, of outstanding strength, but his behaviour was a very different matter . . . he was devoted to choristers, actors, grooms, sailors, and others skilled in similar avocations . . . He was prodigal in giving, bountiful and splendid in living, quick and unpredictable in speech . . . savage with members of his household, and passionately attached to one particular person, whom he cherished above all . . .

(Ranulf Higden, *Polychronicon*)

Edward was the fourth but eldest surviving son of Edward I (by Margaret of France). Though the first English Prince of Wales (1301), he was starved of governmental experience by his father, who distrusted him and disliked his friends. On his accession he renewed his association with Peter Gavaston, a Gascon noble of ability but little discretion. As king, Edward inherited grave problems, notably war with Scotland, tension with France, large debts, and a nobility made mistrustful by Edward I. As a result, the coronation oath (1308) placed added emphasis on the king's obligations and some people even claimed that the crown as an institution was separable from, and more important than, the person of the king. Edward's infatuation with Gavaston provoked a crisis in which the nobles' Ordinances (1311) aimed to limit royal control of finance and appointments and to exile Gavaston. The king's refusal to honour his promises resulted in Gavaston's murder (1312), which made both sides irreconcilable. The Scots' victory at Bannockburn (1314) discredited Edward further, and the nobles, led by the earl of Lancaster, seized power. Lancaster's incompetence and quarrels with certain nobles encouraged the king and his new friends, the Despensers, father and son, to resort to force. They were victorious in a civil war (1321–2) and Edward felt able to rescind the Ordinances and execute Lancaster after his capture at Boroughbridge (1322). Edward was now vindictive to the point of tyranny, whilst French advances in Gascony damaged his reputation further. By 1326 there seemed little alternative to a rising. The queen, Isabella of France, who had taken her son to the Continent, allied with Roger Mortimer and led an invasion against her husband. Edward was eventually captured in South Wales (November 1326). After being forced to abdicate in Parliament in favour of his son, he was imprisoned in Berkeley Castle. An abortive attempt to free him led to his murder (September 1327). The story popularized later by the French and the pope that he had fled to Sicily was propaganda aimed against Edward III.

THE TOMB-EFFIGY OF KING EDWARD II in Gloucester Cathedral. Probably from a London workshop, it has a stylized portrait of the king, seen by the sculptor as he should be rather than as he was at the time of his murder in Berkeley Castle, several months after his deposition in 1327. This tragic end of an anointed king was the basis for the brief cult that arose around the tomb.

There was an uncomfortable paradox between the elevated reputation of a hereditary Christian monarchy and the patent unsuitability of certain kings. One way of resolving the dilemma of those who shrank from assaulting the monarchy itself, and yet felt impelled to oppose unsatisfactory kings was to separate the crown from the person who wore it, regarding the one as inviolable but the other as correctable, even removable. According to this theory, the king was the custodian and the servant of the crown.

There was talk along such lines in the thirteenth and fourteenth centuries when it was relevant to the political crises of Henry III's and Edward II's reigns. The fiction was maintained after 1422 that Henry VI was still the source of executive power in the English monarchy, even though he was a baby; and after the dynastic revolutions of 1461 and 1485 the distinction was carefully drawn between *de facto* kings of the past and *de jure* kings. But discussions on these matters tended to fizzle out by the fifteenth century: usurping dynasties dared not pursue them because they might weaken an already uncertain position. Thus, the least secure of English kings and dynasties, those of the fifteenth century, were the very kings and dynasties which most vigorously promoted the public ideology of Christian kingship and worked to elevate the monarchy high above the common stock. If Richard II, with his high views of kingship, insisted that his subjects approach him on bended knee, the custom was continued in the next century, and Edward IV is said to have popularized the use of 'Majesty' when the monarch was addressed.

In England there was no real alternative to heredity in determining the succession to the throne. Force of arms was hardly conducive to stability and order. A king's nomination of his successor would more likely fuel rivalries than avoid them. Election, which was common in the Church and was practised in Germany and Eastern Europe, seemed out of place in an England where kings were so powerful and could lord it over their nobles and bishops; in any case, the elective German kingship after the death of Frederick II (1250) was no advertisement for effective rule. Parliament, which in any case was the king's creation, certainly did not demand a role in king-making. After 1399 there is no clear sign that Henry IV thought that he owed his position to a Parliament that had co-operated in the downfall of King Richard, or that the descent of the crown in the Lancastrian family was actually established by a Parliament which simply recorded the fact formally (1406). There is no proof that Richard III, after he had seized the crown, sought parliamentary approval for his action; rather did he use Parliament later on to declare his accession and gain acceptance of his kingship. And in 1485, even Henry Tudor, the weakest of all usurpers, made no pretence of acknowledging that he owed his crown to Parliament—though he realized it was unwise to mention heredity either. Henry comes closer than any of his usurping predecessors to attributing his accession to a demonstration of God's will, as vouchsafed on the battlefield. He had adopted the style and title of king in France by November 1484—on what grounds other than sheer pragmatism is not clear, since if anyone of his line had a hereditary claim to the English throne it was his mother, Margaret Beaufort. All God had to do at Bosworth was confirm and vindicate his kingship. No other king had dared so much, though the stories that were circulated in Henry's own interest after 1485—that his step-uncle, the sainted Henry VI, had prophesied his accession as early as 1470—helped to justify the first Tudor's unique effrontery. By his bold and imaginative exploitation of the mystique of kingship, this most unsure of kings laid the foundations for his dynasty's notable development of an ideology of kingship. Ultimately, it was politics that triggered dynastic change in the fifteenth century. It was royal success or failure that mattered, and God's intervention could be summoned by the shameless or the ingenious to justify the unjustifiable. Once stability had been restored, heredity was allowed to determine the succession once again, even to the extent under the Tudors of allowing the accession of a woman for the very first time (1553).

One more paradox may be mentioned. The century that witnessed such dynastic turbulence was also the century in which there was an unprecedented amount of theorizing about the monarchy. This was largely the result of the depositions of 1327 and especially 1399, after Richard II had so flouted English custom and law and the accepted restraints on monarchs. Later in the fifteenth century, lectures on the royal prerogative and powers were being given to students at the Inns of Court. Sir John Fortescue, the most notable contemporary theorist of kingship, contrasted the English monarchy, which he regarded as limited, or 'regal and political' because the subject assented to laws and taxes, with the 'regal' monarchy of France, where the king imposed taxes and made and unmade laws at his will.

Hand in hand with the elevation of monarchy went the broadening of the concept of treason committed by those who attacked the king and his kingship. Edward III's statute of treasons (1352) was the foundation of the law of treason for long after. It defined treason (and therefore the protection given to kingship) quite narrowly: killing the king, his queen, or his heir, violating the king's wife or his eldest unmarried daughter, waging war against the king at home or adhering to his enemies abroad—in other words, overt acts against the king or his kingship. Richard II, a monarch more conscious of his regal station than most, took matters further. In 1397 the king was given wider protection, and treason was extended beyond the overt act to include conspiracy to depose the king or raise war against him. Then, in 1423, further statutory precautions were taken to protect the baby-king Henry VI; and case-law had already encompassed treason by words spoken against the king.

By the end of the Middle Ages, there was a delicate balance between hereditary monarchy in the male line and political pragmatism; between the king as an earthly officer and a semi-religious figure; between the king's prerogative and customary limitations on his power; between these limitations and kingly majesty; between the person of the king and his sacred office. Kings walked a tightrope and fell off more frequently in the fifteenth century than ever before. Yet however they acquired the crown, every king was determined to be no less a king than his predecessors, and in the circumstances some of them—Henry IV, Henry V, Edward IV, and Henry VII especially—were remarkably successful.

Paradox was the keynote of the Scottish monarchy in the later Middle Ages, no less than of the English, though circumstances were often different. The last of the ancient line of kings, Alexander III (d. 1286), and his predecessors had Anglo-French blood in their veins, and so did the later Balliol, Bruce, and Stuart dynasties. Yet their overriding preoccupation during the fourteenth and fifteenth centuries was to keep the aggressive English monarchy at bay and preserve their kingdom's independence. This Anglo-Scottish struggle enabled Robert I Bruce (1306–29) to take the throne from the more senior Balliol line by posing as the champion of the patriotic cause; he spectacularly defeated an English army at Bannockburn (1314), and a letter to the pope (1320) announced that, like another Maccabeus or Joshua, he was the choice of 'the whole community of the realm' as king. More so than that of contemporary English kings, the position of Scottish monarchs in the fourteenth century depended on their acceptance by the notables of the realm. This was indicated, more clearly than in England, by the emphasis placed in discussion and practice on the distinction between the person of the king and his office. The succession dispute after 1290 focused the mind wonderfully and two interregna (1290–2 and 1296–1306) gave this constitutional quandary an immediacy it never had in contemporary England. For all its enthusiasm for Robert I, the Declaration of Arbroath darkly warned the pope:

But were he to desist from what he has undertaken and be willing to subject us or our kingdom to the king of the English or the English, we would strive to expel him forthwith as our enemy and as a subverter of right, his own and ours, and make someone else our king who is equal to the task of defending us.

On several occasions in the fourteenth century the succession to the Scottish throne was declared—even determined—by the secular and religious notables in Parliament. (Henry IV of England relied on a similar statutory declaration after the Lancastrian usurpation in 1399.) The monarchy which they helped to describe was (compared with the English monarchy) pitifully weak. Yet for that very reason, perhaps, it survived as the ultimate source of justice, administration, and patronage in later medieval Scotland, and no one suggested that it be abolished or significantly altered. The position, status, and authority of the

ROBERT I BRUCE

(1306–1329), king of Scots

. . . we in our humility have judged it right to entreat of your highness most earnestly that . . . you desist from persecuting us and disturbing the people of our realm, so that there may be an end of slaughter and shedding of Christian blood . . .

(Robert I to Edward II, 1315)

EARL OF CARRICK in right of his mother (1292), grandson of Robert Bruce, claimant to the Scottish throne (1291), and great-great-grandson of David I, Robert has been the subject of myth-making of large proportions. A man of courage, energy, ambition, and powers of leadership, his character and career seem heroic. The opportunism and rashness of youth turned to patience and vision, which earned him respect among Scots and enabled him to re-establish an independent kingdom that resisted English aggression. At first (1296), Robert sided with Edward I when John Balliol revolted. But during the patriotic resistance movement under William Wallace, he changed sides and became a Guardian of the Realm (1298–1300). Although noble quarrels caused him to submit again to Edward (1302–5), English successes made him plan new resistance: after Wallace's execution (1305) and Robert's murder of his rival, John Comyn, at Dumfries (1306), he seized the throne. Following defeat at Methven, he fled westward, even as far as Rathlin Island off the Antrim coast. The story of the persistent spider dates only from the sixteenth century—and then to fortify the resolve of one of Robert's men, not the king himself. Nevertheless, in 1307–9 he fought in all parts of Scotland, defeating English sympathizers, establishing control north of the Forth, and winning the loyalty of lesser folk. He aimed to eject the English, re-establish peace, and gain recognition as the true king. He made steady progress (from 1309), culminating in the victory at Bannockburn (1314), which showed his military genius. His Irish strategy, in which his brother (and heir) Edward became 'high king' (1316–18), increased the pressure on England. Berwick was captured (1318) and northern England harried until a truce was made (1327). The Declaration of Arbroath (1320) declared his ambitions for Scotland, and in 1323 the pope recognized him as king. He concluded a truce with France (1326) and a treaty with England (1328) which gave him all he had fought for. Though crippled, even in his last years (1327–8) he twice visited Ireland to maintain the links with Scotland. Close to death (possibly, but not certainly, from leprosy), Robert instructed that his body be buried at Dunfermline and his heart be taken on the journey to the Holy Land which he himself had never made. Its guardians were defeated on the way in Spain (1330) and the heart was returned for burial in Melrose Abbey.

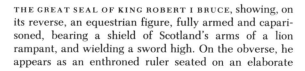

THE GREAT SEAL OF KING ROBERT I BRUCE, showing, on its reverse, an equestrian figure, fully armed and caparisoned, bearing a shield of Scotland's arms of a lion rampant, and wielding a sword high. On the obverse, he appears as an enthroned ruler seated on an elaborate throne. Robert is described as *Deo Rectore Rex Scottorum* ('Under God's Governance King of Scots'). The seal is closely modelled on those of English and Scottish kings as they had developed in recent centuries.

DAVID II

(1329–1371), king of Scots

KING EDWARD III (*right*) CLASPING KING DAVID II OF SCOTLAND BY THE HAND. Each figure is surmounted by his coat of arms. David had been captured at Neville's Cross (1346). He was later ransomed for 100,000 crowns and thereafter adopted a more pacific policy towards England.

THOUGH for much of his life at the mercy of others, he turned out to be clever, tough, and stern. He mastered his kingdom, yet failed to ensure the succession. The only surviving son of Robert I and his second wife Elizabeth, he was four when he married Joanna, sister of Edward III, and soon afterwards (1329) he became king. He was the first Scottish king to be anointed, with great ceremony, at his inauguration (1331), but a series of guardians ruled for him during his minority. He was sent to France for safety (1334) after the English invaded and Edward Balliol challenged his throne. On his return in 1341, he was described as 'stout, young and jolly', committed to a French alliance and to hostility towards the English that led to his wounding and capture at Neville's Cross (1346) and his detention in England. During David's absence, Robert the Steward, who had a claim to be his heir, ruled for him. The treaty of Berwick (1357) imposed a ransom of 100,000 marks which Scotland may have been capable of paying. Thereafter, David reorientated his policy, partly because of a friendship which had blossomed with Edward III and partly because of his growing concern for the succession: he had no children and he disliked Robert the Steward. This produced difficulties with some nobles, even a rising (1363) and the brief arrest of Robert. But David did not impose his ideas for an English succession in 1363–4 (which may not have implied subjection of his kingdom), and during 1357–71 he reformed the machinery of government and asserted his power in the Highlands and the Western Isles. Despite two marriages (and plans for a third), he was the last of his line.

Scottish monarchy were there to be intermittently developed by later fifteenth-century kings.

On the other hand, the mystique of Christian kingship was heightened at this very time of dynastic weakness and political vulnerability. In 1329 the pope conceded that Scottish kings should henceforth be solemnly crowned and anointed, as English kings had been since the Dark Ages, and not simply enthroned at Scone in a mainly secular ceremony. Though he was only seven, David II was the first monarch to have imparted to him (1331), with the sanction of the Church, the full sovereignty in his kingdom which English kings claimed in theirs. This inestimable buttress to kingship in Scotland was consolidated by an unbroken line of Stuart kings between 1371 and the mid-sixteenth century, despite the fact that every fifteenth-century king of Scotland succeeded as a minor. The accession of Mary, queen of Scots in 1542 was a resounding vindication of the independent sovereign Stuart monarchy of Scotland. She was only six days old!

Royal Blood and the Royal Brood

Like the kingship itself, English kings from Henry III to Henry VIII are a bundle of paradoxes. Unlike earlier monarchs, most of them were born in regal surroundings, and yet their lives—certainly their latter years—frequently seem far less secure than those of Norman or Angevin kings. To the layman or amateur geneticist it seems that the more precise the conventions of hereditary succession became, and the more frequently the sons and daughters of kings married English partners instead of foreign ones, the more precarious were their lives and the fewer their children. Although later medieval kings still married foreign princesses (exclusively, up until the second half of the fifteenth century), the seizure of the throne by English noblemen on at least four occasions from 1399 meant that there were more kings of England with English-born parents than at any time since the tenth century; and these English parents came from a small stock of frequently related senior nobles. The royal line of Lancaster from Henry IV was extinguished in 1471, when Henry VI and his only child, Edward, were done to death after the battle of Tewkesbury. The male line of the Tudors from Henry VII failed with the death of Edward VI in 1553, and even the female line from Henry VIII ran into the sand fifty years later. After Edward III, there was only one monarch, Henry VI, who had a mother of non-English stock before the birth of Mary Tudor in 1516.

After the experience of the Lancastrian royal family, in which the four strapping sons of Henry IV produced between them only one legitimate child (Henry VI), Edward IV may not simply have followed the lustful instincts for which he is notorious in choosing Elizabeth Woodville as his wife, the first English-born queen of England since the Norman conquest; he may also have been conscious that he was marrying a widow whose marriage to Sir John Grey had clearly demonstrated that she could mother healthy sons. He chose well: Edward had a crop of children, seven daughters and three sons. He can hardly be blamed for failing to foresee when he married Elizabeth in 1464 that the ruthless ambition of his youngest brother, Richard, duke of Gloucester, would elbow his two surviving sons aside in 1483. Richard III himself, who had married into the great aristocratic family of Neville, produced only one sickly child, Edward, who died in 1484 and thereupon left Richard with no heir to his ill-gotten crown. It is worth noting, too, that none of these later medieval kings produced anything approaching the crop of bastards that Henry I had fathered. After Edward I, who fathered one illegitimate son, only Edward IV and Henry VIII, the most lascivious of kings, made headway in this direction, with one illegitimate son in each case; Richard III's acknowledged bastards, a son and a daughter, were the result of youthful adventures before he gained the crown. The extramarital activities of several contemporary Scottish kings—Robert II and James IV in particular—suggest that neither the moral imperatives of the age nor the force of the Church's teaching imposed significant constraints on them.

Of the thirteen kings of England from Henry III to Henry VIII, six were born in one or other of the royal residences; we may include among them Edward V, who was born in sanctuary in Westminster Abbey (1470), where his mother was cowering from the supporters of the restored Henry VI while her husband, Edward IV, fled to the Low Countries. Henry III was the only later medieval king to be born in the old Anglo-Saxon city of Winchester. His son, Edward I, was born in the newer capital of Westminster—a sign of the changing focus of English kingship. Both Edward III and Henry VI were born at Windsor Castle, the greatest country residence of English kings in the Thames valley, and one which had a new significance for English kingship in the later Middle Ages. Henry VIII was born down river at Greenwich, one of a number of newer palaces which the Tudor kings came to prefer and beautify. Edward II was born during Edward I's tour of conquered Wales in 1284, at Caernarfon, the headquarters of the king's new principality of North Wales. The remaining six monarchs were the sons of noblemen, not of kings, and their place of birth reflects this fact. Henry IV was born at his father's Lincolnshire castle of Bolingbroke, and his son, later Henry V, in the duchy of Lancaster lordship of Monmouth in 1387. Similarly, Richard III was born at the Yorkist family home at Fotheringhay, in Northamptonshire, whilst Henry VII was born even further afield (and posthumously) at Pembroke Castle, which belonged to his uncle Jasper (1457). Most kings, therefore, were born in England (or in an English environment in Wales), and this had not been so for more than two centuries. Moreover, it is striking that none of them was born in the northern parts of the realm—indeed, of those born in England, only two (Henry IV and Richard III) first saw the light of day north of the Thames, and neither of these could reasonably have expected to be king at the time of his birth.

In further stark contrast with previous centuries, only two kings in this period were born in France. Richard II, the surviving son of the Black Prince, was born at Bordeaux in English Gascony, where his father had established his extravagant court; his elder brother, Edward, who died young, was born at Angoulême, somewhat to the north. And Edward IV, the eldest son of Richard, duke of York, was born at Rouen in 1442, while his father was governor of Normandy for Henry VI. The significance which contemporaries came to attach to royal birth in England was expressed by Richard III, admittedly for his own ends. In casting round for any means to justify his usurpation of the throne in 1483, he not only

CAERNARFON CASTLE, GWYNEDD, begun by King Edward I in 1283 after the death of Llywelyn ap Gruffydd, Prince of Wales. It was designed to help ensure the conquest of Llywelyn's principality. Caernarfon had a special role: Edward was conscious of its Roman past, and in 1283 the alleged body of Magnus Maximus, father of the Emperor Constantine, was found there; the castle's towers and walls are reminiscent of those of Constantine's capital, Constantinople. Edward II was born at Caernarfon in 1284, though the cynical declaration to the Welsh attributed to his father that he had thereby given them a prince 'that was born in Wales and could speak never a word of English' is not recorded before the sixteenth century.

denied the legitimacy of his nephews, Edward V and Richard, duke of York, but also claimed that their father, his own eldest brother, Edward IV, had been illegitimate, one proof of which was that he had been born in France. Richard commended himself to the Londoners as being of good, respectable English birth.

It was no easier in the later Middle Ages than in the past to contemplate training kings specifically for kingship, even though hereditary succession in the male line seemed to have been established in 1216. The hazards of childhood would have been enough to defeat any educational plans laid by kings and queens for their children. Edward II was not the eldest son of Edward I, but his fourth, and several of Edward III's offspring did not survive childhood. If the Black Prince had been raised with the expectation that one day he would be king, he was cruelly thwarted by death in 1376, and whatever regal training and education he received was never put to use except as his father's lieutenant in Aquitaine, where his performance was not impressive. As for Henry IV and Henry V, each spent his early years in the household of a great nobleman; as youngsters, they had no expectation of reaching the throne, although when Henry IV (at the age of thirty-two) deposed King Richard in 1399, his eldest son

EDWARD III

(1327–1377), king of England

Then the king leapt on a palfrey with a white rod in his hand . . . he rode from rank to rank, desiring every man to take heed that day to his right and honour. He spake it so sweetly and with so good countenance and merry cheer that all such as were discomfited took courage in the seeing and hearing of him.

(Jean Froissart, *Chronicles*, on the battle of Crécy, 1346)

EDWARD was a distinguished knight, a vigorous and daring commander admired across Europe. Even-tempered, self-confident, and accessible, he and his sons presided over an opulent court. But his preoccupation with the Hundred Years War and chivalric display, including his Order of the Garter (1348), seems adolescent and not always in England's interest. He was quickly declared king when Edward II was deposed (1327). His marriage to Philippa of Hainault (1328) was arranged beforehand. For a few years (to 1330) he was overshadowed by Queen Isabella and her lover, but his *coup d'état* forced her to retire and gave him the reins of power. He was soon embroiled with Scotland, trying to reverse concessions made in his name at Northampton (1328); he encouraged Edward Balliol to seize the Scottish throne. By 1337 he began war with the French and in 1340 adopted the title of king of France. His campaigns showed him to be a fine tactician and made him popular, though his well-publicized victories off Sluys (1340) and at Crécy (1346) and Poitiers (1356) were remarkable more for Edward's luck and defensive tactics than for long-term gain. At the height of his career, he lavished time and money on Windsor Castle, glittering tournaments, and his celebrated Order—just when the plague struck. After an initial period (1338–43) when Parliament and some ministers grumbled about the costs of war and the consequences of his absences, with good sense and a will to remove all obstacles to his military objectives he established a harmonious relationship with his nobility, who eagerly joined his enterprises, and the Commons in Parliament, to whose self-importance Edward pandered in taxation and legislation. During the post-plague years, he buttressed the fortunes of landowners, and with the pope resident at Avignon, he agreed to limit his authority in England. Edward saw eye to eye with his subjects. He personally harried southern Scotland (1356) and besieged Rheims (1359), the coronation site of French kings, but the treaty of Brétigny (1360), whereby he would surrender the French title in return for an enlarged Aquitaine in full sovereignty, failed. Calais was his only lasting territorial gain, and at its siege (1346–7) he all but forgot chivalric ideals in his anger at the stubborn burghers. After Queen Philippa died (1369), his grip on the war and his hold on the affections of his people loosened: he withdrew to Windsor and perhaps became senile; his mistress, Alice Perrers, and corrupt servants squandered the goodwill he had enjoyed. His last years were saddened by the death of his son, the Black Prince, and an outcry against his ministers in the 'Good Parliament' (1376). Edward had lived too long. He had planned another expedition to France (1372) but was frustrated by storms—just as well perhaps. He is said to have died alone, the rings pulled from his fingers by Alice and with only one priest to administer the last rites.

THE GILT-BRONZE TOMB-EFFIGIES OF KING EDWARD III AND QUEEN PHILIPPA (d. 1369), in Westminster Abbey. The king's head, possibly by John Orchard, seems based on a death-mask, though the flowing hair and beard appear stylized. The queen's matronly figure is realistic; the effigy was made in later life, c.1367, by Jean de Liège, who had been employed at the French court.

THE MAGNIFICENT GILT-BRONZE EFFIGY OF EDWARD, THE BLACK PRINCE, eldest son of King Edward III. It lies on his tomb in the Trinity Chapel, Canterbury Cathedral. The embodiment of chivalric virtue, his effigy shows, as the prince's will requested, a knight 'armed in steel for battle with our arms quartered; and my visage with our helmet of the leopard put under the head of the image'. Above the tomb hang his accoutrements.

was twelve and thenceforward could be nurtured as the king-to-be. Indeed, Henry V and his younger brothers were the most extensively and imaginatively educated of all the noble children related to the royal house in later medieval England.

In the fifteenth century, the education of royal sons and prospective heirs (less so of daughters) became more formal and professional and had an eye to the virtues and qualities which, it was felt, ought to be developed in a king. Throughout the Middle Ages, kings had been instructed by tutors or masters once they left the care of nurses. Usually of knightly or even noble rank, these men were expected to guard their charges and teach them the arts and accomplishments, both practical and intellectual, thought desirable in kings' sons; more specialist teaching was always available in the royal households, not least from the clerks who were to be found there. According to his biography, William the Marshal needed a good deal of persuading before he agreed to become Henry III's guardian in 1216. The earl of Chester's opinion was decisive:

'You are so fine a knight, so upright, so respected, so loved and so wise that you are considered one of the finest knights in the world. I say this to you in all sincerity, it is you that ought to be chosen.'

Even so, the Marshal appreciated that the day-to-day care of the king was not his *métier*:

'My lords, behold this young and tender king. I could not undertake to lead him with me about the land. And I cannot stay in the same place, for I shall have to go to the marches of the kingdom to protect them. That is why I ask you to name an upright man to whom the young king shall be entrusted.' . . . Upon which the Marshal entrusted the child to the bishop of Winchester. (*History of William the Marshal*)

Henry VI was placed under the supervision of two of the most senior and respected of his nobles, his great-uncle, Thomas Beaufort, duke of Exeter, and the renowned knight, Richard Beauchamp, earl of Warwick; whilst Edward IV's young son and heir, Edward, was governed by his maternal uncle, Earl Rivers, in accordance with detailed ordinances drawn up by the king himself in 1473.

The nature of the training intended for kings is rarely known in detail. We can be sure that they were taught the military arts, and in 1256 a tournament was specially arranged so that the future Edward I could be 'instructed in military law'. His son, later Edward II, was sent on a campaign to Scotland at the age of seventeen, to learn at least the military side of a king's trade; whilst the Black Prince was first blooded in battle at Crécy when he was even younger—and with such distinction that the vision of the triumphant father and his son on the battlefield would inspire painters of the Gothic revival in the nineteenth century. More intellectual accomplishments, especially a knowledge of languages and an

RICHARD BEAUCHAMP, EARL OF WARWICK (d. 1439) IS MADE MASTER AND GUARDIAN OF KING HENRY VI IN 1428. This scene from *The Pageant of the Birth, Life and Death of Richard Beauchamp, earl of Warwick*, *c*.1485–1500, shows Warwick in the centre with a sword, taking on the charge in Parliament. He is holding his warrant of authority in his left hand; to the left are temporal lords, including presumably the two royal uncles, the dukes of Bedford and Gloucester, wearing coronets; to the right are spiritual lords including three bishops. The king wears a coronated cap of estate and holds an orb with a cross.

ability to read books, are more difficult to detect in the schooling of kings. It is still possible for historians to debate whether some of England's later medieval kings—even the more learned among them, such as Henry V—mastered Latin; Henry VI's only son is known to have been rather poor at it. Only with the spread of Renaissance interests and values in England and Scotland during the later fifteenth century did its popularity in the royal schoolroom return; and then Henry VII made sure that his sons, Arthur and Henry, were taught it to an advanced level. James IV of Scotland was very good at it. Contrariwise, few historians doubt that even fifteenth-century kings, in a patriotic age, could speak (and presumably write) French; the tender scene in Shakespeare's *Henry V*, in which the coy princess, Katherine of Valois, took to teaching the victorious Henry the charms of her language at the French court in 1420 is a reflection of English self-confidence at the end of Queen Elizabeth's reign rather than of Henry's lamentable knowledge of French 150 years earlier. As to their reading, it is easier to enumerate some of the books which kings had on their shelves, or which they were given, or which had prefaces addressed to them, than to be certain that they ever read them, let alone in their youth. This was the age of 'Mirrors for Princes', a genre of moral and educational writing for kings and princes, of which the most popular was *Secreta secretorum* (*The secret of secrets*). Such books were composed for, and presented to, English kings: Henry VI's son Edward had a short life, but before he died in 1471 George Ashby had written a practical and academic manual for his instruction as heir to the English throne; and Sir John Fortescue wrote his famous book on the laws of England specifically for Edward to read. Henry V is said to have read similar works when he was a prince, but we cannot be sure that all the sons of kings did so or learned the kingly craft from them. The programme of study devised by the court poet and historian, Bernard André, for Henry VII's eldest son, Arthur, included the classics and books on the noble and chivalric virtues, and if the prince was at all conscientious, he would have found exemplary reading matter in his father's rich library at Richmond.

The most valuable training that a prospective king could receive was in the practical arts and wiles of kingship. Whether he was given such training depended, in the first instance, on whether he was able to grow up and mature during the lifetime of his father, something which Norman and Angevin kings managed to achieve. It was short-sighted of Edward I to deprive his eldest surviving son of experience of government and politics simply because he mistrusted his son's judgement and was impatient of his eccentric interests and dubious friendships. Fifteenth-century kings were even less fortunate, and the series of usurpations meant that the upbringing of even those kings who snatched the crown from anointed temples was far from ideal. Henry IV and Henry VII spent their early manhood as English nobles, Henry Bolingbroke in the most splendid and influential aristocratic court in late fourteenth-century England; he was raised by his Promethean father, John of Gaunt, who was Richard II's uncle and for much of his reign his senior counsellor. Henry himself became a prominent earl and an enthusiastic crusader, and he was well versed in the labyrinthine corridors of English political life during the troubled reign of his cousin, Richard II. Henry Tudor, by contrast, though he may have picked up the rudiments of a gentleman's education (even a smattering of Welsh) in the Herbert household at Raglan Castle before he was fourteen, was more harshly schooled as an impoverished exile in Brittany; there he relied on the protection of the Breton duke, acquiring little knowledge of England and its kingship except by hearsay and correspondence with political dissidents. Henry was second only to the baby-king Henry VI in having deep chasms of ignorance in his mind about the practical arts of kingship. Even Edward IV, who was king from the age of nineteen, was better prepared, as the eldest son of Richard, duke of York, the richest and highest-born nobleman in Henry VI's England; though born in Normandy, Edward was brought up in England and the Welsh march, and he was made aware of the turbulent politics of the Wars of the Roses during his teens.

Above all, it was Henry V who received the most appropriate training for an English king. He was twelve when his father seized the crown, but before he was seventeen he had been given a measure of responsibility for suppressing the rebellion of Owain Glyndŵr and was introduced to a kind of warfare in the mountains of Wales that demanded qualities of persistence, imagination, and rugged steadfastness against a guerrilla enemy who rarely fell to battle. A few years later, he dabbled in English politics, fearlessly adopting attitudes that were sometimes at variance with those of his father. There is no doubt that the knowledge of government and rulership that Prince Hal acquired in Henry IV's later years, the political associations and antennae which he developed then, and the domestic and foreign policies he gradually formulated were the keys to his robust rule as king. He may well have sowed sheaves of wild oats in his youth, as a mid-fifteenth-century chronicler maintained, only to abandon them as king:

And before he was king, when he was Prince of Wales, he fell and inclined greatly to riot, and drew to wild company. And divers gentlemen and gentle-women followed his will and his desire at his commandment; . . . And then he began to reign as king, and he remembered the great charge and worship that he should take upon him. And at once he commanded all his people who were parties to his misgovernance before that time, and all his household, to come before him . . . they were the homelier and bolder unto him, and did not dread him at all, insomuch that when they were come before him, some of them winked at him, and some smiled, and thus they made foolish grimaces unto him, many of them. But for all that, the prince kept his countenance very serious towards them, and said to them: 'Sirs, you are the people that I have cherished and maintained in riot and wild governance, and here I give you all in commandment and charge you, that from this day forward you forsake all misgovernance and live according to the laws of Almighty God and the laws of our land. . . . And so he . . . charged them all to leave his household, and live as good men, and never come any more into his presence, because he would have no occasion or remembrance whereby he should fall to riot again. (*The Brut Chronicle*)

But Shakespeare's portrait of a prince who exorcized the excesses of his youth by donning a mantle of virtue the instant he succeeded to the throne is a dramatic caricature:

> The breath no sooner left his father's body
> But that his wildness, mortified in him,
> Seemed to die too. Yea, at that very moment
> Consideration like an angel came
> And whipped th'offending Adam out of him,
> Leaving his body as a paradise
> T'envelop and contain celestial spirits.
> Never was such a sudden scholar made;
> Never came reformation in a flood
> With such a heady currance scouring faults;
> Nor never Hydra-headed wilfulness
> So soon did lose his seat—and all at once—
> As in this king.
>
> (*Henry V*, I. i)

Strange to say, one of the least experienced of English kings in the later Middle Ages, Henry Tudor, also proved to be one of the most successful—a fact that helps to put in perspective the significance to be attached to the training of kings (or lack of it). Qualities of character, combined with schooling in practical realities, were more likely to shape a king than assiduous teaching programmes devised by kings or the tutors and masters appointed by them. This being so, the minors among English rulers, notably Henry III, Richard II, and Henry VI, never had a chance. Given little opportunity to develop sound judgement and an independent mind in their formative years, all three were dominated by nobles and factions that were at odds with one another. They became used to dependence and later relied on friends and favourites who were not always worthy of their master's trust. If they asserted themselves, they often did so erratically and petulantly, wilful in their defence of friends even when the winds of criticism blew hard. Some of the theoretical programmes of instruction carefully prepared for prospective kings were ironically reserved for three kings-to-be who were cut down in adolescence: Edward, the son of Henry VI; Edward, the eldest son of Edward IV; and Arthur, Henry VII's first-born. What kind of kings these kings-of-the-classroom would have made is a fascinating but insoluble question.

RICHARD II

(1377–1399), king of England

He was of the common stature, his hair yellowish, his face fair, round and feminine, sometimes flushed; abrupt and stammering in his speech, capricious in his manners ... He was prodigal in his gifts, extravagantly splendid in his entertainments and dress.

(Monk of Evesham, *History of the Life and Reign of Richard II*)

RICHARD is a subject ripe for the psycho-historian. His father, the Black Prince, died when he was nine, his mother, the plump and jolly Princess Joan, when he was eighteen. He had no surviving brothers or sisters, and when his beloved wife, Anne of Bohemia, died (1394) the king was grief-stricken. He relied on friends who were unworthy of his confidence but monopolized his patronage. Edward III's remaining sons, Richard's uncles, may have encouraged his elevated view of kingship. And the Peasants' Revolt (1381), during which Richard had the confidence of the rebels and helped persuade them to disperse, may have nurtured such instincts. He succeeded to the throne (1377) when English armies abroad and royal government at home were discredited, but he did not have the gifts of statesmanship to respond. Criticism of his advisers and favourites outraged him to the point of violence. Parliament in 1386 and 1388, led by 'appellant' lords, attacked his ministers but Richard would not compromise; he even sought French aid. After being threatened with deposition (1387), in 1388 he reluctantly swore his coronation oath again. This rankled and in his last ten years Richard planned revenge rather than accommodation. In 1389 he declared his minority ended and thereafter treated his subjects with harsh suspicion, securing the pope's promise to excommunicate opponents and (1396) French military help if needed. Indeed, his policies of peace with France and Scotland and the restoration of royal power in Ireland were more far-sighted than wise in the circumstances. In 1397–8 he struck at the appellants of 1388, exiling, murdering, or executing them. Though little short of a tyrant, as a patron of fashion and culture his reputation is substantial—and not simply for introducing 'small pieces of cloth ... to carry in his hand to wipe and clean his nose' (i.e. handkerchiefs). Yet by 1399, 'all the good hearts of the realm clean turned' away from him'. When he was in Ireland (1399), his appellant cousin, Henry Bolingbroke, who was exiled in 1398 and deprived of his inheritance (1399), invaded, arresting Richard at Flint and deposing him. He was imprisoned in Pontefract Castle, but risings in his favour probably forced Henry to have him killed. His body was brought to London (1400) for display and then quietly buried at King's Langley. Henry V transferred it (1413) to Westminster Abbey as a mark of reconciliation.

THE GILT-BRONZE TOMB-EFFIGIES OF KING RICHARD II AND ANNE OF BOHEMIA, in Westminster Abbey. They were commissioned in 1395, soon after the queen's death, and executed by Nicholas Broker and Godfrey Prest. According to the contract, the images were to look like the king and queen—even though Anne is known to have been unattractive.

MARGARET OF ANJOU, Henry VI's queen, pictured kneeling at prayer. This is an illumination from her prayer roll, dating from the mid-fifteenth century, with two angels supporting her coat of arms. Henry married Margaret (1445) after the negotiations for one of the count of Armagnac's daughters came to nothing. Margaret's piety is less marked in historians' perceptions of her than her robust political instincts.

Royal marriages in the later Middle Ages were utilitarian. Few kings or the offspring of kings were allowed the luxury of marrying for personal or emotional reasons. Henry V is traditionally said to have fallen in love with Katherine of Valois as soon as he clapped eyes on her, though hard-headed considerations of diplomacy and war were more compelling motives for their marriage in 1420 (and the earlier negotiations that took place before ever they met). His father, Henry IV, received touching and admiring letters from the widowed duchess of Brittany, Joan of Navarre, which were the prelude to their marriage in 1403; but there were also sound political reasons for a link between England and Brittany, and it would be rash to portray Joan as taking the initiative in courting the widower-king whom she claimed to have admired from afar. Even Henry VI was sufficiently interested in the personal side of marriage negotiations to send a painter to Armagnac in 1442 to produce portraits of the two daughters of the count of Armagnac so that he could choose the more attractive of them as a wife. But this proposal, and others which Henry's ministers considered, were designed to provide England with a foreign ally against Charles VII of France, rather than simply to gratify King Henry.

THE MARRIAGE OF KING HENRY V AND KING CHARLES VI'S DAUGHTER, KATHERINE OF VALOIS, at St John's Church, Troyes, in 1420. It is a miniature from Jean Chartier's *Chronicle of King Charles VII* of France. This marriage sealed the treaty whereby Henry became Charles VI's heir. The queen is accompanied by several ladies, perhaps including her mother, Queen Isabella, the king by several attendants, including possibly (with a characteristically large nose) Philip, duke of Burgundy. The archbishop of Sens presided. This book was written in 1487 for Sir Thomas Thwaytes as a gift for Katherine's grandson, King Henry VII. The borders display the Beaufort emblem of the portcullis interspersed with the Tudor double rose; Henry VII's arms appear below.

The most spectacular exception to the list of utilitarian marriages in the later Middle Ages is that of Edward IV. In 1464 he married Elizabeth Woodville, an English widow. Not only was she the first English-born queen to marry an English king since before the Norman conquest, but it was rumoured that Edward was so smitten with her that when she denied him her bed outside wedlock, he blundered into matrimony. Contemporaries, and historians since, heavily criticized the king for sacrificing his greatest asset, his marriageability, with so little thought for the implications, though Elizabeth's large family was later put to good political and social purposes by Edward.

If kings did not marry for love, they sometimes found it later. Edward I was so moved by the death, in 1290, of his first wife, Eleanor of Castile, that he ordered that the route followed by the cortège bringing her body from Nottinghamshire, where she died, to Westminster, where she was buried, should be marked by a succession of 'Eleanor Crosses' that are among the most notable examples of royal architectural patronage in the Gothic age. Edward III, too, became devoted to his queen, Philippa of Hainault, whom his mother had secured for him in 1326 (and whom he married in 1328). No one has claimed that the soldier-king was unfaithful to her in camp or at court before the very last years of her life (and she died in 1369). It is true that Edward sought consolation after 1366 in the arms of a grasping and disreputable mistress, Alice Perrers, the wife of one of his knights. Richard II was utterly inconsolable when his tiny first wife, Anne of Bohemia, died in 1392; the impulsive and capricious king found even the continued existence of the royal manor-house at Sheen in which she had died too much to bear, and it was largely demolished on his orders soon afterwards. Henry VII grew to love his wife, Edward IV's eldest daughter, Elizabeth, whom he publicly promised to marry as early as Christmas 1483 when he had good reason to advertise himself as the unifier of all the factions in England and in exile that were hostile to Richard III. They almost certainly never met before Bosworth, but when Elizabeth died in 1503 Henry 'privily departed to a solitary place, and would no man should resort unto him'; the lonely monarch was desolate for a period—before embarking on the search for a replacement in the courts of Western Europe. Even Henry VIII, who married Catherine of Aragon in 1509

A GOLD MEDALLION COMMEMORATING THE MARRIAGE OF KING HENRY VII AND ELIZABETH OF YORK in January 1486. The obverse (*here*) shows the king and the crowned queen, the reverse the Tudor rose symbolizing the unity of Lancaster and York at the conclusion of the Wars of the Roses.

GILT-BRONZE TOMB-EFFIGY OF ELEANOR OF CASTILE (d. 1290), first wife of Edward I. This and Henry III's tomb effigy were commissioned by Edward in 1291 from a London goldsmith, William Torel. A duplicate of the queen's (now vanished) was ordered for Lincoln Cathedral, where her entrails were buried. The first life-size bronze figure sculptures in England, they were designed to glorify the monarchy and match the effigies of French kings recently commissioned for St Denis. Edward was also moved by genuine affection for his Spanish queen, to whom he was happily married. Note the realistic cushions, decorated with the arms of Leon, Castile, and Ponthieu (a county which passed under Edward's control) and the jewel sockets, which help to make this the finest of medieval royal effigies.

after her first husband, Henry's elder brother Arthur, had died, found his wife quite congenial to begin with, until her incapacity to produce healthy children began to worry him.

In view of the diplomatic and political nature of most marriage alliances, it is surprising that relations between kings and their queens were not more strained than they seem to have been. Deep dislike and vicious quarrels appear to have been relatively rare, although since queens had their own households, it was possible for an incompatible pair to keep their distance from each other. Kings and queens frequently went about their own business, and (to take one example) in the first ten years of their marriage (1445–55) Henry VI and Margaret of Anjou spent only about half their time in one another's company. Relations were spectacularly bad between Edward II and his virago of a wife, Isabella, 'She-wolf of France' (as she was later known). But then it may be that any wife would have found life difficult or distasteful with England's notoriously 'gay' monarch. Even Margaret of Anjou, whose domineering personality places her close in the popular mind to Isabella, may not have lost patience with her unworldly husband,

JOHN, EARL OF SHREWSBURY PRESENTING MARGARET OF ANJOU WITH A BOOK OF ROMANCES (from which this illustration is taken), in the presence of her husband, the crowned King Henry VI, on the occasion of their marriage in 1445. The book was the earl's wedding gift. Both monarchs bear a sceptre. Members of the royal court are also portrayed: the chamberlain with his staff of office, the queen's ladies and, perhaps, wearing a circlet, Humphrey, duke of Gloucester, with other nobles behind him. The royal arms serve as a backdrop for the scene.

Henry VI, until the king's own breakdown (1453) and subsequent incapacity threatened the Lancastrian kingship and the heritage of their son Edward who, when he was born in 1453, went unrecognized by the sick monarch.

> ... at the Prince's coming to Windsor, the Duke of Buckingham took him in his arms and presented him to the King in goodly wise, beseeching the King to bless him; and the King gave no manner answer. Nevertheless the Duke abode still with the Prince by the King; and when he could no manner answer have, the Queen came in, and took the Prince in her arms and presented him in like form as the Duke had done, desiring that he should bless it; but all their labour was in vain, for they departed thence without any answer or countenance saving only that once he looked on the Prince and cast down his eyes again, without any more. (John Stodeley's newsletter, 19 January 1454)

Margaret, 'a strong laboured woman', proved to be a staunch and energetic champion of the dynasty while her husband was a broken reed.

English queens of the later Middle Ages were sought in the same broad arena as in the centuries following Æthelred's marriage to Emma of Normandy—France. The Hundred Years War confirmed this. The marriages of Edward I (his second, 1299), Edward II (1308), Richard II (his second, 1396), Henry V (1420), and Henry VI (1445) accompanied efforts to secure a lasting peace with England's pre-eminent enemy and rival in Western Europe; on each occasion, the objective proved unattainable. Henry V came closest to success with a bold treaty which not only included his marriage to Katherine, daughter of King Charles VI, but also made him Charles's heir. This was the most portentous marriage of any medieval English king; but Henry did not live long enough to preside over the 'dual monarchy' of England and France, for he predeceased his elderly and insane father-in-law by two months in 1422 and left this extraordinary legacy to his nine-month-old son, Henry VI of England and, for those who recognized him, Henry II of France.

Nor were these the only marriages dictated by Anglo-French relations. As in Norman and Angevin days, marriage alliances with the neighbours or nobles of France were regarded as strategic weapons in the armoury of English kings and diplomats, and could offer valuable protection to the English territories in France. Henry III sent his son Edward to Gascony in 1254, at a time when Alfonso X, king of Castile, was threatening the integrity and stability of the duchy. There, Edward married Eleanor, Alfonso's daughter, as one means of diverting the Castilian king's fire and protecting the distant province. The marriage between Edward III and Philippa, daughter of William, count of Hainault, a county on the northern frontier of France, was arranged before Edward's accession by his mother, Isabella. She was so angry when her brother, the French king, refused to offer her and her lover refuge during her exile that she sought shelter with Count William and his help in invading England in 1326

HENRY VI'S CORONATION AS KING OF FRANCE AT SAINT-DENIS, near Paris, 1431. The deteriorating English position in France demanded a public demonstration of Henry's claim to the French throne, but this ceremony lost some of its impact by being held at Saint-Denis rather than at the customary coronation seat of French kings, Rheims. Moreover, the crowning was done by the king's great-uncle, Cardinal Beaufort, bishop of Winchester. The king is shown with the open crown of France and a sceptre; two bishops are touching the crown after the coronation as a sign of fealty.

to topple her husband, Edward II, from his throne. Henry IV's marriage to the dowager duchess of Brittany is also noteworthy as a device to ensure the independence of a great French duchy and to give English diplomatists leverage in their dealings with the king of France.

Among later medieval English kings, Edward I was the only one to be already married when he became king—until the fifteenth century, when dynastic revolution brought to the throne two kings in their thirties, Henry IV and Richard III, who had already taken wives, in both cases English-born ladies. Edward IV

HENRY IV

(1399–1413), king of England

... it is my will that no man think that by way of conquest I would disinherit any man of his heritage, franchises, or other rights that he ought to have, nor to put him out of that he hath and hath had by good laws and customs of the realm ...

(Henry IV's speech to Parliament, 1399)

THE GILT AND PAINTED ALABASTER TOMB-EFFIGIES OF KING HENRY IV AND HIS SECOND WIFE, JOAN OF NAVARRE, duchess of Brittany. Henry is the only post-Conquest king of England to be buried at Canterbury. Queen Joan built an altar tomb over the place in Thomas Becket's Chapel where the king's body was laid to rest (1413), and she also commissioned the effigy. Joan's own effigy was placed beside her husband's after her death (1437).

HENRY's life after deposing Richard II (1399) was devoted to keeping himself and his line on the throne: he was not universally regarded as Richard's right heir. The eldest surviving son of John of Gaunt and Blanche of Lancaster, he was a politician and soldier in the chivalric mould. Earl of Derby (1377) and duke of Hereford (1397), he was one of the appellant lords criticizing Richard's ministers and friends in 1388; in the 1390s he crusaded in Eastern Europe. Reticent, cautious, orthodoxly pious, even studious, he shared the instincts of the nobility and became a good manager of men. Accused of disloyalty by Richard, he was exiled (1398) and his father's inheritance declared forfeit (1399). He defiantly returned (June 1399) while Richard was in Ireland, and his invasion turned into a bid for the throne (September). He desperately, but not without ingenuity, justified Richard's deposition, anxious to disguise his 'conquest' of England. But he faced more threats than any other king—from Ricardians, the disillusioned Percy family, Owain Glyndŵr's Welsh and their French and Scottish allies, even some clerics—which demanded decisive action from Henry and substantial resources from Parliament. He led fruitless expeditions to Wales (1400–5), though his victory over the Percies and Welsh at Shrewsbury (1403) was important, and his execution of rebels at York (including the archbishop, 1405) confirmed his mastery. He faced self-confident Parliaments (1401–6) which aired grievances, criticized royal servants, and resisted taxation, but Henry conceded when he could and sternly avoided inroads on his prerogative. He used Parliament to declare the succession in his Lancastrian dynasty. Incapacitated by illness in his last years (from 1408), his son and heir, Prince Hal, played a greater role in government, even opposing the king on foreign policy. The prince's faction ruled in 1410–11, but Henry reasserted himself; the tension between father and son enabled French writers to report soon after that the prince took the crown from beside his father's bed even before the king expired—a scene turned into fine drama by Shakespeare. Henry IV died in the Jerusalem Chamber in Westminster Abbey, though Caxton, a century later, was the first to link this with an earlier prophecy (1399) that he would reconquer Jerusalem. Henry overcame his unique problems as a usurper without damaging the monarchy.

was the first since the conquest to marry an Englishwoman after becoming king. The first two Tudor monarchs made it almost customary, though in Henry VIII's case not without some of the personal and political problems that had accompanied Edward's match. The self-conscious Englishness of the monarchy in the later Middle Ages was thus matched from 1464 by the inclination of its kings to spurn foreign brides, whatever their diplomatic advantages. If the ability to produce children weighed most heavily with them, Henry VIII's marital record was a reminder to contemporaries that such expectations were at the mercy of the Almighty, not the plans of men.

Queens were generally the passive instruments of policy (though the teenage Margaret of Anjou seems to have been used by her uncle, Charles VII of France, to persuade her husband, Henry VI, to make a truce with him). They were expected to produce children and, as the kings' consorts, to add lustre to a court that increasingly reflected the king's majesty and magnificence. Their coronations rarely seem to have been more than splendid ceremonial occasions; nevertheless, Henry VII was careful, at an especially delicate dynastic moment, to avoid too obvious a reliance on the attractions of unity and political reconciliation implied by his marriage with Elizabeth of York and her coronation (1486) soon after Bosworth. Since few kings were already married when they succeeded to the throne, there were few queens to be anointed and crowned beside their husbands. Rather did most queens' coronations take place in Westminster Abbey after their marriage: Margaret of Anjou's was some weeks after her wedding in Titchfield Abbey, in the New Forest, in 1445; Edward IV's queen was crowned exactly one year after their secret marriage; Philippa of Hainault had to wait more than two years for her coronation; and Elizabeth of York almost as long—indeed, after the birth of her first child, Arthur. Those queens who, like Isabella of France and Margaret of Anjou, were fully capable of appropriating regal powers of government, became distinctly unpopular among influential sections of English opinion.

Life was not easy for queens in the later Middle Ages if they were not English born. They were sometimes distrusted and unpopular, as was Anne of Bohemia, who was also so diminutive as to cause one chronicler to wonder whether 'such a small bit of body' was not a poor bargain for Richard II. Members of their own family rarely accompanied foreign-born queens to England, but when they did so (as happened in Henry III's reign) they were deeply resented. Their foreign servants and advisers were unpopular too, as the Bretons accompanying Queen Joan discovered after 1403. The charge of witchcraft levelled against her and her entourage in 1419, though it may have had a financial motive, may equally have pandered to anti-foreign sentiment. Those queens who found themselves widowed and dowagers, especially when they were still fairly young, had varying fortunes. Edward I's second wife, Margaret of France, spent her widowhood in

THIS SPLENDID AND BEJEWELLED CROWN was probably made in France or Burgundy for Richard II's first wife, Anne of Bohemia (d. 1394), daughter of the Emperor Charles IV (d. 1378). It was in the royal treasury when Henry IV seized Richard's throne (1399). He sent it with his daughter Blanche in 1402 when she married Ludwig, son of Ruprecht, count palatine of the Rhine; it descended to the Wittelsbachs of Bavaria and so to the Munich Residenz Museum, where it can be seen today.

comfort, bringing up her three young children; but no other widowed queen of England in the later Middle Ages fared so well or contentedly. Edward II's fell into disgrace in 1330, when her son seized the reins of power for himself and shunted his intriguing and unpopular mother into obscurity. After Henry IV's second wife, Joan, became the centre of the witch-hunt which her eccentric interest in astrology encouraged, she spent her latter years, first, in protective custody and, then, in private but comfortable retirement. Henry's VI's wife, following her husband's deposition (1461), was a vigorous exile, plotting his return and drumming up support in Scotland and France, before falling into Edward IV's hands. She was eventually returned to France to live in abject poverty. Her last will, composed just three weeks before she died in 1482, is sadly moving:

... however weak and feeble of body ... my will is ... that the few goods which God and [Louis XI] have given and lent to me be used for this purpose and for the paying of my debts as much to my poor servants ... as to other creditors ... And should my few goods be insufficient to do this, as I believe they are ...

Edward IV's queen, Elizabeth Woodville, had a very fraught time indeed at Richard III's hands, and even after Henry Tudor married her eldest daughter she was carefully confined to a nunnery by her suspicious son-in-law, who also coveted her wealth. Only Henry V's widow, Katherine of Valois, led a life that may have been a happy, contented, and fulfilling one; 'unable fully to curb her carnal passions' (as one chronicler maintained), she embarked on a second marriage with the Welsh squire, Owen Tudor.

The comparisons and contrasts to be drawn from the stories of England's and Scotland's queens reflect the fierce independence of the Scottish kingdom and its nervous relationship with England in the later Middle Ages. The flowering of Scottish patriotism at the end of the thirteenth century, and the stiff resistance of the Scots to the threat of English conquest, may well be reflected in the marriage plans of the new Bruce and Stuart dynasties in the fourteenth and fifteenth centuries. Scottish kings from Robert I (who succeeded in 1306) to Robert III (who became king in 1390) were already married when they acquired the crown; of the seven queens between them, five were Scottish born. The preference for English brides which had been set by Malcolm III in the eleventh century was never as strong again. The tense relations between the two kingdoms in the later Middle Ages, and the Franco-Scottish alliance during much of the Hundred Years War, meant that on only two occasions—in 1424, when James I married Joan Beaufort, a kinswoman of King Henry IV, and 1503, when James IV married Margaret Tudor, daughter of King Henry VII—were English marriages negotiated. And both cases were exceptional: James I contracted his marriage while in captivity in England, and Henry VII had fought at Bosworth with a Scottish contingent at his side and began his reign with a sympathetic and quite un-English attitude towards the Scots. More typically, Scottish kings of the fifteenth

HENRY VII'S DAUGHTER, MARGARET TUDOR, who married King James IV in 1503. She is shown, wearing a gold crown and robes decorated with the English and Scottish royal arms, praying to St Margaret, an earlier English bride of a Scottish king. St Margaret was venerated in medieval Scotland and the Book of Hours which Henry VII gave his daughter (in which this illumination appears) offered St Margaret as an inspiration to the new queen. The Tudor arms and supporters, the dragon and the greyhound, are below the picture; the portcullis emblem of the queen's grandmother, Lady Margaret Beaufort, is in the margin.

ROBERT II

(1371–1390), king of Scots

THE son of Walter, hereditary steward of Scotland, and a daughter of Robert I, he was the first Stuart king of Scots. He was regarded by Robert I as his heir (1318) should he fail to produce a son—which he did in 1324. After David's birth, Robert was confirmed as heir apparent (1326) but had to wait until 1371 before succeeding at the age of fifty-five. Most of his energies were absorbed in war with the English and in governing during David's minority and absences (1334–57), and also in producing at least twenty-one children (eight of them bastards). He fell out with David and even rebelled (1363), but his own reign was lethargic and achieved little: he played no part in the war and his sons ruled for him after 1384. Despite settling the succession on his sons by his two wives in turn (1373), the fact that his first wife's children were born out of wedlock created bitterness and bloodshed for long after.

century looked to the continent for their brides and marriage alliances: James II married Mary of Gueldres, and James III Margaret of Denmark, Scotland's nearest neighbour across the sea.

The royal family or kinsfolk—those whom contemporaries identified as having 'blood royal' flowing in their veins—were an invaluable prop of kingship. In later medieval England they had a self-conscious identity that made the king's kinsmen widely regarded as a distinct 'estate' within the English ruling establishment. In the fourteenth and fifteenth centuries, these members of the blood royal became more important than ever before in almost every facet of public life: social, dynastic and military, political, and governmental. From the king's point of view, his kinsmen provided a dependable corps of leaders within the nobility at large. It was the good fortune of Henry V to have the support and companionship, at home and abroad, of his brothers Thomas, duke of Clarence, John, duke of Bedford, and Humphrey, duke of Gloucester, for much of his reign. They took to heart the death-bed exhortation of their father, Henry IV, who reportedly urged Prince Hal to cherish his brothers. It is a scene vividly recaptured by Shakespeare, who has the dying king address Thomas of Clarence thus:

> And thou shalt prove a shelter to thy friends,
> A hoop of gold to bind thy brothers in,
> That the united vessel of their blood
>
> .   .   .
>
> Shall never leak . . .
>
> (*Henry IV*, IV. iv)

From the nobility's standpoint, the royal kin were a privileged circle which others could aspire to join through friendship or marriage or both, and which offered opportunities for increased influence, wealth, and standing in the realm.

Potentially, therefore, the king's relatives were a vital link between crown and nobility that was capable of forging particularly close relationships between the monarch and his greater nobility. Equally, in some circumstances the blood royal could occasionally turn into a quarrelsome company that might undermine the kingship itself or indeed, as in 1483–5, help to extinguish the ruling dynasty. If only Edward IV and his brothers George and Richard 'had been able to live without dissension', lamented the Crowland chronicler, their talents could have been placed unitedly at the service of their family and the crown.

During the fourteenth and early fifteenth centuries the ranks of the English nobility were gradually differentiated, became more distinct, and ultimately were institutionalized in the context of a parliamentary 'House of Lords'. The upper reaches of society were now more closely defined and refined as the English peerage, with a special status and special titles as barons or better. At the same time, the king's kinsmen were more highly esteemed and consciously identified, even though—or perhaps because—the blood royal was now more difficult to define. It was more difficult to do so partly for accidental reasons: first, the propensity of Edward III and Queen Philippa to produce sons (seven of them, five of whom survived to manhood and married); secondly, the extraordinary marriage of Edward III's eldest son, the Black Prince, to a widow, Joan of Kent, whose two sons (the Holands) by her first husband were treated by their half-brother, Richard II, as members of the royal family; and thirdly, the practice

THE SONS OF KING EDWARD III, originally portrayed on a mural behind the high altar in St Stephen's Chapel, Westminster. These paintings of *c.*1355–63 were rediscovered in 1800 but destroyed in the great fire of 1834. The illustration is from a copy made by Robert Smirke RA, *c.*1805. They show the king's five sons bearing the royal arms and kneeling in order of birth behind the crowned king beneath elaborate Decorated canopies; they are being presented by St George to the Virgin and Child. There were companion figures of Queen Philippa and her daughters.

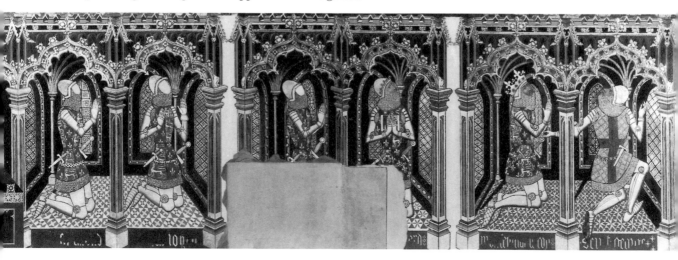

THE ALABASTER EFFIGY OF THOMAS, DUKE OF CLARENCE, brother of Henry V, in St Michael's Chapel, Canterbury Cathedral. He was killed at the battle of Baugé in 1421. He wears the Lancastrian SS collar, denoting loyalty and service to the dynasty, and full plate armour of the early fifteenth century. Though his relations with his elder brother were not always harmonious, he and his other brothers, John and Humphrey, formed a loyal royal family around the king in his great military enterprises in France after 1415.

of granting titles to noblemen who were not the king's relatives, something which Edward II revived when he created his close friend, Peter Gavaston, earl of Cornwall in 1307. During the ensuing century the immediate kinsmen of kings, those with royal blood, were increasingly designated as such, and people from all ranks in society took to distinguishing them from the rest of the nobility.

In stark contrast to the peasants' clamour in 1381 against Richard II's uncle, John of Gaunt, and other ministers, John Cade's rebels in 1450 pleaded with Henry VI 'to take about his noble person his true blood of his royal realm, that is to say, the high and mighty prince the Duke of York [who was Henry's second cousin] . . . Also to take about his person the mighty prince, the Duke of Exeter, the Duke of Buckingham, the Duke of Norfolk . . .' These three dukes were not described as '*high* and mighty' but, like York, they were the king's cousins. Higher in the social scale, the Commons in Parliament in 1450 accused Henry VI's chief minister, the duke of Suffolk, of the 'final destruction of the most noble, valiant true Prince, your right obedient Uncle the Duke of Gloucester . . . and of the abridging of the days of other Princes of your blood'.

The nobility were even more sensitive to the position of the royal kin by the fifteenth century. The lesser among them prided themselves on their loyal service

JOHN, DUKE OF BEDFORD, brother of King Henry V, kneeling before the figure of St George, the patron saint of the house of Lancaster, clad in the robes of the Garter. This rich and delicate illumination is from the duke's Book of Hours, which was commissioned c.1423 for his bride, Anne, sister of the duke of Burgundy, as a wedding present; it was executed under the direction of Pol of Limburg. Bedford's motto is on the banner behind the kneeling duke. The duke's arms, supported by an eagle and an antelope, are in the margin beneath, and his emblem of the tree root and his motto appear in the margins. The book was given by Anne to Henry VI in 1431 on the occasion of his coronation in France.

to the 'true Lords of your noble blood', as did Thomas, Lord Lumley. Disputes over precedence often quoted in evidence nearness to the royal stock and entitlement to bear the royal arms. Noblemen took to commissioning illuminated royal pedigrees on to which their own lineages could be grafted (as did another of Henry VI's cousins, Henry Percy, earl of Northumberland). Royal kinsmen in the fifteenth century were even prepared to use their special blood as a standard of revolt against a royal minister or even against a king who was seemingly himself betraying the blood royal. In 1440 Humphrey, duke of Gloucester, the heir presumptive of his nephew, Henry VI, hit out at Cardinal Beaufort, who dominated the king's counsels and had 'estranged me your sole uncle, my cousin of York, my cousin of Huntingdon, and many other lords of your kin, to have any knowledge of any great matter'. A generation later, in 1469, Edward IV's brother George, duke of Clarence and Richard Neville, earl of Warwick, pointedly reminded Edward IV himself that those conspicuous failures as king, Edward II, Richard II, and Henry VI, had 'estranged the great lords of their blood from their secret Council, And [were] not advised by them; And taking about them other not of their blood, and inclining only to their counsel, rule and advice'. In the eyes of Clarence and Warwick, the welfare of the blood royal could be equated with the welfare of the king and the entire realm.

Even the most authoritative source of legal opinion drew a fine distinction between the blood royal and the rest of the English peerage. When Henry VI's kingship was challenged by Richard, duke of York in the autumn of 1460, the king's justices—who were admittedly nervous about expressing any opinion on the challenge—declared that 'they durst not enter into any communication thereof', for it 'pertained to the Lords of the King's blood, and the peerage of this his land, to have communication and meddle in such matters'.

All these people who portrayed the king's kinsmen as a distinct and superior élite did so for personal, sectional, or political reasons; yet during the fifteenth century the practice was common and well before 1500 it had entered the canon of English constitutional custom. Given the nature of a hierarchical society, we can be certain that it echoed what kings and their kinsmen themselves believed. The proliferation of noble styles and titles in fourteenth- and early fifteenth-century England served, amongst other things, to emphasize the special status of the blood royal. Jealous of the king of France, where the 'princes of the fleur-de-lis' were already a discrete company, Edward I took a significant step towards an English royal identity for the blood royal when, in 1301, he created his eldest surviving son the first English Prince of Wales with a princely patrimony—conquered Wales. It was a formal and high-sounding title henceforward reserved for the eldest son and heir of kings. Edward III took another important step when, in 1337, he created his eldest son the first duke in English history. During the next sixty years, twelve other dukes and one duchess were created, and all

THE PEERAGE

By origin, peers were the military companions and tenants-in-chief of the monarch. Greater definition of their position and privileges became necessary in the thirteenth century with the development of parliamentary institutions, and summons to the House of Lords was accepted as evidence of a peerage. In 1387, during the reign of Richard II, the first peerage by letters patent was created when John Beauchamp de Holt was made Baron Kidderminster. Though the peerage was always regarded as one of the pillars on which the crown rested, during the seventeenth and eighteenth centuries it was credited with a balancing role, preventing the constitution from sliding either into despotism or into anarchy. In 1707,

at the Act of Union with Scotland, a new British peerage was instituted, and changed in 1801, after the union with Ireland, into a peerage of the United Kingdom. In Victoria's reign, life peerages were granted to judges to enable the judicial work of the House of Lords to be carried on, but the institution of life peerages to other persons, to mitigate the party bias of hereditary peerage, was postponed until 1958. One result has been to give a new lease of life to the House of Lords, which probably stands higher in public esteem than at any time during the twentieth century. In the late 1980s, just under one-third of the House consists of life peers, though they take the greater share of the House's debates and business.

DUKE
The title was first reserved for members of the royal family, and though efforts to restrict it have failed, it has been sparingly granted. The first non-royal creations were by Richard II.

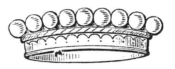

VISCOUNT
The title is derived from the Latin term *vice-comes*, responsible for a county. The first viscount in England, based on French example, was created by Henry VI in 1440.

MARQUESS
Taking its name from the custodianship of marches or borders, it was instituted after French example by Richard II in 1385 when Robert de Vere was created marquess of Dublin.

BARON
The title is of Norman origin. Formal recognition was first by summons to what became the House of Lords, but in 1387 Richard II granted a barony by letters patent to John Beauchamp de Holt as Baron Kidderminster. He did not live long to enjoy his new honour, being executed on Tower Hill in 1388.

BARONET
Baronetcy is a hereditary order of knighthood, founded in 1611 by James I to provide funds for the settlement of Ireland. The original intention not to exceed 200 was soon broken, and there were lavish creations, mainly to raise money, in the Stuart period. An order of Irish and of Scottish baronets was subsequently established, merged in 1707 into baronets of Great Britain, and in 1801 into baronets of the United Kingdom.

EARL
Derived from the Saxon and Danish office of responsibility for a shire, it is therefore, with baron, the oldest title.

HUMPHREY, DUKE OF GLOUCESTER, King Henry IV's youngest son who was protector of England for his nephew, Henry VI. He is shown kneeling at a prie-dieu before the risen Christ, and being presented probably by St David. This miniature illumination appears in the psalter which was made for Humphrey *c.*1415, when he was about twenty-five years old. His own cultural interests, especially through his contacts with Renaissance Italy, are well known. This book was part of his extensive library.

ROBERT III

(1390–1406), king of Scots

ROBERT laboured under three disadvantages. His father, Robert II, and his mother were unmarried when he was born, and legitimation in 1347 did not remove the stigma. His given name of John stirred so many unfortunate memories of kings (not only of John Balliol in Scotland) that on his accession he took the name of Robert III. And in 1388 he was so badly kicked by a horse that he was regarded as unfit to govern for his ineffectual father. Real power was exercised by his forceful brother Robert, earl of Fife and duke of Albany, but the realm slipped into disorder and justice was scarce. The king's eldest son David, duke of Rothesay, was lieutenant of Scotland from 1399 but quarrelled with Albany, who may have murdered him at Falkland (1402). English attacks made matters worse and the gentle monarch retired to the Isle of Bute and, perhaps for fear of Albany, sent his surviving son James to France (1406). James was captured at sea by the English; soon afterwards King Robert died, a pathetic failure.

had royal blood in their veins. Even by the time of Henry VIII's death in 1547, almost all the fifty-two dukedoms created in England had been for the benefit of the royal family—and that was no accident. Moreover, three of the six English noblemen granted the even newer title of marquess, which was initially borrowed from France by Richard II in 1385 and ranked higher than that of earl, were closely related to English kings. Thus, the diversification of the English peerage and the invention of its two senior titles were primarily designed to highlight the blood royal. The comparison with Scotland is meagre but not without interest: the first two dukes in Scottish history, created in 1398, were the sons of kings.

The precision given to the crime of treason pointed in the same direction and at roughly the same time. Edward III's statute of 1352 specifically protected the king, his queen, his eldest son and heir, his eldest daughter, and the wife of his eldest son. Case-law extended its scope to cover Richard II's uncles (1394) and Henry V's brothers (1414)—in other words, all the sons of a king who were then living. And in 1536 Henry VIII declared that even a king's sisters, aunts, and nieces merited special protection under the law of treason. Violation of the blood royal was evidently regarded as of a different order to assaults on any other subject.

The signs and tokens of royalty represented social and political realities in an age before the imperatives of democracy turned them into the picturesque and bizarre. In the chivalric age, the fashion for arms, 'the ensigns of nobility', was a matter of sufficient substance by the fifteenth century for the crown to attempt to control the granting and use of arms. Already the special place of at least the king's male kinsmen had been acknowledged when Edward III, at the outbreak of the Hundred Years War, allowed all his sons to bear the new royal arms of France and England quarterly. Richard II went further to elevate the royal stock in the public consciousness, applying a mind that was fascinated with heraldry and kingly dignity, and besotted with things French. In the 1390s he allowed the male descendants of Edward I, his own half-brothers (the Holands), and the illegitimate children (the Beauforts) of his uncle, John of Gaunt, to use the king's distinctive arms. And when he legitimized the bastard Beaufort children in 1397, Richard referred to them as 'our most dear kinsmen . . . sprung from royal stock'. Like many of Richard's actions, these were both novel and imaginative, designed to enhance his own majesty by honouring the blood royal in a peerage that could add lustre to the crown itself: 'the more we bestow honours on wise and honourable men, the more our crown is adorned with gems and precious stones', he declared on one occasion.

Under the Lancastrians, heraldry continued to mirror the special quality of the blood royal, and Cade's rebels in 1450 believed that Henry VI would be 'the Richest King Christian' if he drew his royal cousins about him. Even Edmund and Jasper Tudor, the sons of Owen Tudor and Katherine of Valois, adopted the royal arms when they were publicly recognized as Henry VI's half-brothers and created earls of Richmond and Pembroke in 1452. They might not be of the blood royal of England, strictly speaking, but they were regarded as members of the royal family and therefore entitled to bear the king's arms. The Yorkists went further still, and in 1474 Henry Stafford, duke of Buckingham, was allowed by the king's heralds to use the royal arms of his ancestor, Edward III's son, Thomas of Woodstock.

The formal style used by some of the closest royal kinsmen in the fifteenth century reflected the same reality. Self-conscious awareness of his position led Humphrey, duke of Gloucester to style himself in his formal letters and on his seal as 'son, brother and uncle of kings' during Henry VI's reign. And this pretentious style was copied by Henry VI's half-brother, Jasper Tudor, who described himself as 'the high and mighty prince, Jasper, brother and uncle of kings, duke of Bedford and earl of Pembroke', following the accession of Henry Tudor in 1485. To trumpet one royal relationship had not been uncommon in the past; to trumpet two or three exhibits the pride of a peacock.

This sensitivity towards the blood royal was sharpened by the rapid succession to the English throne of three cadet branches of the Plantagenets between 1399 and 1485, and it was illustrated by the names chosen for their sons and daughters by the kings of these lines. Of the Yorkists' eleven legitimate children, only two bore a name favoured by the Lancastrians, and that was the name of Edward the Confessor whom all medieval kings had venerated since at least Henry II's day. Likewise, Henry Tudor looked to his own antecedents when choosing names for his sons: Arthur, Henry, and Edmund. And although three of his daughters had names borne by Yorkist aunts (Margaret, Katherine, and Mary), these also commemorated three ladies of the Lancastrian past (including Henry's mother and grandmother). A sense of familiarity, strictly speaking, was present in earlier centuries, but in the fifteenth dynastic developments made it all the stronger. It was the Scandinavian and German connections of Stuart and especially Hanoverian kings that reduced commemorative royal nomenclature to the absurd by introducing double- and triple-barrelled Christian names, so that Charles Philip Arthur George had so many names that his bride got them in the wrong order when they exchanged their marriage vows in 1981!

Some of the reasons for the emergence of the royal family as a distinctive element in the English polity have already been noted. The compelling desire to emulate, rival, and ultimately surpass the French monarchy in reputation created the conviction from Richard II onwards that English kings were the 'Most Christian' kings on earth. To be supported by a blood royal, bearing novel titles of superior honour, lent added distinction to the monarch himself. Moreover, as we have seen, by the thirteenth century English kings ruled dominions beyond the borders of the realm whose common bond was the king's lordship. In an age when London and Westminster were developing as the settled capital of the kingdom and the permanent headquarters of royal government, ruling these dominions placed greater strain on the structures of a personal monarchy. Problems of administrative supervision and of asserting the royal presence could be partly solved by using an acknowledged and respected royal family. Apart from Richard II, no medieval English king visited Ireland after 1210; Edward I was the last king-duke to visit Gascony; few monarchs spent much time in Wales or on the wearisome task of subduing the Scots; and only Edward III and Henry V were prepared to commit themselves to lengthy stays in France. Instead, Edward III's second son Lionel was the first royal lieutenant of Ireland (1361) and he was created England's second duke to underline the significance of his mission. Jasper Tudor, newly created duke of Bedford, a royal title last borne by Henry IV's second son John, was Henry VII's lieutenant of Ireland (1486). Edward III's eldest, the Black Prince, became royal lieutenant in Gascony and so did his younger brother, John of Gaunt; and of the six royal lieutenants there in the fifteenth century, five were close relatives of kings. As for Wales, more than half the country was the patrimony of the Prince of Wales who, after 1301, was the king's eldest son and heir. The fact that few of the Princes of Wales reached manhood as princes emphasizes that it was their royal status, rather than their individual capabilities, which commended them as nominal rulers of the king's Welsh principality. In northern France, too, the blood royal was frequently preferred when the king himself could not cross the Channel to visit his conquered dominions. Even within the realm, the late medieval kings who adopted something akin to French methods of provincial (or apanage) government looked to their sons and kinsmen as their territorial agents: the Prince of Wales and the dukes of Lancaster in the fourteenth century; Richard, duke of

THE ARMORIAL BEARINGS AND BADGES OF FOUR FIFTEENTH-CENTURY KINGS OF ENGLAND—
Henry VI, Edward IV, Richard III, and Henry VII—from Prince Arthur's Book, compiled before 1519.
Each badge, with the arms of France and England quarterly framed by the Garter, is supported by the
crowned lion of England on one side and by the distinctive supporters of the individual kings on the
other—the hog for Richard III, the Welsh dragon for Henry VII. The bearings and coats of arms, too,
belong to the individual kings—St George's Cross to Henry VI, the sun in splendour to Edward IV and
Richard III. Such heraldic displays symbolized the honour and grandeur of kings; subjects adopted them
as expressions of loyalty.

Gloucester in the north under Edward IV; and the duke of Buckingham in Wales
and the west midlands under Richard III. To convey the royal will and substitute
for the royal presence when the king's responsibilities were now so broad, the
royal family was considered best.

The constitutional uncertainties and dynastic rivalries of the fifteenth century
also helped to give the blood royal a high public profile. Henry IV formally
announced in 1399 that he claimed Richard II's crown 'by right line of the Blood
coming from the good lord King Henry the third'. A few years later, Henry twice
declared in Parliament how the crown should pass to his eldest son and his heirs;
and should they fail, to each of Henry's other sons in turn and their respective

THE YORKIST ROYAL FAMILY in the stained glass of the north-west transept window of Canterbury Cathedral. Edward IV and his queen, Elizabeth Woodville, are flanked (*left*) by their sons Edward V and Richard, duke of York ('The Princes in the Tower'), and (*right*) by five daughters, led by the eldest, Elizabeth, who married Henry VII. Dating from *c*.1482, the window may be the design of William Neve, the royal glazier. The window was damaged by Puritans in 1643 and only the king and queen retain their original heads; one of the daughters' is in the Burrell Collection, Glasgow.

heirs—in short, to the royal blood of Lancaster. When this blood ran dangerously thin after the death, without legitimate heirs, of Henry V's three younger brothers, the sole surviving direct male descendant of Henry IV, his grandson Henry VI, took steps to emphasize the dignity of his remaining royal kinsmen, widening the circle of the blood royal to include even his Tudor half-brothers.

For the blood royal had its uses, especially in a turbulent age. English noblemen had often married royal princesses in the past, and Edward I's marital arrangements on behalf of three of his daughters brought political and material benefits to the crown at home. Another three were used to seal diplomatic and military alliances in the Low Countries as a defence against the French. Edward III's five surviving sons married wealthy English heiresses, though two of them later took brides in Spain and Italy. Both Edward IV and Henry VII were therefore behaving traditionally when they arranged royal marriages, though in Edward's case his own offspring were very young and instead he deployed his wife's children by her first marriage. Henry Tudor used, not his own daughters, but those of Edward IV to the same end: social and dynastic control and domestic stability.

In the later Middle Ages more substantial significance was attached to the blood royal than ever before, distinguishing those who had it from those who did not, raising the status of the royal kin within the nobility and emphasizing their value to the king and kingdom. In 1483 Parliament acknowledged this special breed when, for the first time, it banned the wearing of cloth of gold and purple silk except by the king and his queen, the king's mother, his children, and his brothers and sisters. Ironically, later that same year, Richard III reviled the Yorkist royal family and did his best to destroy it. He denounced Edward IV's queen and 'her blood adherents and affinity' for plotting the destruction of

HENRY V

(1413–1422), king of England

... the king himself, wearing a gown of purple, proceeded, not in exalted pride and with an imposing escort or impressively large retinue, but with an impassive countenance and at a dignified pace ... Indeed, from his quiet demeanour, gentle pace, and sober progress, it might have been gathered that the king ... was rendering thanks and glory to God alone, not to man.

(Henry V returning from Agincourt, from *The Deeds of Henry the Fifth*)

ELDEST son of Henry IV and his first wife, Mary Bohun, Henry renewed the Hundred Years War, occupied half of France, and became heir to the dual monarchy of France–England. A dour, stern man, intolerant of opposition and ruthless in pursuit of his ends, he was famed for his sense of justice and concern for rectitude (including in religion). Such qualities inspired respect and devotion, if not liking. Abroad he raised England's reputation to new heights a mere decade and a half after 1399. When his father was exiled (1398), Richard II took charge of Henry, knighted him, and possibly gained his affection. He was well educated and retained an interest in letters and music. As heir to the throne, he was created earl of Chester, duke of Cornwall, and Prince of Wales (1399), then duke of Aquitaine and Lancaster. He had military experience against Glyndŵr (1403–6), but his apprenticeship in politics offended his father over policy towards France (1410–11). The sobering effect of his accession was exaggerated by later writers. To begin with, he had to suppress rebellion and stamp his authority on the realm, rooting out Lollardy (1414–17) and crushing a conspiracy to unseat him in favour of the earl of March (1415). His plans to conquer France rested on Burgundy's alliance and naval power. With a united realm supporting and financing him, he attacked and garrisoned towns and castles in northern France, rather than conducted *chevauchées*; his victory at Agincourt (1415) was won by luck and skill in difficult circumstances. The story of French envoys presenting Henry with a gift of tennis balls was popularized after these victories to ridicule the humiliated French. The fall of Rouen (1419) completed the conquest of Normandy and Henry advanced into the heart of France and, with Burgundy's aid, forced Charles VI to a treaty at Troyes (1420): he was

THE PORTRAIT OF KING HENRY V from the National Portrait Gallery. It was painted *c*.1518–23 as part of a series of fifteenth-century English kings. It is the prototype from which later paintings of the king were derived. The hair-style and dress suggest that it is based on a contemporary likeness.

recognized as heir to the French throne and married Charles's daughter Katherine. The Emperor Sigismund visited England (1416) and he and Henry influenced the Council of Constance to end the Great Schism. He even vowed to go on crusade to the Holy Land when events in the West allowed. At the siege of Meaux (1422), Henry fell ill—perhaps of dysentery— and died at Vincennes. In view of the breadth of his ambitions, his reputation may have benefited from an early death.

himself, the duke of Buckingham, 'and the old royal blood of this realm'. Then, he impugned the legitimacy of his own brother, Edward IV, and his young nephews, Edward V and Richard, duke of York. Soon afterwards he stigmatized Henry Tudor's royal blood as bastard. Arguably it was these affronts to royalty that demolished Richard's own reputation and alienated his subjects. The very circumstances that had defined and elevated the blood royal of England, by the end of the fifteenth century had all but destroyed it: three branches of the Plantagenets perished in the Wars of the Roses. The *coup de grâce* was delivered in the sixteenth century by the failure of the Tudor monarchs—the result of chronic infertility, personal predilection, and political judgement—to do their marital duty.

The Machinery and Projection of Monarchy

The relationship between the crown and the provinces was direct and immediate in a kingdom such as England, which was relatively compact and well centralized. The annual appointment of sheriffs (with their financial, administrative, and judicial duties) and escheators (who were mainly concerned with the recovery of lands); the frequent nomination of justices of the peace and commissioners for a host of other tasks (their activities much extended from the mid-fourteenth century); and the installation of constables in royal castles scattered the length and breadth of the kingdom—all gave the king and his advisers an opportunity to influence and control events in town and countryside. They relied heavily on local lords, knights, esquires, and other worthies, many of whom also received fees from the royal household and were therefore a corps of dependable servants at the king's beck and call for all manner of purposes, both at the centre and in the provinces. There were also lawyers and courtiers who had little or no prior connection with the provincial offices to which they were appointed, yet their presence in the localities gave the crown confidence that its interests would be safeguarded. These were the very people who were elected to Parliament, and by the time of Edward II's dethronement in 1327 it was customary to summon commoners' representatives whenever a Parliament was held. After the Hundred Years War began in 1337, it was usual for the Commons and Lords to meet in Parliament at the heart of royal government in Westminster. By all such means, the king's influence in parts of his realm far from Westminster, London, and Windsor was reasonably assured.

The hub, focus, and fulcrum of English administration was the royal household in the king's court. The great departments of English government had evolved from small, unpretentious beginnings in the household of pre-Conquest days. The king's personal apartments had been transformed into the more public and less personalized offices of the Chancery (or secretariat), the Exchequer and the

AN ALTAR-PIECE, *c.*1505–9, PORTRAYING KING HENRY VII AND ELIZABETH OF YORK, with their children, the sons to the left (Arthur, Henry, and Edmund), the daughters to the right. They are shown kneeling before St George the dragon-slayer, England's patron saint. The royal tents are decorated with Tudor emblems, including the Beaufort portcullis and the double rose. The king is wearing a closed imperial crown.

Treasury, and the Privy (or private) Seal. These had gradually gone 'out of court' and become institutions of the state, leaving the household itself to cater mainly for the domestic needs of the king and his family. These institutions were complex and sophisticated in their organization, and by the later Middle Ages their staff was highly professional and specialized. These administrators worked in permanent offices at Westminster or in the city of London. They administered not only the English shires and towns, but also the king's dominions in the British Isles and overseas, and it is not too fanciful to regard them as civil servants.

PETER CHRISTUS'S PORTRAIT OF EDWARD GRIMSTON, one of Henry VI's servants and ambassador to the Low Countries. The portrait was painted probably in Bruges on an ambassadorial visit in 1446. The SS chain in his right hand symbolizes his Lancastrian service. This is the earliest known panel portrait of an English gentleman and perhaps the finest portrait of an Englishman painted before 1485.

In the latter half of the fourteenth century, the professional civil servant at Westminster and London began to change his character. For long a cleric and therefore literate, he might now be a married layman in a world where literacy was becoming more widespread. By 1430 the beneficed clergyman was the exception in the king's Exchequer and the financial departments of his household. The change took place more slowly in the Chancery, but there too laymen outnumbered clerical bureaucrats by about 1440.

They were all members of a highly trained profession, and many of them served Church and State, king and subject, town and noble estate: they travelled regularly from county to county, and from the capital to the provinces and the dominions. They had a distinctive contribution to make in English government and society. The growing role of the lay civil servant during the fifteenth century accentuated the differences between Church and State and between laymen and clerics. In some respects, it may have weakened the crown because laymen were a heavier burden on its financial resources and its reserves of patronage; perhaps, too, it tended to politicize the king's bureaucracy as laymen felt it prudent to court those who could reward them or had political power. On the other hand, the greater numbers of laymen may have strengthened the crown, for they were almost totally dependent for rewards on the king's generosity. When the Reformation was in the offing, the clerics' hold on the central administration had so loosened that Henry VIII could disregard the opinion of clergymen in the 1530s and be confident that many laymen would support his assault on the English Church.

This highly professional royal administration was largely responsible for the emergence in the fifteenth century of a standard written English that was popularized by the king's Chancery through its mass of letters, writs, and other documents. It amounted to an official written dialect sponsored by the king and capable of bringing uniformity and discipline to English government. Efforts were consciously made to ensure its use as the language of administration even in dominions such as Ireland, Wales, and Calais, where other languages were spoken and written. It was an instrument for tighter royal control and would be used to great effect by the early Tudor kings. At the same time, it helped to make the monarchy and its administrative machine the focus of an increasingly self-conscious and united English nation.

As for the bureaucrats themselves, who moved easily between the offices of the king and the state and those of private institutions and individuals, their activities are likely to have softened personal animosities and promoted co-operation and understanding between the king and his subjects. In such circumstances, they were an aid to political cohesion in the kingdom and in the dominions too.

In the provinces of the realm and the royal dominions the king's local agents formed a much more 'amateur' corps of administrators: men (almost never women) who conducted enquiries, made surveys and assessments, collected taxes, arrayed armed forces, served on juries, and even acted as justices. They served the king for little or no financial reward, but rather out of a sense of obligation to him; though it also suited their purpose to do so because service attracted patronage and favours and offered opportunities for advancement and influence. These were loyal subjects doing their duty, rather than professional bureaucrats, and on their co-operation the effectiveness of English government and royal rule depended hundreds of miles from Westminster. In a country where close and co-operative relations between king and nobility were of the first importance, many of these knights, esquires, gentlemen, merchants, and townsmen were the links between the administrations and bureaucracies of the crown and those of private individuals and institutions, whether nobles or bishops, monasteries, or town councils.

The immense private domains owned by Henry IV (of Lancaster) and Edward IV (of York) at the time they seized the crown gave a new dimension to the royal estate; and Henry Tudor acquired all of these domains in 1485. Many servants and administrators were thereby able to move from the offices of nobles who were now kings into the public departments of the crown in all parts of the realm. The royal family and its extensive estates were also at the monarch's disposal, for 'A well-endowed royal family was an essential attribute of effective kingship' (B. P. Wolffe). The Prince of Wales had great authority and vast lands in distant parts—Cornwall and Chester, not to speak of Wales itself—which were often less amenable to the wishes of Westminster than shires closer to hand. And a well-stocked family such as Edward III's and Henry IV's could be expected to buttress the practical power of the crown where their lands and interests were predominant. Even more valuable in this respect was the queenly estate. The domestic and estate organizations of English queens were an extension of the king's household and court; yet included in the dowers of queens were broad acres situated in many parts of the country, whilst an English-born queen such as Anne Neville was also a considerable heiress in her own right, with private resources to place at the disposal of her husband, Richard III. Some queens, such as Margaret of Anjou and Elizabeth of York, travelled especially widely, taking the face of majesty where the king might never go; others, such as Elizabeth Woodville, took a close interest in the management of their estates and affairs; and yet others, such as Queen Margaret in the late 1450s, energetically exploited the regional influence which their position and lands afforded them.

There was a marked community of development between medieval England and its dominions in terms of administration. English kings had an approach to government in their subject lands which, taking due account of differing time-scales, the vitality of local customs and institutions, and the degree of English

IRISH REVENUE OFFICERS AND THEIR
DISTRAUGHT CLIENTS around a
chequered cloth or exchequer, on
which counters were moved as a mode
of calculation. The drawing is in a
fifteenth-century accounts book. The
Irish Exchequer was modelled on
Westminster's and, like its English
counterpart, it authorized receipts and
disbursements of royal revenue every
year.

infiltration, was remarkably consistent. After all, when Edward I tried to subject
Scotland to English overlordship, it was little more than a century since Henry II
had first launched his conquest of Ireland (1172), less than seventy-five years
since Chester had been absorbed (1237), and less than twenty years since the
principality of Wales had fallen into the king's hands (1282–3). The king's
response to each situation was similar, and on each occasion he added to his store
of governmental knowledge and experience. The English regime in southern
Scotland in the generation after 1296 illustrates some of the lessons in government that had been learnt in England, Ireland, and Wales in the previous
century.

Based at Berwick, this regime was headed by a royal lieutenant, a chancellor,
and a treasurer according to a pattern generally familiar elsewhere. For more
local purposes, the English inevitably relied on existing Scottish arrangements,
but in any case these owed much to Anglo-Norman example: sheriffdoms now
covered much of Scotland, though only in the early sixteenth century were they
introduced in the far north and the Highlands, and in the Western Isles. It is true
that the dynastic and military crises of fourteenth-century Scotland enabled
Scottish nobles to enlarge their estates and usurp regional authority, but in the

JAMES I

(1406–1437), king of Scots

That firm and sure peace be kept and held throughout the realm among all subjects of the king; and if any man presume to make war against another, he shall suffer the full penalties of the law.

(Enactments of Parliament, 1424)

Son and heir of Robert III, James was sent to France by his father (1406), probably to escape the duke of Albany's clutches; but he was captured on the way. His honourable captivity in England (1406–24) was the most influential period in his life. Albany (d. 1420) was not eager for his return, and the English used him in France (1420–1) to discourage Scots from serving in the French armies. He was well educated at the English court, where he wrote *The Kingis Quair*, which ranks him among major Scottish poets; no English (or Scottish) king had achieved such literary distinction since Alfred—but then none had as much available time. The heroine of the romance is Joan Beaufort, Henry V's kinswoman whom James married (1424). At the same time, the king's release was negotiated in return for a £40,000 ransom. James proved a harsh, even vindictive, king who was determined to curb the nobles even in the Highlands, and especially his rivals descended from Robert II. He arrested some, executed a few (including the new duke of Albany), and confiscated estates. He consolidated the royal resources, imposed heavy taxation, bled the Church (despite papal protests), and provided peace. Abuses in government were corrected, justice improved, and James showed genuine concern for his subjects as a whole. Still, some nobles resented him, and in 1437 a group led by the earl of Atholl assassinated him at Perth. His body was buried nearby in the Carthusian monastery which he had founded (1429).

PORTRAIT OF JAMES I, the poet-king. This is one of a series of portraits of the first five Jameses, painted in the sixteenth century by an unidentified painter. It is thought to be based on an earlier portrait now lost. A similar series was commissioned of English kings.

fifteenth century many of these nobles were mastered and their estates confiscated; with greater resources and dynastic stability under the Stuart kings, royal authority was reasserted. At the same time, Edinburgh (and Holyrood) became the favourite residence of Scottish kings. Scone retained its traditional role as the ceremonial focus of Scottish kingship, but the geographical position and commercial wealth of Edinburgh meant that it was slowly emerging as a governmental capital akin to London and Westminster.

English kings and their advisers sought to disseminate their views widely in town and country; and, in a society where sedition often bred violence, they tried to correct rumour and falsehood wherever they flourished. It took about a week to travel from Newcastle upon Tyne to London, and almost as long for the royal messenger service to carry the news of Edward IV's death at Westminster to his son, the Prince of Wales, at Ludlow. Meanwhile, unfounded or malicious rumour could attempt its insidious worst. Thus, in the later Middle Ages, effective channels of communication were essential for effective government by a monarchy whose headquarters were in the far south-east. Traditional and novel methods—administrative, parliamentary, and other—were used to disseminate news and official views throughout the realm. In the political crises of the fourteenth and fifteenth centuries, the rulers of England appreciated in particular the value of education and literacy in shaping popular opinion; and the Yorkists were especially skilled at circulating newsletters and propaganda against their Lancastrian enemies during the Wars of the Roses.

Co-operation between king and subject, centre and provinces, was vital for defence. It was the time-honoured duty of the king's subjects to provide military service in defence of the king and the realm when required—a duty which went back beyond the Anglo-Saxon *fyrd*—and to assist in the preservation of law and order. In the later Middle Ages, protection of the ports and coastline was a responsibility that naturally fell on those who lived in the 'maritime land', and it became a matter of urgency during the 1370s and 1380s, and again in the 1440s, when England was repeatedly attacked by the French and their allies. This system of defence was capable of adaptation, experiment, and reform, with the result that it remained intact until Tudor times. As a co-operative enterprise, it worked well. So did the system of raising armies for the defence of England and English interests abroad. The feudal array of knights and their followers had always been supplemented by shire levies and paid recruits. From Edward I's reign, when England was a society almost perpetually at war, the system was transformed so that it relied more heavily on paid and indentured forces, professional to a degree and provided by the nobles and lesser landowners, whose co-operation in the king's military ventures was still essential for success.

The king's obligation to offer justice to every subject, through the central courts of King's Bench and Common Pleas, which were eventually settled at Westminster by the fifteenth century, and through commissions of lawyers and landowners nominated in each county, was beginning to show signs of strain. The political instability of the fifteenth century was matched by a legal system that was now impeded by the complexities of the law and legal procedures that were the growth of centuries. The distance of counties such as Herefordshire and Cornwall from Westminster, and the proximity of some counties to the turbulent Scottish border and the Welsh marcher lordships were further obstacles to the effective-

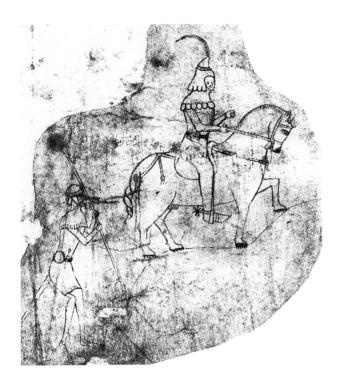

A MOUNTED KING'S MESSENGER, a large plume in his hat, and his more elderly runner carrying a staff and armed with a sword and dagger for his protection, as they travel up hill and down dale conveying the king's instructions. This sketch is from a book of messengers' expenses of c.1360.

ness of the central courts; while Cheshire, Lancashire, and the county of Durham retained the independent jurisdiction that made them 'palatine' counties outside the customary shire system, even though the earldom of Chester and the duchy of Lancaster (at least) were vested in the crown by the fifteenth century. Attempts were made by Edward IV and especially by Henry VII to remedy this state of affairs, and they culminated in Henry VIII's decision to abolish independent franchises and palatinates in 1536, and to unite England and Wales in 1536–43.

Some English noblemen and gentry were less co-operative in upholding the law than their obligations and their role as local officials and commissioners demanded. This was all too apparent when the monarchy itself was engulfed by civil strife in the Wars of the Roses. Some felt that they were victimized and excluded from local positions of influence; others resorted to self-help in resolving disputes rather than endure the frustrations of the law; and some were outraged when kings such as Henry VI and Richard III behaved in a partisan fashion. For a time, especially between 1450 and 1485, the English monarchy appeared to be failing in its duty to offer equitable justice to all the king's subjects and to ensure security and peace throughout the realm.

Those factors which in the past had forged links between the king and his subjects—ties of landholding, the obligations of a feudal society, and traditional military service—were less compelling in the later Middle Ages. Relationships now depended very largely on mutual interest and the readiness to give and receive patronage. Since the king was the greatest and wealthiest patron of all,

A DAY'S BUSINESS IN THE COURT OF KING'S BENCH, which emerged in Henry II's reign and became the senior court of common law. By 1420 it ceased to travel about the country and met permanently in the Great Hall at Westminster. Beneath the royal arms five justices are shown presiding. Below them around the green covered table are the officers of the court, including clerks writing the rolls; of the two ushers with staves, one is administering an oath. The prisoners are marshalled in chains, to appear in turn at the bar of the court.

with the largest resources of all, he had the best means of creating and sustaining such relationships in the service of the monarchy. There was a danger that personal and sectional interests might be preferred by foolish or wilful kings— such as Henry VI who favoured his household servants above all others, or Edward IV who relied on his noble friends—at the expense of the crown's wider needs. The king's lordship had not only to be 'good' but it had to be circumspect and catholic: it was not an easy balance to strike.

HENRY VI

(1422–1461, 1470–1471), king of England

He was tall in stature, and had a slender body, to which his limbs were all in correct proportion. His face was handsome, and continually shone with that goodness of heart with which he was abundantly endowed.

(Polydore Vergil, *English History*)

THE PORTRAIT OF KING HENRY VI from the Royal Collection. It was painted *c*.1518–23 as one of a series of portraits of English kings. Dress (and an original tall hat since obscured) suggests that it was based on a lost contemporary panel portrait of *c*.1450–61. Henry is shown wearing the Lancastrian SS collar, denoting attachment to the dynasty.

ENRY is one of England's most enigmatic kings. Yorkists belittled his abilities and Tudors sought to make him a saint. His mental collapse (1453–5) and deterioration led historians to judge him unfairly by the yardstick of his later years. Rather was he pious, educated, well intentioned, and compassionate, but lacking shrewdness, foresight, and calculation. After a long minority (1422–36), when he was brought up by his mother, Queen Katherine, and dominated by his quarrelsome uncles, Cardinal Beaufort and Humphrey, duke of Gloucester, he was an active ruler during 1436–53. The heritage of Henry IV and Henry V sat uneasily on his shoulders. Dynastic insecurity resurfaced when his marriage to Margaret of Anjou (1445) failed to produce offspring (until 1453); Henry turned to the Beauforts as possible heirs to the throne. The French war and the dual monarchy were beyond England's capacity to sustain and Henry tried radical ways, including surrendering territory and releasing prisoners, to arrange peace—which was unpopular with most. His indulgence towards friends and servants, and his lack of interest in administration alienated powerful nobles; his reliance on the dukes of Suffolk (to 1450) and Somerset (to 1455) angered Richard, duke of York. Yet his imaginative educational and religious ventures— Eton and King's College, Cambridge—reveal clear gifts. By 1450 nobles, commons, and soldiers in France were disgruntled: Cade's rebellion and York's demands for reform caused him to panic. His illness (1453) threw court and country into confusion and civil war (1455). He was wounded at St Albans (May 1455) and thereafter Queen Margaret controlled him and his government in defiant mood. In 1460 he was captured at Northampton by York's allies and forced to accept York as his heir, though when Warwick was defeated at St Albans (1461) Henry was reunited with his wife and son Edward. York's son, Edward, took the throne and Henry and his family fled to Scotland. Captured on a foray in northern England (1465), he was imprisoned by Edward IV in the Tower, only to be brought out, a cypher, and recrowned in 1470. The end came when his son was killed and his queen was defeated at Tewkesbury (1471), for Edward had Henry murdered soon after. His cult now grew. Buried at Chertsey Abbey, Richard III transferred the body to Windsor (1484), perhaps to exploit the king's posthumous popularity. After 1485 his saintly reputation was enhanced by Henry VII, who used it to buttress the Tudor dynasty and persuade the pope to canonize him—without success. A not unattractive figure, he lacked the qualities to manage an awesome inheritance.

English kings and their protagonists were eager to demonstrate and justify the distinctive character of the monarchy—and its superiority over other monarchies, especially those of France and Scotland. They did so gradually, subtly, and not always consciously, by creating a myth focused on the monarchy, elements of which can still be detected today. It was widely accepted that the English monarchy had an ancestry that was at once ancient British and Roman imperial, the two fusing in the person of the Emperor Constantine who, it was alleged, had been born at York of a British mother, whose own forebears had sprung from Brutus, grandson of Aeneas of Troy. From the same line descended the heroic Arthur, who had ruled all Britain, including England, and had attempted to save it from barbarian hordes at the beginning of the Dark Ages. This was the most popular and compelling historical saga current in England (and Wales) after Geoffrey of Monmouth wrote his book, *The History of the Kings of Britain*, about 1130.

Such fabulous stories about the antique origins of kingship in England were admittedly under fire in some quarters, not least from the pen of the Italian historian, Polydore Vergil, whom Henry VII commissioned to write a history of England and its kings; but these stories still had their vigorous champions in the sixteenth century. However, more reliable material was available with which to buttress the English royal myth: there were distinguished Anglo-Saxon predecessors whom kings from the twelfth century onwards were eager to claim among their venerable forebears once the immediate post-Conquest generations had passed. By the time of Henry III, Anglo-Saxon saints and rulers were being venerated, and the king's father, John, was attracted by the Anglo-Saxon saints resting at Worcester, among whom he asked to be buried. After the death of Henry III Westminster Abbey, the shrine of St Edward and the coronation seat of English kings, came to rival the French royal mausoleum at Saint-Denis. Henry's successors continued to favour Anglo-Saxons, and no one was more fascinated by King Arthur than Edward I. Henry VI wanted to have King Alfred canonized, not for his gallant culinary efforts but to celebrate his religious and educational accomplishments, which Henry VI sought to emulate. Henry himself had a vigorous posthumous cult within a few years of his death. It was harnessed by Richard III and especially by Henry VII and Henry VIII, before the campaign to have him canonized foundered in the stormy seas of Reformation politics.

To set off such worthies many monarchies have a scapegoat: Richard III is England's. Richard is one of the most persistently vilified of English kings, surpassing even King John. He is the only crowned king of England since Stephen not to have a surviving tomb; the modest grave provided by his supplanter, Henry VII, in the Grey Friars Church at Leicester, was destroyed in the sixteenth century and Richard's bones cast out and lost for ever. He was, too, the first English king since 1066 to be defeated and slain in battle—itself a sure sign to

THE CROWNED HEAD OF KING RICHARD III, who is pictured in this early sixteenth-century wood-carving on a misericord in Christchurch Priory church, Dorset, holding a sceptre. It also suggests the deformed hunchback of early Tudor invention—though Richard may indeed have had irregular shoulders.

contemporaries that God was prepared to disown a wrongfully anointed king. Henry VII made sure that this message was proclaimed loud and clear. Richard, too, is the only English king to cause such delusions among later generations as to inspire violent and evil acts, even in our own day. In January 1835 the first attempt was made to assassinate an American President, Andrew Jackson. As the President prepared to leave the Capitol in Washington, a figure six feet away drew two pistols and fired point-blank. The reports echoed deafeningly in the famous rotunda, but both pistols had misfired. The would-be assassin, Richard Laurence, was subdued with the help of none other than Davy Crockett. Laurence claimed at his trial that he was Richard III and the rightful king of England. He was declared insane and consigned to an asylum for life. In 1835, Richard III still seemed the embodiment of evil, whose designs were foiled by what contemporary newspapers regarded as God's protective hand; this seemed to be proved by a small-arms expert, who concluded that the odds on two pistols misfiring within seconds of one another was 125,000 : 1. More tragic still was the report just a few years ago of a young Briton who murdered his fiancée because he, too, thought he was Richard III. This durable myth of Richard, the Royal Beast, was carefully cultivated as an essential element of the English royal myth by the ruthless, quarter-Welsh Tudor monarchs, who posed as God's chosen instruments. Their aim was to convince a nation that, after Richard's short and violent rule, the sunny uplands of Tudor England had been reached and the glorious progress of the ancient British monarchy could resume.

One reason for the development of such a myth lay across the Channel in France, and it gathered force from the later twelfth century onwards. The antique myth of England and its monarchy was pitted directly against somewhat earlier but similar French claims. At the council of the Church held at Constance in 1414, the English representatives maintained that England was 'not inferior to the realm of France in antiquity or authority'. They pointed to the antiquity of English Christianity, introduced (they insisted) by Joseph of Arimathea, who had taken the crucified Christ from the Cross. If true, the English claim was unassailably superior to Frenchmen's veneration of a mere St Denis. It was stated that England

is superior in the antiquity of its faith, dignity and honour and at least equal in all the divine gifts of regal power and numbers and wealth of clergy and people. During the second age of the world, the excellent royal house of England arose and it continues in real existence to this date. Among many holy palmers whom it has produced and whom none cannot here well enumerate, there are St. Helen and her son, the Emperor Constantine the Great, born in the royal city of York. They rescued many lands from the infidels and brought the Lord's Cross in faith from the country of infidels to Christian lands.

The English, too, were secure in their belief that their kings had championed the pope in Rome during the Great Schism of the Church (1378–1417), when most Frenchmen had given their support to the rival pope at Avignon.

The most potent royal house of England has never departed from obedience to the Roman Church but has always fought under it in Christian fashion.

An uninterrupted devotion to the faith from its very beginnings was a major justification for English pride in its monarchy and its superiority over all other peoples. The fact that at the very next council of the Church, meeting at Basle in 1436, the Spanish bishop of Burgos was able to explode the myth of Joseph of Arimathea's extensive travels did not impress Englishmen or their kings.

The English saga also had to contend with a Scottish myth which claimed for the Scots and their kings an origin that was even more antique and whose Christian associations were just as venerable. We do not know when it was first formulated, though poets had rehearsed the descent of Scottish kings at royal inaugurations long before the thirteenth century. The Wars of Independence gave this myth more urgent purpose and a wider popularity. It was the opening blast of the Declaration of Arbroath in 1320:

. . . we gather from the deeds and books of the ancients, that among other distinguished nations our own nation, namely of Scots, has been marked by many distinctions. It journeyed from Greater Scythia by the Tyrrhenian Sea and the Pillars of Hercules, and dwelt for a long span of time in Spain among the most savage peoples, but nowhere could it be subjugated by any people, however barbarous. From there it came, twelve hundred years after the people of Israel crossed the Red Sea and, having first driven out the

JAMES II

(1437–1460), king of Scots

ONE of the most distinctive of kings, his large birthmark earned him the description 'of the fiery face'. The only surviving son of James I and Queen Joan, his coronation (at Holyrood, 1437) was the first inauguration of a Scottish king since Kenneth mac Alpin not to take place at Scone. Holyrood was his favourite seat, the scene of his marriage and burial. James's minority was marred by the struggles of rival families for power in the realm and control of the king. Later, especially after marrying (1449) the able and cultivated Mary of Gueldres, he exerted his authority throughout the kingdom, not least by his own extensive travels. He sought to control the nobles, but relations with the powerful Douglases remained uneasy: only after he himself had stabbed the earl to death (1452) was he able to break their power. His resolute government, based on financial resources augmented by noble confiscations, was admired. But his international forays were unwisely belligerent: his demands of the king of Norway were high-handed, and his attempts to seize English border posts, taking advantage of the Wars of the Roses, came to grief at Roxburgh, where James was killed when a cannon near which he was standing exploded (1460).

KING JAMES II, *c*.1460, the only known contemporary portrait, from the diary of a German noble, Jörg von Ehingen, whose travels took him to James's court in 1458. In his youth, Jörg had served James's sister, the wife of Duke Sigismund of Tyrol. The king's facial birthmark is prominently shown.

Britons and altogether destroyed the Picts, it acquired, with many victories and untold efforts, the places which it now holds . . . As the histories of old time bear witness, it has held them free of all servitude ever since. In their kingdom one hundred and thirteen kings of their own royal stock have reigned, the line unbroken by a single foreigner. Their high qualities and merits, if they were not otherwise manifest, shine out sufficiently from this: that . . . our lord Jesus Christ, after his passion and resurrection, called them . . . almost the first to his holy faith. Nor did he wish to confirm them in that faith by anyone but by the first apostle by calling . . . namely the most gentle Andrew, the blessed Peter's brother, whom he wished to protect them as their patron for ever.

The English disdained such lofty pretensions, and the quality of their laws, customs, and methods of royal governance persuaded them that they were justified in doing so. In the mid-fifteenth century, Sir John Fortescue reflected enthusiastically on English institutions in his book, *In Praise of the Laws of England*. He declared them to be far superior to all others, especially those of France. 'There is no gainsaying nor legitimate doubt but that the customs of England are not only good but the best'; and, he added, in accordance with the English myth, this was partly because they were rooted in antiquity. He went further: he equated English law and royal government with the law of nature and, more significantly, with the law of God. England, therefore, was the 'mightiest and most wealthy realm of the world'—a world which, for all the temporary difficulties in which individual kings found themselves, was England's oyster.

England's fortunes in the Hundred Years War, notably its resounding victories over the French and Scots, seemed to confirm the primacy of her kings. The favour of the Almighty, as exemplified by such successes as Crécy (1346), Neville's Cross (1346), Poitiers (1356), and Agincourt (1415), demonstrated to Englishmen—and others were persuaded too—that God was on the side of England and its kings, and that their triumphs were the triumphs of justice. Nor was this conviction confined to kings and courts. Popular songs and poems made the same point. Christ protected the English and their leaders in battle, most obviously when, as at Crécy and Agincourt, and at Neville's Cross against the Scots, the English few were pitted against the hostile many. Even when Edward III suffered embarrassing reverses, the popular mind regarded these as mere temporary set-backs, confident in the knowledge that, like the sinful David, Edward would be punished but not destroyed—in contrast to the French, whose sins were monstrous and their consequent misfortunes crushing.

It has recently been suggested that 'the nationality of God was a touchstone of European nationalism' (J. W. McKenna). If that were so, then in the later Middle Ages God was an Englishman and English kings their most favoured representatives on earth. They certainly claimed to be so. This attitude sprang initially from royal propaganda aimed at undermining the special claims which French monarchs made on God's favour, claims which popes had supported before 1200. Their political ideology embraced sacred kingship and the unique piety of the French people; it seemed to be proved by the wizardry of their kings in performing miraculous cures, by the sacred oil given to their ancestor Clovis for use at French coronations, and by the sacred insignia of the fleur-de-lis and the war banner of the oriflamme; and it was acknowledged most recently and publicly in 1311, at the beginning of the papal residence at Avignon, when the pope gave Philip IV the unique title of 'Most Christian King'. The French were compared to the people of Israel, 'a peculiar people chosen by the Lord to carry out the orders of Heaven', and their king was therefore God's superior instrument.

This was a political ideology that later medieval English kings could not abide, especially during the Hundred Years War. As a result, they consciously sought to match the special qualities the French claimed: from the later twelfth century onwards, they identified venerable figures among the pantheon of Anglo-Saxon and English saints and monarchs; Westminster Abbey became the shrine of English kingship from Henry III's reign; scrofula, epilepsy, and other spasms were cured by the royal touch, probably from Henry II's reign; and in the early fourteenth century it was discovered that Thomas Becket, 150 years before, had acquired holy oil from the Virgin Mary—a more sublime and reliable messenger than Clovis—for use at English coronations. English pretensions to divinity were carefully nurtured and the successes in the Hundred Years War seemed to vindicate them. When, after 1337, Edward III claimed the French crown through his mother, Isabella of France, daughter of King Philip IV, it was likened to Jesus's descent from the house of David. When he introduced new coins as king of England and France after 1340, the snooty motto read 'Jesus, passing through the midst of them, went his way'. And when Parliament met in 1377, immediately after the great Edward's death, the Chancellor was quite explicit:

God would never have honoured this land in the same way as He did Israel through great victories over their enemies, if it were not that He had chosen it as His heritage.

It was powerful propaganda, all the more necessary since England's military fortunes had been on the wane for a decade and more. During the Great Schism in the Church after 1378, it was the English and their kings who were authorized to lead crusades in Flanders and Spain against supporters of the anti-pope in Avignon. They were portrayed as the new Israelites and England as the new Jerusalem—convictions they have never entirely abandoned.

Henry V's reign confirmed that all this was so. In popular propaganda, the great Harry appeared as the 'true elect of God', the celestial warrior. His baby son and successor, Henry VI, was likened to the Christ-child as the saviour of his and God's kingdom; his people were 'that special tribe the English' whose king was 'over all other Christian kings'. Now that Henry V and his successors were also claiming to be kings of France, it was logical to follow Richard II's example and adopt the title 'Most Christian King', which brooked no competitor, not even the French monarch. By 1440, when he received the pope's gift of the Golden Rose, Henry VI was spoken of as 'Most Christian of Christian Kings', even as 'Most Christian and most gracious Prince, our most dread sovereign lord'. Henry VII, whom popes flattered with as many as three Blessed Swords and Hats, used the same style half a century later: when Caxton printed a book for him in 1489, he was addressed as 'the highest and most Christian king and prince of all the world'. What eluded the English was the papal approval long ago accorded to French monarchs. Spurred on by the conferral on the new Spanish king and

EDWARD III INTRODUCED A GOLD COINAGE, in the 1340s, and the design of this splendid gold noble (1348 onwards) publicized the king as commander of the Ship of State. The obverse (*left*) shows Edward brandishing a sword and holding a shield charged with the quartered arms of England and France, which represented his claim to be king of both realms (from 1340). With Edward standing in a twin-castled ship, the coin also perpetuates memories of his sea victory at Sluys (1340) and the description of 'King of the Sea' in which he gloried. On the reverse (*right*), the Christian symbol is interwoven with crowns, English lions and French fleur-de-lis; the motto invokes the New Testament and the name of Jesus as sanction for his grandiose pretensions. (approx. × 2)

queen of the title 'Catholic Majesties', Henry VIII tried to blackmail the pope to secure the title he wanted, but it was not until 1521 that he obtained recognition of the 200-year-old special relationship between God and the English king: the title 'Defender of the Faith', which British monarchs use to this day. This ideology gave England and its later medieval kings parity with, and eventual superiority over, all monarchies of the West, and it encompassed king and nation indivisibly. A young German student, visiting England for the first time in the mid-sixteenth century, noted that good English was spoken only in England, which he described as 'God's heavenly realm'; the English themselves seemed to be 'the blessed and the chosen of God'.

Justification and vindication were just as important at the end of the Middle Ages as they had been in creating the myth of the superior English monarchy; this myth was now extended to encompass the inhabitants of the dominions as well. The king's independent authority that was the later medieval 'empire' of England was accordingly regarded as embracing his far-flung dominions too. A supporting and persuasive myth was popularized by the publicists of the English monarchy. It was based on the legends of a British past, in which Arthur and his predecessors ruled far broader acres than England. British histories and prophecies made lively reading in Wales and Scotland in the later Middle Ages, especially when they reproached the English as descendants of invading Saxons. Yet Edward I, conqueror of the Welsh and 'Hammer of the Scots', showed deep

HENRY VI (*right*), KING AND SAINT, as portrayed on the wooden screen (*c.*1500) of St Catherine's Church, Ludham, Norfolk. Henry is shown with a halo, as well as orb, sceptre, and the closed crown of England. He stands beside the East Anglian saint-king, Edmund, to whom he was closely attached. Such representations of Henry were common at the end of the fifteenth century and reflect Henry VII's efforts to exploit the growing veneration of his step-uncle in order to legitimize and strengthen the new Tudor dynasty.

interest in Arthur as king of Britain, and later English kings proclaimed their descent from the self-same British rulers and appropriated their supposed rights in the British Isles. On occasion, Arthur was portrayed as symbolizing the English 'empire', and Arthurian romance and Brutus legends were popular long before Caxton printed them in the late fifteenth century. They were celebrated in Edward I's reign by a Yorkshire chronicler, who at the same time lauded the achievements of Edward, 'the long shanks':

> Now are the islanders all joined together,
> And Albany [Scotland] reunited to the royalties
> Of which King Edward is proclaimed lord.
> Cornwall and Wales are in his power,
> And Ireland the great at his will.
> There is neither king nor prince of all the countries
> Except King Edward, who has thus united them;
> Arthur had never the fiefs so fully.
>
> (*Chronicle of Peter Langtoft*, 1297)

English and foreign observers referred to 'the island of England', even 'the British island of England', and 'Great Britain' appeared in the official vocabulary of Edward IV and Richard III, well before England became Shakespeare's 'scept'red isle'. Arthur was the imperial forebear of English emperors and his British realm was now reconstituted as the English 'empire'. Determined to make England the best of European nations, later medieval Englishmen and their kings had at the same time taken a significant step towards creating a single British monarchy with a far more ambitious future.

The buildings built by kings, the literary and decorative arts commissioned by kings, and the *objets d'art* collected by kings, these were the visual reflection of monarchy, and they played a larger role in projecting it in the later Middle Ages than at any time in the past, with the possible exception of Alfred's reign. It is not simply that more examples of the cultural patronage of kings survive from these centuries; rather did English kings from Henry III onwards have a keener and fuller appreciation of the value of such patronage in impressing the distinctive, English character of their monarchy on the world at large. Their patronage had a solid utilitarian, as well as an aesthetic, foundation.

Henry III, and probably Richard II, had an unusually refined cultural sense and aesthetic taste. In Henry's case, it is best displayed in the colourful and elaborate schemes of decoration which he ordered for his greatest architectural enterprise, the enlarging of Westminster Abbey; there, the sculptures, statuary, tiles, and mosaics bear the impress of his rich imagination. His passion for collecting jewels, relics, and paintings also testifies to his sophisticated taste. King

JAMES III

(1460–1488), king of Scots

LIKE his father, James was not crowned at Scone, but at Kelso Abbey (1460). His long minority was inevitably troubled by unstable relations with England, and dissident and ambitious nobles. At first, Queen Mary (d. 1463) and Bishop Kennedy of St Andrews (d. 1465) ruled for him; then a group of nobles tried to control him (from 1466). Meanwhile, Edward IV urged the expulsion of Lancastrian exiles from Scotland and even plotted (1462) the partition of Scotland with opposition nobles to gain his ends; a truce was sealed in 1463 to Edward's satisfaction. When James asserted his own authority (1469), he faced great difficulties in restoring strong central government. He was cavalier in his treatment of the nobles, and accused his brothers, Albany and Mar, of treason (1479); Albany fled to England, where Edward regarded him as Alexander IV and put him at the head of an invasion force (1482). James's interest in intellectual, artistic, and religious matters was shared by friends whom he advanced unwisely and who therefore alienated the nobles. Under the strain of war, in 1482 several of these favourites were hanged. Another noble rising in 1488 in the borderland secured the support of James's son and heir, and at Sauchieburn, near Stirling, the king was captured and murdered; he was buried at Cambuskenneth Abbey. James was intelligent but not wise, taking too high a view of his kingly office and paying too little regard to the arts of political management.

AN ALTARPIECE OR TRIPTYCH OF HUGO VAN DER GOES. The inner side of the left panel shows James III and, probably, his son, later James IV; the king is being crowned by St Andrew, Scotland's patron saint, and the red lion badge of Scottish kings is surmounted by a helm. The inner side of the right panel shows James's queen, Margaret of Denmark, at prayer with St George. Whereas the saints are Hugo's work, the royal figures are probably not. The panels were commissioned for the collegiate church of the Holy Trinity, Edinburgh, c.1480, and the donor, Sir Edward Bonkil, provost of Trinity College, appears on the outer side of the left panel. As a painted altarpiece with royal portraits, it has no surviving parallel in fifteenth-century England.

CULTURAL PATRONAGE BY THE MEDIEVAL MONARCHY

IN the Middle Ages art was not an end in itself nor simply an expression of social values. Kings and courts fostered literature and art, architecture, music and science, as did their wealthy subjects; but always with a broader public purpose in mind. Welsh and Irish kings patronized poets for their praise-poems and eulogies; other artistic endeavours promoted religious and political reform in tenth-century England, conquest and regal power in feudal England and Scotland, and the magnificence of monarchy in the later Middle Ages.

Foreign contacts were influential and sometimes introduced new fashions: the Confessor modelled Westminster Abbey on Jumièges, David I copied Durham at Dunfermline, Eleanor of Aquitaine popularized the French lyric, and Anne of Bohemia encouraged 'international Gothic' styles. Individual monarchs had their special tastes: Athelstan collected books and relics; St Margaret enlivened the domestic arts of needlework and embroidery at the Scottish court; Richard I played the troubadour; Henry III loved exotic decoration in painting, jewellery, and sculpture, and Edward II enjoyed 'theatricals'.

Yet cultural developments are more than the sum of individual tastes. Alfred's promotion of education, literacy, book production, and the Anglo-Saxon language went hand in hand with monastic rebuilding and a continuing renaissance in music and the decorative arts which was largely generated by the royal court at Winchester. 'What shall I say [wrote Bishop Asser] of the treasures incomparably fashioned in gold and silver at his instigation? And what of the royal halls and chambers marvellously constructed in stone and wood at his command?' Anglo-Norman and Angevin triumphs put art to political and religious purposes with remarkable results: Romanesque forms inspired royal castle-building (culminating in Henry II's Dover and Richard's Château Gaillard), monasteries such as Henry I's Reading, and Rufus's palatial hall at Westminster. There was intellectual vitality, in science, philosophy, and history, at Henry I's and Henry II's courts, and Lanfranc and Anselm, two of the greatest thinkers of their age, were brought to England by Norman kings: 'with the king of England [Henry II] it is school every day!' (Peter of Blois). Love of literature and fine language at the Angevins' court was the foundation of chivalric culture.

Later medieval English kings and their courts had few rivals as patrons in the British Isles. They might not be cultural innovators, though Henry III's rebuilding of Westminster Abbey and several palaces set an example. The Hundred Years War modified artistic influences from France: Decorated and Perpendicular architecture was distinctively English (witness the realism of royal tomb sculpture, Richard II's work on Westminster Hall, and Henry VII's chapel at Westminster); so were the polyphonic music popularized by the early Lancastrians, and the long-established 'English work' of embroidery. After 300 years when French and Latin dominated, the flowering of English literature from the pens of Chaucer and Gower, Hoccleve and Lydgate owed something to royal patronage, and Henry V's contribution to the English language, which he promoted in government, was second only to Alfred's. The artistic motifs of chivalric culture were ingeniously exploited by Edward I and Edward III, especially at Windsor and in castle- and palace-building; celebrations, festivals, entries, and gift-giving offered opportunities for their display.

Regal interest in intellectual matters was largely conventional, although Edward III had a large library in the Tower. Yet Henry III had encouraged scholars to settle at Cambridge (1229) and Henry VI founded Eton and King's College, Cambridge; and most late medieval monarchs were fascinated by astrology and the arts of prediction. In the fifteenth century, humanistic influences began to seep into English and even Scottish culture—less through royal intervention than through the individual taste of nobles such as Henry V's brother, Gloucester, and Edward IV's brother-in-law, Rivers. Exile sharpened Edward IV's and Henry VII's awareness of continental currents (Henry VII commissioned his tomb from a Frenchman and an Italian, and histories from Bernard André and Polydore Vergil), and both kings patronized Caxton and early printers; but their palace-building and Gothic vaulting (at St George's, Windsor, and at Westminster) were firmly in an English tradition, as was their book-collecting and taste for jewellery, music, and pomp.

Stuart kings from the late fourteenth century to Flodden (1513) encouraged Lowland Scottish poetry, often patriotic and celebratory in tone, from such writers as Barbour, Henryson, Dunbar, and Douglas; but James I wrote the *The King's Quair* during exile at the English court. At the same time, there was royal building at castles (Edinburgh and Stirling) and palaces (Linlithgow, Holyrood, and Falkland). James IV was a flamboyant friend to artists, musicians, and scholars, and was receptive not only to pervasive English influences but also to hints from Renaissance Europe; and he was also interested in medicine and printing at Edinburgh. Kings, their courts, and their capitals might not monopolize developments in arts and sciences, but by the sixteenth century they had the resources, the need, and the will to affect them decisively.

ye And noble prince excellent
My lord the prince, my lord gracious
I humble servant and obedient
vnto your estate hye and glorious
Of whiche I am ful tendir and ful zelous
Me recomaunde vnto your worthynesse
With hert entier and sprite of mekenesse

HENRY V AS PRINCE OF WALES receiving Thomas Hoccleve's *On the Rule of Princes* from its author. Henry was well educated and this book, by a man who was also a government official, was one of a number designed to describe the powers and obligations of a ruler.

Richard may well have had the same love of beautiful things, though in his case it seems to have focused more on literature and books. The chronicler and poet from Hainault, Jean Froissart, presented to the king a fine collection of love poems when he visited England in 1395, confident that Richard would appreciate it; and to judge by Froissart's proud report of the king's reaction, he was not mistaken.

I took it to his chamber, for I had it ready with me, and laid it on his bed. He opened it and looked inside and it pleased him greatly. Well it might, for it was illuminated, nicely written and illustrated, with a cover of crimson velvet with ten studs of silver gilt and golden roses in the middle and two large gilded clasps richly worked at their centres with golden rose-trees. The King asked me what it was about and I told him: 'About love!' He was delighted by this answer and dipped into the book in several places and read, for he spoke and read French very well. (Jean Froissart, *Chronicles*, bk. IV)

Richard asked the English poet, John Gower, to write for him, and whatever cautions may be expressed about exaggerating Richard's artistic nature, it is undeniable that there was a substantial amount of literature of all kinds being read and commissioned around his court. Moreover, he is the first English king known to have appointed a painter laureate, 'the king's painter'.

Looked at much more broadly, the fruits of royal cultural patronage provided the setting for the ceremonies, celebrations, and commemorations of kingship, whether in stone (such as Westminster Abbey and St George's Chapel, Windsor), or in the music of the courts of Henry IV and Henry V. The triumphant Christian monarchy of England was represented, above all, at Westminster. Henry III's building enterprises were royal architectural and sculptural patronage on an unprecedented scale. In 1245 he took responsibility for the design and cost of the new abbey-church adjacent to his palace and the seat of government. He demanded the highest standard of decoration in the latest French style. The abbey's unusual octagonal chapter house later became a regular meeting-place of Parliament and thereby one of the best-known buildings in England. It was the coronation church of English kings and, once Henry had translated the body of Edward the Confessor behind the high altar in 1269, their burial church too. As he intended, it quickly surpassed Canterbury as the most important ceremonial church associated with the English monarchy; the king's piety, aesthetic taste, and sense of majesty combined to make it so.

At the end of the Middle Ages, Henry VII added to the architectural glory and dynastic significance of Westminster by replacing the lady chapel with a new chapel which, with its whiff of Renaissance influences, was the finest late Gothic church in the realm. His motives were similar to those of Henry III. Henry VII's chapel was to be the shrine of his sainted step-uncle and predecessor, Henry VI, and although the latter's body remained at Windsor, the chapel became a Tudor shrine, with Henry VII's tomb and bronze effigy (and those of his queen) at the centre, surrounded by the symbols of family and monarchy. In the centuries in between, kings, queens, and several of their children had been buried in the abbey, their fine tombs and expressive effigies clustered near the Confessor's own tomb-chest in a chapel of kings. Close by was Henry V's chantry chapel, erected by his son in the 1440s to house King Hal's tomb and that of his wife, Katherine of Valois (though Katherine's was never sealed, and on his birthday in 1669 Samuel Pepys went down to the abbey and was able 'to kiss a Quene').

These royal works were designed to rival—even surpass—the material glories of the French monarchy, exemplified by the Sainte Chapelle of France's holiest and most revered monarch, Louis IX. They stressed, too, the dynastic tradition of the English monarchy, which was in the forefront of Edward III's mind when he commissioned decoration and wall-paintings for the palace of Westminster; it was even more prominent in the artistic and architectural expression of dynastic legitimacy by the usurping Lancastrian, Yorkist, and Tudor families. Above all, the cultural patronage of kings reflected the power, prestige, and ambition, the opulence, splendour, and dignity of English kingship, and the royal palaces, castles, and churches were its public forum. At the heart was the king. Life-like tomb-effigies, from John's at Worcester (erected in 1232) to Henry VII's at Westminster (completed soon after his death in 1509) are literally the public face of majesty. From the later fourteenth century, kings had their portraits painted, and the earliest painting of a contemporary English king is that of the youthful Richard II in Westminster Abbey; the picture of the resplendent, kneeling Richard in the so-called Wilton Diptych (now in the National Gallery) may also have been completed in his reign, or very shortly afterwards. Rows of statues of the kings of England stared out from the screens and walls of a number of cathedrals and churches from at least the thirteenth century: a genealogical series of wall-paintings of English kings confronted diners in the abbot's hall at Gloucester by the fourteenth century; and from the painted roof of St Mary's, Beverley, their pictures looked straight down on the congregation below.

For the rare king who was not buried at Westminster, the posthumous attention he received was no less. In 1232 Henry III was present at the public ceremony to inter the body of his father, King John, in the new choir built at Worcester Cathedral with Henry's encouragement; the tomb was placed, as John had wished, between the shrines of two Anglo-Saxon saints. Henry also pursued his cultural interests in the service of the monarchy in more secular surroundings, notably at the two palaces of Windsor and Clarendon; at Clarendon the decoration was lavish, retelling themes of romance, the saga of Tristan and Isolde and the adventures of Richard the Lion-heart. He revealed his fascination with the symbolism and pomp of monarchy in instructions to his artistic adviser, Edward of Westminster, the son of a goldsmith:

WHEN ST MARY'S CHURCH, BEVERLEY, Yorks., was rebuilt in Henry VI's reign (*c*.1445), the chancel roof was painted with pictures of forty English kings (two of the earliest, *left*) from the Anglo-Saxon period to Henry VI himself, and with four legendary ones including Brutus. Congregations looking heavenward (*far left*) were more likely to feel the weight of the medieval English monarchy bearing down on them. In 1939 the portrait of one of the legendary kings was overpainted with that of King George VI!

Because we recall to memory that you told us that it would be more magnificent to make two bronze leopards to be placed on either side of our throne in Westminster, than to make them out of chiselled or sculptured marble, we command you to get them made in metal as you told us.

Edward I's great castle-building ventures added another dimension to the power and prestige of English kings, especially the enormous fortresses in the latest concentric style in North Wales, where the principality of Llywelyn the Last was finally conquered in 1282–3. Edward employed architects and engineers from as far afield as Savoy, and the plan of Caernarfon's new castle (1284–94) and the design of its walls were consciously reminiscent of the Roman imperial grandeur of Byzantium; at Caernarfon the king's son Edward was born in 1284. Perhaps inspired by his father's work at Westminster Abbey, in 1291 Edward began to build a new chapel dedicated to St Stephen in the royal palace close by. He deliberately sought to emulate St Louis's glittering wall of glass in the Sainte Chapelle, and it is a tragedy that all but the undercroft of St Stephen's was destroyed by the great fire that swept through the palace of Westminster in 1834. Edward's sense of the power and dignity of his monarchy was symbolized by a new coronation chair, beneath whose seat was placed the ancient inauguration Stone of Scone which Edward had filched from Scotland in 1296; and the English dynastic tradition was vividly expressed in life-size bronze effigies of his father and mother which he placed close to the Confessor's tomb at Westminster, rivalling those in the French royal mausoleum at Saint-Denis.

Sophisticated artistic taste may be less evident in Edward's patronage than in his father's, although the Westminster effigies are fine examples of the metal-worker's art, and sculptured elegance is the keynote of the Eleanor Crosses erected between 1291 and 1295 where the cortège bringing Queen Eleanor's body from Lincoln to Westminster rested. Their statuary and heraldic emblems were public memorials of English kingship every whit as impressive as the statues being erected in France to the memory of St Louis.

After the civil war of Edward II's reign, the efforts of Edward III to restore the authority and reputation of the monarchy laid stress on regal dignity and the monarchical tradition. Edward himself loved display in dress and jewels, whilst his wife, Philippa, was no mean patron of poets and musicians at court, some of them from her native Hainault. Regal power and magnificence are more evident in Edward's work on the royal palaces. He completed St Stephen's Chapel, Westminster, and its wall-paintings were an iconographical representation of the

THE ELEANOR CROSS AT HARDINGSTONE, NEAR NORTHAMPTON, 1291. This is probably the earliest of twelve fine decorated crosses (of which three survive) erected by Edward I at the resting-places of Queen Eleanor's funeral cortège as it made its way in November 1290 from Lincolnshire to Westminster Abbey, where she was buried. The pedestal is hung with Eleanor's shields of arms and with three open books; above are three statues of the queen. Edward may have been inspired by the crosses erected in 1271 at the resting-places between Paris and Saint-Denis where Philip III of France set down the bones of his father, St Louis, on their way to burial.

king and his family, supported by Old Testament stories in paint and glass. At Gloucester he exploited the curious cult of his father (who was venerated perhaps by royalists opposed to the veneration of Edward II's enemy, Thomas, earl of Lancaster, or perhaps to rival the cult of St Louis in France) by sponsoring the magnificent Perpendicular choir of St Peter's Abbey in the 1330s. Edward II's alabaster tomb became its centre-piece. Most spectacular of all were the new chapel and college buildings of St George at Windsor (1350–7), which were designed as the ceremonial headquarters of his new chivalric Order of the Garter. The foundation and subsequent history of this royal fraternity were a celebration of militant kingship in the company of the English nobility. At a 'solemnity' at Windsor in 1344,

the lord king and all the others stood up together, and having been offered the book, the lord king, after touching the Gospels, took a corporal oath that he himself, at a certain time appointed for this . . . would begin a Round Table, in the same manner and estate as the lord Arthur, formerly King of England, maintained it, namely to the number of 300 knights, a number always to be maintained. (Adam Murimuth, *Continuation of Chronicles*)

Four years later, after the resounding victories at Crécy, Neville's Cross, and Calais, Edward's ideas were given more explicit and permanent shape:

. . . on St. George's Day, the king celebrated a great feast at Windsor castle . . . Along with the king all were clad in gowns of russet sprinkled with blue garters, wearing the like garters on their right legs, and wearing mantles of blue with escutcheons of St. George. In this sort of apparel and bare-headed they devoutly heard mass . . . and afterwards sat in orderly array at a common table, in honour of the holy martyr, to whom they specially dedicated their noble fraternity, calling their company that of St. George of the Garter. (Geoffrey le Baker, *Chronicle*)

The charming story that the ceremony was inspired by Edward's gallantry when the countess of Salisbury's garter slipped at a ball, with the king responding to the smiles of the company with the words 'Honi soit qui mal y pense' (Evil be to him who evil thinks) which later became the motto of the Order, cannot be found earlier than the sixteenth century. Rather was the garter used to symbolize the unity of the king and his chivalric nobility, the motto exhorting them to great feats in promoting Edward's claim to the throne of France. When the fragment of the True Cross (the famous *Croes Naid*, in Welsh), which Edward I had confiscated among Prince Llywelyn the Last's regalia in 1284, was given to St George's Chapel by Edward III at the Order's founding, it marked the appropriation of Welsh princely pretensions, too, by the 'imperial' English monarchy. The presence of the Stone of Scone in Westminster Abbey already implied the subordination of Scottish regal tradition to that of England.

THE ROYAL GOLD CUP made in Paris
*c.*1380, with a stem, decorated with
roses, dating from the Tudor period,
and an inscription of *c.*1604. It was
made for the duke of Berry as a gift
for his brother, King Charles V, but
was never presented to him because
the king died (1380). It was eventually
acquired by John, duke of Bedford,
and when he died in 1435 it passed to
his nephew, Henry VI. It was evidently
regarded as a valuable item of royal
treasure suitable for gift-giving: James
I gave it to Constance of Castile about
the time of the Anglo-Spanish peace
treaty, 1604, as the inscription records.

Kingship was both a business and a calling, and each aspect was present in Richard II's ambitious plan to extend the palace of Westminster by transforming (from 1394) the Norman hall into the largest and finest Gothic hall in Europe and the headquarters of royal government. He commissioned for the hall a series of stone statues (several of which still exist) representing himself and his predecessors as far back as the Confessor, whose cult at Westminster Abbey he encouraged. Richard's chief architect and sculptor was Henry Yevele, who also made the gilt tomb-effigies of Richard and his first wife in the mid-1390s, the king's at least fashioned from life. King Richard, with his high-flown views of the prerogatives and dignity of kings, is probably the first king of England to have his effigy constructed to his own design in his own lifetime. Richard was no artistic philistine; the literary liveliness of his court and the beginnings of royal portraiture in his reign, not to speak of the superb craftsmanship of his effigy, speak otherwise, even though many of the books he owned may have been inherited from his grandfather.

THE ORDERS OF CHIVALRY

THE honours, titles, and distinctions at the disposal of the sovereign have, during the twentieth century, been democratized as the nature of the monarchy itself has changed. Originally reserved for the monarch, his family, and his most immediate aristocratic supporters, they have been broadened into a vast network of public recognition. New orders have been founded, old ones extended in size, and monarchs have struggled to retain much say in their distribution. The biggest expansion by far came, significantly, at a moment of acute peril for the monarchy in 1917, when the lists of the new Order of the British Empire served to balance the endless Rolls of Honour from the Western Front. Henceforward, civil servants, teachers, postmasters, and even academics could aspire to public acknowledgement of their services. At the same time, the Order marked another change in society by recognizing women in large numbers as worthy of acclaim. There were, of course, bitter jibes that medals were being distributed in bucketfuls and *Punch* observed that to remain *un*decorated was a singular distinction. But throughout the ages it has been a common refrain that honours have been cheapened and that the new recipients are unworthy.

The Honours list is scrutinized by a small committee of Privy Counsellors before submission to the sovereign. The committee has access to police and security records. The awards are made at more than a dozen investitures at Buckingham Palace.

The most important orders are:

THE GARTER
Instituted by Edward III in 1348 and limited to the sovereign and twenty-four Knights Companion. The most distinctive features are the Star, the Garter, and the blue diagonal ribbon. The chapel of the Order is at Windsor.

THE THISTLE
Revived by James VII and II in 1687, and refounded by Anne in 1703. Originally established in the fifteenth century, it is restricted to the sovereign and sixteen Scottish knights. The sash is a green ribbon.

THE BATH
Established in 1725 by George I, but with medieval antecedents. It has a civilian and a military division, with three ranks in each class.

ORDER OF MERIT
Established by Edward VII in 1902 with membership limited to twenty-four. There is a special connection with the world of art, literature, and music, and Thomas Hardy and Elgar were early members of the Order.

THE ORDER OF ST MICHAEL AND ST GEORGE
Founded in 1818, it is reserved mainly for diplomats, and the ROYAL VICTORIAN ORDER, founded by Victoria in 1896, is for members of the royal household.

THE ORDER OF THE BRITISH EMPIRE
Announced in June 1917 soon after the change of royal name to Windsor was promulgated. There are five grades—Knight Grand Cross, Knight Commander, Commander, Officer, and Member. Attached to the Order is the British Empire Medal.

THE FIRST GARTER KING OF ARMS, WILLIAM BRUGES (d. 1450), depicted c.1430 in his armorial book, the first book of arms of the Garter knights. Such books and ordinances were compiled for the chivalric orders from time to time. Bruges is shown in a surcoat of the royal arms of England, holding a scroll representing the Garter ordinances, and kneeling before a victorious St George, the Order's patron, who is flanked by two garters, its insignia. St George wears the ostrich feathers favoured by the Black Prince, a founder Garter knight, as his badge, which later Princes of Wales have used down to our own day.

The dynastic revolutions of the fifteenth century were accompanied by a perceptible shift of emphasis in the cultural patronage of English kings. The qualities of monarchy continued to be projected publicly, but greater attention was now understandably given to dynastic legitimacy. Under Henry V and Henry VI English writers of varying talents were recruited to celebrate the achievements of the Lancastrians and to demonstrate their rightful place in the line of English kings; John Lydgate especially became a wearisomely omnipresent poet, recounting Henry VI's lineage. The Lancastrian court made English polyphonic music renowned in Europe, and whatever the innate talents of the Scottish king, James I, he was given opportunity to realize them in *The Kingis Quair* while a captive in England (1406–24). Henry VI's plans for his educational and religious foundations of Eton and King's College, Cambridge, unprecedented as kingly ventures, were only partly complete by the time he lost his wits and, by 1461, his throne, but his personal interest in their architectural details is not in doubt. He also asserted the Lancastrian regal tradition when he built the chantry chapel of his father in Westminster Abbey, portraying in stone Henry V's coronation and his knightly prowess. At Canterbury, where his grandfather, Henry IV, the founder of the dynasty, was buried, Henry VI inspired (and perhaps the loyal Lancastrian archbishop, Henry Chichele, executed) the decoration of the undercroft chapel as a Lancastrian memorial.

Yet it was Edward IV and Henry VII who put cultural patronage wholeheartedly to dynastic purposes. Edward rebuilt St George's Chapel, Windsor, and he may have seen it as a mausoleum for himself and his descendants as kings of England. His new great hall at Eltham Palace displays the confidence and power of the Yorkist monarchy, and his personal aesthetic taste was so tickled by his exile in Flanders (1470–1) that he formed a collection of illuminated manuscripts which is the only manuscript collection of a medieval English king to survive intact (in the British Library).

Material culture as propaganda reached its height under the guiding hand of the king who had greatest need to use every available means to establish himself on the throne and secure popular acceptance of his dynasty: Henry VII. Henry's passion for the literary and artistic fashions of Burgundian Flanders was even greater than that of his predecessors. He resumed the building of King's College, Cambridge, in 1508; he completed St George's Chapel; and he seems to have been an enthusiastic patron of music (including Welsh harpists), literature, printing, and art as an accompaniment to royal ceremonial. At Westminster he took to spectacular lengths the portrayal of Christian monarchy and the Tudor dynasty. The new lady chapel was constructed as a magnificent shrine for himself and his family as successors of the saintly Henry VI; its rich dynastic symbolism and heraldic emblems intermingled with representations of apostles, saints, and

THE GREAT HALL, WESTMINSTER, another of Richard II's striking artistic commissions. Rebuilt *c*.1393–9, it is the most substantial surviving part of the palace of Westminster and in its day was the largest Gothic hall in Europe, 240 feet long by 70 feet wide. It incorporates technical innovations: the hammer-beam roof and the timber vaulting, the work of royal craftsmen.

EDWARD IV

(1461–1470, 1471–1483), king of England

. . . men of every rank, condition and degree of experience in the kingdom marvelled that such a gross man so addicted to conviviality, vanity, drunkenness, extravagance and passion could have such a wide memory that the names and circumstances of almost all men . . . were known to him just as if they were daily within his sight . . .

(The Crowland Chronicle)

ELDEST surviving son of Richard, duke of York and Cicely Neville, Edward was raised as earl of March. After the death (December 1460) of York, whom Henry VI acknowledged as his heir, Edward defeated the Lancastrians at Mortimer's Cross (February 1461) and seized the crown (March). His 'first reign' (1461–70) was turbulent, despite initial support from Warwick 'the Kingmaker', Henry VI's capture (1465), and Queen Margaret's failure to retaliate. Edward was intelligent, approachable, and promiscuous; his self-confidence, secret marriage to Elizabeth Woodville (1464), and differences over French policy alienated Warwick, and Edward's brother Clarence also deserted him. His miscalculations helped put him at Warwick's mercy (1469); yet his refusal to submit to the earl's control forced Warwick to withdraw to France, where he allied with Queen Margaret to restore Henry VI (1470–1). Edward fled to the Low Countries, where his literary, artistic, and printing interests were aroused, to be applied later to regal propaganda. Edward's daring return (1471) exploited divisions in Henry's 'Readeption', and Edward took London, imprisoned Henry, and defeated and killed Warwick at Barnet (April 1471). Henry VI was put to death after a further victory at Tewkesbury (May). Edward had shown himself to be an able, courageous, and ruthless commander, capable of swift reactions. In his 'second reign' (1471–83), he sometimes showed the instincts of a noble rather than a king, and his attitude to government relied heavily on individuals and his own personal control. He was indulgent to his wife's many relatives and Clarence, who persisted in disloyalty; when finally Edward executed him (1478), the legal grounds were dubious. Edward bent the law in his own interest so that his efforts to curb lawlessness were undermined. Concerned to exploit his financial resources, he encouraged trade, made commercial treaties, and reverted to household management of his revenues. His invasion of France (1475) was inglorious if profitable, his search

THE PORTRAIT OF KING EDWARD IV from the Royal Collection. It was painted *c.*1534–40, but a prototype portrait of the king existed by 1472 when an engraving was made, showing the king holding the orb and sceptre and wearing a closed crown. It was doubtless engraved for propaganda purposes, and the present portrait may be derived from it. Edward is here shown holding what may have been the coronation ring. When his tomb was opened in 1789, the skeleton was found to measure 6 ft. 3 in.

for security only part-successful. By 1483 his brother Richard, duke of Gloucester, had great power in the north; his son and heir Edward, in his mother's relatives' charge, ruled in Wales, and his friend, Lord Hastings, dominated the midlands. Edward's life-style damaged his health, and his early death prevented Prince Edward (twelve) from asserting his authority.

THE TERRACOTTA BUST OF
KING HENRY VII (d. 1509) by
the Italian sculptor Pietro
Torrigiano. It was made
c.1508–9 and is the best
portrait of the king towards the
end of his life (though the nose
is later). This is one of several
examples of Henry's
imaginative use of the visual
arts to enhance the dignity of
his kingship.

prophets. Whilst he (and especially his flamboyant son, Henry VIII) continued
to spend money on the older royal residences (Woodstock, Westminster, and
Greenwich) when times were more settled after 1494, he also began to construct
a newer breed of palaces in the lower Thames valley close to London: Sheen
was transformed into Richmond Palace and Whitehall came to replace Westminster, which was gradually taken over by government offices; associated with
them were new religious houses, two at Richmond and two in London. These
residences provided an appropriate setting for magnificent kingship, apart from,
and above, the hurly-burly of the capital and the administrative machine—
reminiscent of French royal châteaux in the countryside outside Paris. Westminster was the seat of government, and the scene of the inauguration and ending of
kings, but it was at their country palaces that kings henceforward lived an
opulent and dignified existence apart from their subjects.

Scottish kings in the fifteenth century preferred their country palaces, at
Falkland and Linlithgow, where they built smart Renaissance buildings, as often
as the older fortresses of Edinburgh and Stirling. James IV and James V especially
impressed their kingship on their subjects by travelling to the far north of their
kingdom and the outlandish Isles, where there were communities that had never
seen the king before—and, in some cases, would not do so again until the
twentieth century.

JAMES IV

(1488–1513), king of Scots

... of noble stature, neither tall nor short, and as handsome in complexion and shape as a man can be ... He speaks the following foreign languages: Latin, very well; French, German, Flemish, Italian and Spanish ... He is courageous, even more so than a king should be.

(A Spanish visitor to Scotland, 1496–7)

For the first time in a century, in 1488 Scotland had a king who took immediate charge of his realm, and James IV's coronation was held at the traditional site, Scone. As a life-long penance for involvement in his father's death, James wore an iron chain round his waist. Under him, the kingdom made major strides towards centralized government. Vigorous and popular, he extended the royal administration to the west and north, and by 1493 had overcome the last independent lord of the Isles. His financial resources were extended, and so was his role in making appointments in the Church. His active foreign policy was designed to win reputation for himself and his kingdom on the Continent, and to this end he reformed his army and navy. To begin with, relations with England were turbulent, and James broke the truce (1495) to support the pretender Perkin Warbeck; even after a new truce was negotiated (1497), border raids continued. The peace treaty of 1502 and James's marriage to Henry VII's daughter Margaret (1503) created greater stability on the border and between the two kingdoms. But when Henry VIII joined the Holy Alliance against France (1512), James revived 'the auld alliaunce' and invaded northern England (1513) in Henry's absence. Despite his large army—perhaps the largest ever to cross the border from Scotland—James was utterly defeated at Flodden; the king and many of his nobles perished. James was enthusiastic if impetuous, a man of great energy and broad horizons which he explored with perhaps too little restraint. He cherished the idea of the crusade,

A PANEL PORTRAIT OF KING JAMES IV, one of a set of portraits of Kings James I–V which were produced in the sixteenth century, presumably to celebrate the Scottish monarchy in the same way as the Tudor series of English kings celebrated the English monarchy.

and at home relished the role of patron of science, literature, education, architecture, and printing. Under his patronage, colleges were founded, whilst one of his sons was sent to Italy to study under Erasmus.

Acceptance of hereditary succession in the male line would seem to imply a stable monarchy. But the fact remains that kings came to a violent end more frequently in the later Middle Ages than ever before. Only six of the thirteen English monarchs between Henry III and Henry VIII died peacefully in their beds at one or other of the royal residences—so far as we know. Henry III, Henry IV, Edward IV, and Henry VIII died at Westminster, Edward III and Henry VII

THE BRONZE GATES OF KING HENRY VII'S CHAPEL, WESTMINSTER ABBEY. They were made between 1503 and 1519 by Thomas Ducheman and incorporate Tudor royal emblems: the Beaufort portcullis, the fleurs-de-lis of France, the lions of England, and the crown and the thornbush which may recall the incident at the battle of Bosworth when Richard's discarded crown was found and placed on Henry's head.

at Sheen (or Richmond). On the other hand, four were murdered after being deposed: Edward II at Berkeley Castle in Gloucestershire, by horrible means known to every student of history; Richard II at Pontefract by means unknown; Henry VI in the Tower of London when Richard, duke of Gloucester was in the building; and Edward V (and his brother Richard) most probably in the Tower, though the bones of two children found there in the seventeenth century are not

RICHARD III

(1483–1485), king of England

If I would speak the truth in his honour, I must say that he bore himself with great distinction like a noble knight despite his small body and slight strength, most honourably defending himself to his last breath.

(John Rous, *History of the Kings of England*)

RICHARD III's defeat and death at Bosworth (22 August 1485) began the destruction of his reputation by Tudor propaganda, crowned by Shakespeare's portrait of Evil Incarnate. The foundations of this vision (including physical deformity) are insubstantial, but should not be swept aside entirely. Youngest son of Richard, duke of York and Cecily Neville, his earliest years saw his father's struggle with Henry VI (to 1460); after Edward IV's accession, he was created duke of Gloucester (1461) and went into exile with the king (1470–1). On their return, he was prominent at the victories of Barnet and Tewkesbury (1471), though there is no evidence that he personally slew the Lancastrian heir at Tewkesbury. His brother Clarence's defection (1469–71) caused a rift which widened when Richard married (1472) one of Warwick's heiresses, for the other was Clarence's wife. He was present in the Tower when Henry VI was murdered, but can hardly be held responsible. In the 1470s he was loyal to Edward and did not engineer the downfall of Clarence—indeed, he seems to have been sorry at the outcome (1478). The Scottish campaign (1482) gave him military experience, and as Edward's lieutenant in the north he attracted loyalty from northerners. When Edward died (April 1483), as protector for his nephew Edward V he felt his position threatened by Queen Elizabeth and her Woodville relatives. He therefore planned to seize the crown: he executed Lord Hastings, Edward IV's chamberlain, and the queen's brother, Earl Rivers, while the queen took sanctuary in Westminster Abbey. Edward V and his brother Richard, duke of York, were put in the Tower and were never seen again (skeletons found there in 1674 may be theirs). They were declared bastards; even Edward IV was said to be illegitimate, as Richard prepared for his coronation (26 June). These illegal acts flawed his kingship. Potentially capable, his reliance on northerners was resented in southern England and his collaborator, Henry, duke of Buckingham, proved unreliable. Buckingham revolted (October 1483) and was executed; thereafter Richard used bribes and skilful diplomacy to persuade the duke of

AN UNFLATTERING PICTURE OF KING RICHARD III AND HIS WIFE, ANNE NEVILLE, daughter of Warwick the Kingmaker. Richard is wearing a closed crown; he carries a sword and an orb with a cross, and the royal arms are on his chest. The queen wears a coronet and a gown displaying the complex Neville arms as well as those of England; she holds a sceptre surmounted by a dove in her left hand. Rumours that Richard plotted Anne's death were so widespread after the queen died in 1485 that the king had to deny them publicly.

Brittany to surrender Richard's remaining rival, the exiled Henry Tudor—and almost succeeded (1484). By 1485 Lancastrians, Tudors, and alienated Yorkists urged Henry's invasion; yet for all the reluctance of several nobles to support Richard at Bosworth, the outcome was uncertain until Richard's brave charge brought matters to an issue. Talented and experienced as a noble, ambition, apprehension, and unchecked ruthlessness made him a bloody usurper who could not survive.

HENRY VII

(1485–1509), king of England

His body was slender but well built and strong; his height above the average. His appearance was remarkably attractive and his face was cheerful, especially when speaking; his eyes were small and blue, his teeth few, poor and blackish; his hair was thin and white; his complexion sallow.

(Polydore Vergil, *English History*)

ONLY son, born posthumously, of Edmund Tudor, earl of Richmond, and Margaret Beaufort, great-great-granddaughter of Edward III. He spent his early years (1461–70) in Yorkist custody, whilst the Tudor myth that Henry VI prophesied that he would be king has no basis other than a possible meeting between them (1470). After the battle of Tewkesbury (1471), he fled with his uncle, Jasper Tudor, to Brittany, where he relied on the duke's charity (1471–84). Richard III's usurpation transformed his prospects: Lancastrians and alienated Yorkists regarded him as the best alternative to Richard. With perseverance, courage, and imagination, he agreed to marry Edward IV's daughter Elizabeth (1483), styled himself king (1484), and secured French aid for an invasion. He was in the thick of the fighting at Bosworth (22 August 1485). Crowned on 30 October, he owed his throne to his own efforts but stressed his parents' Lancastrian and British heritages; his marriage to Elizabeth of York (1486) engaged Yorkist support. Henry had learned the virtues of caution, patience, and thrift; he had seen how disruptive noble power could be, and he had a liking for Brittany and France. After a period of uncertainty and education (Henry was a good learner), he embarked on vigorous rule. Risings (1486–99)—especially of imposters such as Simnel (1487) and Warbeck (1491–7)—were dealt with decisively but with conciliation. He created few peers and relied on trusted servants, many of them companions of his exile; he controlled the nobility by punitive bonds. To establish his dynasty in England and secure its acceptance abroad, he deployed his own and Edward IV's children in marriage; his diplomatic aims were peace, recognition, security, and trade. He refurbished traditional methods of government to assert his rights and increase his revenue; in later years

THE GILT-BRONZE TOMB-EFFIGIES OF KING HENRY VII AND ELIZABETH OF YORK in Henry VII's Chapel, Westminster Abbey. They were made by Pietro Torrigiano between 1512 and 1519 after a design by Guido Mazzoni, based on King Charles VIII's tomb at Saint-Denis, was rejected. The king's face seems more realistic than the queen's (d. 1503). Guardian saints are depicted on the sides of the tomb.

modifications were made to tighten his control of administration and justice and make him richer. His personal application to routine, including daily examination of accounts, became legendary. As a master propagandist, he spent his wealth wisely to reflect his majesty and authority, especially at Westminster and not least in scholarship and culture. He did not seek cheap popularity and became suspicious, secretive, and miserly. He took Queen Elizabeth's death (1503) hard and the death of his heir, Prince Arthur, was a dynastic blow. But in 1509 he had a full treasury and no one opposed Henry VIII's accession.

certainly those of the two unfortunate lads, even if they have been reinterred in Westminster Abbey. The persecutor of the 'Princes in the Tower', Richard III, died on Bosworth Field, and two other kings expired on campaign,. Edward I at Burgh by Sands on his way to Scotland for yet another Scottish campaign, and Henry V as a result of something akin to dysentery contracted at the siege of Meaux in 1422. It is striking, too, that apart from the murder of Richard II, only two of these kings—Edward I and Richard III—died in England north of the Thames; and only Henry V died in France, whence his embalmed body was ceremonially conveyed to Westminster for burial. Hereditary succession did not ensure a peaceful ending or public security.

The burial of later medieval kings was accompanied by solemn ceremony, even the burial of those kings who were deposed and murdered; after all, contemporaries were anxious to cloak their sacrilegious acts with respectability, and therefore even Edward II, Richard II, and Henry VI were treated in death with due respect and honour. The chapel of Edward the Confessor in Westminster Abbey was the pre-eminent shrine of English kingship in the later Middle Ages and in the Tudor period. Of the thirteen kings between Henry III and Henry VIII, seven were buried in the Abbey. There, clustered round the Confessor's tomb behind the high altar (whence it was translated by Henry III), their tombs and magnificent effigies were erected, giving Westminster a royal significance comparable with that of the Anglo-Saxon burial church at Winchester and Saint-Denis in France. Richard II, who had been murdered in Pontefract Castle and whose body was taken to King's Langley for quiet burial, was eventually reinterred at Westminster by Henry V (1413). It was even intended that Henry VI, who had personally indicated the spot for his own burial in the Confessor's chapel—and the mason's marks can still be seen beneath the carpet—should also be buried in the Abbey, though his remains still rest at Windsor.

The popularity of St George's Chapel as a burial place for English kings began with Edward IV, who brilliantly reconstructed Edward III's Garter chapel with the probable intention of creating a Yorkist royal mausoleum. Although Richard III lavished patronage on chantry chapels at the family home of Fotheringhay and in his favoured city of York, it is likely that he too would have been buried at Windsor if he had died honourably in his bed. It was to Windsor that he translated the body of the last Lancastrian king in 1484, from its obscure grave in Chertsey Abbey, symbolizing reconciliation with the Lancastrian dynasty; in any case, by then the murdered Henry VI was becoming a cult figure and Richard may have tried to use this posthumous popularity in support of his own unsure kingship. Although Henry VIII was buried at Windsor, the other Tudors reverted to Westminster as their burial shrine. Henry VII reconstructed the lady chapel to create the most handsome and opulent chantry in England, asserting his credentials as the legitimate king of England by arranging his own and his wife's

KING RICHARD II ON HIS WAY FOR REBURIAL in Westminster Abbey in December 1413. The king died at Pontefract (1400) but in a symbolic act of reconciliation at the outset of his reign, Henry V ordered the body to be ceremonially interred at Westminster. The pall-bearers carry Richard's arms, surmounted by a crown. The black monks of Westminster follow the bier with the crowned king's body (or his effigy) on top to the resplendent tomb which Richard had commissioned for himself and Queen Anne after her death in 1394.

burial there and planning the translation of his step-uncle, Henry VI, while pursuing the cause of Henry's canonization in Rome. He succeeded marvellously in all but the latter design.

Henry IV's is the only other burial that requires explanation. He and his second wife, Joan of Navarre, were interred in Canterbury Cathedral, where their expressive alabaster tomb-effigies still lie. It may be that Henry the usurper could not bring himself to be buried in the Plantagenet shrine at Westminster and preferred to be buried in England's premier church, close to England's premier saint and martyr, Thomas Becket. Whatever his reasoning, his son did not share it. Henry V was buried with great ceremony in Westminster Abbey, where he had translated Richard II's mortal remains in 1413, thereby signalling a determination to declare the legitimacy of the Lancastrian dynasty in the right line of English kings.

As for Edward II, the most agreeable thing about his end was the magnificent surroundings of his last resting place in St Peter's Abbey, Gloucester. The monks of St Augustine's, Bristol, are traditionally said to have shrank from accepting the murdered king's body in 1327 when those who had custody of him at Berkeley Castle approached them; instead, the monks of Gloucester obliged. They doubtless showed more charity than foresight, but the fact that Edward's tomb soon became a place of pilgrimage, as the shrine of a deposed king of England, meant that the offerings of the faithful went straight into Gloucester's coffers and helped to pay for the fine choir of the abbey church which was begun in the 1330s with the full backing of the new king, Edward III. As for Richard III, his body was buried ignominiously in the Grey Friars Church at Leicester, to which it was brought from the battlefield slung naked across a horse and trussed like a sheep. Henry VII contributed modest funds for a tomb, but it was later rifled and broken up, and the remains of the king's body were thrown away, never to be recovered, not even by enthusiastic Ricardians in our own day. Westminster Abbey was the foremost shrine of English kingship, and Henry VII's new chapel enhanced its magnificent setting for royal burials. The century that saw serious turbulence around the throne was also the century during which the throne was elevated as never before in magnificence and majesty.

4. GOVERNING MONARCHY

1509–1689

The Nature of Tudor Monarchy

THE three sections into which the modern period has been divided are, at best, rickety and indistinct signposts. No one word can do more than indicate, in an approximate way, the character of a period, or serve as more than a discussion point. Historical developments are rarely obliging enough as to proceed in an orderly and regular fashion. Though there are undoubtedly significant differences in the nature of the Tudor and Stuart and the Hanoverian monarchies and we can see that the power and importance of Parliament grew greatly, historians do not agree whether the decisive changes occurred in the 1530s, the 1640s, the 1680s, or even later. Though it is clear that, in the course of the nineteenth and twentieth centuries, there was a further diminution of royal power, caused as much by the growth and complexity of public business as by the challenge of party, the shift occurred over more than a hundred years. Above all, there is the difficulty that bulks large in all constitutional analysis, of deciding when certain developments have become permanent and irreversible. Vigorous and determined monarchs can breathe new life into powers that have seemed defunct: feeble and ineffective rulers can let slip powers that had seemed well established.

In the period which we have called governing monarchy, the court was the very centre of political life. The fundamental political decisions—the making of alliances, diplomatic or matrimonial, peace and war, the elevation and dismissal of ministers—were made by the sovereign. To that, one must immediately offer reservations. In practice, the sovereign might be too young, too lazy, too ill, too uninformed to conduct business himself. He might, for long periods, delegate day-to-day business to ministers or favourites. Nevertheless, the potential for exertion was there, even if fitfully employed, and few ministers in this period, however great—Wolsey, Thomas Cromwell, Cecil, Buckingham, Strafford, Clarendon, Danby—doubted that their careers could be ended in a few days if they lost the favour of their sovereign.

Most political commentators of the late fifteenth and sixteenth centuries were at pains to insist that though the powers of the English monarch were formidable, England was not a despotism, and they drew a distinction between the English monarchy and that of most continental countries. Sir John Fortescue's *On the governance of England*, written in the 1470s, began, as we have seen, by contrasting *dominium regale* and *dominium politicum et regale*. In the first, according to Fortescue, the monarch may impose his own laws; in the second, he rules by consent. The distinction offered is therefore between absolute monarchy and limited or constitutional monarchy: England and Scotland were examples to Fortescue of constitutional monarchies, France the chief example of an absolute monarchy. One hundred years later, Sir Thomas Smith offered a similar analysis in *De Republica Anglorum, a discourse on the Commonwealth of England*. Though Smith described in very full terms the powers of the monarch and the awe with which he should be approached, he preceded it with a long exposition of the powers of Parliament which contained 'the whole universal and general consent and authority as well of the prince as of the nobility and commons'. By contrast, Louis XI of France was blamed for bringing that country 'from the lawful and regulate regime to the absolute and tyrannical power and government'.

It is doubtful whether we should regard these statements as accurate constitutional analyses or as examples of the English gift for admiring themselves and their institutions. At first sight, there certainly appears to be a marked contrast between the vigour and prestige of Tudor Parliaments and the effeteness of the États généraux not summoned between 1484 and 1560, and once more dormant between 1614 and the beginning of the Revolution in 1789. French theorists did not, however, see eye to eye with English. Philippe de Commynes, whose *Mémoires* were written in the 1480s and 1490s, denied that the king of France had the right to tax without consent. The mainstream of French comment before Bodin was constitutional in character, arguing that genuine consultation existed between the monarch and the various *parlements*, the notables, the provincial estates, and the Great Council. Claude de Seyssel, whose *La Monarchie de France* was presented to Francis I in 1515, insisted that the French monarchy was superior because the powers of the king were limited by religion, justice, and policy. By 'policy' he meant ordinances to which the agreement of *parlement* was necessary, and though he did not deny that these bridles might be bent, 'they can scarcely be broken'.

With the publication of Jean Bodin's *Six livres de la République* in 1576, political thinking took a new turn. Bodin's message was the indivisibility of sovereignty and the consequent impossibility of limited or mixed monarchies. The primary attribute of sovereignty was the power to give laws to subjects without their consent. Sovereignty, Bodin argued, was in no way affected by the existence of estates: consultation of his subjects by the ruler was a matter of prudence, not of law. The English Parliament was, in his opinion, no better off than the French États généraux, having 'no independent power of considering, commanding or determining, seeing that they can neither assemble nor adjourn without express royal command'.

Bodin's theory has the virtue of simplicity, but it seems peremptory and indiscriminate. An analysis which made no distinction between the monarchies not only of Scotland, France, and England, but also of Ethiopia, Muscovy, Persia, and Turkey, was not terribly helpful. They were all, insisted Bodin, absolute or sovereign monarchies.

In practice, the strength of the Tudor monarchy in England depended more on finance than on political theory. The strongest weapon in the armoury of the House of Commons was its claim that its consent to taxation must be obtained, and this went some way to meeting Bodin's objection that it had no independent right of assembly. But the assumption was still that the monarch should be expected to 'live of his own', looking to Parliament for supply only on extraordinary occasions, such as marriages, coronations, rebellions, or wars. A prudent and parsimonious prince might go for years without the need to summon Parliament, and thereby give little opportunity for public criticism of his policies or his ministers. But the growing cost of warfare, a number of dangerous risings and rebellions, and the insidious effects of inflation were undermining royal finances. Henry VII, a careful and patient ruler, came close to living on his customary resources and built up substantial reserves: Henry VIII made little attempt to do so and, from his reign onwards, financial problems continued to dog the monarchy, limiting its ambitions and provoking constitutional and political clashes.

Where contemporaries differed strongly, it was unlikely that historians would be unanimous, and there has been sharp disagreement on how the Tudor monarchy should be characterized. In the later nineteenth century, the prevailing orthodoxy was that of Bishop Stubbs, who saw promising constitutional progress arrested, or even reversed, by the vigour of Tudor rule. At the beginning of the twentieth century, this view was challenged, notably by A. F. Pollard, who argued that it was during the Tudor period that the foundations for later

HENRY VIII OPENS PARLIAMENT, 1512. Henry's use of Parliament to effect his religious changes and to adjust the succession enhanced its position, though it was still summoned at the royal will and only occasionally. Henry is preceded by the duke of Buckingham, carrying the cap of maintenance and followed by the earl of Oxford bearing the staff of the Lord Great Chamberlain.

parliamentary dominance were laid. More support came from Sir John Neale, one of whose declared objectives was to dispose of the myth of Tudor despotism, and from G. R. Elton, who found in Thomas Cromwell the man responsible for 'the flowering of parliamentary monarchy'.

Something of a swing back to the Stubbs view has been attempted more recently. In 1964 J. S. Roskell argued that Parliament did not gain domination until the later seventeenth century and that during the Tudor period its influence did not much increase. Roskell did not argue that the Tudor monarchy was a despotism, but in 1966 Joel Hurstfield tackled the question head on in a lecture entitled, 'Was there a Tudor despotism after all?' He concluded that 'if the government of Henry VIII failed to establish, in the fullest sense, a Tudor despotism, it was not for want of trying'.

A certain amount turns on semantics. Does a despotism have to be despotic all the time? Does it have to be despotic towards everyone? If it has widespread popular support, does it cease to be despotism? If the despotic acts are accomplished by due process of law, are they no longer despotic? The case against Henry VIII must include the *politique* executions of Empson and Dudley on trumped-up charges of treason at the very beginning of his reign; the callous and mean-spirited discarding of his three leading ministers, Wolsey, More, and Cromwell—the latter two executed, the first hunted into his grave; the judicial murders of the Kildares, after pardon given; the vast extension of the laws of treason, from their tentative beginnings in the later Middle Ages; the relentless hunting down of dynastic rivals, including the sixty-eight-year-old Margaret Pole, countess of Salisbury, butchered in the Tower; the brutal suppression of the

Pilgrimage of Grace, after the usual insincere assurances of pardon; the appropriation of the right to regulate the succession (a claim which even Bodin denied to absolute princes). To such a list, it would be supererogation to add Henry's treatment of his wives.

Most of these acts have been palliated and defended. Many monarchs have refused to keep faith with rebels. Henry VIII is not the only sovereign to abandon ministers who have served their turn, though the seizure of Wolsey's buildings and the execution of Thomas Cromwell a mere three months after his elevation to the earldom of Essex adds a characteristically spiteful flavour. The new definitions of the law of treason were clearer than the reliance upon constructive treason in the past. The settlement of the succession was a matter of great national importance. It was a brutal age. Men in high politics knew that they played for great stakes and neither expected nor showed much mercy.

The argument that most of this was done within the law, much of it by statute, deserves more careful examination. The use of attainder against Thomas Cromwell had the effect of depriving him of any trial or the means of defending himself. Much turns on how independent Tudor Parliaments really were. It is true that there is evidence of opposition to royal policy from time to time. In 1523

HENRY VIII IN MIDDLE AGE. This portrait, attributed to Joos van Cleve, shows Henry at the age of about forty-four. The high-bridged nose was a Tudor characteristic and is found in his daughter Elizabeth. The king is holding a scroll with a quotation from St Mark's gospel.

the House of Commons was extremely reluctant to grant the taxes that Wolsey required, and the Act of Proclamations of 1539 seems to have been substantially modified to meet parliamentary objections. But the circumstances of the time scarcely allowed Parliament to be an effective permanent check upon government. The right of dissolution, as Bodin had pointed out, was a powerful weapon in the hands of the monarch and was still being used with considerable effect at the end of the seventeenth century. The limitations on freedom of speech were considerable. Bishop Fisher was not summoned to the House of Lords in 1534 because he was known to disapprove of the crown's policy. Peter Wentworth's campaigns on behalf of freedom of speech in Elizabeth's reign are well known, but it should not be overlooked that he died in the Tower of London for his outspokenness. The arts of management gave the court a large say in the membership of the House of Commons. But perhaps the main reason why Parliament could hardly be a severe restraint upon government, even had it wished to be, was that its sessions were infrequent. Elton has pointed out that, during 118 years of Tudor rule, Parliament was in session for no more than eight years. During the forty-five years of Elizabeth's reign, there was a Parliament in session for only two and a half years. Of course, it is true that there is little evidence that this state of affairs was resented. Parliaments still meant trouble and taxation, and ministers made a virtue of the fact that the monarch summoned Parliament so little. Nor is it at all clear that most subjects disapproved of strong, even high-handed, rule, unless they were its victims. But that is hardly the same as denying that despotic elements were present in Tudor rule.

The two great centres of power, with a good deal of overlap between personnel, were the Council and the Household. The Council was the executive mainspring, its members appointed and dismissed by the monarch and responsible only to him. Total membership fluctuated considerably, but during the reign of Henry VIII it was forty or so persons. The Council got through a vast variety of business, diplomatic, military, financial, and administrative, together with much judicial work. It met regularly during law terms in the Star Chamber at Westminster, and at other periods a smaller number of councillors accompanied the king on his journeys and progresses.

During the period of Thomas Cromwell, there was a streamlining of Council functions and procedures. A smaller group of about twenty exercised effective power, meeting regularly throughout the year. Since membership of the Council was much coveted by ambitious courtiers, it was difficult to keep numbers down: Edward and Mary failed to do so, but Elizabeth reimposed restraint. The royal secretaryship was a post of growing importance, held by men such as Cromwell, Burghley, and Sir Robert Cecil.

Henry VII appears to have attended Council regularly, Henry VIII and Elizabeth less so. The monarch's life was lived out in the court, dominated by

God saue the Kyng.

THE KING IN COUNCIL. As long as the monarch was the mainspring of government, his regular presence at Council was essential. During the eighteenth century the gradual cessation of attendance at cabinets meant that the sovereign was removed from the process of policy-making and the first minister's position consolidated. The woodcut, by Jacob Faber, appeared in Edward Hall's *Chronicle*.

ceremonies, audiences, and entertainments. In this strange world, the great officers of the Household, such as the Comptroller and the Lord Chamberlain, mixed with peers and aspirants, grave counsellors, doctors, prelates and lawyers, ambassadors and envoys, ladies-in-waiting, the whole swarming with servants and servants' servants, and surrounded by beggars and hangers-on. With something like 1,500 persons to be fed and housed, it was a major Tudor industry. The horrific problems of supply were compounded by the fact that there were usually no less than a dozen residences to which the monarch might move, and regular progresses were made in the summer, at least in the south of England. The monarchy betrayed its origins in the distant past as a southern English kingdom: no sovereign progressed as far as Wales, Scotland, or Ireland, and even the north of England was regarded as unreasonably remote. Progresses had the double advantage of showing Majesty to the people and spreading the burden of supporting it. Royal visits, though a great honour, were a source of vast anxiety and expense. Entertainment for the monarch and court was expected to be spectacular, coping with the numbers involved meant adapting rooms and hiring tents and pavilions, expensive parting presents were also *de rigueur*, and the whole enterprise could go disastrously wrong through rain, illness, or an unlucky word. The excuses proffered to avoid, or at least curtail, a royal visit, verged on the desperate. When Elizabeth threatened to visit the archbishop of Canterbury in Kent in 1573, Matthew Parker replied to Burghley that he was overwhelmed by the honour. Was Her Majesty aware, he added in passing, that there were measles and pox at Canterbury and plague at Sandwich: he 'would be loth to have her person put in fear or danger'. His house had 'but an evil air' and his own infirmity and distemper would make it difficult for him to do justice to the occasion. It was to no avail. Elizabeth was not easily put off and the visit went ahead. A little later, the archbishop had the pleasure of breaking the news to his brother of York that the queen proposed a visit there.

To limit importunity, court life was ceremonious, formal, and dignified. Sir Thomas Smith wrote in 1565 that 'no man speaketh to the prince nor serveth at the table but in adoration and kneeling, all persons of the realm be bareheaded before him; insomuch that, in the chamber of presence, where the cloth of estate is set, no man dare walk, yea, though the prince be not there'. It was an act of quite desperate folly in 1599 when Essex, hot from his Irish campaign, burst into the queen's bedchamber and flung himself at her feet—apart from the imprudence of surprising the sixty-six-year-old monarch without her wig and before she had completed her *toilette*.

Monarchs led conspicuously public lives. In the great empty Tudor palaces there were few private rooms. Significantly, what began in the seventeenth century as the withdrawing room, to enable the sovereign to escape from the throng, became very quickly the drawing room, where he received company. From rising in the morning to retiring at night, the monarch was cocooned in ceremony and formality. Grooms and gentlemen warmed his linen, robed him, combed his hair and escorted him: at the end of the day, with equal formality, the bed was made, the mattress pricked, the night-cap placed, the bed curtains drawn. Meal times were particularly formal. Each dish was placed on the table in careful order, with an appropriate flourish of the hand, and the monarch served on bended knee. Each dish was tasted against poison. Frequently the royal family dined in public under the gaze of a crowd of onlookers. Even the most intimate moments of life—nuptials, childbirth, and death-beds—were played out against a host of observers. It is scarcely surprising that successive generations of rulers loved the chase and the hunt, where the same degree of ceremony could hardly be maintained.

DINING IN STATE (*above*). As part of the process of showing themselves to their subjects, Tudor and Stuart monarchs dined regularly in public. This sketch after Holbein shows Henry VIII eating with great formality. The Hanoverians allowed the practice to lapse, George III in particular relishing private family life. See picture on p. 374.

HENRY PLAYING THE HARP (*left*). Henry VIII was an accomplished musician and had a large collection of lutes. Here he is playing a small Celtic harp known as a clàrsach. His villainous-looking companion is the court fool, Will Sommers. We must take it on trust that he was said to be vastly entertaining and an excellent mimic.

Ceremonies and formal entertainments took up much time. Apart from the grand state occasions, such as coronations, weddings, christenings, funerals, and the opening of Parliament, there were ambassadors to receive and impress, envoys to dispatch, presentations to be made, honours to be bestowed, gifts and petitions to be acknowledged. Most monarchs found some of the occasions trying. At Easter, the sovereign performed the ritual washing of the feet of the poor and distributed Maundy money: Pepys noted on one occasion that Charles II delegated the washing to one of his bishops and no monarch after James II performed that part of the ceremony himself. Two other ceremonies not always welcome to the monarch were the formal levee and touching for the King's evil. As the levee developed, the guests gathered in a circle and the monarch was expected to exchange a few words with everyone in turn. Since the guests were not permitted to initiate subjects, the conversation was often banal and spiritless. Anne found such occasions particularly difficult; Fanny Burney was begged not to reply to George III in monosyllables but to try to get some sort of conversation going, while the young Victoria's artless attempts to converse prompted Charles Greville to irreverent comment.

Touching for the evil was perhaps the most striking manifestation of the claim to sacerdotal or even divine powers since the monarch was credited with the gift of healing scrofula. The ceremony was organized on very formal lines, the monarch stroking the victim with both hands down his cheeks and throat. Since it involved close contact with a large number of diseased and sick people, some monarchs, like James I, did not find it pleasant. Surprisingly, the practice reached a climax during the reign of Charles II, not, one would have thought, the most devout of rulers, but who was credited with having touched no fewer than 90,000 persons during his reign. There were hundreds presented at each ceremony and each received a commemorative medallion or angel.

The mixture of private and public aspiration made the Tudor court a theatre of mankind, with dazzling triumphs and mortifying rebuffs. The importance of catching the royal eye was so great that frowns, smiles, and nods were reported with avidity. Slight signs were analysed with all the attention now devoted to Moscow parades by Kremlinologists. At the 1526 Mardi Gras, Henry VIII abandoned the motto he had worn for Catherine of Aragon—*The Loyal Heart*—and sported instead the more equivocal *Declare I dare not*. In the course of the next year it became clear that the new lady was Anne Boleyn. Similarly, when in 1607 a handsome young page broke his arm while jousting, it was observed that James I's solicitous enquiries exceeded the demands of common politeness: a new planet had emerged, in the shape of Robert Carr, Viscount Rochester within four years, Earl of Somerset within six.

In the unbearably moving last act of *King Lear*, the old king, in defeat with Cordelia, catches the fascination and the pathos of court life:

Come, let's away to prison:
We two alone will sing like birds i' the cage:
When thou dost ask me blessing, I'll kneel down,
And ask of thee forgiveness: so we'll live,
And pray, and sing, and tell old tales, and laugh
At gilded butterflies, and hear poor rogues
Talk of court news; and we'll talk with them too,
Who loses and who wins; who's in, who's out;
And take upon us the mystery of things,
As if we were God's spies: and we'll wear out,
In a walled prison, packs and sects of great ones,
That ebb and flow by the moon.

In addition to his possession of the crown of England, Henry VIII was also lord of Wales, lord of Ireland, and king of France. The reality behind these imposing titles needs explanation. For generations after the Glyndŵr rebellion, Wales was, in effect, an occupied country, its native population subject to severe penal sanctions, yet lawless and remote. But Henry Tudor hailed from the principality and the Red Dragon flew as his standard at Bosworth. Though the Welsh began to bask in royal sunshine and there were soon English complaints of favouritism, Henry VII did not attempt any large-scale reconstruction. His son, in two statutes of 1536 and 1543, incorporated Wales into England, dividing the country up into counties and hundreds, introducing English administration and justice, and giving the Welsh representation in the Parliament at Westminster. Though the insistence upon English as the official language makes the settlement appear an act of colonization, Welshmen were afforded equal rights in England. Among the many who took advantage of these opportunities were the Syssils of Alltyrynys near Pandy, who followed Henry VII into England, set up at Stamford, and produced in William Cecil and his son Robert two statesmen who helped to govern England for fifty years.

In Ireland, effective control was limited to the area of the Pale, around Dublin. There was an uneasy understanding with the great Anglo-Irish lords and little contact with the Gaelic parts of the country. Richard II's two expeditions in the 1390s had met with some success in reasserting royal power. But his second expedition in 1399 was ended by news of Henry Bolingbroke's invasion of England, and the reconciliation Richard had hoped for between the Anglo-Irish and the Gaels did not materialize. The Anglo-Irish continued to regard the native population with contempt and none of their chiefs was summoned to Parliament. Henry IV was faced with Glyndŵr's rebellion in Wales at the beginning of his reign, and his successors, Henry V and VI, were preoccupied with the campaigns in France. The Anglo-Irish were left largely to fend for themselves. Henry VI was warned in 1435 with some exaggeration that the king's writ ran scarcely more than thirty miles from Dublin. Edward IV showed little interest in restoring royal authority, and Richard III, who was more concerned, was never in a position to take action. What authority remained was exercised by the earls of Kildare. After Bosworth, there was some chance of the two countries drifting completely apart, when Lambert Simnel, claiming to be Edward V, was crowned in Dublin. Though the battle of Stoke in 1487 removed him, a second Yorkist pretender, Perkin Warbeck, claiming to be Richard IV, was more difficult to dislodge. Not until 1497 was he captured and eventually executed. Meanwhile, Sir Edward Poynings had restored some royal power, and Poynings law declared that an Irish Parliament could not assemble without express permission nor legislate without prior approval by the Council in England. A large-scale attempt to restore Tudor control was postponed until 1520 when the earl of Surrey, son of the victor of Flodden, took over an imposing army. A further rebellion by Thomas, son of the ninth earl of Kildare, was suppressed by Sir William Skeffington, and in 1541 Henry VIII was declared king of Ireland. Royal authority remained precarious.

It could well be argued—and without offence to Irish nationalism—that the biggest single failure of the British monarchy was its inability either to subdue or to conciliate Ireland—'conquest or reformation', in Thomas Cromwell's phrase. If the southern English monarchy in which it originated had any natural role, it was to transform itself into a monarchy of the British Isles. The long-term failure in Ireland was the product of three factors—tenacity of Gaelic resistance, great distractions elsewhere, often against France, and paradoxically the poverty of the country, which made it probable that any revenue that might be squeezed out of it would be more than swallowed up by the effort required to collect it. The British monarchy never had the resources, the opportunity, nor perhaps the will, for a sustained campaign of conquest. Nor was the alternative policy of reconciliation pursued with determination, though it was spelled out by Henry VIII in a famous instruction to his Lieutenant that government should be by 'sober ways, politic drifts and amiable persuasions founded in law and reason'. Gladstone in 1868 had good precedent for his mission to pacify Ireland. From the support for Perkin Warbeck in the 1490s to the denial of the use of ports in the war against Nazi Germany in the 1940s, the British crown paid a heavy price for its failure of policy.

The kingship of France was an even more doubtful asset than the lordship of Ireland. The Pale left to England was even smaller than in Ireland, and consisted of little more than the port of Calais and its immediate hinterland. All that survived of the great possessions of the Plantagenets and Lancastrians was an area of some 120 square miles, rather smaller than the Isle of Wight. But the claim to the French crown remained heady. Henry VI had been crowned in Nôtre Dame in 1431, and in 1512 Julius II, in one of the many twists of papal diplomacy against Louis XII, recognized Henry VIII as king of France. In fact, a more plausible and promising line of advance was in Scotland. Henry VII's eldest daughter Margaret had married James IV of Scotland, and for many years there was a proposal to marry Elizabeth, Henry VIII's daughter, to James V, with the expectation of a united kingdom for their son.

The resources to support these lofty pretensions were slender. The Tudor standing army consisted of a small force of some 200 Yeomen of the Guard, not all of them fit for service. Armies were mustered largely by reliance upon the great magnates to bring in men—with all the hazards that entailed: during the Pilgrimage of Grace, Lord Ferrers provided 1,000 men and the duke of Norfolk 600. The county levies or militia were of little use and were employed mainly in local skirmishing, though regular training improved their quality later in the sixteenth century. If money was available, mercenaries could be hired. At the beginning of the Tudor period, there was scarcely a navy at all. Henry VIII inherited only 5 ships from his father, though he left 53 to his son. Nevertheless, royal vessels formed only a part of most fleets: of 150 ships sent to Portugal in 1589, only 7 belonged to the queen. There was no regular naval personnel: noblemen or sea-captains took command, with crews of merchant seamen.

The two main sources of supply were the crown lands, built up under Henry VII, and the proceeds from the customs duties, granted for life. They were eked out by feudal dues, such as wardship, the profits of justice, subsidies when Parliament could be persuaded, and loans. They were scarcely enough for prolonged campaigning and supply was a constant preoccupation for Tudor statesmen.

The administrative support was similarly sketchy. The number of full-time officials in the employment of the crown was tiny: in Elizabeth's reign, some 600 servants administered the great offices of state, with perhaps the same number looking after crown lands. In the shires, social and economic regulation and a good deal of the administration of law and order was in the hands of the sheriff, supported by the unpaid justices of the peace, of mixed capacity and zeal. Even when supplemented by the supervisory role of bishops and assize judges, and commissioners appointed for special purposes, it was not a formidable force.

This factor must, to some extent, modify the previous discussion of despotism. Indeed, one may suggest that the Tudor and early modern state pitched its theoretical claims high partly because the reality was so different. By contrast, the modern democratic state has humble political pretensions, claiming to derive its power from popular consent; yet its hand is felt by the subject in almost every walk of life and its regulations enforced to a degree that was quite impossible in Tudor England.

Henry VIII

'Magnificent, liberal, and a great enemy of the French', was the Venetian ambassador's report on the new king on the first day of his reign in April 1509. The auspices could hardly have been better. Henry VIII was seventeen years of age, well built, athletic, and reputed something of a scholar. His was the first peaceful succession to the throne since that of Henry VI in 1422 and there was no sign of disaffection. His father bequeathed him a stable and well-ordered realm and a substantial treasure. The financial position was so strong that for the past five years it had not been necessary to summon Parliament for supplies. Abroad, the great rift between Valois and Habsburg, which had developed after Charles VIII's incursion into Italy in 1494, offered a safe choice in diplomacy between cautious non-alignment or a skilful tilting of the scales.

Henry set off with an admirable determination to take his responsibilities seriously and to keep abreast of the paperwork. It did not last—in which respect he was no different from most monarchs. His passion for hunting and jousting, his interest in music and theology, to say nothing of his demanding love life, meant that documents rarely received the detailed attention Henry VII had given them. Hence, there was an opportunity for a capable minister to make himself indispensable by taking over the burden. We must be careful how to interpret this however. Henry never surrendered the reins totally, and none of his ministers ever forgot that, at any moment, the prince could give them their dismissal. But in the nature of things, Henry's lack of application weakened his position: a good deal of influence slipped out of his hands, even if he retained the final say.

Almost his first action as monarch turned out to have momentous consequences. Within seven weeks of his accession, Henry had married Catherine of Aragon, his brother's widow. Her previous marriage to Arthur in 1501 had lasted a mere five months and had almost certainly never been consummated when he died at Ludlow in 1502 at the age of fifteen. The remaining seven years Catherine had spent in England, formally betrothed to Henry, but in a twilight existence, a diplomatic pawn in constant danger of being sacrificed. Henry's reign falls into three parts. The first, up to 1529, saw the emergence and supremacy of Thomas Wolsey. A royal chaplain at the accession, he was appointed almoner: by 1514 he was archbishop of York, and the following year saw him a Cardinal of the Church and Lord Chancellor. The second period, from 1530 to 1540, carries the imprint of the clear mind of Thomas Cromwell, who moved into the vacuum created by the disgrace and death of the Cardinal. Surviving a few awkward months, when it looked as though he would be sucked down by his former association with Wolsey, Cromwell was a member of the Council by 1531, Chancellor of the Exchequer by 1533, and secretary to the king

ROSE AND POMEGRANATE are the great symbols of Tudor England and Aragon in this woodcut of the coronation of Henry VIII and Catherine. Edward Hall, the chronicler, wrote: 'if I should declare what pain, labour and diligence the tailors, embroiderers and goldsmiths took both to make and devise garments for lords, ladies, knights and esquires, and also for decking, trapping and adorning of coursers, jennets and palfreys, it were too long to rehearse.' The banquet after the ceremony was said to be 'greater than any Caesar had known'.

by 1534. During the last seven years of Henry's reign, after the execution of Cromwell, no leading minister emerged, and with matters of state receiving but fitful attention from an ailing king, it is hard to see much but drift and improvisation.

Christopher Columbus set out on his first great voyage the year after Henry's birth, and throughout his childhood the New World was being opened up by the Spanish and Portuguese. In these developments, Henry showed little interest. His world remained that of western Europe. Foreign affairs consisted of the ever-changing patterns woven by the emperor, the king of Spain, and the king of France, with the kings of Portugal, England, Denmark, and Scotland playing supporting roles. It was natural enough that Henry should wish to measure himself against the young French king, Francis I, who succeeded in 1515, and Charles V, who united Spain and the empire in 1519. Indeed, for the monarch,

CULTURAL PATRONAGE UNDER THE TUDORS AND STUARTS

In short, the wealth and civilization of the world are here; and those who call the English barbarians appear to us to render themselves such. I here perceive very elegant manners, extreme decorum, and very great politeness; and amongst other things, there is this most invincible king, whose accomplishments and qualities are so many and excellent that I consider him to excel all who ever wore a crown.

In the papal nuncio's ecstatic reaction to a joust arranged by Henry VIII to mark the signing of the Holy League in 1517, we see one reason for the lavish displays expected of monarchs—to impress foreigners and subjects alike. At this tournament there were said to be 50,000 spectators and the banquet lasted seven hours. Even Henry VII, reputed careful with his money, had not spared on spectacle. His victory at Bosworth in August 1485 was followed by a grand coronation in October, marriage to Elizabeth of York in January 1486, celebrations for the birth of his son Arthur in September 1486, and the queen's own coronation in November 1487. The festivities were sumptuous and were intended to stamp the image of the new Tudor regime. In similar fashion, rulers were expected to give support for learning and the arts whatever their personal predilections. The constant exchange of presents with foreign princes and their envoys gave opportunities to employ an army of craftsmen and artists of all kinds—painters, miniaturists, sculptors, jewellers, goldsmiths, armourers, clockmakers, silversmiths, and furniture-makers.

Henry VIII took undoubted pleasure in the arts. He built extensively, particularly at Whitehall and St James's, after the palace of Westminster had been severely damaged by fire in 1512; at Hampton Court, where he added the chapel and great hall to Wolsey's building; and at Nonsuch, where he began a completely new palace in 1538. One of Elizabeth's favourite residences, Nonsuch fell into neglect during the civil wars and was pulled down during the reign of Charles II. Henry's patronage of Hans Holbein the younger demonstrates how much a great artist can do to fix an image of royalty for posterity—legs astride, hands on hips, fists clenched, exuding confidence and authority. In 1537 Holbein painted a great fresco of the new dynasty, showing Henry, his mother and father, and Jane Seymour: it hung in the palace of Whitehall and was destroyed in the fire of 1698, only copies remaining. Henry's personal delight was music. He performed and composed, had a good singing voice, collected musical instruments, and brought over to England foreign musicians such as Memo, organist at St Mark's, Venice. Thomas Tallis began his career under Henry's patronage.

Elizabeth inherited her father's artistic interests and talents. She played the virginals, sang, and danced. Her virginals can still be seen in the Victoria and Albert Museum. Her finances did not permit building on the grand scale but the long gallery she added at Windsor now serves as the royal library. Her reign saw the finest achievements in the art of miniature painting, with Nicholas Hilliard and Isaac Oliver among the most outstanding. The royal collection is the largest and the oldest in existence. She extended her patronage to Jonson and Shakespeare, was present at the first performance of both *The Comedy of Errors* and *A Midsummer Night's Dream*, and was, of course, the inspiration for Spenser's poem, *The Faerie Queene*.

The early Stuarts, despite their financial difficulties, were generous patrons. James I used Inigo Jones, whose Banqueting Hall was one of the few buildings to survive the fire at Whitehall in 1698, and whose Queen's House at Greenwich was finished by Charles I. The posts of Master of the King's Musick and of Poet Laureate date from this period. The laureateship started in the reign of James I, when the king gave a pension to Ben Jonson, and was put on a formal footing with the appointment of John Dryden in 1668. Though the talents of some of the laureates were unremarkable and few of the annual birthday odes are memorable, later laureates included Wordsworth and Tennyson. Charles I appointed a Master of Musick in 1626 and the list includes William Boyce, Elgar, Bax, and Bliss.

Charles I was perhaps the best informed of all royal patrons, with a particular interest in painting. In 1628 he purchased, in the face of considerable competition, the great collection of Raphaels, Titians, and Correggios which had belonged to the Gonzagas, dukes of Mantua. Though the collection was sold off during the Commonwealth, many were recovered at the Restoration, and Charles II added the remarkable collection of drawings by Leonardo da Vinci.

At the Restoration a new area for royal patronage emerged with the establishment, under Charles II's sponsorship, of the Royal Society to undertake scientific research. He was also responsible for the building of the Observatory in Greenwich Park. His most important artistic contribution was the support he gave to Sir Christopher Wren. In the early years of the Restoration, Wren designed Chelsea Hospital; after the great fire of 1666 he commenced the building of new St Paul's and many London churches; and the rebuilding at Greenwich which Charles started was finished by Mary after the Glorious Revolution. William III also employed Wren in very substantial rebuilding at Hampton Court and at Kensington Palace, which he had purchased from the earl of Nottingham.

ROYAL JOUST. Tournaments remained a form of display and entertainment well into the seventeenth century. In this encounter at Westminster in 1511, Henry VIII jousts before Catherine of Aragon to celebrate the birth of their son Henry. The young prince died ten days later. Though kings usually did well in tournaments, accidents were possible. Henry himself had a narrow escape in March 1524 when jousting with his visor open, and in 1559 Henry II of France was killed in a tournament when his opponent's lance splintered.

foreign affairs remained something of a family matter right up until 1918. Henry's wife was Spanish, his eldest sister Margaret had been married to James IV of Scotland since 1503, and his other sister Mary married Louis XII of France in 1514. Marriage alliances were an essential arm of diplomacy, even if they rarely produced the benefits expected of them.

Henry's early decision to marry Catherine may have been prompted, to some extent, by strategic considerations. All commentators stress, at the outset of his reign, Henry's antagonism towards the French and his ambition to rekindle the glories of Henry V. A Spanish marriage could be the foundation for a firm understanding with his father-in-law, Ferdinand of Aragon. The pleasant task of dismembering France could then begin.

In fact, Henry's first taste of diplomacy and warfare was humiliating and highly educative. Ferdinand was persuaded to fall in with Henry's plans with gratifying ease. A joint Anglo-Spanish force was to invade France from the south and reconquer Gascony and Aquitaine for England. In the summer of 1512 a very large English army was duly landed in northern Spain and waited only the signal from Ferdinand to attack. It did not come. Ferdinand merely made use of the presence of English troops to protect his flank in an occupation of the independent kingdom of Navarre. Struck down by heavy rain, dysentery, and shortage of beer, Henry's troops mutinied. Ferdinand then complained bitterly to

HENRY VIII'S SUIT OF ARMOUR made towards the end of his life, probably by Erasmus Kyrkenar at Greenwich. It reminds us of the medieval past when monarchs were expected to lead their men into battle. Henry's father had won the throne by conquest and all his life Henry VIII hankered after military glory. The waist was flared out and the thigh and knee armour cut away to accommodate Henry's enormous bulk, which was so great that pulleys had to be used to hoist him up and down.

Henry that the English troops had deserted just when he was about to do terrible things, and Henry, in his innocence, authorized his father-in-law to cut the throats of any English he found running for home.

For 1513 Henry kept the same ally but changed the plan. Ferdinand would strike in the south while Henry landed an expeditionary force in the north. Another mighty army was prepared. This time Ferdinand baled out without a blow struck, leaving Henry to carry on alone. A three months' campaign succeeded in capturing the town of Thérouanne, described unkindly by Thomas Cromwell as an ungracious French doghole, and the important town of Tournai, held for only five years and handed back in the next diplomatic *bouleversement*. A rather straggly cavalry action was dignified as the battle of the Spurs. Meanwhile, Lord Surrey, left behind to guard the border against the Scots, inflicted upon them one of the most crushing defeats of all time at Flodden

Field, where the king, Henry's brother-in-law, and the Scottish nobility were cut down.

Flodden, the credit for which was tactfully yielded to Henry, cast a glow over the campaigns of 1513. But perhaps their most important consequence was to lay the foundations for the emergence of Thomas Wolsey as the king's chief adviser. Though the strategy of the French campaign may have been difficult to perceive, the supply and commissariat, which Wolsey supervised, had proved a brilliant success.

The aggregation of power built up by Wolsey in the next fifteen years made him the greatest subject of modern times: only Oliver Cromwell could rival him. In 1515 Wolsey became Lord Chancellor, and used his position vigorously, both in his own court of Chancery and in the increasing use of the Council's judicial authority in the court of Star Chamber. His appointment as Cardinal in 1515 was followed in 1518 by powers as *Legate a latere*, subsequently granted for life. These enabled him to shunt his colleague William Warham, archbishop of Canterbury, to one side, and to exercise government of the Church in England. He lived in the grandest style, flaunting his wealth and basking in pomp. The state banquet given in honour of the Princess Mary in 1518 was said to be 'the like of which was never given by Cleopatra or Caligula'. His great palaces of York Place in Whitehall and Hampton Court, where he began building in 1515, were far finer than anything the king possessed. His colleges at Oxford and at Ipswich were planned on a stupendous scale: of the former, a don remarked that it was less a new college than a new university. Foreign ambassadors reported that he had the management of the whole kingdom. 'We have to deal', wrote Bishop Fox, 'with a cardinal who is not a cardinal but King.' Henry himself, remarked many observers, knew little of what was going on, content to leave irksome business to the great Cardinal, while he pursued his pleasures.

At times the power of the monarch seemed quite eclipsed. That was an illusion and one from which Wolsey never suffered. Though there has been much discussion of the objectives of Wolsey's policy, and historians have argued that the central theme was the search for European peace or service to the papacy, there is little doubt that all was directed to the power and glory of the monarch. When Wolsey lost royal favour, the edifice he had constructed so carefully collapsed like matchsticks, leaving him a forlorn, bewildered, and frightened man. The first moment of real anxiety came in 1527 when he was in France, arranging for the virtual take-over of the Catholic Church while the pope was in captivity, only to discover that the king had bypassed him with an independent approach to Clement, aimed at hastening divorce from Catherine. The royal messenger had been specifically instructed not to share his secrets with the Cardinal. Although Wolsey recovered from the immediate crisis, for the remaining two years he was struggling desperately against the tide of events.

HENRY VIII

(1509–1547)

King Henry is twenty nine years old, and much handsomer than any other sovereign in Christendom—a great deal handsomer than the King of France. He is very fair, and his whole frame admirably proportioned. Hearing that King Francis wore a beard, he allowed his own to grow, and as it was reddish, he had then got a beard which looked like gold. He is very accomplished and a good musician; composes well; is a capital horseman, and a fine jouster; speaks good French, Latin and Spanish; is very religious; heard three masses daily when he hunted, and sometimes five on other days . . . He is extremely fond of hunting, and never takes that diversion without tiring eight or ten horses, which he causes to be stationed beforehand along the line of country he means to take. He is also fond of tennis, at which game it is the prettiest thing in the world to see him play; his fair skin glowing through a shirt of the finest texture.

(Sebastian Giustinian, *Calendar of State Papers*, Venetian, ii, no. 1287, 1519)

THE sense of power exuded by Henry in his portraits reflects personal and political strength. He was a man of vast proportions, with a magnificent physique until he declined into grossness in later years. He had abundant energy and vitality. In addition, his reign witnessed a remarkable extension in the theoretical claims of the monarchy. The older forms of address as 'Your Grace' or 'Your Highness' were finally laid aside for 'Your Majesty', and there was a marked increase in court ceremony. The chief success of the monarchy was in establishing its claim to represent national sovereignty by extruding any rival authority. First, papal jurisdiction was cut down by a series of Acts, particularly that of 1533 forbidding appeals to Rome, on the grounds that England was an empire, governed by one supreme head and king 'with plenary, whole and entire power'. The next step was to assert royal authority over the Church. Another statute of 1534 recognized that the king was 'the only supreme head of the Church of England called *Anglicana Ecclesia*, with 'full power and authority' to amend or reform any abuses or errors therein.

The early years of Henry's marriage to Catherine appear to have been happy, even idyllic. There was no obvious reason why the birth in 1510 of a still-born daughter should cast too long a shadow. But by 1525 Catherine was forty, and repeated pregnancies had produced only one surviving child, the Princess Mary, born in 1516. The five years by which Catherine was older than Henry were now

THOMAS WOLSEY AND THOMAS CROMWELL steered Henry's ship of state for twenty-two years. Wolsey, born a butcher's son in Ipswich, became one of the most powerful ministers of all time. At the Field of the Cloth of Gold in 1519 he was attended by 300 servants, but failure to secure Henry's divorce brought about his downfall in 1529. Cromwell was Henry's chief adviser from 1532 onwards until destroyed in 1540 by the unlucky Cleves marriage. He is shown here in his mid-forties as a man of business, plainly dressed, and seated at a green-baize table.

apparent, and the queen showed an increasing tendency to plumpness and piety. The succession of Mary as queen in her own right would be without precedent, and, to a sixteenth-century mind, the guarantee of a disputed succession, a civil war, or, at least, domination by a foreign power through marriage. It seemed for a moment in 1525 as if Henry toyed with the idea of grooming for the succession his illegitimate son by Mary Blount: the six-year-old boy was created duke of Richmond and Lord High Admiral, and invested with the order of the Garter. But, in the end, Henry turned towards the thought of divorce and remarriage. Discussion of suitable candidates commenced.

When the question of obtaining a divorce from the papacy was first raised, there was no reason to believe it hopeless. There was, at the least, a respectable case in canon law that the marriage to Catherine had been invalid from the outset. Leviticus 20: 21 was a heavy text: marriage to a deceased brother's wife was specifically prohibited and the couple were warned that they would be childless. Catherine maintained that her marriage to Arthur had never been

JAMES V

(1513–1542), king of Scots

He was called of some, a good poor man's king; of others he was termed a murderer of the nobility, and one that had decreed their whole destruction. Some praised him for the repression of theft and oppression: others dispraised him for the defoulling of men's wives and virgins ... And yet none spake altogether besides the truth.

(John Knox, *History of the Reformation in Scotland*)

JAMES V at the age of twenty-eight.

SON of James IV and nephew of Henry VIII, James was eighteen months old when his father was killed at Flodden. During childhood he was the sport of noble factions, but in 1528 he escaped from the Douglasses and began his personal rule, pursuing his opponents with a severity that bordered on savagery. The rift between Henry VIII and the Emperor gave James the opportunity of playing a balancing role, and he received the Garter from one and the Golden Fleece from the other. In 1537 he married Madeleine, daughter of Francis I and, on her death within a few months, he married Mary of Guise. Partly under the influence of his second wife, James defended the Papacy and put down reformist preachers. In December 1541 he broke an agreement to meet Henry VIII at York and war followed. Late in 1542 James, already ill, despatched a force across the border: it was trapped and forced to surrender at Solway Moss. James, overcome by the news, died the following month, leaving as his heir a week-old daughter, Mary.

consummated, but the papal dispensation granted in 1503, to cover all circumstances, had assumed that it had been. Technically, Henry was asking, not for a divorce, but for recognition that he had never been married at all. Even divorces were by no means unknown. Louis XII had been granted a divorce in 1499. The duke of Suffolk, the king's brother-in-law, had had a marriage annulled by reason of consanguinity in 1507, and Henry's sister Margaret, widow of James IV of Scotland, had a divorce granted in 1527 to end an imprudent second marriage, to Henry's great indignation. Henry may well have believed that Wolsey's vast influence with the papacy would be sufficient to obtain a ruling in his favour. When Wolsey and Campeggio were empowered to decide the matter in May 1529, all seemed to be on course, but in July the pope avoked the cause to Rome. Within three months, Wolsey was dismissed and charged with praemunire.

The years of Wolsey's supremacy were colourful rather than deeply significant. The kind of prestige which the treaty of London or the Field of the Cloth of

Gold brought was, by nature, ephemeral, and there is little evidence that Wolsey had much concern for, or even understanding of, the country's long-term strategic or economic interests. Although he had a phenomenal capacity for work, Wolsey attempted so much that little was systematically pursued, save perhaps in the law. It was been suggested that he showed Henry the potential for controlling the English Church. That may be doubted. Wolsey's unique position postponed the policy of a breach with Rome that was ultimately adopted, since it seemed simpler to exploit his influence with the papacy. But his arrogance, ostentation, and pluralism helped to discredit the Church at a time when it needed all the friends it could get.·

Wolsey's eventual successor as minister, Thomas Cromwell, is sometimes contrasted with the Cardinal, but the differences can be pressed too far. Cromwell was a Wolsey man and came to prominence under his patronage. It is true that Wolsey showed little faith in Parliament, while Cromwell made vigorous use of it. This is partly a matter of circumstances. As a Cardinal of the Church, Wolsey found the anti-clerical attitude of the Commons awkward, while Cromwell could make use of it as a weapon against the papacy. At an earlier stage in his career, however, Cromwell had referred to the Commons disparagingly as a talking-shop.

The 1530s saw so many reforms that the effect has been claimed as a revolution in government. That is perhaps excessive. Yet there is no doubt that Cromwell's attack upon problems was far more systematic than Wolsey's had been. Though the driving force behind Cromwell's innovations was undoubtedly the divorce, his reorganization extended much further—into the incorporation of Wales described earlier and the attempt to delineate a clearer policy towards Ireland.

Cromwell was not firmly established in power until after More's resignation in May 1532. His successor as Lord Keeper was Thomas Audley, a close colleague of Cromwell's. Cromwell succeeded not only to Wolsey's position but also to his problems. The attempt to obtain the divorce through pressure on the papacy had stalled: the military successes of Charles V meant that Catherine's nephew had the Pope *en prise*. Much of 1530 had been devoted to a fruitless attempt to obtain opinions from the universities of Europe. Even had they been unanimous which, predictably, they were not, it is far from clear how their views could have unlocked the door. Cromwell's key was a bold change of policy, using the power of Parliament to decide the issue.

The first step in the evolving strategy was an attempt to soften up the clergy by indicting fifteen of them, including eight bishops, on a charge of praemunire. Though it was not followed up with much vigour, a request to Convocation in January 1531 for a subsidy hinted that all the clergy might have been guilty of praemunire. In exchange for recognition of his position as Supreme Head of the Church of England, Henry offered a pardon. The clergy managed to salvage some dignity by submitting 'so far as the law of Christ allows'.

FOR POPE, READ KING. One of the greatest steps in the development of royal power was Henry VIII's seizure of spiritual authority from the papacy and the assumption of the title 'Head of the Church'. In this woodcut, Henry, assisted by Cranmer and Cromwell on his right, rests his feet on the prostrate body of Pope Clement VII, to whom Bishop John Fisher gives comfort.

The following year, an Act against Annates struck against the pope's financial position, insisting that 'great and intolerable' sums of money had been drained from the kingdom. The statute was suspended during the king's pleasure, that is, it was intended *in terrorem*. Progress towards a complete breach with Rome was slow. In August 1532 the death of Warham, who had crowned Henry and Catherine, enabled Henry to promote Cranmer to the archbishopric of Canterbury. With papal confirmation received in the spring of 1533, things speeded up. In May of that year, one of the first actions of the new archbishop was to declare Henry's marriage invalid, and a week later Anne Boleyn, pregnant with the future Elizabeth, was crowned queen. The pope's response of excommunication was met by a salvo of parliamentary legislation. An Act in restraint of appeals to Rome declared that the king possessed 'whole and entire' authority within the realm, and that no judgements, interdicts, or excommunications from Rome were valid. It was followed by an Act of Submission of the clergy and an Act of Succession, while an Act of Supremacy repeated Henry's claim to be Supreme Head of the Church of England. The most famous victim of the new legislation was Sir Thomas More, executed in the summer of 1535, trapped under the provisions of a new Treasons Act.

The repudiation of papal authority and the insistence upon imperial status, though of great symbolic importance, did not in themselves materially alter the

HENRY VIII'S WRITING BOX is preserved in the Victoria and Albert Museum. The Tudor rose is prominent on the front of the box and the inscription is that of the Garter—*Honi soit qui mal y pense.*

HENRY TO ANNE BOLEYN ON HIS HOPES FOR A DIVORCE. In this letter of September 1528, Henry informs Anne that Campeggio, the papal legate, 'aryvyd att Parys on Sonday or Munday last past, so that I trust by the next Munday to here off hys aryvall att Cales, and then I trust within a wile after to enjoy that whyche I have so long longed for, to God's pleasure and owre bothe comfortes. No more to yow at thys present, myne owne darlyng, for lake off tyme, but that I wolde you were in mine armes or I in yours, for I thynk it long syns I kyst yow.' But Campeggio had been warned to hasten slowly and the marriage did not take place for another four years.

crown's position. The vast sums said to have found their way to Rome as Annates were a mere trickle. But the breach was followed by an action which could have tipped the balance of domestic power decisively in favour of the monarchy. The dissolution of the monasteries and the expropriation of monastic lands have been called a revolution in landownership comparable only to that effected by the Norman Conquest.

Action against some of the smaller houses had preceded the breach with Rome. Wolsey had closed twenty-nine small communities between 1524 and 1529, using the proceeds to support his new foundations. After the compilation of the *Valor ecclesiasticus* in 1535/6 another 200 smaller monasteries were dissolved by statute, and the remaining greater houses followed in 1538–40. Large sums of money poured into the royal coffers and for a few years the ordinary crown revenues were more than doubled. But by the end of the reign more than half of the properties had been sold off, the proceeds swallowed up by the abortive war against France. The monastic estates found their way, in the end, less to new men than to ambitious families already well established in county society.

The driving force against Rome and the monasteries was Cromwell, whose supervision gave a coherence and purpose to the years 1530–40, singularly lacking in the rest of Henry's reign. For years, Cromwell seemed to be the great survivor, too useful to be cast aside. In his rise, he had dexterously side-stepped the fall of his patron, and promoted the king's wishes in the divorce and the marriage to Anne Boleyn. The death of Catherine in January 1536 and the miscarriage which followed two weeks later spelled Anne's death-warrant, since the king was now free to make a new and undisputed marriage, and his eye had already lighted upon Jane Seymour. Cromwell presided over the charges of adultery and Anne, her brother, and four others met their death. Later the same year, the Pilgrimage of Grace called for Cromwell's dismissal and 'condign punishment': the rebels were put down and Cromwell escaped. In 1539 his position appeared to be badly shaken when the Act of Six Articles signified the return to a more conservative doctrinal stance, away from the Reformation views favoured by Cromwell. He recovered once more, and in the autumn of 1539 was busily arranging Henry's fourth marriage to Anne of Cleves, after Jane Seymour's death in childbirth. The tragicomedy of that celebrated non-event finally proved Cromwell's downfall. Elevated to the earldom of Essex in April 1540, he was peremptorily arrested less than two months later, and executed within six weeks. The charges against him were grotesque. One does not know whether to marvel more at Henry's ingratitude or his stupidity.

Henry never found another servant remotely approaching Cromwell's capacity. The greatest influence belonged to the elderly duke of Norfolk, uncle to the king's fifth wife Catherine Howard, until he in turn fell foul of the king in the dying months of the reign. The main event of these years was a return to Henry's

HENRICVS DEI GRA REX ANGLIE

HENRY VIII IN OLD AGE. This engraving of Henry at the age of fifty-three by Cornelis Massys eschews the heroic in favour of candour, the head bald, eyes lost in folds of fat. Nevertheless, Henry clambered on to horse the same year to make one last throw for military glory in France.

adolescent dreams of conquest. As usual, Henry was let down by his allies, and an enormous army of 40,000 men, assembled at appalling expense, succeeded in capturing only the town of Boulogne, handed back to the French ten years later. The war was paid for by a variety of desperate expedients, subsidies, forced loans, borrowing, depreciation of the currency, and alienation of the monastic properties. They combined to fuel a roaring inflation, which was well under way when Henry died in January 1547.

It is curiously difficult to strike a balance sheet for Henry's reign. The conventional interpretation suggests an enormous strengthening of the crown's position, the papacy excluded, the clergy brought under control, the nobility cowed, the wealth of the monasteries acquired, the administration reformed, Wales incorporated. But a closer look raises doubt. If the primary objective of Henry's policy was to secure the succession, he could hardly have done worse. Six marriages had produced one sickly son, and two princesses, whose inheritance had been placed in jeopardy by bastardization and reinstatement. A temporizing doctrinal policy had produced, not harmony, but deep and dangerous religious schism. The proceeds of monastic lands had gone to build up the economic strength of the gentry and nobility and place them in a position to resist the crown. The use of Parliament to effect the religious and dynastic changes had handed it a weapon with which to confront the monarchy in the future.

THE WIVES OF HENRY VIII

HENRY VIII's matrimonial adventures owed as much to politics as to passion. He was betrothed to Catherine of Aragon, his brother's widow, when he was eleven years of age, and married her as soon as he succeeded to the throne at seventeen. The motive seems to have been a mixture of chivalry and inability to repay the dowry which had been received. Their first son lived only a few days in 1511, and a series of miscarriages and still births followed. The only surviving child was the Princess Mary, born in 1516. By the 1520s, Henry's mind was turning towards divorce. In 1527 formal proceedings for an annulment of the marriage were instituted, by which time Henry's attentions had moved on to Anne Boleyn, younger sister of a former mistress. Catherine resisted great pressure to retire to a nunnery and negotiations continued until 1533, when Cranmer's appointment as archbishop coincided with Anne's pregnancy. At the coronation in June 1533, Anne was six months with child, and the Princess Elizabeth was born in September. By January 1536, when Catherine died at Kimbolton, Henry's passion for Anne was spent, and his eye had been taken by Jane Seymour, a lady-in-waiting and sister of the future Lord Protector. Anne's miscarriage later that month sealed her fate, and in the summer she was accused of incest and adultery and beheaded. The betrothal to Jane followed a day later. Henry's third marriage lasted sixteen months, and in October 1537 Jane died giving birth to Prince Edward. The fourth marriage, to Anne of Cleves, was purely diplomatic, and was intended to rally Protestant Germany against the emperor. Henry hastened to Rochester to greet his bride, whom he had never seen, but recoiled in dismay, complaining that he had been deceived by her portrait. To Cromwell, he confided: 'if it were not that she is come so far into England, and for fear of making a ruffle in the world, and driving her brother into the Emperor and the French king's hands, I would never have her: but now it is too far gone, wherefore I am sorry.' Closer inspection merely confirmed the king's anxieties and a few months later, the marriage was annulled on grounds of non-consummation. Anne was assured that she would be treated as a sister, was given a generous settlement, and remained in England until her death in 1557. A month later, Henry married Catherine Howard, an attractive and vivacious seventeen-year-old, but who had formed previous attachments. After little more than a year, she was accused of adultery and beheaded, dying in the Tower with composure and dignity. Henry's sixth wife was Catherine Parr, twice-widowed and aged thirty-two. Older and more mature than her predecessors, Catherine got on well with Henry's mixed brood of children, created something of a home, survived him, and married a fourth time a few months after his death. She died in childbirth at Sudeley Castle in September 1548. Henry's lifelong desire for a secure succession produced three legitimate adult children, none of whom had offspring.

THE WIVES OF HENRY VIII. Catherine of Aragon, Anne Boleyn, Jane Seymour, Anne of Cleves, and Catherine Parr; there is no authentic portrait of Catherine Howard.

Henry's Heirs: Edward, Mary, and Elizabeth

After the vicissitudes of the previous twenty years, it is a tribute to the residual strength of the Tudor dynasty that the succession of Edward VI in 1547 passed off as quietly as that of Henry VIII had done. Yet the prospects were bound to be doubtful. Edward was nine years of age—three years younger than the previous boy-king, Edward V, who had come to the throne in 1483. On that occasion, it had been but a matter of three months before the young monarch was elbowed aside by his uncle, Richard III. Even if Edward VI was luckier and survived, the probability was that the nobility would use the period of Regency to strengthen its position against the crown. The opening days of the new reign appeared to run true to form. Since it had no intention of obeying the will of the late king, the Council at once announced that it would be implemented 'in every part and article'. It then declared the earl of Hertford, uncle to the new king, to be Protector of the Realm. Within a fortnight the new Protector had, in turn, declared himself duke of Somerset, and awarded both estates and promotions to his brother Thomas Seymour and his other followers.

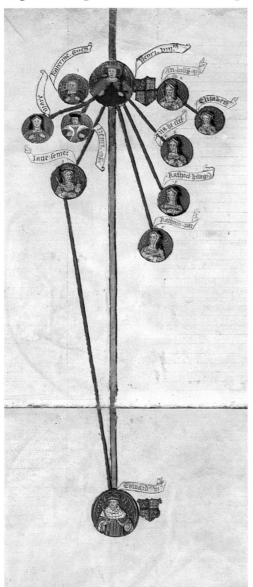

Edward was pale, thin, under-sized, and intelligent. His mother, Jane Seymour, had died at his birth, and his father must have been a terrifying, if distant, figure. He grew up, not surprisingly, with a cautious and reserved manner. His education had been mainly a grounding in the classics, and he continued his father's interest in theological speculation. He revealed, at an early age, an inclination towards the Reformed religion.

THE TUDOR PEDIGREE continued from p. 177. The problem is what to make of 'Henri obi', next to Mary on the Catherine of Aragon stem. Their son Henry, born in January 1511, died after eight weeks. But the portrait is that of a young boy. Henry VIII's son Henry by Elizabeth Blount was born in 1519, created duke of Richmond (a royal title) in 1525, and given the Garter. Further honours were showered upon him and it looked as if the king had decided to make him his heir. But instead Henry's thoughts turned to divorce and Richmond died in 1536, aged seventeen.

There was plenty of unfinished business from the previous reign for the Protector to tackle. Inflation was running at crisis proportions, there were troubled relations with the kingdom of Scotland, and religious drift and uncertainty. Within two and a half years, Somerset went from spectacular triumph to total disaster. His first decision was to settle the Scottish problem by a hammer-blow, thereby redeeming two inconclusive campaigns he had waged there in 1544 and 1545. In September 1547 at Pinkie Cleugh, just outside Edinburgh, he crushed a superior Scottish force. But he was unable to follow up the victory and impose satisfactory peace terms. His religious policy marked a stride towards Protestantism: the Act of Six Articles was repealed, the marriage of clergy allowed, and the first book of common prayer introduced, changing the Latin service to an English one. The last innovation contributed towards his fall. The attempt to impose the English service in Cornwall in June 1549 led to a serious rising, in which Exeter was besieged, and it was followed a month later by Ket's rebellion in Norfolk. Sixteen thousand rebels camped out on Mousehold Heath for six weeks, twice occupied Norwich, dispensed their own justice, and were defeated only by a major military campaign, backed by foreign mercenaries, and led by the earl of Warwick. Though the government regained control of the situation, Somerset's days were numbered. By October 1549 he was in the Tower, and though, rather surprisingly, he was released in 1550 and readmitted to the Council, his final overthrow and execution were merely postponed until January 1552. His uncle's downfall was watched by the young king with no elaborate show of grief: 'Today,' he wrote coolly in his diary, 'the Duke of Somerset had his head cut off on Tower Hill.'

Somerest's successor in power was John Dudley, earl of Warwick, the victor of Dussindale, where Ket's followers had been cut to pieces. The office of Protector was allowed to lapse and Dudley, raised to the dukedom of Northumberland in October 1551, operated as Lord President of the Council. In an effort to restore domestic stability, the Council invented the office of Lord Lieutenant, charging the holder with the maintenance of order in his shire. Under Northumberland's auspices, the speed of the religious changes was increased. A number of the more conservative bishops were deprived of their sees, and the second book of common prayer, issued in 1552, was markedly more reformist than the first. But Northumberland's position depended upon an understanding with the fiercely Protestant young king. By the spring of 1552, Edward's health was giving cause for concern, and a few months later the signs of tuberculosis were apparent.

The threat to Northumberland's position prompted plans which, in retrospect, may have seemed more hopeless than they really were. Edward's heir was his eldest sister, the Princess Mary who, through all the changes, had clung tenaciously to her mother's religion. A strict interpretation of the nullity of Catherine's marriage must however imply that Mary was illegitimate. Anne

EDWARD VI

(1547–1553)

Edward was the offspring of Henry's third marriage to Jane Seymour, who died when he was born in October 1537. He was given a largely classical education by Richard Coxe and Sir John Cheke. He succeeded his father in 1547 at the age of nine, survived measles and smallpox in the spring of 1552, but died of tuberculosis in July 1553. Though his journal is factual rather than personal, it conveys something of the preoccupations and activities of a sixteenth-century ruler.

Summer, 1549 The people suddenly gathered together in Norfolk and increased to a great number, against whom was the Lord Marquis Northampton sent with the number of 1060 horsemen, who, winning the town of Norwich, kept it one day and one night, and the next day in the morning with loss of 100 men departed out of the town, among whom the Lord Sheffield was slain . . . with which victory the rebels were very glad. But afterward, hearing that the Earl of Warwick came against them, they began to stay upon a strong plot of ground upon a hill near to the town of Norwich.

17 May 1550 Removing to Westminster from Greenwich.

11 June 1550 Order was given for fortifying and victualing Calais for four months; and also Sir Harry Palmer and Sir Richard Lee were sent to the frontiers of Scotland to take a view of all the forts there and to report to the Council where they thought best to fortify . . .

10 January 1551 Three ships, being sent forth into the Narrow Seas, took certain pirates and brought them into England, where the most part was hanged.

18 March 1551 The Lady Mary, my sister, came to me to Westminster, where after salutations she was called with my Council into a chamber where was declared how long I had suffered her mass in hope of her reconciliation and how now, being no hope, which I perceived by her letters, except I saw some short amendment, I could not bear it. She answered that her soul was God's and her faith she would not change, nor dissemble her opinion with contrary doings. It was said I

constrained not her faith but willed her as a subject to obey. And that her example might breed too much inconvenience.

8 July 1551 At this time came the sweat into London, which was more vehement than the old sweat. For if one took cold, he died within three hours, and if he escaped, it held him but nine hours or ten at the most. Also, if he slept the first six hours, as he should be very desirous to do, then he raved and should die raving.

22 August 1551 Removing to Windsor.

Boleyn's daughter, the Princess Elizabeth, had also been bastardized and reinstated. By the will of Henry VIII, the descendants of his eldest sister, Margaret, widow of James IV of Scotland, had been set to one side, but those of Mary, his younger sister, had been specifically recognized. After her brief marriage to Louis XII of France, Mary had married Charles Brandon, duke of Suffolk. Their daughter Frances, born in 1517, married Henry Grey, marquess of Dorset and duke of Suffolk. Their eldest daughter, Lady Jane Grey, was in 1553 fifteen years of age. When, in May 1553, she was married to Guildford Dudley, the only unmarried son of Northumberland, the outlines of the plot became clear. Six weeks later, Edward VI was dead.

Northumberland's chief hope was the will of Edward, made three weeks before his death, in which, largely to thwart any restoration of the old religion, he bequeathed the crown to Lady Jane. After considerable hesitation and much pressure, the Council recognized her claim and instructions were issued for proclaiming her throughout the kingdom. Only King's Lynn and Berwick on Tweed responded. On news of the death of her brother, Mary fled to Framlingham and was proclaimed rival queen. Northumberland then placed himself at the head of troops to apprehend her, but by the time he reached Cambridge, the strength of Mary's position had become apparent. Bowing to the inevitable, Northumberland disbanded his men and, outside Great St Mary's, pledged himself to Mary. By 3 August, Mary was in London, welcomed and fêted: Northumberland, his son, and daughter-in-law were prisoners in the Tower.

The reign of Mary Tudor, which began with so striking a demonstration of loyalty, is the most tragic, publicly and personally, in English history. On the character of Mary, historians differ. What to some is steadfast courage in adversity is to others no more than stubborn bigotry, nor perhaps are the two always far apart. The streak of self-righteousness that gave her the strength to endure appalling persecution hardened during her reign and helped to bring it to its pitiful close. For much of what went wrong during the short five years, the blame must be placed on the monstrous treatment meted out to her by her father, which made her dogged, obstinate, and secretive.

Her birth in 1516 was a source of great joy to her parents after so many disappointments, and the early reports were of a bright, cheerful, and affectionate little girl. At the age of ten, the shadow of her parents' divorce fell across her. She was left for several years in the care of her mother, but in 1532 they were parted, and Henry refused permission for them to meet again, even during Catherine's last illness at Kimbolton. In 1533, by act of Parliament, Mary was declared illegitimate, deprived of her right to the succession, and ordered to abandon the title of princess. She clung to her links with her cousin, the Emperor Charles V, who alone could offer her some measure of protection. In 1536, after Catherine's death, relentless pressure was brought upon her to subscribe to her own illegitimacy and to acknowledge Henry's supremacy over the Church. Her submission, after an agony of resistance, brought her a grudging toleration, and in 1544 she was reinstated in the succession, after Edward. But the succession of her half-brother brought a new period of persecution, in which she was urged to abjure the mass. In 1551 the imperial ambassador warned the English court that

ANNO DNI · 1544.

LADI MARI · DOUGHTER TO
THE MOST · VERTUOUS PRINCE
KING HENRI · THE EIGHT

THE AGE OF · XXVIII YERES

THE PRINCESS MARY. By 1544 Mary had survived the humiliations subsequent to her mother's divorce and was restored to her place in the succession in February. She represented the hopes of all traditional Catholics. This portrait was probably painted in the summer or autumn, since Mary's privy purse accounts for November record a payment to 'one John that drue her Grace'.

further interference with her liberty would mean war with the emperor. As Edward grew up, his increasingly Protestant views created fresh barriers between them, and almost his last act was to strike her out of the succession once more. His death in 1553 found her an embittered woman of thirty-seven, prematurely aged, possibly beyond child-bearing, and convinced that only her faith in the true religion could have caused her to be spared among so many perils and dangers.

She was, as the imperial ambassador pointed out, a novice in government and was given little time to learn. Her reign has three interrelated themes—the return to Rome, her marriage, and the war against France.

It was inevitable that, after her sufferings, she should turn for advice to her Spanish relatives and their envoys. The purely ecclesiastical side of the reconciliation with Rome was effected without undue difficulty. It began with a campaign against priests who had taken wives. The bench of bishops was filled once more with Catholics, Catholic doctrine and practice restored, and the title of Supreme Head of the Church abandoned as soon as practicable. In November 1554, Cardinal Pole, Mary's cousin, in a formal ceremony, absolved the realm for its sin of schism. But even in this, Mary was only partly successful. The gentry and aristocracy made it clear that under no circumstances were they prepared to part with the monastic lands they had purchased, and though Mary began the reintroduction of the monastic orders, progress was slow. The campaign of persecution which accompanied and was intended to buttress the changes was ill-judged. Nearly three hundred, of whom the most famous were Cranmer, Latimer, Hooper, and Ridley, were burned at the stake, and the experience stitched itself into the national consciousness.

Marriage was an urgent necessity if Mary was to have any chance of bearing a Catholic heir and avoid leaving the crown to her sister, Elizabeth. As a young girl, Mary had been on the point of betrothal to Charles V, and in 1553 her hopes fastened on his son, Philip, eleven years her junior but already a widower. Personally and politically, the marriage was a disaster. Philip stood out for the title of king, though it was hedged about with limitations, and was to lapse in the event of Mary's death. He arrived in July 1554 and between Spaniards and English disenchantment was mutual. Philip performed his duties with sufficient ardour to enrapture Mary, and within a few months she was convinced that she was with child. After just over a year, Philip left for the continent and his return was postponed time after time. When he did return in the summer of 1557 it was a short and, on his side, a cold visit. Once more Mary went through all the delusions of a false pregnancy.

The object of the marriage, from the Spanish point of view, was to engage the English in the emperor's struggle against the French. Mary was quite willing to see her country play such a role. War was declared in June 1557. In January 1558

MARY I
(1553–1558)

MARY's marriage to Philip of Spain in July 1554 was celebrated in great style, as this contemporary commentator wrote:

This marriage being ended and solemnized, which was declared and done by the said Lord Chancellor both in Latin and in English, his Lordship also declared there that the Emperor's Majesty signed under his Imperial Seal the Kingdoms of Naples and Jerusalem to his son, Philip, Prince of Spain, whereby it might well appear to all men that the Queen's Highness was then married not only to a Prince but also to a King.

The Queen's marriage ring was a plain hoop of gold without any stone in it, for that was her pleasure, because maidens were so married in old times.

There was for certain days after this most noble marriage such triumphing, banqueting, singing, masquing, and dancing as was never in England heretofore. Wherefore, to see the King's Majesty and the Queen sitting under the cloth of state, in the hall where they dined, and also in the chamber of presence at dancing time, where both their majesties danced, and also to behold the dukes and noble men of Spain dance with the fair ladies and most beautiful nymphs in England, it should seem to him to be another world.

(John Elder, *Copie of a letter sent in to Scotlande*)

A less ecstatic view of the proceedings was taken by the Spanish gentlemen, who did not envy Philip his duty. Ruy Gómez described Mary in patronizing terms as 'a very good creature, though rather older than we had been told'. Two days later, he added:

I believe that if she dressed in our fashions, she would not look so old and flabby. To speak frankly with you, it will take a great God to drink this cup. I have made every preparation for doing my share; and the best of it is that the King fully realises that the marriage was concluded for no fleshly consideration, but in order to remedy the disorders of this kingdom and preserve the Low Countries.

The following month, another gentleman reported to a friend in Salamanca:

Their Majesties are the happiest couple in the world, and more in love than words can say. His Highness never leaves her, and when we are on the road, he is ever by her side, helping her to mount and dismount. They sometimes dine

together in public, and go to mass together on holy days. The Queen, however, is not at all beautiful: small, and rather flabby than fat, she is of white complexion and fair, and has no eyebrows. She is a perfect saint, and dresses badly.

(*Calendar of State Papers, Spanish*, vol. xiii)

Philip spent less than a quarter of their married life in England. To the emperor, Philip's father, Mary wrote: 'I confess I do unspeakably long to have him here.' During the last year of her life, when she was ill and fancied herself pregnant, he remained abroad. In December 1558, he wrote, pleasantly, 'I felt a reasonable regret for her death.'

the French, after a quick campaign, recaptured the town of Calais, after more than two hundred years under English rule. A third visit by Philip failed to materialize. Ten months later, without child, without husband, without hope,

Mary died, and was buried, not in robes of state, but dressed as a member of a religious order.

To what extent did these events damage the crown? Jane Grey's interregnum was a mere hiccough, serving, if anything, to confirm the strength of Mary's position. Wyatt's rebellion, six months later, was a more serious affair: the rebels, 4,000 in number, reached Westminster and were thwarted only by the Lord Mayor of London, who refused to open Ludgate to them. But in any case, even if successful, the probable effect of the rising would have been to place Elizabeth on the throne: the dynasty itself was not in jeopardy. The loss of Calais, though a personal and national mortification, was a blessing in disguise, ending the wild dreams of a French empire, and opening up the possibility of colonial development overseas. In other ways, too, Mary handed over a strengthened throne. The melodrama of her personal disaster must not obscure the steps towards an improved administration. Her Council began to tackle some of the economic difficulties, a review of customs duties provided a substantial increase in revenue, most of which went to ease Elizabeth's task, and a start was made on improving the condition of roads, which would greatly facilitate trade and good government. Against this, the restoration of those Church lands still in the possession of the crown further weakened its position in relation to the gentry and nobility, who pointedly declined Mary's invitation to give back their own lands voluntarily. Mary had also to recognize that an unquestionable reconciliation with Rome depended largely on the use of Parliament, thus confirming the increase in prestige that its vigorous role in the 1530s had given it.

As is often the case, the question to which one would most like the answer eludes historians—whether a longer period of Catholic rule would have produced a permanently Catholic country. The imponderables are too many for dogmatism and the hypotheses cancel each other out. There is little doubt that the original impetus of Protestantism was declining and the Counter-Reformation organizing itself: one cannot rule out the possibility that a sustained campaign of persecution would have proved as successful in England as it was in Bavaria and Bohemia. On the other hand, there is evidence of serious and growing discontent with Mary's policies, together with a dangerously eligible alternative to hand in Elizabeth. The key problem is to know what length of Catholic rule to postulate and here, ironically, the crucial decision may have been Henry's marriage to Jane Seymour, which produced Edward. Had Mary inherited in 1547, she would have taken over a country still basically Catholic in doctrine and would, at the age of thirty-one, have had much better prospects of a long reign for herself, and a Catholic heir.

The question of the succession, unresolved despite Henry's preoccupation with it, dominated much of Elizabeth's reign, colouring, if not dictating, her attitude towards marriage, foreign relations, and the religious settlement. Like other mortals, Elizabeth had a marked distaste for contemplating her own extinction— gazing on her own shroud was her apt description. This was not mere human weakness but an awareness that a named successor would undoubtedly become a focus for all the disappointed and discontented in her realm.

The succession itself passed off without mishap. In the last few months of her reign, Mary came to accept that her sister would succeed her. Philip of Spain was already contemplating the possibility of marriage to Elizabeth, found it unlikely that his overtures could be rejected, and flattered himself that his support had brought about her peaceable succession.

Mary's reign had done little to reconcile conservative men to the idea of female rule. Fortunately for Elizabeth, most of her immediate rivals were also female. If the prohibition of the Scottish line was upheld, next in succession was Lady Catherine Grey, younger sister of Lady Jane and granddaughter of Mary, younger sister of Henry VIII. But after the catastrophe of 1553 it was improbable that the Greys would make another push. Lady Catherine's sister had perished at the block in 1554, and her mother had remarried a ginger-haired groom, sixteen years her junior. If the claims of the Scottish line were allowed, the successor was Mary, child of James V, who had become queen of Scotland when she was seven days old. Now aged sixteen, she was married to the dauphin of France. Though by adopting the style of queen of England, Mary threw her hat into the ring, she was not for most Englishmen an attractive candidate. Not only would her succession have brought the distinct possibility of the country falling under French domination just as it was congratulating itself on having escaped from Spanish, but the union of France, Scotland, and England in a powerful western bloc must mean warfare on the grand scale against the Habsburgs in Spain, Germany, and Italy.

The uncertainty over the succession was emphasized in October 1562 when Elizabeth fell victim to smallpox and for several days was believed to be dying. William Cecil, Secretary of State, favoured summoning Lady Catherine from the Tower to be queen. Mary, widowed since 1560 and maintaining a precarious hold upon her Scottish kingdom, found few supporters. Another Scottish descendant of Margaret Tudor was Margaret, countess of Lennox. With her the succession seemed assured, since she had a seventeen-year-old son, Henry, Lord Darnley, whose physical charms had already been appraised and whose intellectual defects were not yet fully apparent. A Yorkist candidate was Henry, earl of Huntingdon, and great-great-grandson of that George, duke of Clarence, elder brother of Richard III, who had ended up in a butt of malmsey wine. Aged twenty-seven, Huntingdon's sex and Protestant inclinations made him a plausible candidate, but the moment passed, and he settled down as one of Elizabeth's more useful supporters.

MARY QUEEN OF SCOTS' marriages produced one child and little happiness. At fifteen she married the future Francis II of France, who succeeded to the throne unexpectedly in 1559 but died a year later. In this portrait by François Clouet she is shown as dauphiness. Her second marriage to Lord Darnley ended after eighteen months when he was mysteriously killed. Almost at once she married the earl of Bothwell, who, after a few weeks, fled to Denmark; he was incarcerated for years at Dragsholm, where his body is still preserved. Mary spent nearly half her life in captivity in England before her execution in 1587. Her son by Darnley, James, united the crowns of England and Scotland in 1603.

Like her half-sister Mary, Elizabeth had been brought up in a hard school, but had reacted differently. To an even greater extent she had been in mortal danger. For much of Mary's reign, her execution had been urged upon the queen. After the Wyatt rising, she had spent two months in the Tower, while the conspirators were racked to provide evidence against her. But after a few youthful indiscretions with Thomas, Lord Seymour, Elizabeth had discovered the wisdom of prudence, a low profile, and dissimulation. By comparison with Mary, she had three advantages. At the age of twenty-five, the question of marriage was less urgent. There was no attractive rival within sight. Thirdly, while there is little evidence that Mary was above average in intelligence, it soon became clear that the new ruler was a woman of character, ability, and determination. It is true that she was much given to tergiversation, particularly as she grew older, but often this was a balancing act between factions, and sometimes it reflected her understanding that the issues were more complex than some of her more robust advisers understood. What is remarkable is the evidence, after years of chaos and

THES BE THE SONES OF ʤ RIGHT HONERABLES ʤELLE OF LENOXE AD
ʤE LADY MARGARETZ GRACE COVNTYES OF LENOXE AD ANGWYSE.

1563

CHARLLES STEWARDE
HIS BROTHER. ÆTATIS. 6.

HENRY STEWARDE LORD DAR
LEY AND DOWGLAS, ÆTATIS, 17.

HENRY, LORD DARNLEY, was a great-grandson of Henry VII. At the time of this painting, which shows him with his younger brother, he was seventeen. Mary Queen of Scots, recently widowed as queen of France, was much taken with his tall and slender appearance and married him in July 1565. His time as king of Scotland was disastrous. He became impossibly arrogant and played an equivocal part in the murder of Mary's musician, David Rizzio. In February 1567 he was himself murdered at Kirk o' Fields.

misjudgement, of a first-class intelligence at work, weighing problems, anticipating rather than reacting to difficulties, and with a cool judgement that contrasted sharply with the fitful and choleric outbursts of her father and the sullen tenacity of her half-sister. Above all she was endowed with one of the rarest of political gifts—the more remarkable in a woman of autocratic and imperious temper—the instinct to know when to give way and how to do it gracefully.

The progresses for which Elizabeth was celebrated served a variety of functions. Their main intent was to show the sovereign to her people and to enable her to win acclaim by graceful and considerate actions. But there were more utilitarian motives. The standard of Tudor sanitation meant that the royal palaces became unbearable after several weeks of occupation and the court's absence for several months in the summer gave an opportunity to clean up. Such large numbers of persons had to be transported, together with vast quantities of luggage, clothing, furnishings, and supplies, that the royal convoy moved extremely slowly and twelve miles was a very reasonable day's journey. Consequently, progresses were limited to the south and the midlands. Elizabeth made at least twenty-five progresses in her forty-five years on the throne. A very high standard of ceremony and entertainment was expected. The sheriff and gentry welcomed their sovereign at the boundaries of each county and the mayor and corporation at each borough. The streets were decorated with flags and bunting, church bells rang, fireworks were set off, pageants prepared, and orators licked their lips in preparation for lengthy speeches. Elizabeth was adept at both the gentle and the florid touch. At Warwick, in 1572, where she had been warned that the Recorder would be more than commonly nervous, she beckoned him with 'Come hither, little Recorder . . . you were not so afraid of me as I was of you, and I now thank you for putting me in mind of my duty.' Six years later, at Norwich, when the Mayor presented her with a cup of money, she protested that

ANOTHER PART OF THE FOREST. Elizabeth's picnics were elaborate affairs, the queen still surrounded by courtiers and served on bended knee. Leicester wrote to Burghley in 1575 of a disaster on the queen's progress to Kenilworth: 'even by and by Her Majesty is going to the forest to kill some bucks with her bow . . . God be thanked, she is very merry and well-disposed now. But at her first coming, being a marvellous hot day, at her coming hither, not one drop of good drink for her . . . But we were fain to London with bottles, to Kennilworth, to divers other places where ale was . . . It did put her very far out of temper.' Victoria's picnics from Balmoral, three hundred years later, were less formal, the queen relishing a nip of whisky provided by John Brown.

what she really valued were 'the hearts and true allegiance of our subjects'—
though, characteristically, she did not return the money.

For her religious settlement that picked a careful path between the extremes of
Catholicism and Puritanism, she has been much praised. But in fact her room for
manœuvre was limited. Submission to the papacy must logically mean accepting
that her father's divorce had never been valid and that she was a bastard with no
claim to the throne. Consequently, Parliament was used to reinvest her with the
Supreme Governorship of the Church—the change of title from Supreme Head

being a gesture of conciliation. But the total opposition of the bench of bishops to her renewed breach with Rome (she was hard put to it to find a bishop to crown her and had to be content with the bishop of Carlisle) pushed her into a less conservative posture than she might have wished. On the other flank, there was little in the Puritan or Calvinist position to commend itself to a monarch. She disliked the fanatical character of the movement, its long and reproachful sermonizing, and its presumption that the secular arm should be directed by the spiritual. One who could barely stomach bishops was unlikely to revere presbyters. John Knox, who had been considered for a bishopric in 1552, insisted that 'the punishment of such crimes as idolatry, blasphemy and others that touch the majesty of God, doth not appertain to kings and chief rulers only, but to the whole body of that people', and he specifically denounced the doctrine of obedience to the monarch in all things as horrible blasphemy.

The chances of the religious settlement taking root depended mainly upon Elizabeth herself surviving until a new generation of subjects had grown up, by whom the new services were taken for granted, or even admired. The prospects of the queen reigning for forty-five years must have appeared distinctly remote. Her immediate predecessors had lasted six and five years respectively. In an age of violence and political assassination, the odds were not good. In Scotland, Darnley was proclaimed king in 1565 and blown up eighteen months later. Four successive Regents met violent deaths—Cardinal Beaton in 1546, Moray in 1570, Lennox in 1571, and Morton in 1581. In France, the duc de Guise was shot in 1563 and his son killed in 1588, the duc de Condé in 1569, Henri III in 1589, and Henri IV in 1610. William the Silent, Dutch stadtholder, was assassinated in 1584. Elizabeth survived the rising of the northern earls in 1569, but her position was made infinitely more hazardous in 1570 by the publication of a papal bull, specifically releasing her subjects from their allegiance. The Ridolfi plot of 1571, in which her cousin the duke of Norfolk was involved, was followed by the Throckmorton plot in 1583, Dr Parry's plot in 1585, and the Babington plot in 1586.

Even if Elizabeth survived dagger and poison, there remained the chance of foreign intervention to place Mary Queen of Scots on the throne. A grand coalition of France and Spain to restore a Catholic monarch was by no means out of the question, and Elizabeth's object had to be to weaken both powers and to reduce the chances of their acting together.

High among strategic considerations was bolting the back doors. From Wales, Ireland, and Scotland, invasions had been repeatedly launched. The reorganization of Wales during her father's reign had brought that country firmly under control. But England's hold upon Ireland remained precarious and the fact that Protestantism made little progress among the native Irish added religious to national animosities. Elizabeth did not have the resources to effect any permanent improvement there and the country remained an easy target for Spanish activity. For the most part, the English continued to regard the native population with horror: 'it is the fatal destiny of that land,' wrote Edmund Spenser, 'that no purposes, whatsoever are meant for her good, will prosper or take effect': perhaps, he mused, God had reserved that land 'for some secret scourge that shall come by her into England'. All through the early years of Elizabeth's reign there were rebellions and risings. The Irish door was never firmly shut and, at the end of her reign, swung open dangerously to let in the Spaniards.

If Ireland was the natural hunting-ground for the Spaniards, Scotland was traditionally that of the French. Flodden and Pinkie Cleugh had demonstrated England's superiority in arms, but a turbulent feudal nobility, growing Presbyterian interest, and a volatile queen made Scotland an unstable and uncomfortable neighbour. At the accession of Elizabeth, Scotland was virtually a French satellite, with Mary living in France as the dauphiness, and her mother Mary of Guise acting as Regent in Scotland. The treaty of Cateau-Cambrésis in 1559 brought to an end the long Franco-Spanish conflict and opened up the possibility of a French–Scottish–Spanish Catholic alliance. This threat was removed by the events of 1559–60 when, in the name of Protestantism, the Scottish lords rebelled. With great hesitation, Elizabeth intervened to assist them and the resultant treaty of Edinburgh formed the basis for a changed relationship. Mary abandoned her claim to the English throne (though remaining a possible successor), the French troops were sent home, and papal jurisdiction was replaced by a Presbyterian form of Church government. Though the problem of Mary continued to exercise Elizabeth for a further twenty-six years, Scotland itself had been brought permanently into the English orbit.

Among the leading political questions to be settled was the problem of Elizabeth's marriage. In the conditions of the day, it was impossible that a husband, foreign or English, would not attempt to exercise real authority. That, more than any mystical attachment to virginity, was probably at the heart of Elizabeth's own reservations. But the difficulties in choosing a husband were genuine enough. A foreign prince, if he was of adequate rank, would almost certainly seek to use England for his own ambitions as Philip of Spain had done. A native subject, even if one of sufficient distinction could be found, would drag the queen into factions. There was the further complication that Elizabeth regarded the question as personal and prerogative, while her subjects, with some justice, regarded it as a matter of vast public importance, on which they were entitled to air their opinions.

As early as February 1559, when she had been on the throne no more than three months, the House of Commons reminded her of her duty to marry. She offered a wordy and ambiguous reply, assuring them that she would never marry to the prejudice of the realm. After that, for nearly thirty years, suitors swam

ELIZABETH AGED THIRTY-SIX
One of the many fine portraits
by Nicholas Hilliard, the best
miniaturist of the age. It was
drawn from life, since Hilliard
later recorded that the queen
asked him about the use of
shadow and chose carefully
where to sit.

about her and aspirants languished, often in Latin. Philip of Spain put in his bid at once and was assured by his envoy that should the queen marry a foreigner 'she will at once fix her eyes on Your Majesty'. But when the suit was further pressed, Philip was reminded that marriage to a dead brother's wife had caused complications in the past and marriage to a dead sister's husband might do no less.

She had some lucky escapes. The Archduke Charles was a front runner in the early years of her reign. But he was said by his detractors to have a head even bigger than the earl of Bedford's and since he refused to come to England to allow comparisons to be made, the suit did not prosper. The earl of Arran, who had a claim to the Scottish throne, was put forward as a candidate in 1560 and rejected: he subsequently went insane. Erik XIV of Sweden waged a long and ardent campaign in the 1560s but, after defeat, married the daughter of a common soldier and was deposed as a homicidal maniac in 1568.

Among the native population, Sir William Pickering, a nubile ambassador, held the stage for a few brief months in 1559. The earl of Arundel, another candidate, was forty-six at Elizabeth's accession, and twice widowed. But the leading contender, for many years, was Lord Robert Dudley, grandson of Henry VII's minister, son of the duke of Northumberland who had brought forward Lady Jane Grey, and himself raised to the peerage by the queen in 1564 as earl of Leicester. Confident and personable, there was no doubt that Elizabeth was greatly attracted to him. But Dudley was married to Amy Robsart and though her mysterious death in 1560 cleared that difficulty, the manner of it made it almost impossible for Elizabeth to marry him. Such a marriage would have provoked the most bitter opposition, not least from William Cecil, appointed Secretary of State on the first day of her reign. In the end, Elizabeth remained the only unmarried ruler, of marriageable years, among the forty-one monarchs since William Rufus.

Marriage was used by Elizabeth, in the time-honoured way, as a weapon of diplomacy. She had seen the reputation of her half-sister speedily reduced by injudicious policies and she gave to the retention of her own popularity a very high priority. This necessitated the avoidance of heavy taxation which, in turn, ruled out an ambitious policy abroad. Her personal caution in such matters was reinforced by her early experiences. Though she got out of the Scottish intervention in 1560 with gratifying results, it had been an expensive business. Her second adventure, in France, was less gratifying and even more expensive. The outbreak of open warfare between the Huguenots and the Catholic Guise faction promised the opportunity to weaken that kingdom, strike a blow for Protestantism, and either regain Calais or an equivalent. In 1562 she promised the Huguenot leaders substantial subsidies, and an army of 3,000 men was dispatched under Dudley's brother, Warwick, to seize and hold Le Havre. The result was disaster. The French factions made peace in 1563 and joined forces to besiege the English. Decimated by plague, Warwick had no alternative but to capitulate.

Throughout the 1560s and 1570s the miserable French religious strife continued under two feeble monarchs, Charles IX and Henri III. But whatever wry pleasure might be felt at the discomfiture of an old enemy was mitigated by the realization that it rendered France incapable of offering effective resistance to the apparently growing power of Spain. Indeed, the understanding between the Guise faction and the Spaniards offered a worse scenario—of joint action by them in support of the Counter-Reformation. The ludicrous drawn-out marriage negotiations in the 1570s and 1580s between Elizabeth and the French princes of the blood—first Anjou and then Alençon—owed as much to the need to keep on terms with the French as with Elizabeth's personal desire to preserve as long as possible the pleasures of dalliance and courtship. 'If I were a milkmaid with a pail on my arm', she told Sir John Harington in 1576, 'I would not match with the greatest monarch.' But two years later, the Alençon match was on again, with her night-cap sent to him as a token of encouragement to do his wooing in person. Against all the odds—Alencon was small, half her age, and had a deformed nose—his visit in August 1578 was a great success. In 1580 French envoys to discuss the marriage terms were entertained by a pageant in which the Fortress of Perfect Beauty was assailed by Desire. The assault failed. By this time, diplomatic considerations were more important than ardour. Subsidies from his bride-to-be enabled Alençon to carry on desultory warfare against the Spaniards in the Low Countries. Slowly the match cooled, Elizabeth promising to be a sister to him. When he died in 1584, marriage for the purpose of an heir was out of the question. Nevertheless, Elizabeth was greatly affected by the news.

By this time, there were more desperate matters to worry about. The Dutch had risen in revolt against their Spanish rulers and appealed for help from Protestant Europe. Elizabeth responded with great caution, partly because she did not wish to encourage rebels against their lawful sovereign. The most she would permit at first was the dispatch of 'volunteers' in 1572 and 1578. But by 1584 it looked as if such modest measures would not prevent the Dutch from being totally overthrown. The Spaniards had acquired a considerable boost in resources in 1580 with the acquisition of Portugal, and the assassination of William the Silent in 1584 threatened to tear the heart out of Dutch resistance. In August 1585 the queen accepted the necessity of a formal treaty in support of the Dutch and an expedition was sent out under the command of Leicester.

The conflict between Philip and Elizabeth brought Mary Queen of Scots into play once more. Since 1567 she had been a captive in English custody, the Scottish throne being occupied by her young son, James VI. Philip's obvious move was to effect her rescue and place her on the throne by force of arms. In August 1586 Walsingham picked up the Babington conspirators, whose evidence made Mary's complicity in the plot abundantly clear. Mary was tried in October and found guilty. The following month Parliament begged Elizabeth to proceed to execution. In February 1587, after an agony of indecision, Elizabeth had her cousin beheaded.

By this time, Philip's plans for the Enterprise of England, the great knock-out blow, were well advanced. Though greatly scaled down in the course of preparation, and seriously disrupted by Drake's brilliant raid on Cadiz in the spring of 1587, the Armada, when it set sail in July 1588, was the largest expeditionary force in history. A fleet of 130 ships, manned by 8,000 sailors, were to escort some 20,000 men to a junction off the coast at Calais with another 20,000 troops from Parma's forces, and land them on the Kent coast. Their landing would coincide with a rising of the English Catholics, urged on by the dispersal of copies of Cardinal Allen's *Admonition to the Nobility and People of England*, calling upon them to overthrow the usurper and restore the true faith.

Preparations on this scale could not be made in secret and the English had had months to look to their defences. The objective had to be to prevent a Spanish landing: once ashore, the outcome would be doubtful. Since 1578, Hawkins had been getting the navy into shape, building smaller and faster vessels and equipping them with heavy long-range guns. Augmented by private vessels and converted merchantmen, the English could expect a rough parity in ships, inferior in tonnage but superior in handling. There was no standing army. The bulk of the

MARY

(1542–1567), queen of Scots

'I am myself a Queen, the daughter of a King, a stranger, and the true kinswoman of the Queen of England. I came to England on my cousin's promise of assistance against my enemies and rebel subjects and was at once imprisoned.'

Mary at her trial, October 1586

'You have planned in divers ways and manners to take my life and to ruin my kingdom . . . I never proceeded so harshly against you; on the contrary, I have maintained you and preserved your life with the same care which I use for myself.'

Elizabeth to Mary, October 1586

MINIATURE OF MARY, later in her captivity in England.

THE situation which faced Mary when she returned to Scotland in 1561 after the death of her first husband Francis II would have taxed the most experienced statesman. The Scottish nobility was turbulent and factious, Protestantism had made great strides, and her mother, Mary of Guise, had ended her Regency and life besieged in Edinburgh castle. Mary was still only nineteen and had been brought up in France since she was five.

Had she concentrated totally on Scotland, it might have been possible to restore much of royal authority. But the lure of the English throne, either by replacing or succeeding Elizabeth, wrecked the prospect. It was in part responsible for her disastrous second marriage to Darnley, great-grandson of Henry VII. After Darnley's murder and Mary's hasty marriage to one of his assassins, Lord Bothwell, Mary's credit was exhausted. She left in 1568 to seek refuge in England. There she remained for nineteen years until the discovery of the Babington Plot against Elizabeth sealed her doom. Elizabeth's ministers demanded execution: 'as long as life is in her, there is hope: so they as they live in hope, we live in fear.' After great hesitation, Elizabeth signed the death warrant at Greenwich on 1 February 1587, and Mary was beheaded at Fotheringhay a week later. As the executioner lifted the head, the thick auburn tresses parted, revealing grey cropped hair.

forces available were the shire levies, organized by the Lords Lieutenant, and of dubious quality. The more formidable fighting men were provided by the nobility and gentry—Hatton bringing 400, Essex 300, and Walsingham 260. At Tilbury, where the main force gathered, Leicester had no more than 12,000 men, with perhaps another 1,000 as a bodyguard for the queen.

The two other supreme factors were money and commanders. Elizabeth had some advantages in that her credit was better than Philip's, who had already sustained two bankruptcies, but it was essential to husband her slender resources. Leicester's campaigns in the Low Countries had already made a severe dent in Elizabeth's treasure-chest. To keep the army at readiness in the field cost some £80,000 a month, and the navy an additional £12,000. These

ELIZABETH I

(1558–1603)

ELIZABETH took more than common pains with appearances: she had hundreds of dresses and a vast collection of jewellery. In 1563, after she had been on the throne for five years, she issued a proclamation against inferior or debased representations of herself, promising that 'some special person' would be allowed to finish a portrait to act as a copy for all others. Thirty-three years later, the queen's Serjeant Painter was ordered to destroy all unseemly portraits of her. In the course of time a formalized portrait emerged. Horace Walpole wrote in the eighteenth century that 'a pale Roman nose, a head of hair loaded with crowns and powdered with diamonds, a vast ruff, a vaster fardingale, and a bushel of pearls, are the features by which everybody knows at once the pictures of Queen Elizabeth'.

Since she lived to be, by Tudor standards, an old woman, the gap between myth and reality widened year by year. At the end of her reign, young courtiers swooned at the feet of a bony and arthritic woman, with bad teeth and a red wig: 'England's Astrea, Albion's shining sun.' She became a legend in her own lifetime. But however much the queen enjoyed flattery, her feet remained firmly on the ground, as the Essex crisis demonstrated. In 1600 Essex, in disgrace after his behaviour in Ireland and fearful of losing the farm of the sweet wines on which his fortune depended, bombarded her with appeals for forgiveness: 'if Your Majesty will vouchsafe to let me once prostrate myself at your feet and behold your fair and gracious eyes . . . though afterwards Your Majesty punish me, imprison me, or pronounce the sentence of death against me . . . I shall be most happy.' To Francis Bacon, Elizabeth remarked, with laconic bitterness: 'My Lord of Essex has written me some very dutiful letters, and I have been moved by them, but what I took for the abundance of the heart, I find to be only a

suit for the farm of sweet wines.' Essex, in a rage, declared that the queen's mind had become as crooked as her carcase, and, tempted into treason, ended on the block.

were prohibitive figures. Walsingham's intelligence service assured her in the summer of 1587 that the Spaniards could not come until the summer of 1588; she raised £75,000 by a forced defence loan, borrowed £35,000 from the city in March, and a further £26,000 in August. Nevertheless, the drain of money was a major preoccupation, and the fleet had to be disbanded within a month of the decisive encounter.

To command the naval forces, Elizabeth chose Lord Howard of Effingham, not the most experienced of her captains, but level-headed and conciliatory. He was given wide powers of discretion and handled his spirited captains with skill. Medina-Sidonia, the Spanish commander, was not without talent, but he was ill, dejected, and handicapped by precise and inviolable instructions.

The queen was at her favourite palace of Richmond when the Armada was first sighted on 19 July. She moved to St James's at the end of the month, and on 8 August, while the danger was still not past, went to Tilbury to review her troops. The following day she addressed them in one of her most famous speeches. Picking up the threat to her person contained in Allen's foolish pamphlet, she began by telling them that she had been warned not to commit herself to armed multitudes for fear of treachery: 'but I assure you, I do not desire to live in distrust of my faithful and loving people,' and ended by never doubting 'that by your obedience to my general, by your concord in the camp and your valour in the

ROBERT DEVEREUX, EARL OF ESSEX, emerged as the leading favourite of Elizabeth after the death of his stepfather Leicester in 1588. But he got into financial difficulties and after the failure of his Irish expedition in 1599 engaged in a half-hearted and amateurish rising. He was executed on Tower Hill on 25 February 1601 at the age of thirty-four.

THE GARTER PROCESSION OF 1576 by Marcus Gheeraerts. The revived cult of the Garter, with its Arthurian and heroic implications, fitted in well with Tudor aspirations and Elizabeth made much use of it. The annual feast was invariably imposing and the occasional degradation of a knight melodramatic. Elizabeth, at the rear, is preceded by a nobleman bearing the sword of state. In front of them are two gentlemen ushers; Sir Thomas Smith, principal secretary of state with the bishop of Winchester; Usher of the Black Rod, the Registrar (Dean of Windsor) and Sir Gilbert Dethick, Garter King of Arms; the Emperor Maximilian, on the right, was not present but is included by artistic licence.

field, we shall shortly have a famous victory over these enemies of my God, of my Kingdom and of my People'. Not until the speeches of Churchill in the 1940s was rhetoric to play a more important role nor fit the occasion so exactly.

Meanwhile, the vast Armada made its way slowly up the Channel, the English ships snapping at its heels, picking off the odd vessel, but not inflicting a mortal blow. At the end of the week it lay off Calais, waiting for Parma's men. Overnight, Howard sent in eight large fire-ships, with devastating effect. The Spanish vessels cut their cables and ran, losing their cohesion as a fighting force. After a sharp action the following day, Medina-Sidonia resolved to make for Spain by way of the Scottish and Irish route. Forty-four of his ships, including many of the largest, never reached home, and two-thirds of his men perished. The English losses were incredibly light—not one ship and no more than a hundred men, though disease, as usual, took its grim toll. Not one invader reached the shore of England.

The defeat of the Armada was the prelude to a long and gruelling struggle. Philip had both the will and the resources to strike again and again. Protestant prospects appeared to improve once more when Henri III of France was assassinated in 1589 and succeeded by Henri of Navarre. But Henri IV, despite help from Elizabeth, had much difficulty in establishing his claim, and in 1593

took the step of converting to Catholicism. Naval operations against the Spaniards in the 1590s found it hard to repeat the successes of former years and were just as easily diverted from strategic purposes to loot. Twice in the later 1590s Philip mounted further Armadas, and twice the English were saved by the weather rather than by their own exertions. But the most menacing aspect of the continued warfare was the increasing success that the Spaniards achieved in stirring up revolt in Ireland.

The English position in Ireland had long been hazardous. Money was not available to make subjugation possible, plantations had failed, disorder was endemic, and there had been revolts of the great Irish families every decade of the reign. But Tyrone's rising of 1595 was on a totally different scale and threatened to overthrow England's position completely. The Spaniards supplied him with arms and money and at the Yellow Ford in 1597 he inflicted a major defeat on the English forces, killing their commander. Elizabeth was determined that the defeat be avenged and the command, in 1599, was given to Essex, Leicester's stepson and Cecil's rival at court. Essex's conduct defied belief. The one quality of fighting courage he did possess deserted him and most of his vigour was devoted to the wholesale creation of knights. Nothing could persuade him to give battle to Tyrone in his Ulster stronghold. Instead he met Tyrone for secret

THE CULT OF ELIZABETH. Hans Eworth's painting of 1569 is an early example of the transformation of Elizabeth into a figure of transcendental beauty, radiance, and majesty. In this new judgement of Paris, the three goddesses are routed, Juno taking her defeat particularly badly, Venus unconcerned. In the background is a glimpse of Windsor Castle.

talks and arranged a truce. 'Perilous and contemptible' was Elizabeth's terse comment. Essex's last throw was on a par with the rest of his judgement—a headlong dash from Dublin to throw himself, mud-bespattered, at the queen's feet at Nonsuch. The following day he was under arrest. It was left to Mountjoy in 1601 to defeat both Tyrone and the 5,000 men the Spaniards had landed.

Essex's revolt, in February 1601, was as ill-organized and irresolute as his Irish campaign had been—a mere spasm of faction. Yet it cast shadows over the last years of Elizabeth's reign and has contributed to the view of them as years of decline and decay: 'crisis and desperation' is the verdict of one historian, the years in which everything went sour. Certainly the 1590s were difficult, with poor harvests, financial strain, restive Parliaments, and a Puritan movement becoming increasingly dissatisfied with the line Elizabeth's bishops were taking. The war against Spain dragged on, with no conclusion in sight. Yet the portrait of decay is surely overdrawn. Some power was bound to seep from the queen as age overtook her and prudent men calculated on her successor. But she handled the Irish crisis with resolution, never flinched at the Essex rising, and in her golden

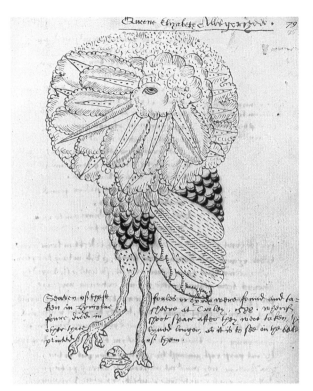

A STRANGE BIRD TAKEN AT CROWLEY IN 1588 (*left*). Not all representations of Elizabeth were flattering and in this drawing her ruff is swollen up into an image of vanity. The title is 'Queen Elizabeth allegorized'. The text relates that seven of these birds were found and taken at Crowley (Crowland) in Lincolnshire; four died in great fear after they were taken but three lived longer.

THE QUEEN'S UNIVERSE (*right*). In this representation from John Case's *Sphaera civitatis*, published in 1588, Elizabeth presides over a Ptolemaic system. To her are attributed Majesty, Prudence, Fortitude, Religion, Clemency, Eloquence, and Abundance.

speech to MPs in November 1601, dealing with the protests against monopolies, showed herself at her disarming best.

Elizabeth's concept of her own position and powers was lofty and she did not shrink from expounding it. In 1566, under presure from both Houses to take action about the succession, she summoned thirty members of each to her presence, and warned them: 'I am your annointed Queen. I will never be by violence constrained to do anything. I thank God I am endued with such qualities that if I were turned out of the realm in my petticoat, I were able to live in any place in Christendom.' When she dismissed that Parliament, two months later, she advised them 'never to tempt too far a prince's patience'. In 1571, the House of Commons was told to 'meddle with no matters of state but such as should be proposed to them'. She used freely her power to veto legislation: fifteen bills that had got through in the 1585 session bit the dust.

In the struggle between Elizabeth and her Commons, honours were, by and large, even. The prolongation of the war after 1588 made the summoning of Parliaments more necessary and the need for extraordinary supply gave the Commons a sharp weapon. In the debate over monopolies, the queen was forced to retreat. Yet though she could not always prevent them from discussing her marriage, the succession, or the religious question, their deliberations did not necessarily have much effect upon policy.

For decades to come, men looked back at the reign of Elizabeth as a golden age. In 1588, the nation, against what appeared to be all the odds, had survived a moment of extreme peril. Both the outcome and the manner of its achievement helped to identify people and ruler as seldom ever before. Elizabeth's Church settlement, largely the product of expediency in her early years on the throne, rooted itself and grew strong: fortified by the polemical defence by Richard Hooker, the Church of England attracted to itself, in the course of time, a passionate loyalty and became one of the chief props to the monarchy. Elizabeth herself, by the end of her reign, was a legend and an institution, the pride of her people and a source of amazement to Europe. Only old men and women could remember any other ruler: it was the longest reign since Edward III and she was the oldest monarch ever to sit on the throne of England.

Her formal portraits, in growing contrast to reality, presented a queen of majestic, serene, and imposing appearance, unscathed by the passing of time: *semper eadem* had always been one of Elizabeth's favourite mottoes. Her decision not to marry became a deliberate act of self-sacrifice, a mystical virginity denoting her total devotion to her people. Great poets and artists competed to flatter her. In Hans Eworth's painting of 1569, Juno, Minerva, and Venus were routed by Elizabeth in a new judgement of Paris. To Edmund Spenser in the *Faerie Queene* she was Gloriana; Ben Jonson saluted her as 'Queen and huntress, chaste and fair'; for Shakespeare she was 'a pattern to all princes living with her and all that shall succeed'. More simply, but perhaps with greater sincerity, the street ballads called her 'the great lionness'.

She was fortunate in her death. As late as 1602, she was still dancing with enthusiasm, both publicly and privately at Hampton Court. Her temper became fiercer than ever and she was, from time to time, the prey to melancholy, brooding on Essex and the past. But in February 1603, when the new envoy from Venice was due for an audience, the old queen put on a vintage performance. First his visit was postponed at the last minute, which, he reported sedately, was a fairly routine piece of haughtiness. A week later he was summoned by a Gentleman Pensioner and introduced into the presence chamber by the Lord Chamberlain:

The Queen was clad in taffety of silver and white trimmed with gold; her dress was somewhat open in front and showed her throat encircled with pearls and rubies down to her breast. Her skirts were much fuller and began lower down than is the fashion in France. Her hair was of a light colour never made by nature, and she wore great pearls like pears round the forehead; she had a coif arched round her head and an Imperial crown, and displayed a vast quantity of gems and pearls upon her person.

She conducted the audience in Italian, one of the nine lauguages she was said to command, and which included Irish, Cornish, and Welsh, and reproached the envoy gently that the Venetian Republic had been so slow in establishing diplomatic contacts. At the end of the audience, she offered her hand to be kissed, and, with pardonable vanity, remarked: 'I do not know if I have spoken Italian well, still I think so, for I learnt it when a child, and I believe I have not forgotten it.' Six weeks later she was dead, quietly and peacefully: 'as easily as a ripe apple from a tree', observed one onlooker. She died, wrote the Venetian envoy, 'A Queen who had lived for long both gloriously and happily in this world.'

At her death, in 1603, she left her successor very serious problems. Most monarchs do. But there is nothing to suggest that they were more intractable than the ones she had faced at her accession in November 1558. That the monarchy itself was in peril in 1603 would have struck most Englishmen as absurd. Its weakness was one which her own success had illuminated—that personal monarchy at this level demanded a combination of skills and character that was extremely rare, and unlikely to be repeated.

James I and Charles I

While Elizabeth lay embalmed in the palace of Whitehall, James VI of Scotland flung himself south to claim his inheritance with all the dignity of a smash-and-grab raid. Learning the news on 26 March, he was over the border by 7 April, leaving his pregnant wife and three children to follow. At Berwick, he inspected the massive fortifications built in the 1550s to keep out the Scots. At Doncaster, he rewarded the landlord of the Bear Inn by granting him the reversion of a lease on a manor-house, hanged a thief without trial at Newark under the impresssion that it was legal, made promises galore, created knights by the dozen, and talked incessantly. His new subjects rushed to meet him and were charmed at his generosity and lack of reserve.

There was admittedly some excuse for haste. It was uncertain how the English would take to receiving a monarch from a country so often their bitter enemy. The infanta of Spain had a claim to the throne through her descent from John of Gaunt's daughter, Philippa, though it was not prosecuted. There was no opposition. For some years, the inevitability of the Scottish succession had been acknowledged, and from 1601 Sir Robert Cecil, Burghley's son and successor, had been in secret correspondence with James, sending him information and advice.

The first few months of James's accession, exploring his new palaces and estates, were probably the most happy of his life which, to that point, had hardly been of much tranquillity. He was six months in his mother's womb when Rizzio, the musician, was dragged from her at Holyrood and stabbed to death. Rumour hinted that Rizzio was actually James's father. When he was eight months old, his father, Darnley, was blown up and strangled, almost certainly with the complicity of his mother. Before he was a year old, Mary had married his father's murderer, the earl of Bothwell, and James never saw her again. When he was one year and one month, she was forced to abdicate and James was declared king. During his childhood, there were four Regents. The first, Moray, was shot when James was three; the second, Lennox, was killed in a skirmish when he was four; the third, Mar, died, believed poisoned, when he was five; the fourth, Morton, lasted several years, but was deposed in 1578, and executed three years later. In 1582 James, then sixteen, was kidnapped by Lord Gowrie and his supporters and held for eleven months against his will. In 1586 his mother was executed at Fotheringhay. James was then twenty. He grew up nervous, mistrustful, and with a reputation for dissembling: if his later portraits suggest a fearful disposition, it was not entirely without reason.

By the later 1590s, he had established some sort of order in his kingdom. In 1589 he made his one foreign visit, to Denmark, to marry the Princess Anne, stayed at Kronborg, and found the Danes hard drinkers. Though the marriage produced rather languid delight, it ensured the succession with the birth of Prince Henry in 1594 and Prince Charles in 1600. In the mean time, James had survived a conspiracy of the North Berwickshire witches, who had made waxen images and killed cats to effect their diabolical design, and between 1591 and 1594 he suffered repeated attempts by the earl of Bothwell to intimidate him by a show of force. Though he did not crush the nobility, James was gradually able to exert some authority, and after 1596 had gained the upper hand in his struggle against the presbytery. Nevertheless, the precarious nature of his position was demonstrated once more in August 1600, not much more than two years before his accession to the throne of England, by the Gowrie conspiracy. According to his own testimony, James was lured to their house by the sons of the Gowrie who had kidnapped him, and escaped only at the last minute another attempt to murder him in cold blood.

His English subjects were naturally interested to know the opinions of their new monarch and James was by no means unwilling to oblige them. His theoretical position had been established in two treatises in 1598 and 1599—the *Trew Law of Free Monarchies* and *Basilikon Doron*. The argument was a fairly simple assertion of divine right kingship, remarkable more for being spelled out than for any novelty. 'Kings', he insisted in the first book, 'are called Gods by the prophetical David because they sit upon God his throne in the earth and have the

THE HOPE OF ENGLAND. The eldest son of James I and Anne of Denmark, Henry was created Prince of Wales in 1610 when he was sixteen. 'He was of a comely, tall, middle stature,' wrote a friend, 'a strong, straight, well-made body (as if Nature in him had shewed all her cunning) with somewhat broad shoulders and a small waist . . . a most gracious smile with a terrible frown, courteous, loving.' Though the allegory in Robert Peake's painting shows the prince seizing Time by the forelock, he died of typhoid at the age of eighteen, leaving his less gifted brother Charles as heir to the throne.

count of their administration to give unto him.' Rebellion against a king, whether godly or not, was both unlawful and blasphemous. In *Basilikon Doron*, the same message was spelled out in verse form:

> God gives not kings the style of Gods in vain,
> For on his throne his sceptre do they sway,
> And as their subjects ought them to obey,
> So Kings should fear and serve their God again.

That these remained James's formal views may be surmised from his observations in March 1610 to an assembly of Lords and Commons in a two-hour harangue:

Kings exercise a manner of resemblance of divine power on earth . . . they have power of raising and casting down; of life and death; judges over all their subjects and in all causes, and yet accountable to none but God only.

In practice such lofty pretensions could not be maintained, either in Scotland or in England. It is difficult to assess the position of the Scottish monarchy in the century before the personal union of the crowns because, for much of the time, it was in minority: James V was eighteen months old when he succeeded after Flodden; Mary was only six days old when James V died, and her son, James VI, was just over a year old when his mother was forced to abdicate. Under these circumstances, it was not easy to distinguish the permanent power of the crown from a recovery as the young monarch took up the reins.

Conventional wisdom insists that the Scottish monarchy was a good deal stronger than the English. It is not easy to see that, except in the seventeenth century. First of all, the comparison is extremely awkward, since both monarchies and both Parliaments were evolving and changing all the time. The Scottish Parliament probably caused fewer problems to their monarchs. There was one chamber, which meant that the representatives of the royal burghs were overshadowed and intimidated by the great magnates. The development of the institution of the Lords of the Articles from the fifteenth century onwards meant that business was digested and legislation prepared before Parliament itself met. There was no debate and no power of initiating legislation. But Scottish kings had also to deal with the Kirk and the magnates, and here they were markedly less successful. As the new Kirk developed after 1560, it made determined claims to intervene in secular matters and was most unwilling to be brought under episcopal control. 'You are brought in extreme danger both of your life and crown,' warned one minister to James's face in 1596. It was only in 1597 that, his opponents having overplayed their hands, James gained command of the situation and began to restrict the powers of the General Assembly. With the greater nobility he had even more trouble. There were large parts of the country—particularly in the north and west—where allegiance was but a token, and lords such as Bothwell and Huntley moved around the country accompanied by armed bands, engaged in savage blood feuds. On 27 December 1591 Bothwell pursued James to Holyroodhouse itself, forcing him to take refuge in a tower, while Bothwell's followers ransacked the rooms. During the 1590s, as he waited for an inheritance that must have seemed infinitely postponed, there was danger that the royal table would be unprovided, guests at receptions were asked to bring their own food, and when salvation arrived with news of the death of Elizabeth, James had to borrow money from his Edinburgh subjects to make the journey south. The extreme sentiments of *The Trew Law of Free Monarchies* and *Basilikon Doron* may be read as what James would have liked his subjects to think, rather than as a sober description of the political situation in Scotland. Rarely have theory and practice been so far apart.

The union of the two crowns added enormously to the power of each country. The other country, so often a bitter enemy and at best a hesitant friend, was now a reliable ally. The energies which had so frequently been devoted to thwarting

JAMES OUTDOES SOLOMON. In the 1630s, Rubens was at work on canvases for the ceiling of Inigo Jones's new Banqueting Hall. One panel (*detail*) celebrates the union of the crowns of England and Scotland. James, seated as Solomon, outdoes the wisdom of his predecessor in a new judgement, ordering unity rather than division. Two scantily dressed ladies, representing England and Scotland, assisted by Minerva-Pallas, place a crown on the head of a robust infant, Charles, who tramples on discord. By a remarkable irony, a decade later Charles stepped from the Banqueting Hall to the scaffold erected outside.

JAMES VI AND I. The predominant trait in these three likenesses of James is wariness, the eyes watchful, if not suspicious. Nor, in the light of James's early experiences, is it surprising. The first shows him at twenty-nine in 1595 before he succeeded to the throne of England; in the second, in middle age, he is enjoying his new splendour; the third, in 1622, is an engraving of him at fifty-eight, towards the end of his life, hanging on, battered but defiant.

each other were now channelled in the same direction. But the increase of strength was potential rather than real and was scarcely realized before another 150 years had passed. The Seven Years War (1756–63), with the union an established reality and the Jacobite menace a thing of the past, was perhaps the first time that the full weight of the union was brought to bear.

James's attempt to turn the union of the crowns into a full governmental union was one of his earliest failures, though the blame was not entirely his. He may have misjudged the timing of the initiative: given twenty years for the old enmities to die, union was plausible. But in the immediate wake of his succession, the main feeling of his English subjects was intense irritation at the number of indigent Scots who had followed their king southwards.

James's handling of the problem shows him at his best and worst. The advantages to be gained by a union were worth contending for. But his tactics were deplorably inept and, in the end, helped not only to defeat the project but to discredit himself in the process. He introduced it in his first address to his English Parliament in March 1604. After dwelling repeatedly on the blessings his succession had brought to the kingdom and the inexpressible joy with which he had been received, he proposed that the two countries should henceforward be known as Great Britain. In case there was doubt where his sympathies lay, James explained that only those 'blinded with ignorance or transported with malice' would dare oppose: it would be spitting in the face of God. Nevertheless, Parliament, and the House of Commons in particular, was unenthusiastic: the grand old name of England would be heard no more, all advantage would fall to the needy Scots. James addressed them a second time in an even more maladroit speech. He had not expected so much discourse and dispute, he warned them:

True, it was that England was famous, victorious and glorious, but she had been conquered: Scotland never had. His ancestors, when they were lions and not sluggish, were ever victorious.

To a nation which had won Flodden, Solway Moss, and Pinkie Cleugh in the previous hundred years, this was ill-advised: from a monarch trying to heal national differences plain silly. Even this did not do the trick. England was too overcrowded to receive hordes of Scots: would a border Englishman, extradited to Scotland, get a fair trial? The most the Commons would do was to appoint commissioners to meet with the Scots and consider the matter further. Instead of gratitude at some modest progress, James rewarded them with reproach. In Scotland, he had been treated always as a wise counsellor:

Contrary here, nothing but curiosity from morning to evening, to find fault with my propositions. There all things warranted that came from me. Here all things suspected. . . . He merits to be buried at the bottom of the sea that shall think of a separation, where God hath made such a union.

The commissioners could not reach agreement and the project foundered. Frustrated by Parliament's attitude, James then introduced the name of Britain, a new flag, and arrangements for border extradition by prerogative action, thus injecting a fresh constitutional grievance into the struggle. The first session of his new English Parliament had revealed some of James's less amiable qualities—relentless loquacity, insufferable vanity, intemperate language, ineradicable self-righteousness, and total inability to comprehend opposition.

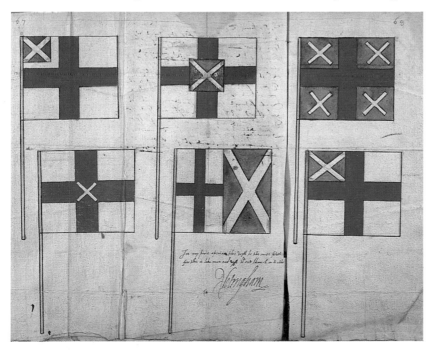

THE FLAGS OF ST ANDREW AND ST GEORGE. James failed in his attempt to follow up the personal union of the two crowns by a full governmental union. The earl of Nottingham had designs for a common flag sketched out, writing on the version *bottom middle*, 'In my poore opinion, this will be the most fittest for this is like man and wife, without blemish unto other'.

A second major reform, which could have affected the position of the monarchy, was the proposed Great Contract of 1610. Steady inflation, eighteen years of warfare with Spain, and rebellion in Ireland had wrought havoc with royal finances, even under a queen so careful that she was habitually accused of parsimony. She left a debt of some £100,000. James had a reasonable chance of recovering the situation. True, he had a family to support. But the rebellion in Ireland was over and since as king of Scotland he was not at war with Spain, one of his first actions was to make peace on behalf of his new kingdom. But his generosity with other people's money knew no bounds. Elizabeth's wardrobe, for all her fine gowns, had cost £9,000 p.a.: James was soon spending £36,000. The inherited debt of £100,000 had risen by 1608 to £600,000.

Parliament gave a remarkably generous grant in 1606. It was swallowed up. Salisbury tried to deal with the deteriorating situation by prescribing economy: James was incapable of practising it. Royal lands were sold off and revenue raised by impositions—that is, customs duties based on prerogative action. Still the gap widened. In 1610 Salisbury came forward with a proposal for a Great Contract between monarchy and Parliament: as it finally emerged, Parliament was to provide a regular income to the crown of £200,000 p.a., plus a special grant of £600,000, half of which would be devoted to redeeming the accumulated debt. In return, James would abandon the practice of purveyances, whereby the court purchased for its needs at artificially low prices, and would modify the exercise of wardship, which had for many years been an irritant to gentry and nobility. After much debate and a good deal of manœuvre, a preliminary understanding was reached by the summer recess.

During the autumn, doubts crept in. The court wondered whether £200,000 would prove adequate, particularly in a period of inflation, and began to edge up its demands. On the other side, it was pointed out that purveyancing affected only the southern counties, where the court moved, and though wardship was a grievance, it concerned comparatively few subjects. The political strategists in the Commons argued that a regular supply would give the monarchy financial independence, which must reduce the liberties of the subject and the chances of redress of grievance. What guarantee was there that James would not take the money and run up fresh debts? 'The royal cistern', commented John Hoskyns, 'has a leak, which, till it were stopped, all our consultation to bring money unto it was of little use.' When Parliament reassembled, the moment had passed and the contract was abandoned. Its failure spelt eclipse for Salisbury, who died two years later.

One can exaggerate the importance of the Great Contract. It would not have removed those financial difficulties which were to haunt the Stuarts and the readjustment of the £200,000 would have been a tedious business. Nevertheless, it was a step towards financial reality, recognizing that the old concept of the crown living off its own resources could no longer make sense in a modern world of large navies and standing armies. There was the making of a political compromise. Sir Julius Caesar had grave reservations about the contract: to abandon prerogative rights in exchange for parliamentary revenue was, he suggested, the high road to a democracy. That was shrewd. It would have been even shrewder to perceive that the other road led to ship money, the eleven years' tyranny, the civil war, and the scene outside the Banqueting Hall in Whitehall.

By 1610 there was a good deal of disenchantment between James and his new subjects. He found them ungrateful, narrow-minded, and suspicious: they found him garrulous, opinionated, coarse, and lacking in dignity. There was a cruel contrast between his public appearances and Elizabeth's; she had revelled in such occasions, with an instinct for the right gesture, the appropriate response: James was frightened of crowds and viewed them with mistrust. Though he talked a great deal about the heavy burden of state which he carried, ministers were all too well aware that he could scarcely be persuaded to attend to business, spending his days in hunting. 'He seems to have forgotten that he is a King,' wrote the Venetian ambassador, 'except in his kingly pursuit of stags, to which he is quite foolishly devoted.'

There were, of course, far more specific reasons for disillusion. Catholics and Puritans had looked forward to James's accession to bring some improvement in their position. Both were disappointed. Catholic bitterness produced the Gunpowder Plot of November 1605 and though it was the work of a tiny group of extremists, it dealt a terrible blow to English Catholicism. With more reason, moderate Puritans had looked for some relaxation and had approached the Hampton Court conference in 1604 with optimism. Though the conference was not a total fiasco, no general shift in the position of the Church took place, and Bancroft's appointment as archbishop in succession to Whitgift implied that none was likely. The first session of James's first Parliament in 1604 ended in ominous controversy. There had been a running battle over the right of the Commons to decide their own elections and though, in the end, James gave way, he delivered on 30 May a sharp reproof, reminding the Commons that their privileges were a mere matter of grace. The Commons retorted with their Apology, entered in their own Journals, in which they insisted that their privileges were of right:

The prerogatives of princes may easily and do daily grow. The privileges of the subject are for the most part at an everlasting stand . . . being once lost are not recovered but with much disquiet.

The eclipse and death of Salisbury deprived the crown not only of a sound and experienced adviser, but of a man who had been listened to in Parliament with respect, having served a long apprenticeship there. He was replaced by Robert

JAMES VI AND I

(1603–1625)

THOUGH the malice in Sir Anthony Weldon's account of the king is transparent and has been attributed to the loss of his post at the Board of Green Cloth, many of the details of his pen-portrait are confirmed by other sources:

He was of a middle stature, more corpulent through his cloathes than in his body, yet fat enough, his cloathes ever being made large and easy, the Doublets quilted for stiletto proof, his Breeches in great pleats and full stuffed: He was naturally of a timorous disposition, which was the reason of his quilted Doublets: His eyes large, ever rolling after any stranger came in his presence . . . His Beard was very thin: His Tongue too large for his mouth, which ever made him speak full in the mouth, and made him drink very uncomely, as if eating his drink, which came out into the cup of each side of his mouth: His skin was as soft as Taffeta Sarsnet, which felt so, because he never washed his hands, only rubbed his fingers ends slightly with the wet end of a napkin: His Legs were very weak . . . that weakeness made him ever leaning on other men's shoulders . . .

A more balanced, indeed antithetical, description is given by David Hume in his *History of Great Britain*:

Many virtues . . . it must be owned, he was possessed of, but no one of them pure, or free from the contagion of the neighbouring vices. His generosity bordered on profusion, his learning on pedantry, his pacific disposition on pusillanimity, his wisdom on cunning, his friendship on light fancy and boyish fondness . . . His capacity was considerable, but fitter to discourse on general maxims than to conduct any intricate business . . . Awkward in his person and ungainly in his manners, he was ill-qualified to command respect; partial and undiscerning in his affections, he was little fitted to acquire general love.

Carr, a Scotsman, who owed his position to James's appreciation of his good looks. His rise was spectacular: Groom of the Bedchamber at the age of twenty in 1607, given 'a tablet of gold set with diamonds' the following year, viscount in 1611 and earl of Somerset in 1613. Rochester had few pretensions to statecraft and much of his energies were devoted to his complex private life. Meanwhile, things drifted. In 1612 Prince Henry, heir to the throne and by all accounts a personable youth, died of typhoid, leaving his younger brother Charles as next in line. Debts mounted and when, at length, a new Parliament was summoned in 1614 it was rancorous and utterly abortive—the Addled Parliament.

In the course of 1615 it became apparent that the king's eye had strayed to another and younger gilded youth, George Villiers. Rochester's days were numbered, particularly since he had grown argumentative and overbearing. His fall was sensational. Late in 1615 he and his wife were accused of poisoning Sir Thomas Overbury, a former follower, when he had been prisoner in the Tower two years before. Both were convicted and though James pardoned them, the rest of their lives were spent in the Tower or in retirement.

The rise of Villiers, dazzlingly handsome, was even quicker then Rochester's had been. He was made cup-bearer in 1614 at the age of twenty-two, Gentleman of the Bedchamber in 1615, Viscount Villiers 1616, earl of Buckingham 1617, marquess 1618, and duke in 1623. James was besotted with him. 'I love the Earl of Buckingham more than anyone else,' he told his surprised Council in 1617, 'and more than you who are here assembled . . . Jesus Christ did the same and therefore I cannot be blamed. Christ had his John, and I have my George.' The king's pet-name—Steenie—was after St Stephen who, according to the Bible, 'had the face of an angel'.

Villiers's climb to influence was contrasted by many with the treatment meted out to Sir Walter Ralegh. Ralegh had himself been a rising star of the court in the 1580s and remained high in the queen's favour. But Cecil and Howard, in their correspondence with James before his accession, maligned him without mercy and at the accession he was dismissed from all his offices. Late in 1603 he was accused of a ludicrous conspiracy with the Spaniards to place Arabella Stuart on the throne, sentenced to death, and reprieved. For twelve years he languished in the Tower, writing his *History of the World*. In 1616 he was allowed out to make his last voyage—a desperate search for gold in the Orinoco river. It was a disaster: there was a brush with the Spaniards, his son was slain, and he returned home in June 1618 with no gold. James, beside himself with rage at the risk to good Anglo-Spanish relations, offered to hand Ralegh over to Philip III for execution in Spain—the most disreputable suggestion ever made by a British monarch. Philip politely declined the offer and Ralegh was executed on Tower Hill, dying with consummate bravery. The man who sent him to his death was a notorious poltroon.

Among James's dearest principles, on private and public grounds, was love of peace. He came to the conclusion that it was best found by alliance with the power of Spain. To this conclusion, he was assisted by the Spanish ambassador, Gondomar, who arrived at court in 1613 and soon established over James the most extraordinary ascendancy. He is 'day and night at the palace of Whitehall', wrote the French ambassador, 'where the most secret counsels are confided to him and where they listen to his advices and follow them almost to the letter'. But after a brief interlude of peace, the European situation was boiling up once more for a gigantic convulsion.

In 1613 James's daughter Elizabeth had married Frederick, the Elector Palatine, both at the age of sixteen. Five years later, Frederick plunged into events over his own head, by imprudently accepting the throne of Bohemia, in defiance of the Habsburgs. The emperor and his Spanish allies united to crush this impertinence, and in 1620 the Spaniards invaded the Palatinate, while the emperor's troops recovered Bohemia. Frederick appealed for help to Protestant Europe in general and his father-in-law in particular.

For James, the irruption could hardly have come at a worse time. For several years he had been pursuing a *rapprochement* with Spain and negotiating for a marriage between Charles, his heir, and the Spanish infanta. The war rapidly became a European struggle, for in 1621 the twelve years' truce between the Spaniards and the Dutch came to an end, with both sides willing to resume hostilities. As usual, the key to an active foreign policy was finance, and the advent of Buckingham had done nothing to improve James's position. It would be necessary to summon a Parliament, and the House of Commons would press for a Protestant crusade.

PEACE WITH SPAIN. One of James's first successes was to wind up the inconclusive and protracted war with Spain. Henceforward he followed a pro-Spanish line and was anxious to promote the marriage of his son Charles to the infanta. At the peace conference at Somerset House in 1604, the Spanish delegation is to the *left*; opposite them (*foreground*) Robert Cecil leads the English delegation. On his *right* are the earls of Northampton, Devonshire, Nottingham, and Dorset.

The Addled Parliament of 1614 had lasted a mere eight weeks. The Parliament of 1621 lasted longer but was, if anything, an even greater disaster. During the second session, late in the year, James departed to Newmarket, and conducted a kind of bombardment from a safe distance. True to form, the House of Commons demanded war with Spain, firm measures against the Catholics, and a Protestant marriage for the Prince of Wales. James retorted that 'fiery and popular spirits' had been led to debate matters 'far beyond their reach or capacity'. Gondomar threatened to leave the country unless James took a strong line with his Parliament. James obliged and advised the Commons that 'we feel ourselves very free and able to punish any man's misdemeanours in parliament as well during their sitting as after, which we mean not to spare hereafter'. Since several members had been arrested and imprisoned after the Addled Parliament had been dissolved, this was no empty threat. The Commons refused to be cowed and countered with a protestation, declaring that their liberties were of right. Gondomar advised dissolution and James, after some hesitation, agreed. In the Banqueting Hall from which his son was to step to the scaffold, James called for the Commons Journals and tore out the protestation. Gondomar assured him that it was the best thing that had happened for a hundred years. Gratifying though it may have been to tear out the protest, it did not provide a revenue.

The later years of James's life saw a strange and complex triangular relationship between the king, Buckingham, and the Prince of Wales. Prince Charles, who emerged from the shadows after his brother's death in 1612, was something of an unknown quantity: he was small, shy, prim, and rather stolid. For some years he was on bad terms with his father's favourite and there was a series of petty quarrels. In 1618 a serious clash led first to an imposed reconciliation and then to a close friendship. Secure in the affection of both monarch and heir, Buckingham grew more assertive. Insofar as James had any coherent foreign policy left after 1621, it was to cling to the Spanish connection, in the hope that Philip IV would use his good offices with the emperor on behalf of Frederick. He therefore pushed ahead with the marriage proposal while the Spaniards constantly raised their terms. In 1623, exasperated at the delay, Buckingham and Charles hit upon a wild scheme to dash to Madrid incognito and carry all by romantic ardour. Even James could see that this was not very prudent and would put the Spaniards in an impossibly strong position. 'Here are Baby Charles and Steenie,' he moaned feebly to a courtier, 'who have a great mind to go by post to Spain to fetch home the Infanta.' Charles and Buckingham brushed aside his objections and departed, travelling under the uninspired pseudonyms of Jack and Tom Smith, and eked out with false beards. Their disguise was so impenetrable that they reached Gravesend before they were stopped. James dispatched letter after letter to his 'sweet boys' from their 'poor old dad'. Philip IV, scarcely able to credit his luck, offered the most ferocious terms: the king of

GEORGE VILLIERS, DUKE OF BUCKINGHAM. These two portraits suggest the transformation from royal favourite to man of business. The first was painted soon after his arrival at court in 1615. He was twenty-four, but looked younger. Ten years later, the second portrait shows a man of wide experience, with a commanding, even imperious, countenance. He was murdered at Portsmouth in 1628.

England must remove all disabilities upon his Catholic subjects, promise never to reimpose them, and obtain parliamentary guarantees. There was not the remotest chance of Parliament doing any such thing. Charles signed. Having signed, he waited a further three months before getting cold feet, and leaving without his bride-to-be, but with a stylish and genuine Spanish beard.

Buckingham and Charles returned changed men. They now talked violently of war with Spain and a French marriage. James demurred and was once more brushed aside. The 'sweet boys' demanded a Parliament, which would no doubt support them. They would get their bellyfull of Parliament, James retorted. But he agreed to summon one for February 1624, and in his opening remarks tried to be conciliatory: 'he was their own kindly king', they could freely advise him. 'I now hope, after the miscarriage of the last [Parliament], that this may prove happy.' There was no harm in hoping. Parliament rejected with indignation the suggestion by the Spanish ambassador that Buckingham should be executed for his insolent behaviour while at Madrid and advised the king to have no more dealings with Spain. The most notable victim was Lionel Cranfield, earl of Middlesex, who had laboured for some years as Lord Treasurer to curb royal extravagance and had made many enemies in the process. With the connivance of Charles and Buckingham with whom he had quarrelled, he was dismissed, fined, and sent to the Tower. Parliament was prorogued in May, never to meet again in James's lifetime. It had certainly proved more harmonious than most of James's Parliaments, largely because the prince and Buckingham were, in effect, leading the opposition to James's pro-Spanish policies.

James died in March 1625 of a complication of disorders. The funeral was exceptionally lavish and the climax of the sermon was a sustained panegyric on the British Solomon. Power had long since passed into other hands. There was nothing in 1625 to suggest that the political differences were irremediable. But the danger signs were clear enough. The kingdom was on the brink of war with Spain, its finances shattered, and the House of Commons restive and suspicious. The situation called for all the skill and delicacy that Baby Charles could bring to bear.

In many ways Charles was an improvement on his father. He had far greater dignity of bearing, with a marked distaste for coarse or drunken behaviour. Whereas James was talkative to excess, Charles was reserved, and a residual stammer made him appear taciturn. In sexual morality, he was above reproach. He was regular and serious in his devotions. He had a love of music, a good command of languages, was fond of drama and the masque, and had an excellent

HALCYON DAYS. In this painting by Adrian van Stalbent, Charles and Henrietta Maria stroll in Greenwich Park, not far from the spot where the Observatory was built in his son's reign. Inigo Jones's new Queen's House stands in front of the old palace, which was replaced by the present buildings after the Restoration. After the Civil War, Henrietta Maria looked back to the 1630s as a golden period: 'I had a husband who adored me', she wrote.

knowledge of painting. Relief in the country at the collapse of the Spanish match had given him a transient popularity. There was not a plausible rival claimant within sight. In three important respects, however, he was very much his father's son: his concept of royal authority was just as high, he was equally devoted to the duke of Buckingham, and, most unfortunate of all, he was, if anything, even more self-righteous than James—without even the pawky Scottish humour that occasionally brought James down to earth.

The year before his accession, when he had in practice been in command, revealed both a lack of judgement and a lack of scruple. To facilitate the marriage to the infanta he had pledged himself to concessions to the Catholics that he knew could not be implemented. Having escaped from a disastrous Spanish Catholic marriage, he embarked within weeks of his return upon negotiations for a disastrous French Catholic marriage, to the Princess Henrietta Maria, daughter of Henri IV. The French, not to be outdone in zeal by the Spaniards, insisted on similar concessions for their co-religionists. This was a little awkward since, in April 1624, Charles had pledged himself in Parliament that were he to marry a Catholic wife, there should be 'no advantage to the recusants at home'. The concessions asked for were therefore made in a secret clause, added to the marriage treaty.

Charles's position as monarch deteriorated with surprising speed. Within two years he was on very bad terms with Parliament, reduced to such financial straits that he attempted to pawn the crown jewels, and engaged in war, at one and the same time, with France and Spain. The war did not go well. An attack upon Cadiz, led by Sir Edward Cecil, in an attempt to emulate Drake's exploits, ended in fiasco. Twenty months later, Buckingham himself led an expedition to the Île de Ré, in an effort to relieve the Huguenot town of La Rochelle, in rebellion against Louis XIII and Richelieu. It was repulsed with heavy losses.

The ill-success of these ventures, together with the dislike Buckingham had engendered as royal favourite, dragged Charles into a series of damaging confrontations with his Parliaments. The first, summoned in June 1625, revealed a suspicious attitude by granting tonnage and poundage, normally given for life, for one year only. The meeting at Oxford, to which Parliament was adjourned because of the plague, was soured by accusations that there were secret clauses attached to the marriage treaty and Charles dissolved it after no more than a week. The next Parliament in February 1627 was worse, even though leading opponents of the ministry had been pricked as sheriffs to render them ineligible. Sir John Eliot launched an attack upon the inept expedition against Cadiz: 'our ships are sunk, our men perished, not by the sword, not by an enemy, not by chance, but by those we trust.' Within a month, the Commons had prepared a formal indictment of Buckingham. Charles reminded them sharply that Parliaments were 'altogether in my power for their calling, sitting and dissolution . . . it is not a way to deal with a King'. Buckingham himself begged for moderation: 'it is no time to pick quarrels one with another ... we have enemies enough already.' Each side was becoming dangerously exasperated. Ministers professed not to understand how Parliament could allow the war effort to be crippled for want of supply: their opponents would not grant money to be squandered by incompetence. Tempers flared. The Commons proceeded to an impeachment of Buckingham: the king retorted by committing Digges and Eliot to the Tower. Buckingham's advice to the king was to persevere with the Parliament, but in June Charles decided to dissolve. This solved one problem at the cost of a worse—how to conduct a war without parliamentary subsidies.

The third Parliament in March 1628 met in the aftermath of the failure to relieve La Rochelle. After much urging, a grant of five subsidies was made. But the hunt after Buckingham was as relentless as ever. In a Petition of Right, the duke was named as 'the chief cause of these evils and dangers to the kingdom'. In June Charles prorogued once again.

Buckingham then turned his full attention to another attempt to relieve La Rochelle. A new expedition was assembled at Portsmouth and there, in August 1628, Buckingham went to assume command. He was stabbed through the heart at the Greyhound Inn by John Felton, a solitary fanatic with a private grievance. La Rochelle surrendered two months later.

Buckingham's position has been misunderstood by those who have seen him merely as a royal favourite. They have not acknowledged the change in his position from a mere courtier and man of pleasure under James, to the mainspring of government under Charles, a hard-working man of vast political and military power. The melodrama of Buckingham's end may distract attention from two emerging long-term problems. The first was over the monarch's right to choose his own ministers. Nobody disputed that this was an essential part of the royal prerogative, but it was assumed that the ministers would be acceptable to Parliament. If they were not, there was opportunity for repeated confrontations. Secondly, it was increasingly clear that large-scale warfare could hardly be carried on in the face of parliamentary disapproval. Throughout Europe, the escalating cost of war produced clashes between princes and their representative institutions. In France and Spain the États généraux and the Cortes went under; in Bavaria and Brandenburg, Scandinavia and Russia, the rulers carried the day. *Salus respublicae* was the supreme law. In the crisis of the first four years of Charles's rule were laid out the themes that were to dominate English political life for the next ninety years.

The meeting of Parliament in January 1629 offered proof that Buckingham had been not the cause, but the symptom of mistrust. 'The grievance of grievances', the 'great author of our misfortunes' was no more, yet harmony did not prevail. 'Let us not be jealous of each other's action', appealed Charles. But the result was

CHARLES AND HIS QUEEN AS APOLLO AND DIANA (*above* and *facing*). This picture brings together two of Charles's interests—painting and the masque. It was made in 1628 by Gerrit van Honthorst and is now at Hampton Court. The king and queen appear as Apollo and Diana, with the duke of Buckingham as Mercury presenting the seven liberal arts. Since the king was usually accorded a heroic role in masques, it would be strange if they did not help to corrupt his judgement and fend off reality. In 1637 when the judges pronounced in favour of the crown over ship money, Henrietta Maria danced a ballet in a masque entitled *Luminalia or the Festival of Light*, celebrating the defeat of darkness by light. It was not as simple as that.

violence on an unprecedented scale. The Commons again postponed supply pending redress of grievance. When the Speaker, on Charles's instructions, attempted to adjourn the House, he was held down in his chair. After seven weeks, Charles dissolved his third Parliament and arrested Holles, Valentine, and Sir John Eliot.

Clearly the old constitution was close to stalemate. Some of the causes of the discontents were traditional—the desire of members to see a vigorous government policy with rather less desire to will the means. But the factor that was increasingly poisoning relationships was religious strife. The wider European context was crucial. In 1618 James's son-in-law, in a direct challenge to the

Habsburgs, had accepted the throne of Bohemia. The succeeding years saw him driven out of his new kingdom and then expelled from his native Palatinate. Dynastic, religious, and balance-of-power considerations prompted the English to demand his restoration. But the European conflict which developed went badly for the Protestant cause and in 1626 Christian IV of Denmark was decisively beaten at Lütter, partly because his English subsidies were months in arrears. Until the intervention of Gustav Adolf of Sweden, it looked as though Protestant Europe might be drowned in a rising Catholic tide.

In this menacing situation, small suspicions cast huge shadows. To a later generation, anti-Catholic hysteria might seem bigotry and intolerance. But the

grandfathers of the members of the 1629 Parliament had seen plot after plot against Elizabeth after the papal excommunication, and their fathers had seen a papist attempt to blow up king, Lords, and Commons. In this context, Charles I's marriage to Henrietta Maria was ominous, especially since her ardent Catholicism was well known: each English defeat or set-back could be explained by treachery at the very heart of government. Bishop Laud's endeavours to promote Arminianism were seen by many as but the prologue to Catholicism. Charles's willingness while in Madrid to discuss conversion was remembered. 'There is a general fear in your people', he was told by the Commons in June 1628, 'of some secret working and combination to introduce into your kingdom some innovation and change in our holy religion ... even when the same is, with open force and violence, prosecuted in other countries, and all the reformed churches in Christendom either depressed or miserably distressed: we do humbly appeal to Your Majesty's princely judgement, whether there be no just ground of fear that there is some secret and strong cooperating here with the enemies of our religion abroad, for the utter extirpation thereof.' Once mistrust had reached this level, compromise was almost out of the question. If supplies were granted and an expedition fitted out, against whom would it be used, the enemies abroad or the opposition at home?

The first consequence of the breakdown was the abandonment of any attempt to recover the Palatinate by force of arms. Peace was made with France in 1629 and with Spain the following year. In 1632 the Elector died, still in exile. The shortage of money was, in some ways, a blessing in disguise, forcing Charles to adopt a more realistic foreign policy.

In the end, it was eleven years before Parliament was again summoned. The decision to make do without Parliament may have been against the spirit of the constitution, but no one could deny that the prerogative belonged to the monarch. The absence of a Parliament was less of a grievance to most subjects than the systematic efforts to raise revenue by non-parliamentary means—impositions, forced loans, distraint of knighthood, exploitation of the forest laws, wardship, and, above all, ship money, extended in 1635 from the coastal counties to those inland. Even if the yield from these expedients could be maintained, the political damage was serious, alienating many of the gentry and nobility who were the natural supporters of the crown. The earls of Salisbury and Southampton were fined for infringement of the forest laws; the earl of Bedford was forced to compound for his development at Covent Garden. Sir Gervase Markham was first fined for not taking up knighthood, then for refusing ship money. John Hampden, a wealthy Buckinghamshire landowner, was taken to court over ship money. William Prynne, member of Parliament and antiquarian, had his ears twice cropped, and was stripped of his academical and legal degrees. John Bastwick, a Cambridge graduate and doctor of Padua, lost his ears and was

CHARLES I

(1625–1649)

CHARLES became heir apparent on the death of his elder brother Henry in 1612. In 1625 he married the fifteen-year-old Henrietta Maria, daughter of Henri IV of France. After a difficult beginning, the marriage became one of deep affection, particularly after the death of the duke of Buckingham. In her later years in France as a widow, Henrietta Maria wrote of the 1630s as a time when she had 'every pleasure the heart could desire'.

The Civil Wars divided men so deeply that a balanced and dispassionate assessment of Charles after 1640 is difficult to find. To his adversaries he was increasingly the man of blood, too deceitful to trust or do business with; to his supporters, he finished as the spotless martyr of *Eikon Basilike*. The following extract is from 1637 when the waves were beginning to run high but the denouement remained uncertain. Anzolo Correr was Venetian ambassador at the court of St James's, knew the king well, and had had several lengthy audiences and conversations with him. He was reporting to the Senate in Venice:

Charles the first of his name, King of Great Britain, was born in 1600 and is therefore in the flower of his age . . . He is pacific, but by necessity, as certain indications show his inclination for war. He would make it if he had not been compelled to abandon the idea to avoid subjecting himself to the indiscretion of his subjects. He is not prodigal like his father, but neither is he illiberal, when the limits of his treasury are not the cause. He has no vices or lusts, he is just but he is rather severe and serious than familiar. He does not grant pardons readily, except in matters of life and death, provided the case is not extreme. He handles arms like a knight and his courser like a riding master. He is not subject to amours, and since the death of the Duke of Buckingham he has had no favourites. He selects his ministers not from affection but from his opinion of their capacity. He is extreme in nothing, except that he persists with his sentiments, and anyone whom he has once detested may be sure that he will never recover his favour. He has literary erudition without ostentation, possessing what befits a king . . . As he has given up governing by Parliament, as his predecessors did, it remains to be seen if he will go on and if he will be able to do by the royal authority what former kings did by the authority of the realm. This is a difficult matter and the more perilous, seeing that if it be true that the estates are perturbed about the two great causes of religion and the diminution of the liberty of the people, he has perturbed both, and will be very fortunate if he does not fall into some great upheaval.

sentenced to life imprisonment for his attacks on the bishops. Provided that the crown never needed help, the policy made sense.

The monarchy split on a forgotten rock—Scotland. Charles had had little trouble with his native kingdom and had given it scant attention. He had left it at the age of three and did not return until 1633 for a belated coronation. In the meantime, it had been administered by the Scottish Privy Council. The Scottish Parliament, overshadowed by the General Assembly of the Kirk and rivalled by

CHARLES I DINING AT WHITEHALL PALACE. The respect and deference offered to the monarch was essential for the maintenance of royal dignity. To deprive him of these was to deny his authority. At Windsor, just before his trial, Parliament ordered that no ceremony should in future be permitted at the king's meals: no trumpets should sound, the dishes should not be covered, nor should they be presented on bended knee. Charles refused to accept the changes and took his meals in private. See p. 307.

the Convention of Scottish burghs, offered little resistance. Clarendon remarked later that there were few in England who had heard of any disorder in Scotland, 'nor anything done there that might produce any'. But there were signs that Charles's touch was not sure. The brief coronation visit was, in the eyes of many Scots, marred by his insistence on an Anglican form of worship. The trial of Lord Balmerino for presenting grievances to the king was imprudent and provocative. A Revocation Edict of 1625 took back all grants of land made by the crown since 1540, and though it was subsequently modified, landowners were alarmed at the threat.

In 1634, in his search for religious uniformity, Charles ordered the preparation of a new Scottish prayer book, closely modelled on the English one. When the dean of St Giles tried to use it on 23 July 1637, the congregation rioted. Charles ordered repression and by 1638 the situation was out of control. A General Assembly met at Glasgow, a national covenant was signed, and the bishops fled.

The king decided upon force and told Hamilton, his chief minister, to gain time by flattery. Slowly Charles gathered an army and the following summer moved to York to direct operations. But the confrontation on the Tweed turned into anticlimax and insincere negotiation. At this juncture Charles remembered his strong man in Ireland and summoned Strafford. 'Come when you will,' he wrote, 'you shall be welcome to your assured friend.' It was Strafford's death warrant.

Without parliamentary subsidies, there could be no second attempt to bring the Scots to heel. Strafford was confident that he could manage a new Parliament. A meeting of the Irish Parliament in March 1640 went off well: Strafford presided, and the Houses were as loyal as could have been wished, providing both troops and money. But the English Parliament ran true to form. The speech by Lord Keeper Finch on 15 April was a masterpiece of ineptitude: His Majesty had 'graciously sequestered the memory of all the former discouragements in preceding assemblies'. Laying aside 'the shining beams of Majesty, as Phoebus did to Phaeton', the king offered members 'the honour of working together with himelf'. More specifically, he wanted money and quickly. Next the Lord Keeper revealed that, shocking to relate, some Scots, 'men of

CHARLES I. The juxtaposition of these two portraits suggests how much a great artist can do to impose his own style and interpretation. In the first, by Daniel Mytens, Prince Charles is a rather glum and unimpressive figure. In the second, by Peter Lely after Van Dyck, King Charles, kitted out with a trim beard and embellished by the Garter, is majestic, cultivated, and imposing. The viewer could be forgiven for forgetting that His Majesty was very short and stuttered badly.

Belial', had repaid His Majesty's trust with disaffection and even defiance. The House of Commons was not moved. Harbottle Grimston, whose father had been imprisoned for refusing to contribute to a forced loan, asked whether there were not urgent grievances in England also, and John Pym joined in with a catalogue of complaints. Within three weeks, the Parliament had to be dissolved. The king blamed 'the malicious cunning of some few seditious affected men'. The needle was stuck in the groove of 1629.

But from the end of the Short Parliament, events tumbled over themselves, with men trying to find a footing as best they could. The Scots disobligingly refused to wait to be crushed, advanced over the Tweed, brushed aside light resistance, and occupied Newcastle. Strafford dragged his crippled body north to stiffen resistance, but was forced back on York. By the treaty of Ripon, signed in October 1640, the Scots stayed in occupation of Northumberland and Durham, and received payment of £850 a day, pending a settlement. At last Parliament had its guarantee.

The Long Parliament was summoned for the following month. 'It shall not be my fault', declared the king handsomely, 'if this be not a Happy and Good Parliament.' It was happier for some than for others. Strafford's head was off his shoulders within six months: 'stone-dead hath no fellow', observed the earl of Essex pleasantly. When the preposterous impeachment against Strafford had shown signs of faltering, Pym hurried through a bill of attainder, which did not allow for examination of the evidence or permit a defence. Charles refused his consent to Strafford's execution, then, in the face of menacing crowds, took advantage of Strafford's letter releasing him from his promise, to allow it.

The Long Parliament set about making up for lost time. Laud followed Strafford to the Tower and the royal government disintegrated. Sir Francis Windebank fled to France, Lord Keeper Finch to The Hague. A Triennial Act in February 1641 provided that no more than three years could elapse between Parliaments. On the day that Strafford, in his own words 'stepped from time to eternity', Charles agreed that the Parliament could not be dissolved without its own consent—an almost unthinkable breach in the armoury of prerogative. Reforms followed in shovelfuls. Ship money was declared illegal, fines for knighthoods abolished, the forests redefined, High Commission and Star Chamber dissolved, and the Council of the North (Strafford's old power base) and the Council of Wales suppressed. The structure of prerogative government was torn down. In May 1641 the Commons moved on with a bill to abolish episcopacy: it ran into opposition in the Lords. At last there was a chance to halt the slide. 'If we make a parity in the church,' observed Sir John Strangeways, 'we must at last come to a parity in the Commonwealth.'

In October 1641 came news that changed the situation at a stroke. The native Irish had risen and were butchering the English 'sparing neither sex nor age'.

MASSACRE OF PROTESTANTS IN ULSTER. England's divisions in 1641 were the signal for the native Irish to try to drive the new Protestant planters from Ulster. This representation of a particularly ugly incident at Portadown depicts Catholic priests blessing the massacre of women and children. But Charles's opponents dared not trust him with an army to restore English control.

Once again Charles miscalculated. He had presumed in 1640 that the Scottish rebellion would unite all Englishmen in detestation of their old enemy: instead, the parliamentary leaders had shown a keen awareness of the tactical assistance the Scots had given them, together with much sympathy for Scottish constitutional and religious demands. Charles thought it inconceivable that the English would stand aside to watch Irish papists drive their fellow countrymen into the sea. But the Irish rising brought up a question on which compromise was almost impossible—who would command the army sent to restore English rule and what use would be made of it if victorious?

Pym, as usual, seized the initiative with a Grand Remonstrance, reiterating the grievances, and followed it by a Militia Bill, authorizing troops to be raised only under officers approved by Parliament. Charles retorted with a proposal to the Lords to raise 10,000 volunteers under his command. At the same time he prepared a coup, the signal for which was to be the arrest of five of the Commons' leaders. It misfired totally. On 4 January 1642 the king forced his way into the Commons to demand the five members. They had left by the back door. 'I assure you,' said Charles weakly, 'I never did intend any force.' Pym's answer was to turn the Militia Bill into an ordinance which would carry royal authority even if the king, by bad counsel, refused it. Charles withdrew to York and in June 1642 exchanged with Parliament the Nineteen Propositions and the royal answer. It is a key document of British constitutional history, much studied in subsequent years. At the time it was little more than a tactical manœuvre for moderate support in an armed struggle which both sides saw as inevitable.

On 22 August 1642 at Nottingham Charles raised the royal standard and called upon all loyal subjects to support him. The ceremony was symbolic in that, behind the majesty, was muddle and incoherence. The royal standard had to be hastily made. A declaration was concocted, to which the king made last-minute additions. In pouring rain, the ink ran and the herald could scarcely decipher the message. That night, in a gale, the standard blew down.

Civil War and Interregnum

The first question was whether the king, having abandoned his capital, could raise an army large enough to recapture it. The immediate response was disappointing. Many men, perhaps the vast majority, were reluctant to commit themselves, out of prudence or incredulity, that fighting was at hand. Money was in short supply. Peers and courtiers made personal gifts; the two universities gave their college plate; Shropshire recusants paid their fines for three years in advance; the queen, dispatched to Holland in February, managed to pawn the crown jewels. At Nottingham, Charles got together a thousand men and began a recruiting march through Derby to Shrewsbury. Meanwhile, Parliament raised an army of 13,000 and placed it under the command of the earl of Essex. The first blows were exchanged in September at Powick Bridge, just south of Worcester, where Rupert, the king's nephew, won a cavalry skirmish.

By October, Charles had collected a sizeable army and began an advance through the midlands. He eluded Essex but then turned to face him at Edgehill, north-west of Banbury, drawing up his troops at the top of the ridge. Though the superiority of the royalist cavalry was evident, the battle was inconclusive. Charles gave up the chance of beating Essex to London in favour of a ceremonious entry into Oxford, where, characteristically, many students abandoned their studies at once 'and could never be brought to their books again'. By the time Charles resumed his advance, the moment had passed. Essex's forces, reinforced by the trained bands of the city, barred his way at Turnham Green, near Brentford. The king returned to Oxford, which he made his capital for the rest of the war.

The first round having been inconclusive, long-term considerations came into

THE WAR YEARS. Charles took personal charge of the royalist armies during the Civil War and conducted the Lostwithiel campaign in 1644 with considerable skill. Here he is seen in the field dictating dispatches to Sir Edward Walker.

play. When allegiances settled down, the king retained the north, west, and south-west, Parliament London, East Anglia, and the south-east. Everywhere there were pockets of resistance, and much of the war consisted of picking off or reinforcing local garrisons. A serious blow to the king, before hostilities commenced, had been his failure to secure Hull, which had ammunition and was a valuable link with the continent. Bristol, Portsmouth, Gloucester, and Plymouth also held out for Parliament, curbing the mobility of local royalists, who were not anxious to abandon their homes and families to forays if they joined the king. An even more severe set-back to Charles was that the navy, on which he had lavished great attention, followed the lead of the earls of Warwick and Northumberland, joined his adversaries, and helped to cut him off from continental aid.

The great European powers, in the midst of a gruelling and bloody struggle themselves, had neither incentive nor spare capacity to intervene in English affairs. Charles's resources did not permit him to hire more than a few mercenaries, and even weapons and ammunition were hard to come by. The most likely way of tipping the internal balance was therefore to bring in Scottish or Irish auxiliaries. Charles had already taken steps to come to terms with his rebellious Scottish subjects. In August 1641 he had visited Edinburgh and formally accepted the most sweeping constitutional and religious changes, establishing a Presbyterian form of government and a severely limited monarchy. But to engage the Scots on his side was another matter. It was difficult to decide whether to bid for the support of the predominant Presbyterian group or to rely upon their traditional opponents from the Highlands, nor did it take Pym long to realize that the Scots could turn the scales. The covenanters were more natural allies of Parliament than of the king, and in September 1643, after a summer of military defeats, Parliament reached an agreement with them. The Solemn League and Covenant provided for an armed alliance, to be co-ordinated by a Committee of Both Kingdoms, with a pledge to introduce a reformed system of Church government into England. But the campaigning season was drawing to a close and intervention could not take place until 1644. Charles had little alternative but to back Montrose and his Highlanders, and for a year or so it looked as though he had made the better choice.

The situation in Ireland was even more confusing. Scottish covenanters, English parliamentarians, and English royalists were equally determined that the native Irish must be put down. The impetus of the rising had almost carried all before it, and the royal army hung on desperately in Dublin and a few garrison towns. Ormonde, appointed commander-in-chief as soon as the rising occurred, managed in 1642 to launch some counter-attacks, though the rebels insisted that they were acting on behalf of the king. In April 1642 a Scottish army landed at Carrickfergus and began a rescue operation on behalf of Scottish settlers in Ulster. It soon became clear that a complete subjugation of Ireland would be a long affair. Charles could not afford to wait and sent urgent instructions to Ormonde to make terms so that he could ship his troops across the water. Though the political odium of negotiating with Catholic rebels was damaging, Charles could not be squeamish. In September 1643—the same month as the Solemn League and Covenant—a truce was signed. It was then a question of whether Charles's Irish reinforcements would prove more effective than his covenanting opponents.

The decisive year—1644—began with a political offensive by the king, somewhat belated and not well handled. It had been a mistake to allow his opponents to appropriate for themselves the authority of Parliament. In January, Charles repaired some of the damage by summoning his own Parliament to Oxford where, in deep snow, it met in the hall of Christ Church. The attendance was at least respectable—well over 100 members of the Commons and 44 peers were present, with another 57 members and 38 peers affirming allegiance, but unable to appear. The Westminster assembly by comparison numbered some 200 members and 20 or so peers. Charles might have used it for a major peace initiative. It granted forced loans and excise, though how many would pay was another matter, and then became involved in a quarrel with its Westminster counterpart. Charles soon tired of it and prorogued it in April, thanking the members fulsomely for their 'great and unanimous expressions of affection'. His private opinion was more laconic—'a mongrel parliament'.

Ormonde got his troops from Ireland into action first. Late in October 1643 two regiments landed at Minehead and Bristol: the following month, another 2,000 landed at Mostyn and were placed under Lord Byron to liberate Cheshire and Lancashire. They proved a sore disappointment and Fairfax routed them at Nantwich in January 1644. In the later months, Charles thought of bringing over native Irish soldiers, but few arrived, and those who did were treated by the parliamentary forces with savage brutality.

The Scottish intervention turned out to be a more substantial affair. It was bound to be a serious anxiety to the king since the duke of Newcastle, commander in the north, would be caught between converging forces. Leven led his men across the Tweed in January 1644 and began the siege of Newcastle upon Tyne. Fairfax extended his grip on Yorkshire and the northern royal army was squeezed into Durham. By April Newcastle had been forced south to York and was treating to surrender the city. Rupert then led a relieving force across the Pennines from Lancashire, saved York, but acting under peremptory orders offered battle at Marston Moor, though heavily outnumbered. The result was a crushing defeat and Rupert himself was obliged to hide in a beanfield. York and the north had to be abandoned, and the duke of Newcastle fled to the Continent. Marston Moor was by far the heaviest blow that the royal cause had suffered. Yet there were enough victories on the king's side to offset the damage and carry the war into another year. First Charles beat Waller at Cropredy Bridge, north of Oxford, and then, pursuing Essex into Cornwall, outmanoeuvred him at Lostwithiel, forcing the surrender of 6,000 men, abandoned by their general.

Though the king's forces did not permit another direct challenge to the Scots in the north of England, it was possible that diversionary attacks in Scotland might force them to return home. An invasion of Galloway by Montrose in April proved abortive. But a week after Marston Moor, a small force of native Irish landed at Ardnamurchan on the extreme west coast of Scotland. Montrose, without troops, left Carlisle to join them, linking up at Blair Atholl. Together they smashed through a larger covenanting force and occupied Perth. Next Montrose took Aberdeen. When Argyll set off in pursuit, Montrose took to the mountains. In December he burst out of the hills into the Campbell country. Two months later he inflicted a second humiliating defeat on Argyll's forces at Inverlochy, just outside Fort William, with Argyll watching the disaster from his galley on the loch. At the start of 1645 Charles's cause seemed in better shape than had been imaginable after Marston Moor: 'my affairs begin to smile on me again', he wrote in May 1645 to Henrietta Maria.

It was an illusion. Montrose's brilliant successes were heartening but peripheral, nor was it reasonable to expect that he could indefinitely snatch victory against heavy odds. During the winter of 1644, Parliament at Westminster had taken steps to put its house in order. The self-denying ordinance enabled them to weed out some of their weaker commanders, and Cromwell, who had distinguished himself at Marston Moor, helped Fairfax to organize the new Model

RUPERT'S POODLE 'BOYE' became something of a mascot to the royal army. The painting is believed to be by Rupert's sister, Princess Louise.

Army, with improved training and discipline. The collapse of desultory peace talks at Uxbridge convinced nearly everyone that it must be a fight to the finish. Nevertheless, the train of events started with a royalist initiative in May, Rupert leading a successful attack upon Leicester, which could be followed either by an incursion into the very heart of parliamentary resistance in the midlands and East Anglia, or by an attempt to recapture control of the north. Fairfax and Cromwell united their forces and at Naseby outnumbered Rupert and the king by two to one. After early successes, the king's troops were overwhelmed by numbers and the defeat was total. Charles's correspondence fell into the hands of the enemy and was at once published to demonstrate his perfidy.

Naseby was followed in quick succession by blow after blow. The following month, Goring was badly beaten by Fairfax at Langport. In September, Rupert was forced to surrender Bristol, to the king's indignation; and Montrose, after two more victories at Alford and Kilsyth, was crushed at Philiphaugh. With some

RUPERT'S HEAVY DEFEAT AT MARSTON MOOR turned the scales against the king. According to this hostile woodcut, Rupert was reduced to hiding in a beanfield. His enemies ransacking his baggage find crucifixes while dead on the field of battle lies his dog.

difficulty Charles held out the winter at Oxford, still hoping for Irish troops who never came, or for French forces which the queen was trying to raise. On 21 March 1646 the last royalist army in the field, under Lord Astley, surrendered at Stow-on-the-Wold. Astley, who had been in command at the first battle at Edgehill, was there at the last. The fall of Oxford could no longer be postponed and on 26 April 1646 Charles left, disguised as a servant. On 5 May, after a strange journey through the Fenlands, he arrived at Southwell to place himself in the hands of the Scottish army.

Charles had two and a half more years of his life left. Since most of the time he was a prisoner, though treated with respect, it is all too easy to see him as a bird fluttering in a cage, desperate to escape. In fact, for most of the time, the king was

THE ROYAL CHILDREN. 'That which pleased His Majesty most', wrote Clarendon, 'was that his children were permitted to come to him, in whom he took great delight.' This painting by Hoskins was done at Hampton Court in the summer of 1647 while the king was in captivity. Their sad expressions tell the story. James, duke of York, the future James II, was thirteen: he escaped to the Continent in April 1648. Henry, duke of Gloucester, was eight: he died of smallpox in 1660, a few months after the Restoration. Princess Elizabeth, already ill, died at Carisbrooke Castle in 1650.

fortified by a serene conviction that things were moving his way. He had no doubt that monarchy was the sole prop of the social order: 'you cannot be without me: you will fall to ruin if I do not sustain you,' he told the parliamentary commanders. Events were to prove that the vast majority of his subjects agreed with him, but too late to save him from the scaffold. Though he often talked of dying rather than yielding, it was only in the last few months, after the second Civil War, that the shadow of the axe fell across him.

Though the journey to Southwell looked like surrender, nothing was further from the king's mind: he intended by diplomacy to recover the ground lost by force. He was acutely aware of the divisions between his opponents: consequently he combined an unshakeable regard for his ultimate objective with a degree of duplicity conceivable only in the high-minded. Each of his kingdoms was split into contending factions. In Ireland, four groups jostled for power—the old royal government, a group recognizing Parliament, a Scottish covenanting expeditionary force, and the native Catholic Irish, bound together in a formidable Confederation. In Scotland, the Presbyterians had gained the upper hand against the royalists, but were in danger of further division among themselves. In England, Parliament showed signs of division between Presbyterians and independents, and both were in danger of parting company from the army, where the growth of radical and levelling doctrines threatened the authority of the commanders. With the increased possibility of foreign intervention as the Thirty Years War gradually ground to a halt, there was ample material for Charles's fatal addiction to diplomacy.

His first negotiations were, perforce, with the Scots, who assailed him with batteries of indefatigable Presbyterian ministers. They failed to persuade him to sign the Covenant: it would mean 'the absolute destruction of monarchy', he declared. After nine months, the Scots handed him back to the English Parliament, in return for arrears of payment. Parliament removed him to one of his own houses at Holdenby in Northamptonshire, and resumed negotiation. After six months at Holdenby, he was seized by the army, now dangerously at odds with Parliament, taken to Royston and Hatfield, and thence to Hampton Court. Further negotiations took place. In November 1647 he escaped to Carisbrooke Castle in the Isle of Wight, only to find himself in increasingly close captivity. Attempts to escape were betrayed or botched. By December 1647, the wheel had come round again, and he was once more in discussion with the Scots, on the basis of 'the Engagement': the Covenant was to be imposed on England, a Presbyterian system established pending a final Church settlement, the army disbanded. In the event of Parliament refusing, the Scots would provide an army to restore Charles to enjoyment of rights, including command of the militia and choice of ministers.

The outcome was the second Civil War, which began in the spring of 1648 with a series of uncoordinated royalist risings, but became formidable when Hamilton led an 'Engager' Scottish army across the border. Cromwell's victory at Preston brought the second Civil War to a close and settled Charles's fate. The army, first the rank and file, and then the leadership, had come to the conclusion that permanent peace would be impossible while the king lived. They therefore resolved to put the man of blood on trial. In December 1648 Colonel Pride purged the House of Commons of some 150 members, leaving a tiny rump of some eighty or so, totally dependent upon the army leaders.

Cromwell and his fellow generals, having come to the conclusion on 16 November that Charles must be executed, wasted little time. A fortnight after, the king was moved to Hurst Castle, and, just before Christmas, back to Windsor. In the first week of January, Parliament established a High Court of Justice, under the presidency of John Bradshaw. The trial began on 20 January in Westminster Hall, where Strafford had been heard seven years earlier. Charles, predictably, refused to plead: 'I would know by what power I am called hither— I mean lawful, there are many unlawful authorities in the world, there are robbers and highwaymen.' By the authority of the people of England, retorted Bradshaw. Under what law was he being tried, persisted the king, 'for if power without law may make laws, I do not know what subject he is in England that can be sure of his life'. On the 27th Charles was sentenced to death as a 'Tyrant, Traitor, Murderer, and public enemy to the good people of this Nation'.

CHARLES'S DEATH WARRANT. Charles refused to recognize the High Court of Justice, presided over by John Bradshaw, and after a week was condemned to death. Fifty-nine members of the original 135 commissioners signed the death warrant, Bradshaw first, then Lord Grey, then Oliver Cromwell. At the Restoration in 1660, forty-one of the fifty-nine were still alive. Fifteen fled abroad and, in all, nine were put to death. The bodies of Cromwell, Ireton, and Bradshaw were removed from Westminster Abbey and hanged at Tyburn before burial in a common pit. Thomas Harrison, one of the proudest of the regicides, told his judges, 'This was not a thing done in a corner.'

THE EXECUTION OF CHARLES I. The many engravings and representations of the execution helped to fasten the scene into national consciousness. The scaffold was erected outside the window of the Banqueting Hall in Whitehall. Charles asked his gentleman to give him an extra shirt: 'the season is so sharp as probably may make me shake, which some observers may imagine proceeds from fear.'

His execution, on a scaffold outside the Banqueting Hall in Whitehall, took place three days later. After acknowledging the 'unjust sentence' he had permitted on Strafford, the king reiterated his case with great clarity: 'If I would have given way to an arbitrary way, to have all changed according to the power of the sword, I had not have come here.' To the few people on the scaffold who could have heard, he repeated:

I must tell you that the liberty and freedom [of the people] consists in having a government, those laws by which their life and their goods may be most their own. It is not for having a share in government, Sir, that is nothing pertaining to them. A subject and a sovereign are clear different things.

Then, after a short declaration of Anglican faith, Charles placed his head on the block. It was taken off at one blow.

Eikon Basilike, a strange concoction of polemic and prayer, based upon Charles's own writings, became one of the most influential books of all time, and established, as he had hoped, Charles as a martyr for his people. After the head had been sewn back to the body, the coffin was moved to Windsor, and laid in the vault in the place that had been reserved for Catherine Parr. Charles's final resting-place was therefore next to his great-great-uncle, Henry VIII.

Charles's behaviour during the last few years of his life is not easy to interpret. At times he seems to have watched the drift towards disaster to such an extent that some historians have invoked a death-wish. It is not an area where it is wise to be too confident. Certainly he had a taste for theatricals and he mused often about death. But it would be hard for any man to go through four years of war without remarking that he would rather die than give up his principles, while his sense of drama seems to have pushed him towards optimism rather than despair. As late as November 1647 he wrote to Parliament, 'Let me be heard with Freedom, Honour and Safety, and I shall instantly break through the clouds of retirement, and show myself ready to be *Pater Patriae.*' It is a scene in a masque rather than real life. The marked passivity may have been in part the product of exhaustion, and partly that, cocooned by ceremony and etiquette, Charles found it hard to make decisions, preferring to have them made for him. Hence, in

THE ROYAL MARTYR. This embroidery was based upon the crude engraving by William Marshall printed as frontispiece to *Eikon Basilike*, published soon after the king's death. Charles grasps a crown of thorns but his vision is of eternal glory. *Eikon Basilike* went through thirty-five English editions within a year and fixed the image of Charles as martyr.

captivity he plotted persistently to escape, and when presented with the chance, demurred or bungled it. To escape from Hampton Court in order to finish up in captivity on the Isle of Wight near Parkhurst suggests incompetence on the grand scale.

What did Charles die for? His answer at the trial was that he stood for the rule of law against the power of the sword, on which the so-called Court of Justice was based. But everyone in the conflict stood for the rule of law: the issue was what the law said, and how it could be upheld. Pym's most famous speech had been on the supremacy of the law, ironically while putting the case for Strafford's attainder. Civil war was, by definition, a matter of force, and Charles had drawn the sword in the first place. Had his armies prevailed and allowed him to hang Essex, Manchester, Cromwell, and Bradshaw, would it have been any the less the triumph of force?

A second answer would be that Charles died to save the monarchy, together with the Church of England and its hierarchy on which that monarchy was, in his view, irrevocably based. Indeed, through all the shifts, manœuvres, and ter-giversations forced upon him, Charles clung to his ultimate objective with total determination. But it does not answer the question. Hardly one of his opponents denied the need for monarchy, and the brief republican movement was the result of his downfall, not the cause. It is true that, from early days, Charles was convinced that his opponents aimed to subvert monarchy, but this was merely one of his many over-simplifications. The truth is almost the reverse—that until the very last moment, after the second Civil War, hardly any man of property or rank could conceive how a stable and tolerable society could survive except on the basis of monarchy.

At issue, therefore, was what Charles and his opponents took monarchy to mean, and with what powers they would endow it. One could trace the various assertions and concessions through the events of 1641, the Nineteen Propositions of the summer of 1642, the treaty of Uxbridge, the treaty of Oxford, the treaty of Newcastle, and so on. But these negotiations were all distorted by tactical considerations, the product of the king's perceived strength or weakness. It may be better to consider his views at the moment of apparent triumph or at the moment of impending death, with no cause to dissemble and nothing more to hope in this life but a speedy ending.

Throughout the 1630s, when Charles appeared in command of the situation, his attitude towards Parliament scarcely changed. It was hateful to him, 'odious', 'abhorred'; he was determined not to humiliate himself before it, he could not bear to hear the word mentioned. And on the scaffold, with ten minutes to live, he repeated his solemn conviction that the subject was entitled to no share in government.

What place did that leave for Parliament in the constitution? Here we run into historiographical difficulties, for the tendency of much recent scholarship—and scholarship of a high level—has been to deny any long-term significance in the struggle and to accuse proponents of such a view of naïve teleology. There is by now an almost ritual denunciation of Samuel Rawson Gardiner as a historian of simple Whiggish views, who regarded the clash as a necessary step in the evolution of Victorian parliamentary democracy. Of course, it is not hard for any historian to demonstrate muddle, incoherence, and improvisation in human affairs, but to stress long-term or comparative factors is by no means the same as practising teleological history. And if Gardiner stands charged with contamination by the Victorian values of his own day, may one not suggest that an undue emphasis on immediate, ephemeral, and contingent factors may itself be an indication of a decline in intellectual confidence among twentieth-century British academics.

It has been observed that '*with hindsight*, it is tempting to see the constitutional motif of the first part of the seventeenth century as King versus Parliament, as absolutism against law and representative government'. With respect, there can hardly have ever been an issue where hindsight was less necessary. Almost without exception, contemporaries attached long-term significance to their struggles and described them as confrontations between monarchy and Parliament. Far from imposing our own patterns on the past, we are merely taking heed of what contemporaries said. 'We are', observed Sir Robert Phelips in 1626, 'the last monarchy in Christendom that yet retain our ancient rights and privileges.' His opponents on the royal side did not dispute his interpretation of the struggle, but argued that Parliament was the aggressor: 'seeing the turbulent spirits of their parliaments', explained Dudley Carleton '[monarchs] began to stand upon their prerogatives, and at last over threw the parliaments throughout Christendom, except only here with us.'

There is no doubt that an institution summonable at will, and sitting for perhaps a few weeks at intervals of years, could play no regular part in the *routine* of government. But too much emphasis on the weakness and ephemerality of early seventeenth-century Parliaments merely confronts the historian with a different predicament—to explain how the authority of Parliament was so massively and speedily established in the 1640s, and how it managed to survive schisms, purges, and humiliations. Nor did the Restoration of the monarchy in 1660 mean that Parliament was packed off to the junk-room of history, as the États généraux and Zemsky Sobor were.

The explosive mixture of the 1630s and 1640s was a compound of constitutional disagreements with religious animosities. Few denied that it was a parliamentary right to vote supply, and government without supply was no government at all. Charles, if he accepted the need for Parliament, maintained that it should vote supply and ask no questions. In an age of profound religious passions and with a

ORDER DESTROYED. In this cartoon of 1649, the royal oak, symbol of authority and stability, is chopped down under the supervision of a very lifelike Oliver Cromwell. The common herd graze regardless, being fattened for slaughter. Hell gapes beneath Cromwell, who looks suprisingly unconcerned. Magna Carta and the rule of law go down with the tree.

royal government well below average in competence, that was naïve. Charles, like his father, was very willing to testify to his own high principles: it did not readily occur to either of them that other people might have principles as well. At the very heart of Puritanism was a deep and painful preoccupation with individual responsibility to God, which was bound to lead some of its adherents to question the rightness of government policy, at home and abroad.

To stress long-term issues is not to seek to exonerate Charles. He had a poor hand to play and he played it badly. The contrast with his predecessors and successor is instructive. Cromwell also had great difficulties with his Parliaments: Charles attempted to arrest the five members and Cromwell dismissed the Rump. But even in his dying months, Cromwell never lost control of the situation: he had a natural authority and a massive common sense denied to Charles. As for Charles's great predecessor Elizabeth, it is customary now to dwell upon the problems she faced in her later years—or, perhaps more properly, refused to face. But can one seriously envisage her abandoning London and raising the royal standard in some provincial town against one of her Parliaments?

The new king, the eighteen-year-old Prince of Wales, received the news of his father's death at The Hague, where his sister Mary was married to William of Orange. The royal family was scattered. Henrietta Maria was in France, with her youngest daughter Henriette-Anne, and had just been joined by James, duke of York, who had escaped from parliamentary captivity in 1648. Henry, duke of Gloucester and the Princess Elizabeth were still held by the Parliament.

In the interval between sentence and execution, the House of Commons had rushed through an Act, forbidding any person to proclaim another monarch, and the office of king was formally abolished on 7 February 1649. Charles II was proclaimed in French in Jersey, by Ormonde in Ulster, and by the Estates in Edinburgh, who pointedly referred to him as king of Great Britain, France, and Ireland. His resources were meagre indeed, a few ships, and some outposts such as the Isles of Scilly and the Isle of Man. He had, of course, relatives in high places on the continent. But Louis XIV, his young cousin, had himself been forced to flee his capital by the Frondes in the course of 1648, and William of Orange, who had succeeded his father in 1648, died unexpectedly of smallpox two years later.

The only possible areas for royal military action were therefore Ireland and Scotland. In the former, Ormonde maintained a royalist presence and was in negotiation with the Catholic Confederation. In September 1649 Charles moved to Jersey to prepare for an expedition. His republican opponents moved quicker, and a week before Charles entered St Helier, Cromwell had crushed Irish resistance at Drogheda, bolting the door.

It was now a question of what the Scots would do for their king. The price to be paid would without doubt be high—recognition of the Covenant and the virtual abandonment of Montrose. Negotiations started at Breda in April 1650, with the Scots insisting not only that Charles accept the Covenant and limited kingship in Scotland, but impose Presbyterian Church government on England. With few cards to play, Charles slowly capitulated. Early in July he arrived in Scotland, to find Argyll and his friends harsh, fanatical, and prolix. Cromwell, the bane of the Stuarts, followed him across the border three weeks later, and in September 1650 defeated the covenanting army, against the odds, at Dunbar.

Though badly beaten, Leslie, the Scottish commander, managed to stabilize his line on the north side of the Forth, enabling Charles to retain the northern part of the kingdom. On 1 January 1651 he was crowned at Scone, in a Presbyterian ceremony. But when campaigning resumed in the summer, Cromwell outflanked

THE SCOTS HOLD CHARLES II'S NOSE TO THE GRINDSTONE. As part of his settlement with the Scots, Charles II was obliged in 1650 to accept a Presbyterian form of Church government and subscribe to the Covenant. From Scotland he launched the desperate invasion which ended at the battle of Worcester in 1651. In an accompanying verse, the presiding cleric remarks: 'We for our ends did make thee king, for sure; not to rule us, we will not that endure.'

the Scots to the east, pushing Charles into the desperate venture of his invasion of England.

Charles crossed the border on 31 July, followed by Cromwell a week's march later. From the outset, things went badly. Carlisle refused to surrender, so Charles had to be proclaimed at Penrith. The English royalists, cowed by repeated defeats and suspicious of Scottish invaders, did not rally in anything like the expected numbers. A month's march found Charles and the Scots in the old royalist stronghold in the west midlands at Worcester. Here they were trapped by a superior parliamentary force and routed. Cromwell's 'crowning mercy' came a year to the day after Dunbar.

The night of 3 September 1651 was the nadir of Charles's fortunes. After a vigorous and courageous day, he was swept out of the north gate of Worcester with the remnants of his beaten army. His extraordinary Odyssey of the next six weeks took him into Shropshire where he hid in the Boscobel Oak, near Tong, and thence cautiously via Stafford and Bristol into Somerset and Dorset, thence into Wiltshire, Hants, and Sussex, hiding in orchards, ditches, and priests holes. A parliamentary notice described him as 'a long dark man, above two yards high' and offered a £1,000 reward for his capture. But though forty or fifty people at different times knew of his whereabouts, he was never betrayed. But his crossing, from Shoreham to Fécamp, though a miracle of fortitude, resource, and good fortune, left him totally dependent upon foreign charity and foreign intervention.

The year 1651 was a disaster for the royalist cause. Monck, left in command in Scotland when Cromwell headed south, received the surrender of Stirling and stormed Dundee before the battle of Worcester had been fought. The Isles of Scilly surrendered in May 1651, the Isle of Man in October, and Jersey in December. For the next nine years there was no place in his three kingdoms on which Charles could set foot in safety. He lived the miserable life of exile, his tiny court moving from place to place as credit ran out, buoyed up by rumour, dogged by disappointment, with little diversion save amatory exploit. A Scottish rising in 1652 captured Inverness and subsided: a more substantial one, organized by Middleton, ended in July 1654 at Dalnaspidal in Glen Garry. In 1655 an ambitious English rising went off at half-cock, leaving John Penruddock to hold Salisbury for the king for a few hours before being rounded up at South Molton.

Meanwhile, Britain had a king *de facto* in Cromwell. Of him, Clarendon wrote that, 'without the name of king, but with a greater power and authority than had been ever exercised or claimed by any king; he received greater evidence and manifestation of respect and esteem from all the kings and princes in Christendom than had ever been showed to any monarch of those nations'. Cromwell's string of victories in three kingdoms had given him the complete confidence of the army and from 1647 when it had moved upon London, the army had commanded the state. Cromwell's experience as a member of Parliament, stretching back to 1628, gave him a better chance of building some bridge between army and Parliament than any other senior officer had.

Though Parliament, or more properly those members remaining in the Commons at Westminster, had been conducting the affairs of half the kingdom from the outbreak of war until 1649, the execution of the king and the abolition of the monarchy demanded formal changes in the machinery of government. The House of Lords had, of course, gone down with the monarchy, being voted 'useless and dangerous' on 6 February 1649; three peers were subsequently elected as members of the House of Commons. It followed that the approval of the remaining House was all that was needed for a bill to become law. The executive of the Commonwealth was to be a Council of State of forty-one members, chosen by the House of Commons. The first contained five peers, of whom one, Lord Grey of Wark, did not sit. Cromwell took the chair at the first meeting of the Council. Much of the next two years he spent campaigning. In April 1653 he put an end to the Rump Parliament and summoned, in its place, the Little or Barebones Parliament, a nominated assembly of 140 members. While the new body plunged into a whirlpool of reform, a reconstituted Council of State continued to administer the government. But in December 1653 the conservative majority of the Little Parliament organized their own coup and surrendered power back to Cromwell.

The army leaders were not unprepared for this eventuality. Back in December 1651, in a discussion after Worcester, Cromwell's opinion had been for a government 'with somewhat of a monarchical power' in it. His views were probably those of the great majority of Englishmen. At that time, the most likely outcome seemed the crowning of Henry, duke of Gloucester, youngest brother of Charles II and still in parliamentary hands, with Cromwell as Regent or Protector. Henry's father had foreseen this possibility and at a meeting with him and the Princess Elizabeth the day before his execution had impressed upon him

CROMWELL HAS HIS OWN DIFFICULTIES. The Rump was all that was left of the original Long Parliament after repeated purges. Attendances were down to well under one hundred members. In April 1653 Cromwell dismissed them with the words: 'you have sat here too long for the good you do.' That night a poster appeared outside the palace of Westminster: 'This House is to be let: now unfurnished.'

the need for total loyalty: 'sweetheart, now they will cut off thy father's head; mark, child, what I say; they will cut off my head and perhaps make thee a king; but, mark what I say; you must not be a king so long as your brothers Charles and James do live.' But early in 1653 Henry had been allowed to leave for the Continent, where he was reunited with his mother, Henrietta Maria.

The arrangements introduced in December 1653 under the Instrument of Government marked a shift back towards authority. It was a principle of the new constitution that executive power was to reside in a single person. Cromwell refused the title king, but served as Lord Protector, the position previously held by Somerset during the reign of Edward VI. His residence was to be the palace of Whitehall. He was to be assisted by a smaller Council of State. Parliament was to consist of one house of 400 members, was to meet at least once every three years, and could not be dissolved within five months of its assembly. The Lord Protector and Council could issue ordinances during Parliament's recess but they were to be confirmed as soon as Parliament met, and the Protector was to have no power of veto. The Instrument of Government was as close to a balanced constitution as it was possible to devise in the 1650s. Scotland and Ireland were allotted seats in Parliament and, for the first time, there was a governmental union of all three kingdoms.

As soon as the new constitution was put to the test, it failed. Elections were held in the summer of 1654 and the new House of Commons assembled in September. It insisted at once on its own supremacy, began to dispute the nature of the constitution, demanded control of the armed forces, and encroached upon that restricted religious toleration which Cromwell regarded as one of the fundamentals of the constitution. After less than a week, Cromwell descended upon the House in some anger to insist that the fundamentals of the Instrument must be accepted. The ardent republicans, led by Haselrig and Bradshaw, withdrew rather than deliberate under duress. In January 1655, as soon as he was allowed to, Cromwell dismissed Parliament.

Before the next meeting of Parliament, Cromwell resorted to the least popular of all his expedients, the rule of the Major-Generals. After the Penruddock rising of 1655, the country was divided into ten districts, in a species of martial law. In the summer of 1656, fresh elections were held for a new Parliament. Though Cromwell had been criticized for not taking pains to manage his Parliaments, the preliminaries could hardly have been more closely supervised. The Major-Generals were encouraged to see that supporters were returned, one hundred of the members were debarred as unreliable, and a further sixty or so refused to continue under such obvious military domination. The purged House then urged Cromwell, in the Humble Petition and Advice, to assume the kingship. After protracted discussions, he declined to do so, but agreed to a further strengthening of the executive.

OLIVER CROMWELL

I saw him dead, a leaden slumber lyes,
And mortal sleep over those wakeful eyes:
Those gentle rays under the lids were fled,
Which through his looks that piercing sweetnesse shed;
That port which so majestique was and strong,
Loose and depriv'd of vigour, stretch'd along:
All wither'd, all discolour'd, pale and wan,
How much another thing, no more that man?
Oh! humane glory, vaine, oh! death, oh! wings,
Oh! worthlesse world! oh transitory things!
Yet dwelt that greatnesse in his shape decay'd,
That still though dead, greater than death he lay'd;
And in his alter'd face you something faigne
That threatens death, he yet will live again.

This excerpt from Andrew Marvell's 'A poem upon the death of O.C.' is a reminiscence of the lines on Hector in Book II of Virgil's Aeneid.

OLIVER I was the king England never had. But for a few weeks in the spring of 1657 it looked a probability. Cromwell emerged from the ruck of parliamentary generals in the later years of the first Civil War, and consolidated his position by his victory at Preston in the second Civil War, and the subjugation of Ireland and Scotland. He was instituted as Lord Protector in December 1653 with royal splendour, moving into the palace of Whitehall. In January 1657 Sindercombe's plot to assassinate him prompted his supporters to beg him to accept the crown, partly to give him more protection under the law of treason. In March, the Speaker of the House of Commons offered him the title in the Banqueting Hall. After a delay of five weeks, Cromwell declined, to the consternation of his close associates: 'His Highness's refusal,' wrote Colonel Jephson, 'hath so amazed his real servants as I know not what to write or say concerning it . . . God direct us to something which may preserve these nations from total ruin.' But the offer in any case had come too late and the following year Cromwell was dead. He was buried in great state in Westminster Abbey. At the Restoration his body was exhumed, dragged to Tyburn and beheaded. His head was stuck on a pole outside Westminster Hall, where it remained for more than twenty years. Blown down in a gale in the reign of James II, it passed at length into the possession of his Cambridge College, Sidney Sussex, where it is buried near the chapel.

Two features of the Humble Petition which demonstrated the gathering movement back to the old constitution was the clause empowering the Protector to name his successor, and the decision to bring back a second chamber, under the curiously feeble title of 'the Other House'. This was to be, not hereditary peerage, but a nominated body of not more than seventy, who would then co-opt on vacancies. Cromwell's nominations were largely his own family, the leaders of the army, and such members of the old peerage as would serve, to add a pinch of dignity. But the Humble Petition did not put an end to constitutional wrangling. When Parliament reassembled in January 1658 the House of Commons, ever tenacious of its own authority, at once launched an attack upon the Other House, declaring it unconstitutional. After sixteen days, Cromwell dissolved the Parliament once more.

Cromwell's refusal of the kingship has been much debated. But he had little to gain from it. Armed with the power to name his successor, and supported by an Upper House which he himself would control, he had all the attributes of monarchy. The title itself, while alienating many of his supporters, particularly in the upper ranks of the army, would add little to his power. Though it is entertaining to ponder what the House of Cromwell would have been like, there is little reason to believe that the final outcome would have been any different. In the absence of a competent and tough son to succeed Oliver, one must suppose that Richard IV's reign would have collapsed as easily as did that of Richard the Lord Protector.

Behind Cromwell's persevering if naïve attempts to find a lasting settlement was a genuine desire to divest himself of military power. It returned to him again and again, like a boomerang seeking its thrower. But this was because, despite his undoubted integrity, he was not prepared to abandon all power and hand everything to a parliamentary majority, if it meant watching that majority humiliate the army and encroach upon religious toleration. Not unnaturally, he did not succeed in solving the conundrum of how to give up power while keeping it. It was this deeply felt desire to get back to civilian and parliamentary rule that justified placing Cromwell's statue outside Westminster in 1899, even though, superficially, he was a man who had treated Parliaments with scant respect.

The difficulties between the Lord Protector and his Parliaments did not do much to assist Charles II, to whom Cromwell referred amiably but disparagingly as 'the young gentleman'. Strife between ruler and Parliament was, after all, a rather routine expectation to mid-seventeenth-century man. Provided that Cromwell retained control of the army—a matter on which he was no more willing to compromise than Charles I—he was impregnable. Even if, against the odds, his parliamentary opponents such as Scott, Bradshaw, and Haselrig had gained the upper hand, they were classical republicans, and even less likely to do a deal with the royalists than Cromwell. Though Cromwell's government, like all those of the seventeenth century, suffered from acute financial difficulties, it was in other respects massively competent. Its military and naval strength made it much courted by the rest of Europe. The fortunes of the House of Orange were in eclipse in the Dutch Republic after 1650 and Charles's relatives could do little to help. Mazarin, restored to power after the Frondes, sought Cromwell's assistance against the Spaniards. Spain was not unwilling to support Charles II, by way of diversion, but her diplomacy was sluggish and her resources too limited to defend her own empire, let alone take on fresh commitments.

Under these circumstances, Charles could do little but watch. His main

DANCING AWAY THE HOURS . . . For nine years after his escape from Worcester, Charles II was in exile, with little to do save to hope, and to avoid blunders. Cromwell's regime seemed impregnable. Here the king dances at The Hague with his sister Mary.

concern was to avoid some stupendous blunder that would rule him out for good. Though it was tempting in discussion with the papacy and the Catholic states to remember Henrietta Maria's devotion to her religion and his amiable intentions towards his Catholic subjects, Charles was extremely careful to avoid the charge of personal conversion. When Henrietta Maria, having got Prince Henry back into her care, showed signs of attempting to convert him, Charles reacted with uncharacteristic speed and sharpness: 'if Your Majesty has the least kindness for me, I beg of you not to press him further in it.' To Henry he wrote that if he disobeyed, 'you must never think to see England or me again'.

In the summer of 1658 Charles's cause looked bankrupt. The forces sent by Cromwell to collaborate with the French against the Spaniards won a decisive victory at the battle of the Dunes, and Dunkirk was handed over to the British. In

September Charles II was in Holland, playing tennis, when he received the news he must have waited for with growing impatience—Cromwell was dead, on 3 September, the anniversary of his great triumphs at Dunbar and Worcester. He had named as his successor his eldest son, Richard.

The next few months were among the most dispiriting of Charles's life. Nothing happened. Richard's accession as Lord Protector passed off without a murmur. 'The King's condition never appeared so hopeless, so desperate,' wrote Clarendon, 'for a more favourable conjuncture they could never expect than this, that had blasted all their hopes, and confirmed their utmost despair.' True, the new Lord Protector was a gentle and ineffective man, with none of the force of character of his father. But should he be overthrown, the probability seemed that

'SOME HAVE GREATNESS THRUST UPON THEM . . .'. Richard Cromwell survived as Lord Protector less than a year. Clarendon wrote of him: 'thus the extreme pusillanimity of the son suffered himself to be stripped in one moment of all the greatness and power which the father had acquired in so many years with wonderful industry, courage and resolution.' Richard fled to the Continent at the Restoration but returned to live a secluded life at Cheshunt in Hertfordshire and died aged eighty-eight in 1712.

power would fall to one of the military men, Fleetwood, Lambert, or Monck, commanding the army in Scotland. For six months, Oliver governed from the grave. Then, in January 1659, as soon as Richard met his first Parliament, the weakness of his personal position became apparent. A strange coalition of republicans and crypto-royalists launched bitter attacks upon the military, whom they could not forgive for purging the Rump. The army, in its turn, accused the civilians of ingratitude, and demanded its arrears of pay. In April the army leadership forced the Protector to dissolve Parliament. By doing so, Richard placed himself entirely in the army's hands. Once more the nature of military despotism was obvious. The lesser army officers then urged the recall of the Rump and were joined by the republicans. In May the old Speaker and forty members returned, and began dismantling the Protectorate—the rule of one person, the other house, and so on. On 25 May Richard bowed to the inevitable and resigned.

Army and the Rump, old adversaries, snarled at each other. The Council of State, civilian dominated, ran the government of the day. The royalists, misreading the signs, got a rising off the ground, but it was confined to Cheshire and put down by Lambert with no great difficulty. Jealous of Lambert as the new Cromwell, the Rump cashiered him in October 1659. Lambert prudently got his blow in first, sent in his troopers, and threw out the Parliament. In the absence of Oliver, the army was now thumping around like unsecured cargo in the holds of the ship of state. A Committee of Public Safety was appointed to carry on the government.

At this point, the army split. On receipt of the news of the coup, Monck in Scotland prepared to intervene to support Parliament—the fourth time a Scottish army had moved south. Lambert moved north to confront him. The threat was enough to get the Rump restored once more late in December. On 1 January 1660, Monck's army began its long march. Lambert's forces melted away, and on 3 February, Monck's men moved into London.

Everything now depended on this stolid, cautious man. It was extremely difficult to know his intentions, partly because he had been in Scotland in command since 1651. If he was a secret well-wisher to the Stuarts he dissembled remarkably well, and as late as March 1660 the exiled court was in despair. The probability is that he was guided by events and that the strength of support for the monarchy slowly moved him. Relations between the Rump and their saviour deteriorated fast, and in February Monck insisted that they allow the secluded members to return and set a term to their own existence.

In April 1660 fresh elections were held and a Convention met on the 25th, together with the old House of Lords. They found an adroit letter to the Speaker from Charles at Breda, together with a Declaration, promising pardons, arrears of pay for the army, confirmation of land purchases, and liberty to tender consciences in religious matters. In his letter to the Speaker, Charles wrote of his deep affection for Parliaments: 'None of our predecessors have had a greater esteem for Parliaments than we have, in our judgement, as well as from our obligation. We do believe them to be so vital a part of the constitution of the kingdom and so necessary for the government of it that we well know neither prince nor people can be in any tolerable degree happy without them.' This handsome testimonial performed wonders, and Parliament at once sent a cordial invitation to return. On 26 May 1660 Charles II set foot in England at Dover, having spent more than eight years abroad. By an unhappy chance, the vessel sent to collect him was called the *Naseby*: it was hastily renamed the *Royal Charles*.

KINGMAKER MONCK. When George Monck marched his army across the Tweed in January 1660, it seemed likely that he would seize power for himself. But he used his influence to bring about the Restoration of Charles II and, as duke of Albemarle, was an important figure at court in the 1660s. The unfinished water-colour is by the miniaturist Samuel Cooper.

The Restoration

Superficially, the restoration of the monarchy was the work of one man, George Monck, who was at once kitted out with the Garter and a dukedom. In fact, it reflected the deep attachment to the monarchy felt by the great majority most of the time. The execution of the king and the abolition of monarchy had never had much support, outside the ranks of the army. During the republic, there was a steady drift back to monarchical forms—the emphasis on a single person, the restoration of a second chamber, and the offer of the throne to Cromwell. The fact that Monck was both cautious and apolitical means that he was a sound reflection of general opinion, a politician by instinct rather than ideology. It is more surprising that the Restoration had been so long delayed, and that is a tribute to the extraordinary military and political ability of Oliver Cromwell, the one man who could hold the army together. As soon as his funeral had taken place, the struggle between his successors was bound to let in their royalist opponents.

Evidence of the strength of monarchical feeling was that, after twenty years of bitter dispute about the relations of executive and legislature, Charles was restored within three weeks, with no specific conditions, other than those he chose to give in the Declaration of Breda. To the royalists, this was almost miraculous: they had assumed, as a matter of course, that any restoration would be preceded by detailed negotiations on the lines of Charles I's exchanges with Parliament. Gratifying though it was for Charles II to come back with his hands free, it also meant that the points at issue remained unresolved, and were to dominate the next thirty years.

What was the balance sheet after twenty years of turmoil? The need for monarchy had been widely accepted and the king restored with most of his powers intact. The case that monarchy alone provided a barrier against military despotism and the overthrow of the social order seemed to have been proved. Yet Parliament did not emerge from the contest discredited. It had demonstrated a capacity for adaptation and an ability to carry on the government of the country in very difficult circumstances. If the faith of many people in the restoration of a monarchy in 1660 looked naïve, there was a corresponding faith that a free Parliament would end the nation's miseries, and it was a Parliament, in the shape of the convention, that had summoned back the king. The example of the trial and execution of Charles I could never be forgotten, and James II in particular seems to have had his father's fate in mind in the course of 1688. The outcome was stalemate.

Those issues which had been of such consequence in 1640 were settled, piecemeal, in various ways. Charles was determined not to lose control of the armed forces and the Militia Act of 1661 vested authority firmly in the crown. The financial difficulties which had caused so much trouble before the Civil War continued afterwards. Parliament sanctioned an annual revenue of £1,200,000, but since it fell short on collection by at least £200,000–£300,000, there was a persistent deficit. It could hardly be met by reviving distraint of knighthood, benevolences, and the like, and the Court of Wards had not been restored: some of the contortions of Charles II's foreign policy derived from this fundamental financial weakness. In religious matters, the exigencies of the Civil War had moved the crown over from a policy of uniformity towards toleration: Parliament had moved in the opposite direction, and the religious settlement which emerged was a parliamentary one.

Two pieces of legislation remedied the work of the Long Parliament in 1641 and 1642. The bishops were, after some discussion, restored to their seats in the House of Lords. The Triennial Act of 1641 was also repealed: though the king was still under an obligation to meet Parliament at least once every three years, no mechanism for enforcing the new Act was provided. Since the monarch retained both his right of veto and the right of prorogation and dissolution, Parliament was still in a difficult position should it come to a direct confrontation once more.

There was no certainty in 1660 what the religious settlement would prove to be. Charles was still, at least in theory, pledged to the Solemn League and Covenant and the Presbyterians were among his most devoted supporters. But

CHARLES II CROWNED. Pepys devoted several pages of his diary to the coronation in April 1661. On the 22nd there was a secular procession from the Tower to Whitehall. Pepys put on a new velvet coat and had a good view from Cornhill, regaling himself with wine and cakes: 'The King, in a most rich embroidered suit and cloak, looked most nobly . . . The streets all gravelled; and the houses, hung with carpets before them, made brave show, and the ladies out of the windows. One of which, over against us, I took much notice of and spoke of her, which made good sport among us. So glorious was the show with gold and silver that we were not able to look at it, our eyes at last being so much overcome with it.' He did not see so much of the service in the Abbey the following day, partly because of the throng and partly because 'I had so great a list to pisse that I went out a little while before the King had done all his ceremonies.' But, like most of his fellow countrymen, Pepys ended the day horribly drunk.

THE RESTORATION OF CHARLES II in 1660 also meant the restoration of Scottish independence after the brief union during the Commonwealth. This statue of Charles was erected in Parliament Square in Edinburgh in 1685. For many years, Charles shared the square with a statue of John Knox, the divine—surely the strangest of juxtapositions. Knox's tomb was in the old churchyard immediately beneath the hooves of Charles's horse.

a religious conference at the Savoy in the spring of 1661 failed to reach a compromise and Anglican opinion soon hardened. The second Parliament of the Restoration, meeting in May 1661, lost no time in ordering that the Solemn League and Covenant be burned. The Act of Uniformity of 1662 insisted that the clergy should subscribe to Anglican doctrine and more than 1,000 clerics lost their livings. The Clarendon code erected a series of defences of the Church of England's supremacy. The outcome was that dissent became a persistent part of the religious and political life of the country.

In Scotland, the Restoration brought back not only the native monarchy but national independence. The legislative union was abandoned, with little regret on either side. The Scottish Estates, meeting in 1661, by an Act Rescissory, which cancelled all legislation subsequent to 1633, handed back to the crown all those constitutional concessions granted by Charles I on his visit in 1641. Aided by a generous financial settlement, the result was that Charles II's position was much stronger in Scotland than in England. After some hesitation, Episcopacy was reintroduced into the Kirk and those ministers who could not accept the changes were forced out in 1663.

Charles made no coherent and sustained effort to establish an absolute monarchy, lacking both the application and determination. Pepys, who knew both Charles and James, duke of York, wrote in 1667 that 'the design is, and the Duke of York is hot for it, to have a land army and so make the government like that of France; but our princes have not brains, or at least care and forecast enough to do that'. But circumstances pushed Charles in that direction, as did his memories of exile in France when his hosts jeered at the English monarchy as no monarchy at all. Revealing was his candid comment in Parliament after the repeal of the Triennial Act that neighbouring princes would now see that England was really a monarchy.

At the age of thirty, more than half his life spent, Charles returned home, world-weary, good-humoured rather than merry, with a wariness inclined to melancholy. His fairly demanding pursuit of distraction and pleasure—hunting, racing, sailing, womanizing—left little time for high politics, and his attention

CHARLES II BY CANDLELIGHT. There are many excellent likenesses of Charles II, most of which catch his swarthy and saturnine appearance. This representation by Samuel Cooper is in chalk. John Evelyn, the diarist, witnessed the sitting in January 1662: 'I had the honour to hold the candle whilst it was doing; choosing to do this at night and by candlelight, for the better finding out the shadows; during which His Majesty was pleased to discourse with me about several things relating to painting and graving, etc.'

to government, though intelligent, was fitful. He was more than content to let Edward Hyde, the companion of his exile, run the country as earl of Clarendon. Since the dominating object of his existence had been to recapture the throne, it is understandable that it became an end in itself, and there was not a lot he wanted to do when he got it. He tended to react to events and to exert himself when forced into a corner. It is significant that the only development which moved him to decisive and sustained action was towards the end of his life when the threat to the succession of his brother, James, duke of York, touched an old chord. But for much of the rest of his life he was an amused observer.

The first crisis of his reign was the second Dutch War, which began in May 1665. For most Englishmen, the commercial and colonial rivalry offered by the Dutch outweighed regard for them as fellow Protestants. The first Dutch War had originated with the Navigation Act of 1651, a direct challenge to the Dutch carrying trade, and had ended, inconclusively, in April 1654. Charles had even less reason than his subjects to admire the Dutch, since the Regent regime took pains to exclude the House of Orange from power. Nevertheless, he was not one of the ardent advocates of war. Persistent clashes about the right of search and saluting led to a declaration of war in February 1665, after Parliament had voted a subsidy of £2½ million. The most far-reaching episode took place before the formal declaration of hostilities: the Dutch settlement of New Amsterdam on the Hudson river was overrun and named New York. In the first major engagement, off Lowestoft in June 1665, the English fleet, commanded by James, duke of York, fared much the better. But thereafter was a slow drift to disaster. The year 1665 was Plague Year, with 70,000 dying in London alone: the court withdrew to Oxford and Parliament was summoned to meet there. The subsidies to support the war proved hard to collect and ran out depressingly quickly. In January 1666 France and Denmark came to the assistance of the Dutch. There was more heavy and bloody naval warfare in the summer of 1666, without decisive advantage to either side. In September 1666 the Great Fire of London left St Pauls, 87 churches, and 13,000 dwelling houses destroyed. By the end of the year the English were ready to sue for peace and, hard pressed for funds, began demobilization. In June 1667, in one of the most daring of all naval exploits, the Dutch sailed into the Thames Estuary and up the Medway to Chatham where the greater part of the English fleet was at anchor. The seamen refused to serve for arrears of pay, and Pepys, fearing the worst, made his will, sent his wife and father into the country, and buried his gold in the garden. Despite desperate attempts by Albemarle to erect some makeshift defences, the Dutch burned the *Royal James* in harbour and towed away the flagship, the *Royal Charles*.

While these disasters were overtaking the country, at court La Ronde went on with its usual vigour. In April Charles was plunged into gloom when La Belle Stewart, one of the queen's maids of honour, for whom he had sighed in vain for some months, eloped with the duke of Richmond. In July Pepys heard that Nell Gwynn had been bought up by Lord Buckhurst and abandoned the stage for £100 p.a.: by August she was said to be 'poor and deserted' and made a reappearance at the Theatre Royal. The same summer, Lady Castlemaine was said to be pregnant and determined that the king should recognize the child. Pepys reported:

She hath told the King that whoever did get it he should own it; and the bottom of the quarrel is this: she is fallen in love with young Jermin, who hath of late lain with her oftener than the King, and is now going to marry my Lady Falmouth. The King, he is mad at her for entertaining Jermin, and she is mad at Jermin's going to marry from her, so they are all mad; and thus the kingdom is governed.

ROYAL MISTRESSES. Charles II and his brother James vied with each other in sensuality but, by common consent, Charles's mistresses were more comely: indeed, James's were so ill-favoured that his brother suggested that they must have been prescribed as a penance. Nell Gwyn (*left*) was born in Hereford and came to Charles via the Theatre Royal, Drury Lane; Louise de Kéroualle (*right*) was sent over by Louis XIV on approval. They helped to replace the services of Barbara, Lady Castlemaine. On 4 November 1670, John Evelyn saw Louise, 'that famed beauty, but in my opinion of a childish, simple and baby face'. Her emotional outbursts earned for Louise from Nell Gwyn the nickname 'the weeping willow'.

Things were managed so badly, thought Pepys, that 'most people that I meet with agree that we shall fall into a commonwealth in a few years whether we will or no'.

The Dutch exploit did not prevent peace terms being signed at Breda in July 1667. The consequences of the war were considerable. The first victim was Clarendon, adviser to Charles during the long years of exile, and Chancellor since the Restoration. Though he had little direct responsibility for the conduct of the war, he was a convenient scapegoat, and Charles was tired of him. No attempt was made to protect him, and, faced with an impeachment, he fled to France, where the last years of his life were devoted to finishing his *History of the Great Rebellion* and writing his autobiography. Appeals to Charles for permission to return to his native country went unacknowledged. Of long-term significance was that the Commons extended their claims, insisting on a committee to investigate the national finances. The ecstatically loyal Parliament of 1661 was fast developing a much more questioning stance towards the royal government.

The diplomatic realignment after the second Anglo-Dutch War had consequence for England. The Dutch had little reason for gratitude towards their French allies, whose intervention had been half-hearted. England had been made acutely aware of its diplomatic isolation. Louis's alliance with the Dutch was hardly likely to survive the revelation of his long-term plans against the Spanish Empire, based on the claims of his wife. In 1667 he attacked in Flanders, overrunning several important border towns. The Dutch responded by organizing a Triple Alliance with England and Sweden to restrain French aggrandisement. At first sight the alliance was a great success, since Louis at once made peace at Aix-la-Chapelle on significantly moderate terms.

Louis's moderation was only tactical. His resentment at Dutch intervention was great, and accompanied by all the moral indignation people often feel against those they have injured. He was urged on by his minister Colbert, determined to smash Dutch prosperity, if necessary by war. Louis's first step was to undermine the Triple Alliance and isolate the United Provinces, and to this end he began, in 1669, negotiations with Charles. But a new and sensational point soon emerged from the discussions—a proposal that Charles should declare himself a Catholic, in return for money, and if necessary, troops to put down any resistance. Admittedly, there was no suggestion that Catholicism was to be established as the national religion, but in a period in which the principle of *cuius regio, eius religio* was widely accepted, it was a thin distinction to draw. England and France were to wage war on the Dutch *à l'outrance*; their power was to be crushed, their pride humbled, and the English rewarded by bases on the Continent. In May 1670 Charles's sister Henriette-Anne visited him at Dover to conclude the signing of the secret treaty. Its preamble declared that the intention was perpetual friendship between France and England, and that a treaty of such importance had rarely been made in human history. Knowledge of the secret treaty was given only to two of the cabal who formed Charles's ministry— Clifford and Arlington, both Catholics—and its existence was to be masked by a public treaty, omitting the Catholic clauses.

The secret treaty of Dover has been much debated. Efforts have been made to represent it as a master-stroke of policy, whereby Charles obtained good money out of Louis in exchange for worthless promises. The declaration of personal Catholicism was to be made at Charles's discretion, and was never forthcoming. It is not a lofty defence, nor does it stand up to scrutiny. It is true that secret treaties were commonplace. But the treaty ran counter to the national interest: shrewd observers were already alarmed at the evident growth and ambition of France, and it was scarcely sensible to support that aggrandisement in order to spend fifty years restraining it again. Secondly, the treaty involved Charles in a downright and categorical lie to Parliament. In January 1674 the king declared:

I cannot conclude without showing the entire confidence I have in you. I know you have heard much of my alliance with France; and I believe it hath been very strangely misrepresented to you as if there were certain secret articles of dangerous consequence . . . I assure you there is no other treaty with France, either before or since, not already printed, which shall not be made known.

Witnesses remarked that at this point, the king was seen to fumble with his notes, as well he might. If he became increasingly seen as a man not to be trusted, he had but himself to blame. The rumours of secret Catholic diplomacy did much to prepare the soil for the ludicrous allegations of the Popish Plot, with which he had to wrestle in the last years of his life. Finally, it placed Charles at Louis's mercy. The king of France had only to reveal the secret clauses in order to bring about a fair chance that Charles would be forced on his travels again. In his meaninglessly tricky diplomacy, Charles revealed himself very much his father's son.

It is difficult to fathom his motives, particularly since the Catholic clauses were his own suggestion. The French very sensibly doubted whether they could be implemented and were concerned lest a premature declaration should cause such unrest in England that the joint attack upon the Dutch would be impeded. Had the proposal come from James, duke of York, it might well have been the product of religious enthusiasm. Charles's interest in religion was fitful and inclined to scepticism. A recent commentator has argued that the Catholic clauses were but a 'temporary and comparatively unimportant tactical move', designed to make sure of the alliance with France. If that were so, the proposal was sillier than ever. The advantage gained was trifling compared with the risks run, and Louis was so avid to strike down the Dutch that no such concession was needed. Whether seventeenth-century Englishmen, had they been told the truth, would have regarded the matter as 'comparatively unimportant' may be doubted.

Morality aside, the consequences of the secret treaty were uniformly disastrous to Charles's own intentions. The co-ordinated onslaught on the Dutch in 1672 failed to bring them to their knees and financial difficulties once more forced Charles to withdraw, leaving Louis to carry on the war alone. An early consequence was the overthrow of the De Witt brothers, the destruction of the Regent regime, and the promotion of William of Orange to supreme power in Holland. Gratifying though it was for family reasons to see his nephew in such a distinguished position, William might also prove a very dangerous rival should Catholicism once more become an issue in England. The other part of the treaty was equally unfortunate since it ensured that Catholicism *could* become an issue. Common prudence prevented Charles from declaring himself a Catholic and he faced some pointed reproaches from James and those Catholic powers in the secret. He therefore decided to do something for his Catholic subjects by a declaration of indulgence, coinciding with the outbreak of war, by which he used his prerogative powers to suspend the penal laws against Catholic and Nonconformist dissenters. The timing was utterly maladroit. Two months before war was declared, the Stop on the Exchequer—the equivalent of a declaration of bankruptcy—had ruined the government's credit, and placed it totally at the mercy of Parliament to vote supplies to carry on the conflict. But an Anglican Parliament would neither agree to suspend the penal laws nor see religious matters taken out of its hands and governed by prerogative. By 1673 Charles had to withdraw the Declaration of Indulgence. By way of counter-attack, Parliament passed the Test Act, which instituted an oath against transubstantiation for all office-holders, which no Catholic could take. James, duke of York, who had been converted to the faith in 1669, was forced to resign his post as Lord High Admiral. But this raised, in the most public fashion, the question how a man who could not be trusted to serve in office under the crown, could be allowed to succeed as king of England. As year after year went by without Catherine of Braganza having children, the problem of the heir apparent's Catholicism became dominant. The ultimate result of Charles's initiative was to put back the cause of Catholic toleration in England by some 150 years.

The peace with Holland in 1674 gave Charles a few years of respite. His new Lord Treasurer, Thomas Osborne, earl of Danby, showed some skill in building up a royalist group in Parliament, and a substantial rise in the revenue from customs duties, coupled with an economy drive, gave Charles some relief from his financial troubles. But the spectre of Catholicism refused to go away. No doubt Protestant Englishmen were too suspicious, and politicians in opposition, such as Shaftesbury and Buckingham, were willing to play upon their anxieties. They presumed, as a matter of course, that a Catholic ruler would aim at absolute monarchy, based upon a standing army: the fires of Smithfield would be rekindled. At the safe distance of 300 years it is easy to chide them for their bigotry. But the private language of James would have done little to reassure them, while across the Channel Louis XIV, whose armies marched from victory to victory, was clearly losing patience with his Protestant subjects. At home, the king himself was suspect, his mother, sister, brother, and wife were or had been Catholics, as was Louise de Kéroualle, his favourite mistress since 1671. After the death of Anne Hyde in 1671, James married an Italian Catholic, Mary of Modena. In a somewhat desperate attempt to restore the balance and assert his Protestant stance, Charles in 1677 married off James's daughter Mary to William of Orange. Relations with the now ageing Cavalier Parliament remained tense however. They complained continually that the penal laws were not being enforced: the papists of London and Middlesex had been given the absurd assessment of £100. 13*s.* 4*d.*, of which only the 13*s.* 4*d.* had been paid. In foreign policy, Charles lurched from one side to the other. In 1678 he resolved to intervene to help the Dutch and an army was dispatched to Flanders. The combatants promptly made peace. Parliament voted £200,000 to disband the army. Charles diverted it to other purposes, and the slowness with which the army was dismantled encouraged suspicion that it had, all the time, been intended for domestic use.

In this atmosphere of growing mistrust, rumour, and suspicion, burst, in August 1678, the Popish Plot, a lurid allegation that Jesuit priests were conspiring to murder the king and take over the country. It was not clear whether Charles was to be poisoned, shot, or stabbed, or all three, but he was certainly to be done to death. The two persons who stepped forward to unmask these fiends did not inspire confidence: Israel Tonge was an eccentric clergyman with an obsession with Jesuits; Titus Oates was a renegade Jesuit novice aged thirty, who had been expelled from almost every institution to which he had belonged. They were assisted, however, in floating their plot by two pieces of good fortune. The magistrate before whom Oates had sworn his testimony, Sir Edmund Berry Godfrey, was found dead in October 1678 in circumstances that have never been fully explained. Secondly, Oates had mentioned that an investigation of the papers of Edward Coleman, former secretary to the duke of York, might well prove revealing. Coleman's letters did not, in fact, confirm the existence of the plot at all, but did include wild and inflammatory correspondence with foreign Jesuits, in which he declared that the chances of 'the utter subduing' of the pestilential Protestant heresy of the three kingdoms had never been better since the days of Queen Mary.

For Protestant Englishmen, this was confirmation of their worst fears. Why the Jesuits should wish to murder someone who was at least very sympathetic to Catholicism and probably their best hope was obscure, but it was a rebuttal that Charles himself could hardly put forward. A frenzy of fear possessed London. The House of Commons declared *nem. con.* that the existence of a 'damnable and

CHARLES II
(1660–1685)

A character of King Charles II by George Savile, first marquess of Halifax, usually known as the Trimmer, was first published in 1750, many years after his death. It portrays a prince who was watchful and unsentimental.

H<small>E</small> had but little Reading, and that tending to his Pleasures more than to his Instruction. In the Library of a young Prince, the solemn Folios are not much rumpled, Books of a lighter Digestion have the Dog's Ears. Some pretend to be very precise in the time of his Reconciling (to Rome) . . . Whispers went about, particular Men had Intimations; *Cromwell* had his Advertisements in other things, and this was as well worth his paying for. There was enough said of it to startle a great many; So much, that if the Government here, had not crumbled of itself, his Right alone, with that and other clogs upon it, would hardly have thrown it down. I conclude that when he came into *England* he was as certainly a *Roman Catholick*, as that he was a Man of Pleasure; both very consistent by visible Experience . . .

It may be said that his Inclinations to Love were the Effects of Health, and a good Constitution, with as little mixture of the *Seraphick* part as ever Man had: And though from that Foundation Men often raise their Passions, I am apt to think his stayed as much as any Man's ever did in the *lower Region*. This made him like easy Mistresses . . . his Patience for their Frailties shewed him no exact Lover . . .

He lived with his Ministers as he did with his Mistresses; he us'd them, but he was not in love with them . . . The present use he might have of them, made him throw Favours upon them . . . but he tied himself no more to them, than they did to him, which implied a sufficient Liberty on either side . . .

The thing called *Sauntering*, is a stronger Temptation to Princes than it is to others. The being galled with Importunities, pursued from one Room to another with asking Faces; the dismal Sound of unreasonable Complaints, and ill-grounded Pretences; the Deformity of Fraud ill-disguised; all these would make any Man run away from them; and I used to think it was the Motive for making him walk so fast. So it was more properly taking Sanctuary . . .

It must be allowed he had a little Over-balance on the well-natured Side, not Vigour enough to be earnest to do a kind Thing, much less to do a harsh one; but if a hard thing was done to another Man, he did not eat his supper the worse for it. It was rather a Deadness than Severity of Nature, whether it proceeded from a Dissipation of Spirits, or by the Habit of Living in which he was engaged.

hellish plot' had been proved, ordered the cellars to be searched, gave instructions for coffins to be opened lest they contained arms: from all parts of the country came reports of masked men galloping through the night. Best of all, from Oates's point of view, dozens of volunteers rushed to report suspicious circumstances and sinister conversations overheard: each allegation had to be investigated, and for some weeks the business of the country was at a standstill, while half the citizens wrote down the testimonies of the other half.

From melodrama, the plot moved into high politics. Though Oates had, in his opening statements, insisted that James, duke of York was also to be a victim if he would not go with the plot, the revelations from his secretary were an acute embarrassment. Another of Oates's named conspirators was Sir George Wakeman, physician to the queen, who had agreed to poison the king. By November, Oates, whose memory was improving step by step, recalled seeing a letter from Wakeman which made it clear that the queen would play her part, in revenge for the 'violation of her bed' by Charles. This new evidence Oates imparted to the king on 24 November, in an audience which must have had its awkward moments. By the following month, the chase had moved on to the Lord Treasurer, Danby, who was impeached and accused of attempting to conceal the plot. An examination of his secret correspondence with the English ambassador to France made it clear that Charles had sought large subsidies in order to avoid having to summon Parliament.

On 3 December 1679 the plot claimed its first victim when Coleman was hanged, drawn, and quartered at Tyburn. In the following months took place a series of trials, with Oates as chief witness, and groups of Jesuits and priests as defendants. Charles refused to credit the accusation against the queen, but

SWINGS AND ROUNDABOUTS. The triumph of Charles II after the Oxford Parliament and the succession of his brother James brought bad times for Titus Oates, principal author of the Popish Plot, seen here being flogged through the streets of London in May 1685. After the Glorious Revolution he was given a small pension and died in 1705.

James, duke of York could not be shielded in the same way. Soon after Parliament met it was proposed to remove him from the king's presence and councils. In January 1679 Charles at last dissolved his Parliament, now out of control, but the new one which assembled in March 1679 was, if anything, more zealously Protestant than ever. Charles tried conciliation. The Privy Council was re-modelled and several members of the opposition, including Shaftesbury and Essex, appointed. James was persuaded, much against his will, to absent himself awhile, and chose Brussels: by way of quid pro quo and to safeguard his interest in the succession, he demanded that Charles should formally declare that James, duke of Monmouth, product of the king's relationship in exile with Lucy Walters, was not his legitimate son. This Charles did in a written note to the Privy Council, one of the quainter royal documents.

Charles met his new Parliament with an appeal for unity, hoping their proceedings would be calm and peaceful. In return, the Commons resumed their impeachments of Danby, who resigned. When Charles pardoned him, the Commons voted the pardon illegal. Next they resolved that James's succession would imperil English liberties. Charles offered to agree to restrictions on his successor's powers, provided that the succession itself was assured. In May, a bill excluding James from the succession in England, Ireland, and Scotland was brought in, the two latter being included in case their own legislatures forgot to do so. At this juncture, Charles decided to dissolve his third Parliament.

The confrontation between king and Parliament was ominously reminiscent of 1641 and civil war was frequently predicted. For a year Charles managed to avoid summoning a new Parliament, reducing the opposition to harassing tactics. In June 1680, at Shaftesbury's instigation, James was indicted as a papist recusant and the countess of Portsmouth as a common prostitute: Lord Chief Justice Scroggs directed the jury to discharge the suit. In October 1680 Parliament was summoned again, Charles driven by shortage of supplies for Tangier—part of his wife's dowry, which was being attacked by the Moors. The eyes of Europe, Charles declared, were upon Parliament: 'Let us therefore take care that we do not gratify our enemies, and discourage our friends, by any unseasonable disputes.' But the storm over the duke of York would not die down. The Commons immediately reintroduced a bill stripping him of the succession and threatening him with a charge of treason if he returned to England. When it was defeated in the Lords, they turned back to the plot and impeached Lord Stafford, one of the five Catholic peers in custody since October 1678. Accused of hiring an assassin to murder the king, he was found guilty and beheaded in December 1680. Charles's supporters argued that the fears of the nation could be met by restrictions on James's future conduct, but the majority insisted on total exclusion, and on 7 January 1681 resolved not to grant supply until an Exclusion Bill had been passed. Charles dissolved them once more.

DIVINE RIGHT OF KINGS

Let every soul be in subjection to the higher powers; for there is no power but of God, and the powers that be are ordained by God.

Therefore, he that resisteth that power, withstandeth the ordinance of God; and they that withstand shall receive to themselves judgement. (*Romans* 13)

THE doctrine of the Divine Right of Kings, with the corollaries of passive obedience and non-resistance, was promulgated in the sixteenth and seventeenth centuries, largely as a consequence of the religious struggles of that period. It had, however, a long pedigree. The theory of the God-King was central to Egyptian civilization, and the pyramids testify to the strength of that belief. The anointing of Hebrew kings marked them as agents of Yahweh and sacrosanct. Capetian kings of France introduced the practice of touching for the king's evil, and this claim to supernatural healing powers was soon adopted by their English rivals. Regular and formal ceremonies continued to be held until 1714 when the Hanoverians abandoned them, though in France they continued until the reign of Charles X in the 1820s.

In the sixteenth century, the doctrine was further developed into the proposition that subjects had no right of resistance to lawful rulers: even a tyrant must be left to divine retribution. But however attractive to rulers, the theory had severe limitations. It could scarcely be presented as more than an assertion, while the blanket endorsement of power—as in Romans 13—would apply equally to usurpers. In the shrill version expounded by James I—that kings were not merely granted divine powers but were themselves Gods—it smacked of blasphemy. An important statement of the case was Sir Robert Filmer's *Patriarcha*, written in the later 1630s, but printed in 1680, during the Exclusion crisis. It was singled out for refutation by

CHARLES II touching for the evil.

Whig theorists of contract, such as Algernon Sidney and John Locke. A doctrine which relied so heavily upon biblical authority was bound to suffer damage in the age of reason.

Charles summoned a new Parliament to meet at Oxford in March and began urgent negotiations with Louis for a subsidy that would give him room for manœuvre. Louis agreed to provide £400,000 over three years so that Charles could dispense with Parliament. Under these circumstances, Charles could meet his Parliament with some composure. The opposition trooped into Oxford, a royalist stronghold, as defiant as ever. Charles addressed them in the Geometry School: he would listen to any reasonable expedient to preserve the government

RACING AT WINDSOR. Charles II took a keen interest in horse-racing and during his reign more formal rules were drawn up. At Windsor, races were held on Datchet Mead until Anne changed the venue to Ascot in 1711. The king watches from a small and rather makeshift royal box.

in Protestant hands, but he must remind them that, without the monarchy, neither religion nor property was safe. Charles's supporters offered a permanent Regency, to be exercised by the princess of Orange on James's behalf. It was rejected. Shaftesbury counter-proposed that Monmouth be recognized as successor. That was an unwise move, splitting the forces of the opposition. The Commons then resolved to introduce yet another Exclusion Bill. Charles dissolved them after a week with the laconic remark that 'we are not like to have a good end'.

Considering that Shaftesbury and his supporters claimed repeatedly to be defending the cause of Parliaments, they have not won very much respect, and are often portrayed as a desperate faction, supported by an ignorant and bigoted rabble. Shaftesbury had the misfortune to collide with a poet of genius, Dryden, and went down to posterity as the false Achitophel, 'resolved to ruin or to rule the state'. The opposition's association with the unsavoury Oates smeared their cause with innocent blood. But there is another side to the argument. They were right to doubt the sincerity of Charles's repeated declaration of his devotion to the Church of England, and their fears of what James would do if he succeeded were shown, in a few years, to be anything but fanciful. They were accused, as a matter of course, of aiming at the destruction of monarchy itself. But when Sir

William Coventry in 1679 charged them in the Commons with wanting to bring back a commonwealth, they denied it with indignation. Shaftesbury, a man of broad Dorset acres, held the traditional view that monarchy was the very foundation of the social order telling Evelyn that he would support the principle of monarchy to his last breath, 'having seen and felt the misery of being under a mechanic tyranny'. Nor were they in a position to demand extensive restrictions on the royal prerogative, which would alienate their two candidates, Monmouth or William of Orange. They maintained that all that they wanted were adequate guarantees against popery. Sir Henry Capel's father had been beheaded during the Civil War for his loyalty to the crown, a fact which Sir Henry did not often allow the Commons to forget. Nevertheless, he moved steadily into opposition, finishing up as a supporter of Exclusion. 'I have a great deal of reason to be sensible of the miseries of '41', he told the House: 'I would have the world see that we have no intention to eclipse the monarchy by meddling with the militia or the prerogative.' The Exclusion Bill was 'our whole, our all'.

The French subsidy enabled Charles to trump Shaftesbury's ace, and he gathered up the rest of the tricks smoothly. Interest in the plot was waning at last, while the threat of civil war was enough to bring many sober men back to the crown. A declaration published in April 1681 and ordered to be read in all churches assured Charles's subjects that he was still resolved to have frequent Parliaments, but, in fact, the Oxford Parliament was the last of his reign. Shaftesbury was arrested in July 1681 on a trumped-up charge of treason and held in the Tower until November: though acquitted, the threat was clear enough and Shaftesbury took himself off the following year to die in exile in Holland.

The Whigs were in total disarray. Several of them dabbled in real treason and the Rye House Plot in the summer of 1683 was a conspiracy to assassinate Charles and his brother on their way back from Newmarket. Essex cut his throat in the Tower: Lord Russell and Algernon Sidney, two of the leading Exclusionists, finished up on the block. Danby was released from the Tower. James, called home from Scotland where he had been acting as High Commissioner, took more and more control of royal policy. He even managed to pay off a few old scores when, in 1684, he brought an action against Oates and was awarded £100,000 damages, with twenty shillings costs. The sincerity of Charles's and James's belief in toleration may be judged from the fact that in 1683 and 1684, free at last to pursue whatever policy they wished, persecution of the dissenters had never been fiercer.

The success of the Whigs in three general elections between 1679 and 1681 had demonstrated what party propaganda and organization could achieve. The king's riposte was a remodelling of the parliamentary boroughs so that friendly members of Parliament would be returned. Charters were called in for inspection

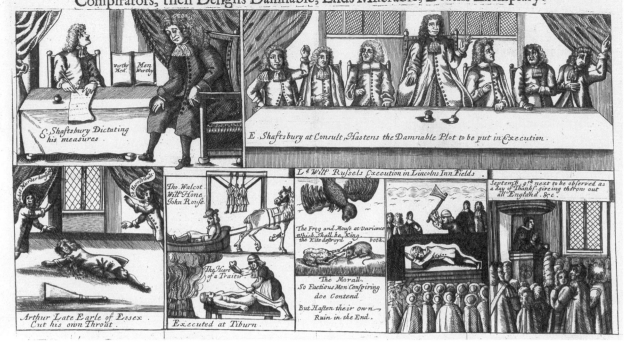

A History of the New PLOT: Or, A Prospect of
Conspirators, their Designs Damnable, Ends Miserable, Deaths Exemplary.

THE RYE HOUSE PLOT, 1683. Some of Charles's opponents, desperate after their defeat in 1681, turned to conspiracy. A rather half-hearted plan to assassinate Charles and his brother on their way back from Newmarket at the Rye House, near Hoddesdon, Hertfordshire, was discovered in 1683. The Frog and the Mouse in the broadsheet, contending to be king, are presumably Monmouth and William of Orange. The Kite destroyed them both.

and new ones issued, with Whigs and their supporters excluded from the corporations. Shaftesbury's old power base in London was destroyed. Though the manipulation of the boroughs by the crown would, had it been sustained, have dealt a serious blow at the independence of Parliament, it was also a harbinger of eighteenth-century methods, and more subtle than the previous practice of prorogation and dissolution.

The price to be paid for four years without the pleasure of parliamentary advice was a subdued role in European affairs. The French subsidy, even when augmented by the improvement in the yield from the customs, scarcely permitted a vigorous foreign policy. Louis was therefore able to proceed with his forcible reunions unchecked by the English, while Tangier, too costly to be defended, was abandoned in 1684, after France and Portugal had declined to buy it.

Charles devoted much of his later years to rebuilding. The new St Paul's rose slowly from the ashes of the Great Fire. Windsor Castle was extensively rebuilt and became his favourite residence. At Winchester, a vast new palace was begun, intended to rival Versailles. It was never completed, and mouldered away, being used in the Seven Years War to house French prisoners. In February 1685 at Whitehall, Charles suffered a stroke which left him for five days at the mercy of his doctors. Towards the end, a priest was smuggled into the apartment—Father Huddlestone, who had helped the king to escape after Worcester, thirty-four years before—and Charles was received into the Catholic Church.

Charles's most celebrated biographer turned his last years into a pastoral idyll: 'Charles was now master of as great a power as any king of England had wielded—the sweeter that it was founded, with little help of arms or money, on his people's love. . . . Never had the English people known such a king.' It was founded on French subsidies and deceit. True, Charles had triumphed over great difficulties—largely of his own making. He had struggled with considerable skill to preserve the throne for his brother James. It was scarcely worth the effort.

THE GREAT FIRE OF 1666 was attributed by many to the papists and an inscription condemning the 'treachery and malice of the popish faction' remained on the Monument until 1830. Charles and his brother James helped to direct operations to curtail the spread of the fire.

James II and the Glorious Revolution

James II got off to a splendid start. After all the excitement of the Exclusion crisis, his succession was declared without protest of any kind. William of Orange sent dutiful congratulations to his father-in-law: Monmouth, in exile in the Low Countries, contemplated joining the emperor in his campaign against the Turks after the rescue of Vienna. James's first speech to the Privy Council was a model of tact and common sense:

I have been reported to be a man for arbitrary power, but that is not the only story has been made of me, and I shall make it my endeavour to preserve this Government, both in Church and State, as it is now by law established.

How had James acquired such a reputation? The death of their father had made an overwhelming impression on each of the brothers, but they drew from it different conclusions. Charles inferred that opposition should be handled with subtlety and patience, James that any concession merely prepared the way for the next. 'Compliance', he insisted, had been 'the fatal rock on which his father miserably split.' His career confirmed his leaning towards authority. After serving in the armies of Louis XIV, he commanded the royal navy from 1660 to 1673, fighting with gallantry in several bloody encounters. He was therefore essentially a military man, while Charles remained a civilian. After his conversion to Catholicism in 1669 and the slow development of the Exclusion crisis in the following decade, he had been obliged to watch while Charles handled the situation, uncertain to what extent he could rely upon his brother and suspicious of the growing influence and popularity of James, duke of Monmouth. Exclusion he understandably regarded as striking at the very heart of monarchy: the arguments which could be offered to set aside the lawful heir to the throne might, with equal plausibility, be used against the king himself.

At the height of the Exclusion crisis, from November 1679 until March 1682, he was in Scotland, where he pursued a policy of 'thorough'. The Scottish Parliament was induced to declare formally that the religious views of the heir to the throne were of no consequence. The Covenanters, who had risen in rebellion in 1679, had been put down by Monmouth, who was subsequently accused of undue leniency: James did not make the same mistake and used, with equanimity, torture, allowed under Scottish law. Though he has been credited with advanced views on religious toleration, his conduct in Scotland suggests that his sole concern was to pursue Catholic advantage. In 1686, the Scottish Privy Council was ordered to relieve Catholics from the penal laws, while maintaining them against Covenanters. The French ambassador, Barillon, commented that James was 'very anxious that only the catholics shall be granted the free exercise of their religious rites'.

James came to the throne at the age of fifty-one with far greater experience of government than any monarch of modern times. He was more inclined to business than his brother Charles, though his passion for hunting, combined with his odd addiction to piety and promiscuity, made inroads on his time. He had strong, even dogmatic views, and his stiff manner contrasted with the easy urbanity of Charles. 'He has all the faults of the king his father', wrote the French envoy Bonrepaus, 'but he has less sense and he behaves more haughtily in public.'

His position was a strong one. There were standing armies in his three kingdoms of nearly 20,000 men, built up over the previous twenty years. The improvement of trade had been sustained and with a revenue of about two millions, James was much better off than Charles had been, with a token £1,200,000, much of it impossible to collect. In addition, Louis sent at once another instalment of the French subsidy. The remodelling of nearly one hundred parliamentary boroughs held out the prospect of a friendly and generous Parliament.

James's first move was conciliatory and sensible. Two days after his succession,

JAMES II'S CORONATION, 1685. Though James's political position disintegrated quickly, his early months as monarch were triumphant. His Parliament was loyal and generous (the two do not always go together) and his coronation particularly lavish. The banquet in Westminster Hall was, judging by this engraving, more decorous than most. At the service, the archbishop of Canterbury presided but James did not receive Communion.

he announced his intention of summoning a Parliament to meet him in May 1685. During the last year of his reign, Charles II had been in technical breach of the Triennial Act of 1664. James's prompt action allayed misgivings and Parliament was more likely to be generous before problems had begun to pile up. Besides, the new king was a great believer in firmness: 'I know the English,' he told Barillon, 'one must not show them at the start that one is afraid of them.'

By and large, the move was a success, though James's opening speech ended with a menace: 'The best way to engage me to meet you often is always to use me well.' The tough stance appeared to be justified. On its first day, the Commons voted the same revenues that Charles had had, but for life, and with a much greater yield. But when, in committee, they demanded that all laws against dissenters be put into effect, the honeymoon cooled. James took them to task, and the House recanted, satisfied to rely upon his gracious word.

In June 1685 Monmouth landed at Lyme Regis with a force of some eighty men. William of Orange did nothing to help him. If Monmouth established himself as king, William's claim through Mary would be set aside. The Monmouth invasion lasted a mere three weeks. He failed dismally to attract much support from the gentry or aristocracy and his ill-equipped army of peasants was butchered by the king's regular troops at Sedgemoor. Monmouth, captured hiding in a ditch, was taken to London where he pleaded in vain with James for his life.

The ease with which Monmouth's adventure was defeated indicates how superior professional soldiers had become to ordinary citizens, most of whom

THE REBELS ROUTED. In the absence of newspapers, radio, and television, other means of representing events and influencing opinion assumed greater importance. This pack of cards took as its unconvivial theme Monmouth's rebellion in 1685. The six of clubs shows Monmouth's entry into Lyme Regis; the seven of spades shows the duke's fate; and the five of diamonds that of his followers.

were no longer accustomed to carry arms. On James the effect seems to have been to cause him to overestimate the strength of his position. When Parliament reassembled in November 1685 there was growing anxiety at the number of Catholic officers to whom James had granted commissions. The king made it clear that he was not prepared to dispense with their services. When the Commons begged him to remove the apprehensions of his loyal subjects, James replied reproachfully that he deserved better confidence. 'We are all Englishmen', declared John Coke, the member for Derby, 'and we ought not to be frighted out of our duty by a few high words.' This was too outspoken for the House, which dispatched him to the Tower. But the complaints rumbled on, and 20 November James suddenly prorogued the Parliament. It did not meet again during his reign.

James's campaign to promote the Catholic cause now gathered pace, with attacks upon the main bastions of power, the Law, the Church, the army, the universities, and the commission of the peace. As a preliminary to establishing his right to appoint Catholic army officers, the king dismissed six judges early in 1686: after a collusive action against Sir Edward Hales, a Catholic officer, the remaining judges upheld James's right to dispense with the penal laws in particular cases. The following month, after Compton, bishop of London had refused to suspend a cleric for delivering an anti-Catholic sermon, an Ecclesiastical Commission was appointed, which immediately suspended him from his ecclesiastical functions. In October 1686 a heavily revised commission of the peace was issued, a large number of Catholic justices being added. Charles's campaign against the parliamentary boroughs was reactivated by *quo warranto* proceedings. The two universities received similar treatment. The vice-chancellor of the University of Cambridge was dismissed and a Catholic master forced on Sidney Sussex, the Catholic master of University College, Oxford, allowed to retain his post, another Catholic appointed dean of Christ Church and the Fellows of Magdalen College, Oxford expelled after they had refused to elect a Catholic president at James's insistence. In August 1687 the Lords Lieutenant of the counties were asked whether they would support the withdrawal of the penal laws and those who refused were replaced.

It has many times been argued that James had no wish to establish a Catholic despotism and that his Protestant subjects were very wrong to suspect his motives. But it should be remembered that in August 1685 James's ally Louis had revoked the Edict of Nantes which gave protection to French Protestants. One can only wonder what more James could have done to alarm his subjects or how long they were to wait before opining that all was not well. The main positions of power were, one by one, entrusted to Catholic hands. Tyrconnel was appointed commander-in-chief of the army in Ireland and then Lord Deputy. In Scotland, power went to Lord Perth and Lord Melfort, brothers recently converted to Catholicism. The command of the Channel fleet was given to a Catholic, Sir

Roger Strickland. The important garrison town of Portsmouth was put under the governance of James's illegitimate son, the duke of Berwick. Lord Sunderland, the leading minister, trimmed his sails to the prevailing wind and announced his conversion. Five Catholics were admitted to the Privy Council in the summer of 1686: Lord Belasyse became head of the Treasury and Lord Arundel of Wardour became Lord Privy Seal. Father Petre, a Jesuit, became one of the king's closest advisers: it was rumoured that he was to succeed to the archbishopric of York, which was held vacant, and James urged the pope to make him a cardinal. James even attempted to nominate Lord Carlingford, another Catholic, to the command of the six regiments which were in Dutch service, though William refused to agree.

Within three years, the great majority of James's subjects had been alienated. Two events in the summer of 1688 brought matters to a crisis. In April 1688 James issued a second Declaration of Indulgence, repeated the terms of that of 1685, and, for good measure, insisted that it be read in all churches. When seven bishops petitioned James to reconsider the matter, they were charged with seditious libel. On 30 June they were acquitted, amid scenes of widespread rejoicing. The second event was the birth of a son to Mary of Modena, James's second wife, after a childless marriage of fifteen years. Protestants who had comforted themselves with the thought that, by the nature of things, the throne

THE SEVEN BISHOPS RELEASED. A Dutch engraving of the departure of Archbishop Sancroft and his six colleagues from the Tower after their acquittal on 30 June 1688 on the charge of seditious libel. They were given a rapturous farewell with the bells of the city pealing. James's decision to prosecute the bishops was the last straw for many loyal Anglicans.

must soon be in the hands of Mary and her formidable Protestant husband, could now look forward to a line of Catholic monarchs. In desperation they invented and popularized one of the most absurd of all royal stories—that the new prince was a changeling, smuggled in to the bedchamber by Jesuit intriguers while the warming pan was being fetched.

The day after the acquittal of the seven bishops, an appeal was dispatched to William of Orange to intervene to protect English liberties. It was signed by Shrewsbury, Devonshire, Danby, Compton, Lumley, Edward Russell, and Henry Sidney, a cross-section of the aristocracy, and it assured William that he would be welcomed by nineteen out of twenty Englishmen. July and August, William devoted to the preparation of a fleet and some 14,000 men, though he was successful in concealing the exact purpose for a few critical weeks.

The precariousness of James's position now became apparent. He had alienated, by his attacks upon the Church of England, almost all of the natural leaders of the kingdom, the gentry and aristocracy. In exchange, he depended upon an ill-assorted and inadequate alliance of inexperienced Catholics and those dissenters who were disposed to take his conversion to the cause of religious toleration at its face value. On paper, the army he had assembled at Hounslow was formidable, but James himself had been present to hear the outburst of cheering when the acquittal of the bishops was known. In the navy, on which he had lavished much care, there was widespread dissatisfaction at the introduction of Catholic officers and popish practices. After the revolution, in a conversation in exile, James remarked how much he had spent on the army and navy, whereat his wife retorted, testily, that it had not done him much good.

Under these circumstances, James's best hope was that Louis would make some diversion that would prevent William from leaving Holland. Although Louis obliged by warning the Dutch that he would come to James's aid if he was attacked, in September he launched a major offensive in Alsace against the emperor, thus letting William off the leash. James was therefore abandoned to his own devices, which could scarcely be encouraging.

At this juncture, James flung his political machine into reverse. It was a move that smacked of desperation and, in itself, constitutes a remarkable commentary on the folly of his earlier proceedings. In August he announced that a new Parliament would meet in November. Two months later, he abandoned the Ecclesiastical Commission, promised to restore Compton to his see, gave London back its forfeited charter, abrogated all proceedings against the boroughs from 1679, and, in new commissions of the peace, began the process of weeding out the new Catholic justices and their dissenting allies, and reinstating the Lords Lieutenant, Deputy Lieutenants, and justices who had been ejected. Even the Fellows of Magdalen were allowed back to their delightful college.

William sailed from Holland on 20 October and, almost at once, was forced

JAMES II

(1685–1688)

> A great king, with strong armies and mighty fleets, a vast treasure and powerful allies, fell all at once; and his whole strength, like a spider's web, was so irrecoverably broken with a touch that he was never able to retrieve, what for want both of judgement and heart, he threw up in a day.
>
> (Gilbert Burnet, *A History of my own Times*, bk. IV.)

JAMES II is almost certainly the least popular of English monarchs, the strange mixture of arrogance and weakness, piety and debauchery having found few admirers. Born in 1633, he was named after his grandfather. He grew up in exile after the civil wars, became involved with Anne Hyde, daughter of the earl of Clarendon, and married her in 1660 when she became pregnant. The marriage produced two daughters, Mary and Anne. In 1669 James was converted to Catholicism. After the death of his first wife in 1671, he married Mary of Modena, aged fifteen. No living child was born until James Francis Edward in 1688. James survived the attempt to exclude him from the throne and succeeded his brother in 1685. His brief reign was dominated by his endeavours to advance Catholicism, checked by the successful invasion by William of Orange in 1688. James fled to France and lived the rest of his life in exile, dying in 1701. He is one of a small number of rulers since the Conquest the whereabouts of whose body is not known. His remains were buried in the church of the English Benedictines in Paris, but the grave was desecrated during the French Revolution. James's Memoirs were also destroyed in the Revolution.

back by fierce gales. His declaration made no mention of claiming the crown, but fell back on that trusted panacea for the nation's grievances, a free Parliament. After a second attempt, he eluded the English fleet, landing at Torbay on 5 November. A diversionary rising, organized by Danby, got under way in Yorkshire, and another in Cheshire. Torbay was perilously close to the place where Monmouth had landed three years before, and for a fortnight it remained doubtful whether the Dutch invasion would stall in the same way. But James's counter-measures were hesitant and leisurely. He joined his army at Salisbury on the 19th, was incapacitated for two days by a nosebleed, and after five days, resolved on retreat. Lord Cornbury, son of Clarendon, John Churchill, and Prince George of Denmark, husband to Princess Anne, then went over to William. On James's return to London, he discovered that Princess Anne herself had left to join Danby in the north. One by one, the nobility dropped off. William was left to make a slow unopposed march towards London.

James's mind turned increasingly to thoughts of his father's fate and he resolved on flight. This should have presented no difficulty, since William was only too anxious not to be encumbered by his father-in-law. But in the distracted state to which James was now reduced, he succeeded in bungling an escape which his enemies were all too ready to facilitate. The queen and young prince were first packed off. Then, in heavy disguise, James got as far as Faversham, where he was held by a group of suspicious and disrespectful fishermen. He was back at Whitehall on 16 December, William having advanced to Windsor. Three days later, James made a second and successful departure, getting as far as Rochester. From there he took ship for France, explaining, somewhat unnecessarily, to Lord Ailesbury, 'I retire for the security of my person.'

Within six weeks, James's world had crumbled. After months of preparation for resistance, he surrendered his kingdom without a blow. Unnerved and confused by the desertions, he persuaded himself that he was in mortal danger, trapped in a web of intrigue and deceit. But his haughty and imperious manner had always masked the brittleness of a weak man. Louis received him with great kindness and placed Saint-Germain at his disposal: the French courtiers were less charitable—'when one listens to him, one understands why he is here.'

William had two immediate tasks—to establish what his constitutional position was, and to eliminate Jacobite resistance in Britain, so that the country could join the Dutch in resisting French aggrandisement. At one stage, a Regency on behalf of James had seemed a possibility. But apart from the inherent absurdity of the situation, it would run into difficulties over the infant Prince of Wales, since it was an article of faith on the winning side that the child was not the rightful heir. Nor was William prepared to stand aside and see his wife declared queen by herself, since it would give him no standing should she predecease him. The Convention which met in January 1689 resolved that by his flight James had abdicated: Mary and William were then declared joint rulers, a precedent being found in the days of Mary and Philip of Spain.

James, in the meantime, accommodated himself easily to his new life at Saint-Germain, resuming hunting and his devotions with renewed vigour. After some weeks, he had to be reminded that there remained one kingdom he had not yet lost and, without much enthusiasm, he left Brest in March 1689, accompanied by French arms and advisers, to pay his first visit to Ireland, which Tyrconnel was holding for him. Though the vast majority of his Irish subjects were Catholic, their interests and James's did not necessarily coincide. James saw the country as a stepping-stone to Scotland and England. The ambition of the native Irish and the Old English was to use the opportunity to throw off dependence on England

Gulielmus & Maria
D.G. Angl: Scot:
Fran: & Hiber: Rex
& Regina &c.

Vander Gucct sculp.

WILLIAM AND MARY CROWNED. The awkward constitutional position following James's flight was solved by offering the crown jointly to William and Mary. William's personal situation, should Mary predecease him, was safeguarded by Anne agreeing, with considerable reluctance, to postpone her claim to the throne.

WILLIAM'S LANDING AT TORBAY. William's expedition was a hazardous business since James had devoted much attention to his navy and a royal fleet, under Lord Dartmouth, was stationed to intercept. On the first occasion, William was driven back by storms, but when he sailed again Dartmouth was penned in the Thames estuary by an east wind and, when he finally emerged, was prevented from a close pursuit by a shift of wind to the west. William landed unopposed on 5 November, Thanksgiving Day for the Gunpowder Plot, and stepped ashore at Brixham. Many detected in 'the Protestant Wind' the hand of God at work.

and establish an independent Ireland. While perfectly willing to welcome James, they were no more anxious than the English to arm him with absolutist powers.

The French advisers were appalled when they beheld their new Irish allies. Tyrconnel's army, though large, particularly on paper, was totally deficient in discipline, training, and equipment. Since no money was available, officers had been told to pay their own troops. Loyalty was therefore personal. At Derry, when one captain was killed, his men at once left: the French commander was obliged to fire on them to remind them of their duty, but had first to borrow the muskets.

James spent the early summer getting his army into some kind of shape. A Parliament summoned at Dublin in May proved to be more Catholic than the king. An Act of Attainder named more than 2,000 of their opponents and decimated the Protestants; the land settlement based upon the Act of 1667 was overturned; and the authority of the English Parliament over Ireland denied. These measures did not do much to persuade James's English subjects to entrust themselves to him once more. Meanwhile, the attempt to starve out Derry, the last important Protestant stronghold, failed. In August the Huguenot general Schomberg landed in Ulster, and the following summer was joined by William himself. James advanced to the Boyne, thirty miles north of Dublin, to give battle. In blazing heat, on 1 July, with William directing the battle in person, the Catholics were defeated. James departed in some haste. 'I do now resolve to shift for myself', he told his courtiers, and was at Duncannon, on board for France, before William had entered Dublin.

William's position was now assured, though the subjugation of the west of Ireland took time. In Scotland, a convention offered the throne jointly to William and Mary, though conditional upon the abolition of Episcopacy and the

THE SIEGE OF LONDONDERRY. Though the fighting in England at the Glorious Revolution was no more than skirmishing, in Scotland and Ireland there were sustained campaigns. The turning-point in the latter kingdom was the relief of Londonderry after a siege of 105 days. On 28 July 1689 supply vessels broke through the boom across the Foyle and three days later the besiegers struck camp.

ENGRAVED GOBLET depicting William's victory at the battle of the Boyne and inscribed: 'To the glorious and immortal memory of King William and his Queen Mary and perpetual disappointment to the Pope, the Pretender and all the enemies of the Protestant religion.' These glasses were probably used for ceremonial drinking at Orange clubs, particularly on the anniversaries of the battle (1 July) and William's birthday (4 November). This specimen belonged to Charles Cobbe, archbishop of Dublin from 1743 until his death in 1765.

institution of a Presbyterian Church order. Viscount Dundee succeeded briefly in rallying the clans for James, and inflicted a defeat upon William's general Mackay at the pass of Killiecrankie in July 1689. But Dundee died in the moment of victory, nobody else could hold the clans together, and the Jacobite challenge fell apart.

The first constitutional task after the departure of James II was to secure the throne against any Catholic successor. The Bill of Rights recounted at length James's misdeeds and insisted that 'It hath been found by experience that it is inconsistent with the safety and welfare of this protestant kingdom to be governed by a popish prince.' No person embracing Catholicism or married to a Catholic was eligible to succeed to the throne. The right of free petitioning was reinstated, the suspending power condemned, the dispensing power 'as used of late' declared invalid, and a standing army forbidden in peacetime, save by parliamentary consent. The Toleration Act of 1689, though far from complete, rewarded the Protestant dissenters for their refusal to side with James. The hereditary principle was just about maintained by the pretence that James had abdicated the throne, and Princess Anne's rights were safeguarded by the stipulation that she would take precedence over any children born to William of a second marriage. William was to have the right of administration.

The Glorious Revolution has always been a subject of controversy. It was worshipped by eighteenth-century Whigs such as Burke, who saw it as the foundation on which political liberalism and parliamentary supremacy had been erected. Macaulay turned it into the central event of modern British history, claiming that Britain in the nineteenth century was spared the convulsions and revolutions that shook the continent because she had had a conservative and moderate revolution in 1688. As political viewpoints changed, so interpretations shifted. Twentieth-century historians wondered whether so bloodless a revolution could really be a revolution at all—though the absence of bloodshed in England was pure luck, and blood in plenty was spilled in Ireland and Scotland. Marxist commentators objected that there was no social element to the revolution and dismissed it as a mere *coup d'état*. Other historians, when they discovered that it had been effected largely by the aristocracy, felt that it could not have amounted to much: an American historian dismissed it as 'the respectable revolution', as though that was sufficient to prove its inadequacy. Over recent years, the argument has rolled on, with the conservative and radical aspects of the revolution being stressed in turn.

One reason that the Glorious Revolution is difficult to get into focus is that there are really two revolutions rolled into one, or perhaps, more moderately, two aspects of the same revolution. It was in origin a protest against what was taken to be Catholic despotism. But as soon as the task of crushing popery had been completed, the underlying rhythms of English political life re-emerged, much as they had done in the 1650s. William was anxious to preserve the position of the monarchy, while many members of the Commons could not pass up the chance they had of strengthening their own powers. The Exclusion crisis and the last four years of Charles's reign had demonstrated how potent a weapon was the power of prorogation and dissolution. William was victor in the first revolution, victim in the second.

The crucial question in 1689 was supply. William was understandably anxious to have the customs granted for life—as had all kings in Tudor and Stuart times, save Charles I in 1625. The Commons, with great deliberation, granted it for four years only, and their total financial settlement was at a level bound to fall short of the crown's needs, even in peacetime. That this was far from inadvertent may be seen by the parliamentary debates in the spring of 1689. 'When princes have not needed money,' declared Sir Joseph Williamson, 'they have not needed us.' Sir Thomas Clarges was in complete agreement: 'if you give this revenue for three years, you will be secure of a parliament.' They followed their financial pressure with a Triennial Bill, and though it was defeated in the Lords in 1690, William was forced to accept it in 1694. William was extremely bitter at the ungenerous treatment he had received and spoke towards the end of 1690 of returning to Holland and abandoning the ungrateful English.

The result was an important and permanent shift in the balance of power between monarchy and Parliament. From 1688 onwards, Parliament had to be summoned annually. The fact that William's main objective in coming to England had been to engage her resources in the struggle against France merely confirmed his weak position in relation to parliamentary supply.

In this way, therefore, the Revolution did produce an important change in the constitution. The monarchy remained of central importance, but Parliament was promoted from an intermittent to a permanent feature of political life. The old weapons of prorogation and dissolution decayed, the right of veto dropped into disuse, while the more subtle methods of management and leadership came to be primary political considerations. There was still room for a persistent tug-of-war between monarch and Parliament, particularly over the choice of ministers, and the crown retained formidable weapons in its armoury. But the context of the political and constitutional struggle had been permanently altered.

It was a remarkable demonstration of the extent to which the old commonwealth ideal had withered that not even the foolishness of James II could revive it. Edmund Ludlow, the old regicide, left his safe refuge in Switzerland in 1689 and journeyed to England under the impression that his time had come: he discovered that he had totally misjudged the situation and was obliged to depart hastily. But though monarchy survived, it survived in different form. The year 1688 was the first step on that gradual retreat from real power that, in the end, enabled monarchy to come to terms, first with liberalism, then with democracy. But the extent of the decline in royal power was, for many years, masked by the fact that national power was growing so fast. The damage to the royal position done by the Triennial Act of 1694, the Act of Settlement of 1701, and the Septennial Act of 1716 has to be measured against the great successes in the wars against France, the steady increase in empire, and the eventual achievement of union with Scotland in 1707. The limited monarch of a united country turned out to have as much or more power in the world than the quasi-absolutist monarch of a weak and divided country. Charles II, in a powerful constitutional position in the 1660s, watched his flagship towed away by the Dutch: George II, a limited monarch, enjoyed a last year in which the church bells were worn out with ringing for victory. From 1603 to 1688, the Stuarts rowed doggedly against the national tide, persistently misjudging the interests, the mood, and the prejudices of their country. From 1688 onwards, despite many quarrels and crises, the monarchs rowed with the tide of national opinion. Thirty years of maladroit politics left James II in 1689 exactly where his brother had been in 1659—in exile in France: forty years on from 1689 saw the country in the safe hands of Sir Robert Walpole, most famous of all the parliamentary managers, poised on the very brink of industrial and imperial greatness.

5. MIXED MONARCHY
1689–1820

The Later Stuarts: William, Mary, and Anne

PRINCESS MARY's marriage to William of Orange in 1677 had been very much an affair of state. The bride was fifteen, twelve years younger than her husband; she wept copiously when acquainted with his offer and on leaving her native land. William was a short, sallow-complexioned man, with a stoop, a persistent cough, and a dry and reserved manner. The posthumous son of William II of Orange, he had been involved in high politics since his birth. While the Regent's regime in Holland lasted, the Prince remained in shadow. But in 1672, when William was twenty-one, Louis launched his great onslaught designed to cripple the Dutch. William was summoned to save his country as Stadholder, Captain-general, and Admiral-general. So began his life's work—the confinement and diminution of French power.

The marriage, after an inauspicious start, grew into a solid and affectionate partnership. There were no children, and Mary much resented William's mistress, Elizabeth Villiers, unflatteringly described in later years by Swift as 'squinting like a dragon'. William slowly became aware of his wife's political judgement and, according to Burnet, a barrier was removed in 1686 when Mary made it clear that, should she succeed to the throne of England, she would be prepared to be guided by her husband. In 1688, fed by her sister, the Princess Anne, on stories of Mary of Modena's false pregnancy, she accepted the legend

MARY II

(1689–1694)

I N 1688 Mary's Protestant upbringing and loyalty to her husband led her to take his part against her father, James II. She was also determined that William should share the throne with her. In the remaining six years of her life, she took a more active part in government. But in 1694 she died, at the age of thirty-two, from smallpox and was buried in Henry VII's chapel in Westminster Abbey, in an impressive ceremony, immortalized by Purcell's sombre funeral music. In the two extracts that follow, the insensitivity of her conduct in February 1689, as perceived by John Evelyn, is explained by the account given by Mary herself in her Memoirs.

23
QUEEN MARY.   WISSING.

22 Feb. 1689 I saw the new Queene and King, so proclaimed, the very next day of her coming to Whitehall, Wednesday 13 Feb. with wonderful acclamation and general reception, Bonfires, Bells, Gunns, etc. It was believed that they both, especially the Princesse, would have showed some (seeming) reluctancy at least, of assuming her Father's Crowne and made some Apologie . . . But, nothing of all this appeared; she came into W-Hall as to a Wedding, riant and jolly, so as seeming to be quite transported; rose early on the next morning of her arrival, and in her undresse (as reported) before her women were up; went about from roome to roome, to see the Convenience of Whitehall: Lay in the same bed and apartment where the late Queene lay: and within a night or two, sate down to play at Basset, as the Q(ueen) her predecessor used to do: smiled upon and talked to everybody: so as no manner of change seemed in court, since His Majestie's last going away . . .

The next day after I came, we were proclaimed, and the government put wholy in the prince's hand. This pleased me extreamly, but many would not believe it, so that I was fain to force my self to more mirth than became me at that time, and was by many interpreted as ill nature, pride, and the great delight I had to be queen. But alas, they did little know me, who thought me guilty of that; I had been only for a Regency and wished for nothing else . . . but the good of the public was to be preferred and . . . I have had more trouble to bring my self to bear this so envied estate than I should have had to have been reduced to the lowest condition in the world.

of a suppositious Prince of Wales, and took her husband's part against her father. There was an emotional and dramatic parting when William sailed on his expedition. Should he die in the adventure, he told her, she must marry again, but he added, sententiously and characteristically, not to a papist.

William brought to the throne in 1689 a sharp intelligence and a very wide experience of European affairs. But gratitude to the saviour of the country's liberties evaporated with considerable speed, particularly as the English discovered that their enhanced role in foreign affairs would have to be paid for by taxation. A long-term factor which increasingly weakened the position of the monarchy was the growth of party. There had, of course, been groups or factions in Tudor and early Stuart Parliaments, usually based on an aristocratic patron or a family alliance. But the shortness of the sessions and the long intervals between Parliaments did not encourage organizational developments. The remarkable length of the Cavalier Parliament permitted the gradual growth of more permanent associations, and Shaftesbury's opposition in the 1670s developed many of the characteristics of organized party—a headquarters at the Green Ribbon Club on the corner of Chancery Lane, attention to pamphleteering and propaganda, party lists, and some electoral co-ordination. At the same time, the terms 'Whig' and 'Tory' came into use, the former supporting contract or limited monarchy and stressing the right of resistance, the latter advocating strong monarchy and preaching the doctrine of non-resistance. Much of the support for the Whigs came from the dissenters, who hoped for a measure of religious toleration, while the Tories leaned on the Church of England and religious exclusiveness. The conduct of James II, by using the prerogatives of the monarchy to undermine the established Church, placed a great strain on Tory consciences. In 1688 most Tories put loyalty to the Church first.

After 1688 there was a rapid development of party. The length of parliamentary sessions increased markedly, while the Triennial Act ensured frequent general elections and put a premium on electoral activity in the constituencies. Though the Tories had given full support to the Revolution, the Whigs moved quickly to appropriate it to themselves. William, anxious to preserve his freedom of action, adopted a non-party posture, and his first ministry was a balanced one. Shrewsbury, a Whig, held the seals as Secretary of State for the North, and had Whig colleagues at the Treasury in Monmouth and Delamere. Nottingham, the other Secretary of State, was a Tory, along with Danby (now Carmarthen) as Lord President of the Council. Halifax, the trimmer, was Lord Privy Seal. Whig members of the Convention were anxious to drive home the advantage they felt they had, and Carmarthen and Halifax were soon under fierce attack. William dissolved the Convention Parliament after a year. To his next Parliament, in March 1690, he addressed an appeal, begging them to compose their differences and take into consideration a union with Scotland. Both appeals fell on deaf ears.

In 1693 Godolphin put the king's predicament aptly in a memo. The Tories, traditional supporters of the crown, were not sure that William was the lawful monarch, while the Whigs, who had supported him, were traditional critics of monarchy.

The Tories, who are friends to prerogative, are so mingled with Jacobites that they are not to be confided in during the war; and the Whigs, who are for that reason of necessity to be employed to support your cause against the common enemy, will at the same time endeavour all they can to lessen your just power.

Moreover, the existence for more than sixty years of an active rival monarchy in exile could hardly help but weaken the position of the crown.

Another problem was the relationship between William and Mary and the Princess Anne. Anne had been the immediate successor to Mary and, under normal circumstances, would have succeeded to the throne in 1694 on Mary's death. The offer of the crown jointly to William meant postponing Anne's claims, should Mary die before her husband. This was an awkward situation and made more tense by the natural inclination of persons who resented Dutch favourites and Dutch ways to cluster round Anne as the English reversionary interest. There were unpleasant disputes early on about Anne's revenue and her apartments at Whitehall, and Anne could not forgive William for not having a higher opinion of the talents of her husband, the amiable but sluggish Prince George of Denmark. The root cause of the quarrel, however, was undoubtedly Sarah Churchill, a close friend of the princess since childhood. Lady Marlborough was pretty, intelligent, spirited, dominating, and totally dedicated to the advancement of her husband. William did not dispute Lord Marlborough's military ability, but mistrusted him, remembering that he had been among the first to desert James. Marlborough took himself into opposition, moving in 1691 that the king be asked to dismiss all foreigners. Marlborough's bitterness tipped over into treason and he wrote to James at Saint-Germain making his peace. William dismissed him from his post as commander-in-chief in the Netherlands. But Anne doggedly refused to dismiss Lady Marlborough and preferred to withdraw from court altogether. After angry exchanges, Mary and her sister never met after the summer of 1692. Though after Mary's death in 1694, William succeeded in re-establishing formal and polite relations with the princess, and reinstated Marlborough in 1698, she and Lady Marlborough continued to refer to him in private as Caliban or the Dutch monster.

The subjugation of Scotland, though less bloody than Ireland, produced one atrocity which, even after the horrors of the twentieth century, shocks and disgusts—the massacre of the Macdonalds of Glencoe in February 1692. Two circumstances made the butchery peculiarly odious—first, that the enemies of the small clan exploited a legal technicality to take their vengeance; second, that the soldiers who shot and bayonetted their victims had been quartered upon them and had lived with them on terms of friendship for eleven days. In August 1691 William had agreed to pardon all enemies who had made their peace by 1 January 1692. McIan, chief of the Macdonalds, surly and disaffected, had left it to the last possible minute and had then presented himself at Inverlochy in appalling weather, only to find he must report to Inverary sixty miles away. He arrived six days late, and though William's instructions specifically allowed for discretionary leniency, Sir James Dalrymple, Secretary of State for Scotland, chose to regard the clan as outlaws. After the east and west ends of the glen had been sealed, the soldiers turned on their hosts. Only incompetence and a blinding snowstorm allowed some of the men to escape over the hills. William undoubtedly signed the order that the rebels be extirpated: how much he read of the instructions we will never know. After Jacobite pamphleteering had forced a public inquiry in 1695, Dalrymple was dismissed, but William gave him an indemnity and showed no great zeal in punishing the guilty.

William's main preoccupation—the struggle against Louis XIV—met with fitful success. The aggressive policies of the forcible reunions in the 1680s, coupled with the Revocation of the Edict of Nantes, alerted Europe to Louis's ambitions, and it was not difficult to form a coalition to restrain him. In the Nine Years War, from 1688 until 1697, England, Scotland, the Dutch, the Emperor, Spain, Savoy, Bavaria, Saxony, Brandenberg, and Brunswick were lined up against France. But to co-ordinate the allies' activities and keep them in the field was another matter. William's first stinging defeat was a naval battle off Beachy Head in July 1690. It was made worse by the fact that the English and Dutch vessels did not support each other. It gave the French temporary command of the channel at a time when William was in Ireland and opened up the possibility of invasion. Not until the naval victory off La Hogue in May 1692 was the danger removed. On the continent William suffered defeat at the hands of Luxembourg at Steenkirke and Neerwinden in 1692 and 1693, but the severity of the French casualties prevented them from following up their advantage.

At home, William was forced increasingly to rely upon the Whigs, who were more determined to support the war, and by 1694 the ministry was overwhelmingly Whig in composition. The death of Mary from smallpox in December 1694, as well as causing great grief to William, weakened his political position. But within eighteen months, the revelation of a serious Jacobite plot to assassinate the king reminded the English how much they had to lose. There were widespread declarations of support and associations were formed, in which subjects pledged themselves to protect their ruler.

The campaigns of 1694 and 1695 were inconclusive and in the spring of 1697 peace negotiations began in earnest. The treaty of Ryswick maintained the *status quo ante bellum*, but Louis was forced to recognize William as king of Great Britain and Ireland. The peace settlement, rather than removing William's problems, transferred them to Westminster. His English subjects regarded peace as an opportunity to reduce the burden of taxation; William was extremely concerned not to lower his guard, particularly at a time when the eventual succession to the throne of Spain was coming to the fore.

Hardly had the celebrations for peace been concluded than the parliamentary counter-attack on William's position began. In December 1698 a motion was carried limiting the army to a mere 7,000 men, all of whom must be English. It was a studied insult, not merely to the Dutch, but to many Huguenots who had

DYING IN PUBLIC. There was little privacy in the birth or death of monarchs. Mary died of smallpox at the age of thirty-two in 1694. Burnet wrote that William's 'spirits sunk so low that there was great reason to apprehend that he was following her'. In this Dutch engraving, Mary is shown lying in state.

fought on the allied side. 'I am so upset ... about the troops that I can't think of anything else,' William wrote to his minister Heinsius. At one stage, the king drafted an abdication speech and prepared to return to Holland: he was persuaded not to deliver it. In March 1699 his Dutch Blue Guards, who had been with him since 1688, were forced to leave the country. A final appeal to the Commons to find some way of continuing them in his service 'which His Majesty would take very kindly', was indignantly refused—the king, retorted the House, should entrust his safety to his own subjects. In 1700 it was carried to resume all the Irish lands which the king had granted to his supporters and the Commons begged him to dismiss from his counsels all foreigners save Prince George of Denmark.

On top of these slights came another crushing blow. In July 1700 the eleven-year-old prince, William, duke of Gloucester, son of Princess Anne, died. He had been a bright and talkative little boy, fond of playing at soldiers, and a great admirer of his uncle William. The direct line of succession was broken. Anne was only thirty-five, but in poor health, and unlikely to have more children. William was fifty and could have remarried. But his own health, never strong, was giving way and he suffered from swollen legs. He showed only desultory interest in eligible princesses and, indeed, his preference for male company, particularly

ANNE'S LAST HOPE. William Henry, duke of Gloucester, seen here at the age of ten, was the only surviving child of Princess Anne and Prince George of Denmark. He was devoted to his uncle, William III. His death in July 1700, five days after his eleventh birthday, brought to an end the Stuart succession. The Act of Settlement then placed the crown with Sophia, Electress of Hanover, and her heirs.

Keppel, often led to spiteful rumours. Consequently the Act of Settlement, jumping the Catholic heirs, provided for the crown to pass to the Princess Sophia, Electress of Hanover, daughter of Elizabeth, queen of Bohemia, and a granddaughter of James I. Since she was already seventy it was improbable that she would live to succeed, but she had a forty-year-old son George Ludwig, and a seventeen-year-old grandson George Augustus. The royal line was assured.

But the Act of Settlement was more than a solution to the dynastic problem. It provided yet another opportunity for the House of Commons to wage war against the powers and prerogatives of the crown, and further restrictions were, somewhat incongruously, tacked on. Parliamentary consent was to be necessary before the monarch could engage in war or leave the country, the Privy Counsellors were to sign their advice, so that they could be held responsible. No foreigner, even if naturalized, was to be allowed office or a seat in Parliament. No person holding a pension or office of profit under the crown could be a member of the House of Commons. Judges were to hold office on good conduct and not at royal pleasure, and pardons were not to be pleaded against impeachment proceedings.

These provisions were a very mixed bag indeed, and reflected current preoccupations as well as long-term aspirations. The conduct of James II in closeting and dismissing judges had brought the independence of the judicature to the forefront of politics, and though William had, from the start of his reign, appointed on good conduct, the Commons seized their chance to establish judicial independence as strongly as possible. In fact, they established it a little too strongly, since a judge could in future be dismissed only by addresses from both Houses of Parliament. There was therefore no easy method of dismissing judges who had become senile or markedly eccentric, and there was some embarrassment at later periods.

The clause against placemen was part of the struggle by the House of Commons to protect itself from government control through patronage. The great expansion of the army, navy, and civil service had given ministers more offices and commissions to dispose of than ever before. A good deal of general legislation failed to become law between 1689 and 1701, and in 1694 William vetoed one bill, but specific prohibitions passed against Collectors of the Land Tax, Commissioners of the Salt Duty, and Commissioners of Customs and Excise. The provision in the Act of Settlement was so sweeping that, if implemented, it would have meant the exclusion of ministers from Parliament: executive and legislature would have been separated on something like the American pattern. But the legislation was not to come into effect until Anne's death and in 1706 it was modified by the Regency Act, which allowed office-holders to retain their seats provided that they offered themselves for re-election. Though this put them to trouble and expense and was not repealed until as late as 1926, only very occasionally did it result in the office-holders' defeat, since the convention was soon established that it was ungentlemanly to oppose a member seeking re-election. But periodic sallies to eliminate placemen continued. In 1742, after the fall of Walpole, Commissioners of the Navy and Victualling Office were added to the list of proscribed persons, and in 1782, after the fall of Lord North, government contractors were also disqualified.

The legislation against foreigners and the limitations on the monarch's travel abroad reflected irritation at William's evident preference for his fellow country-men and his own country, together with apprehension about the Hanoverian future. Of more importance were the provisions which attempted to tighten the legislature's grip on the appointment of ministers. This was one of the most central of the prerogatives of the crown, and the battle raged throughout the eighteenth and nineteenth centuries. It was the essential point at issue between political parties and the monarch, the former insisting that only a united ministry could work efficiently, the latter defending his right to refuse ministers he did not trust or who were personally offensive to him. The main weapon in the Commons' armoury at this stage was impeachment, and it had been used against Buckingham, Strafford, Clarendon, and Danby. But it suffered from certain defects. The process of presenting the victim by the Commons to the Lords for trial invited disagreement between the Houses. It was a massive and cumbersome piece of machinery, better at bringing to justice great malefactors than as an instrument of routine control. Impeachments lapsed with the dissolution of Parliament. It was not easy for prosecutors to identify the particular advice a minister was said to have given, and the crown might interpose a pardon or indemnity. Recent impeachments in 1701 against Lord Somers, Orford, Portland, and Halifax had collapsed. The weapon of impeachment was little used in the rest of the eighteenth century, and disappeared with the celebrated prosecutions of Warren Hastings and Viscount Melville.

Some of the constitutional points in the Act of Settlement which may appear of little interest attracted attention at the time because they were caught up in a great debate on the conduct and control of foreign policy. After the treaty of Ryswick, genuine attempts were made by the great powers to avoid another immediate conflict when the question of the Spanish succession fell due. Given the state of health of the decrepit Charles II, that could only be a matter of a few years. By the first partition treaty, to which William was a party, Spain, the Indies, and the Netherlands would go to a compromise candidate, a young Electoral Prince of Bavaria, while the Habsburgs would be compensated with Milan, and the French with Naples and Sicily. The treaty was not communicated to Parliament and Somers fixed the great seal to it in secret. With the unexpected death of the Electoral Prince in February 1699, a revision became necessary, and a second partition treaty was negotiated. This time, the Archduke Charles, on behalf of the Habsburgs, was to take Spain, the Indies, and the Netherlands, with the dauphin of France retaining his original share. When the existence of the treaties became known, there was great indignation in Parliament that it had not been consulted: the negotiation, declared the Commons, had been 'transacted in the most irregular manner'. The clauses in the Act of Settlement insisting upon signed advice and that a pardon could not protect against impeachment were efforts to bring this vital area of public business under parliamentary scrutiny.

Meanwhile, the substantive foreign policy question had flared up again. In November 1700 the hapless Charles II died. leaving a will in which the undivided Spanish inheritance was offered to Philip of Anjou, second son of the dauphin, and grandson of Louis XIV. Louis, tempted at the prospect of so vast an addition to his family's influence, accepted on behalf of his grandson. In

WILLIAM III

(1689–1702)

WILLIAM's thirteen years as king of England were by no means pleasant. The death of Mary caused him great grief and he wore a lock of her hair under his clothes for the rest of his life. The outcome of the great struggle against Louis XIV remained doubtful, the chances of a Jacobite restoration were not negligible, and the English showed themselves fiercely resentful of his Dutch friends and supporters. Daniel Defoe, who admired William, wrote a stinging attack upon the ingratitude of the English in his satire *The Consolidator*, published in 1705.

His Majesty left a quiet, retired, completely happy condition, full of honour, beloved of his country, valued and esteemed, as well as feared by his enemies, to come over hither at your own request, to deliver you from the encroachments and tyranny, as you called it, of your prince.

Ever since he came hither, he has been your mere journeyman, your servant, your soldier of fortune; he has fought for you, fatigued and harassed his person, and robbed himself of all his peace for you; he has been in a constant hurry, and run through a million of hazards for you; he has conversed with fire and blood, storms at sea, camps and trenches ashore, and given himself no rest for twelve years, and all for your use, safety and repose. In requital of which, he has always been treated with jealousies and suspicions, with reproaches and abuses of all sorts and on all occasions, till the treatment . . . ate into his very soul, tired it with serving an unthankful

nation, and absolutely broke his heart; for which reason I think him as much murdered as his predecessor was, whose head was cut off by his subjects.

September 1701 he compounded the offence by assuring James II on his deathbed that he would recognize his thirteen-year-old son, Prince James Edward, as the rightful king of England. A new European convulsion was now inevitable, with the Spanish succession as the main prize, and the English succession reopened.

William did not live to see the commencement of the war. In February 1702, while riding in Hampton Court, his horse stumbled and threw him, causing a broken collar-bone. A fortnight later, he died of an inflammation of the lungs. His health by that time was so bad that he could not, in any case, have survived much longer. It is clear that, in the course of his reign of thirteen years, the crown suffered an important erosion of power. In part this was the direct consequence of the Glorious Revolution, and in part the weakening of his political position by his determination to make intervention in Europe his priority. The constant need for fresh supplies to support the escalating demands of warfare did more to assist the Commons than either the annual Mutiny Act or the Triennial Act. One possible way of escaping from the financial strait-jacket which the Commons imposed was for the crown to raise money by borrowing. The Bank of England, established in 1694 as one of the weapons of war, proved enormously successful. The existence of a national debt gave thousands of people a stake in the continuation of the revolutionary settlement and regime. But since the national debt depended upon parliamentary guarantees, it did not really improve the crown's tactical situation.

It is hard to review William's reign without feeling sympathy for his difficulties. It is true that he had neither an easy nor ingratiating manner. But his intervention in 1688 had been decisive, the policies he pursued were in the national interest at home and abroad, and the slights to which the Commons in particular subjected him were unworthy and disreputable. Gratitude is never a commodity much to be relied upon, but in the 1690s its life-span was peculiarly short. The Privy Council ordered a monument in the Abbey: it was never erected. William's funeral, at midnight, was private to the point of obscurity. His subjects turned with relief to their new queen who, with predictable bad taste, assured them that her heart was 'entirely English'.

Though the reign of William saw a significant shift in the balance of power between monarch and Parliament, and a number of prerogative powers disappeared, it is important not to exaggerate or anticipate the extent of royal decline. As we have seen, the crown devised new methods of dealing with new problems. If the powers of suspension and dispensing had gone, and the right of veto and punitive dissolution were in decay, much of the ground could be recovered by influence. The bribery and corruption, with which the eighteenth-century system was once credited, was the inevitable consequence of the changes after 1688. Since Parliament could no longer be ignored or defied, it had to be controlled. The longest and most stable administrations—those of Walpole, Pelham, North, and the younger Pitt—were when the crown found a minister who could both serve its needs and command the Commons.

The crown remained the centre of the executive, and the phrase, much used by eighteenth-century politicians—'carrying on the king's government'—was a reality. The monarch retained special power over the army, navy, and the Church, and in foreign affairs his position was strengthened by the fact that his ministers were, in many cases, dealing with his uncles, cousins, and in-laws. He was the fount of honour, distinction, and pension in a period when these things counted for a great deal. Even in that most important of areas, the choice of ministers, though often limited by party pressure, eighteenth-century monarchs retained great power. It was a very brave politician, sure of himself, his friends, and the public, who set out to 'storm the closet' and thrust himself on the monarch. One of the most independent of ministers was William Pitt, earl of Chatham, who, in his early days, had made himself *persona non grata* to George II by his attacks upon Hanover. In 1754, only three years before his famous ministry began, Pitt wrote of the hopelessness of his situation:

The weight of the irremovable royal displeasure is too heavy for any man to move under ... it has sunk and exanimated me; I succumb under it, and wish for nothing but a decent and innocent retreat ... where I may no longer seem to stick fast aground ... and to have the mortification to see every boat pass me that navigates the same river.

From this predicament, the Seven Years War rescued him.

The life of Anne, the new queen, had been difficult. Her mother, Anne Hyde, had died when she was six years of age. Her father's conversion to Catholicism placed a barrier between him and his two Protestant daughters. The princess grew up a simple and shy woman, short-sighted to an awkward extent. She surrounded herself with a few close friends, to whom she was fiercely attached, and in unpleasant circumstances took refuge in stubborn silence. Her marriage in 1683 to Prince George of Denmark was a great success and she was devoted to her stolid Dane. But the succession of still-births, miscarriages, and false pregnancies which followed undermined her health, and by her mid-thirties she was a semi-invalid, able to walk only with difficulty. The events of James's reign placed her in a cruel dilemma. She was one of the first to refuse to believe that her stepmother's pregnancy was genuine, clearly allowing her own interest to sway her judgement. At the revolution, Prince George abandoned James soon after the Salisbury fiasco, and Anne fled to Nottingham, under the protection of Henry Compton, bishop of London. The settlement of the throne was a great strain to her. Though ultimately obliged to recognize that William must be king, she resented giving up her precedence to him, and, indeed, her bad health meant that there was a serious chance that he would outlive her and that she would never be queen. By 1691 she had made her peace with her father in exile in a letter expressing contrition for her undutiful conduct. Her lurches of attitude scarcely suggest a strong mind at work—rather a woman preoccupied with her own situation, turned in upon her grievances.

In March 1692, when Princess Anne was resisting William and Mary's demands that she should dismiss Lady Marlborough, she wrote to her 'dear Mrs. Freeman': 'never believe your faithful Mrs. Morley will ever submit, she can wait with patience for a Sunshine Day, and if she does not live to see it, yet she hopes England will flourish again.' 'Sunshine Day' was now come, and her friends basked in its golden rays. As queen, Anne inherited William's war, and her reign, more than any other, was concerned with events in Europe. The formal declaration of war came within two months of her accession, and peace was made only thirteen months before her death. Her little circle of close friends became

ANNE. This portrait of Anne in middle age suggests a plain, plump woman, somewhat lacking in vivacity, but conscious of her own dignity and with a certain determination. At the revolutionary settlement in 1689 she was obliged to postpone her claim to the succession in favour of her brother-in-law William. This caused ill feeling and she referred to him privately as 'the Dutch monster'.

the nucleus of the war group. Sidney Godolphin, 'Mr Montgomery' to the friends, was an experienced financier who had commanded the Treasury in the later years of Charles II and from 1690 to 1696 under William. He was now recalled to office. The second and third of the group, Mr and Mrs Freeman, otherwise Sarah and John Churchill, were showered with honours and appointments. Within a week of William's death, Marlborough was given the Garter and dispatched to Holland as Captain-general of the Army, Master-general of the Ordnance, and Ambassador-extraordinary. On his arrival in Holland, he was appointed deputy Captain-general of the Dutch forces. Sarah became Groom of the Stole, Mistress of the Robes, and Keeper of the Privy Purse, all well remunerated, and two of her daughters were appointed Ladies of the Bedchamber. The change of fortunes was signalled by Lady Marlborough replacing Portland, William's former friend, as Ranger of Windsor Great Park, with her own residence. By the end of the year, after a first successful preliminary campaign in the Low Countries, Churchill was created duke of Marlborough.

One of the most urgent problems Anne inherited from William was that of relations with the kingdom of Scotland. One might have expected the Glorious Revolution to have brought the two countries closer, since each had repudiated James and invited in William. The establishment of a separate Church organization in Scotland and the abandonment of attempts to establish Episcopacy removed one area which had caused severe disagreement ever since the personal union of 1603. But, in fact, relations between the two kingdoms had deteriorated to an alarming extent. The Scottish Parliament had, like the English Parliament, asserted itself after 1688, attacking the power of the Lords of the Articles, a kind of steering committee which arranged business, and showing unwonted independence. The scandal over the Glencoe massacre was followed almost at once by the disaster of the Scottish settlement in Darien, into which vast Scottish hopes and much money had been invested. It was true that the English had thrown obstacles in the way of the settlement, partly because they did not want Scottish competition, and partly because William was not anxious to see a clash with Spain, which had claims on Darien, at just the moment that the Spanish succession was becoming an issue. By the end of his reign, it appeared that the two horses which Stuart monarchs had to ride were galloping off in opposite directions. The establishment of an independent Jacobite Scotland could not be ruled out, and though there was little doubt that England, with its superior resources, could defeat and subdue the Scots if necessary, it would be a crippling diversion of resources at a time when the English were straining to hold Louis XIV's France in check.

William's last message to his Parliament eight days before he died had included an invitation to consider the union of the kingdoms, and Anne repeated it in her first message. But detailed negotiation in 1702–3 broke down, and the Scottish Parliament retorted with an Act of Security, which declared that, on the death of Anne, they would not choose the same monarch as the English unless arrangements had been agreed 'to secure the honour and independency of the crown of this kingdom, the freedom, frequency and power of Parliament, and the religion, liberty and trade of the nation, from English or any foreign influence'. Anne refused her consent, but, with the Scottish Parliament threatening to withhold supplies in the middle of the war, she was obliged in 1704 to give way. The case of Thomas Green, an English captain who had put into port in Leith and was subsequently hanged on the most flimsy charge of piracy, showed how serious the breach between the two countries had become. James Hodges, in a pamphlet entitled 'War bewixt the two British kingdoms considered', argued the case for a 'perpetual settlement'.

By 1705 therefore, relations between England and Scotland had reached their lowest ebb. The path ahead could lead only to complete separation or complete union. In the light of the animosities, it may seem hard to understand why union was chosen. But the alternative, however gratifying to Scottish pride, would have solved none of the country's difficulties. Her exports to England would still have been handicapped and she would still have no access to the English colonies. However humiliating the fiasco of Darien had been, looked at coolly it offered little support for those who argued that Scotland should go it alone.

The Aliens Act passed by the English Parliament in February 1705 was intended to bring the state of tension to a crisis and did so. Unless by December 1705 the Scots had either accepted the Hanoverian succession or were in negotiation for a Union, they would be treated as aliens, and trade with Scotland prohibited. Negotiations were recommenced in April 1706 and concluded with some speed. England's object was security, Scotland's economic advancement, and on this basis the Union was achieved. The Scottish Parliament was abolished and Scotland given representation in the Parliament of Great Britain, to meet at Westminster. Scotland was to have forty-five MPs and sixteen elected peers in the Lords. There was to be a common flag and common coinage, but the ecclesiastical settlement in each kingdom was undisturbed. Since Scotland would be taking on responsibility for the much larger English national debt, she was given a cash payment of £400,000, most of which went to the losers in the Darien adventure as compensation. The Scottish land tax was to be one-fortieth of the English and the Scots were given economic equality with England. The Hanoverian succession was jointly adopted, and on 1 May 1707 the union of the two kingdoms took effect. One of the longest aspirations of the crown had been achieved, largely under the pressure of war.

For years the union was unpopular. Scots complained that they had been sold, and though economic progress was made, it came slowly. The English disliked Scots who came south, just as they had done in the 1600s. The uprisings of 1715 and 1745 provided evidence that security was not easily to be obtained. Nevertheless, the foundations of stability had been laid. By mid-century, Scotland had became an asset and, more and more, Scots, instead of going off to join Swedes or French, fought side by side with the English. The result was a crucial shift in the European balance of power, and it is no coincidence that Britain's great leap forward in the Seven Years War came when, for the first time for decades, there was no risk of subversion from Scotland.

Meanwhile, John Churchill was revealing to the world military genius of the highest order. In 1703 he had to be content with tactical successes, but the following year a French thrust across the Rhine towards Vienna forced Marlborough to hazard a brilliant and daring interception. When the armies met at Blenheim on the Danube, Marlborough's victory was overwhelming. Twenty-eight French regiments surrendered on the field of battle, and the commander-in-chief, Tallard, finished as Marlborough's prisoner. To his wife, Sarah, the duke scribbled in pencil a hasty note:

I have not time to say more, but to beg you will give my duty to the Queen, and let her know her army has had a glorious victory. Monsieur Tallard and two other generals are in my coach, and I am following the rest. The bearer, my aide de camp Collonel Parker will give her an account of what has passed. I shal doe it in a day or two by another more at large.

VICTORY. Marlborough's hasty note to Sarah announcing his glorious victory over the French at Blenheim was scribbled on the back of a tavern bill. The following day, in a longer note, he wrote that she would forgive his vanity in adding that 'within the memory of man there has been no victory as great as this'.

The queen gave Marlborough her estate at Woodstock and Parliament voted to build him a palace fit to commemorate the greatest victory of English arms since Agincourt. Two more crushing successes, Ramillies in 1706 and Oudenarde in 1708, exposed France to the prospect of invasion and brought Louis to sue for peace.

The queen who presided over this astonishing run of victories was a sorely afflicted woman. Harassed unmercifully by politicians and scolded incessantly by the duchess of Marlborough, she watched with dismay the collapse of the health of her husband Prince George under a series of debilitating asthmatic attacks. Her own state of health was pitiful. Sir John Clerk, one of the commissioners for the union with Scotland, saw her during the summer of 1706 and the spring of 1707, and wrote an account which was sharp but not lacking in compassion:

THE FALL OF LILLE. Marlborough was anxious to bring the war of the Spanish succession to a close by an invasion of northern France and in 1708 laid siege to Lille, Vauban's masterpiece of defensive fortification and believed to be impregnable. It was taken in December 1708 though at heavy cost. This representation is from the celebrated tapestries at Blenheim, completed by Judocus de Vos in 1715.

THE DUKE AND DUCHESS OF MARLBOROUGH. Sarah Jennings married John Churchill in 1678 after a tempestuous courtship. She became a Lady of the Bedchamber to Princess Anne in 1683 and a great favourite, but her violent quarrel with Anne when queen in 1710 helped to undermine her husband's position. Kneller's portrait, soon after 1700, hints at her pert vivacity, while Klosterman's painting of the duke shows him handsome and self-possessed. In 1743, at the age of eighty-three and long a widow, Sarah read over the letters she had exchanged with Churchill before marriage 'desiring to burn them, but I could not doe it'. Her husband she thought 'handsome as an angel'.

Her Majesty was labouring under a fit of the gout, and in extreme pain and agony, and on this occasion everything about her was much in the same disorder as about the meanest of her subjects. Her face, which was red and spotted, was rendered something frightful by her negligent dress, and the foot affected was tied up with a poultice and some nasty bandages ... Nature seems to be inverted when a poor infirm woman becomes one of the rulers of the world ... She appeared to me the most despicable mortal I had ever seen in any station.

If her reign had brought Anne glory beyond imagination and a popularity with her subjects unequalled since the reign of Elizabeth, it brought her little peace of mind. Her deep friendship with Sarah Churchill turned sour under the duchess's incessant demands and strident reproaches. In letter after letter, at intolerable length, Sarah complained that the queen would not support those to whom she owed everything. Beneath her timid and diffident manner, the queen had strong views of her own and was resolved never to place the crown at the mercy of one party. Devoted to the Church of England, she could not yield to Sarah's simple demonology in which all Tories were Jacobites at heart and only Whigs fit

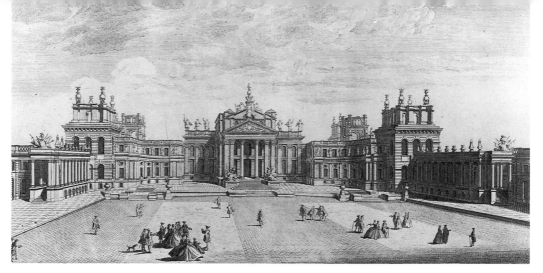

BLENHEIM PALACE. Built by Vanbrugh and landscaped forty years later by Capability Brown, Blenheim is the grandest non-royal residence. Marlborough took great delight in it but his wife thought it 'a wild, unmerciful house'. After his death, she added the Arch from Woodstock and the Column of Victory, with a twenty-five-feet-high statue of her husband.

to be trusted with power. In vain the queen tried repeatedly to close the subject or to divert Sarah's frantic argumentation. Each concession brought fresh demands, each resistance another hysterical accusation of ingratitude. Honours were showered on the duke. They were not enough. He was Captain-general—it must be for life: he was given a pension of £50,000 p.a.—it must be extended to the Churchills in perpetuity.

Slowly the queen's patience wore thin. As early as 1703 the duke and duchess were threatening resignation. The queen replied

Give me leave to say, you should a little consider your faithful friends and poor country, which must be ruined if ever you put your melancholy thoughts in execution. As for your poor unfortunate faithful Morley, she could not bear it, for if ever you should forsake me, I would have nothing more to do with the world but make another abdication, for what is a crown when the support of it is gone? I never will forsake your dear self, Mr. Freeman nor Mr. Montgomery, but always be your constant and faithful servant, and we four must never part, till death mows us down with his impartial hand.

Sarah hammered on. The queen tried reasoning: 'I am very sorry to find that everybody who are not whigs, must be reckoned Jacobites.' In 1706 the Churchills demanded that their son-in-law Sunderland should replace Sir Charles Hedges as Secretary of State. Anne demurred, defending her personal freedom and her monarchical position:

All I desire is my liberty in encouraging and employing all those that concur faithfully in my service, wherether they are called whigs or tories, not to be tied to one, or the other, for if I should be so unfortunate as to fall into the hands of either, I shall look upon myself, though I have the name of Queen, to be in reality but their slave.

Sunderland was nevertheless appointed. In August 1708, ironically on the way to a thanksgiving service at St Pauls to mark the victory at Oudenarde, queen and duchess had a blazing row in the royal coach, which culminated in Sarah's hissing 'Be quiet' to Anne. 'Your Majesty', wrote Sarah, 'chose a very wrong day to mortify me.' 'After the commands you gave me on the thanksgiving day,' replied the Queen icily, 'of not answering you . . . I do not say anything to that nor to yours which enclosed it.'

Trapped by the impossibility of dispensing with the duke's services while the war continued, the queen looked desperately for support and found it in Robert Harley and Abigail Hill. Harley, the son of a parliamentarian supporter from the Hereford–Welsh border, entered the House of Commons in 1689 as a country Whig, acquired a reputation as an organizer, and was elected Speaker in 1701. He took a prominent part in guiding the Act of Settlement through the Commons, and in May 1704 was brought forward by Marlborough and Godolphin to replace Nottingham, a High Tory, as Secretary of State. But he had moved politically into a moderate Tory position and his dislike of extremism chimed well with the queen's fear of party domination. Abigail Hill was a first cousin of Sarah Churchill and a second cousin to Harley. The family was impoverished and in 1697 Sarah obtained a post for her as bedchamber woman to the princess, a humble position, but one which gave easy personal access. As Sarah's frequent absences from court and termagent behaviour when she was there undermined their friendship, Anne turned to Abigail for companionship.

Marlborough and Godolphin, unwilling to credit that the queen had a mind of her own, searched for a prompter behind the scenes. The rancour came to a crisis in 1707 and 1708. First, Sarah discovered that Abigail had made a secret marriage with the queen's assistance. Her rage was towering, and she did not hesitate to accuse the queen of lesbian tendencies: Anne's regard for Abigail, warned Sarah, was 'strange and unaccountable, to say no more of it'; an inclination to none but her own sex must damage the queen's reputation. In the mean time, Marlborough and Godolphin had identified Harley as the secret influence at work to stiffen the queen's resistance and in February 1708 tendered their resignations, rather than work with 'so vile a creature'. The queen seems to have considered promoting a Harley ministry but he could not obtain the necessary parliamentary support. This placed her in Marlborough's hands. Harley was dismissed, taking with him his young follower Henry St John. St John's place as Secretary at War was taken by a rising young Whig, Robert Walpole.

These were to be the last of Godolphin and Marlborough's triumphs, political or military. The queen's favour was dangerously alienated and her relations with the duchess were at freezing point: on 25 October 1709 the queen wrote of the duchess to Marlborough—'I desire nothing but that she would leave off teasing and tormenting me.' Worse still, the allied war effort faltered. Their efforts to install the Habsburg candidate, Charles III, on the throne of Spain, which had started so well, ran into increasing difficulties. After a severe defeat at Almanza in April 1707 they were hard pushed to retain a foothold in Catalonia. The peace terms which the allies offered Louis after Oudenarde were so severe that he could scarcely accept them, though the condition of France was pitiful. Philip of Anjou was to get no territory at all and Louis was asked to pledge himself to assist, if necessary, in removing his grandson from Spain. Louis rejected them and threw himself on his country in an unprecedented appeal to the French nation. The fourth of Marlborough's great battles, at Malplaquet in September 1709, was at best a dubious victory, but so bloody and indecisive an encounter that the French also claimed the honours of the day. With total victory an ever-receding horizon, a great wave of war weariness in both England and the Dutch Republic threatened to undermine support for the grand alliance.

Under these circumstances, Harley's way back to power was clear. The Whig cry of 'No peace without Spain' seemed more and more unrealistic and the case for a negotiated settlement inescapable. This fitted the domestic political situation, for as long as the war continued, Marlborough was indispensable. In January 1710 an initial clash came when the queen ordered Marlborough to appoint Abigail's brother, John Hill, to a regiment. Marlborough refused and threatened a parliamentary motion asking the queen to dismiss Abigail. Anne was outraged at interference with her private Household and Marlborough's friends warned him that he was on weak ground. The motion did not appear and Hill had to be content with the promise of a pension in lieu of his regiment. It was a shaky compromise.

The discontent with Whig policy found an unexpected channel of expression. In November 1709 Dr Henry Sacheverell, a High Tory divine with Jacobite leanings, preached a sermon defending strict hereditary succession, and, by

SACHEVERELL'S TRIUMPH. The prosecution of Dr Sacheverell for preaching a High Tory sermon became a grand inquest on the meaning of the Glorious Revolution and helped to bring down the Whig ministry. The modesty attributed to him on this playing card was not much observed by most of his acquaintance.

Others would Swell with Pride, if thus cares'd,
But he bears humble Thoughts within his Breast.

QUEEN ANNE IN HER STATE COACH. Accompanied by an escort of the Household Cavalry and Yeomen of the Guard, the queen is approaching Old Horse Guards on her way to open Parliament.

implication, impugning the parliamentary settlement of the succession after the revolution. The printed version became a best seller and the Whig ministers decided to impeach the doctor. A vast surge of opinion supported him, counties and boroughs petitioned for the dissolution of the Whig-dominated Parliament, while the mob roamed menacingly in London. Though the government scraped a conviction, the sentence—a three years' suspension from preaching—was the most lenient possible. With the Whigs discredited and her lines of communication with Harley restored, the queen could launch a counter-attack. In April 1710 she had a last painful audience with the duchess. Next she dismissed Sunderland, whom she had never liked and whose intrusion upon her in 1706 she had bitterly resented. Marlborough protested that the dismissal of his son-in-law would be interpreted as a sign of waning confidence and would damage his standing in European affairs. The queen replied sharply to Godolphin:

It is true indeed that the turning a son-in-law out of his office may be a mortification to the Duke of Marlborough: *but must the fate of Europe depend on that*, and must he be gratified in all his desires?

Harley was now seeing the queen frequently and begging her to stand firm. In August 1710 she took the decisive step of dismissing Godolphin, though with the promise of a pension to soften the blow. His post went to Lord Poulet, with Harley as Chancellor of the Exchequer, a minor post but the major influence. The question was whether Marlborough would put into effect his repeated threat to resign if Godolphin went. He did not. Godolphin can scarcely have been delighted to receive from his ally the offhand remark—'I have taken the resolution of troubling my head as little as is possible with politics, but apply my thoughts wholly now to finish this campaign.' In the miserable fag-end recriminations that led to Sarah's own dismissal, the duke remarked wearily that 'a man must bear with a good deal to be quiet at home'. In September 1710 the queen dissolved Parliament and called a general election.

The last four years of Anne's reign were of tortuous and tangled manœuvre, at home and abroad. She had escaped from one predicament only to plunge into another. She was once more delivered over to party rule. The Whigs retained only slight influence at court through the duchess of Somerset, who had succeeded to the duchess of Marlborough's offices, and through the Lord Chamberlain, the duke of Shrewsbury, who adopted a non-party stance. But Harley himself was in a tight situation. The general election of 1710 had returned a massive Tory majority, but many of the new members were High Tories, who formed themselves into the October Club, to keep an eye on signs of moderation.

Two events, in quick succession, reinforced the case for peace. In December 1710 Stanhope was beaten in Spain at Brihuega and it became apparent that imposing the Archduke Charles was beyond the allies' strength. Four months later, the archduke succeeded to the Habsburg dominions: to labour in the face of great odds to place him on the throne of Spain meant reconstituting the gigantic empire of Charles V. There remained only the hope that Marlborough, who had outmanœuvred the French armies in 1711, would be able, by occupying Paris in 1712, to land a knock-out blow. Harley, aware that the destruction of the Grand Alliance would alienate the Hanoverians, took out an insurance by opening secret discussions with the Pretender. By the late autumn of 1711, preliminary articles had been agreed with the French, whereby Philip was to succeed in Spain and the Indies, in exchange for a promise that the thrones of France and Spain should never be united. Marlborough remained convinced that one last push would finish the job, and to keep him quiet the ministers encouraged accusations against him of peculation.

It was doubtful, however, whether Harley could carry so enormous a volte-face. In December 1711, his ministry was defeated in the Lords on a motion that no peace would be honourable if Spain and the Indies went to a prince of the House of Bourbon. But Harley, now ennobled as Oxford, was too far advanced to retreat. Three weeks later, after evidence had been laid against him before the Commons, Marlborough was dismissed. He was replaced as commander by the duke of Ormonde, whose duties, it transpired, were not to be onerous. To overcome the Whig majority in the Lords, Oxford persuaded the queen to create twelve peers at once, including Samuel Masham, husband of Abigail Hill. When, in the spring of 1712, the peace negotiations at Utrecht were protracted, the ministry found itself in the strange position of fearing an allied victory and ordered Ormonde not to engage. For good measure, copies of the orders were sent to the French commander Villars, who was thereby enabled to engage the Dutch and the Austrians, win the battle of Denain, and turn the tide. The Dutch had then no alternative but to make peace as well. The final settlement in April 1713 confirmed England's possession of Gibraltar and Port Mahon, gave her territorial concessions in North America, and access to the Spanish slave trade. Louis recognized Anne's title and the Pretender was ordered out of France. The emperor and his German allies, including Hanover, continued the struggle for another year. At the settlement, the Habsburgs took over the Spanish Netherlands to give greater protection to the Low Countries.

In her deep desire for peace, the queen made three very serious errors. The dismissal of Marlborough on trumped-up charges was unworthy. 'The affair of displacing the Duke of Marlborough will do all for us we desire,' wrote Louis silkily. Swift, who had thrown himself into the propaganda struggle on behalf of Oxford, retained some sense of human dignity: 'I do not love to see personal resentment mix with public affairs.' The shameless abandonment of Britain's allies and the disreputable restraining orders to Ormonde stained the country's honour. Her agreement to create peers for party purposes represented a crucial weakening of the royal prerogative. It was not forgotten. In 1831 William IV was forced to give a similar pledge, and George V another in 1910.

No sooner had the ministry achieved its great object of peace than its cracks began to show. Henry St John, seventeen years Harley's junior, and Secretary of State for the North since 1710, was not content to wait his turn. In June 1712 he was mortified, on receiving a peerage, to be granted only a viscountcy when he demanded the earldom of Bolingbroke. Abigail Hill, Lady Masham, changed sides and abandoned Harley. Though the Tories managed to increase their majority at the general election of 1713, the party showed every sign of splitting into Jacobite and Hanoverian wings. Harley's nerve began to go, he drank heavily, spoke incoherently, and lost his grip on business.

The queen's attitude to the succession was much canvassed and the Jacobites professed great hopes of her. But it was impossible for her to recognize James Edward's claims without conceding that for twelve years she had usurped the throne. In December 1713 she had a serious illness and the issue of the succession became urgent. Harley and Bolingbroke began independent and rival negotiations with the Pretender, and in January 1714 Harley sent him a memo advising him to declare at once his conversion to the Church of England. James refused point blank: 'it is for others to change their sentiments', he replied loftily. Oxford and Bolingbroke were left high and dry: their struggle for power more and more resembled that of men fighting in the tumbril. For good measure, the Whigs demanded that the Electoral Prince of Hanover be brought over at once to take his seat in the House of Lords as duke of Cambridge.

ANNE
(1702–1714)

An abiding theme of Anne's life was her devotion to the Church of England. It produced the breach with her father in 1688 and, less directly, with her oldest friend, Sarah, duchess of Marlborough. The second daughter of James, duke of York, by Anne Hyde, she was born in 1665. When her father converted to Rome and married a Catholic as his second wife, Anne was brought up as a member of the Church of England, under the supervision of Henry Compton, bishop of London. During James's reign, she was concerned that pressure would be directed to force her to Rome: to her sister Mary she wrote in April 1686, 'I abhor the principles of the Church of Rome as much as it is possible for anyone to do.' The following year, she assured Mary that 'I am resolved to undergo anything rather than change my religion.' Of Mary of Modena, James's second wife, she wrote: 'she is a very great bigot in her way, and one may see by her that she hates all Protestants.' She was quick to express doubts about Mary's pregnancy, writing in March 1688: 'I can't help thinking Mansell's wife's great belly is a little suspicious.' At the Revolution, she fled to Nottingham and threw in her lot with William and Mary.

After her succession in 1702, her regard for the Tories, 'the Church party', led to difficulties with her childhood friend the duchess of Marlborough, who was a passionate Whig. 'I know the principles of the Church of England,' she wrote, 'and I know those of the Whigs, and it is that and no other reason which makes me think as I do of the last. And, upon my word, my dear Mrs Freeman, you are mightily mistaken in your notion of a true Whig; for the character you give of them does not in the least belong to them, but to the Church.' She supported the Act against Occasional Conformity, took a keen interest in ecclesiastical appointments, welcomed the proposal to establish the queen's bounty by transferring the crown's tenths and first fruits to clerical purposes, and greatly approved the bill to build fifty new churches in London. She was buried in Henry VII's chapel next to her husband, Prince George of Denmark.

Though lacking in confidence and not a ready speaker, Anne could defend her point of view with tenacity. 'Everything I say', she told the Duchess, 'is imputed either to partiality or being imposed upon by knaves and fools. I am very sorry anybody should have either of those characters given them for any fault in my understanding, since all I say proceeds purely from my own poor judgement, which, though

it may not be so good as other people's, I'm sure is a very honest one.'

The statue of Anne, erected at Blenheim by the duchess of Marlborough, represents the triumphant queen 'under whose auspices John, Duke of Marlborough conquered' rather than the harassed woman with whom Sarah quarrelled so bitterly. 'I am going to Rysbrack', wrote the duchess, 'to make a bargain with him for a fine statue of Queen Anne, which I will put up in the bow window room at Blenheim with a proper inscription. It will be a very fine thing and though but one figure will cost £300.' Privately, Sarah wrote of Anne: 'she certainly, as is said on the inscription, meant well and was not a fool; but nobody can maintain that she was wise, nor entertaining in conversation. She was in everything what I described her: ignorant in everything but what the parsons had taught her as a child.'

In June 1714 the Electress Sophia died at the age of eighty-four: she had failed by two months to become queen of England. The new heir apparent, George Ludwig, asked for a member of his family to be permitted to reside in England. The mere thought of it agitated the queen greatly and she refused permission. The scene was apparently set for civil war.

On 27 July Oxford was dismissed, though no successor as Lord Treasurer was appointed. Three days later and before any decision had been reached, Anne suffered a stroke. The ministers hastily nominated Shrewsbury and the queen recovered sufficiently to indicate her consent. On 1 August she died. 'I believe sleep was never more welcome to a weary traveller than death was to her,' wrote Dr Arbuthnot.

Anne is one of the saddest of our monarchs, the contrast between public glory and private misery almost too cruel. The majestic statue at Blenheim, erected after her death by a half-repentant Sarah, disguises a harassed and worried woman. Her insecurity and lack of confidence made her unduly dependent upon personal friends and that in turn exposed her to constant importunity and exploitation. During her reign, public and private matters were mixed even more completely than usual. 'She was born for friendship', wrote Johnson, 'not for government.' Nevertheless, she defended the prerogatives of the crown with some tenacity and only her concession on the peerage creation was really damaging. The right of veto lapsed during her reign and subsequently atrophied, but it was at best a cumbersome weapon, certain to produce a storm, and susceptible to outflanking movements like tacking. Later monarchs developed more subtle ways of controlling Parliament—by building majorities in the Commons or using the Lords as a constitutional longstop.

Anne was the last of the Stuarts on the throne and one of the more agreeable members. Louis XIV called them an unlucky family, but most of their bad luck they brought on themselves. Common sense was not their strong suit. With the last of the Stuarts disappeared strict indefeasible hereditary right and much of the mystical power of kingship. Anne was the last ruler to touch for the evil. In March 1712 she touched a very small boy, Samuel Johnson, a sufferer from scrofula. It did not do much good.

The Early Hanoverians: George I and II

August 1714 is one of the grand anti-climaxes of British history. Everything pointed to a desperate race for the throne, George Ludwig from Hanover, James Francis Edward from Lorraine. The Pretender's previous attempts to recover his inheritance had not been particularly encouraging. In 1708 Louis had fitted out an expedition to convey James to Edinburgh, whence he would occupy Scotland, dissolve the union, and storm south to regain his throne. The unfortunate young man promptly fell ill with measles. When the fleet did get to the Firth of Forth and waited for some signal from the shore, none came. They then moved to Inverness but the wind preventing them from landing, they went home again. James did not actually set foot on Scottish soil. He then served with the French army against Marlborough and, according to Sir Charles Petrie, undermined the loyalty of the English troops by riding up and down on a white horse. The English commander arranged a rendezvous, but when the time came, the Pretender was in bed with a cold. 'The course of history might well have been changed,' wrote Sir Charles sympathetically.

But 1714 gave the Pretender a chance to redeem himself, and George Ludwig made it a very sporting contest by making his own preparations for departure with great thoroughness and taking a mere six weeks on the journey. The Pretender decided on a policy of masterly inactivity. After years of melodramatic

THE SAME SYMBOL BUT RIVAL INTERPRETATIONS. On the *left*, the coronation medal struck in 1715 showing the Saxon horse uniting the Electorate of Hanover with the kingdom of Britain. On the *right*, a Jacobite medal of 1721 in which the Saxon horse savages the British lion and unicorn, while Britannia weeps beneath a stunted oak. The good representation of London shows new St Paul's.

plotting and scheming, the succession passed off without incident. Even Inverness, which had declared for James in 1702, kept quiet on this occasion, though there were reports of stones thrown at Aberdeen.

The new monarch, who arrived at Greenwich in September 1714 was fifty-four years of age. He had a fluent knowledge of French and at least some command of English. He was an experienced soldier and diplomat and had been Elector since

1698. It was his second visit to England. Late in December 1680, when twenty years old, he began a four months' stay, which, it had been rumoured, was a reconnaissance to see if a marriage to Princess Anne was a possibility. It did not materialize and in 1682 he married a cousin, Sophia Dorothea. The marriage was a disaster. An heir, George Augustus, was born in 1683 and a daughter, Sophia Dorothea (who later married Frederick William I of Brandenburg-Prussia) four years later. But by 1691 George Ludwig had taken a regular mistress, Melusine von der Schulenberg and Sophia began an affair with Count Philip von Königsmarck, a Swedish soldier in the Hanoverian service. In 1694 the second couple were surprised, Königsmarck killed, Sophia Dorothea divorced and then kept in strict though comfortable seclusion in her native Celle. The Hanoverian family closed ranks but could not stifle rumour. The episode was a gift to Jacobite propagandists who portrayed George as a savage and gloomy tyrant, holding his innocent wife in a dungeon while he paraded his mistress to the world.

Hanover, or Brunswick, was a medium-sized German state in 1688. Though it could not compare with Saxony, Bavaria, or Brandenburg in importance, it had escaped relatively lightly from the miseries of the Thirty Years War. The core of the inheritance was Calenberg around Hanover itself, but an elder brother ruled Celle to the north. A symbol of the growing importance of the duchy was its elevation to electoral status in 1692. Celle took possession of Lauenberg in 1689, other territories were acquired by purchase, and in 1705 the two main territories were reunited. The total population was then about 400,000. In 1714 Hanoverian ambition aimed at the acquisition of Bremen and Verden to the north-west, offering access to the sea. They remained part of the empire which Charles XII of Sweden was desperately struggling, against enormous odds, to defend, but they were also coveted by Denmark, which had Holstein to the north and Oldenberg to the west. One great advantage of the new dynastic link with Britain was that British influence, and particularly naval strength, could be brought to bear.

The situation that faced George was complex. Though he insisted that he reigned by hereditary right, there were more than fifty Catholic relatives whose claims were better. The king's speech to his first Parliament skirted over the difficulty by declaring that it had pleased God to call him to the throne of his ancestors. The new monarch had the normal mistrust of party as a mechanism for limiting royal choice, and it would have been foolish not to declare that he would lay aside party distinctions and employ men on their merits. Yet the behaviour of the Tory party in the previous four years—their flirtation with the Pretender and their betrayal of the Grand Alliance—had deeply offended him. George's first action was to restore Marlborough to the command of the army. As soon as the queen was dead, the sealed instructions were opened naming the Regents who were to hold power until George arrived: they included a large majority of

Whigs, but four Hanoverian Tories, and four Tory ministers who continued to serve ex officio. But the Regency was only a holding operation. Greater significance attached to George's first ministry: Bolingbroke and Oxford were at once discarded. Shrewsbury continued as Lord Chamberlain, Cowper replaced Harcourt as Lord Chancellor, and Halifax presided over the Treasury in commission. The crucial position of Secretary of State for the North, whose sphere of activity included Germany and the Dutch Republic, went to Viscount Townshend, a Whig who had negotiated the barrier treaty to protect Holland from future French aggrandisement. His colleague for the south was another Whig, Stanhope, who had held command of the army in Spain. The king hoped to persuade some Tories to take office and Nottingham was appointed Lord President. But William Bromley and Sir Thomas Hanmer, two Hanoverian Tories, refused to serve, suspecting that they would be isolated. Hence, the ministry which finally emerged was far more emphatically Whig than George had intended. Its first task was to prepare for a general election, since the existing House of Commons contained a large Tory majority. The royal proclamation in January 1715 called, pointedly, for the return of members who had supported the Protestant Succession, 'when it was most in danger'.

The general election returned a substantial Whig majority, and the Tory position began to look desperate. Bolingbroke bolted for France to join the Pretender and was joined some months later by Ormonde. Oxford stood his ground, faced impeachment for his part in the peace of Utrecht, and was committed to the Tower. Meantime, the cabinet reshuffle after the death of Halifax brought Robert Walpole to the Treasury, combined with effective leadership of the House of Commons.

James Francis Edward, who had so signally missed the bus in 1714, decided on a bold stroke a year later. The '15 was a strange business. Neither Louis XIV nor his successor in government, the Regent Orléans, was prepared to give assistance. The British government had plenty of warning, suspended Habeas Corpus, and called in reinforcements. The earl of Mar then jumped the gun and declared James III at Braemar, rallying the clans. The intention was to concert with a rising in the north of England and another in the west country. Neither was much use. Thomas Forster raised some support in Northumberland, captured Holy Island for one day, moved around rather vaguely, marched into Lancashire, was bottled up in Preston and surrendered. But compared with the western rising, the northern enterprise was deadly. Wyndham, who was to have given the signal in Somerset, was arrested in bed. Hart, who was to have delivered up Bristol, was also arrested. Maclean whose task was to capture Plymouth very sensibly joined the government. The Pretender was duly declared at St Columb and there was shouting in the streets of Oxford. At Bath the government captured the arsenal of the insurrection, 3 pieces of cannon, age

uncertain, 11 chests of fire-arms, a hogshead of swords and 200 horses. The latter, remarks the Jacobite historian solemnly, were 'to have mounted the Jacobite cavalry'. The only leader with much military experience was Ormonde who was dispatched to the coast of Devon to contact local sympathizers. After lights had repeatedly been flashed from his vessel, the splash of oars was heard, but it turned out to be customs officers asking if he had anything to declare. Ormonde went home. Mar, denied diversionary support, had the usual small successes in the Highlands, fought a bitter but indecisive battle at Sheriffmuir in November and found his troops beginning to desert. With the sense of timing that distinguished the Jacobite cause, James landed in Scotland in January 1716 and was at once struck down by a heavy cold—caused, says Sir Charles Petrie, by the inclement weather. When he recovered, it was doubtful whether he was more dispirited at the sight of his followers or they at him. 'Our men began to despise him', wrote one Jacobite, 'some asked if he could speak.' After five weeks, James left for France. It was his only visit to Britain.

In Hanover, the estates remained but had little power. In his new dominions, relations with Parliament and the need to obtain supply were an ever-present concern to George. But though he could not hope to escape from a parliamentary context, George was as anxious as previous monarchs to retain freedom of action. The financial settlement was a generous one, with £700,000 p.a. allocated to the civil list, and arrangements made to wipe off arrears. In 1715 the clause in the Act of Settlement which forbade the king to go abroad without parliamentary sanction was repealed, and subsequently George visited Hanover often and for long periods. The Septennial Act of 1716, though primarily a party measure, enabled him to keep a Parliament for seven years, though the gain to royal power was somewhat offset by the encouragement the measure gave to the development of parliamentary experience and techniques.

The Whig ministry became even more monolithic after Shrewsbury resigned in July 1715 and Nottingham and Aylesford in February 1716. But party domination did not give the sovereign peace and quiet. With the Tories almost eliminated as contenders for power, the Whigs could afford to quarrel among themselves. The king's visits to Hanover provided good opportunities for dissension. The ministers who accompanied him wondered what was going on behind their backs: those who stayed in England wondered whether their colleagues were ingratiating themselves with the monarch. In 1716, the rebellion crushed, George made his first visit home, taking Stanhope and then Sunderland with him, and leaving Townshend and Walpole behind. The personal friction took political shape in a sharp disagreement about foreign policy. George, as Elector of Hanover, was at war with Charles XII of Sweden, Bremen and Verden being the prize. English naval power in the Baltic could tip the scales, but, under the terms of the Act of Settlement, could not be used directly. A fleet was dispatched to protect British trade, with instructions to the admiral to use his discretion in collaborating with the Danes. Townshend objected to the development and to the growing *rapprochement* with France, and was demoted from Secretary of State to Lord Lieutenant of Ireland. In the spring of 1717 the ministry appeared to be using Swedish intrigues with the Jacobites to force a declaration of war on Charles XII. Walpole and his friends opposed in the Commons, and when, the following day, Townshend was dismissed, Walpole resigned.

From 1717 to 1720, the dissident Whigs conducted a formal and sustained opposition to their former colleagues. They were not at all scrupulous, opposing matters they had previously supported, and openly attempting to collaborate with the Tories. An early consequence of Whig disunity was that Oxford escaped from the impeachment proceedings against him, though he never again played a major political role. Walpole's parliamentary skill enabled him to inflict embarrassment and occasional defeat upon the ministers. The Whig opposition clustered round the Prince of Wales at Leicester House, thus repeating the pattern of William's reign and anticipating that of the rest of the century.

Identification with the heir apparent had several advantages: it offered some limited patronage while in opposition, held out promise for the future which grew in force year by year, and, above all, removed any taint of Jacobitism that opposition might bring. The peak of Walpole's effort came in 1719 when Stanhope and Sunderland reintroduced their peerage bill. The number of peerages was to be carefully limited in future and the House of Lords turned into an almost closed body. The ministers' objective was to preserve their majority in the Lords against a change of ministry on the prince's accession. George I seems to have given the measure unenthusiastic support, perceiving clearly enough the damage it would do to the prerogative, but comforting himself with the thought that the brunt of the inconvenience would be felt by his son. For identical reasons, Leicester House was violently opposed to the bill. Walpole, in a brilliant debating speech, pointed out that it would place the House of Lords in an impregnable position and slam the door on the hopes and ambitions of many gentlemen of family. Its rejection in December 1719 by the overwhelming majority of 269 to 177 forced Sunderland and Stanhope to concede that they must do a deal with their Whig critics.

An important part of the new understanding was an effort to reconcile George I and the Prince of Wales, whose differences had reached embarrassing heights. At the succession of the House of Hanover, George Augustus was thirty-one and had been married for nine years to an intelligent princess, Caroline of Ansbach-Bayreuth. He was given an income of £100,000 p.a., and took his place in the cabinet and Privy Council. But in 1716, though appointed Regent for George's absence in Hanover, the prince was discontented with the limitations on his powers, which included a prohibition of the creation of peers. Thence, the prince moved into more open opposition, playing the English card just as the Princess Anne had done against William: it was put about that he was not much concerned about the fate of Bremen and Verden. Resentment exploded into a public quarrel with an absurd incident at the christening of the prince's baby son, George William, in November 1717. The duke of Newcastle, as Lord Chamberlain, claimed traditional right to act as godfather, to the prince's displeasure. After the ceremony there was a violent quarrel, in which the timorous Newcastle gained the impression that the prince was offering to fight him. George ordered the prince to move out of St James's at once, leaving his children behind him. The unfortunate little prince, cause of the commotion, died after three months so that the godfathership was no fearful burden. But when the king went to Hanover in 1719 and 1720, the prince was not named Regent and power was delegated to a Regency Council. At one stage of the quarrel, relations were so bad that Sunderland suggested to the king that the prince could be transported and never heard of more. If it is to the king's credit that such suggestions were ignored, it is less creditable that Sunderland escaped a charge of high treason.

GEORGE I

(1714–1727)

GEORGE was fifty-four when he landed at Greenwich in 1714 to claim the English throne under the terms of the Act of Settlement, and had another thirteen years to live. His claim was through his maternal grandmother, Elizabeth of Bohemia, daughter of James I. He had been ruler of Hanover since 1698 and had taken an active part in the war against Louis XIV.

The English found their new ruler an unglamorous, elderly gentleman, set in his ways: his natural reserve was reinforced by his imperfect command of English and by his preference for his German friends and servants. Lady Mary Wortley Montagu's description of him was hard:

In private life, he would have been called an honest blockhead . . . he was more properly dull than lazy, and would have been so well contented to have remained in his little town of Hanover that if the ambition of those about him had not been greater than his own, we should never have seen him in England . . . he was passively good-natured and wished all mankind enjoyed quiet, if they would let him do so.

In fact he had a good knowledge of diplomacy, an interest in science, and a deep affection for music. Horace Walpole, as an old man, recalled that as a boy of ten, not yet imbued with republican notions, he begged his father to allow him to see the king, and was brought in to the duchess of Kendal's apartments in St James's Palace at ten o'clock one night:

We found alone the King and her. I knelt down & kissed his hand, he said a few words to me, and my conductress led me back to my mother. The person of the King is as perfect in my memory as if I saw him but yesterday. It was that of an elderly man rather pale & exactly like to his pictures and coins; not

tall, of an aspect rather good than august, with a dark tye wig, a plain coat, waistcoat and breeches of snuff-coloured cloth, with stockings of the same colour, & a blue ribband over all. So entirely was he my object, that I do not believe I once looked at the Duchess; but as I could not avoid seeing her on entering the room, I remember that just beyond His Majesty stood a very tall, lean, ill-favoured old Lady; but I did not retain the least idea of her features, nor know what the colour of her dress was.

The bad relations between George I and the Prince of Wales became confused in the minds of some historians with the king's proposal to bring to an end the personal union between Britain and Hanover. Since the matter was for decades shrouded in secrecy, it was assumed that the suggestion was part of a vendetta against the prince, to rob him of his inheritance. But, in fact, the prince's interests were completely safeguarded. George I was concerned that the union might render the Hanoverians unpopular in Britain and give the Jacobites an opportunity: he also foresaw possible clashes between British and Hanoverian ministers. In a will dated 1716 he therefore proposed that Hanover should go to any second son whom his grandson Frederick might have. British ministers were unenthusiastic, perceiving constitutional and legal difficulties. One of George II's first actions on succeeding in 1727 was to pocket the will. The matter dropped and the union continued until Victoria's accession to the throne in 1837.

The ministerial reconstruction of 1720 brought Walpole and Townshend back as Paymaster and Lord President of the Council. A reconciliation of sorts was effected between the king and his son, though the first meeting was strained. With all four leading ministers in their mid-forties, a further struggle for personal supremacy could hardly be long postponed. The event which decided that question—and at one time appeared to threaten the stability of the new dynasty—was the South Sea Bubble.

It was fortunate for the Hanoverians that the Bubble burst at a moment when the Old Pretender was not in a position to exploit his opportunity. Bereft of support from France after the death of Louis XIV, he had turned to minor powers. Charles XII, fighting a losing battle to preserve his own empire, could make use of the Jacobites to put pressure on Hanover and help to retain Bremen and Verden. After Charles was shot dead in Norway in 1718, James Edward Stuart turned to Spain. Philip V equipped a small force in 1719 which made a landing in the Western Isles, but received little local support, and surrendered at Glenshiel.

The long war against France during Anne's reign had resulted in a massive increase in the national debt. The interest payable swallowed up nearly one-third of all annual revenue. In 1711 Harley had established the South Sea Company and charged it with the redemption of part of the debt by conversion into South Sea stock. In 1720 the Company extended its operations to redeem more than half the national debt of £50 million. The terms were attractive, and for some months the face value of company stock roared upwards, carrying with it a considerable number of smaller companies and enterprises. Company stock worth £100 was selling at £130 by April 1720, and more than £1,000 by July. In mid-autumn, prudent investors began to pull out and the crash was even faster than the rise.

The panic which ensued caught the king on one of his visits to Hanover, from which he returned at speed. The royal family was deeply involved, personally and publicly. British credit was an important weapon in European diplomacy. The king was governor of the Company and had invested substantial amounts. His mistress, the duchess of Kendal, had been given stock to the value of £15,000 in return for her favour, and the king's half-sister, the countess of Darlington, had received the same. All the ministers had invested: Sunderland held £50,000 of stock and Craggs, the Postmaster-General £30,000.

The explosion that resulted shattered the government. Stanhope suffered a stroke in the Lords while replying to taunts and died next day. The younger Craggs, one of the Secretaries of State, died from smallpox and his father

SPECULATOR'S PARADISE, 1720. For six months, the frenzy prompted by the South Sea Company scheme provided magnificent opportunities for projectors and bucket-shop proprietors. George I, his friends, and associates were heavily involved. When the bubble burst, the prestige of the new dynasty was shaken but their Jacobite opponents failed to seize the opportunity.

committed suicide a few days later while under investigation. Aislabie, Chancellor of the Exchequer, was expelled from the Commons and sent to the Tower. Sunderland, First Lord of the Treasury, managed to stave off a Commons censure by 233 votes to 172, but was crippled by the scandal and resigned in April 1721.

Economic recovery after the Bubble was slower than political. There can be no doubt that the experience dealt a blow to credit, though not to the extent of the Mississippi scheme in contemporary France, and it has been suggested that industrialization may have been put back decades by the loss of confidence. Politically, the recovery was surprisingly swift. The Jacobites managed to get a plot together in 1722, by which the king was to be murdered on his way to Hanover, but it was uncovered at an early stage. Walpole replaced Sunderland as First Lord of the Treasury and began the longest running administration in British history. One of his avowed objectives was to see off the Jacobite challenge and it is significant that the Jacobites' last throw, in 1745, came three years after his resignation.

The last few years of George's reign were smoother. The Great Northern War, which had raged for twenty years, came to an end at Nystadt in 1721, with Sweden surrendering almost all her Baltic empire. With Walpole, George soon established cordial relations and his new minister's mastery of the Commons made for a quiet life. The king had more time to supervise the landscaping of Kensington Gardens and to listen to the music of George Frederick Handel. Then, in June 1727, on a visit to Hanover, he was struck down unexpectedly and died at Osnabruck, where he had grown up as a boy.

It used to be customary to stress the grossness and the corruption of Hanoverian life. That there was greed the Bubble showed only too well. But there is another side to the coin. Quite rapidly the country began to leave behind the melodrama and turbulence of Stuart England. Plots and conspiracies became a thing of the past, and political life less frenetic and vindictive. It is as difficult to imagine Newcastle being sent to the Tower in 1755 as Danby and Harley had been, as it is to imagine a conspiracy to assassinate George III on one of his country walks. Sanity was breaking in.

The succession of George II went off without a murmur. The conduct of the Old Pretender on that occasion was so subtle that the historian is baffled. On receipt of the news of George I's death, he went at once to Lorraine where he remained incognito for three weeks. Any threat to the new stability came, not from the Pretender, but from George II himself. The reconciliation with his father had never been more than formal and he had no liking for George I's ministers: Newcastle, who had succeeded Carteret as Secretary of State in 1724, had been the butt of George's anger at the christening quarrel. When Walpole reported the news of his father's death, George II ordered him abruptly to take his instructions

CULTURAL PATRONAGE UNDER THE HANOVERIANS AND THEIR SUCCESSORS

On Wednesday evening (the 17th.), at about 8, the King took water at Whitehall in an open barge, wherein were also the Dutchess of Bolton, the Dutchess of Newcastle, the Countess of Godolphin, Madam Kilmanseck, and the Earl of Orkney. And went up the river towards Chelsea. Many other barges with persons of quality attended, and so great a number of boats, that the whole river in a manner was covered; a city company's barge was employed for the musick, wherein were fifty instruments of all sorts, who played all the way from Lambeth (while the barges drove with the tide without rowing, as far as Chelsea) the finest symphonies, composed express for this occasion by Mr Hendel; which His Majesty liked so well, that he caused it to be played over three times in going and returning. At eleven, His Majesty went ashore at Chelsea, where a supper was prepared, and then there was another very fine consort of musick, which lasted till 2; after which, his Majesty came again into his barge, and returned the same way, the musick continuing to play till he landed.

Daily Courant, 19 July 1717

Contrary to popular belief, the Hanoverians were by no means a philistine dynasty. Their keenest interest was in music. George I donated £1,000 to the Royal Academy of Music in 1719 and though George II was said to have 'hated all poets and painters', he was a great admirer of the works of Handel. Frederick, Prince of Wales, was a keen cello player and his son George III was so devoted to music that he confessed to Fanny Burney that it was as strange for him to meet people who had no ear for music as it was to meet people who were dumb. The harpsichord was his great solace during the long years of mental derangement at the end of his life.

Nor did they neglect other arts. George I was responsible for the extensive redecoration of Kensington Palace and the grounds were landscaped by Henry Wise and Charles Bridgeman: a number of small ponds were run together to form the Serpentine. George II and Queen Caroline patronized Michael Rysbrack, the sculptor, whose equestrian statue of William III stands in Queen Square, Bristol. Frederick was more than commonly interested in artistic matters. The barge in which he gave concerts on the Thames is preserved in the National Maritime Museum. He was a discerning collector of paintings, including those of Van Dyck, Rubens, and Holbein, and his son added to the royal collection pictures by Vermeer, Bellini, and Canaletto. George III was a keen collector of books and made handsome gifts to the British Museum, founded in 1753. He had also an intelligent interest in science and technology: his own microscope is in the Science Museum at Kensington and he encouraged Herschel to construct at Windsor what was then the world's largest telescope.

With George IV, art was a passion. His devotion to building and interest in painting kept him in acute financial difficulties for much of his life but earned him a posthumous tribute from Wellington as 'the most distinguished and the most munificent patron of the arts in this country, and in the world'. He purchased Rembrandts and Rubens as well as the contemporary painters Stubbs and Gainsborough. The Brighton Pavilion is the best known of his building projects, but he was also responsible for the complete remodelling of Buckingham Palace, for Nash's great complex centred on Regent's Street, and for the vast rebuilding of Windsor Castle under the supervision of Wyatville.

Victoria had no deep appreciation of art, though she sketched very competently and sang sweetly. But Prince Albert was both accomplished and informed and, under his influence, she bought paintings as often as she could, being particularly fond of Winterhalter and Landseer. Albert was a good amateur musician and composer and Mendelssohn was a frequent visitor to Windsor. The prince enjoyed arranging concerts and it was at Windsor in 1844 that Schubert's Great C Major symphony received its first performance in England.

Though Albert helped to design Osborne and Balmoral, money for building on the grandest scale was no longer available and there were new demands upon royal time and attention. He chaired the committee that organized the Great Exhibition of 1851 and, a few days before the opening, confessed himself 'more dead than alive from overwork'. It was an enormous success: there were six million visitors, the queen went thirty-four times, and there was even a sizeable profit at the end.

Albert's work for the Great Exhibition marked the beginning of a change in the nature of royal patronage. Of course collections continued to be made and commissions placed: Queen Alexandra began the collection of the remarkable work of the Russian goldsmith Carl Fabergé; George V's great joy were his hundreds of volumes of postage stamps, starting with a penny black; while the royal family's collection of photographs has now become an important archive. Royal patronage and approval continues to be of great importance to individuals. But support for artists and writers has increasingly given way to sponsorship of and work for humanitarian and charitable organizations, British and international. George VI, as duke of York, devoted much time to the Industrial Welfare Society, Prince Philip sponsored the Duke of Edinburgh's award scheme as a challenge to young people, and Anne, the Princess Royal has travelled thousands of miles in the interests of the Save the Children Fund.

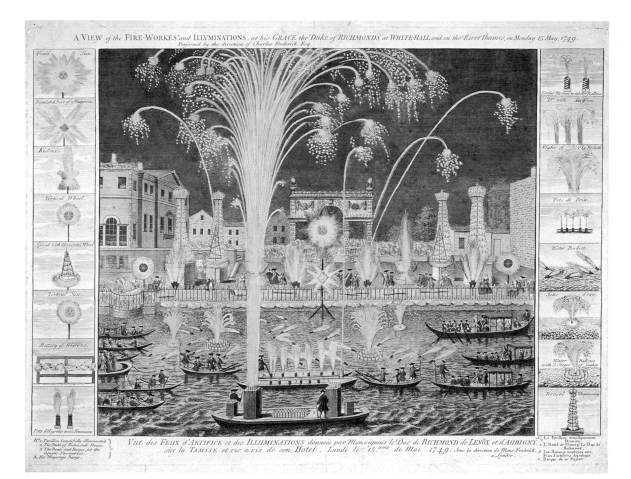

THE PEACE OF AIX-LA-CHAPELLE IN 1749 was celebrated by a grand fireworks display in Green Park, for which Handel provided the music. The Duke of Richmond put on his own display a month later, which Horace Walpole described: 'you can't conceive a prettier sight. The garden filled with everybody of fashion. The King and Princess Emily were in their barge under the terrace, the river was crowded with boats, and the shores and adjacent houses with crowds.'

from Spencer Compton, Speaker of the House and Treasurer to the prince. Walpole seems to have taken advantage of Compton's lack of experience, won over the new king with the offer of a generous civil list of £830,000 p.a., and cemented his position by an understanding with Queen Caroline.

George II was forty-four when he succeeded. Despite an absence of personal papers, he is one of the best known of all monarchs, though it should be remembered that in Lord Hervey and Horace Walpole he had the misfortune to pick up two very acid and gifted critics. He was short, fierce, and bustling: according to Hervey, he prided himself upon a fine leg. He had few pretensions to intellectual or artistic prowess. A succession of mistresses did not prevent him being on good terms with Queen Caroline, a woman of education and taste, with an interest in theological matters. His personal courage was undoubted. He had fought with distinction at Oudenarde under Marlborough and, at the age of sixty, led his troops, sword in hand, at Dettingen in 1743, with the words, 'Now, boys, fire and behave bravely, and the French will soon run.'

The succession and coronation over, court life soon settled down into a predictable routine. The early decision to continue with Sir Robert Walpole freed the king from major political problems for the next fifteen years of his reign. Much of his time was spent with his mistresses, particularly Mrs Howard, and the rest devoted to stag-hunting or card-playing. From this routine, George and his court were relieved by his periodic visits to Hanover, to which he became

WALPOLE'S LENGTHY PERIOD AT THE TOP stemmed from his ability to deal with George I and II while commanding the confidence of the House of Commons. In this engraving by A. Fogg (*c.*1730) after Sir James Thornhill, he chats to the Speaker of the House, Arthur Onslow, a staunch ally.

ROYAL QUARTET. Though Frederick, Prince of Wales has not won golden opinions, he was a keen musician and a discriminating collector of paintings. Philippe Mercier was appointed painter to the prince in 1729 and produced this portrait of him with his sisters Anne, Caroline, and Amelia. This version has the Dutch House at Kew in the background: another version sets the scene at Hampton Court.

devoted. The uncertainty of the royal temper made attendance at court a mixed pleasure:

His Majesty stayed about five minutes in the gallery; snubbed the Queen, who was drinking chocolate, for being always stuffing, the Princess Emily for not hearing him, the Princess Caroline for being grown fat, the Duke for standing awkwardly, Lord Hervey for not knowing what relation the Prince of Sultzbach was to the Elector Palatine, and then carried the Queen to walk, and be re-snubbed, in the garden.

It is not easy to draw up a balance sheet on the position and influence of the monarchy over the thirty-three years of George's reign. At first sight, it might be supposed that, for all his bluster, the king was ineffective and that a serious erosion of royal power took place. Sir Robert Walpole's opinion, according to Hervey, was that the king was a great political coward and governed by others. Horace Walpole wrote that the 'dimunition of majesty' was notorious to all the world. At times, George II was inclined to agree. 'Ministers are the kings in this country', he remarked in 1744, and in 1755 the thought of his return to England from Hanover provoked the outburst:

GEORGE II AT DETTINGEN IN 1743. At the age of sixty George II took the field for the last time, defeating the French at Dettingen. The other officers in the painting are George's son, the duke of Cumberland, and Lord Holdernesse. This was the last flicker of the ancient tradition of the king as warrior-chief. No subsequent monarch led his troops in person, though George IV on occasion suffered from the delusion that he had.

There are kings enough in England. I am nothing there. I am old and want rest, and should only go to be plagued and teased there about that damned House of Commons.

He certainly sustained some serious political defeats. In 1727 his own first choice, Sir Spencer Compton, did not become minister. He was unable to keep Walpole in office in 1742 or to sustain Carteret in 1744. Two years later, when tired of the Pelhams, he suffered a most severe set-back when he imprudently tried to launch a Bath–Granville administration. No one was willing to serve, and the wits complained that it was not safe to walk the streets for fear of being pressed into the cabinet. The Pelhams came back on their own terms. In 1756 he was unable to keep out William Pitt, whom he detested because of his attacks on the Electorate of Hanover.

But this is far from the complete picture and we must remember that in a reign of thirty-three years, there are bound to be ups and downs. Each of the defeats may be analysed and qualified. In 1727 it was George's judgement that was at fault, not his power. The withdrawal of Walpole in 1742 may be seen as a check to royal influence, but the root cause was that Walpole, at sixty-six and after twenty-one years at the helm, had no longer stomach for the fight. Carteret, whom the king liked, partly because he spoke German, was forced out in 1744,

GEORGE II

(1727–1760)

T HE memoirs of Lord Hervey, vice-chamberlain at the court, offer an incomparable portrait of the king, though clearly spiced with malice. In this excerpt, George II had been forced in 1735 to return from Hanover which, together with a painful attack of piles, had put him into 'an abominable temper':

Whilst the late King lived, everybody imagined this Prince loved England and hated Germany; but from the time of his first journey, after he was King, to Hanover, people began to find, if they had not been deceived in their former opinion, at least they would be so in their expectations; and that his thoughts, whatever they might have been, were no longer turned either with contempt or dislike to his Electoral dominions. But after this last journey, Hanover had so completed the conquest of his affections, that there was nothing English ever commended in his presence that he did not always show, or pretend to show, was surpassed by something of the same kind in Germany. No English, or even French cook could dress a dinner; no English confectioner set out a dessert; no English player could act; no English coachman could drive, or English jockey ride; nor were any

English horses fit to be drove or fit to be ridden; no Englishman knew how to come into a room, nor any English-woman how to dress herself; nor were there any diversions in England, public or private; nor any man or woman in England whose conversation was to be borne . . . Whereas at Hanover all these things were in the utmost perfection; the men were patterns of politeness, bravery and gallantry; the women of beauty, wit and entertainment, his troops there were the bravest in the world, his counsellors the wisest, his manu-facturers the most ingenious, his subjects the happiest; and at Hanover, in short, plenty reigned, magnificence resided, arts flourished, diversions abounded, riches flowed, and every-thing was in the utmost perfection that contributes to make a prince great or a people blessed . . .

In truth, he hated the English, looked upon them all as king-killers and republicans, grudged them their riches as well as their liberty, thought them all overpaid, and said to Lady Sundon one day as she was waiting at dinner, just after he returned from Germany, that he was forced to distribute his favours here very differently from the manner in which he bestowed them at Hanover; that there he rewarded people for doing their duty and serving him well, but that here he was obliged to enrich people for being rascals, and buy them not to cut his throat.

BUSTS OF GEORGE II AND QUEEN CAROLINE by Michael Rysbrack in terracotta, now at Kensington Palace. Lord Hervey also described the scene at Caroline's death-bed, when she urged George to remarry. 'Wiping his eyes, and sobbing between every word, with much ado, he got out this answer, *"Non, j'aurai des maîtresses"*.'

but rewarded with the Garter in 1749 and brought back as Lord President of the Council in 1751 for the rest of the king's reign. Though the exigencies of war forced George to accept Pitt in 1756, royal displeasure had kept him out of office or in subordinate positions for many years, and the outcome was that from 1757 onwards he was obliged to share power with Newcastle. Pitt himself certainly did not draw the moral that royal favour was of little account: on the contrary, he was famous for obsequiousness in the closet where, according to one eye-witness, he bowed so low that his hooked nose could be seen from behind between his bowed legs.

There were other important areas in which George II maintained a very high profile. He was keenly interested in the army, well informed about regiments and their colonels, and most reluctant to allow political intervention: according to his brother Horace, Sir Robert Walpole was told very firmly that he did not understand military matters. Newcastle, likewise, was warned by the king not to interfere in Bedchamber questions: it is 'a personal service about myself, and I won't suffer anybody to meddle in'. The king was determined not to dilute the value of the peerage by wholesale increases, and he resisted the importunities of candidates and ministers so effectively that there were fewer peerages granted during his reign than in any comparable period since Elizabeth. He took an active interest in foreign affairs, where the possession of Hanover gave him an independent base. It is true that Walpole managed to resist the king's wish to take part in the war of the Polish succession in the 1730s, but there the king chose his ground badly. It was not easy to suggest that the question whether a Russian puppet or a French puppet should preside over the battered hulk that was eighteenth-century Poland was a vital British interest.

In maintaining his power, George was handicapped by his own lack of application. He 'used often to brag of the contempt he had for books and letters; to say how much he hated all that stuff from his infancy'. Characteristically, he took out his irritation on Caroline, who was fond of reading, telling her she was a pedant, and that she spent her time more like a schoolmistress than a queen. But, in the routine business of politics, it put him at a disadvantage against his ministers that he was often under-briefed. Two other factors also worked against him. The first was the continued existence, for the greater part of his reign, of an active Jacobite cause. By making him extremely reluctant to employ Tories, it weakened his room for political manœuvre. The second factor was the existence of a reversionary interest at Leicester House. From the mid-1730s, Frederick, Prince of Wales, commanded an independent political squadron, and though he died in 1751, in the later 1750s Prince Geroge's court emerged once more as a centre of potential opposition to the crown.

After the inactivity of James Edward in 1727 it might have seemed that the Jacobites had shot their bolt. Walpole helped to insure against any revival by his understanding with France, first through the Regent, then through Cardinal Fleury. One reason for his reluctance to become involved in the war of the Polish succession was the opportunities that European conflict might afford the Stuarts. But he was unable to prevent the drift into war with Spain in 1739 and from 1742 onwards the British engaged in the war of the Austrian succession, as supporters of Maria Theresa. George II was an enthusiastic supporter of intervention, partly to hold the balance of power against French aggrandisement and partly because of his cordial detestation of his nephew Frederick II of Brandenburg–Prussia, challenging Habsburg power in the empire.

The danger to the Hanoverian succession was that renewed conflict in Europe coincided with the growing up of the Young Pretender, Charles Edward Stuart. James Edward, at the age of thirty-one, had married a princess of the Polish house of Sobiewski. Though the marriage lasted but a few years, it produced two sons, Charles Edward, and his brother Henry, who became a cardinal, and, in Jacobite reckoning, succeeded his brother as Henry IX of England. A substantial expedition in 1744 ran into storms and was forced back. But in June 1745 the young prince, aged twenty-four, sailed from Nantes, with a tiny following, on what looked like a forlorn hope. Landing at Eriskay, he was at first disappointed by the small response of the clans. George II, on another protracted visit to

WILLIAM, DUKE OF CUMBERLAND, the victor at Culloden, was the favourite son of George II and Queen Caroline, whose dislike for the Prince of Wales was notorious. Cumberland's later military career in the Seven Years War was undistinguished, though he was emerging as an important political force when he died in 1765 at the early age of forty-four.

Hanover, returned to England in August 1745, and refused to be dismayed. But the following month, Charles captured Perth and Edinburgh, declared the Union dissolved, defeated Sir John Cope at Prestonpans, and with an army grown to 5,000 men clearly presented a real threat. By November, he had crossed the border, captured Carlisle, and was heading south into Lancashire, where he hoped for an enthusiastic welcome from Catholic and Jacobite sympathizers.

In the end, the '45 was decided by political action, or rather inaction. The Hanoverians mustered three armies, one under Cumberland in the west

A VERY YOUNG PRETENDER. This portrait of Prince Charles Edward, from the studio of Antonio David, painter to the Old Pretender, shows him in 1729 at the age of ten. He wears the star and ribbon of the Garter, and (partly concealed) the jewel of the Thistle on a green ribbon. It was probably of this portrait that his father wrote in November 1729 that 'I have had my children's pictures lately done, which are very like.'

midlands, a second under Wade east of the Pennines, and a third gathering to the north of London. But, in all the march to and from Derby, there was scarcely any serious fighting. The decisive factor was the almost total refusal of the English, Jacobite or not, to rally to Charles Edward. Lancashire, in particular, proved a bitter disappointment, with only Manchester providing a few hundred recruits of poor quality. At Derby took place the famous council of war in which the prince was overruled and it was resolved to retreat. Lord George Murray and the majority were right that ahead lay certain defeat at Northampton or some other town: Charles Edward was equally right that, in retreat, lay ultimate catastrophe. Victory was not for the taking: the bitter choice was between ruin and disaster.

After the battle of Culloden, in April 1746 despite attempts to regroup at Ruthven, the Jacobite cause was broken for ever. The prince escaped to France, drifted into marital difficulties, took to the bottle, and died in 1788. The remaining rebels were hunted down with great severity, the great majority being transported to the colonies. A series of new fortifications pinned down the Highlands while the power of the clan chiefs was smashed by the Act abolishing heritable jurisdictions.

Perhaps the most surprising thing about the Jacobite movement was that it persisted for more than fifty years in the face of continuous disappointment and adversity. From Culloden, the Hanoverians gained in three separate ways. First, their claim to the throne was no longer in dispute and they were under less pressure to make concessions. Secondly, the dissociation of the Tories from

JACOBITE WINE-GLASS. The rose and bud represent the Old Pretender and the Young Pretender, and the thistle Scotland. The inscription 'AUDENTIOR IBO' means 'I will go more boldly.'

Jacobitism meant that they could once more be regarded as within the body politic, and thus the monarchs gained greater freedom of action. Thirdly, Scotland was transformed from the liability it had been to a source of strength and, for the first time, the union approached its full potential. Under these circumstances, the Hanoverians could afford to be indulgent. When Charles's brother, Henry IX, fell upon hard times during the Napoleonic wars, George III gave him a small pension. The cardinal reciprocated by leaving the crown jewels

REBELLION JUSTLY REWARDED, a nice laconic piece of eighteenth-century prose. The medal was struck in 1745 to commemorate the duke of Cumberland's successes against the Jacobite invaders led by Prince Charles Edward. The British hero was known to his friends as 'Sweet William' and to his foes as 'Stinking Billy'.

which James II had taken away to the Prince Regent, who, in turn, arranged in 1819 for Canova to erect a monument in St Peter's, Rome to the Old Pretender and his two sons.

The emergence of a Prince of Wales's party as a feature of the political landscape for much of the eighteenth century was, in part, an attempt to overcome the taint of impropriety, or even disloyalty, which adhered to a formal opposition. While government was still conceived and spoken of as the king's, formed opposition must remain suspect. The rivalry between monarchs and their sons may be seen therefore less as a freak of Hanoverian family life than as a step in the eventual legitimization of the concept of opposition. There were, of course, issues of allowances and the personnel of the prince's court which were bound to contribute to personal rancour. The animosities between George I and his son and George II and his may have been extreme, but it should be remembered that the Princess Anne had soon found herself at odds with her deliverer, William of Orange, after 1688.

Frederick Lewis was seven years old at the time of the accession of the House of Hanover. He was brought up in the Electorate and remained there until 1728, being created Prince of Wales the following year. Almost at once, relations with his parents became strained, partly over his allowance, and partly because their preference for his younger brother, William, duke of Cumberland, was so apparent. In 1736 he married Augusta of Saxe-Coburg, and his political friends moved in Parliament for an increased allowance, without success. In 1737 when the princess was pregnant, the queen clearly suspected some plot to bring in a surreptitious child and cheat Cumberland of his inheritance. When the princess began labour at Hampton Court, her husband bundled her into a coach and drove to St James's. The result was a public breach with his father and mother. Told to remove himself from the palace, the prince took up his father's old headquarters at Leicester House.

It is something of a mystery to understand why Frederick was so detested. Hervey thought he had not one grain of wit, Walpole that he had neither sincerity nor regard for truth. But the royal family ransacked language to express their hatred. 'The nauseous beast', declared his sister Caroline, 'cares for nobody but his own nauseous self,' while the queen, red with rage, hissed 'there he goes— that wretch, that villain—I wish the ground would open this moment and sink the monster to the lowest hope in hell'.

Frederick's political following was based upon his court, and augmented by a certain amount of electoral influence through his possessions in the duchy of Cornwall. Though he could never boast many members, they played some part in the overthrow of Walpole in 1742, and he carried on a sustained opposition to the Pelhams in the later 1740s. In a testament to his son, the prince outlined his political programme, advising him to regard himself as an Englishman, not a

Hanoverian, and to revive the plan to separate from Hanover as a means of vanquishing Jacobitism. Party distinctions should be laid aside and the Tories encouraged to look once more to royal favour and employment. In February 1748 the prince reached a formal understanding with the Tories, with an agreement to bring in a Place Bill and a Militia Bill. At the prince's accession, the Tories were to be offered both high office and honours. But in 1751, when the prince was forty-four and his father sixty-eight, he died suddenly, possibly of an unsuspected abscess.

Prince George was nearly thirteen when his father died. His mother, Princess Augusta, immediately came to terms with the court, and was appointed Regent in the event of the prince succeeding while under age. But from 1756 onwards, after the prince had attained his majority at the age of eighteen, Leicester House resumed its former role as a centre of opposition. Prince George took over, not only his father's policies, but many of his former advisers. Dodington, once Frederick's chief adviser, was too old for active service but still hoped for a peerage; the second Lord Egmont, an Irish peer who had been first minister designate at the time of Frederick's death, remained in favour; Lord Bute, who had served Frederick as a Lord of the Bedchamber, was made Groom of the Stole in 1756 and marked down as the coming man of the future reign. The main anxiety of the young prince was that his military uncle, the duke of Cumberland, might seize power by a coup: according to Walpole, the prince feared the worst when, on a visit, his uncle drew his sword to amuse the boy.

George II was far from popular in the early years of his reign. He travelled little in England and his preference for Hanover was too marked to go unobserved. Soon after the queen's death, he brought over a German mistress, Madame Walmoden, soon elevated as Lady Yarmouth: the liaison was a butt for satire and caricature. But, as often happens, longevity slowly kindled respect. Since 1714 there had been a substantial increase in population and a great growth of exports and imports. The 1750s were years of considerable prosperity, and though the Seven Years War began disastrously with the loss of Minorca, it ended in a blaze of victory, with the conquests in India by Clive and of Canada by Wolfe.

Horace Walpole, who started off by disliking George II intensely, finished by according him a grudging respect, paying tribute to his moderation and lack of rancour. His faults—fussiness, pomposity, irritability—were largely on the surface: beneath was common sense and judgement. He did not seek to undermine the constitutional settlement which had brought his family to the throne, and though there were sharp and persistent quarrels with ministers, they were legitimate disagreements about the extent and use of the royal prerogatives. The support over many years given to Walpole and the Pelhams suggests steadiness of purpose. Though he showed marked favour to Carteret, that

VAUXHALL PLEASURE GARDENS. This painting by Canaletto shows the Grand Walk in 1751. The gardens were opened just after the Restoration and closed in July 1859 after they had fallen into disrepute. Vauxhall and its rival Ranelagh were places of enchantment and diversion, particularly at night, with coloured lights in the trees, fireworks, fountains, taverns and dining-rooms, dancing and puppet-shows, music and private boxes. Ranelagh was the more exclusive and had a reputation for good music. The nearest modern equivalent are the Tivoli Gardens in Copenhagen.

statesman was without question a man of scholarship and ability, and after the episode of 1746 showed that he could not be supported, George did not pursue the vendetta against the Pelhams. He disliked Pitt, but Pitt had gone out of his way to be personally offensive to the king, and until the end of the Seven Years War it was by no means obvious that that strange man was more than an opinionated rhetorician.

In June 1760 the victory of Prince Ferdinand at Minden wiped out the shame of the capitulation in 1757 at Klosterseven, which had brought ill-feeling between the king and his favourite child, William, duke of Cumberland. On 25 October 1760 George rose at his usual time of six o'clock, called for his chocolate, retired to the privy and suffered a massive heart attack, which killed him on the spot. Among those who knew him well, there was a good deal of unanimity of opinion. He had a clear but unsubtle mind, a fierce but forgiving temper. His painful honesty was at the bottom of his appalling rudeness: he never learned to dissemble, and deviousness was not among his failings. 'He might offend,' wrote Lord Charlemont, 'but he never deceived.' Waldegrave admitted that the king's predilection for Hanover, where his authority was unquestioned, had not been allowed to influence his conduct in Britain. He was nearly thirty-one when he first landed in England and he remained all his life something of an observer of its strange ways. To Lord Waldegrave he remarked in 1757:

We were angry because he was partial to his electorate, though he desired nothing more to be done for Hanover than what we were bound in honour and justice to do for any country whatsoever when it was exposed to danger entirely on our account. That, we were indeed, a very extraordinary people, continually talking of our constitution, laws and liberty. That as to our constitution, he allowed it to be a good one, and defied any man to produce a single instance wherein he had exceeded his proper limits.

Horace Walpole, who had never much liked George II, gave him an elegiac farewell:

What an enviable death! In the greatest period of the glory of his country and of his reign, in perfect tranquillity at home, at seventy-seven growing blind and deaf, to die without a pang.

GEORGE II. George, Viscount Townshend, a soldier and member of Parliament, was also an accomplished caricaturist. This ink drawing of George II in the 1750s is a good likeness, with receding forehead, protruding eyes, and a slightly self-important air.

DECORATED MUGS AND VASES of naval and military heroes were particularly popular in the eighteenth century. In this example from the Royal Worcester collection, George II is offered a laurel wreath of somewhat inadequate size.

George III: the search for stability

The accession of George III was long accorded an importance in British historiography which is difficult to justify. The element most clearly apparent is continuity rather than innovation. In his famous declaration that he gloried in the name of Briton, the new king echoed the words of Anne, and acted upon the advice of his father: since he was the first of the Hanoverians to be born in this country, it is almost inconceivable that he should not have played this card. In his avowed detestation of party, he was at one with every ruler since the Glorious Revolution. Like George II he began by affecting a dislike of Hanover, ignored advice to make a separation, and ended with vast theoretical affection for his Electorate. In his claim to be rescuing the crown from oligarchy, he was repeating his father's ambitions in 1747. The elevation to high office of Lord Bute, though imprudent and as it transpired unfortunate, was, in itself, no more remarkable than Anne turning to the Churchills, George II promoting Sir Spencer Compton, or Prince Frederick's intention to hand over administration to Lord Egmont.

Three factors combined, however, to strengthen the new king's position. The substitution of a monarch aged twenty-two for one aged seventy-seven was enough to discourage most politicians from rash opposition: they were unlikely to outlive the king. Secondly, since George was still unmarried, it would be at least twenty years before there was the possibility of a princely opposition to the crown, such as had plagued his grandfather and great-grandfather. Thirdly, he was the first monarch since 1689 not to have to face dynastic rivalry. With the death of Jacobitism, there was no longer any reason for a ban on the Tories, and their traditional sympathy for Church and king made it easy for them to move out of opposition.

George III's boyhood, and particularly his adolescence, is well documented. There is no truth in Walpole's insinuation that he was very backward, unable to read English at eleven. Though not gifted, he was of average ability. His main weakness, which he admitted, was sluggishness and indolence. He was brought up with his brother Edward, which was not altogether an advantage, since the younger brother was brighter and seems to have been more of a favourite with their parents. As he grew older, he developed an admiration for Bute, his tutor, bordering on idolatory. The merest hint that Bute might not wish for the political lead when their time came was enough to send the young prince into paroxysms of melodrama—'I should with an eye of pleasure look on retiring to some uninhabited cavern.' It was not a very practical suggestion for a Prince of Wales to make. Bute, to his credit, tried to hint that George might feel differently towards him once he was married: the prince would not hear of it: 'I shall never change in that, nor will I bear in the least to be deprived of your company.'

Nevertheless, at the age of twenty-one, the prince was obliged to confess that

he had grown grave and thoughtful: 'it is entirely owing to a daily increasing admiration of the fair sex, which I am attempting with all the philosophy and resolution I am capable of to keep under, I should be ashamed after having so long resisted the charm of those divine creatures now to become their prey.' When the curtain was eventually lifted on this sighing and panting, the lady turned out to be, of all things, the fifteen-year-old niece of Henry Fox, one of Leicester House's most hated opponents. Prince George, in his ecstasy, threw grammar to the wind:

I was struck with her first appearance at St. James's, my passion has been increased every time I have since beheld her; her voice is sweet she seems sensible has a thorough sense of her obligations to her sister Lady Kildare, in short she is everything I can form to myself lovely. I am daily grown unhappy, sleep has left me, which never was before interrupted by any reverse of fortune: I protest before God I never have had an improper thought with regard to her . . .

Bute told him firmly it would never do, and with remarkable speed, the prince got over it, countering with the suggestion that they might look through the almanack for suitable German princesses. A few days later he reported that an evening's researches had produced 'three new ones ... as yet unthought of'.

The legend that George came to the throne filled with prerogative principles, fed to him by Bute and his mother, can be traced back to Horace Walpole. There is no truth in it. Bute's exposition of the constitution seems to have been quite unimpeachable. George's own explanation of Bute's unpopularity was that he had shown himself an enemy to despotism:

My friend is also attacked in the cruel and horrid manner, not for anything he has done against them, but because he is my friend, and wants to see me come to the throne with honour and not with disgrace and because he is a friend to the blessed liberties of his country and not to arbitrary notions.

Far from planning aggrandisement, Bute and George were afraid of being victims of a coup by 'myrmydons of the blackest kind', plotting to 'establish despotism here'.

But though George must be acquitted of any sinister intentions, he possessed some unfortunate qualities. Deprived of the company of people of his own age, he grew up solemn, priggish, and censorious. Taught by Bute to view the world as full of plots and conspiracies to dethrone him or entangle him, he was mistrustful and suspicious. Though he cured his early indolence and replaced it by meticulous and mechanical activity, he never got over the feeling that he was surrounded by bad and wicked men, and the depravity of the age in which he had had the misfortune to be born was one of his most constant themes.

His first action as king demonstrated both his taste for melodrama and his utter reliance on Bute. Riding over Kew Bridge, he was stopped by a messenger with news of his grandfather's death. To Bute he wrote at once: 'I have ordered all the servants that were out to be silent about what had passed as they valued their employments, and shall wait till I hear from you to know what further must be done.'

George III had two immediate objectives—to bring Bute into the administration and thus inaugurate a reign of virtue, and to make peace. The second aim was in part humanitarian. But the king was also convinced that the war served mainly Hanoverian interests and that Britain was being ruined by the vast increase in the national debt, against which his father had specifically warned him. It was also apparent that, while the war continued, Pitt's services were indispensable. It was not dissimilar to the problem Anne had faced with Marlborough.

A hint of the difficulties that lay ahead came on the very first day of the reign. At six in the evening, at the Privy Council, the king declared his desire to see an end to the bloody war. Pitt at once bridled at the implication and insisted that the speech be amended before it was given to the world. In the published version, the awkward formula 'expensive but just and necessary war' showed how difficult it had been to keep the domestic peace.

Lord Bute was sworn into the Privy Council on 27 October and in March 1761 replaced Lord Holdernesse as Secretary of State for the Northern Department. The promotion of Bute did not raise new constitutional issues but it brought up, in acute form, the old one of the king's right to choose his ministers. Previous royal favourites since the Glorious Revolution had at least been men of experience and some ability. Sir Spencer Compton in 1727 had been an MP for nearly thirty years and Speaker of the House of Commons since 1715; Granville in the 1740s had been a peer since he was five, and had served as ambassador, Lord Lieutenant of Ireland, and Secretary of State for both North and South. Bute, by contrast, was

TUTOR AND FRIEND. He 'would make an excellent ambassador in some proud little court where there is nothing to do,' was Frederick, Prince of Wales's dismissive summary of Lord Bute, one of his Lords of the Bedchamber. Bute stayed in the household of Princess Augusta after Frederick's death and became tutor and Groom of the Stole to Prince George in 1756. Though accused of instilling into the future George III absolutist notions, Bute's advice was moderate. The new king promoted him to be first minister, but within a year public scorn and derision forced him out of politics.

almost totally without political experience, having served for four years as a representative Scottish peer in his twenties. In Newcastle and Pitt he was challenging two politicians of vast experience, who presided over the most successful ministry of the century. As the political excitement grew, each side retreated to rather extreme constitutional positions. The king's supporters argued that he had the right of every gentleman to choose his own servants: their opponents countered, in the words of the *Annual Register*, that the spirit of the constitution required that the crown should be directed in the exercise of this public duty by public motives, and not by private liking and friendship. Neither argument can really stand up to scrutiny. It was hardly sensible to regard the first minister of the crown as a personal servant. Yet where should 'public duty' be expressed if not in Parliament, where Bute received overwhelming support. This, in turn, prompted the answer that Parliament was seriously out of touch with public opinion and that royal influence had undermined its independence. Thus, out of a rather simple adolescent affection, emerged a series of profound political and constitutional questions.

But before political battle was joined, there were domestic matters to be attended to. Matrimony was clearly an urgent necessity. In his confession to Bute, George had conceded 'how strong a struggle there is between the boiling youth of twenty-one years and prudence, the last I hope will ever keep the upper hand, indeed if I can weather it, marriage will put a stop to this combat in my breast'. Since Bute had ruled out a native product and the princess had to be Protestant, Germany was the place to look. Lists were drawn up and discreet enquiries made. The Princess Philippina of Brandenburg-Schwedt was 'stubborn and ill-tempered'. Princess Frederica of Saxe-Gotha was of a philosophical turn of mind, which George did not much fancy. The Princess Caroline of Hesse-Darmstadt was too big, and had 'a strange father and grandfather', suggesting that there might be something in the blood. The princess of Anhalt-Dessau's grandfather had married an apothecary's daughter, while the princess of Brandenburg's mother was under a cloud for having had an affair. The winner in this none too competitive field was Charlotte of Mecklenburg-Strelitz, aged seventeen, not a beauty, but reported sensible. Throughout the summer of 1761 the young king waited with growing impatience. On 7 September the bride landed at Harwich. His only wish, wrote George dutifully to Bute, was that the marriage would prove fruitful. The following day she arrived at St James's in the afternoon and was married that evening. George's wish was granted abundantly. The first of their fifteen children, the future George IV, made his appearance in August 1762.

Peace talks with France began early in 1761. Pitt insisted on draconian terms. France refused and reached a compact with Spain to enter the war. In October 1761, when the cabinet refused a pre-emptive strike against the Spaniards, Pitt resigned. Since the king had already wondered whether 'that mad Pitt' ought not to be dismissed, it was not inconvenient, though the parting with Pitt was surprisingly emotional and protracted. George Grenville, Pitt's brother-in-law, was to have the lead in the House of Commons, no sinecure if Pitt was in baleful mood. Three months later, the cabinet was forced to declare war on Spain.

Newcastle followed Pitt out in May 1762 in protest against the refusal to honour obligations to Frederick of Prussia. The king had little liking for 'that proud, overbearing prince'. As for Newcastle, he had frequently threatened resignation—'what if he does?' the king had written. But it might have occurred to a more experienced ruler that he was closing down his political options fast, and becoming dangerously dependent upon Bute, who was himself far from steady. Bute replaced Newcastle as First Lord of the Treasury, but was already expressing dismay at the effect that the rough and tumble of politics had upon his stomach. 'Vigour and the day is ours', declared the king splendidly, but it was not his stomach.

After eighteen months on the throne, George III was a strange mixture of ferocious opinions (at least on paper) and numbing diffidence. Bute's approbation was still sought on the most trifling personal matters. 'The Queen', wrote George, 'wishes very much I would give her my picture in enamel to wear at her side instead of a watch; I see no impropriety in it but wish he would if he sees any send me word.' The king seemed to have little idea of the difficulties of presenting government policy to the Commons and Bute was hardly the man to advise him. Charles Townshend, difficult but talented, was 'that vermin'; for Henry Bilson Legge, the king had nothing but contempt—he was as 'obnoxious' as Pitt. Of Grenville, still technically leading for the government, the king wrote that he had 'never yet met with a man more doubtful or dilatory'. In order to ease peace negotiations with France, the king conspired with Bute and Egremont to send a private message to the French that the island of St Lucia would be given back, though the majority of the cabinet thought otherwise. Grenville, who would have to defend the peace, was not in the secret. It was left to the French to suggest a mode whereby the disunity in the British cabinet might be overcome. On 26 July the king's letter to Bute was concerned with the disarray in the cabinet and (at greater length) the king's alarm that a 'very ill-looking fellow', for once not a member of the government, had been found loitering outside the queen's bedchamber.

By the autumn of 1762 peace terms had been agreed with the French. Pitt was certain to fall upon them in the Commons. Bute persuaded the king to offer the lead to Henry Fox. It was a sad admission of political realities on George's part, since Fox was one of the politicians he most distrusted. But 'bad men', observed the king, 'must be called in to govern bad men'. The reign of virtue was postponed yet again.

At least Fox did the job, even if he was not squeamish about his methods. Though Pitt delivered the anticipated onslaught against a craven and inadequate peace, it was not easy to make a settlement which guaranteed British supremacy in both India and North America seem totally unsatisfactory, and the majority of 319 against 65 in the Commons was more than ample. But Lord Bute was not enjoying political prominence. He was jostled in the streets, lampooned viciously as a Scottish favourite and lover of the Princess Dowager, and hanged in effigy. It was now Bute's turn to pine for the uninhabited cavern: 'if I had but £50 p.a. I would retire on bread and water, and think it luxury, compared with what I suffer,' he wrote. After less than a year as first minister of the crown, he insisted on tendering his resignation. The king was horrified. 'I own I had flattered myself when peace was once established that my dear friend would have assisted me in purging out corruption . . . then when we were both dead our memories would have been respected and esteemed to the end of time.' Beneath the politics one detects the sense of betrayed affection.

Bute was determined to retire, putting forward Henry Fox as his successor. The king protested strongly, not merely on grounds of 'personal dislike' but because the whole winter had been 'nothing else but a scene of corruption'. Though Bute talked the king into it, Fox refused, and in desperation, the lead was

FAMILY LIFE. Queen Charlotte (*left*) with her eldest daughter, Charlotte, the Princess Royal. At the age of thirty-one, she married Frederick of Würtemberg and died without children in 1828. (*Facing*) George, Prince of Wales with his brother Frederick, duke of York. They are painted in the second drawing-room or the warm room at Buckingham Palace by Zoffany. Frederick followed a military career and was heir to the throne when he died in 1827.

offered to George Grenville, who accepted. But if Bute in office had raised constitutional difficulties, Bute out of office raised even more, since he continued to offer advice to the king as a 'minister behind the curtain'. Grenville had every reason to be uneasy about his own position, demanded public proofs of the king's confidence, and insisted that all recommendations for patronage should be directed through him. At stake was not merely the principle that only ministers could tender political advice but the powers and influence of the first minister himself.

Grenville's ministry, which lasted two years, was a nightmare for the king. There were few strictly political differences between the two men. Each advocated a strong policy towards John Wilkes, charged with seditious libel, and towards the Americans, who resented Grenville's attempt to raise revenue by means of the Stamp Act. But Grenville's uneasy mixture of arrogance and timidity, fed by his suspicions of Bute's continuing influence, and expressed with that unstoppable loquacity to which all his acquaintance paid awed tribute, soured relations between king and minister. 'When he has wearied me for two hours,' complained the king, 'he looks at his watch to see if he may not tire me for an hour more.' Soon Grenville was more intolerable than Pitt or Newcastle had ever been. Even the appointment of court painter, Grenville demanded, must be under ministerial control. For a monarch who had begun with the intention of rescuing the crown from toils, George had proved singularly unlucky. It was an indication of the desperation to which he had been reduced that in 1765, when he

decided he could bear it no longer, the king turned for advice to the duke of Cumberland, the uncle who had been the demon of his youth.

Cumberland hoped to bring back the Pitt–Newcastle coalition. When Pitt refused to serve, Newcastle and his friends came back alone, headed by the young marquess of Rockingham. But they were almost as obsessed with Bute as George Grenville had been. When government supporters showed some reluctance to join in the repeal of the Stamp Act which had been passed a mere two years before, it was inevitable that Rockingham and his friends should look for secret influence at work. Though they carried repeal, Pitt remained aloof, Grafton decided he could not carry on without him, and the ministry broke up in June 1766.

The king's overwhelming concern was still to avoid Grenville at all costs and this time he turned to Pitt. It was an astonishing reversal of attitude. In May

1760 Pitt had been 'the most dishonourable of men ... the blackest of hearts'; by October he was 'a true snake in the grass'. But in 1765 it was 'my friend, for so the part you have acted deserves from me'. Publicly, there was little to divide them. Pitt had always been something of a loner in politics, with little trust in parties. His move to power in 1757 had been the signal for many of the Tories to transfer their support to government. He was therefore in many ways the ideal man to take up the king's crusade to extirpate party. This time he responded to the invitation with alacrity: 'happy could I change infirmity into wings of Expedition,' he replied, in his inimitably florid style.

The first six years of George's reign were an incomparable tragicomedy. George's immaturity can scarcely be denied. He was full of schemes for turning people out without much corresponding desire to invite others in. He had little understanding of the importance of managing the Commons, though it had been a critical question while he was Prince of Wales. His low opinion of all politicians made him less than open towards them, and he had few of the arts of conciliation which a constitutional monarch needs. It is of course by no means unusual for young men in their twenties to see things in black and white and to be impatient with compromise. What is unusual is for them to find themselves on a throne. Had Frederick lived a normal life-span, George would have inherited in his forties, a more mature man. Even with Victoria, who succeeded at an earlier age, there were difficulties in separating public and private concerns. But Victoria had an almost ideal mentor in Lord Melbourne—sensible, experienced, relaxed, amusing, and tolerant. George had Bute.

In many respects George was the victim of his good qualities. He was far too conscientious. The incessant appeals by Bute as tutor to banish indolence produced an over-reaction. With no mistresses to distract him George devoted many of his hours to political manœuvre, to the detriment of his own health and well-being. The attention he paid to affairs of state was almost too great for him personally and for the precarious balance of the eighteenth-century constitution. At the last crisis of the Rockinghams in May 1766 he wrote to Bute:

I can neither eat nor sleep, nothing pleases me but musing on my cruel situation ... Indeed, if I am to continue the life of agitation I have these three years, the next year there will be a Council of Regency to assist in that undertaking.

But, amid all this agitation, there were signs that George was learning. He was parting with the Rockinghams, he told Bute, 'without any quarrel', being resolved, as much as possible, to make no new enemies: 'for it is very unpleasant to be afterwards obliged to appear forgetting what one has suffered.'

With the return of Pitt, George had every reason to believe he was in clear water. All contact with Bute was at an end. 'I have for ever done with this bad public,' he wrote to the king in a final letter, 'my heart is half broke and my health

SKETCH OF SYON HOUSE BY PRINCE GEORGE. The prince studied drawing under John Joshua Kirby, who lectured and wrote on perspective. When he came to the throne, George III paid for the plates in Kirby's edition of *The Perspective of Architecture*, published in 1761.

ruined, with the unmerited barbarous treatment I have received.' To a friend, he wrote, 'I know as little, save from newspapers, of the present busy scene as I do of transactions in Persia.' Pitt retained much of his wartime prestige and had demonstrated that he could break, if not make, ministries. Grafton stayed on from the previous administration and moved to become First Lord of the Treasury, though nobody, least of all Grafton himself, doubted that real power lay with Pitt. Henry Seymour Conway and Lord Shelburne were Secretaries of State, the former leading in the Commons. Pitt himself moved to the Lords as earl of Chatham, taking the nominal office of Lord Privy Seal.

It is often said that Pitt's move from the Commons proved fatal to his influence. There is some truth in it. But the careers of Liverpool and Salisbury in the nineteenth century demonstrate that it was not impossible to conduct an effective government from the Lords, and Pitt's administration was not overthrown by the Commons. It collapsed as a consequence of the bizarre breakdown of Chatham himself.

Further indication of the king's growing maturity was his treatment of Chatham, which could hardly have been more tactful and patient. The ministry got off to a lively start. Harking back to his previous period of office and fearing a Bourbon resurgence, Chatham made overtures to Frederick of Prussia for a renewal of their wartime alliance. It was refused. The remnants of the Rockinghams who had stayed in found Chatham's dictatorial manner increasingly intolerable, and by the end of the year most of them had resigned or been dismissed. Another visit to Bath in October 1766 was needed to get the great man into shape for the parliamentary session, and as soon as it was ended, he was back at Bath, leaving Grafton to carry on as best he could. Problems piled up. The East India Company was in financial trouble, the Americans unappeased by the repeal of the Stamp Act. In February 1767, after one false start, Chatham set out for London, reached the Castle Inn, Marlborough, and remained for three weeks prostrate. The opposition took advantage of his absence to inflict a sharp defeat on the government, reducing the Land Tax by a shilling in the pound. Early in March, Chatham reached London. 'Now you are arrived in town,' wrote the king cheerfully, 'every difficulty will daily decrease.' Instead, Chatham collapsed into total seclusion. The king suggested horse-riding or a change of doctor, and offered to visit him: Chatham declined, pleading 'utter disability'. Day after day he sat in a darkened room, his food passed through a hatch by the servants, his hands and limbs shaking, his grasp of conversation distressingly fitful. Grafton managed to effect running repairs on the ministry, replacing Charles Townshend, after his unexpected death, by Lord North, and bringing in the Bedfords for support. At last, in October 1768, convinced that he had been abandoned by those he had himself abandoned, Chatham tendered his resignation. If his health ever recovered, every moment of his life, he assured the king, would be dedicated to His Majesty. The 'able and dignified' ministry on which the king's hopes of extirpating party had rested, ended in complete confusion.

Grafton soldiered on for another fifteen months, plagued by the issues arising from Wilkes's election for Middlesex, and tormented by the sardonic newspaper attacks of the unknown Junius. The last straw came in January 1770 with the re-emergence in the House of Lords of Chatham, miraculously restored to health, and condemning his former colleagues with all his old vigour. His first salvo carried away his ally, Lord Chancellor Camden. Chatham's explanation of his own failure was impudent in the extreme: he had been undermined by the same secret influence that had brought down his predecessors. Bute's influence, he declared, was as potent as ever. At the end of the month Grafton insisted on resigning, much to the dismay of the king who reproached him with desertion in the moment of battle.

Faced with an apparently triumphant opposition coalition of Grenville, Rockingham, and the Chathamites, the king looked desperately for someone to lead a forlorn hope. His eye lighted upon Lord North, a junior minister still and only thirty-seven, but with sixteen years' experience of the House of Commons. North was fat, good-humoured, imperturbable, a good man of business, and an incomparable debater. George's letter of appeal was not a masterpiece of tact:

'you must easily see that if you do not accept, I have no peer at present in my service that I could consent to place in the Duke of Grafton's employment.' The first division was encouraging and yielded a government majority of forty. The king cheered up at once: 'believe me, a little spirit will soon restore a degree of order in my service.' For once George was right and had, at long last, backed a winner.

The opening years of George's reign were turbulent and difficult. The king paid a heavy price for his initial blunder in perceiving vast talents in Lord Bute, and a more ruthless man would have dropped the encumbrance quicker than George did. Yet the retribution—politically and posthumously—seems out of proportion to the offence. The post-war years were bound to be difficult. In Europe, the overwhelming triumph of Britain at the peace of Paris set up a counter-move to preserve the balance of power and the country became dangerously isolated. Demobilization caused a good deal of distress, food shortages produced some sharp riots in 1765 and 1766, and there were unpleasant financial crises. The mood of the country seemed strange—excitable, suspicious, unsteady. The enormous growth in newspapers, London and provincial, testified to the increase in a reading public, and Wilkes and Junius took advantage of it to launch spectacular journalistic careers. The attacks on Bute and the Princess Dowager were of persistent ferocity and unfairness. Even the king was not spared. 'Remember', Junius told him, in the famous letter of December 1769, 'that a throne acquired by one revolution may be lost by another.' 'It is not, however, too late', added Junius with the effortless effrontery that was his trademark, 'to correct the error of your education . . . Discard those little, personal resentments, which have too long directed your public conduct.' But if George's behaviour was not always wise, that of the leading politicians contributed greatly to the discontents, as though they were determined to earn the shabby opinion George had of them. Wilkes's irresponsibility was, of course, quite deliberate. He had explained cheerfully in 1768 that his alternatives were to raise a dust or die in a gaol. Grenville, who had taken a very firm line against Wilkes when in office, changed sides completely in opposition, and though he laboured indefatigably to persuade the Commons of his utter consistency, few were impressed. The alliance of Grenville, who had passed the Stamp Act with the Rockinghams who had repealed it, looked a trifle opportunistic. Chatham's conduct remains inexplicable save possibly in psychological terms: his accusation of secret influence, though seized upon by the opposition as proof absolute of all their allegations, was wildly at variance with the repeated efforts the king had made to coax him back into action, and the deference the king had shown to his opinions.

THE NOBLE LORD IN THE BLUE RIBBON. Though this portrait by Nathaniel Dance of Lord North as Chancellor of the University of Oxford was formal, it catches something of his relaxed, sleepy, imperturbable manner. His mastery of the Commons made the opening years of his administration easy. But he was not the man to deal with the American crisis, as he was the first to admit. 'Let me not go to the grave', he begged George III, 'with the guilt of having been the ruin of my King and country.' The king refused to allow him to resign. The most criticized of all prime ministers, North was a man of decency, honour, integrity, and wit.

George III: America and India

The first years of Lord North's administration were among the easiest that George enjoyed throughout his long reign. His new minister's command of financial detail was a great asset. His political judgement was good. He showed no wish at all to pursue the Wilkes issue with any vigour and, as had often been predicted, neglect proved a more effective way of dealing with Wilkes than persecution had been. By the middle of 1770, the opposition were quarrelling among themselves. As an added bonus, the king found North as agreeable to work with as did most other people. In June 1771, after only eighteen months as first minister, the king offered North the Garter—one of the few examples of that honour going to a commoner. In 1774 the *Annual Register* observed that the ministry 'had so long carried everything with so triumphant a sway that no common event seemed capable of endangering its security'.

The king's anxieties at this time were personal rather than political. The year 1772 was particularly trying. First came news that the king's younger sister, Caroline, queen of Denmark, had been arrested for adultery, her lover Struensee executed, and she herself imprisoned in Kronborg. Though George was able to negotiate for her an honourable retirement to Celle in Hanover, she remained a source of concern until her early death in 1775. In February 1772, George's mother, the Dowager Princess of Wales, died of cancer in her early fifties: contrary to much speculation, contemporary and subsequent, there is no evidence that she wielded any significant political influence. The king also had troubled relations with his brothers. Edward, duke of York, with whom he had been brought up, lived a demanding life, and died at Monaco in 1767 at the age of twenty-eight. Henry, duke of Cumberland, attracted unfortunate notoriety in 1770 when Lord Grosvenor brought an action for crim. con. against him and was awarded damages. The duke's ardent letters to Lady Grosvenor were produced in evidence, causing the fashionable world to debate which were worse—the duke's morals or his grammar. From the Scylla of adultery, His Royal Highness plunged at once into the Charybdis of matrimony, making an imprudent secret marriage with Anne Horton, a widow, and a member of the unloved Luttrell family. The king refused to recognize the duchess and insisted on the introduction of the Royal Marriages Bill, which is still in force. This forbids the marriage of a member of the royal family, under the age of twenty-five, without the formal consent of the sovereign. It was bitterly opposed. Charles Fox, taking over his father's old feuds, resigned office in order to speak against it, and Chatham denounced it in private as 'wanton and tyrannical'. No sooner had the bill become law than another brother, William, duke of Gloucester, confessed that he had long been married to the illegitimate daughter of Sir Edward Walpole. Neither duchess was ever received at court.

North's administration, which lasted twelve years, was the first to be dominated by colonial questions. In the hundred years between the restoration of Charles II and the accession of George III, England had been transformed from a minor colonial power, scrambling with Prussians, Danes, and Swedes for the remnants left by Spaniards, French, and Dutch, into the leading world empire.

At the end of the Tudor period, there were no plantations, other than in Ireland, since Ralegh's settlements in the New World had not survived. Substantial emigration during the reigns of James I and Charles I established footholds on the east coast of America, which developed into Virginia, Maryland, Massachusetts, and Newfoundland. Bermuda, occupied in 1612, and Barbados were the nucleus of the British West Indies, augmented in 1655 by the conquest of Jamaica from the Spaniards. The aggressive mercantilist policy of the Commonwealth, exemplified by the Navigation Act of 1651, was sustained under Charles II with the foundation of the Carolinas, and the granting of charters to Rhode Island, Connecticut, and New Jersey. James, duke of York, took an active part in the conquest of New Amsterdam from the Dutch in 1664, and became proprietor of the new colony. To the north was established the Quaker settlement of Pennsylvania, and further north again were settlements on Newfoundland and in the Hudson Bay area. By 1700 the total population of the British mainland colonies was more than 200,000. To the north and west were French territories, running from the St Lawrence, down the Great Lakes and along the Mississippi to the Gulf of Mexico. Imposing in extent, they were thinly populated, with no more than 12,000 settlers in 1700, despite persistent efforts by Colbert to promote emigration. The remainder of the continent, including Florida, was claimed by the fading power of Spain.

Between 1700 and 1763, the issue in North America was decided by three wars, together with the successful plantation of yet another British colony, Georgia, in the 1730s. In each of the wars, the colonial element was increasingly important, and the proportion of regular troops committed to the struggle rose steadily. Britain's intervention in the war of the Spanish succession was to a great extent inspired by commercial motives, lest the advantages of trade with the vast Spanish empire should be monopolized by France. It was the first war in North America to show the balance beginning to tip in Britain's favour. Fighting was largely restricted to skirmishing and privateering, and the one major British effort to take Quebec, supported by 5,000 troops and 60 ships, failed because of the difficulties of navigating the St Lawrence. But at the end of the conflict, Acadia passed under British control, and was renamed Nova Scotia, with the chief town called Annapolis. Spain too was forced to make concessions—the first breach in her colonial monopoly. The Asiento—the right to supply negro slaves—was handed over to the South Sea Company for thirty years, with the right also to send one ship a year of 500 tons to Portobello.

All these arrangements led to more strife. In North America, boundaries were still ill-defined. The South Sea Company soon discovered that the Asiento—circumvented by smuggling on the grand scale—was less lucrative than had been expected. The Portobello ship led to protracted disputes. The Spaniards placed difficulties in the way and the voyage was made on only eight of the possible thirty occasions. The ship itself presented an extraordinary spectacle. Normal practice was for the vessel to call first at Jamaica, where it was stripped of everything that could be removed—food, water, ammunition, personal belongings. Then, stuffed with goods, it tottered 500 miles to Portobello, a floating warehouse. So amazed were the Spaniards at the quantity of goods that continued to pour from its holds that it was rumoured the vessel was filled up each night from attendant small craft.

Between the treaty of Utrecht and the War of Jenkins' Ear, which began in 1739, the British position was strengthened by the settlement of Georgia. The area was to the south of the Carolinas, running up to the borders of Spanish Florida. The whole territory was claimed by Spain and a seventeenth-century attempt to colonize it had been destroyed by Spanish intervention. The renewed

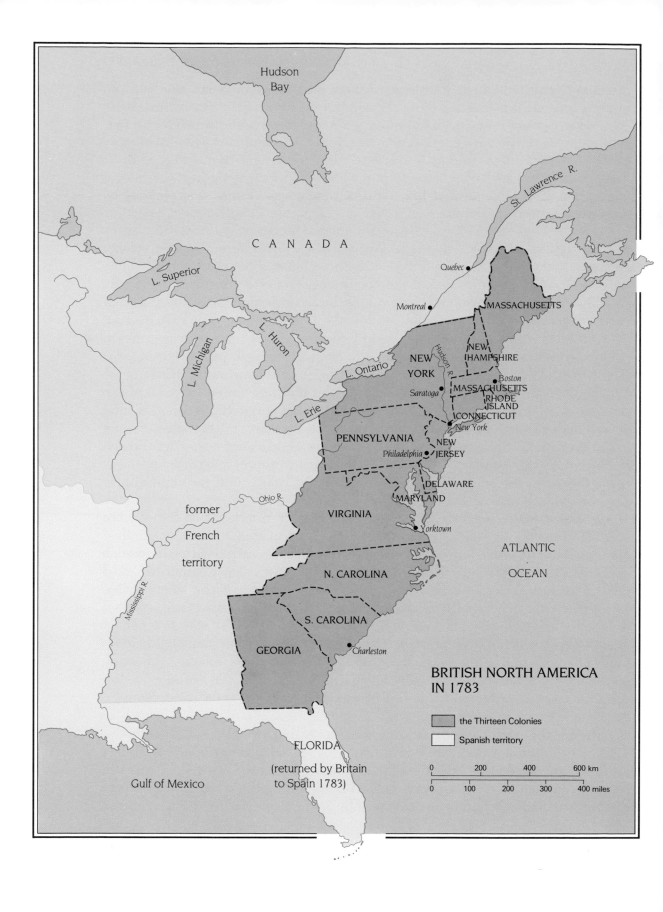

Hudson
Bay

CANADA

L. Superior

St. Lawrence R.

Quebec

L. Michigan

L. Huron

Montreal

MASSACHUSETTS

L. Ontario

NEW
YORK

NEW
HAMPSHIRE

L. Erie

Hudson R.

Boston

Saratoga

MASSACHUSETTS

RHODE
ISLAND

CONNECTICUT

New York

PENNSYLVANIA

NEW
JERSEY

Philadelphia

DELAWARE

former

Ohio R.

MARYLAND

French

VIRGINIA

territory

Yorktown

ATLANTIC

Mississippi R.

OCEAN

N. CAROLINA

S. CAROLINA

GEORGIA

Charleston

BRITISH NORTH AMERICA
IN 1783

the Thirteen Colonies

Spanish territory

FLORIDA

(returned by Britain
to Spain 1783)

Gulf of Mexico

0		200		400		600 km
0	100	200	300		400 miles	

attempt in the 1730s was a mixture of piety and imperialism. General James Oglethorpe and Lord Egmont, two of the principal founders, hoped to send out people released from debtors' prisons in order to give them a new start in life. The government saw the colony as a barrier to Spanish attacks on the cultivated lands of the Carolinas, or as an advanced base from which Florida might be overrun. Certain settlers were discouraged in the interests of military efficiency. Catholics and slaves were mistrusted as potential subversives, and a group of German pacifists were not what the authorities were looking for. But emigrants from the Scottish Highlands were promising material and were given the place of danger near the Spanish frontier. Though the population grew slowly, by 1760 it was at about the 6,000 mark, with a considerable number of negro slaves in addition.

The foundation of Georgia, and continued difficulties about trading rights, helped to bring about war with Spain in 1739. After a sensational start in which Portobello was captured a month after the declaration of war, the British war effort faltered. In 1744 the French came in and succeeded in threatening Acadia. A counter-attack seized Louisbourg, the fortress built to protect French Canada, but it was handed back at the treaty of Aix-la-Chapelle in 1748 in exchange for Madras.

Though the peace held formally for eight years, there were persistent clashes between French and English in the Ohio valley. In 1754 a force under George Washington was obliged to surrender, and General Edward Braddock, sent out to retrieve the situation in 1755, was ambushed and killed.

The Seven Years War saw the employment on the American continent of the largest forces ever seen there. James Wolfe had at his disposal 8,000 regulars, 48 warships, and 119 transports, while Montcalm, the French commander, had eight batallions and large numbers of Canadian and Indian auxiliaries. Montcalm's offensive was first held and then slowly pressed back. In 1758 Louisbourg was captured again, preparing the way for an assault up the St Lawrence river. The following year was decisive. A three-pronged attack, with Wolfe leading the main assault, resulted in the capture of Quebec, and though the French regrouped, their naval defeat at Quiberon Bay cut them off from reinforcement. In September 1760 they surrendered and New France came to an end. In the Caribbean, too, the British were successful. One by one, the lucrative sugar islands fell. After 1762 the Spanish were discomforted by the capture of Havana, capital of Cuba, and by the success of an expedition from Madras against Manila, in the Philippines.

The constitution of the thirteen British colonies varied considerably, according to their original foundations and subsequent vicissitudes. Virginia had been a crown colony from the beginning under a charter of 1633 granted to Lord Baltimore, a Catholic, who had proprietary rights. The attitude of James II to the

THE ATTACK UPON QUEBEC (1759). This print shows Wolfe's men scaling the Heights of Abraham and outflanking Montcalm's defences. The attack was in fact by night and conducted in total silence. Told that Wolfe was mad, George II is reported to have replied, 'I wish he would bite my other generals.' Wolfe died in the action with lines from Pope's translation of the *Iliad* in his pocket: 'Brave tho' we fall, and honour'd if we live, Or let us Glory gain, or Glory give!'

colonies sheds some light on his ambitions in England. He had no liking for representative institutions and refused to grant an assembly to New York, of which he was proprietor. The charter of Massachusetts was revoked by Charles II in 1684 and joined with New York and New Jersey to form the Dominion of New England, with no representative rights. The Glorious Revolution was too good a chance for the colonists to miss. Massachusetts declared against the king and resumed its former rights; New York did the same; Maryland repudiated its papist proprietor and made common cause with William's supporters. The eighteenth century saw increasing pressure from colonial assemblies on royal governors until it was a commonplace of the 1750s that the colonies were, in effect, independent states, united only by allegiance to the common crown.

Responsibility for colonial affairs in England was shared. Technically, the Privy Council had charge, considered appeals, and moderated colonial legislation. In practice, business was delegated to a committee for colonial affairs. Correspondence passed through the Secretary of State for the South, who had an Under-Secretary for American affairs. The President of the Board of Trade and

Plantations also had considerable influence, though the Board was advisory. In addition, many colonial questions involved the Admiralty, the Treasury, and the Customs. The colonies themselves appointed agents, often merchants acting on retainers, to represent their interests and lobby at Westminster. It was a confused and overlapping system, which had barely managed to co-ordinate the small empire of the early eighteenth century, and could certainly not be expected to deal with the strains imposed on it after 1763.

The other great centre of colonial activity was India, still not under government control. The original East India Company, established by Elizabeth in 1600, had struggled against strong Dutch competition. In the course of the century, it acquired bases at Madras, Surat, and Hooghly, later moved to Calcutta. The French established themselves at Pondicherry and at Chandernagore, near Calcutta. The gradual collapse of the Mogul empire, which claimed sovereignty over the subcontinent, hastened the intervention of the European powers. With little chance of the emperor providing effective law and order, the companies established their own forces, and raised revenue to support them. In 1739 the utter defeat of the emperor at the hands of the Persians led to the sacking of Delhi and the disintegration of his remaining authority. The fighting in the war of the Austrian succession was limited and the French, under Dupleix, had the better of it. Madras was regained by Britain at the peace only by surrendering Louisbourg in exchange.

Though administration was still in the hands of the Company, the British government had dispatched regulars in the 1740s to reinforce the company troops. It was therefore unlikely that the Company's affairs would remain unregulated for long. The French and British were already at war as auxiliaries of the native princes in 1756 when the Seven Years War broke out. Clive followed up his success at Plassey against Suraj-ud-Daula by seizing Chandernagore. A French counter-attack against Madras failed and Pondicherry itself was besieged and captured in 1761. Though the French retained bases after 1763, effectively their power in India was broken.

After the war, the Company drifted into financial difficulty as administrative costs rose. In 1767 it was also required to make an annual contribution of £400,000 to the national Exchequer: the strain that this placed upon the Company's resources, exacerbated by a severe famine in Bengal, brought it in 1772 to the brink of bankruptcy. Though North had little desire at this stage to assume direct responsibility for the Indian empire, he was forced to intervene to avoid a credit crisis of alarming proportions. His Regulating Act of 1773 offered a substantial loan in exchange for some measure of control. The Governor of Bengal was given precedence over the others as Governor-General, to promote better co-ordination, and a council of four established to advise him.

The immediate origin of the American conflict which developed during

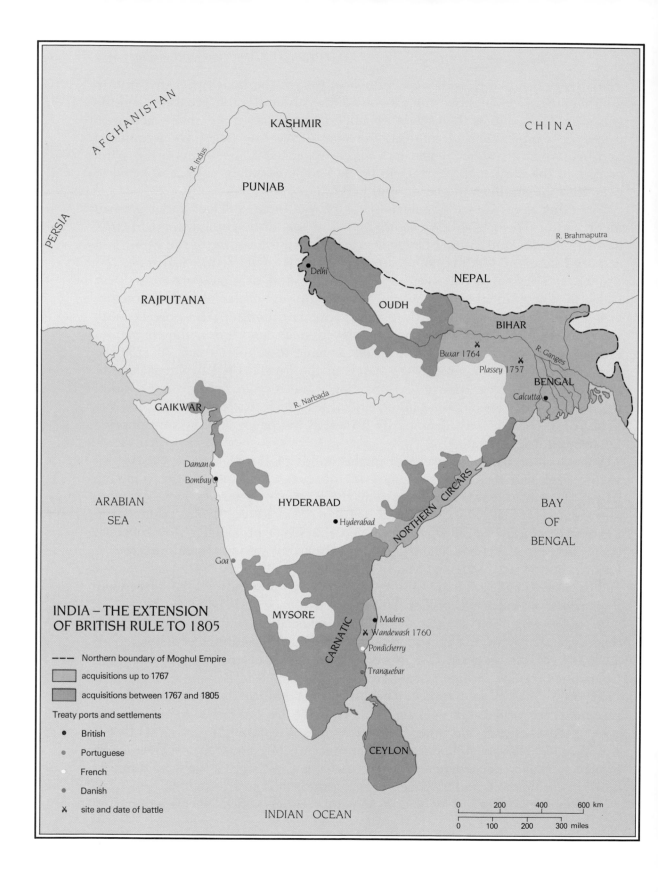

AFGHANISTAN

PERSIA

KASHMIR

CHINA

R. Indus

PUNJAB

RAJPUTANA

Delhi

NEPAL

OUDH

BIHAR

R. Brahmaputra

Buxar 1764

Plassey 1757

R. Ganges

BENGAL

Calcutta

GAIKWAR

R. Narbada

Daman

Bombay

ARABIAN
SEA

HYDERABAD

Hyderabad

NORTHERN CIRCARS

BAY
OF
BENGAL

Goa

MYSORE

CARNATIC

Madras

Wandewash 1760

Pondicherry

Tranquebar

CEYLON

INDIA – THE EXTENSION
OF BRITISH RULE TO 1805

- - - Northern boundary of Moghul Empire

acquisitions up to 1767

acquisitions between 1767 and 1805

Treaty ports and settlements

● British

● Portuguese

○ French

● Danish

✕ site and date of battle

INDIAN OCEAN

| 0 | 200 | 400 | 600 km |

| 0 | 100 | 200 | 300 miles |

North's administration was the heavy cost of the war, to which George III had referred. The national debt had almost doubled and required an annual revenue of £4 million to service it. Since this was nearly half the normal peacetime revenue, retrenchment and economy were inescapable.

The vast expansion of territory brought under the British crown in America meant a substantial increase in the cost of garrisons. An estimate in 1763 suggested the need for 10,000 men, at an annual cost of £225,000, and a formal minute to the Board of Trade asked for a discussion of some contribution 'least burdensome and palatable to the colonies'. To the American claim that they were already contributing through the operation of the mercantilist system, the British retorted that smuggling was on such a scale that hardly any revenue came in. An estimate of tea imports in 1763 suggested that only one-tenth paid the legal duties, while Lord North pointed out that for every sixpence the Americans paid in taxation, the British paid twenty-five shillings. The total yield from the American customs was put at a derisory £1,800 p.a.

A serious Indian rising in 1763—the conspiracy of Pontiac—added to the problem. The colonial governments gave little help in restoring order and British regulars had to be employed. To prevent further clashes with the Indians, the British government imposed a ban of expansion west of the Alleghenies.

Each ministry in turn came back to the question of raising an American revenue. Grenville's immediate response was to tighten up customs regulation and order officials to their posts. To encourage a more zealous discharge of their duties, they were promised one half of the value of any cargo seized as contraband. The Sugar Act of 1764 aimed at raising an additional £45,000 p.a.: the tariff on foreign molasses was reduced to 3*d.* a gallon, but new impositions were placed on wine, coffee, and sugar. American merchants complained that the new rates were excessive and, in an ominous move which elevated the disagreement to a constitutional dispute, the assembly of Massachusetts protested that its fundamental right to consent to its own taxation was being invaded.

The following year, Grenville carried his second proposal—to extend to America the stamp duties paid in Britain on items such as newspapers and legal transactions. A formidable campaign of protest was mounted: stamps were burned, collectors tarred and feathered, a trade embargo on British goods attempted, and a congress summoned at New York to co-ordinate resistance. British merchants complained that the dislocation of trade was ruining them.

Until this time, the king had accepted the advice of his ministers on what appeared to be largely a technical matter. He was uneasy at the Rockinghams' proposal in 1766 to repeal the Stamp Act after less than a year in operation, but when Rockingham demanded assurances of the king's support, he was given them. The ministers, sensitive to the charge that they were retreating in the face of pressure, accompanied the repeal by a Declaratory Act, reaffirming Britain's right to legislate for the colonies in all cases. This eased the tactical problem of steering repeal through Parliament, though at the risk of negating any gratitude the Americans might feel.

Chatham, who took over in 1766 from the Rockinghams, inherited their difficulties. During the repeal debates he had come forward as the friend of America, denying Parliament's right to impose taxes. But his administration had still to raise a revenue. From Bath, Chatham wrote that his whole mind was 'bent on acquiring such a revenue as must give strength, ease and lustre to the King's reign'. These were admirable sentiments, but vague. Under the circumstances, his Chancellor of the Exchequer, Charles Townshend, took the initiative. When, in the early months of 1767, it became apparent that the cost of the military establishment in America would be of the order of £400,000 p.a., Townshend cheerfully pledged himself to raise the necessary revenue from the colonists themselves. His colleagues had little idea what he had in mind, and it was in flagrant contradiction to Chatham's previous attitude. The following month, the ministry's defeat on a Commons motion to reduce the Land Tax by one shilling deprived them of some £500,000 p.a. in taxes, and made the position even more urgent.

In May, Townshend brought forward his proposals. He avoided internal taxes in America, and proposed to impose port duties on tea, glass, paper, painters' colours, and red and white lead. In addition, by suggesting that in future colonial governors should be paid by the crown, and not by their assemblies, he offered a blow at the increasing financial control the colonies could exercise. Having lit the fuse, he promptly died.

The colonists replied with defiance. The assembly of Massachusetts adopted a circular letter, denouncing the new duties as illegal and rejecting any suggestion of representation—thus promoting the suspicion that they were more attached to the first than second part of their slogan, 'No taxation without representation'. Officers of the crown were helpless; revenue men were obstructed, juries would not convict, and the Townshend duties brought in the merest trickle. At Boston, troops were ordered into the town to restore order, and clashes led to the Boston massacre in March 1770, in which five colonists were killed. This was the situation facing Lord North when he took over the government.

With tempers flaring on both sides of the Atlantic, North's room for manoeuvre was extremely limited. Even Chatham deplored the 'demon of discord' evident in New York: 'they are doing the work of their worst enemies themselves. The torrent of indignation in Parliament will, I apprehend, become irresistible.' Nevertheless, North embarked upon a policy of conciliation, offering in March 1770 to remove all the Townshend duties save the tax on tea. His initiative was overtaken by news of the Boston riots, and though the proposals were implemented, the ministry had no choice but to strengthen military and naval presence in America. In June 1772 Rhode Island colonists seized and burned the revenue cutter *Gaspée*: attempts to identify the culprits failed completely.

The measure which sent the precarious situation sliding into war was an over-ingenious device by North to help the stricken East India Company. Politically it was impossible to remove the 3*d.* tax on tea, but if the Company were allowed to export direct to the colonies, avoiding British dues, it could undercut the smugglers. It would have the further advantage that by persuading thousands of colonists to buy cheap tea, it would induce them to accept the principle of commercial regulation. The insidious attractiveness of North's proposal alarmed the militants and prompted them to a pre-emptive strike in December 1773. The Boston tea-party left forty tons of company tea floating in the harbour. Most of the British were utterly exasperated at the latest instance of American ingratitude and violence. 'The ministry appears stronger than ever', Burke warned his American correspondents, and Chatham was appalled at so 'criminal' a defiance.

Any further hesitation was ended by news in April 1774 of a repetition of the Boston outrage. Four coercive acts went through with massive majorities—to close the port of Boston, suspend the charter, arrange for the trial of British soldiers and officials elsewhere, and provide for adequate billeting. General Gage was sent back as governor, though with instructions to 'quiet the people by gentle means'. A fifth act, to settle the new territory of Canada, added to the tension. The grant of civil rights to French-Canadian Catholics brought out all the old Puritan prejudices of New England, while the extension of the boundaries south into the Ohio valley threatened to cut off the colonies from what they regarded as their natural hinterland. The king moved with the tide of British public opinion. Nothing less than the authority of Parliament was at stake. 'The die is now cast,' he wrote to North in September 1774: 'the colonies must either submit or triumph. I do not wish to come to severer measures, but we must not retreat.'

Attempts persisted on each side to avoid a showdown. A continental congress, meeting in Philadelphia in September 1774, petitioned the king for protection against designing ministers. Even if he had been sympathetic to congress, which he was not, it is hard to see how the king constitutionally could have gone against a policy overwhelmingly endorsed by Parliament. North, for his part, brought in measures to restrain the trade of New England, but accompanied them with a proposal not to exercise the right of taxation if the colonists themselves would provide for administration, justice, and defence. The suggestion was overtaken by news of the skirmish at Lexington in April 1775. It was followed two months later by the first substantial engagement at Bunker's Hill, where a thousand British casualties testified to the fierceness of the fighting.

Until then, spokesmen for the colonies had placed the blame on corrupt and tyrannical ministers. But the publication of Tom Paine's *Common Sense* in

MASSACRE AT BOSTON, 5 MARCH 1770. The massacre was rather less deliberate than this print suggests. Relations between the redcoats and the inhabitants of Boston had been strained for some time. On the evening of the 5th, an exchange of insults and some snowballing led to a small detachment being cut off. When they opened fire, five were killed and six others wounded.

January 1776 speeded up a change of mood. Paine let loose all his pent-up republican sentiments, insisting that hereditary monarchy had undermined the independence of the House of Commons and aimed at despotism at home and abroad. George III was dismissed as 'the royal brute'. The charge was repeated, though in more elegant language, in Thomas Jefferson's Declaration of Independence, published in July 1776. The reign of George III had been 'a history of repeated injuries and usurpations' and the king had shown himself 'unfit to be the ruler of a free people'. It was unfair. Every measure against the colonies had been carried in Parliament by large majorities: 'I am fighting the battle of the legislature,' declared the king in September 1775.

The outbreak of war pushed the king into an active role in government. The army was by tradition a sphere of direct royal concern. Five batallions of Hanoverian troops were hired and a considerable number from other German states. A letter to Catherine the Great in the king's own hand received a dusty answer. The raising of regiments by individual noblemen or cities also involved the king greatly. But much of his effort went into propping up his first minister. Though North was prone to bouts of despondency, he remained a valuable political asset, and his departure might open the door to the Rockinghams or Chathamites. 'You are my sheet anchor,' George wrote to him in November 1775. Even in the early years when the war was going well, North was too sensible to take pleasure in it. In 1776 New York was captured and in 1777 Philadelphia also. 'I am very melancholy,' he wrote in November 1777; 'my idea of American affairs is, that if our success is as great as the most sanguine politician wishes or believes, the best use we can make of it is to get out of the dispute as soon as

DIFFERING VIEWS ON AMERICA. In the anti-court cartoon (*above*), America is held down by Lord Sandwich and Lord Mansfield while North forces tea down her throat, Bute hovering, as always, in the background. Britannia turns away, grieving. Spain and France ponder their opportunity. (*Left*) 'News from America or the Patriots in the Dumps' depicts North flourishing news of Howe's capture of New York, while Wilkes and the opposition listen in dismay.

GIBRALTAR UNDER SIEGE, 1782. Though the entry of France and Spain into the war in 1779 tipped the scale in favour of American independence, it also imparted to the struggle a patriotic character it had previously lacked. Rodney won a great victory over a Spanish fleet off Cape St Vincent in 1780 and two years later forced De Grasse, a French admiral, to surrender in the battle of the Saints. Meanwhile, General Eliott, later ennobled as Lord Heathfield, conducted a successful resistance to a four-year siege of Gibraltar. The Spanish floating batteries, seen here in this Austrian print, were believed to be unsinkable and uninflammable. But when they were tried in September 1782 they were totally destroyed by red-hot shot with the loss of 2,000 men.

possible.' It was already too late. Burgoyne's master-stroke—a bold march from Canada down the Hudson valley to cut off New England from the other colonies—had come to grief at Saratoga in October 1777. The defeat brought in France, then Spain, and changed the whole character of the war. North's appeals to be allowed to resign became piteous. The king would not hear of it. It would mean placing him in the hands of men who would enslave the crown, men who had rejoiced in their country's misfortunes.

North survived Saratoga: he could not survive Yorktown in October 1781. It has been part of the standard indictment of George III that his obstinacy kept the war going long after its futility was apparent. That is hardly true. After Saratoga, the prospect of war with the French stiffened national resistance and recruiting ran at a high level. As late as 1781, George Washington wrote: 'we are at the end of our tether.' Even after Yorktown, the British were capable of inflicting smart defeats on their adversaries to improve their bargaining position at the peace table—the conquest of St Eustasius from the Dutch, Rodney's brilliant victory over the French at the battle of the Saints in April 1782, or the heroic defence of Gibraltar against Spanish attacks in 1782. And what eighteenth-century monarch would have watched the loss of the greater part of his empire without struggling against it to the very last minute?

At one point it looked as if the mortification would be too much for the king to bear. On 27 February a motion against the further prosecution of the war in America was carried in the Commons. The king's mind turned to his Hanoverian dominions, once despised, and he drafted a declaration of abdication in favour of his son:

His Majesty is convinced that the sudden change of sentiments of one branch of the legislature has totally incapacitated him from either conducting the war with effect or from obtaining any peace but on conditions which would prove destructive to the commerce as well as the essential rights of the British nation.

His Majesty therefore with much sorrow finds he can be of no further utility to his native country which drives him to the painful step of quitting it for ever.

It was never delivered.

George III: the Later Years

At a later period, when monarchy was less secure, defeat on such a scale might have meant the fall of the dynasty. The Hanoverian throne did not tremble for a moment. If anything, the king's stout defence of what he saw as the national interest identified him more closely with his people.

It was widely predicted that the loss of America must mean the end of national greatness. The Habsburg emperor, Joseph II, who had a gift for getting things wrong, may on this occasion be forgiven for presuming that Britain was now a second-rate power. George III himself was sure that the loss would annihilate the European position of the kingdom. Horace Walpole could see 'little or no prospect of its ever being a great nation again'. They were all wrong. Britain shook off the defeat with remarkable ease and moved into a period of stupendous industrial and commercial expansion. From 1780 to the end of the century the increase in exports was greater than in any previous period, and by 1800 was 80 per cent above the pre-war figure. The king, though greatly agitated at welcoming John Adams as American ambassador in June 1785, managed a speech that was decent and dignified:

I will be free with you. I was the last to consent to the separation; but the separation having been made and having become inevitable, I have always said, as I say now, that I would be the first to meet the friendship of the United States as an independent power.

Nevertheless, the political fall-out at Westminster from North's resignation produced a convulsion that lasted two years. Reminiscent in many ways of the

BALL AT ST JAMES's in June 1782 to celebrate the king's birthday. The Prince of Wales opens the dancing. Court etiquette remained very stiff. 'If you find a cough tickling your throat,' wrote Fanny Burney in 1785, 'you must arrest it from making any sound: if you find yourself choking with forbearance, you must choke, but not cough . . . You must not sneeze. If you have a vehement cold, you must take no notice of it . . . You must not, upon any account, stir either hand or foot. If, by chance, a black pin runs into your head, you must not take it out. If the pain is very great, you must be sure to bear it without wincing.'

turbulence of the 1760s, it tested once more many of the prerogatives of the crown—its right to intervene, to grant peerages, to choose ministers, to dissolve Parliament. At one stage in the crisis over the India Bill, it was even suggested that George should resurrect the right of veto, but use it this time against his own ministers. The outcome was to demonstrate how much strength remained in the crown, provided its powers were used with judgement and determination.

It required from North a very formal statement of constitutional proprieties before he could induce the king to allow his resignation:

Your Majesty is well apprized that in this country the Prince on the Throne cannot with prudence oppose the deliberate resolution of the House of Commons.

To the king, the opposition was both political and personal. The main group, led by Rockingham, was committed not only to independence for America but to a programme of economical reform. Brooding over their misfortunes in 1766, they had reached the conclusion that the independence of the House of Commons had

ROYAL VISIT TO THE ACADEMY, 1789. The formation of an academy of painting was much discussed in the 1750s and in 1760 an exhibition was held under the auspices of the Society for the Encouragement of the Arts. The following year the painters exhibited as the Society of Artists. In 1768 the Royal Academy was founded with Reynolds as its first president. In 1780, the king offered them rooms at old Somerset House. On this visit the king was accompanied by the Prince of Wales and several of his other children.

been undermined. Their great triumph in 1780 had been to carry a motion that the influence of the crown had increased, was increasing, and ought to be diminished. Curiously, they do not seem to have comprehended how reluctant that policy might make the crown to employ them. Few of the Rockinghams had adopted the new policy with greater enthusiasm than Charles Fox, whose debating talents had carried him during the 1770s into the front rank of the opposition. 'Provided that we can stay in long enough to deliver a good stout blow to the influence of the crown, I do not care how soon we go out,' he remarked cheerfully in the spring of 1782. The king disliked him as much as he had his father: 'odious and contemptible' was an early opinion. The feeling was mutual. Charles Fox referred to the king as a 'blockhead' and 'Satan', and on taking office in 1782 remarked: 'Certainly things look well, but he [the king] will die soon, and that will be best of all.'

Rockingham shared the premiership with Shelburne, leader of the surviving Chathamites. In opposition, their partnership had been strained: in office rifts soon appeared. The economical reform programme went through in three instalments—one to exclude government contractors from the House of Commons, another to disfranchise revenue officers, and a third, entrusted to Burke, to establish more effective control of civil list expenditure. A number of economies in the Royal Household did more to irritate the king than help the taxpayer. Burke's reform proved unworkable and the civil list was soon in substantial arrears. The crucial sources of power—the grant of peerages and the existence of rotten and pocket boroughs—were not those which the Rockinghams, an aristocratic party of borough patrons, were anxious to curb. Direct royal influence was in fact already diminishing, from long-term factors over which the Rockinghams had little control, though it remained strong enough to give a good stout blow to the Rockinghams themselves within eighteen months.

The death of Rockingham after only three months in office merely brought to a head the disagreements that had been accumulating. The king gave his support to the less offensive of the two groups and Shelburne succeeded as first minister. Fox and his friends then resigned, joined forces with North and his supporters, and turned Shelburne out on the peace preliminaries in February 1783. To the king, North's action was apostasy of the blackest kind. But with a House of Commons divided into three blocs, North could not avoid a coalition with somebody if he was not to watch his following melt away.

George III was in despair at the humiliating position to which he had now been reduced. The previous abdication draft was taken out, dusted, and refurbished. For five weeks he rang the changes on all possible alternative ministries, as well as some impossible ones. The essential difficulty was to find a politician prepared to face in the House of Commons an opposition which would include Fox, North, Burke, and Sheridan. Only the twenty-three-year-old William Pitt, son of Chatham, might have the courage and skill to do it, and twice he refused. At length the king 'to end a conflict which stops every wheel of government' gave way, though protesting that he hoped 'many months will not elapse before the Grenvilles, the Pitts and other men of abilities and character will relieve me'.

The coalition in the spring of 1783 must have appeared overwhelming. It had handsome majorities and a splendid array of administrative and debating talent. But the king's captivity lasted no more than nine months. From the beginning, George offered neither private nor public signs of confidence. In particular, by refusing to discuss peerages, he advertised in the most public fashion his disapprobation. But an effective counter-stroke depended on two things. There must be some public issue which gave him a pretext for dismissing the coalition and he must find a plausible first minister. His opportunity came with the India Bill, drawn up in the late summer of 1783.

North's Regulating Act of 1773 had not solved the problems of India, where the company was responsible for the government of at least twenty million people.

Carlo Khan's triumphal Entry into Leadenhall Street.

THE COALITION IN SEARCH OF PLUNDER. James Sayers's cartoons did considerable damage to Fox and North in their struggle against the king in 1783. Here Charles Fox as conqueror takes over the East India Company, riding a bemused North and heralded by Edmund Burke. The king used Fox's India Bill to turn out the coalition.

The Governor-General, Warren Hastings, quarrelled bitterly with his Council, which tried to have him recalled; in the Madras Presidency, the governor had been deposed and imprisoned. The financial shape of the Company was little better. Some form of government intervention was urgently needed.

The bill which Burke finally produced instituted political control through seven commissioners, appointed in the first instance by Parliament. As some protection against rapid changes of ministry at Westminster, they were to hold office for a minimum of three years. Since the commissioners named were all supporters of administration, the obvious accusation was that the coalition was concerned with patronage. But in fact the risks, of which Fox and North were perfectly aware, far outweighed any additional support the bill might provide.

The new session of Parliament opened in November 1783 with the opposition in disarray. On its second reading the bill passed with 229 votes to 120. Under normal circumstances, a defeat in the Lords was most unlikely, since the government of the day could usually command a safe majority, helped by the votes of the bishops and the Scottish representative peers. On 1 December Thurlow had an audience with the king and begged him to make known his opposition to the bill. But a more important question was whether Pitt had changed his mind since the spring and was prepared to form an alternative ministry. In secret negotiations, Pitt agreed, provided that 'the great Patriot's sentiments' were communicated to all who might be attentive to them. On 11 December, just before the second reading, the opposition sprang its mine. Lord Temple, Pitt's cousin, emerged from an audience with the king authorized to say that anyone voting for the bill was not only not the king's friend, but would be considered an enemy. The bill went down by nineteen votes. The following night, Fox and North received notes dismissing them.

Neither Pitt nor his supporters ever attempted to defend the king's action: they pretended it was baseless rumour. Though the use of the king's influence to support his ministers was not unusual, its use against them struck at the heart of ministerial responsibility. Carried to its logical conclusion, it implied an end to the balanced constitution, and a return to absolute, even whimsical, government. Burke, always ready to believe the worst, was convinced that there was a 'settled plan' to destroy the independence of the House of Commons. That was untrue. It was the desperate act of a monarch who confessed that he felt himself very near the precipice. There was no scheme of royal aggrandisement. Nevertheless, the situation was extremely tense. French observers believed that the country was on the brink of revolution and that Fox would be king. Even a sober lawyer such as Lord Camden saw it as 'little less than a declaration of open war between the king and his servants'.

Pitt's fledgeling ministry had three weeks over Christmas to prepare to face Parliament. The king's total commitment to the new ministers was signalled by

GEORGE III

(1760–1820)

I do not pretend to any superior abilities, but will give place to no one in meaning to preserve the freedom, happiness and glory of my dominions and all their inhabitants, and to fulfill the duty to my God and my neighbour in the most extended sense.

EORGE III has attracted more strictures than almost any other ruler in modern times. He was unlucky to fall foul of two sharp critics, Horace Walpole, who maintained that there was a settled plan in 1760 to reassert royal authority, and Edmund Burke, whose *Thoughts on the cause of the Present Discontents* in 1770 insisted that a secret cabal planned to undermine ministerial responsibility. Junius and Lord Shelburne, the latter of whom had been something of a royal favourite in 1782, agreed that the king was a hypocrite and a dissembler. George was also denounced by nineteenth-century liberal historians, who held him responsible for the loss of America and deplored his lifelong resistance to Catholic Emancipation. Lecky described him as 'a sovereign of whom it may be said without exaggeration that he inflicted more profound and enduring injuries upon his country than any other modern English King', while Sir George Otto Trevelyan declared, magisterially, that George 'invariably declared himself upon the wrong side in a controversy'.

Contemporary historians are less certain that there was a right or wrong side to controversies and little of these charges remain. George's view of the beauty of the Hanoverian constitution was a conventional one, and if he allotted the crown a prominent role in its operations, so did most of his subjects. The difficulties of his early years as monarch were less the result of political ambition than his adolescent dependence upon Lord Bute. His besetting sin was not lust for power but a certain censoriousness: 'he has rather too much attention to the sins of his neighbours', wrote Lord Waldegrave in a penetrating analysis before George came to the throne. Far from being an insincere politician, he was perhaps not subtle enough, and never learned to give way with much grace. Nor is it surprising that the third ruler of a family brought in expressly to defend the Protestant constitution in Church and State should have great doubts whether Catholic Emancipation would not destroy that constitution.

his willingness once more to grant peerages, the first going within the week to Pitt's cousin, Thomas. 'They are crying peerages about the streets in barrows,' wrote Horace Walpole with pardonable exaggeration. Nobody could be sure to what extent all the activity behind the scenes had succeeded in whittling down the coalition's majority in the Commons.

On the first major division in January 1784 Fox won by fifty-four votes. That was indecisive. He used his majority to try to block any sudden dissolution of

Parliament, but in the course of the next eight weeks the coalition's support slid until, on 8 March, it stood at one. The king dissolved. At the subsequent general election, the electorate's detestation of the coalition and endorsement of the king's actions was overwhelming. Pitt returned as first minister, to hold that office for another seventeen years: Fox came back to spend all but the last six months of his life on the opposition benches.

The crisis pointed in different directions. It had confirmed how potent was the magic of peerages, how critical the king's power to choose and dismiss ministers. To that extent it underlined that royal power was still a reality. But it had also emphasized the need for a minister who could command the House of Commons. Throughout 1783, most politicians recognized that Pitt held the key to the situation. Had he been tempted into joining the coalition, as Fox hoped in the autumn of 1783, there would have been no alternative government and the king would have been helpless. A historiographical controversy arose whether Pitt was more dependent upon the king or the king on Pitt. It is somewhat arid. In the balanced constitution of Hanoverian England, they depended on each other. Pitt could see what the absence of the king's confidence had cost the coalition: the king never forgot that, without Pitt, he was back to the tender mercies of Charles Fox.

At the time of his marriage, George III had purchased the Queen's House, on the site of the present Buckingham Palace, and it was adapted as well as possible for his growing family. St James's Palace was used mainly for ceremonial occasions. But the king did not much like London—'I am never a volunteer there,' he remarked in 1785. For a country residence, he at first used Kew, which his mother had leased, and which he purchased in 1782. But gradually he became fond of Windsor, and it was his favourite residence in the later years of his life. His informal excursions into the park were well known, and hundreds of his subjects were either terrified or enchanted by casual meetings, in which George, no doubt to cover shyness, shot questions at them with gatling rapidity.

The private enjoyments of the king were hunting and card-playing, though he visited the theatre, enjoyed music, and built up a fine library. Engulfed in the preoccupations of a large family and the demanding ceremonial of court life, he had little time or taste for travel. Queen Charlotte never revisited her native land, and George neither visited his Hanoverian Electorate nor crossed the Channel. Scotland, Ireland, and Wales were unknown to him. Even in England, journeys were confined to the southern counties. He never witnessed the great industrial developments in the midlands and the north during his reign. The most hazardous of journeys was the annual seaside holiday at Weymouth during the 1790s. Romantic scenery passed him by: he was not fond, he admitted, of mountains or 'the wild beauties of nature'. It is strange that a king of England, in

ROYAL WALKABOUT SPREADING TERROR (*left*). George III was famous for his indefatigable interest in things and his habit of shooting abrupt, staccato questions at people, accompanied by Eh? Eh? Here, as Farmer George at Windsor, he has reduced one of his farm-workers to gibbering fright.

MORE DECOROUSLY (*below*). A representation of the entire royal family promenading at Windsor. Onlookers were expected to bow respectfully and back away.

a reign of sixty years, never saw the cathedrals of Norwich or Lincoln, York or Durham, nor visited the universities of Oxford and Cambridge.

But even if the king was seen by only a tiny proportion of his subjects, there were constant reminders of his authority. His image was on the coins of the realm and, when postage stamps were introduced, on them too. In the weekly sermon, the parson often dwelt on the need for obedience to the powers that be, a message reinforced on the grand scale at regular Assize sermons. Office-holders

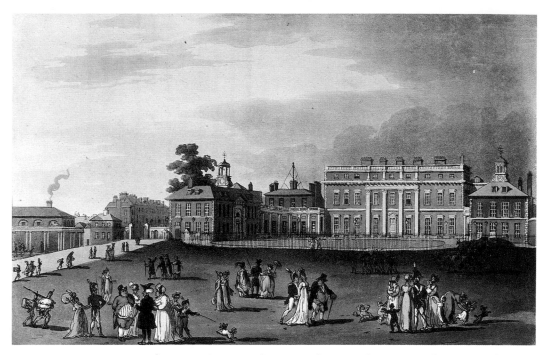

BUCKINGHAM PALACE was known in George III's reign as the Queen's House. In this view in the 1800s it was still of moderate size and in rural surroundings. It was extensively enlarged by George IV in the 1820s and given its present appearance during the Edwardian period.

were required to take an oath to uphold royal authority. Justice was administered in the king's name and the roads referred to as the king's highways. The national anthem, popularized after the Jacobite rebellion of 1745, was orientated towards the king rather than the nation itself. Societies vied with each other for royal patronage, and, on a humbler level, tavern signs depicted the King's Head, the Crown, or the George. Sylas Neville, one of the few republicans left in the 1770s, was disgusted at having to put up at the Royal Oak.

By 1784 the king's family was complete and growing up. The eldest of seven sons, George, Prince of Wales was twenty-two years of age: the Princess Royal was eighteen and had six sisters, of whom the youngest, Amelia, was a baby. George and Charlotte were fortunate enough to lose only two of their children, Prince Alfred, who died at two in 1782, and Prince Octavius, who died at the age of four, in 1783, to his father's great grief. The royal family was regular in worship and sober in tone. The king's hunt after princesses in 1761 had produced an ideal partner: Charlotte suited him well and he was devoted to her. She had little interest in politics, but was fond of music and literature. The Prince of Wales was already a cause of deep anxiety to his parents. Bright, but hopelessly self-indulgent, he took naturally to fast life. By the time he was eighteen, public scandal was narrowly avoided when his mistress, 'Perdita' Robinson the actress, threatened to publish their letters. The king gloomily paid £5,000 to recover them, adding, unnecessarily, 'I am happy to say that I never was personally engaged in such a transaction.' When the prince's attention turned to politics, he was inexorably attracted to Fox and his set. Fox's attempt in June 1783 to obtain an allowance of £100,000 p.a. for the prince almost overturned the coalition ministry before it had time to consider India. 'Indignation and astonishment' was the king's reaction to the proposal. He deplored 'a shameful squandering of public money', and taxed the prince with 'want of even common civility to the Queen and me . . . and total disobedience of every injunction I had given'. The prince had to be content with £50,000 p.a., with another £60,000 to pay off his debts. He took his seat in the House of Lords in November 1783 in time to cast his first vote for the India Bill on its first reading.

But the prince was merely warming to his task. He spent lavishly on his new establishment at Carlton House and by the end of 1784 had run up another £150,000 of debt. Having got out of several more amatory scrapes, he fell madly in love with a widow, Maria Fitzherbert, a Catholic. When she fled to Holland, the prince was in agony, declaring that he would elope with his beloved to America. Fox warned him against any plan of marriage, and the prince agreed: then in December 1785 he went through a secret ceremony, conducted by a parson released from the Fleet prison and promised a bishopric in the next reign. He thereby forfeited his succession to the throne twice over—once under the terms of the Royal Marriages Act and a second time under the Act of Settlement which forbade marriage to a Catholic. Meanwhile, to ensure that his debts

IN HIS EARLY FORTIES, the Prince of Wales retained much of his youthful good looks. He is still part of the younger generation who had abandoned wigs in favour of their own hair. Henry Bone, appointed painter to the prince in 1800, specialized in enamel work.

THE ROYAL LIBRARY

The King's [George III's] library struck me with admiration. I wished for a week's time, but had but a few hours. The books were in perfect order, elegant in their editions, paper, binding, etc., but gaudy and extravagant in nothing. They were chosen with perfect taste and judgment: every book that a King ought to have always at hand.

(John Adams, first American ambassador to the Court of St James, 1783)

MOST monarchs collected or inherited books, but it was only in Edward IV's reign that a permanent royal library was created which has been in continuous existence ever since. Predominantly religious in character before the age of printing, with histories, romances, and books of instruction added in the later Middle Ages, many medieval acquisitions were beautifully illuminated. Under Burgundian and French influence, Edward IV and Henry VII extended their collections of illuminated manuscripts, and Henry appointed the first known keeper of the library, which he installed at Richmond. Henry VIII built up a second library at Whitehall and augmented it with manuscripts from monastic libraries. Although James VI and I left his library in Scotland in 1603, he developed the English royal library at St James's Palace. Having survived the Commonwealth (when it was hoped to turn it into a public library), the collection was partly destroyed when Whitehall Palace was burned (1698); it was restored when Sir Robert Cotton bequeathed (1703) his books and manuscripts to it. George II made a munificent gift of the manuscripts ('the Royal Manuscripts') to the new British Museum (1757). His grandson, George III, was England's greatest bibliophile and virtually started a new royal collection: his interests extended to music and botany as well as traditional subjects, and among his purchases were the Thomason Tracts relating to the Civil War. His library at Buckingham House was open to scholars, and more than 65,000 of his books and manuscripts ('the King's Manuscripts') were donated to the British Museum by his son, George IV. Victoria and Albert, both compulsive writers themselves, formed their own library at Windsor; this now includes the royal archives in the Library, which is open to scholars.

ROYAL LIBRARY, WINDSOR CASTLE. The library at Windsor was originally a gallery which Queen Elizabeth had made so that she could get exercise indoors in bad weather. The magnificent stone chimney-piece to the right is original: the plaster ceiling is a copy made during restoration in 1831.

FILIAL PIETY. The Prince of Wales led a dissolute and extravagant life and his support for Fox and the Whig opposition did nothing to help relations with his father. In this Rowlandson print of November 1788, the prince, accompanied by his cronies Sheridan and Hanger, bursts into the king's sick-room, shouting 'Damme, come along . . . I'll see if the Old Fellow's——or not.' A scandalized bishop is interrupted reading prayers for recovery. The picture of 'The Prodigal Son' on the wall holds out hope of a reformation.

remained adequate, the prince commenced building a massive pavilion at Brighton. In 1787 a meeting of his Whig friends agreed to approach Parliament for financial assistance. He assured Fox that the rumours of a secret marriage were false, and when Fox passed on the assurance to the House of Commons, begged Grey to modify the impression. Grey refused. Parliament was then persuaded to increase his annual allowance, find £161,000 to pay off debt, and advance £20,000 to complete Carlton House.

The closing stages of the American war and the political troubles that followed it, coupled with great anxiety over the conduct of the Prince of Wales and his brothers, placed great strain on the king in the 1780s. In the summer of 1788, he suffered several days of abdominal pain, and spent five weeks at Cheltenham recuperating. But on his return to Windsor, he became worse, talking incessantly, fidgeting awkwardly at concerts, his pulse racing. Early in November, his physicians reported 'entire alienation of mind': he believed he could see Hanover through a telescope, was saving London from floods, and at times his attendants

GEORGE III AND QUEEN CHARLOTTE. In 1807, at the time of these portraits by Peter Edward Stroehling, George and Charlotte had been married forty-six years. For most of that time, their relations had been very close and in 1779 Mrs Delany wrote that they seemed to have but one mind. Charlotte wrote sedately: 'my taste is for a few select friends whose cheerfulness of temper and instructive

reported indecent conversation. By December he was in a strait-jacket, with the doctors at violent odds about the chances of a recovery.

The political consequences were serious. If the king continued unable to perform public duties, the Prince of Wales must be made Regent, and it was presumed that he would at once dismiss Pitt to bring in his Whig friends. Lists of future appointments were circulated and printed. When Parliament met in December, Pitt's tactics had to be to protract discussions on the Regent's power to appoint to office or grant peerages: Fox, in a strange but understandable reversal of attitude, argued for full sovereign powers. But by the middle of

conversation will pass the time away without leaving any remorse for what is passed.' But she was clearly terrified during the king's illness of 1804 by his violence and passion, and subsequently refused to be alone with him. It was sad, wrote Lord Hobart, 'to see a family that had lived so well together for such a number of years completely broken up'.

February, the king was clearly recovering, the bill was abandoned, and the Foxites settled back into their accustomed opposition benches.

In the nineteenth century, it was presumed that the king's illness was lunacy. With the arrival of Freudian analysis, other historians considered it as a severe case of sexual repression. In recent years, the illness has been identified as porphyria, a hereditary disease of the blood, which produces many of the symptoms from which the king suffered. But the haphazardness of the incidence of porphyria seems almost as mysterious as the condition it is designed to explain.

The illness left the king weak and exhausted. To Pitt he wrote that, for the rest of his life, he would 'only keep that superintending eye which can be effected without labour or fatigue'. But even in an older and feebler George III, the 'superintending eye' could be gimlet-like. Within a fortnight of his recovery, he was reminding Pitt to see to the transfer of the dean of Gloucester to St Asaph, and to make the necessary arrangements when the Clerk of the Works at Hampton Court should die. Nor did European developments encourage a life of ease. While George was confined, elections to the French États–généraux had been taking place, and the French slide into revolution gathered pace in the summer of 1789 while the king was recuperating at Weymouth, amid fervent demonstrations of loyalty. By 1793, the two countries were at war, and the following year Portland and the conservative Whigs joined Pitt's administration, leaving Fox to lead a small rump in hopeless opposition.

Neither royal illness nor French Revolution could check the Prince of Wales's round of pleasure. By 1794 his debts were more than £500,000. In desperation, the prince abandoned Mrs Fitzherbert and proposed marriage to his cousin, Princess Caroline of Brunswick. The prince's reception of his bride did not quite match up to his pretensions to civility and elegance: 'I feel faint, a glass of brandy if you please,' was his reported speech. There was an awkward moment in the ceremony when the archbishop paused significantly at the question 'any lawful impediment'. But it was an inspired choice and the prince and his wife tormented each other for the next twenty-five years. In the short term, the marriage served its purpose. Parliament, with painful reluctance, increased his allowance once more, though so much had to be set aside for redemption of debt that the prince had less ready cash than before. The king, in his pious way, had hoped for 'numerous progeny': the princess was delivered of a daughter nine months after the wedding. Five months after that, the prince was complaining of his wife's 'personal nastiness', referred to her as a 'vile wretch', demanded a formal separation, and drafted a will leaving all his possessions (largely debts) to his 'true wife' Mrs Fitzherbert, and but a shilling to Princess Caroline.

The long war with revolutionary France drew attention once more to the state of Ireland, and the political complications arising from it dominated the remaining years of the king's active life. During the American War of Independence, the Irish had raised volunteer forces to defend the country against the French. This had not proved necessary but the volunteers found a use against the English. In 1782 the Rockinghams were forced to concede Irish legislative independence. Another concession in 1793 gave the vote to Irish Catholics. Further the king was not prepared to go, believing that Catholic Emancipation must lead to the separation of the two kingdoms, and that his coronation oath to uphold the Protestant constitution in Church and State could not be broken. But in 1798 a massive Irish rebellion accompanied by a French invasion persuaded Pitt that security demanded a union of the two kingdoms. Catholic Emancipation

HEROES. Wellington was forty-six at Waterloo, Nelson forty-seven at Trafalgar. Their fates were strangely different. Nelson died in the hour of victory, leaving his country to shower honours on his brother. Wellington lived another thirty-seven years to enjoy his ducal rank and to play an important political role, first as prime minister, then as elder statesman. In their one chance meeting, in Lord Castlereagh's ante-room in September 1805, Wellington was not at first impressed: 'he entered at once into conversation with me, if I can call it conversation, for it was almost all on his side, and all about himself, and, really, in a style so vain and silly as to surprise and almost disgust me.' But as soon as Nelson discovered that Wellington was *somebody*, the conversation changed: 'all that I thought a charlatan style had vanished . . . He talked like an officer and a statesman. . . . I don't know that I ever had a conversation that interested me more.' A month later, Nelson was dead.

was to be the price of Irish consent. The union went through, but when, early in 1801, Pitt moved to introduce Catholic Emancipation, the king repeated his formula of 1783, that any man who voted for it would be his enemy. Pitt resigned, though remaining on good terms with the king. The episode coincided with, and may have contributed to, a second severe attack of illness, in the course of which the doctors despaired of the king's life. It was of shorter duration than that of 1788, but even after the king had resumed his formal duties, he was forced to spend a month in isolation and under medical supervision. Only a threat by George to sign no more documents brought about his release.

Superficially the 1801 intervention repeated that of 1783. In fact there were important differences which must mitigate censure of the king on the second occasion. It is clear that Pitt had not discussed Catholic Emancipation with the king in advance and several of the other ministers had great misgivings on the subject. Pitt may even, after seventeen years in office, have been not unwilling to resign. But, above all, the king was entitled to regard his coronation oath as something not to be taken lightly, and so fundamental a change in the constitution as a matter on which the monarch's opinions must be taken into account. His intervention was not intended to blow up the ministry and he made strenuous efforts to persuade Pitt not to go, but to prevent the legislation.

Pitt was replaced by Addington, who negotiated with the French the short-lived peace of Amiens. In 1803 war was resumed and George drew up plans, in the event of a French invasion, to place himself at the head of his troops, sending the queen and princesses to Worcester. He suffered a third attack early in 1804, which necessitated recourse once more to a strait-jacket, and though the attack was much shorter than the previous ones, he was slow to recover from it. Though capable of exerting himself on public business, he was tired and difficult with his family. To add to his miseries, his eyesight was rapidly failing. With the queen, his relations were now purely formal. His violent paroxysms had clearly terrified her and she refused to allow him to sleep in her bedchamber. She too became irritable and the royal princesses, in what they called their nunnery, led a tedious and dispiriting existence.

The resumption of war meant the recall of Pitt as soon as he was ready. He made a somewhat half-hearted attempt to bring Fox into a government of national unity, but the king would not hear of it. But on Pitt's death in January 1806, Fox came in as Foreign Secretary in the Ministry of All the Talents under Grenville, son of the George Grenville who had harangued the king in the 1760s. The king greeted Fox easily: they should bury the past. Within six months Fox was dead. In February 1807 the ministers put forward a proposal to allow Catholics to hold commissions in the army and navy. Though they withdrew the measure when the king expressed his disapproval, he insisted on an assurance that they would recommend no further concessions to the Catholics. They refused and George called on Portland to form a ministry. Two years later, when Perceval succeeded Portland, the king sought similar assurances but was satisfied by a general disavowal. Deeply devoted to the Church of England all his life, the king protected its privileged position to the end of his days, even at the cost of pushing his constitutional rights to their limit.

In 1810, at the age of seventy-two, the king suffered his final attack. It began, like the others, with hasty and incoherent conversation, and soon degenerated into violence. After three months a Regency Bill was passed and was given the royal assent by the Lord Chancellor. The king's person was to be the responsibility of the queen, with a small council to advise her. At first he had lucid moments but would then lapse into plans to escape to Denmark and avoid the flood, or assertions that he was secretly married to Lady Pembroke. He claimed to be able to summon the dead and engage them in conversation: 'in short', reported the physicians, 'he appears to be living in another world, and has lost almost all interest in the concerns of this.'

For nine years, until January 1820, the agony continued. Napoleon occupied

Moscow, escaped from Elba, fought at Waterloo, was dispatched to St Helena. It meant nothing. In 1818 the Queen died and was succeeded as guardian by the duke of York. Sightless and increasingly deaf, the king roamed his rooms at Windsor in an old violet dressing-gown, his beard down to his chest. Hour after hour he smashed out airs on the battered harpsichord that had once belonged to Handel. Sometimes he would pause and explain to his attendants that it was a favourite piece of the late king, when he was alive.

'AND, TO DEAL PLAINLY, I FEAR I AM NOT IN MY PERFECT MIND.' After serious bouts of illness in 1789 and again in 1801, George III became permanently deranged in 1810. He was confined in the custody of Queen Charlotte and, on her death in 1818, in that of the duke of York. He spent his time at Windsor, blind and deaf, increasingly cut off from the world. This portrait sees him as Lear.

6. POPULAR MONARCHY
1820–1988

The Decline of Royal Power: George IV and William IV

In the nineteenth and twentieth centuries, the monarchy has accommodated itself to the transition from an aristocratic to a liberal, and thence to a democratic society. In the process, it moved from sharing government to a share in government, and ultimately to a largely advisory role. There is no neat phrase which will describe this transformation. 'Democratic monarchy' would exaggerate the speed of change: Victoria, as we shall see, was adamant that she would never be the queen of a democracy. 'Titular monarchy' would exaggerate the completeness of the loss of royal power: the monarch retains certain reserve powers which could still prove of importance. The least misleading term may be 'popular monarchy', not in the sense that the monarchy has always been popular—at times it went through periods of considerable unpopularity—but that it compensated increasingly for the loss of formal political power by adopting a less remote attitude, by appealing to a wider range of its subjects, and by concerning itself greatly with its public image. Perhaps the crucial change came, significantly, at a moment of acute danger during the Great War, the storm that swept away so many of the old dynasties of Europe, when George V changed the name of the family to Windsor, in an effort to identify more closely with the nation and its history.

Since the change from the early Hanoverian monarchy was effected neither by revolution, nor, for the most part by legislation, it is impossible to date it with exactitude. But the convergence in the early nineteenth century of a number of general factors reduced the power of the crown substantially.

One of the first of these was the increased power of the prime minister. In the early eighteenth century there was reluctance to accept the need for a first minister at all, and it was a charge against Sir Robert Walpole that he aspired to that position. In time of war the need for such a position was more apparent, and since warfare occupied a large part of the century, the office grew. Chatham was accepted as a directing or co-ordinating minister during the Seven Years War. The absence of an equivalent during the American War worried Lord North, who told the king in 1778:

Your Majesty's service requires a man of great abilities, and who is confident of his abilities, who can choose decisively, and carry his determinations authoritatively into execution. Such should be the character of your ruling minister.

In 1803, during another war, Pitt put the same argument even more forcibly:

There should be an avowed and real minister possessing the chief weight in council and the principal place in the confidence of the King. In that respect there can be no rivalry or division of power. That power must rest with the person generally called the First Minister; and that minister ought, he thinks, to be the person at the head of the finances.

But one of the first objectives of such a minister would, as Pitt went on to say, be to have in the cabinet only persons acceptable to him. What then would happen to the king's right to choose ministers? And if the first minister was, as increasingly happened, also the leader of the largest party in the legislature, what room for manœuvre was left to the king?

Other factors were social and economic. Between the Glorious Revolution and 1810, England had changed profoundly. The population had doubled. In 1688 the provincial centres were still towns of five or six thousand inhabitants: by 1810 Manchester and Birmingham had nearly 90,000 people, Glasgow and Liverpool more than 100,000.

One consequence of the enormous increase in both population and prosperity was a vast expansion of informed public opinion. The political nation of Pope's day was small and aristocratic and his satires catered to their taste. One hundred years later, thousands of the middle and professional classes took an interest in politics, and more and more of the working classes. In 1700 there was no London newspaper, nor any provincial newspapers. At the accession of George III, there were four London papers and at least thirty-five provincial ones. In 1793 there were thirteen London dailies, and by 1836 there were said to be 135 papers printed outside London. While early Hanoverian newspapers sold in hundreds, Cobbett's *Political Register* in 1816 claimed 44,000 for each edition. Political

A CHANGING SOCIETY. George III's reign from 1760 to 1820 saw the beginning of that transformation of England from a country of villages and cathedral and market towns to one of great industrial cities. Birmingham had a population of 35,000 in 1760 and more than 100,000 sixty years later. Turnpikes and canals changed the pace of transport. The iron foundry established at Cyfarthfa in 1765 was producing 4,000 tons a year by the time of this picture in 1795. Merthyr Tydfil, the centre of the Welsh iron industry, grew at a remarkable speed and by 1831 outnumbered Swansea, Cardiff, and Newport together.

comment which in the earlier period, unlike caricature, had been restrained, was outspoken to the point of offence. In 1812 the *Examiner*, provoked by a description of the Prince Regent as 'an Adonis of loveliness', offered a rival portrait:

This delightful, blissful, wise, pleasurable, virtuous, true and immortal prince, is a violator of his word, a libertine over head and heels in debt and disgrace, a despiser of domestic ties, the companion of gamblers and demireps, a man who has just closed half a century without one single claim on the gratitude of his country or the respect of posterity.

Increased political participation also showed itself in the growth of petitioning. After the Restoration, the right to petition had been severely limited. In the early years of George III's reign, a campaign of twenty or thirty petitions was regarded as impressive. Economical reform attracted thirty-eight petitions in 1780. But nineteenth-century petitioning was on a completely different scale. The repeal of the Test and Corporation Acts produced 5,000 petitions, and Catholic Emancipation in 1828 was said to have led to 28,000. Some of them claimed 80,000 signatures. Here was a vast awakening force, which a shrewd monarch would treat with some caution.

Two other factors also helped to diminish royal power. Though the economical campaign of the Rockinghams in the 1780s did not do much damage, it was followed by a persistent crusade by Pitt and subsequent ministers against pensions, places, and perquisities. The patronage at the disposal of the crown, which had traditionally been used to construct parliamentary majorities, was substantially eroded, and though party loyalty went some way to compensating as an attractive influence, obligation was felt more towards the party leadership than to the monarch.

The reduction in patronage bit deeper because it was accompanied by a slow deterioration in the crown's financial position. In 1714 George I had been granted a basic civil list provision of £700,000. Walpole's deal with George II in 1727 substituted the full hereditary revenues, which were based upon the customs and the post-office, and therefore expanded with trade. Frederick, Prince of Wales, in 1747, had accepted the need for a fixed revenue and his son, George III, again influenced by his father's wishes, settled for £800,000. It was never adequate, and by 1769 there was accumulated debt of more than £500,000. In 1777 Parliament raised the fixed revenue to £900,000. It remained insufficient, and every application to Parliament gave opportunities for disagreeable innuendoes and demands for more rigorous accounting. 'Is there no feeling for the suffering of this impoverished country?' demanded Wilkes, of all people, in 1777.

The second factor was the growth in the volume and complexity of public business. The most obvious indication of this was that legislation, hardly a trickle in early Hanoverian days, became a steady stream and then a flood. Much of the new business of government, particularly in financial and economic matters, was of a technical nature. In the Commons, the gentleman politician whose attendance might be only intermittent, slowly made way for the full-time professional. The problem for the monarch was similar. Effective exercise of power depended on a thorough mastery of detailed proposals, which it was hard for even the most conscientious ruler to achieve.

The assumption of power by the Prince Regent in 1811 was a critical moment for the British monarchy. In the previous twenty years there had, for the first time, been manifestations of reviving republicanism, derived mainly from the French Revolution. Monarchy and aristocracy, declared Paine in *The Rights of Man*, would not last another seven years. Hereditary kingship was a mere burlesque, a contradiction in terms. The crown, observed Paine, signified a nominal office of a million sterling a year, 'the business of which consists in receiving the money'. George III's infirmities were not spared—'even the physicians' bills have been sent to the public to be paid'. Paine's broadside was followed up in 1793 by William Godwin's *Enquiry concerning Political Justice*, which had a remarkable, if ephemeral, success, and condemned all kings as would-be despots. The protracted warfare against first revolutionary, then Napoleonic France produced heavy taxation and widespread distress on which resentment could build.

At this inauspicious time, the popularity of the royal family was at a low ebb. The homely virtues of the old king were much admired and his descent into helplessness was regarded with pity. But dislike for the Regent was widespread. His total inability to live within his income at a time of national hardship, his gross and gaudy figure, his shallow insincerities made him the butt of cartoonists and caricaturists. In 1796 the *True Briton* wrote: 'we have long looked upon his conduct as favouring the cause of Jacobinism and democracy in this country more than all the speeches of Horne Tooke.' The support demonstrated for his wife, the Princess Caroline, was less because of her virtues than because it was the easiest way of annoying the Regent. Nor were his brothers much better. In 1809 there had been a parliamentary enquiry into accusations that Mrs Clarke, mistress of the duke of York, commander-in-chief, had accepted bribes to procure commissions in the army. The duke was forced to resign. In 1810 there was an appalling incident in which the duke of Cumberland was found in bed covered in blood, while his valet had had his throat cut. Though a jury determined that the valet, after attempting to murder the duke in a frenzy, had taken his own life, others insinuated that the duke had been the aggressor and that his injuries had been caused by his valet's resistance.

As far as health and cool judgement went, the Regent did not seem, at times, much of an improvement upon his father. Drink and laudanum in large doses was a heinous mixture. In November 1811 he was very ill and rumours were rife that his mind was gone. 'What will become of us,' wrote one agitated subject, 'if as well as our King our Regent goes mad.' A more relaxed observer thought that the obvious solution was to recall the king as sub-Regent. His first political problem was whether to dismiss the ministers and bring his old Whig friends into office. The Regent demurred. At first it was presumed that he hesitated lest the king recover: then because he was still restricted in his powers. When, in 1812, the restrictions were removed and no offer came to the Whigs that they could accept, their rage was unbounded. The change of attitude was by some attributed to the Regent's current mistress, Lady Hertford, and Grey complained yet again of unseen influences at work behind the scenes. 'A madman, doomed from his personal character alone, to shake the throne,' was Creevey's opinion. Spencer Perceval continued in office and on his assassination later in the year, was succeeded by Lord Liverpool, whose long administration saw the country through to the end of the war with France.

Though the twenty-year struggle against revolutionary France caused severe hardship, it helped to unite the nation by giving it a distinctive role and a sense of purpose. Those Whigs who had opposed the early resistance to the Directory fell silent as the full extent of Napoleon's egotistical ambition became apparent. There was little to rejoice at in the opening campaigns, but first Trafalgar, then the Spanish successes and, finally, Waterloo, gave Britons pride in their arms and institutions. Generations of schoolboys were brought up on Gillray's famous cartoon 'The Plumb Pudding in danger' which showed Pitt and Napoleon dividing the world, Napoleon seizing western Europe while Pitt quietly appropriated the rest. The great commanders on land and sea, Wellington and Nelson, became the best known of national heroes, and the establishment moved fast to enlist their glory in its service by bringing them into the peerage. George III had misgivings about a title for Nelson on the grounds that he had insufficient property: it was, he wrote, 'out of the question'. But Pitt insisted, and a grateful nation endowed Trafalgar house in Wiltshire and, for Wellington, Stratfield Saye, near Basingstoke.

Despite the efforts of George III and Queen Charlotte to secure the succession by producing fifteen children, by January 1815 the royal line was distinctly precarious. The Prince Regent's unlucky marriage had produced one daughter, Charlotte, who was then nineteen. There was no other direct lawful issue at all. The duke of York, married to the Princess Royal of Prussia, had no children and, as George III remarked, they lavished their affection on their dogs. William, duke of Clarence, had no less than ten children, but had omitted to marry their mother, Mrs Jordan, the actress. The duke of Sussex had made an invalid marriage in 1793. The other three dukes, Kent, Cumberland, and Cambridge, were as yet unmarried, though the youngest of them was over forty. Of George III's daughters, Princess Amelia had died in 1810. Augusta, Elizabeth, Maria, and Sophia were still unmarried, and lived a tedious life under the reproachful eye of Queen Charlotte. The Princess Royal was married to Frederick of Württemberg, but had no children.

The marriage of Princess Charlotte was therefore a matter of some urgency, and there was an additional reason in that she showed distressing signs of developing rather like her mother. The first suggestion was that she should marry the prince of Orange, whom she rejected. But in May 1816, she was married to Leopold of Saxe-Coburg. In November 1817 she died in childbirth, having had a stillborn child.

In the meantime, the duke of Cumberland had married but had no children. In the course of 1818 there developed an extraordinary rush to the altar by the remaining unmarried royal dukes. Financial advantage vied with duty to their country. First to engage was the duke of Cambridge, in May 1818, to whom a son was born in March 1819. But his ace could still be trumped by his elder brothers. In July 1818, having broken with their respective mistresses, the dukes of

SHAKESPEARE AND THE MONARCHY

'Was there ever such stuff as a great part of Shakespeare,' confided George III nervously to Fanny Burney, 'only one must not say so! What? What?' A vast number of his subjects must have owed whatever knowledge they possessed of the monarchy and its vicissitudes to Shakespeare's history plays. Especially compelling was his portrayal of English regal and political history from Richard II's decline and fall (1397–9) to Henry Tudor's victory (1485). Like most dramatists, Shakespeare sometimes allowed himself considerable liberty with historical accuracy: though Prince Hal and Hotspur are represented in *Henry IV*, part 1, as rivals and contemporaries, they were in fact sixteen and thirty-nine respectively at the time of the battle of Shrewsbury; Queen Margaret, widow of Henry VI, appears in *Richard III*, though she was already dead. The attitude towards monarchy which Shakespeare adopts is, for the most part, respectful, if not adulatory, with an emphasis on order and hierarchy (*Troilus and Cressida*), on the sacred nature of kingship (*Hamlet, Richard II*), on the responsibility which monarchs bear (*Henry V*), and on the fickle behaviour of the masses (*Coriolanus, Julius Caesar, Henry VI*, part 2). In *Henry VIII*, first performed in 1613, he allowed Cranmer, with uncanny prescience, to forecast that when the infant Princess Elizabeth comes to reign, 'every man shall eat in safety under his own vine what he plants' and that she would die a virgin. Cranmer was prudently allowed to add that Elizabeth's successor would be yet another mighty monarch, 'the greatness of whose name shall make new nations'. But Shakespeare permitted a counter-theme to emerge at times. Monarchs are not infrequently portrayed as villains (*King John, Richard III, MacBeth*) and Michael Williams in *Henry V* is given a remarkable speech on the king's responsibilities:

But if the cause be not good, the king himself hath a heavy reckoning to make; when all those legs and arms and heads, chopped off in a battle, shall join together at the latter day and cry all 'We died at such a place.'

EDMUND KEAN AS RICHARD III IN 1814

Clarence and Kent were married at a double ceremony at Kew. The Clarence marriage remained childless. The Kent marriage, to Victoria of Saxe-Coburg, Leopold's sister, produced in May 1819 the Princess Victoria, born in Kensington Palace.

In January 1820 the old king died at last and the Prince Regent became George IV. One of the earliest and least agreeable consequences was the

CAROLINE OF BRUNSWICK was niece to George III and first cousin to George, Prince of Wales, whom she married in March 1795. According to her own testimony, their marital relationship was confined to one night, and since their daughter Charlotte was born on 7 January 1796, this was probably true.

reappearance of a figure from the past, his wife Princess Caroline, returned from abroad to claim her rightful place at his side as queen of England. After her brief spell of married bliss, she had led a frenetic and colourful existence. In 1806 rumours that she had given birth to an illegitimate child led to the 'delicate investigation', conducted by four members of the House of Lords. She was cleared of the accusation though the evidence of her way of life was lurid. In 1814, to the Regent's great relief, she left for a protracted stay on the Continent, finishing up in Italy in the company of a handsome Italian, Bartholomew Bergami, whose relatives made up the greater part of her court. In June 1820, rejecting the offer of £50,000 p.a. to stay away and not press her claim to the title, she landed at Dover. The public greeted her with tempestuous enthusiasm and she much enjoyed her role of an injured woman: her supporters were able to rehearse the catalogue of the king's infidelities. George IV insisted that Liverpool introduce a bill into the House of Lords to deprive her of her rank and declare the marriage dissolved. The evidence was derived from a secret commission, dispatched to Italy in 1818, and made it clear that if she were not an adulteress, she had taken unusual pains to appear so. Her supporters, to spite the king,

CAROLINE'S REVENGE. In Robert Cruikshank's cartoon of February 1820, George IV sees his wife's face in the mirror. She returned after many years on the Continent to claim her position as queen when her husband succeeded to the throne. The scandal was enormous and George IV's coronation was marred by Caroline's attempts to gain admission to the Abbey. She died shortly afterwards. George IV is said to have misunderstood the message when told of Napoleon's death in the words, 'Sire, your greatest enemy is dead', and to have replied, 'Is she, by God?'

retorted that the witnesses had been suborned, and feeling in her favour even led to some disaffection among the guards. When the bill passed its second reading by the narrow majority of 123 to 95, Lord Liverpool was obliged to withdraw it. Parliament awarded her £50,000 p.a., and she attended a thanksgiving service in St Paul's. But her attempt to gain access to the Abbey for her husband's coronation in July 1821 was ill-judged and led to a mixed reception. She died the following month. Even then, George had not heard the last of her. Her supporters insisted that the funeral cortège be routed to Harwich through the city of London, amid scenes of considerable disorder.

It was inevitable that George IV's conduct and personality should weaken not only the public esteem of the crown, but its position in relation to the cabinet. As soon as he became Regent, he asked the cabinet to find £550,000 to pay off debts and another £150,000 for 'Regency services'. It was 'the decided and unanimous opinion' of the cabinet that he must pay his own debts, and for services only

£100,000. Liverpool was particularly hard on him. In 1816, in the middle of great post-war distress, the Regent was still building at Brighton: his ministers, he was warned, 'are perfectly convinced that Parliament will never vote one shilling for defraying such expenses'. Though he could be difficult over appointments, he had neither the stamina nor probably the interest for long political battles. Soon after he became king, Liverpool insisted on bringing in Canning as foreign secretary to replace Castlereagh who had committed suicide. George IV could not forgive Canning for supporting the Princess Caroline, yet, in the end, he had to make 'the greatest sacrifice of my opinions and feelings that I have ever made'.

Even when doing battle on questions closely affecting the court, George IV suffered repeated defeats. In July 1821 he wished to appoint Lord Conyngham, husband of the king's current mistress, as Lord Chamberlain, insisting that the appointment was 'quite independent of the control of any minister whatever'. Liverpool refused and the duke of Montrose was appointed, though Conyngham received compensation. The king was again defeated when he promised a canonry at Windsor to the tutor of Lady Conyngham's sons. He consoled himself for his defeats with petulance and rudeness: 'ministers', remarked Canning, 'have to endure without answering back the epigrams by which a King seeks to avenge himself for his impotence.'

If the king could not command a Windsor canonry, it was unlikely that he would take many tricks in the realm of major policy. He was thoroughly out of sympathy with the 'new political liberalism' of the 1820s but was quite unable to prevent Canning from recognizing the South American states that had rebelled against Spain. Had the government quite forgotten the meaning of the French Revolution, he demanded? But all he could do was to refuse to read the king's speech on the grounds that he had lost his false teeth. His political dilemma was that he could not rid himself of the Liberal Tories without falling into the hands of the Whigs, who were worse: in short, he was so badly out of touch with public opinion, that he had run out of alternatives. In 1828, when the election of O'Connell for county Clare forced once more the question of Catholic Emancipation, the king pleaded his coronation oath and the respect he had for his father's opinions on the matter. He threatened abdication, could not stop talking about the question, and was reported to have worked himself into a frenzy. In the end, after an audience of several hours, he dismissed Wellington's government, climbed down in the evening, and gave way.

A remarkable example of George IV's fitful concern for the powers of the crown, despite his protestations to the contrary, occurred in the spring of 1827. On 17 February Lord Liverpool collapsed with a stroke and for weeks the king hesitated about a successor. 'Nothing could induce him to come to any determination,' wrote Greville. At length George suggested that the cabinet should resolve the matter for him. It was left to the horrified Tories to point out

THE KING'S CHAMPION OFFERS BATTLE. The role of the champion was to fling down the gauntlet at the coronation banquet and offer to fight any rival claimant. Since the offer was never accepted (though there were rumours of a Jacobite challenge in 1761), duties remained light. At the coronation of George IV, the office of Champion, which was hereditary in the Dymoke family by right of the manor of Scrivelsby in Lincolnshire, was performed by Henry Dymoke, since his father was a clergyman. He was accompanied by the duke of Wellington as High Constable and Lord Anglesey as High Steward. According to Mrs Arbuthnot, 'the king behaved very indecently: he was continually nodding and winking at Lady Conyngham and sighing and making eyes at her'.

PUBLIC MONARCHY. George III's preference for private life and his later years of total seclusion gave the monarchy a low profile. George IV changed that, with a programme of tours, visits, and receptions, at least until the last years of his reign. The painting is entitled 'A correct representation of the company going to and returning from His Majesty's drawing room at Buckingham Palace, St James's Park', and was done in 1822.

that he was abandoning a vital prerogative. Peel 'objected on principle to the delegation by the King of this act of royalty', and Wellington, in his more blunt fashion, declared that it was 'the only personal act the King of England had to perform'. Professor Arthur Aspinall, in his detailed analysis of the formation of Canning's ministry, called the whole episode 'an important stage in the long process whereby the quasi-"personal" monarchy of George III was transformed into the constitutional monarchy of Queen Victoria'.

Charles Greville's opinion of the king was that he was 'a spoiled, selfish odious beast'. He was not, however, without talent. He was intelligent and quick-witted, well read, and had an interest in painting and architecture. He was a discerning patron of literature, admired Scott and Jane Austen, and his patronage of artists included Lawrence, Wilkie, and Chantrey. His love of building produced not only the Brighton Pavilion, but massive reconstructions at Windsor and of Buckingham Palace. His support for John Nash, in the face of severe criticism, encouraged the splendid complex stretching up from Trafalgar Square to Regent's Park, now the home of quangos. He was capable of thoughtful and considerate gestures. On form, he had an easy and affable manner and could

THE CORRIDOR IN WINDSOR CASTLE. The early Hanoverians were not particularly fond of Windsor, preferring Kensington Palace and Hampton Court, but George III began a long process of restoration in the 1770s. George IV decided upon a grand reconstruction and the project was put out to competition. The main feature of the proposals by Jeffry Wyatt, the winner, was to heighten the Round Tower by thirty feet to make it more imposing. He also suggested a grand corridor inside the Upper Ward court to link a number of rooms and provide better access. Joseph Nash, a fine water-colour artist, published a volume of lithographs of Windsor in 1848: if the girl with the dog is genuine, she might be the Princess Royal, who was about seven when Nash made his sketches.

make graceful, if rather florid, little speeches. Under the influence of pain, laudanum, and brandy in his declining years, his reminiscences grew more extravagant, and he would embarrass his listeners with stories of his prowess as a cavalry commander at Salamanca.

The essential frivolity of his reign masks some significant developments. Though undertaken much against his will, Catholic Emancipation began the process of emancipating the monarchy from the revolutionary settlement, in which it was a bulwark of the Protestant establishment, and enabled it to play a more national role. His marked love of pageantry and spectacle, in contrast with his father's taste, helped to develop the ceremonial side of the monarchy. The anniversary of the succession of the House of Hanover was marked in 1814 by a

BRIGHTON PAVILION. 'More the pomp and magnificence of a Persian satrap seated in all the splendour of oriental state than the sober dignity of a British prince', was one Member of Parliament's description of George IV's new palace. More laconically, Sydney Smith thought that it looked as though the dome of St Paul's had gone down to the sea and pupped. The illustrations are of the great kitchen and the music room.

GEORGE IV

(1820–1830)

He was, indeed, the most extraordinary compound of talent, wit, buffoonery, obstinacy and good feeling—in short a medley of the most opposite qualities, with a great preponderance of good— that I ever saw in any character in my life.

(The Duke of Wellington)

Wellington's private opinion of George IV was somewhat at variance with his public eulogy in the Lords in 1830 when he declared that the late monarch's understanding and accomplishments far surpassed all his subjects': 'no man ever approached His Majesty who did not feel instructed by his learning, and gratified by his condescension, affability and kindness of disposition.'

Born at St James's in August 1762, the prince soon showed himself bright and lively, but, as the *Dictionary of National Biography* observed sombrely, 'addicted to lying, tippling and low company'. By the time he was eighteen, he was well acquainted with most of the pleasures of the town, and for years Carlton House was a rallying-point for opposition. He escaped from unwise liaisons into an even more unwise marriage, and the scandal after his accession in 1820 when he tried to divorce the queen almost brought the monarchy to its knees. Mrs Arbuthnot, who was in close touch with Lord Liverpool's government, noted on 28 June 1820:

Mr Arbuthnot told me that, at Lord Liverpool's, they had been discussing the state of the country and the public mind, and Lord Liverpool said that the aversion to the King was risen to the greatest possible height, that the Guards in London were all drinking the Queen's health and had the greatest possible contempt for the King from thinking him a coward and afraid of showing himself amongst them. Lord Liverpool said that, if it was found impossible to prevail upon him to come out a little, that it would be advisable to endeavour to prevail upon him to go over to Hanover for a time while the storm here blows over, and have a Regency here. We should soon become tranquil here with the Duke of York for our Governor. In this sad state of things how much

have we cause to bless the memory and mourn the loss of our good old king, whose personal virtues shed lustre on the throne and were an honour to the nation he ruled over ...

Though the queen's death in 1821 removed the immediate problem, George IV never regained much popularity, and his later years were spent in seclusion at Windsor.

giant fireworks display in Green and Hyde Parks, complete with balloon ascent and mimic naval battles on the Serpentine. Even then, his bad luck held, and the Chinese pagoda in St James's Park caught fire and tumbled into the lake. Another development was the resumption, after decades of neglect, of royal visits and travels. Hanover, which had not seen its ruler since the 1750s, gave him a warm reception in 1821. He was the first monarch since Richard II to pay a visit to

Ireland, though of only a few days: 'his heart had always been Irish', he assured his listeners implausibly. On his visit to Scotland, the following year, he adopted Highland dress, and, despite drenching rain and some satire, the visit was counted a success. By comparison, the tone of his father's reign seemed domestic, remote, and limited.

The vitality of the early years of his reign could not be sustained. Increasingly embarrassed at his enormous bulk, he spent his declining years in virtual seclusion and died in June 1830, at the age of sixty-seven. The usual conventional tributes were made, Wellington testifying to his remarkable fitness for the high station he had occupied. Less conventional was *The Times* the day after his funeral:

There never was an individual less regretted by his fellow creatures than this deceased king ... What eye has wept for him? What heart has heaved one throb of unmercenary sorrow ... for that Leviathan of the *haut ton* George IV ... Nothing more remains to be said about George IV but to pay, as pay we must, for his profusion; and to turn his bad conduct to some account by tying up the hands of those who come after him in what concerns the public money.

It was rather a large sledge-hammer for so small a nut. When his attendants began the melancholy task of going through his personal possessions, they found bundles of old love-letters, ringlets, and locks of hair, and dozens of pairs of ladies' gloves, '*gages d'amour* which he had got at balls, and with the perspiration still marked on the fingers'.

Greville's description of the new reign was a *tour de force*:

Never was elevation like that of King William the Fourth. His life has been hitherto passed in obscurity and neglect, in miserable poverty, surrounded by a numerous progeny of bastards, without consideration or friends, and he was ridiculous from his grotesque ways and little meddling curiosity. Nobody ever invited him into their house, or thought it necessary to honour him with any mark of attention or respect, and so he went on for above forty years ... King George had not been dead three days before everybody discovered that he was no loss, and King William a great gain.

The new king enjoyed his succession greatly. At George's funeral, he behaved 'with great indecency', chatting to all his friends 'incessantly and loudly'. He spent much of the opening days of the reign driving round in an open carriage, bowing to the onlookers. He had never expected to be king. From 1796 his niece Charlotte had been next in succession to her father. On her death, the duke of York became heir apparent. It was only his death in 1827 that brought William into the direct line of succession.

His early years had been spent in the navy. He was packed off at the age of thirteen in 1779, got his first ship in 1786, and retired in 1790. His reputation was as an odd, unpredictable, boisterous, uncouth man, a caricature of the 'blunt, honest tar', an awkward mixture of martinet and crony. In 1789 he was made duke of Clarence. From 1791 he lived a quiet life at Bushey Park with Mrs Jordan, the actress, and their growing family. She continued her stage career and it was a matter of speculation in the press who kept whom. In 1811, overwhelmed by debt, William resolved on matrimony, separated from Mrs Jordan, and began the search for a wife. He was turned down by a depressing number of ladies until 1818, when his prospects had improved, and he was accepted by Princess Adelaide of Saxe-Meiningen. The marriage was extremely successful, though two daughters died soon after birth. In 1827 Canning appointed him Lord High Admiral, partly to give the future king some experience of public life. He spent most of the time in violent quarrels with his advisers and resigned the following year.

First impressions of the new monarch were that he was erratic but well-meaning, and pointed comparisons with his deceased brother were made. One commentator decided that though he was either mad or very foolish, he was 'an immense improvement on the last unforgiving animal, who died growling sulkily in his den at Windsor'. His naval habits did not pass without remark: 'His Majesty has an easy and natural way of wiping his nose with the back of his forefinger', observed Washington Irving. A rather greater embarrassment to ministers were his tipsy dinner speeches. Louis Philippe, new king of the French, was described as 'an infamous scoundrel' and the French themselves as 'the natural enemies of England'.

But his political views were far less unsophisticated than his manner might have suggested. It was rather too late in the day to carry on with George III's crusade to extirpate party, and William moved to the next best position—a hankering after coalition, which he frequently urged. The repeated accusations against secret influence at court persuaded him to try to limit political conversation: Croker, who had no particular cause to admire him, wrote that William had 'a very constitutional scruple against receiving advice except from a constitutional adviser'. He had some concept of the role of the monarch as constitutional chairman and, during the protracted crisis over the Reform Bill, he played a difficult hand with considerable finesse.

It was, however, inevitable that a reign dominated by the Reform crisis should see a further weakening of the position of the crown. It began almost immediately when Wellington's Tory government, which William had continued in office, lost the general election of August 1830. This was the first time that it can be said that an administration, with royal support, had lost an election and was an indication of the inroads that decades of economical reform had made on government patronage. Wellington's ministry was defeated in the new House and Grey came in pledged to a measure of parliamentary reform. Croker, surveying the election results, remarked glumly that he saw in them 'the seeds of the most troublesome and unmanageable Parliament since that of 1640, which overturned the monarchy and beheaded the monarch'.

Though William admitted that some reform was inescapable, the Act as it finally passed undermined the crown's position. The considerable extension of the franchise meant a vast increase in the role of public opinion. The elimination of much aristocratic influence made it more difficult to construct a majority by the use of crown patronage and honours, while some of the crown's remaining direct influence went when boroughs such as Queenborough were deprived of representation. William had to be content that his worst fears—a shortening of the septennial Parliaments or even the introduction of secret ballot—had not been realized.

The passage of the legislation placed the king in some very delicate positions. After Grey had been defeated in April 1831, he demanded a dissolution, though it was little more than six months since the previous election. William had already warned the ministers that he was not prepared to grant one, fearing that an election on such an issue would plunge the country into convulsions from John O'Groats to Lands End. His decision was, declared his private secretary, 'final and conclusive'. The Tories prepared to resume office. But, in the end, the king gave way. To Grey, he wrote that, as an individual, he would probably have taken

'A GREAT ACTOR REHEARSING HIS PART.' During and after the reign of William IV, John Doyle produced a large number of brilliant political cartoons under the initials HB. The element of caricature was slight and the representations remarkably lifelike. During the protracted Reform Act crisis, William IV had a difficult role to play and was denounced in turn by each side.

WILLIAM IV

(1830–1837)

WILLIAM IV was one of the most colourful of English monarchs, excitable, undignified, frequently absurd, but with enough common sense to accept political advice. The third son of George III, he became heir apparent at the age of sixty-two, when his elder brother the duke of York died. His character and behaviour had been formed largely by his life at sea. At thirteen, he was sent to join the navy: 'I desire he may be received', wrote George III, 'without the smallest marks of parade . . . The young man goes as a sailor, and, as such, I add again, no marks of distinction are to be shown unto him.' When he gained his own ship, he acquired a reputation as a severe disciplinarian and a difficult man to work with. Retiring in 1790 he settled down at Bushey with Mrs Jordan, the actress, who presented him with a large family. This did not prevent the duke intervening in a debate in the Lords in 1801 to express his detestation of adultery. His only experience of public office was a disastrous year as Lord High Admiral in 1827/8, when he quarrelled violently. 'He distinguished himself', wrote Greville, 'by making absurd speeches, by a morbid official activity, and by a general wildness which was thought to indicate incipient insanity.' His accession in 1830 was marked by excessive affability and an absence of reserve that involved him in scrapes. Mrs Arbuthnot commented:

The King is somewhat *wild* and talks and shews himself too much. He walked up St James's Street the other day quite alone, the mob following him, and one of the common women threw her arms round him and kissed him. However, I hope he will soon go out of town and be quiet.

During the protracted reform crisis, which took up the early years of his reign, he was credited with being an ardent advocate and an implacable opponent of reform, but in practice the strength of public opinion and

the absence of an alternative government left him little room for manœuvre. In the end, he accepted Lord Grey's advice, granting a dissolution in 1831 with reluctance, and promising in 1832 to create enough peers to carry the bill, with even greater reluctance.

a different view: 'as a sovereign it was his duty to set those feelings and prejudices aside.' This was a remarkable admission. George III had made no such distinction when sabotaging the India Bill nor George IV when resisting Catholic Emancipation. From this action, the reformers inferred, erroneously, that William was a keen supporter of the bill. The Tories were horrified. Wellington did not think a king of England had taken any step so fatal to the monarchy since

Charles I had given his consent to the bill depriving himself of the power of dissolving the Long Parliament.

From the Tories' point of view, worse was to follow. The election returned a massive pro-reform majority, but a second crisis developed in the spring of 1832 after the Lords had rejected a revised version of the bill. Ministers resolved to introduce a third bill and to seek assurances from the king that he would, if necessary, create enough peers to carry it. William was extremely reluctant to give such a pledge. When the bill was defeated in committee, Grey asked for the creation of fifty or more peers, was refused, and tended his resignation. But the failure of the Tories to form an administration in May 1832 forced William to surrender and give categorical assurances. They were not, in fact, needed, for Wellington, seeing that the game was up, persuaded most of the Tories to absent themselves. But yet another royal prerogative had been greatly damaged. Control of peerages, which George III had used so successfully against the coalition in 1783, had been snatched from the monarch's hands and used as a party weapon. The influence which the crown had traditionally had in the House of Lords, and which George III had used in the same crisis, was now of little avail, since the Lords themselves could be browbeaten into submission by the Commons.

Subsequent events confirmed how much royal power had been shaken. Grey resigned in 1834 and made way for Melbourne. The new prime minister was no firebrand, but the king was concerned at some of his more radical colleagues, and particularly Lord John Russell and Brougham. In November 1834 when Althorp succeeded his father in the Lords, Melbourne proposed to replace him as leader of the House of Commons by Russell. The king refused, dismissed Melbourne, and sent for Peel to form a Tory administration. Even this reassertion of power misfired. The king pointed out to his new ministers that in 1784 Pitt had faced a hostile House of Commons but had won through, with royal support, to found a long-lived ministry. It was a false parallel. In 1784 government, with the backing of the crown, could still guarantee to win an election. When Peel went to the country in January 1835, as he was forced to do, he was beaten: it was, admitted the king, 'a direct censure upon His Majesty's conduct'.

William understood the theory of the more limited monarchy: the practice he found difficult. 'We all of us mean well,' he told Russell in an amiable moment, 'I have my view of things, and I tell them to my ministers. If they do not adopt them, I cannot help it. I have done my duty.' This very proper anticipation of Bagehot's doctrine that the monarch should advise and warn, did not prevent continued and violent clashes with his Whig ministers, who resumed office in determined mood. In conversation with the new Governor of Canada, the king shouted that the colony must not be placed in hazard: 'I do not consider the present cabinet as mine ... By God, if they adopt any such dangerous course, I will have them impeached.' But most of his anger was reserved for his sister-in-law, the widowed duchess of Kent. Although there were rumours that Queen Adelaide was pregnant, it had been apparent for years that Princess Victoria would succeed. The duchess took no pains to disguise how much she looked forward to that joyous event. She tried hard to keep her daughter away from the king, lest she be contaminated by the swarming FitzClarences. A quarrel over precedence kept both the duchess and her daughter away from the coronation in 1831. She offended the king greatly by taking the princess on a series of progresses that were almost regal in character. In August 1836 there was a violent explosion of wrath at a birthday banquet at Windsor, attended by the princess and her mother. By way of an after-dinner speech, the king begged that he might survive another nine months, so that the country would be spared a Regent, 'incompetent to act with propriety'. He got his wish, with almost a month in hand. Princess Victoria came of age on 24 May 1837: on 20 June, Waterloo day, William IV died.

Victoria

The first result of Victoria's accession was that, after 123 years, the connection with Hanover was at an end. Under the terms of the Salic law, women could not inherit, and the Hanoverian throne passed to her uncle, the duke of Cumberland. His reign there was eventful. One of his earliest actions was to suspend the constitution which his brother William had granted. He survived the revolutions of 1848 and died aged eighty. His only son, blind from an early age, fought on the Austrian side in 1866 and lost his kingdom to the Prussians as a consequence.

Victoria's mother, the duchess of Kent, was another princess of the House of Saxe-Coburg, the elder sister of Leopold, husband of Princess Charlotte. She was widowed with two children, a boy and a girl. Her marriage to the fifty-year-old duke of Kent lasted a mere eighteen months. Six months after the birth of his daughter, he caught a chill on his way to Sidmouth in winter, developed pneumonia, and died in January 1820. Henceforth the duchess devoted her whole existence to bringing up her children. It was a very sheltered life for the young princess. She had little contact with other children, save for her half-sister Feodora, to whom she was devoted. But she married when Victoria was nine and went off to Germany, leaving the princess alone in a world of grown-ups, seeking solace with her dolls. She grew up with social accomplishments, but short of intellectual stimulus.

The change of scene in 1837 could hardly have been more theatrical. The three previous monarchs had been stout, elderly gentlemen of uncertain temper. The new queen was eighteen, tiny, with a clear voice, and a composed and dignified manner. The effect on the equally elderly gentlemen who composed her Privy

Council was remarkable: allowing for a willingness to salute the rising sun, they were bowled over. 'There never was anything like the first impression she produced', wrote Greville, 'or the chorus of praise and admiration which is raised about her manner and behaviour . . . She bowed to the Lords, took her seat, and then read her speech in a clear, distinct and audible voice, and without any appearance of fear or embarrassment.' 'She filled the room,' said the duke of Wellington simply.

Scarcely less dramatic was the transformation taking place in her kingdom. The population of the United Kingdom had now risen to 25 million, some 8 million in Ireland. Since 1801 London had doubled in size and was now 2 million. Birmingham, Manchester, Liverpool, and Glasgow, about the 70,000–80,000 mark in 1801, were now well over 200,000. Bradford, a mere 17,000 in 1801, was a town of 60,000. Seventy years of canal-building and turnpiking had transformed the internal communications of England, and the railways were in turn transforming that transformation. The Liverpool and Manchester railway, opened in 1830, was paying good dividends and had just opened a new terminus at Lime Street. The first Great Western train left Paddington for Maidenhead on 31 May 1838: the return journey, after a good lunch, was completed at a breathless 33 m.p.h. The first all steam crossing of the Atlantic had taken place in 1827. A month after Victoria's accession, Brunel's *Great Western* was launched at Bristol.

The previous ten years had seen great changes also in government and administration. The repeal of the Test and Corporation Acts in 1828, followed by Catholic Emancipation in 1829, had removed most of the remaining religious disabilities. The snug parliamentary boroughs of the old regime—Dunwich, Heytesbury, Gatton, Hindon, and the rest—had been swept away in schedule A, and the great towns of Manchester, Leeds, Sheffield, and Birmingham brought into the representation for the first time. Under the terms of the Municipal Corporations Act of 1835 the large towns had been given elected councils. London had its own metropolitan police force, and the larger boroughs were in the process of establishing their own forces.

Queen Victoria's coronation, which took place in June 1838, was a splendid mixture of majesty and muddle. It was without adequate rehearsal and the clergy, in particular, distinguished themselves by their ineptness. The queen's own version of the occasion was in her inimitable style:

I was awoke at four o'clock by the guns in the Park, and could not get much sleep afterwards on account of the noise of the people, bands, etc. etc. Got up at seven, feeling strong and well; the Park presented a curious spectacle, crowds of people up to Constitution Hill, soldiers, bands, etc.

Driving to the Abbey amid 'millions of my loyal subjects', she arrived to 'deafening cheers'. Lord Melbourne hovered protectively throughout the ceremony. Lord

Rolle, in his eighties, rolled down the steps while attempting to pay homage, whereupon the queen, with some presence of mind, advanced to forestall another attempt and another fall. The wags endeavoured to persuade foreign guests that all Lords Rolles were expected to behave at coronations in this way as acknowledgement of their title. After the anthem, the queen withdrew to St Edward's Chapel:

which, as Lord Melbourne said, was more *un*like a chapel than anything he had ever seen; for what was *called* an *Altar* was covered with sandwiches, bottles of wine, etc., etc. The Archbishop came in and *ought* to have delivered the Orb to me, but I had already got it, and he (as usual) was *so* confused and puzzled and knew nothing, and went away.

The archbishop, who had a bad day, then proceeded to squeeze the ring on to the queen's wrong finger, causing considerable delay while, with some pain, it was eased off. Back at the palace, the queen remarked that there had been very few viscounts: 'there are very few Viscounts,' explained Melbourne, 'that they were an odd sort of title and not really English.' By this time, Melbourne was back in high spirits, telling the queen that he had been one of the first to arrive:

He said there was a large breakfast in the Jerusalem Chamber where they met *before* all began; he said, laughing, that whenever the Clergy, or a Dean and Chapter, had anything to do with anything, there's sure to be plenty to eat.

The first year of Victoria's reign was something of an idyll, with politics rarely intruding. William IV had left her some political advice—never to make categorical pledges, to ask for propositions in writing, and not to make hasty replies—which was sensible enough, though limited. Her uncle Leopold, now king of the Belgians, sent over an adviser, Baron Stockmar, to assist her: he was, wrote Leopold rather forbiddingly, 'a living dictionary of all matters scientific and politic that happened these thirty years'. Meanwhile, Leopold filled in the gaps with long letters of his own: she was to repeat as often as possible how English she was—it would go down well with her subjects who were 'almost ridiculous in their own exaggerated praises of themselves'. She should try to preserve what little influence the crown still possessed: 'the trade of a constitutional sovereign, to do it well, is a very difficult one.' But letters could not be of day-to-day use and her real political education came from Melbourne, with whom she was soon on the most affectionate terms. Melbourne, still handsome, was a Whig of the old school, amused, nonchalant, unenthusiastic, ironic, his cheerfulness shot through with melancholy. The contrast between him and Bute, mentor to George III, could hardly have been greater. Bute was censorious, Melbourne charitable. Bute taught his charge to deplore the wickedness of men: Melbourne encouraged Victoria to shrug off human foibles. Just before her marriage to Albert, the duke of Wellington enraged her by carrying an amendment to the address confirming that the prince was a Protestant. Victoria refused to ask him to the wedding. Melbourne wrote twice to insist that she should, adding, 'I don't think he means any disrespect. It's his conscience.'

Lord Melbourne was also responsible for most of her historical education. It may seem surprising how little Victoria seemed to know about her own ancestors until one remembers that, up to her accession, her life had been totally dominated by two foreigners, the duchess and Baroness Lehzen, neither of whom probably had much interest in or knowledge of English history. Melbourne was almost the ideal teacher, neither systematic nor profound, but chatting about the past with a happy familiarity that brought it to life. Did she know that Lord Holland's grandfather had seen the duchess of Portsmouth, Charles II's mistress? Mary Queen of Scots was 'quite right to have (Darnley) knocked on the head'. George IV had seemed to be a Whig, 'but he did it from opposition and not from

LORD MELBOURNE was Victoria's first prime minister, unofficial tutor, and close friend. After their first audience, the queen wrote: 'I like him very much and feel confidence in him. He is a very straight-forward, honest, clever and good man.' Her affection for him involved her in considerable unpopularity and produced, in the Bedchamber dispute of 1839, a serious constitutional crisis.

principle'. 'Talked of Henry VIII. Lord M. said, "Those women bothered him so." I observed he had ill-treated Catherine of Aragon so. "That was his conscience", said Lord M. funnily, "he thought he was living in a state of concubinage, not of marriage".' The young queen's grasp of history was not strong:

Talked of Henry VIII behaving very ill to (Anne of Cleves); he called her 'A Flanders mare'; of his using other wives so ill; Jane Seymour, I said, narrowly escaped being beheaded. 'Oh no, he was very fond of her,' said Lord M., which I denied . . . And poor Catherine of Aragon he ill-used, I said; 'He got tired of her,' said Lord M., 'she was a sad, groaning, moaning woman,' which made me laugh.

It was certainly not Melbourne's fault that the queen was so partisan. She must try to get over her dislike of Peel, he warned her. Lord John Russell had too much 'bitter personal feeling', observed Melbourne. 'I don't dislike the Tories,' said Lord M., 'I think they are very much like the others.'

In the queen's first important political test she did not show much skill, mainly because Melbourne was so much involved in it. In May 1839 his government was defeated and he was forced to tender his resignation. The queen, greatly attached to him, was desolate: 'all, ALL my happiness gone', she confided to her diary. Peel asked that some of the Ladies of the Bedchamber, many of whom were relatives of Whig ministers, should be changed as a mark of confidence in the new Tory administration. Victoria refused, insisting that she never talked politics to her ladies, and that it had never been asked before. That, explained Peel, was because she was a queen regnant. She still refused, the Whigs took office again, and Peel's opportunity had to wait another two years.

It was a dramatic episode, much debated, and Victoria's transparent partisanship made her temporarily very unpopular with the Tories. But the issue was of no real consequence. It was easily accommodated in 1841 and subsequently changes of the Bedchamber ladies were not demanded. It was a curiously old-fashioned issue in many respects. It would hardly have come about had Peel been sure of his majority and had the queen's known attachment to Melbourne not made him fear treachery at court. But in fact it made too much of the importance of royal confidence. No one disputed that it was much more agreeable to have the monarch's sympathy and goodwill, but it was no longer decisive as it had been in George III's reign. The basic irrelevance of the Bedchamber crisis was shown in 1841 when Melbourne went to the country, and was beaten decisively. Once again, the message of 1830 and 1835 was repeated: the electorate gave the prime minister to the monarch and in 1841 the electorate chose Sir Robert Peel.

The queen came in the course of time to feel great confidence in Peel, but by 1841 Melbourne had, in any case, been overtaken as adviser to the queen by a rival against whom he could not hope to compete—Prince Albert. He was Victoria's first cousin, three months younger, and nephew of Leopold of the Belgians. The suitability of a match had been obvious from the beginning and there was an informal understanding. In 1836 a visit by Albert and his brother Ernest had gone well: 'allow me to tell you', the princess wrote to Leopold, 'how much I like him in every way . . . he has, besides, the most pleasing and delightful exterior and appearance.' Succession and the coronation drove matrimony out of Victoria's mind for a while, but by 1839 continued strains in her relationship with her mother brought it up again. Even then, Victoria was by no means certain. There was the obvious danger of exchanging one tyranny for another. She was anxious not to have a large family, and her attitude to babies was not at all sentimental: their bald heads and jerky limb movements she found disagreeable. In October 1839 Albert came over on a second visit. He had matured into a slim and attractive man. Despite the fact that he had suffered agonies with seasickness, one look was enough to convince the queen: 'it was with some emotion that I beheld Albert', she wrote in her journal, 'who is *beautiful*.' To Leopold, she wrote: 'Albert's beauty is most striking, and he is so amiable and unaffected—in short very *fascinating*.' To Melbourne she remarked, artlessly, that seeing Albert had a good deal changed her mind as to matrimony.

FROM VIRGIN QUEEN TO GRANDMOTHER OF EUROPE. The portrait by Aaron Penley in 1840 shows the queen aged twenty-one. In the photograph, taken in her Golden Jubilee year, she is in her late sixties. When she died in 1901, she had thirty-one grandchildren living.

After the marriage in 1840, it was inevitable that the queen should lean more and more on Albert's advice. He was an intelligent and cultivated man, with a strong sense of duty. The arrival of seven children in the first ten years of married life placed a great physical and emotional strain on the queen and some assistance in the performance of her public duties was essential. Nevertheless, the influence of Prince Albert on the development of the constitution may have been somewhat overrated. In warning the queen not to be partisan, his advice was sound. But she would certainly have cured herself of that attitude, to a considerable extent, in due course. Her attachment to Melbourne was personal rather than political. Peel, whose manner she had found so cold at first, became in turn a firm favourite. Disraeli, whose attacks upon Sir Robert the queen thought odious, also succeeded in the course of time to the royal favour. During her long widowhood, however, she forgot the lesson the prince had inculcated and, as age settled upon her, she was as strong a partisan of the Conservatives as she had once been of the Whigs.

If Albert's insistence on strict neutrality was an acceptance of the logic of the

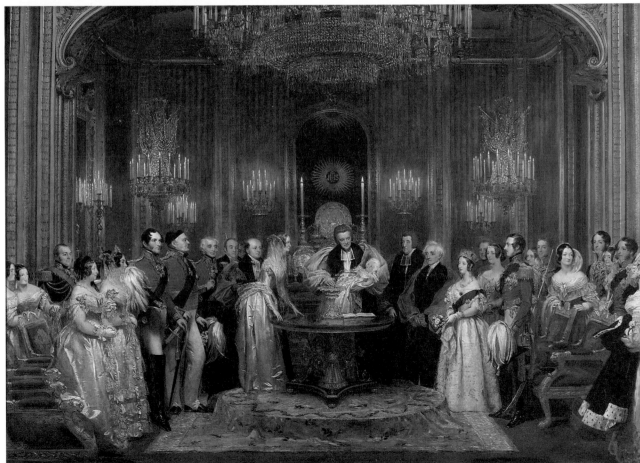

MATERNITY. (*Above*) Victoria's confinement in November 1840. She was, she wrote, 'Not at all nervous once it began' . . . 'Dearest Albert hardly left me at all and was the greatest comfort and support.' But the queen was not pleased to find herself pregnant again almost immediately. (*Below*) Her first child, Victoria, the Princess Royal, later empress of Germany, was christened in Buckingham Palace in February 1841. The baby, known until then rather oddly as 'Pussy', behaved with 'great propriety'.

VICTORIA

(1837–1901)

VICTORIA herself would have been in no doubt that the central event in her life was her marriage to Albert. The progress of her feelings in 1839 from reserve to ecstasy can be charted in the pages of her journal.

Friday 12 July

Talked of my Cousins Ernest and Albert coming over,—my having no great wish to see Albert, as the whole subject was an odious one, and one which I hated to decide about; there was no engagement between us, I said . . . 'Certainly better wait for a year or two', (said Lord M), 'it's a very serious question.' I said I wished if possible never to marry. 'I don't know about *that*,' he replied.

Friday 11 October

Albert really is quite charming, and so excessively handsome, such beautiful blue eyes, an exquisite nose, and such a pretty mouth with delicate moustachios and slight but very slight whiskers; a beautiful figure, broad in the shoulders and a fine waist.

Sunday 13 October

I said seeing them had a good deal changed my opinion (as to marrying), and that I must decide soon, which was a difficult thing. 'You would take another week', said Lord M.

Tuesday 15 October

At about $\frac{1}{2}$ past 12 I sent for Albert; he came to the Closet where I was alone, and after a few minutes I said to him, that I thought he must be aware *why* I wished them to come here,—and that it would make me *too happy* if he would consent to what I wished (to marry me). We embraced each other, and he was *so* kind, *so* affectionate. I told him I was quite unworthy of him,—he said he would be very happy 'das Leben mit dir zu zubringen,' and was so kind, and seemed so happy . . .

DRAWINGS BY VICTORIA HERSELF.

development of events, the same can hardly be said about his views on the role of the crown. It was not in his power to turn the clock back and increase the influence of the crown substantially. But Saxe-Coburg was ruled autocratically and it was natural that Albert should take a high view of the monarchy's position. Disraeli's comment that if the prince had lived longer, 'he would have given us, while retaining our constitutional guarantees, the blessings of absolute government' does not make sense, as reported, but it undoubtedly implies that the

THE ROYAL CHILDREN PLAYING UP. The photograph is from about 1851. The Princess Royal, on the right, at the age of eleven, is on her best behaviour, as befits the eldest. The Prince of Wales, aged ten, is striking poses. The other three, Princess Alice, aged eight, Princess Helena aged five, and Prince Alfred aged seven seem to have had enough.

prince's attitude was assertive. Albert emphasized the 'immense moral responsibility' on the shoulders of the sovereign to 'watch and control' the government. He rejected the idea that the crown could stay out of politics, arguing that the monarch was '*necessarily* a politician'. He claimed that his own position as head of the family meant that he was also the private secretary to the queen and her 'permanent minister'. That was a dangerous illusion. He was not a minister and was not responsible to Parliament. To behave like one meant running the risk of bringing the crown's conduct into collision with the genuine ministers, which, sooner or later, would lead to a serious constitutional crisis.

Albert did not, in practice, put his more ardent aspirations to the test, contenting himself with a restrained and conciliatory role. The presence, side by side, of in effect two sovereigns, intelligent and with a deep sense of duty, seeing eye to eye on most issues, was bound to lead to a temporary enlargement of the authority of the crown, and political circumstances contributed to that. The rift in the Tory party over the repeal of the Corn Laws brought about a confused parliamentary situation, with the Peelites and radicals making a third and fourth group in possible permutations. At the end of 1852, when Derby resigned after his short ministry, he recommended that the queen should send for Lord Lansdowne. The prince pointed out that 'constitutionally speaking', Derby's advice was not needed, and in the end Lord Aberdeen was approached and formed a ministry. In 1855, when Aberdeen resigned, there was considerable shuffling, with Derby and Russell unwilling or unable to form ministries, before Palmerston did so. But the monarch's position was more that of chairman or negotiator than superintending authority.

Albert and Victoria found Palmerston as much of a handful as did most of his associates. In the 1830s Victoria had thought him rather amusing, but with the coming of Albert, a note of deep moral disapprobation entered. Albert and the queen found Palmerston's offhand manner infuriating. They complained repeatedly that they were not adequately briefed and consulted, and that Palmerston's dispatches to foreign courts were unnecessarily offensive. There was a long-running disagreement between Palmerston and Albert over the Schleswig-Holstein question, in which Albert supported his German compatriots. In 1848 the queen remarked to Lord John Russell, the prime minister, that she did not know how long she could put up with Palmerston as minister. A series of incidents throughout 1851 brought matters to a head: in December Palmerston imprudently and uncharacteristically congratulated Louis Napoleon on his successful *coup d'état*, and was dismissed by Russell. It has been called 'the most successful exertion of royal power during the Queen's reign'. To that, there must be three severe reservations. The crucial factor was not the queen's disapproval, which for several years had been ineffective, but Russell's decision to stand no more from his colleague. Secondly, Palmerston could not have fallen had not his own prime minister torpedoed him by revealing the queen's previous correspondence complaining of discourtesy. Palmerston, not surprisingly, declared he would never forgive Russell. Thirdly, if it was victory, it did not last long. Within a year Palmerston was back as home secretary in Aberdeen's coalition. In 1855, at the age of seventy-one, he took over as prime minister to bring a little zest to the war effort. The following year he received the Garter, and he spent nine of the last ten years of his life as prime minister, dying in 1865. For a man who had incurred the profound disfavour of the monarch that was not bad. By contrast, Charles Fox, who incurred the disfavour of George III in 1772, spent more than thirty-two of his remaining thirty-four years in opposition.

The personal popularity of the queen and Albert fluctuated a good deal. At the beginning, admiration for a young married couple of considerable charm overcame the habitual mistrust towards foreigners. Albert's genuine concern for the condition of the lower orders won approval, and the Great Exhibition of 1851, which he master-minded, was an enormous success. In 1849 there was a royal visit to Ireland, which was still recovering from the hideous effects of the famine. The journeys were carefully limited to Cork and Dublin, and the queen can have seen little of the extent of the disaster. But she drove without escort in Dublin— an act of considerable courage, coming three months after a deranged Irishman had shot at her on Constitution Hill. Their first visit to Scotland in 1842 was so successful that in 1847 when the estate of Balmoral became available, it was purchased to add to Osborne in the Isle of Wight. In each place the prince built to his own design, Scottish baronial for Balmoral, Italian classical for Osborne. The development of the railway network meant that Victoria was able to visit on a scale none of her predecessors could have envisaged.

THE GREAT EXHIBITION, 1851. The growing network of railways made possible the enormous success of the Exhibition, which was open for five months and attended by more than six million people. Paxton's Crystal Palace was moved from Hyde Park to Sydenham, where it burned down in 1936. The 100,000 exhibits ranged from stained glass to stuffed cats. Henry Mayhew wrote of the opening day: 'as the morning advanced the crowds that came struggling along grew denser and denser, till at last it was one compact kind of road, paved with heads. On they went, fathers with their wives and children skipping jauntily along and youths with their sweethearts in lovely coloured shawls and ribbons. All London and half the country and a good part of the world were wending their way to see the Queen pass in state to open the Great Exhibition of all the nations.'

The nadir of the prince's reputation came in 1854 at the beginning of the Crimean War. He had never been popular with certain sections of the nobility, who were irritated by his German mannerisms and austere habits; not much of a sporting man, his bookish and artistic interests were derided. In the long run-up to the Crimean War, it was suggested that his pro-Russian sentiments had led him to prevent Palmerston leading the country into war. In January 1854 rumours that he was to be charged with high treason were so rife that crowds gathered outside the Tower to see him brought in. Though it was silly stuff and soon evaporated, for the victim it was a disagreeable experience.

In February 1855, when Palmerston formed his ministry, the general opinion was that he was well over the hill, very deaf, going blind, and unfit for business. The prince was then aged thirty-five. Ten years later Palmerston was still at Number 10, and Albert had been dead for four years, struck down at Windsor by typhoid in December 1861. His last act, probably his most important, had been to moderate a dispatch to the United States, when the country was on the brink of war over the Trent affair. There followed not so much a decline in the powers of

ALBERT

Sunday 10 November 1839
I sat on the sofa with Albert and we played at that game of letters, out of which you are to make words, and we had great fun about them. Albert gave '*Pleasure*', and when I said to the people who were puzzling it out, it was a very common word, Albert said, But not a very common *thing*, upon which Lord M. said, 'Is it truth, or honesty?', which made us all laugh.

(Diary of Queen Victoria)

ALBERT was a cultivated, intelligent, gifted, and sensitive man, with a streak of melancholy. He was born at the Rosenau, outside Coburg, in August 1819. When he was five, his father divorced Albert's mother, and he never saw her again: he remained devoted to her memory and after her death arranged for the body to be brought back to Coburg. He was brought up by his grandmothers and formed a close friendship with his uncle Leopold, later king of the Belgians.

Though deeply moved by Victoria's affection in 1839, he could not quite match her ecstasy: he was by nature more reserved and very conscious that, by his marriage, he would be giving up his native land. A letter to his stepmother revealed a slightly priggish resignation: 'Life has its thorns in every position, and the consciousness of having used one's powers and endeavours for an object so great as that of promoting the welfare of so many will surely be sufficient to support me.' He performed his tasks as consort with considerable skill. Though he wrote later that his object was 'to sink his own individual existence in that of his wife . . . to make his position entirely a part of hers', such self-effacement did not come easily. He plunged into a remorseless round of good works and by 1852 had become, in his wife's words, 'a *terrible* man of business . . . and so preoccupied'. Hard work took a heavy toll. He aged rapidly and shortly before his last illness confessed, 'I do not cling to life . . . I am sure if I had a severe illness, I should give up at once, I would not struggle for life.' He compared himself wryly with the donkey at Carisbrooke: 'He, too, would rather munch thistles in the Castle moat than turn round the wheel at the Castle well; and small are the thanks he gets for his labour.' In December 1861 he caught typhoid and died at the age of forty-two. Like Falstaff on his death-bed, he babbled of green fields—the fields of his beloved Saxe-Coburg.

the crown as a total eclipse. For several years the queen was overwhelmed with grief, incapable of performing public duties, and paying but fitful attention to private ones. To Palmerston she wrote that she could look forward to nothing but 'a pleasureless and dreary life': she longed to join her husband whom 'she would have followed barefoot over the world'. At the height of their row over his conduct of the foreign office in 1851, Palmerston had pointed out that some 28,000 dispatches were sent out each year. The amount of attention that a desolate widow, deprived of her husband's support, could give to such matters was small. But, unable or unwilling to perform her own duties, Victoria was determined neither to abdicate nor to share any matters of importance with the Prince of Wales, whose judgement and discretion she completely mistrusted.

In these circumstances, a republican movement slowly flickered into life. It started as little more than facetious comment—posters that Buckingham Palace was to be let. *Punch*, in September 1865, made the same point more elegantly with a cartoon of the queen as Hermione in *The Winter's Tale*, beseeched by Perdita–Britannia to 'Descend: be stone no more'. *The Times* on 1 April 1864 printed a report that the queen was about to re-emerge into public life and warned that 'they who would isolate themselves from the world and its duties must cease to know and to care'. Victoria was stung to reply, anonymously but in her own handwriting, with some dignity:

She would do what she could . . . to meet the loyal wishes of her subjects; to afford that support and countenance to society, and to give that encouragement to trade which was desired of her. More the Queen could not do, and more the kindness and good feeling of her people would surely not exact of her.

The Times returned to the charge eight months later:

It is impossible for a recluse to occupy the British throne without a gradual weakening of that authority which the sovereign has been accustomed to exert . . . It may be that in time London may accustom itself to do without the Palace, but it is not desirable that we should attain that point of Republican simplicity.

She was persuaded to open Parliament in person in 1866, though it was a frightful ordeal for her. In January 1868 she complained bitterly that 'from the hour she gets out of bed till she gets into it again, there is work, work, work . . . Her brain is constantly overtaxed.' She was in great danger of forgetting an ancient rule of monarchy—that the sovereign was expected to show himself to his subjects and to impress.

By the 1870s royalists were showing signs of alarm. The queen was still insisting that she was too unwell and fatigued to undertake public engagements. A grant of £30,000 for a dowry for Princess Louise went through without difficulty in early 1871, but the proposal for an annuity of £15,000 for Prince

MOURNING FOR ALBERT. Though there can be no doubt that Victoria was genuinely afflicted by the early death of her husband, her grief had also a melodramatic and theatrical element. The Prince Consort's room was left untouched and a special mausoleum built at Frogmore for his remains. In this heavily posed photograph, the queen and Princess Alice mourn beneath a larger-than-life bust of the departed.

Arthur in July ran into considerable criticism. An amendment to reduce it to £10,000 collected fifty-one votes in the House of Commons, and one radical member insisted that the ever-increasing cost of the royal family was causing 'a large amount of republicanism' among working people. An obvious response was to bring the queen more before the public, but that was far from easy. The Princess Royal, now married to the Crown Prince of Prussia, drew up a round robin on behalf of the royal family, begging the queen to recognize the dangers. Gladstone confided to Sir Henry Ponsonby, the private secretary, that his efforts to talk the queen out of seclusion had been his most 'sickening' experience in forty years of public life: '*worse* things may be imagined, but smaller and meaner causes for the decay of thrones cannot be conceived.' He did not see how the fund of credit on which the monarchy had been existing could be replenished, and thought the outlook 'very melancholy'. The queen retreated to Balmoral, where she was thoughtfully provided with the latest radical pamphlet entitled 'What does she do with it?' Disraeli's attempts to help were no more successful than Gladstone's. He loyally seconded the vote for Prince Arthur's grant, but he made a remarkable blunder when he explained in September 1871 that the queen was 'physically and morally incapacitated' from performing her duties. In view of the family's medical history, this kindled rumour that she was insane. Bradlaugh addressed the newly founded London Republican Club in October 1871, on the theme: 'Is the Queen physically and morally incapacitated? If yes, what ought the People to do?' His booklet *Impeachment of the House of Brunswick* sold in large numbers. Its attacks upon 'these small German breast-bestarred wanderers' echoed the tone of Tom Paine: 'in their own land, they vegetate and wither unnoticed: here we pay them highly to marry and perpetuate a pauper race.'

In November 1871 the question flared up higher with a speech by Sir Charles Dilke at Newcastle upon Tyne. His declaration that a republic was only a matter of education and time was received with loud applause: '*if* you can show me a fair chance that a republic here will be free from the political corruption that hangs about the monarchy, I say, for my part—and I believe that the middle classes in general will say—Let it come.'

Dilke's remarks were widely reported. But the excitement died away rapidly in 1872. Dilke was one of the first to trim, explaining a fortnight later that he had meant no discourtesy to the queen. Most of the leading radicals—Bright, Chamberlain, Cowen—hastened to dissociate themselves. Though on paper the National Republican League and the National Republican Brotherhood were formidable, in fact their numbers were small. In December 1871 the Prince of Wales's very serious illness, if it did not end the criticism, summoned up reserves of loyalty and affection. Dilke moved in March 1872 for an inquiry into the civil list, recognizing that dislike of the expense of the royal family was a major concern, but his motion was defeated by 276 votes to 2.

For a few months, something approaching panic seems to have touched some of the royal family. In October 1871 Princess Alice complained bitterly of her mother's curious impassivity: 'she thinks the monarchy will last her time . . . and we must sit quietly and let the approaching calamity crush us without an effort.' Things were not as bad as that. The republican movement was not a serious menace, but it was a warning that public confidence could be alienated and a clear indication of what was needed to restore it.

Republicanism proved to be no more than a spasm, though an unpleasant one for Victoria, and even more so for her children who did not share her invincible confidence. By 1880 it was remarked that none of the republican clubs remained in existence. A new mood of developing interest in imperial matters could be detected. Despite the loss of the American colonies, the acquisition of colonial territories continued steadily. Many of the loyalists who had finished up on the losing side in America moved north to Canada and Nova Scotia, until British settlement began to catch up with French. The first settlement in Australia began in 1788 on the site of Sydney, with the beginnings of settlement in western

Australia in 1829 and New Zealand in 1839. The end of the Napoleonic Wars saw important additions, largely at the expense of the Dutch. The Cape of Good Hope was retained, Ceylon acquired, and the development of Singapore by private exploitation started in 1819.

At the accession of Victoria, in 1837, Canada was on the brink of rebellion. It had survived invasions from America during the war of 1812, but both Upper and Lower Canada had grown increasingly dissatisfied with the controls to which they were subject. The rebellions in 1837 were militarily of little consequence, but Melbourne's government sent out Lord Durham in 1838 as Governor-General and to report. His recommendations were to unite the two provinces and to grant responsible government, reserving important rights of foreign policy and land settlement to the imperial government. Responsible government was not in fact implemented immediately, but slowly became the practice, particularly under Lord Elgin as Governor-General. The rapid growth of population in Ontario upset the delicate balance between British- and French-speaking Canadians and led, in 1867, to the negotiation of Dominion status, on a federal basis, bringing in New Brunswick, Nova Scotia, and, later, Prince Edward Island. The role of the Governor-General was then close to that of the monarch in Britain, and the crown provided the formal and legal link between the two countries. In the event of constitutional disputes between the provinces and the federal government, the judicial committee of the British Privy Council was to be the final court of appeal. The original intention of establishing the new government as the kingdom of Canada was abandoned, partly to avoid provocation to the United States, and the term 'Dominion' adopted.

While these developments were taking place, there had been a transformation in the government of India, of even more consequence to the position of the crown. The Seven Years War, though it decided the ultimate colonial command in India, left the East India Company with a large region in Bengal, but comparatively isolated areas elsewhere. The next ninety years saw a steady expansion of British power. Wellesley's Governor-Generalship saw the power of Tipu Sultan in Mysore broken, and company authority extended into the Carnatic, Tanjore, and Oudh. Further extensions under Hastings brought in most of the remaining territories, save for Punjab and Sindh in the north-west. The disaster of the ill-judged intervention in Afghanistan in 1839 and the subsequent annihilation on the retreat from Kabul, was redeemed in 1849 by the annexation of the Punjab also. But the hold of the British over all their Indian territories was threatened by the events of 1857, when for a time the ferocity of the outburst pushed British troops into isolated pockets struggling desperately to survive. Though the situation was redeemed, Company rule could not continue. In 1858 formal sovereignty over British India was assumed by the crown, with the Governor-General upgraded to the position of Viceroy. The queen watched the unfolding events of the mutiny with the same frozen horror as the rest of her subjects. The constitutional settlement she regarded in highly personal terms. In November 1857 she noted a general wish that India should 'belong to *me*', and a little later summarized Palmerston's intentions as '*all* to be mine'. Fourteen years later, the elevation of William to be emperor of Germany seems to have prompted the thought that her own claims were not inferior. To her private secretary she wrote that she had often been referred to as empress of India: why had she never formally adopted the title? The replacement of Gladstone by Disraeli in 1874 cleared the way to introducing a bill and in May 1876 Victoria became queen-empress. Though in theory the imperial status applied only to India, the queen used it quite indiscriminately and with relish.

For most of her reign, the six colonies in Australia pursued their separate paths. But discussions on a federation began in the 1890s and a bill creating the

DIAMOND JUBILEE, 1897. The Indian cavalry were especially eye-catching and served to remind onlookers of the extent to which the empire had grown. The procession is passing into King William Street, heading for London Bridge. There was a short service outside St Paul's since the queen was too infirm to manage the steps. 'No one ever, I believe,' she wrote, 'has met with such an ovation as was given to me through those six miles of streets . . . the cheering was quite deafening and every face seemed to be filled with real joy. I was much moved and gratified.'

Commonwealth of Australia passed in the summer of 1900. New Zealand declined to join the new federation and was granted Dominion status in 1907. Responsible government was established in Cape Colony in 1872 and, after the Boer War, the Union of South Africa was set up in 1910.

By the end of her reign, Victoria had 10 million white subjects in Canada, Australia, and New Zealand, another 5 million of all races in South Africa, and more than 250 million in India. The effect was partly to offset and mask the political decline of the monarchy at home by providing it with an important and eye-catching role abroad. Victoria herself took a keen interest in colonial development. The Jubilee of 1887 was enlivened by reports of celebrations in far-off lands, even if, like the opening of the Queen Victoria burial ground in a town in Sindh, they occasionally took strange forms. The number of Indian princes attending to pay their respects and the Indian cavalry escort when the queen drove to the Abbey to give thanks attracted much attention. At the Diamond Jubilee in 1897, eleven prime ministers of self-governing dominions were in attendance at St Paul's.

After the 1887 Jubilee, Victoria acquired an Indian servant, the Munshi, and, according to her journal, began learning a few words of Hindustani. The queen was relatively free from class prejudice and retorted to courtiers who complained that the Munshi had been promoted above his station that she recalled an archbishop who was the son of a butcher. Her knowledge of the lower orders was confined largely to servants and retainers on the royal estates, for whom she felt and expressed great affection. Her long and embarrassing friendship with John Brown showed how little in her own life she regarded rank. Her general view of the lower orders was somewhat sentimental, and more than a little tinged by her disapproval of the lounging and dissolute ways of some of the nobility:

The Lower classes are becoming so well-informed—are so intelligent and earn their bread and riches so deservedly that they cannot and ought not to be kept back—to be abused by the wretched ignorant highborn beings, who live only to kill time.

She declared herself categorically against emphasis on class divisions—an attitude 'she was always labouring to alter' and one of her reasons for disliking Gladstone so much, as she admitted after his death, was that she believed he stirred up class antagonism.

In other matters, her views were less advanced. She greatly disapproved of the campaign for Women's Rights—'it was dangerous, unchristian and unnatural', 'this mad, wicked folly'. It was, she wrote, a subject on which the queen could not contain herself. Nor had she much more affection for democracy, towards which great strides were made in the course of her reign. The second Reform Act of 1867, elementary education in 1870, secret ballot in 1872, the Corrupt Practices Act of 1883, the extension of the franchise in 1884, the local government reform of

LOYAL ELY. Coronations, royal weddings, and jubilees afford splendid opportunities for communal junketing. This painting, by J. W. H. Southby, for many years a verger in the cathedral, shows the festivities at Ely on the occasion of the Prince of Wales's wedding in 1863. If the illustration is accurate, the organizers of this luncheon in Dean's Pasture were meticulously efficient.

1885 and parish councils in 1894 indicated clearly enough which way events were moving. The queen did not move with them. To W. E. Forster, she wrote in 1880:

She cannot and will not be the Queen of a democratic monarchy; and those who have spoken and agitated, for the sake of party and to injure their opponents in a very radical sense must look for *another monarch*; and she doubts they will find one.

Once she had recovered from the immediate impact of the Prince Consort's death, the queen's major preoccupation was the supervision of her burgeoning family. Her relations with the Prince of Wales were rather awkward, though she was fortunate that conditions no longer allowed him to form a political opposition as his eighteenth-century predecessors had done. As a boy he was inattentive and had an unamiable propensity to bully the younger children. In 1861, when he paid a visit to Ireland at the age of nineteen, his cavalry officer hosts arranged for him to be initiated by a local actress. His father discovered the affair and his last

AWFUL VISIT. Max Beerbohm's cartoon burlesques the duty visits to Windsor paid by an ageing Prince of Wales to his even more aged mother. Relations between the two were at their worst immediately after the death of the Prince Consort, for which Victoria held Bertie partly responsible. Though they subsequently improved, the queen continued to deplore the fast set in which the prince moved and was reluctant to share duties with him.

visit, before he was struck down by typhoid, was to Cambridge to sort out the matter. Victoria at first blamed the prince for her husband's death, but gradually relations improved. In 1863 he married the Princess Alexandra of Denmark, a willowy beauty, of whom the queen became very fond. Their first child, Albert Edward, duke of Clarence, was born in 1864 and Prince George in 1865. The Prince of Wales moved in a fast set and his unpopularity in certain circles helped to fuel the republican movement of the early 1870s. In 1870 he was obliged to appear as a witness in the Mordaunt divorce case and though there was no evidence that, at least on this occasion, he was guilty, he was subjected to frequent hisses and booing. Victoria was totally unwilling to share any responsibility with him, doubting both his capacity and his trustworthiness. Slowly he settled into the role of an ageing playboy.

The Princess Royal, named Victoria after her mother, was by contrast a bright and clever child, with a gift for languages. She was very close to her mother all her life. In 1858, at the age of seventeen, she married Frederick, later Crown Prince of Prussia, and in 1859 had her first child, Wilhelm, the future German emperor. The Crown Princess adopted the loyalties of her new country and there was a period of very strained relations between her and the Prince and Princess of Wales during the Schleswig-Holstein crisis of 1864, when Prussia and Austria confronted Denmark. Fritz and his wife became in due course the resolute opponents of Bismarck and the hope of liberal Germany. But when he succeeded to the throne in 1888, Frederick III was dying of cancer, and after only three months was succeeded by Wilhelm. The new German emperor's attitude towards England, which he visited often, was ambivalent—a mixture of admiration and rivalry.

Her other children were three boys and four girls. Prince Alfred, her second son, married a Russian princess, Marie, daughter of the Tsar Alexander II. He inherited the duchy of Coburg but predeceased the queen, dying of cancer of the throat in 1900. Arthur, duke of Connaught, married a Prussian princess and was the last of her children to die, during the Second World War. Her youngest son, Leopold, created duke of Albany, was a haemophiliac, and died in 1884, at the age of thirty-one. Princess Alice, her second daughter, was the first of her children to die, catching diphtheria in 1878: 'I was so proud of my 9', wrote the queen simply. Princess Helena and Princess Beatrice married German princes. Princess Louise at the age of twenty-two married Lord Lorne, heir to the duke of Argyll: the queen took a highly practical view of the arrangement, explaining that since the family had 'such swarms of children', they could hardly afford to marry penniless Germans. The children went on swarming. The nine marriages produced thirteen boys and twenty-two girls. In the 1880s great-grandchildren began arriving. In 1894 Alix, daughter of Princess Alice, married the Tsarevitch Nicholas, who succeeded to the Russian throne almost immediately as Nicholas II; in the same year her great-grandson Edward was born, giving Victoria three generations of direct successors.

FOUR GENERATIONS. Photograph of 1894 showing the queen with the Princess of Wales, the duchess of York, and Prince Edward (later Edward VIII) at the prince's christening at White Lodge, Windsor. Victoria wrote: 'it seems that it has never happened in this country that there should be three direct heirs as well as the sovereign alive.'

FOREIGN POTENTATE. The queen was understandably apprehensive about the Shah of Persia's state visit in 1873, having been warned that he usually took his meals on the carpet, threw the food about, and could not be trusted with the ladies. But when he revealed that he had had *Leaves from the Journal of our Life in the Highlands* translated into Persian, all was forgiven.

So vast a family absorbed all Victoria's abundant energy and zest. Willy, Vicki's first-born, had a deformed left arm; Princess Beatrice at the age of eight threw all the milk over herself; Princess Alice had not written for her sister's birthday; Prince Eddy, eldest son of the Prince of Wales, appeared to be outgrowing his strength. Her correspondence became a stream of advice, enquiries, presents, and cards. Her connections with most of the ruling families of Europe, in an age of dynasticism, made her life a strange mixture of public and private, grand and domestic. Prince Alfred's father-in-law, Alexander II of Russia was blown up by a terrorist bomb in St Petersburg; 'Sandro', one of the Battenburg princes, reminded Victoria greatly of Albert and caught the eye of her granddaughter Vicki—he abdicated the shaky throne of Bulgaria and married a singer; Marie, Prince Alfred's daughter, who was intended for Prince George, married the heir to the Romanian throne instead, though the queen was sure that 'society' in Romania must be dreadful. Her personal knowledge of the crowned heads of Europe and her lengthening experience of international relations gave the queen a distinct advantage in matters of foreign policy.

Visitors to Balmoral, Osborne, and Windsor could not be certain that the experience would prove unmixed delight. Balmoral, in particular, was something of an acquired taste. Sir Henry Ponsonby thought that the atmosphere was curiously like a school, while Lady Dalhousie declared that she never saw anything more uncomfortable or that she coveted less. Disraeli was not greatly taken with life in the Highlands, where on his first visit in 1868 he suffered a stomach upset, and on his second in 1874 he caught a severe chill. It is a remarkable indication of his privileged status that he was excused further visits. The queen herself pined for even more seclusion than she had at Balmoral and built herself a small villa in the late 1860s on the shores of Loch Muick, where she spent a good deal of time. Routine at the great house was stuffy, dull, and repetitive. Many visitors found the presence of the invaluable John Brown disagreeable and disliked his habit of slapping ministers on the back. At the ghillies' ball, which seemed to many to come round with unnecessary frequency, Brown presided as MC which gave him an opportunity to order people around. Prince Leopold, the queen's youngest son, had the temerity in 1878 to declare an 'intense aversion' to Balmoral and a point-blank refusal to stay there. To Victoria

GHILLIES' BALL AT BALMORAL. For many years, the ghillies' ball was a great moment for John Brown, Victoria's Scottish servant, who acted as MC. Victoria's reliance upon Brown produced much malicious gossip and, after his death in 1883, she had to be persuaded not to proceed with a third volume of the *Journal* in his honour. She contented herself with commissioning a large number of busts.

this was close to treason. Leopold's conduct, she wrote, was 'wayward and undutiful', a challenge to 'the authority of the sovereign and the throne'.

At Windsor, the arrangements were more formal and the diversions limited. Victoria had always been conscious that her early education had been scarcely adequate and she was rarely much of a conversationalist. 'I must have dined a great many times at the Queen's dinner party,' wrote Lord Ribblesdale, 'and I personally never heard her say anything at dinner which I remembered next morning. Her manners were not affable; she spoke very little at meals; and she ate fast and seldom laughed.' Her hearty appetite was commented on by many observers. Since plates were cleared as soon as the queen was finished, newcomers were given a friendly warning to press on with their feeding and let the conversation take care of itself. The new duchess of Marlborough, an American heiress, found dinner 'a most depressing function' in 1898, with the old queen an inhibiting presence. Two years later, the Aga Khan found Victoria more animated, and noted that her accent was a curious mixture of German and Scottish. Her conversation was punctuated with the German 'tso', the bequest presumably of Mama and Albert. 'In spite of her age,' remarked the Aga Khan, 'the Queen ate and drank heartily—every kind of wine that was offered, and every course, including both the hot and iced pudding.'

Since the queen carried on a life-long vendetta against overheated rooms, visitors often shivered in silence. On the mantelpiece of each room was a thermometer to remind them of their duty. Since routine was geared to the needs of an elderly widow, who preferred the company of her ladies and unmarried daughters, the gentlemen were frequently bored. The queen disapproved strongly of smoking and in earlier days notices prohibiting it were pinned on the walls of rooms. Only in the billiards room was smoking permitted. The king of Saxony, fortified by rank, drew on a large cigar all the way up the grand staircase, to the horror of the court, but lesser mortals like Count Hatzfeldt were reduced to sneaking off to their bedrooms and puffing cigar smoke up the chimney.

It is far from easy to make a sober assessment of the political importance of Victoria's frenzied activities. She was undoubtedly a factor not to be ignored, and within the limits of the advance towards democracy which she could not resist, she defended her rights with tenacity. She won some notable victories. On Gladstone's final retirement in 1894, which the queen bore with fortitude, she offered the premiership to Lord Rosebery rather than Harcourt. Chamberlain and Dilke were allowed into office only after they had explained away their republican past. She refused to have Labouchere in the cabinet in 1892 unless he gave up his connection with the radical paper *Truth*, which he was not willing to do. In 1895 she expressed a strong desire that Henry Mathews should not be reappointed as home secretary, and Salisbury wrote that he had obeyed Her Majesty's wishes. She was flagrantly partisan in her attitude to Disraeli in the

1870s and to his successor as leader of the Tory party, Lord Salisbury. She kept up correspondence with the former after he had resigned in 1880 and in 1894 when she was angry with the Liberals for attacking the House of Lords she enquired from Salisbury, leader of the opposition, whether 'the Unionist party is fit for a dissolution *now*'. On the death of Gordon at Khartoum in 1885 she caused great embarrassment to Gladstone by sending an open telegram: 'to think that all this might have been prevented and many precious lives saved by earlier action is too frightful.' The fact that she was right did not make it easier for Gladstone to bear.

Nevertheless, there are serious reservations. In a reign of more than sixty years, a constitutional monarch is bound to win some skirmishes. Her dislike of Palmerston in the first half of her reign did very little to halt his political progress, and her deep detestation of Gladstone in the second half did not prevent him becoming prime minister four times and carrying on to the age of eighty-four. Her posture was essentially a defensive one: she could resist and protest and obstruct, but it was hard for her to initiate. Only the Public Worship Bill of 1874—to cleanse popish practices from the Anglican Church—was the result of her direct intervention. Even the veto on the employment of certain ministers could only work provided their colleagues were not unwilling to acquiesce. If the prime minister and cabinet were prepared to fight, she was well aware that, because she could not resign, her position was weak. In 1881 she was indignant that the draft queen's speech proposed to evacuate Afghanistan. Harcourt insisted that the speech was understood to be that of the ministers and only in the formal sense of the sovereign. She consulted Beaconsfield privately, who encouraged her to resist. But she had to give way. In 1895 a similar point emerged when Rosebery wished to include references to Welsh and Scottish disestablishment. Salisbury supported her right to withhold approval. But the queen's speech contained references just the same.

One of the best-known analyses of the Victorian constitution, by Walter Bagehot, offered the proposition that the dignified part of the constitution, the monarchy, disguised the efficient part, including prime minister and cabinet: 'A Republic has insinuated itself beneath the folds of a monarchy.' But Bagehot seriously underestimated the surviving influence of the crown in his own day: 'the Queen must sign her own death warrant if the two Houses unanimously send it up to her' is a *bon mot* rather than a sensible appraisal. One must remember that Bagehot's essays first appeared in 1865 when the queen had not recovered from her bereavement: hence she and the Prince of Wales are introduced, somewhat irreverently, as 'a retired widow and an unemployed youth'. Bagehot was hardly in a position to know how much influence the queen exerted. His famous aphorism, that a constitutional monarch has the right to be consulted, to encourage, and to warn, is a little too pat. The queen did not merely warn: she raged. Ministers would probably have added to Bagehot's list the right to harass

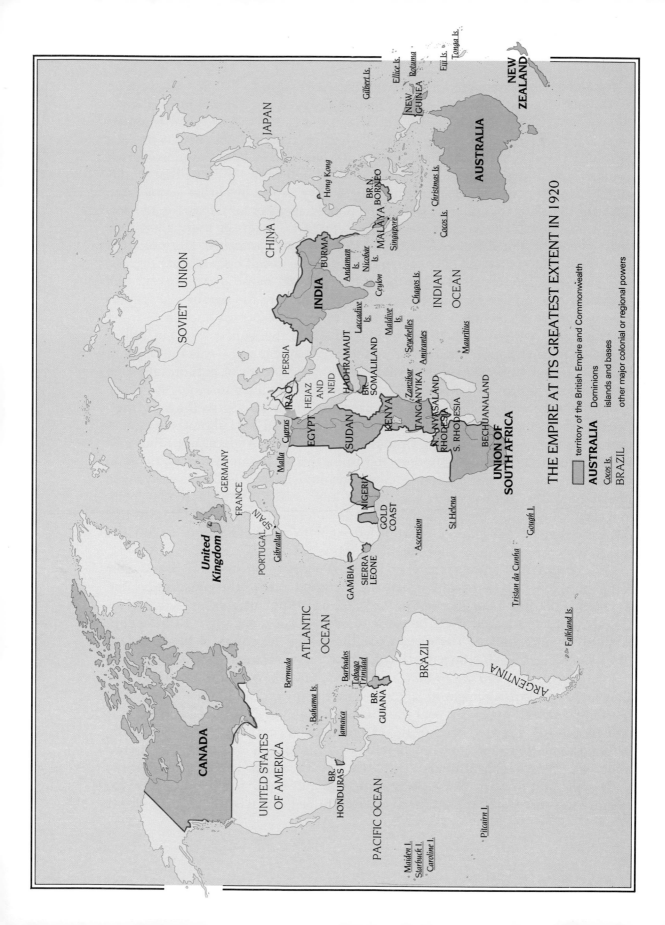

THE EMPIRE AT ITS GREATEST EXTENT IN 1920

territory of the British Empire and Commonwealth

AUSTRALIA   Dominions

Cocos Is.   islands and bases

BRAZIL   other major colonial or regional powers

CANADA

UNITED STATES
OF AMERICA

United
Kingdom

PORTUGAL

SPAIN

FRANCE

GERMANY

SOVIET UNION

JAPAN

CHINA

PERSIA

IRAQ

HEJAZ
AND
NEJD

HADHRAMAUT

EGYPT

SUDAN

BR.
SOMALILAND

KENYA

TANGANYIKA

N. NYASALAND
RHODESIA
S. RHODESIA

BECHUANALAND

UNION OF
SOUTH AFRICA

NIGERIA

GOLD
COAST

GAMBIA

SIERRA
LEONE

Gibraltar

Malta

Cyprus

INDIA

BURMA

Andaman
Is.

Nicobar
Is.

Ceylon

Laccadive
Is.

Maldive
Is.

Chagos Is.

Seychelles

Amirantes

Zanzibar

Mauritius

INDIAN
OCEAN

Hong Kong

MALAYA
BR. N.
BORNEO

Singapore

Christmas Is.

Cocos Is.

NEW
GUINEA

Gilbert Is.

Ellice Is.

Rotuma

Tonga Is.

Fiji Is.

AUSTRALIA

NEW
ZEALAND

St Helena

Ascension

Tristan da Cunha

Gough I.

ATLANTIC
OCEAN

Bermuda

Bahama Is.

Jamaica

BR.
HONDURAS

Barbados

Tobago
Trinidad

BR.
GUIANA

BRAZIL

ARGENTINA

Falkland Is.

PACIFIC OCEAN

Maiden I.

Starbuck I.

Caroline I.

Pitcairn I.

and obstruct. In 1883 even the long-suffering Gladstone was driven to complain that the queen was 'enough to kill any man', while Salisbury—whom the queen was trying to help—remarked that he ran four departments, 'the prime ministership, the foreign office, the Queen, and Randolph Churchill, and the burden of them increases in that order'. But the power to harass and obstruct is not real power, and some of Victoria's evident exasperation may have stemmed from her recognition of that fact.

Bagehot did, however, perceive that the overall influence of the crown was not necessarily diminished by the erosion of its strictly political rights. He took note of the social and psychological influence that the monarch possessed, analysing it in four categories. First was the idea of a royal family, with all its many activities: the marriage of the Prince of Wales, he remarked, was treated as though it was a great event. Secondly, its religious and mystical character enabled the crown to act as a symbol of national unity: 'it is commonly hidden like a mystery and sometimes paraded like a pageant.' Thirdly, the monarch was the unchallengeable head of society, eliminating that competition for supremacy which would otherwise have taken place. Lastly, the crown had become the head of the moral order, setting the tone of society and the country.

Bagehot undoubtedly exaggerated the political neutrality of the crown, describing future rather than existing practice. He wrote too early to be fully aware of the potential of the crown as the symbol of imperial unity. Soon after Victoria's death, Balfour expounded this function to her successor:

The King . . . is now the greatest constitutional bond uniting together in a single Empire communities of free men separated by half the circumference of the globe. All the patriotic sentiment which makes such an Empire centres in him . . . Its citizens know little and care less for British ministries and British party politics. But they know, and care for, the Empire of which they are members and for the Sovereign who rules it.

Victoria died at Osborne in January 1901, aged eighty-one, after a slow and undramatic weakening of mind and body. Joseph Chamberlain remarked in 1898 that the queen was now the beneficiary of that veneration for 'ripe old age' that had, in turn, brought national regard for the duke of Wellington and Mr Gladstone. In December 1899 a spectacularly disastrous week at the start of the Boer War brought from her a characteristic show of spirit: 'please understand', she told Arthur Balfour at Windsor, 'that there is no one depressed in this house. We are not interested in the possibilities of defeat: they do not exist.' In the spring of 1900 she made a state visit to Dublin—'entirely her own idea', she told her daughter—though she had earlier vetoed a proposal to purchase a royal residence in Ireland, ostensibly on the grounds that the climate was unhealthy. Just before her eighty-first birthday, news of the relief of Mafeking showed that the tide in South Africa had turned. She stayed the course to the end, receiving

General Roberts in the last month of her life and conferring on him an earldom and the Garter for his victories over the Boers. The journal, which she had kept for sixty-nine years, was abandoned only four days before she died. On her deathbed, she was supported by her grandson Willy, the Kaiser, with his good arm. But the international family network which, for most of her reign, had been a source of strength, was beginning to look hazardous: if continental autocracy was in peril, would it drag down the British monarchy with it?

Her long reign had demonstrated that not even the most determined monarch could prevent the draining away of direct political power. Slowly the balance had tipped to the electorate, the parties, the cabinet, and the prime minister. But there were compensating advantages and alternative possibilities. Political power is not the only form of power and its exercise, in an increasingly democratic world, threatened to involve the crown in damaging confrontations. There was a different role to which the response to her own period of seclusion had drawn attention. In the later decades of the century, the royal family travelled and were seen on a scale never before possible. The continued spread of newspapers, journals, and magazines, the invention of photography and moving pictures gave the illusion of access to millions of ordinary people. H. G. Wells's mother, in her housekeeper's room at Uppark, was not the only Victorian to follow the life of her queen with fascination.

The changes that had made possible the greater public awareness of the monarchy also pointed to an important new role. When the queen was born, stage coaches lumbered up and down the Great North Road as they had done for decades: by the time she died, a great network of railways was in existence, and Langley and the Wright brothers were on the brink of success with their flying machines. To many people, the monarchy became a rock of stability and security in a world of constant and bewildering change. This imparted to it an essentially conservative function—of anchor—but it also facilitated the acceptance of change, particularly among the upper classes. Of course it was to some extent illusory. The institution that appeared unchanging amid change had itself survived mainly by demonstrating a remarkable capacity for change within existing forms and ceremonies. Rationally, the death of an old tired lady could be of no possible consequence to most of her subjects, who had not known her and had never met her. But since they thought it was, it was. Nor was it only the poor and unsophisticated who were bewildered by news of her death: Henry James, the novelist, celebrated for his dissection of feelings, wrote, 'we all feel a bit motherless today: mysterious little Victoria is dead and fat vulgar Edward is king'.

Edward VII

The moment which many members of his family had awaited with ill-concealed apprehension was now at hand—the accession of Albert Edward, Prince of Wales. His first action, like that of his mother's in 1837, was a private declaration of independence. She had given orders for her bed to be removed from Mama's room for the first time in her life: the new king announced that he would rule, not as his parents had fondly wished, as Albert I, but as Edward VII.

The reasons behind the apprehension are not hard to detect. From the earliest age, the sluggishness of the prince's mental equipment had been an embarrassment. His tutors found it extremely hard to engage his attention, and he was prone to fits of ungovernable rage. He had little power of concentration, was easily bored, and never developed any taste for reading. It has, of course, often been suggested that Bertie's shortcomings were the product of an unimaginative and relentless education and routine, enforced by over-anxious and earnest parents. Such a regime was not extraordinary by mid-Victorian standards, nor were his tutors unaware that it was bad for him to be surrounded only by adults. Unfortunately, when boys of his own age were brought across from Eton to meet him, the prince treated them so abominably that their parents refused to send them again, and the Provost wrote to complain of the prince's apparent enjoyment in inflicting pain. He was, decided the Prince Consort, indescribably lazy: 'I never in my life met with such a thorough and cunning lazybones,' he wrote to his eldest daughter; 'it does grieve me when it is my own son, and when one considers that he might be called upon at any moment to take over the reins of government in a country where the sun never sets.' But the prince continued indefatigably indolent, self-occupied, and pleasure-seeking. His sense of humour remained that of a retarded schoolboy, pouring brandy over the heads of his guests or stubbing out the butt of his cigar in the palm of some unsuspecting crony. One of the least amiable of his traits was his willingness to drop rank with others and his resentment if they dropped rank with him. Genial and expansive one moment, he could turn icy, and tipsy, pert guests at the billiard table could be told to pack their bags.

His appearance improved considerably as he got older. He was short in stature and as a youth, his weak chin and hang-dog expression irritated his mother considerably. He grew fat rapidly, sported a beard, and could pass as a jolly, jovial gentleman. It is certainly true that, despite appeals from both the prince and ministers of the crown, the queen adamantly refused to take him into her confidence on matters of state or offer him any share in government. But this was mainly because she did not trust his discretion. Lord Granville, foreign secretary during the Franco-Prussian war, complained that he had passed on confidential information to the prince only to be warned that he had shown the note to dinner guests the same evening. Not until 1892, when he was over fifty, was he given

SHOOTING PARTY AT SANDRINGHAM. Among the attractions of Sandringham was that the light sandy soil was excellent for breeding game birds. The slaughter of animals and birds was gigantic. A day's shooting could dispatch 3,000 birds or 6,000 rabbits. The king was much impressed by a *battue* on the estate of Baron von Hirsch auf Gereuth at St Johann where ten guns in ten days killed 20,000 partridges. The ladies were expected to watch and admire. In this photograph, Queen Alexandra is on the king's left, the Prince of Wales (the future George V) stands second from left, and the Princess of Wales (the future Queen Mary) is seated third from left. Mrs George Keppel is just behind the king's right shoulder.

access to the range of state papers. Consequently, the prince spent his life in a round of cards, horse-racing, parties, shooting, and the pursuit of women. Dilke, who had shrugged off his republican past and become acquainted with the prince, thought that he had 'less real brain power than the queen': it was not impossible to influence him, though he did not much listen and talked incessantly. He was not totally without interest in public questions. He became a member of the Royal Commission on the Housing of the Working Classes and in 1884 once spent a whole morning visiting the slums of St Pancras, before returning to Marlborough House for luncheon. He followed the experience with a short speech in the Lords explaining how well the tenants at Sandringham were looked after.

The country estate of Sandringham in Norfolk had been purchased for the prince just before his father died. The house was unremarkable, but the estate was large and the shooting good. Victoria thought the whole area bleak when she visited it for the first time, but the occasion was a bleak one, being her winter visit to the prince at the time of his serious illness in 1871. The prince and his wife were devoted to the place, and it became the centre of their lives, with large weekend parties and massive shoots.

Princess Alexandra, elegant and distinguished, acquired very wide popularity. Her command of English was at first somewhat inadequate and placed her at a disadvantage, and from an early age she was afflicted with increasing deafness. This contributed towards a rather vague and aloof manner in public, and was partly responsible for her concentration on family concerns. She and the prince were affectionate, though he soon found other women, of whom Lily Langtry, Lady Brooke, and Mrs Keppel were the best known.

Contemporaries were inclined to credit the king with great political influence, particularly in foreign affairs. This was an illusion. He had never acquired habits of disciplined work, and, coming to the throne at the age of fifty-nine, was unlikely to learn them. Sir Frederick Ponsonby wrote that he would never make the slightest effort to go into the details of anything that bored him, and Sir John Fisher, who had every reason to be grateful to the king for his support of naval reform, remarked that no impression was lasting upon him—'he can't grasp details'. If Victoria, industrious to the very end, had failed to stem the tide, it was impossible for Edward, in an even more complex world, to do so. Though he had

QUEEN ALEXANDRA IN CORONATION ROBES. At her coronation in 1902, Alexandra was still an elegant and beautiful woman. She did not seem greatly concerned at her husband's attentions to other women and outlived him by sixteen years, dying at Sandringham in 1925.

strong and conventionally Tory political views, he had not enough understanding of political matters to make much impression on ministers. Balfour and the Tories treated him particularly casually. In September 1903 Balfour moved to fill the vacancies caused by resignation over the preference issue while the king was at Balmoral. Edward replied by telegram that the resignations should not be announced before he had had the opportunity to discuss them with the prime minister, only to be told that they had already been announced. The king retorted that Arnold-Forster was quite unacceptable as War Minister: he was appointed. Six months later, the king demanded to be consulted before questions were put to cabinet: 'it is impossible for us to yield in a matter of this kind', wrote Balfour.

His high reputation as a European diplomatist was based largely on a hugely successful visit to Paris, which he had always loved, in 1903, and on his meeting at Reval in 1908 with the Tsar, which were held to have cemented the Triple Entente. The comment of an Italian ambassador—'he is the arbiter of Europe's destiny'—shows a total misunderstanding of the British constitution and of the character of the king. Though excellent at public relations, Edward took little part in the formation of policy and none at all in the detailed negotiations. In 1901, to the dismay of his officials, he handed over to the Kaiser his briefing notes on the meeting. Balfour, prime minister in the early years of his reign, remarked that the king never made suggestions on any large aspect of policy and Sir Edward Grey, foreign secretary in the Liberal administration, observed that the king rarely made comments.

In two areas, however, the king had a contribution to make. His support for reform of the armed forces was constant and might have turned the scales in 1914. He was a staunch advocate of improvement of the army medical service and in 1908 stood by Haldane in his campaign against cuts in the army estimates. His advocacy of naval rearmament was even more marked, and he was a complete believer in Fisher's crusade for dreadnoughts.

His second success was in raising the profile of the monarchy, bringing it into the public eye, and obtaining for himself vast and genuine popularity. To a great extent, the retreat from real power was covered by a smokescreen of public acclaim. His appearance was impressive and unmistakable; he delighted in ceremony, possessed a good memory for people, could command graceful gestures, and exuded a general air of affability. His womanizing was, by most of his subjects, regarded amiably as a sign of manliness and spirit: 'Where's Alice?' shouted the crowd outside the opera in 1902. His pursuits and habits of life were those of many of his people. In 1896 he won the Derby with Persimmon. In 1900 he went one better and won both the Derby and the Grand National. In 1909 he won the Derby again with Minoru, amid scenes of frantic enthusiasm. He was larger than life, a king to be proud of. On his accession to the throne, he resumed the practice of opening Parliament in person, which his mother had allowed to lapse.

EDWARD VII

(1901–1910)

He had a most curious brain, and at one time one would find him a big, strong, far-seeing man, grasping the situation at a glance and taking a broad-minded view of it; at another one would be almost surprised at the smallness of his mind. He would be almost childish in his views, and would obstinately refuse to understand the question at issue.

(Sir Frederick Ponsonby, *Recollections of Three Reigns*)

THE greater part of Edward VII's life was spent in the pursuit of pleasure, or perhaps the avoidance of boredom. He had few resources of his own, though he enjoyed the theatre, played bridge, and was devoted to the pleasures of the table. Like many underemployed people, he fussed about trifles, and had an eagle eye for decorations wrongly worn, buttons out of place, and similar lapses of sartorial propriety. His joviality was genuine, but untrustworthy, sunshine and showers in rapid succession: 'there can be no doubt', wrote Sir Frederick Ponsonby, 'that even his most intimate friends were all terrified of him.' He liked to travel incognito but was irritated when the consequence was that he did not receive royal attention. Nevertheless, his personal characteristics enabled him to supply an important new dimension to the monarchy, which achieved a much higher profile than had been possible in the later decades of an elderly widowed queen. He travelled indefatigably, performed his public duties with skill and zest, and left an impression of benevolent royalty. Hence the monarchy emerged from his short reign on a more public footing than before, which coincided with the arrival of the popular press and the cinema.

EDWARD aged about twenty.

On his thirtieth birthday.

In his fifties.

During the last year of his life, the king was involved in a crisis as dangerous for the monarchy as that of 1832. Edward's sympathies had never been with the Liberals and he watched their great electoral victory in 1906 without enthusiasm. Churchill and Lloyd George he found particularly trying. In July 1909 Lloyd George made a famous speech at Limehouse in which he remarked that 'a fully-equipped Duke cost as much to keep up as two dreadnoughts' and was less easy to scrap. The king denounced it as socialism at its worst, 'an insult to the sovereign'. In November the House of Lords rejected Lloyd George's budget, which, in order to pay for old-age pensions and naval rearmament, proposed death duties and a surcharge or supertax on large incomes. It was the first time for more than two hundred years that the Lords had intervened in money matters and it produced a grand confrontation. Slowly the king was pulled into the dispute. Asquith demanded a dissolution and was granted it. He then enquired whether, in the event of the Lords again rejecting the budget, the king would be willing to create enough peers to swamp the Tory majority and allow a Parliament Bill, curtailing the Lords' powers, to pass. The king had already explained that such a request would place him in an awkward position. It would be tantamount to destroying the Lords and he would consent to it only after a second election had placed the matter before the country.

The proposal to emasculate the House of Lords carried an obvious threat to the monarchy. Victoria had been adamant that hereditary peerage and hereditary monarchy went together. To Gladstone she had written in 1884 that 'to threaten the House of Lords is, in fact, to threaten the monarchy itself'. But there was a further and equally dangerous dimension to the crisis. Gladstone's first administration, for all his good intentions, had signally failed to pacify Ireland. The Prince of Wales took the full force of Irish disaffection in 1885 when, on an ill-judged visit to Cork, he was pelted and hooted: 'no one who went through that day', wrote one of his aides, 'will forget it. . . . It was like a bad dream.' Gladstone's attempt at Home Rule in 1886 split his party, forcing the Liberal Unionists into collaboration and then merger with the Conservatives. When he tried again in 1893, the measure was defeated in the Lords by 419 votes to 41. The 1910 election gave the Irish nationalists their chance. The Liberals came back with 275 seats against 273 for the Conservatives, leaving them dependent upon Irish support for Parliamentary survival. A Parliament Bill could now be used to push through Irish Home Rule. Conservatives saw in the crisis of 1910 not only the seeds of class warfare but the beginning of the dismemberment of the British Empire.

In April 1910 a Parliament Bill was introduced, formally preventing the Lords' rejection of any money bill, arranging for the passing of other bills after three successive rejections, and reducing the duration of Parliaments from seven to five years. The king did not live to see the denouement. Decades of smoking twelve cigars a day, eked out with cigarettes, accompanied by gross overeating, caught up at last with his staunch physique. He returned at the end of April from a two months' stay at Biarritz crippled with bronchial trouble, and succumbed on 6 May after a series of heart attacks. In the last conversation between them, the Prince of Wales told him that his horse had won the 4.15 at Kempton Park. 'I am very glad,' murmured the king.

Edward VII was the last monarch of whom it could be said that he was the

AT DRURY LANE. After Victoria's private and secluded existence, it was a novelty to have an extrovert monarch, who enjoyed public appearances. Edward VII is here shown with a party in the royal box at Drury Lane in 1909.

centre of society. It is not merely that his four successors, in their different ways, were neither greatly interested in nor suited to such a role. Society in the old sense scarcely survived the Great War. The eclipse of the gentry and aristocracy, long predicted, finally came to pass, and though garden parties and the presentation of debutantes were still there in the world of social democracy and the great dictators, they seemed increasingly shadows. Edward was lucky in his death: he did not have to see his world in pieces. 'We have always been an aristocratic country', he had written to his mother, 'and I hope we shall always remain so, as they are the mainstay of this country.' In similar fashion, the Great War swept away the crowned heads of Europe, Kaiser, Tsar, Emperor, and all the little kings and princes of Germany. Edward VII's role as 'the uncle of Europe' no longer existed. This sense of a vanished past gave to his reign, in the course of time, an elegiac quality, an Elgar-like *nobilmente*, which it did not perhaps quite merit.

George V

The new king, George V, was a sailor by upbringing and temperament. On rising in the morning and retiring at night, he tapped the barometer. His speech was blunt and his voice loud. He had little taste for society and one of the charms of York Cottage at Sandringham, where he remained until the Queen Dowager died, was that its small size afforded splendid excuse to avoid entertaining. The two great recreations of his life were collecting stamps and shooting. Unlike his father, he was a crack shot and did not need to be fed with easy targets. He was ill at ease on public occasions with a deep dislike of ceremony: the state opening of Parliament in February 1911 he described as 'the most terrible ordeal I have ever gone through', though his speech was of course written by his ministers and the crowds lining the streets gave him a very friendly reception.

Like his predecessor as sailor king, William IV, he had not expected to find himself monarch. He had an elder brother, Albert Victor, known to the family as 'Eddy', and created duke of Clarence in 1890. There seems little doubt that Eddy's difficulties were physical in origin: his tutors reported him to be indolent and unenterprising. He served a spell at sea with his younger brother but in the

PRINCE GEORGE was sent to the naval training ship *Britannia* at Dartmouth in 1877 at the age of twelve. He was small and, as he later remarked, 'got a hiding time and again'. One fight made his nose bleed: 'it was the best blow I ever took, for the doctor forbade my fighting any more.'

army the commander-in-chief complained that he was unable to learn even elementary drill movements. He showed rather more enterprise in getting into amatory scrapes and in 1890 his father wrote, more in hope than experience, that 'a good sensible wife' was urgently needed: 'his education and future have been a matter of some considerable anxiety to us, and the difficulty of rousing him is very great.' The choice fell upon Princess May of Teck, brought up in England, daughter of the queen's first cousin. The prince's secretary wrote, unromantically, that Eddy should be 'told he *must* do it—that it is for the good of the country, etc. etc.'. In December 1891 the engagement was announced. The following month Eddy died at Sandringham of influenza turning to pneumonia.

Prince George took over, not merely his brother's role, but his fiancée as well. After a decent interval, they were married in July 1893. Though the marriage could hardly have been more a matter of state, it became one of great affection. George was essentially a shy and private man, devoted to family life. His relations with his parents were warm and intimate. Despite their considerable differences in taste and temperament, he got on well with his father, who wrote that he had always regarded George more as a brother than a son. Princess Alexandra, his mother, showered him with love though, in her vague way, scarcely seemed to acknowledge that he grew up. The prince seems not to have resented it, signing himself 'your loving little Georgy'. At the age of twenty-five, in command of a gunboat, he received from his mother a letter with 'a great big kiss for your lovely little face'.

Superficially the prince was badly equipped for what was to prove one of the most turbulent reigns in modern British history. He had no command of languages at all. He had scarcely any interest in art or music. But his father, determined that his own son should not suffer the disadvantages inflicted on him, made sure that he saw the most important state papers and at Windsor, during Edward's reign, they worked side by side on matters of state. His knowledge of the world picked up during his naval career was augmented by visits to Australia in 1901 and India in 1905. Above all he possessed a basic integrity, a determination to do his duty, which carried the unmistakable impression of his grandmother.

In 1910 the new king was plunged at once into a most protracted and difficult political and constitutional crisis, during which he was frequently assured that the future of the monarchy was at stake. His task was made the more difficult by the fact that his private secretaries, on whose advice in constitutional matters the sovereign greatly relies, were at variance.

Though the House of Lords had retreated on the budget, there remained the question how ministers proposed to get the Parliament Bill through the Lords. In June 1910 Asquith and Balfour began talks to see if a compromise could be reached. Five months of discussion proved abortive. Asquith then asked for

TIGER SHOOTING, 1912. George V had paid a very successful visit to India in 1905 when Prince of Wales and, as soon as he became king, decided to repeat it. There was a great coronation Durbar at Delhi, after which he wrote: 'rather tired after wearing the Crown for $3\frac{1}{2}$ hours, it hurt my head, as it is pretty heavy.' But, for the king, the high spot was a fortnight's shooting. 'As probably this will be the last and only time in my life when I shall get big game shooting of this kind, I naturally wish to have as many days in Nepal as possible.' In his fortnight, he shot 21 tigers, 8 rhino, and one bear. This, he remarked, was a record.

another dissolution, together with a private pledge from the king that after the election he would, if necessary, create enough peers to carry the bill. It was presumed that, if Asquith and his colleagues resigned before the election, Balfour would not be willing to form a minority government. Knollys advised the king to give the pledges asked for, lest the monarchy, by refusing the advice of its ministers, be dragged into 'the vortex of our political controversies'. Bigge, the other secretary, tendered the opposite advice: the request was both unreasonable and unconstitutional; there was no case for a contingent guarantee, whatever the ultimate outcome might be. Indeed, Asquith was on record that 'a blank authority for an indefinite exercise of the royal prerogative' was a request which no statesman should ask for nor any sovereign be expected to grant. If the promise was to be genuinely secret, it is not clear what advantage accrued to the Liberals from obtaining it. Nevertheless, Asquith and Lord Crewe, leader of

THE PRIVATE SECRETARY

T HE post of private secretary to the sovereign developed in the nineteenth century. In the early decades of George III's reign, the volume of business was comparatively small and the king wrote his own letters and minutes. But failing eyesight forced him in 1805 to seek assistance and he appointed a soldier, Sir Herbert Taylor, thus establishing a long military tradition. During the Regency, Taylor acted for Queen Charlotte, but was recalled by William IV and played an important intermediary role during the crisis over the Great Reform Act. Melbourne paid tribute to Taylor's influence: 'I don't believe the King could have carried it on without Taylor,' he told Victoria. 'Taylor was a very fair man; *upon my honour*, I don't see how it could have gone on; the King used to go and talk to Taylor, and Taylor softened matters.' Victoria had no private secretary for the first years of her reign. The services of Baroness Lehzen, her former governess, were eked out by Baron Stockmar, sent over specially by Leopold of the Belgians as constitutional adviser. After their marriage, Prince Albert acted increasingly as secretary, indeed, at times, almost as joint sovereign. General Charles Grey, son of the prime minister, performed the more routine secretarial duties. On Grey's death in 1870 Victoria appointed another soldier, Sir Henry Ponsonby. His letters, published by his son, indicate the pains he took to keep the queen in touch with public opinion. He was deeply concerned at the unpopularity which the queen's seclusion was bringing upon the monarchy: 'if she is neither the head of the executive, nor the fountain of honour, nor the centre of display, the royal dignity will sink to nothing at all.' Ponsonby suffered a stroke in 1895 and was replaced by Arthur Bigge, who had greatly impressed the queen when reporting the cir-

cumstances of the Prince Imperial's death in South Africa in 1879. For fifteen years, Bigge had acted as Ponsonby's assistant.

Edward VII, on succeeding to the throne, continued with his own secretary, Francis Knollys, and Bigge moved on to serve the heir to the throne. For three years from 1910, George V had two secretaries, Bigge and Knollys. It was not an easy arrangement and in the great constitutional crisis of the autumn of 1910, they offered conflicting advice. Knollys retired in 1913, leaving Bigge, ennobled as Lord Stamfordham, in undisputed charge until his death in 1931. His successor, Clive Wigram, had also served as assistant secretary. He was a soldier and a sportsman, and sprinkled his letters with sporting metaphors: 'my first Test match' was his description of the events leading to the National Government. 'It seems to take a good deal to make him understand things,' wrote Reith of the BBC loftily. Edward VIII appointed Alexander Hardinge, who had also served as Wigram's assistant. It fell to him, in the early days of his post, to address a candid warning to the new king that his relations with Mrs Simpson were causing great speculation. Hardinge continued in office under George VI, retiring in 1943 on grounds of health. His successors in office were Sir Alan Lascelles, Sir Michael Adeane, Sir Martin Charteris, and Sir Philip Moore. Secretaries of intelligence and long experience, such as Taylor, Ponsonby, and Bigge, were in a position to wield considerable constitutional influence, particularly in moments of crisis, when the advice of the politicians might be confused or at odds. There is no suggestion, however, that any of them aimed at, or were credited with, power behind the throne.

GEORGE V and Lord Stamfordham, his private secretary, in the grounds of Buckingham Palace, June 1918.

the House of Lords, in an audience on 16 November, forced the king to give the assurances sought.

George V never forgot the episode and strongly resented the pressure applied to him. It is hard to resist the conclusion that Asquith took advantage of the king's inexperience to rescue himself from the predicament he was in as a result of implying that he would obtain assurances. William IV's advice to Victoria, drawn from a very similar situation, would have helped his successor greatly—never to give pledges, ask for proposals in writing, and insist on time to consider. Nor is it clear how Asquith could have justified refusing to allow the king to consult Balfour, when the question whether an alternative government could be formed was both important and obscure. The second election produced a slightly increased Liberal majority and the Parliament Bill was reintroduced. Enough Tory peers absented themselves or voted with the Liberals to get it through the Lords, partly to avoid placing the king in an impossible dilemma, partly to prevent their majority being swamped by up to five hundred Liberal creations.

The resolution of one crisis merely prepared the way for the next. The Parliament Act opened the door to Irish Home Rule, the price which Redmond and his nationalists demanded for supporting the Liberals. Since resistance in the House of Lords was now out of the question, Ulster began arming to prevent incorporation and the Nationalists to impose it. The king watched the drift into civil war with great dismay, particularly since Asquith seemed somewhat unconcerned. Bonar Law, who had replaced Balfour as leader of the Conservatives, argued that now the House of Lords had been forced into submission, the royal veto could once more be employed. But for the king to veto a measure supported by his responsible ministers and passed with large majorities in the Commons would, in 1914, have been a suicidal course. Harcourt, one of the Liberal ministers, warned that royal intervention could 'reduce the throne to a hopeless ruin'. In the autumn of 1913, with a touching faith in the goodwill of politicians, the king fell back upon that other panacea, a conference of parties. Asquith warned him against allowing himself to be talked into a veto:

We have now a well-established tradition of 200 years that, in the last resort, the occupant of the Throne accepts and acts upon the advice of his ministers. The sovereign may have lost something of his personal power and authority, but the Crown has been thereby removed from the storms and vicissitudes of party politics . . . the Crown would (otherwise) become the football of contending factions.

Nevertheless, Asquith agreed to talks with Bonar Law. They broke down. In the spring of 1914 Asquith offered a compromise—that Ulster be excluded for six years. Carson and his Ulstermen rejected a mere stay of execution. Disaffection among army officers came to a head with the Curragh incident, when some sixty cavalry officers resigned rather than coerce Ulster. The king was 'grieved beyond words'. In July 1914 another conference took place, at Buckingham Palace. Radicals and Irish nationalists much resented the king's intervention, which Charles Trevelyan hoped would turn working men towards republicanism. Again the conference collapsed, this time on the question of the borders of an excluded Ulster, lost, in Churchill's phrase 'in the muddy by-ways of Fermanagh and Tyrone'. But, in August 1914, the Irish crisis was swallowed up by the crisis to end all crises.

The Great War was the time of the breaking of monarchies. Before 1914 they formed the dominant system, challenged only in France, the United States, and Latin America: after 1918, they were an endangered species, clinging on mainly to the outer extremities of Europe.

Throughout most of the nineteenth century, monarchy seemed, if anything, to be gaining ground. Emergent nations seeking recognition in a dynastic world chose monarchs as a badge of respectability. Leopold of Saxe-Coburg, Victoria's uncle, turned down the throne of Greece in 1830 and became king of the Belgians the following year. Prince Otto, one of the Wittelsbachs, then took the Greek throne. Prince Alexander of Battenberg, whose brother was married to Queen Victoria's granddaughter Victoria, became king of Bulgaria in 1879 and Albania chose Prince Wilhelm of Wied in 1913. Serbia and Montenegro both chose native princes. One of the last kingdoms to be established was Norway, which broke away from Sweden in 1905 and invited Prince Karl of Denmark to become king as Haakon VII. He was married to Maud, Edward VII's youngest daughter. The crowned heads of Europe looked down upon this new dynasty and the coronation was not well attended. The English Prince of Wales and his wife went over to support George's sister, though Princess May commented: 'the whole thing seems curious but we live in *very* modern days.'

The widespread hatred towards the Germans which the war produced posed problems for the royal family, with their very strong German links. Edward VII and Queen Mary both spoke English with a trace of German accent. Prince Louis of Battenberg, a cousin of the king, was an effective First Sea Lord: the run against him was so severe that he was obliged to resign. The alliance with Tsarist Russia was also an embarrassment, since it inhibited the case that the war was one of democracy against autocracy. The royal family threw themselves into the war effort. The Prince of Wales went off to France, though he chafed at being kept away from the front line. Prince Albert served in HMS *Collingwood*, and saw action in the battle of Jutland. In 1915 the king, to the dismay of many of the court, imposed a ban on alcohol in the palace during the war to set an example to the nation. In 1917 George decided to change the royal family's name to Windsor. Prince Louis took the name Mountbatten, and was ennobled as marquess of Milford Haven: the duke of Teck, the queen's brother, was made marquess of Cambridge. The king also told the Council that in future members of the royal family would be permitted to marry into British families. Purists and extreme royalists raised their eyebrows at so democratic a gesture, but the majority welcomed the closer identification of monarchy with nation.

The king and his advisers were well aware that defeat in the struggle might bring about the fall of the monarchy. They had been concerned before the war at the growth of trade union militancy, the progress of the Labour Party, and the spread of socialist and syndicalist doctrines. In August 1917 Lord Esher confided to the king's private secretary that if they failed to beat the enemy 'we shall be lucky if we escape a revolution in which the Monarchy, the Church and all our "Victorian" institutions will founder ... I have met no one who, speaking his inmost mind, differs from this conclusion.' One cannot, of course, be certain. It is possible that a defeated nation might have rallied round the monarchy as the Japanese did in 1945, or that a victorious Kaiser might have extended protection to his cousin, not out of sentiment, but in the interests of monarchical solidarity. In the event, the monarchy emerged from the war stronger than before. In the testing time, the wisdom of constitutional monarchy, with the sovereign's role severely limited, contrasted with the disasters that overtook the great European autocracies. The Kaiser had taken a prominent part in the formulation of pre-war German policy and could hardly expect to survive defeat. Nicholas II of Russia

WALKABOUTS. (*Right*) George V makes a better shot at a walkabout than his great-great-grandfather on p. 519. He is talking to a young lad at Sunderland during the Great War. (*Facing*) Accompanied by Queen Mary on a visit to Shadwell in 1922.

blundered by taking personal charge of the Russian army in August 1915, thereby associating himself with the military catastrophe that was to follow.

In March 1917 George V heard, with despair, that his cousin the Tsar had been forced to abdicate. Russia's allies were greatly agitated that the revolution would take her out of the war, leaving them to face the whole weight of German power. Making the best of a confused situation, Lloyd George telegraphed to the provisional government, pointing out that, more than ever, the war had become a struggle between popular governments and autocracies. The British government prepared to offer asylum to the Romanov family, though prudently adding that they should try to bring financial support with them. But the king sounded a warning note 'on general grounds of expediency', leading Balfour to reply that the invitation could hardly be withdrawn. Stamfordham, on behalf of the king, retorted that the Tsar's arrival would place the royal family in a very awkward position, and that public opinion, particularly on the left, was already hostile to the suggestion. The British ambassador in St Petersburg agreed that it would not be wise to risk an 'anti-monarchist' movement in Britain. The following year, the Russian royal family was butchered at Ekaterinburg. George V had placed the

claims of constitutional monarchy before those of family loyalty or even personal friendship, distancing himself from Tsarist autocracy, which was doomed.

The Irish question, which had been placed in cold storage in 1914, had not stayed frozen. Home Rule was postponed while war lasted, but at Easter 1916 the Irish Republican Army attempted to seize independence by force. At the general election of 1918, Sinn Fein captured seventy-three of the Irish seats, refused to attend Westminster, and established a provisional government. For some months British troops tried to suppress it. But in 1920 legislation was passed establishing two governments, one at Belfast and the other at Dublin. George V opened the Belfast assembly in June 1921 calling upon the Irish to 'forgive and forget'. Though the speech was couched as a personal appeal from the sovereign, it was a ministerial statement. De Valera, on behalf of Sinn Fein, refused to recognize the government in the north, and further negotiations took place. The king's role was limited to urging patience and restraint, and in December 1921 an agreement was signed for an Irish Free State in the south, with Dominion status.

George V has been credited by some writers with very considerable political influence, particularly after the war, when his prestige was high and his experience increasing. But the extreme claims that there was a reassertion of royal power can hardly be sustained. On two occasions, in 1923 and in 1931, he appeared to have considerable discretion over the choice of prime minister, and on both occasions his decisions were sharply criticized. In October 1922 the coalition broke up and Lloyd George resigned. His place was taken by Bonar Law and at the subsequent general election, the Conservatives gained a handsome majority over all other parties. But by May 1923 ill health had forced Bonar Law to resign. The choice lay between Lord Curzon, foreign secretary, and the relatively unknown Stanley Baldwin. The king appointed Baldwin, much to Curzon's chagrin, largely on the grounds that the prime minister should be in the House of Commons. However unpalatable to Curzon, the king's decision was common sense, particularly since five of the existing six Secretaries of State sat in the Lords. The king was unable to get advice directly from the retiring prime minister, who was too ill, but the arguments in favour of Baldwin were passed on through Bonar Law's private secretary and reinforced by Balfour, the senior statesman of the Conservative party. The king's action was careful, proper, constitutional, and based on the best advice he could obtain.

The situation in 1931 was more complex. The second Labour government split over the question of cuts in unemployment benefit, needed, it was argued, to prevent a crippling run on the pound. Ramsay MacDonald went to Buckingham Palace to tender his resignation but was persuaded by the king to stay on and preside over a National government, with Conservative and Liberal participation. MacDonald was repudiated by most of the parliamentary Labour party and the king was widely accused of partisanship. Herbert Morrison charged him

GEORGE V

(1910–1936)

GEORGE V, the second son of Edward VII and Queen Alexandra, was a shy, gruff man of plain and simple tastes, with an interest in shooting and stamp-collecting. His naval upbringing encouraged an excessive zeal for punctuality and routine. In 1893, he married Princess May, who had been engaged to his elder brother Eddy just before his death: she devoted herself to her husband's comfort and he was at his happiest in family and domestic life. They made their home in York Cottage at Sandringham, of which Harold Nicolson wrote:

For him Sandringham and the Sandringham ways of life represented the ideal of human felicity. 'Dear old Sandringham', he called it, 'the place I love better than anywhere in the world.' . . . Compared to York Cottage, all the palaces and castles of the earth meant little more to him than a sequence of official residences. It was at Sandringham that he spent his happiest hours; to Sandringham that in later years he would escape from the burden of his official labours; at Sandringham that he died.

After four years on the throne, the Great War broke out. George V flung himself into his duty, reviewing, inspecting, exhorting, and encouraging. In 1915, to set an example to the nation, he banned alcohol from all palaces for the duration: 'the Earl of Rosebery and the Rt. Hon. A. J. Balfour have left the Castle', wrote the Court Circular in happy juxtaposition. The austerity practised in the palaces was not greatly relished by his staff, as the following extract from Sir Frederick Ponsonby's *Recollections* demonstrates:

The King and Queen had decided to take the rations very seriously and at breakfast those who were late got nothing. When I say late, the ordinary meaning of the word hardly conveys the wonderful punctuality of the King and Queen. One was late if the clock sounded when one was on the stairs, even in a small house like York Cottage . . . There was just enough and no more for everyone, but as most people helped themselves too generously, there was nothing for the person who came last.

Godfrey-Faussett was kept on the telephone one day and came into the dining-room after everyone else had sat down. He found nothing to eat and immediately rang the bell and asked for a boiled egg. If he had ordered a dozen turkeys, he could not have made a bigger stir. The King accused him of being a slave to his inside, of unpatriotic behaviour, and even went so far as to hint that we should lose the war on account of his gluttony.

SAILOR KING, 1924. As well as being an accomplished shot and an informed philatelist, George V was a good sailor. He is seen here at Cowes in 1924 at the helm of his yacht *Britannia*.

with having drawn the monarchy into politics 'and pretty dangerous politics at that'. Harold Laski went further, insisting that MacDonald was 'as much the personal choice of George V as Lord Bute was the personal choice of George III'. It was a ludicrous comparison, and convicts Laski himself of poor scholarship as well as partisanship. MacDonald was a twice prime minister, holding office, and in the midst of a national crisis: Bute, by contrast, had no political experience, nor was there any political reason for his elevation. George V was certainly anxious to continue with MacDonald, whom he liked, and to see a government of national unity, after which sovereigns not infrequently hanker. But he acted strictly on constitutional advice. He consulted MacDonald who was both prime minister and leader of the Labour Party, and Samuel and Baldwin, the leaders of the other two parties, who were united in advising him to form a national government.

Of more genuine political significance was the attitude of the king to the first Labour government in 1923. Much depended on whether Labour, as the spearhead of radical change, could be reconciled to the existing parliamentary and political system. In the early days of the Labour movement, the Nonconformist strand predominated over the Marxist one. In 1910, when Edward VII was dying, the Labour MP Will Crooks described him as 'the greatest statesman that the world possesses', adding that the king was 'above men, above party . . . he is father to the lot of us and smiles down upon us all'. MacDonald soon modified his early views on the monarchy, writing in 1911 that the case for republicanism was 'of abstract interest only': provided that there was democratic control of government, 'Socialism does not consider republicanism of essential importance'. Maisky, a future Bolshevik, spoke for many foreign ideologists when he complained of the Labour Party in 1913 that 'Marxist ideas just did not get through to them'. The Bolshevik Revolution of 1917 caused an upsurge of radicalism, but an attempt in 1923 to shift the party ended in disaster. At the party conference, a motion that the royal family was no longer necessary as part of the constitution was defeated by nearly ten to one in votes. A few months later, the issue was put to the test. Baldwin's ill-judged dissolution resulted in a split Parliament, with 258 Conservatives, 191 Labour, and 159 Liberal members. Baldwin refused to revive the old coalition, Asquith refused to support the Conservatives, and the king decided that the Labour party must be given its chance. The king instantly struck up a good relationship with MacDonald. MacDonald wrote that the king was 'human and friendly' and Clynes that he was 'genial, kindly and considerate'. He agreed that ministers who disliked court

THE DELIGHTS OF BOGNOR. George V suffered a severe illness between November 1928 and April 1929 with a serious chest infection and abscesses placing strain upon his heart. Threatened with a trip abroad to recover, he preferred Bognor. As late as June 1929 he was obliged to receive Macdonald to form the second Labour government wearing a Chinese dressing-gown, and it was not until his cursing returned to its normal naval vigour in the autumn that his staff knew recovery was complete.

IN 1935 GEORGE V CELEBRATED HIS JUBILEE AT ST PAUL'S and was given an enthusiastic reception. The rather stylized painting is by Frank Salisbury. His granddaughter's jubilee in 1977 was seen on television by an estimated audience of more than five hundred million.

dress could appear in evening dress, and his private secretary pointed out helpfully that suitable attire could be hired from Moss Bros. To his mother the king wrote in February 1924 that his new ministers took things seriously and 'ought to be treated fairly'. In October 1924, after MacDonald had been defeated in the House of Commons, the king granted a dissolution without difficulty. He parted from MacDonald with the words, 'You have found me an ordinary man, haven't you', adding privately, 'I like him and have always found him quite straight'. Ardent radicals will reflect that by such stratagems are reformers tamed, but most Labour politicians drew the moral that the monarch would not present an obstacle to their programme.

Of direct political influence the king had little, though he dealt with his boxes punctiliously. Even in the granting of honours, he struggled to carry his nominations. In 1921 he proposed to give the Order of Merit to Gilbert Murray: though the award was a personal favour of the king, Lloyd George refused to agree to it on the grounds that Murray had been a pacifist. In 1930 the king suggested a knighthood for E. S. Saunders, the inventor of flying boats, to be told by MacDonald that others had better claims. But by the end of his reign the personal prestige of the monarchy was at a new height. For this there was a variety of reasons. No scandal of any kind attached to his name. Many of his prejudices—against foreign travel, or against demanding art or music—were shared by many of his subjects. He struck a remarkable balance between dignity—he was always immaculately turned out—and pomp, which he disliked. The spread of the cinema made him and the queen known to millions and from

1932 onwards an annual Christmas broadcast won him a large audience. Somehow his subjects gathered the impression of a decent man, determined to do his duty honestly. At his silver jubilee, in May 1935, he was greeted by vast crowds. The service at St Paul's he thought 'wonderful', marred only by a superfluity of parsons. To the two Houses of Parliament, he addressed in Westminster Hall, where Charles I had been tried, a speech composed by George Macaulay Trevelyan, great-nephew of Macaulay and custodian of the Whig tradition. 'The crown', he declared, was 'the historical symbol that unites this

THE PUBLIC FACE. A significant development of the twentieth-century monarchy has been greater opportunities for communicating with subjects. In 1932 (*left*) George V was persuaded to make a Christmas broadcast, the text of which was written by Rudyard Kipling. It was highly successful.

great family of nations and races, scattered over every quarter of the globe . . . the perfect harmony of our parliamentary system with our constitutional monarchy has survived the shocks that have in recent years destroyed other Empires and other liberties. . . . The complex forms and balanced spirit of our constitution were not the discovery of a single era, still less of a single party or a single person. They are the slow accretion of centuries, the outcome of patience, tradition and experience : . .' The speech was well received, and in answer to a parliamentary question the First Commissioner of Works announced with pride that fifty-two extra men had been employed collecting litter from the London parks during the festivities, but that no damage of any kind had been done to the flower beds. Nine months later George V was dead, tired out by bronchial trouble which led to a weakening of the heart.

Abdication and recovery: Edward VIII and George VI

Like many, if not most, monarchs, George V had worried about the qualities his successor would bring to the throne. To Baldwin, he remarked that 'after I am dead, the boy will ruin himself in twelve months'. Archbishop Lang wrote of George V that 'his closing days were clouded with anxiety for the future'.

George V and Queen Mary's relations with their children were not free from difficulty. Despite his basic kindliness, the king was fussy, domineering, and, at times, highly critical: Queen Mary seems to have devoted most of her affection to the king, leaving little for the children. Their relations with David, the eldest, were particularly tense. Small and tough, he spent several years at Naval College with his brother Albert, followed by two years at Magdalen College, Oxford. During most of the Great War he was on the western front. In the years after the war, he made successful visits to Canada, New Zealand, Australia, and India, together with a few days in New York, where he was given an ecstatic reception. He was well aware that his journeys were watched from afar by his father with a keen eye. During the Canadian visit, he received a letter of 'warmest congratulations' on the tour, 'due in a great measure to your own personality and the wonderful way in which you played up'. That was gratifying. But on the New Zealand visit, the prince received a sharp reproof for wearing a turned-down collar while in uniform—'anything more unsmart I never saw', and in India the prince was pursued by a letter, 'I am surprised to see that you and your staff are wearing blue overalls with your white tunics. A most extraordinarily ugly uniform. . . . The regulations ought never to have been altered without my approval . . .'

The prince regarded his father's devotion to ceremony as tedious and misguided, out of touch with the mood of the post-war world, which was more relaxed and carefree. Their life-styles were also markedly different. The king was above all a family man, enjoying the security of routine: the prince was unmarried, showed few signs of wanting to marry, restless, and attracted to what the king regarded as the smart set. Though he rode with dash and enthusiasm, played golf, and shot, his real taste was for dining and dancing, and he was regularly to be seen in London night-clubs. The alternation of generations could hardly be more apparent, with George an image of the domestic earnestness of his grandmother Victoria, and the prince an updated version of his grandfather, Edward VII.

The new king was a complex character. The testimony to his charm as Prince of Wales is overwhelming. Like his grandfather, he had, when he tried, an easy and considerate manner. His fair hair, blue eyes, and slight build seemed a new ingredient in the rather ponderous Hanoverian stock, and for all his sturdiness and gaiety there was a sense of fragility about him, a sadness behind the eyes, which was appealing. But along with these amiable qualities, there were others: he could also be impatient, self-occupied, obstinate, and morose. He never managed successfully to cultivate that most necessary of royal attributes, not to allow boredom to show: indeed, he scarcely tried.

EDWARD VIII BORED. The new king made little effort to disguise the tedium he felt on official occasions. Here he scowls at a 1936 debutante.

Lord Crawford remarked on the prince's inconsiderate and disruptive behaviour when he agreed in 1930 to become a Trustee of the National Gallery:

The Prince of Wales turned up at the National Gallery board meeting today. He fairly amazed us. About halfway through our proceedings, which happened to be extremely important, he got bored and began to smoke . . . He began to talk to his neighbours Sassoon and D'Abernon . . . [it] made business practically impossible. We were quite bewildered by the time our meeting ended. So far as I could make out, the chatter was chiefly about racing and society.

There was a repeat performance in May 1931 when the prince 'scarcely stopped chattering from beginning to end . . . it is almost impossible to conduct our business'.

It is sometimes said that he did not wish to be king. That is untrue. He greatly enjoyed the privileged life which his position gave him and it would be more accurate to say that he wanted to be king on his own terms, which included a marked downgrading of the ceremonial side of things. His friends argued that this was a deliberate move towards a more democratic and egalitarian monarchy. That was to put too purposeful and ideological a gloss on what was, basically, no more than personal predilection. He shared in fact some of the impatience towards democratic processes which were not uncommon in the 1930s: in exile, after the abdication, he was greatly concerned about titles, honours, decorations, and money, while any egalitarian zeal he possessed was not allowed to get out of hand to the point of allowing his secretary to sit down while taking dictation.

It has also been suggested that he was deliberately forced off the throne by a series of political manœuvres in which Stanley Baldwin, as prime minister, played a co-ordinating role. This is impossible to sustain. The king did not have serious political views and, despite sensitive remarks about the plight of the poor and unemployed, had no definite plans. He later described his views as 'distinctly conservative'. He seems to have had scarcely any understanding of the role and functions of a constitutional monarch, not because his father held him at arms' length, but because he had little interest in such matters. What, in the years before his accession, had caused some anxiety was the prince's tendency to isolate himself, mixing with a small and select band of friends. Fort Belvedere, in Windsor Great Park, which he developed in the early 1930s, was both a refuge and a symbol—a retreat from the world, a defensive redoubt ringed with guns, but, in fact, a sham, a make-believe world. It held dangers both to the prince and the monarchy. It distorted the prince's judgement, never strong, until he was close to believing what he wanted to believe, and the experience of his great-grandmother's reign suggested that, whatever the masses wanted, an invisible monarchy was no part of it.

The new reign started, as most new reigns start, with a tiny but significant episode. George V's mania for punctuality had led him to keep all the clocks at Sandringham half an hour fast. It was an absurd but venial foible. While the old king was dying, his eldest son gave orders for the clocks to be put right, and the neighbouring clockmaker was summoned by taxi to carry out the orders. For the first few weeks of the reign, Edward VIII made some effort to deal with the flow of papers contained in the boxes, but by the summer his staff had been obliged to invent stratagems for imposing some order and safeguarding confidentiality. The economy drives that the new king introduced at Windsor, Buckingham Palace, and Balmoral contrasted strangely with the extravagant gifts of emeralds and rubies he lavished upon his constant companion, Mrs Wallis Simpson.

At the accession of King Edward, Mrs Simpson was thirty-nine years of age, twice married, and once divorced. Born in Maryland as Wallis Warfield, she was dark, carefully groomed, and expensively turned out. Her first marriage to an American airman during the Great War ended quickly, and in 1928 she married Ernest Simpson, born in New York of mixed Anglo-American parentage, but a British subject and a businessman of means. Introduced to the Prince of Wales in 1930, Mrs Simpson visited Fort Belvedere in 1932 for the first time, and by 1934 had a monopoly of the prince's attention. Lady Furness and Mrs Dudley Ward, who had previously shared his affections, were dropped.

Readers of American and continental newspapers followed the developing friendship with interest and much speculation. A gentleman's agreement kept the matter out of the British press for the greater part of 1936. In the summer, the king, Mrs Simpson, and other friends took a Balkan holiday and a cruise along the Dalmatian coast, greeted with enthusiasm and pursued by photographers. On their return, in the autumn, Mrs Simpson filed an action for divorce against her husband.

The constitutional position should the king wish to marry was not clear. The only formal limitation on his decision was that the Act of Settlement forbade marriage to a Catholic. But since his wife automatically would become queen, his marriage was a matter of legitimate public concern. The cabinet had the right to warn against it and, if their advice was rejected, to tender their resignations. It would then depend whether anyone else could form an administration. If they attempted, the king's intentions were bound to become the subject of a prolonged discussion. If they failed, the king would have to abandon the proposed marriage, or abdicate. In addition, there was doubt whether the Church of England, which did not officially accept divorce, could take any ceremonial part in such a marriage.

In the middle of October, Baldwin made an effort to head off the approaching crisis. In an audience, he gave the king a file of foreign press cuttings which left no doubt about the nature of the gossip and, according to his own version, given

EDWARD VIII

(1936 abdicated)

I love you more & more & more each & every minute & miss you so terribly here. You do too don't you my sweetheart?

(Edward to Mrs Wallis Simpson, Easter 1935)

Other people's passions often seem inexplicable and other people's love-letters embarrassing. Even so, the banality of Edward's letters to Mrs Simpson seems remarkable. His frequent use of the third person is awkward and contorted: 'HE is terribly excited about new hair pin and HE hopes SHE is too.' At the age of forty-one, his references to himself as a boy are coy and hardly redeemed by vitality of expression: 'A boy is holding a girl so very tight in his arms tonight. He will miss her more tomorrow because he will have been away from her longer.' Nevertheless, his affection for her was deep and unflinching.

The eldest son of George V and Queen Mary, Edward was a complicated personality. The formative period of his life was the years he spent on the Western Front as a young officer in his early twenties. Though he was kept out of danger as much as possible, his equerry and his driver were both killed, and he knew at first hand the horrors of trench warfare. He shared many of the feelings of the post-war generation, contempt for politicians, impatience with routine, a sense of precarious survival, and a determination to live life to the full. 'He obviously means to have fun', noted Lady Cynthia Asquith in March 1918 on seeing him at a dance. One consequence was that he was cut off from the usual establishment which he disliked, and which in turn regarded him as vulgar and flash. It put him at a serious disadvantage should he ever need to gauge public opinion, and A. J. P. Taylor remarked that he 'exaggerated the decline in traditional standards of behaviour'.

Edward won great popularity in the 1920s through his successful Commonwealth and foreign tours and his apparent sympathy for ordinary people. But in one of the main obligations of a Prince of Wales—to safeguard the dynasty—he showed little interest. His relationships were almost invariably with married women, suggesting not merely a certain dependence, but a lack of concern for matrimony. When, in the mid-1930s, his thoughts did turn that way, his choice of Mrs

THE KING ON HOLIDAY WITH MRS WALLIS SIMPSON in Dalmatia, August 1936

Simpson was disastrous. Apart from doubts about her personal fitness to be queen, she had had no children by her two former marriages. To this Edward could reply, as he did when warned that he might be killed in the trenches, that he had brothers. Cut off from reality and deeply in love, he showed an almost total lack of tactical skill in handling the issue in 1936 and, in the end, ran out of alternatives. A similar lack of judgement marked the remaining thirty-six years of his life as duke of Windsor, which were spent largely in France.

later to the House of Commons, read the king a neat little historical essay. The monarchy, he argued, by losing its prerogative powers, had made itself more dependent upon its reputation and integrity. The respect that had been built up patiently could easily be lost, and though moral standards were, in general, lower than before, more was expected from the monarch. It was a curious fencing match, in which the king pointed out that he could not bring pressure to bear on Mrs Simpson to withdraw her divorce action, while Baldwin did not feel able to put the question direct, whether the king intended to marry her.

During the next weeks Baldwin sounded out the leaders of the Labour and Liberal parties, who were in total agreement that Mrs Simpson was quite unacceptable as queen. Meanwhile, it became increasingly unlikely that the press silence could be much longer maintained. On 13 November the king's private secretary, Major Hardinge, sent him a brave and incisive letter, pointing out that if Baldwin resigned on this issue, nobody else would form a government. He warned the king that at any moment the press would break ranks and urged that Mrs Simpson leave the country immediately. Hardinge's reward for his devotion to an extremely unpleasant duty was to be ignored by the king. Hardinge's letter he dismissed as an impertinence. But on 16 November he told Baldwin that he was prepared to abdicate in order to marry Mrs Simpson. A fortnight later, the story broke in the most ironic fashion. On 1 December Bishop Blunt of Bradford delivered an innocuous sermon, intended merely to remind the king of his spiritual responsibilities: 'some of us', concluded the bishop sententiously, 'wish that he gave more positive signs of such awareness.' The *Yorkshire Post* the following day linked the sermon with rumours from America: 'Dr Blunt must have had good reason for so pointed a remark.'

With that, the whole affair became public knowledge. The prime ministers of the Dominions were consulted by Baldwin and concurred with his views. An effort by some of the king's friends to float the idea of a morganatic marriage was rejected by the cabinet. In a last desperate gamble, the king told Baldwin that he wished to make a broadcast which, in effect, would have been an appeal to the nation against the government of the day: not surprisingly, Baldwin and his colleagues refused to sanction it, arguing that they retained responsibility for the king's conduct. A week later, on 10 December 1936, Baldwin made a statement in the House of Commons. The following evening, the king broadcast a farewell message to the people, appealed for support for his brother Albert, boarded a destroyer, the *Fury*, at Portsmouth, and disappeared into the darkness.

It was widely presumed that the abdication of King Edward had dealt a mortal blow to the institution of monarchy, and even the duke of York, in November 1936, wondered whether 'the whole fabric' would not crumble under the strain. In fact the crisis revealed how little republican feeling there was in the country. Indeed, the main danger in December was the formation, not of an anti-monarchical movement, but of a king's party. Briefly, Winston Churchill and Beaverbrook tried to stem the tide against the king, but they were swept aside. Few people denied the king's right to marry whom he pleased, but even fewer thought that Mrs Simpson would make an acceptable queen. Only in the House of Commons was there a brief flicker of republicanism. James Maxton, the member for Glasgow, Bridgeton, declared that monarchy had lost its usefulness, and Willie Gallacher, communist member for West Fife, warned the House that, whatever it did, it could never repair the damage to the monarchical institution. But Maxton's motion for a republic was lost by 403 votes to 5. In the *Political Quarterly*, an over-excited commentator told his readers that the struggle between king and Commons was 'similar in all essentials to that which was fought out in the seventeenth century'. A more inapt comparison would be hard to find. His conclusion was equally plausible—the monarchy could probably never recover the position it had held under George V. Its recovery was, in fact, swift and complete.

One reason that the monarchy's permanent position was so little damaged by these events was identified by Edward VIII in his last broadcast. The decision had been less difficult because of the knowledge that his brother was ready to succeed—'and he has one matchless blessing, enjoyed by so many of you and not bestowed on me—a happy home with his wife and children'. Prince Albert, who chose to reign as George VI (thus finally, one presumes, frustrating the grand design of Victoria), was shy and in awe of his new obligations but second not even to his father in devotion to duty. The new queen, Elizabeth, was one of the first and most splendid results of the relaxation of policy towards royal marriages announced by George V in 1917. Born in Hertfordshire, Lady Elizabeth Bowes-Lyon was the youngest daughter of the earl of Strathmore, of Glamis Castle. In

CHARMING AT SEVEN. Lady Elizabeth Bowes-Lyon is said to have met Prince Albert for the first time when she was five and he was ten: she gave him the cherries from her cake. Here she is seen two years later. After the Great War, she took time to consider his proposal of marriage, but on 13 January 1923 he telegraphed his parents, 'All right. Bertie.'

1922, after some hesitation, she accepted the duke of York's offer of marriage. It was one of the greatest strokes of luck the royal family ever had: for more than sixty years, as duchess of York, queen, and Queen Mother, her kindness has captivated people. George V, her formidable father-in-law, was an instant convert: 'everyone fell in love with her here', he wrote from Balmoral. The two princesses, Elizabeth and Margaret Rose, were ten and six at their father's accession.

George VI was a year and a half younger than his brother, and in their early years they had been inseparable. At the age of six, he joined his brother in a curious makeshift schoolroom at Sandringham, presided over by Mr Henry Hansell, an Oxford history graduate. He made rather slow progress and developed a stammer which became a serious embarrassment to him. In 1907 Prince David departed to Naval College, Osborne, and was replaced in the schoolroom by Prince Henry, with Prince Albert promoted to the giddy heights of school captain, to imbue in him a proper sense of responsibility. Mr Hansell seems to have taken the arrangements with undue solemnity and at the end of 1907 reported sadly that Prince Albert had failed to appreciate his position. He followed his brother to Naval College and on to Dartmouth. During the war, he served in the navy, despite repeated bouts of ill health, and then transferred to the Royal Air Force, where he learned to fly. After the war, he went to Trinity, Cambridge, where, like his father, he read Bagehot on the English Constitution. He gave vigorous patronage to the Industrial Welfare Society and the annual duke of York's boys camps were an offshoot from this interest in promoting social harmony and understanding. In 1927 he and the duchess undertook a very long visit to New Zealand and Australia: he was supervised from afar in just the way his brother had been, and, at the age of thirty-one, received from his father the urgent admonition for his arrival home at Victoria Station—'when you kiss Mama, take your hat off'.

Although George VI felt very acutely his lack of political and constitutional experience, he was well travelled and by no means out of touch with public life. His first task was to re-establish confidence in the monarchy. Though the outcome of the Abdication crisis was to demonstrate the underlying strength of support for the crown, this could not be assumed at the time. The scandal and gossip had been extremely unpleasant. Since it had been clearly established that, in the matter of his marriage, the king must be guided by his ministers, yet another power had been removed, even if the chances of a confrontation on similar lines were fairly remote. Southern Ireland took advantage of the crisis to sever its remaining links with the crown. The constitutional loss was modest, since it largely recognized the existing position, though the abandonment of the treaty ports was to have serious consequences in the war that lay ahead. The remaining royal influence on day-to-day policy had suffered a set-back, since the melodramatic events of 1936 had allowed little time for the boxes or for the routine happenings of political life.

An early decision was to proceed with the coronation as planned for Edward VIII, and it took place in May 1937. The new king's broadcast went off well: careful treatment over the years had reduced his stammer to an occasional hesitation, through which his listeners willed him to continue. The coronation service showed that the clergy were very worthy successors of those who had so confused the king's great-grandmother. Though the king had a very deep personal religious faith and took seriously the spiritual significance of the coronation service, his diary account reminds one inescapably of Victoria's ninety-nine years before:

I had two bishops, Durham and Bath and Wells, one on either side to support me, and to hold the form of service for me to follow. When this great moment came, neither Bishop could find the words, so the Archbishop held his book down for me to read, but horror of horrors, his thumb covered the words of the oath. . . . The supreme moment came when the Archbishop placed the St. Edward's crown on my head. I had taken every precaution as I thought to see that the crown was put on the right way round, but the Dean and the Archbishop had been juggling with it so much, that I never did know whether it was right or wrong . . . As I turned after leaving the Coronation Chair I was brought up all standing, owing to one of the Bishops treading on my robe. I had to tell him to get off it pretty sharply as I nearly fell down.

Two factors helped to make the recovery from the constitutional crisis swift.

The first is that, for ordinary people, it was over in a few days. Though members of the establishment had watched for months the development of Edward's friendship with Mrs Simpson, few Britons knew of it until the first week in December, by which time the decisions of the different parties had been made. There was little time for either a royalist or a republican reaction to develop. Secondly, the menace of the international situation, with the obvious possibility of war, deflected attention from purely domestic concerns.

The behaviour of the duke of Windsor, the title accorded to the former king, continued to be a source of embarrassment to the royal family for some time. The duke and Mrs Simpson married in June 1937 and set up house in France. Relations with the royal family were soured by the new king's refusal to grant the duchess the title of Royal Highness. The duke's political naïvety, which had led him to express some admiration for the totalitarian regimes of Europe, soon brought him into another scrape. In October 1937 he and the duchess visited Germany, ostensibly to study labour conditions, met Himmler, Hess, Goering, and Goebbels, and were received at Berchtesgaden by Hitler. It was a splendid propaganda coup for the Nazi leaders, who spread the impression that the duke had been turned off the throne because of his pro-German sympathies, and docketed him as a possible collaborator. The duke had intended to follow up his German trip with one to America, where he hoped to see the President and proposed to issue a declaration placing himself at the head of a world-wide peace movement. Not unnaturally, the new king regarded this activity as designed to embarrass and upstage him. The British ambassador in Washington, Sir Ronald Lindsay, was summoned to Balmoral, where George VI complained that his brother was 'dropping bombshell after bombshell'. With considerable difficulty,

THE DUKE AND DUCHESS OF WINDSOR IN ODD COMPANY. Shortly after his marriage, the duke announced a personal enquiry into labour and housing conditions, starting in Germany. He and the duchess were warmly received by the Nazi leadership and received by Hitler at Berchtesgaden. Hitler later remarked of the duchess that 'she would have made a good queen'.

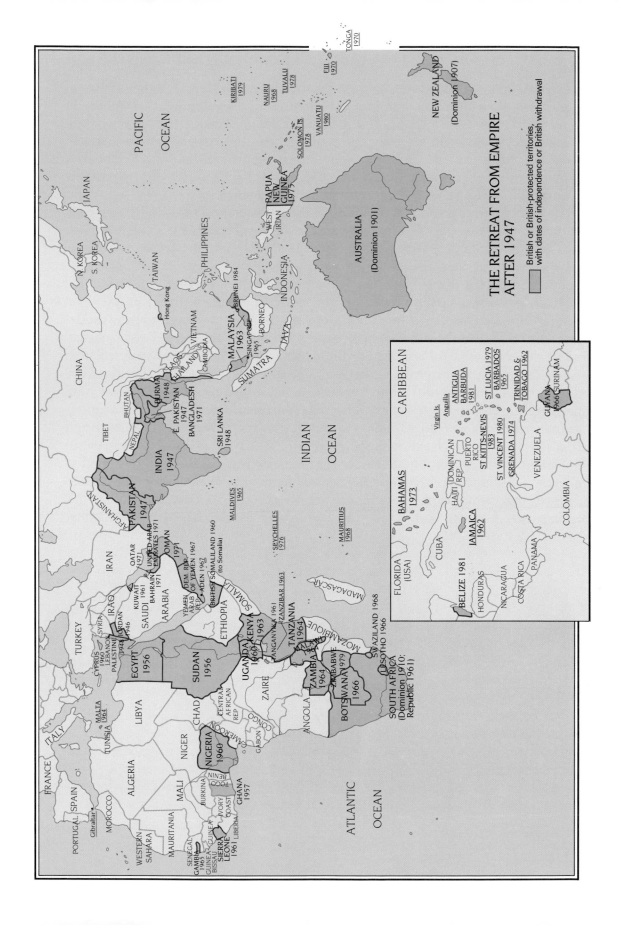

THE RETREAT FROM EMPIRE
AFTER 1947

British or British-protected territories,
with dates of independence or British withdrawal

the duke was persuaded to cancel the tour. But Sir Ronald noted that 'the King does not yet feel safe in his throne, and up to a certain point he is like the medieval monarch who has a hated rival claimant living in exile'. George VI was bound to feel 'uneasiness as to what is coming next, sensitiveness—suspicion'.

Baldwin gave way to Neville Chamberlain as soon as the coronation was over. With his new prime minister's policy of attempting to avoid war by appeasing Germany, George VI was in general agreement, as indeed were the majority of his subjects. At the time of Eden's resignation in February 1938, the king protested vigorously that he had not been kept informed but he continued to support the prime minister. With the skies darkening rapidly, it was time to look to the country's alliances, and the king and queen paid two important state visits, one to France, before the Munich crisis, and another to the United States, in the summer of 1939, when a cordial relationship with Franklin Roosevelt was established. But the king's suggestion of personal appeals to Hitler, the king of Italy, and the emperor of Japan was not approved by the cabinet.

The outbreak of war helped to re-establish the prestige of the monarchy by giving the royal family a very clear role to play. The king took to uniform at once, and as soon as she was eighteen, Princess Elizabeth joined the ATS. The decision to remain in Buckingham Palace was of critical importance: it received direct hits from bombs while the king and queen were in residence and demonstrated more clearly than rhetoric their willingness to share the dangers facing their people. Their visits to bombed cities—Coventry, Sheffield, and the East End of London—brought them face to face with people they would otherwise hardly have met, and in 1942 the king's younger brother, the duke of Kent, was killed in an air crash in Scotland. Political problems were manageable. In 1940, when Neville Chamberlain was forced out of office by the failure of the Norwegian campaigns, his recommendation and the king's inclination was to send for Lord Halifax, who had replaced Eden as foreign secretary. Halifax felt that the prime minister had to be in the House of Commons and Churchill was summoned instead. Churchill's career had been volatile and he had been one of the closest advisers of Edward VIII during the Abdication crisis. After a cautious start, the king developed a liking for and confidence in his new minister.

During the early months of the war, the position of the duke of Windsor continued to cause anxiety. Returning to England on a destroyer in September 1939, the duke accepted a post as liaison officer at Gamelin's Headquarters, was in France at the time of the collapse in the summer of 1940, and escaped first to Spain, then to Portugal. Thence he telegraphed that he was not prepared to return to Britain unless his wife was accorded the title she sought. Meanwhile, the Germans planned to kidnap him and possibly to reinstate him on the throne should their invasion of Britain be successful. Another protracted exchange with the British government took place on the question whether the duke could retain

LONDON, 1940. Even more important than the king and queen's visits to bombed towns was the fact that they remained in London. The two princesses were sent to Windsor. At the suggestion that they might be sent to one of the Dominions, the queen replied, simply, 'the children won't leave without me; I won't leave without the King; and the King will never leave'.

WAR EFFORT. Princess Elizabeth is seen here with Princess Margaret in January 1943 buying savings certificates at a country post office. In 1945 she joined the Auxiliary Territorial Service as 'No. 230873, Second Subaltern Elizabeth Alexandra Mary Windsor: Age: 18. Eyes: blue. Hair: brown. Height: 5 ft. 3 ins.'

his army batman. At length, the duke was persuaded to leave and take up an appointment as Governor of the Bahamas.

Before the war against the Japanese had been brought to a close, the general election of July 1945 produced the first Labour government to command an absolute majority in the House of Commons. Clement Attlee, the incoming prime minister, had been deputy to Churchill during the war, and was well known to George VI. The size of Labour's majority removed any doubt about the electoral verdict. Attlee's initial audience was somewhat hasty since he was due back within twenty-four hours at the Potsdam Conference. For the key post of foreign secretary, Hugh Dalton's name was mentioned, the king counter-proposed Ernest Bevin, and Attlee agreed without further discussion. The king found his new prime minister's dry and terse manner a striking contrast to Churchill's ebullience, and their relations were at first correct rather than cordial.

Despite the king's orthodox conservative views, there were few difficulties with the Labour government. He was dismayed at the scope of their nationalization programme and the vigour with which it was forced through. In 1947 the king accepted without demur proposals to grant independence to India, Pakistan, Burma, and Ceylon, and Lord Mountbatten was dispatched as the last Viceroy, to preside over the separation. When India declared itself a republic, there was discussion by what means she could remain in the Commonwealth, but she agreed to recognize the king as Head of the Commonwealth, though not as head of state.

Though the reign of George VI, unlike those of his predecessors, was free from major constitutional controversy, the king kept a wary eye open for encroachments upon his authority. He persuaded Attlee, with little difficulty, that the Order of the Garter should be regarded as personal to the sovereign and should not be used for party political purposes. After the general election of February 1950, when the Labour government retained office with a tiny majority, the king was concerned lest he be asked to grant another dissolution within a few months: his private secretary wrote pseudonymously to *The Times* on 2 May to express, presumably the royal view, that under such circumstances, the monarch would have the right to see whether an alternative administration could be formed and to consider the 'true interest' of the country. As it happened, Attlee managed to hold on until October 1951, when he was allowed a dissolution but was defeated at the polls. The incoming prime minister, Churchill, wished to name Eden as deputy prime minister as well as foreign secretary. George VI objected that this, by establishing an apparent order of succession, would limit the royal prerogative, though from time to time a minister has been designated to act as deputy prime minister for short periods.

The four members of the inner royal family were a close-knit group. The king and queen were affectionate parents, and the king in particular seemed a little

GEORGE VI

(1936–52)

To No. 10. Tea in the drawing room with Mrs. Baldwin just back from a week-end at Sandringham, where she sat next to the King at all meals . . . (He) craved for time to adjust himself to his new station and its duties. All his life he had been outshone by his brilliant brother and there had been times when as a boy he had felt envious that eighteen months should make so much difference. The King is 'a family man', and he hopes he may keep his lodge at Windsor as a retreat from the public glare.

(Diary of Thomas Jones, January 1937)

GEORGE VI, the second son of George V, had a similar upbringing and shared many of his father's characteristics: the change of name from Albert to George at his accession in 1936 was significant. He was brought up in the navy and served during the Great War. In 1920 he was a sharp enough tennis player to win the Royal Air Force doubles. He was devoted to country life, took great pleasure in Sandringham, where he was born and died, and was happiest with his family. The abdication of his elder brother in 1936 found him extremely diffident about the problems facing him, though he had travelled widely and had considerable knowledge of public life through his interest in industrial welfare. But understanding of his difficulties and respect for the way he faced them produced a very deep public affection. His short reign was dominated by war: the diplomatic moves before 1939, six years of warfare, during which the king and queen remained in London, and the years of post-war reconstruction. During the last four years of his reign, his health deteriorated rapidly, first from arteriosclerosis and then from lung cancer.

TEA AT WINDSOR, 1950.

disinclined to acknowledge that his daughters were growing up. But in the end, Princess Elizabeth was granted permission, at the age of twenty-one, to marry Philip, nephew of Lord Mountbatten. After the ceremony at Westminster Abbey in November 1947, the king wrote to his daughter: 'our family, us four, the "Royal Family" must remain together, with additions of course at suitable moments! . . . your leaving us has left a great blank in our lives but do remember that your old home is still yours.' Prince Charles was born a year later. During the next few years, with the king's health deteriorating sharply, the princess and her husband took on more of the burden of public engagements. In October 1951 they embarked on a tour of Canada and the United States, and in January 1952 they left for a tour of East Africa, Australia, and New Zealand. From this they were recalled while on the first section in Kenya by the news that George VI had died at Sandringham in his sleep. In his first months as king, he had written that he hoped he would be allowed time 'to make amends for what has happened'. He had accomplished just that.

Elizabeth II

Elizabeth II was twenty-five years of age at her accession, with two children, Prince Charles and Princess Anne. In taste and character, she was at one with her father and grandfather, devoted to country life, and with a powerful sense of public duty. She made remarkably few changes in personnel from her father's advisers and the continuity of three reigns of dignified domestic monarchy, scarcely interrupted by the short reign of Edward VIII, became increasingly apparent.

At the time of her birth in 1926, there had been little reason to believe that she would inherit the throne. Her uncle, the Prince of Wales, was in his early thirties

THREE QUEENS MOURNING. At the funeral of George VI in 1952, his mother Queen Mary, his widow Queen Elizabeth, and his daughter Elizabeth II together. A classic photograph.

and might be expected to marry: her parents, next in line, might well have had a son who would take precedence. The abdication made her heir presumptive and focused upon her much more public attention. She had been educated privately by a governess, along with her younger sister Margaret Rose. At the outbreak of war she was thirteen and, until she joined the ATS, had led a rather sheltered life. Her marriage to Philip in 1947 was followed a year later by the birth of her first son. The early death of her father at the age of fifty-six meant that she had very little semi-private life before coming to the throne.

Though the crown she inherited was severely limited in its routine powers, the reserve powers were still of importance and, at times, provoked controversy. On two successive occasions, the leadership of the Conservative Party, carrying with it the prime ministership, caused dissension. Churchill, the prime minister she inherited in 1952, retired in 1955 and was replaced by Anthony Eden, crown prince since the war. But early in January 1957, soon after the Suez crisis, Eden himself retired because of illness, advising the queen to consult Lord Salisbury, Lord President of the Council, about a successor. Salisbury, and the Lord Chancellor, Kilmuir, then polled the cabinet to ascertain its views, which produced a sizeable majority in favour of Harold Macmillan rather than R. A. Butler, who had deputized as prime minister during Eden's absences. Their opinions were confirmed by Churchill and by the chairman of the 1922 committee. But the public, which had taken Butler's succession for granted, were surprised when Macmillan was summoned to the palace, and there were insinuations that the queen had been deceived by a Tory clique. Queen Elizabeth had, in fact, consulted very properly and acted upon the advice received, though the position would have been more awkward had the testimony been less decisive or had Butler been willing to cry 'foul'.

On Macmillan's own resignation in 1963, also as a result of unexpected illness, there was an even more complex situation. The leading contenders were Butler and Lord Hailsham, though Reginald Maudling, Iain Macleod, and Edward Heath were also possibilities. On this occasion, the queen consulted the outgoing prime minister at his hospital bed, who advised her to send for Lord Home as the candidate most acceptable to the party. There was, in fact, a good deal of opposition to the proposal, and Macleod and Enoch Powell refused to serve under Home. But the chances of the queen being drawn into another contentious dispute were removed in 1965 when the Tory Party followed the Labour Party in introducing a formal mechanism for electing the party leader. Though the result was the disappearance of one of the few remaining prerogatives of the crown, it was a prerogative that the queen was probably glad to do without.

It seems unlikely that the choice of prime minister will present difficulties for the monarch in future. Nevertheless, the establishment of the Alliance in the 1980s raised once more the question of the use of the prerogative in a hung

Parliament. That the queen could do other than send for the leader of the largest party, even though he might not command an overall majority, seems hard to envisage, since it would invite the charge of royal prejudice. Should he at once decline to form an administration, the queen might perhaps avoid being dragged into a constitutional dispute. But it is more probable that he would form a government, sustain a defeat in the Commons at an early stage, and ask for a dissolution. The queen would then be in the predicament that William IV found so worrying in 1831 when Lord Grey, having been defeated on the committee stage of the Reform Bill, asked for and was granted a dissolution less than a year after the previous general election. Should she refuse a dissolution, it would not be clear upon whose advice she was acting, and the dangers to which Asquith drew attention in 1913 would be imminent. That this is by no means a purely theoretical possibility is suggested by the situation after the general election of 1974 when Edward Heath, outnumbered by Labour, remained in office for some days while attempting by a deal with the Liberals to construct an overall majority.

If the role of the crown in domestic politics has remained unobtrusive during Elizabeth's reign, its contribution in imperial and international affairs has continued to grow, along the lines sketched out by Edward VII and George V. At the accession of the queen, India, Pakistan, and Ceylon had already been granted full independence, but had opted to remain within the Commonwealth. The

COMMONWEALTH PRIME MINISTERS IN LONDON, 1962. Post-war decolonization meant a new sphere of activity for the Crown as Head of the Commonwealth, a role to which Elizabeth II has devoted particular attention. Prominent in the photograph are Harold Macmillan (prime minister of Great Britain), John Diefenbaker (Canada), Robert Menzies (Australia), Jawaharlal Nehru (India), and Archbishop Makarios (Cyprus). The main issue at the conference was Britain's intention to apply for membership of the Common Market.

"Mr. Wilson! Now that, after all, we had to withdrawn from Ulster—then
Scotland, then Wales, then Cornwall . . . just WHAT am I left to be Queen of?"

CARTOON BY CUMMINGS, 1974. The resurgence of Scottish nationalism, discussion of devolution, and the pace of decolonization raised the question whether the monarchy would be pushed back to its Wessex origins.

queen, as head of the Commonwealth, was the only remaining formal link. Malaysia, Ghana, Nigeria, Uganda, Kenya, Singapore, Zambia, Zimbabwe, and many other states followed the same path, until, at the jubilee of 1977, no fewer than thirty-six states were members, some of them recognizing the queen as head of state, others accepting her only as head of Commonwealth. Burma had declined to join the Commonwealth in 1948, South Africa withdrew in 1962 as a consequence of its policy of apartheid, Aden refused to join in 1967, and Pakistan withdrew in 1972 when Bangladesh was admitted, after the war with India. The Commonwealth continued to grow, as former colonies, some of them very small, achieved independence, until by 1986 some forty-nine states, accounting for nearly one-quarter of the population of the world, were members.

Opinions vary about the importance of the Commonwealth and the part played in it by the monarchy. A fierce exchange in the columns of *The Times* was triggered off in April 1964 by 'A Conservative', writing on 'A party in search of a pattern'. The Commonwealth he dismissed as 'a gigantic farce':

If the monarchy is a precious and irreplaceable heritage of the people of Britain—and most Conservatives believe that it is—it is dangerous to prostitute to the service of a transparent fiction the subtle emotions of loyalty and affection on which that heritage depends. A great and growing number of the people of these islands do not like to see the sovereign whom they regard as their own by every claim of history and sentiment playing an alien part as one of the characters in the Commonwealth charade.

G. A. Johnson, a former editor of the *Statesman*, retorted that the Commonwealth was 'a unique experiment in human relations', and Sir Richard Nugent, Tory MP for Guildford, called it 'the first practical attempt at a world-wide multi-racial society of nations'.

The queen and her husband took their Commonwealth responsibilities extremely seriously and spent months in arduous goodwill tours. These were not, of course, without occasional embarrassment or even hazard. In 1961 the British government was concerned lest a royal visit to Ghana, where Kwame Nkrumah was precariously in power, should place the queen in danger but, at her insistence, the tour was made. A similarly delicate visit was made three years later to Canada, at a time when the agitation for Quebec independence was at its height. In 1986 a visit to New Zealand produced demonstrations on behalf of Maori rights, in the course of which the queen received a direct hit from an egg at point-blank range.

Apart from any personal feelings the queen might have, there are particular reasons why the Commonwealth connection should be of importance to her. It is certainly one of the most prominent surviving responsibilities of the crown. The queen's many tours mean that she almost undoubtedly knows much more about the Commonwealth and its leaders than any of her ministers do. The Governors-General report directly to her, and their appointment—on the advice of the

ROYAL VISIT TO AUSTRALIA, 1963. This photograph of the teeming crowds gives some impression of the stamina that Commonwealth tours demand and the security problems that they pose.

prime minister of the Commonwealth country concerned—does not directly concern the British government. The prerogatives which the Governors-General exercise on her behalf may draw her into political controversy just as the British prerogatives can do. Sir John Kerr was appointed Governor-General of Australia on the advice of the Labour prime minister Gough Whitlam. This did not prevent a storm of protest when, in the constitutional crisis of 1975, the Governor-General dismissed Whitlam and called upon Malcolm Fraser to form a government. Fraser was then granted a dissolution and won the subsequent general election. The queen refused to intervene or to dismiss Kerr arguing that she must, at all times, act upon proper political advice. The Governor-General's robust action was, by many Australians, thought to strengthen the case for the adoption of a republican form of government. It was a curious reminiscence of an earlier episode in 1926 when Lord Byng, the Governor-General of Canada, had refused a dissolution to Mackenzie King but granted one almost immediately after to his opponent Arthur Meighen.

It may not be without significance that the two occasions when there were rumours of strong differences between the queen and Margaret Thatcher concerned Commonwealth matters. In 1983 the queen was reported to be incensed that the United States had launched an invasion of Grenada, of which she was head of state, without any notification to its ally, and the foreign secretary, Sir Geoffrey Howe, had an uncomfortable time in the House of Commons, where the question of the queen's position was raised. In 1986 there were strong newspaper reports, denied from the palace, that the queen was distressed at the strain which Mrs Thatcher's refusal to endorse sanctions against South Africa was placing upon the Commonwealth. It is not possible for the historian, dealing with such recent events, to know the truth of the matter, but it is difficult not to believe that, at the very least, the queen was exercising her right, in Bagehot's famous phrase, to advise and warn.

The opening decade of Elizabeth's reign was at times uncomfortable. The naïve expectations of a New Elizabethan Age, largely promoted by the newspapers, turned sour rather quickly in the face of the country's continuing economic and financial difficulties. The queen herself, relatively inexperienced, appeared at times austere, unsmiling, and remote. Controversy erupted in 1957 when Lord Altrincham complained that the queen was socially isolated in a tweedy clique and that her speeches came over as those of a 'priggish schoolgirl'. Malcolm Muggeridge, journalist and TV personality, joined in the fray, objecting that true religion was in danger of being driven out by 'the royal soap opera . . . a sort of substitute or ersatz religion'. Both men were assaulted, vilified, and ostracized. The borough of Altrincham hastened to repudiate the views of the noble lord and protested its own loyalty to the crown. There was a good deal of genuine indignation felt at attacks upon a woman who could not answer back, but when the smoke of battle rolled away, the more thoughtful members of the royal entourage accepted that there was some truth in the criticisms, and in the 1960s there was a significant relaxation in royal protocol and a determined attempt to broaden the contacts which the palace had with ordinary people.

The difficulties of adjusting the views of the monarchy to swiftly changing social attitudes were also underlined by the question of the marriage of Princess Margaret. In 1953 the princess told the queen that she wished to marry Group Captain Peter Townsend, Comptroller of the Queen Mother's Household and a man of thirty-nine. He was extremely personable with a distinguished war record as a fighter pilot. He was also the innocent party in a divorce granted in December 1952. The palace's views on divorce reflected the teachings of the Church of England and were severe. For many years, even the innocent party in a divorce was not allowed admission to the royal enclosure at Ascot and guilty parties were not invited to royal functions at all. Since the princess was twenty-three she would, under the Royal Marriages Act of 1772, require the queen's permission to marry. Her nearness to the throne made it a public matter and it was put to the prime minister, Winston Churchill. His initial, and characteristic, reaction was all in favour of 'a gallant young airman', but he was persuaded to tender the opposite advice. Townsend was posted to Brussels as air attaché to see whether a two years' absence would solve the problem which, predictably, it did not. In 1955 the issue was once more put to the cabinet. Lord Salisbury, as custodian of the country's conscience, threatened resignation if approval were given; the Churches repeated their warnings, and *The Times*, in an astonishing editorial, declared that if the princess went ahead, she would be entering into a union which 'vast numbers of her sister's people . . . cannot in conscience regard as a marriage'. Under this pressure, the princess announced that the marriage would not take place. It is a distasteful episode and the sequel showed how foolish the objectors had been. In 1960 she married Anthony Armstrong-Jones, a photographer, who was at once given an earldom. The marriage barely lasted a decade and in 1978, after a period of separation, they were divorced.

A persistent criticism of the monarchy that surfaced again in these years was its cost. There had been complaints in the 1770s when George III had asked for an increase in the civil list, reproaches, with more justification, in the 1810s at the extravagance of the Prince Regent, and strictures in the 1870s at the way in which Victoria had been able to add to her privy purse by savings on the civil list. In the twentieth century two somewhat conflicting developments took place. The exemption of the monarch from income tax and death duties, which bit deeply into aristocratic fortunes, meant a considerable increase in the fortune of the crown relative to that of its wealthier subjects. But after the Second World War, the gathering pace of inflation eroded the value of the civil list, from which the salaries of officials are paid. Appearing on American television in 1969, Prince

THE ROYAL MAUNDY

THIS ceremony, traditionally held annually on the Thursday before Easter, 'Maundy Thursday', commemorates Christ's washing of the feet of his disciples; it takes its name from Christ's injunction to the disciples, *Mandatum novum do vobis* ('A new commandment I give to you'). It became increasingly common from the fourth century, not only (or first) in England, though English kings, with their intimate links with the Church, had adopted the practice of washing the feet of poor people on this day before 1066. In deference to Elizabeth I's sensibilities, yeomen of the royal laundry did the washing for her, though her successors until James II resumed the practice. William III delegated it to his almoner, who continued to wash feet until 1754; indeed, the Lord High Almoner organizes the event today. Since 1754 the washing has been replaced by a gift of Maundy Pennies to as many poor men and women (or, more delicately today, senior citizens) as the sovereign has years. Commemorative coins were first struck under Charles II. The ceremony was formerly held in the Chapel Royal, Whitehall, and then in Westminster Abbey until, under Elizabeth II, it began to perambulate the country. Her Majesty still carries a posy of flowers, which was originally designed to counteract the effect of smelly feet.

DISTRIBUTING THE ROYAL MAUNDY: Elizabeth I *c.*1560; and Elizabeth II in Worcester Cathedral, 1980.

Philip remarked that the palace was 'in the red', and added 'we may have to move into smaller premises next year'. His remarks led to a Select Committee the following year, as no doubt they were meant to. Payments by way of the civil list, which were by then completely inadequate, were augmented by services provided through departmental estimates, such as the maintenance of the royal yacht, the royal train, and the queen's flight. The queen had at her personal disposal the substantial income from the property of the duchy of Lancaster, and the Prince of Wales commanded the income from the duchy of Cornwall. Half of this he had, however, agreed to surrender to the Treasury as voluntary taxation. In addition, the queen had in theory great wealth in jewels, paintings, and furniture but, as was pointed out on her behalf, these were held in trust for the nation and were not realizable assets.

The debate that followed was, at times, cantankerous, but raised important questions about the kind of monarchy subjects wished to see. William Hamilton, Member of Parliament for West Fife, acted as counsel for the prosecution: 'the most insensitive and brazen pay claim made in the last two hundred years' was his comment. The most telling blow for the defence was perhaps that by Andrew Duncan who pointed out that, even taking into account the departmental contributions, the upkeep of the monarchy was no more than the bill for tranquillizers on the National Health Service. There was no doubt that royal finances were intricate and complex. But one important source of dispute was removed by the queen agreeing that, in future, no savings on the civil list would accrue to the privy purse, and another source of embarrassment was to be avoided by regular review of the civil list, instead of resort to extraordinary requests to Parliament. Clearly, if the full weight of redistributive taxation were to fall upon the sovereign, it would only be a matter of time before Sandringham

THE QUEEN INSPECTING A GUARD OF HONOUR AT SAN DIEGO on her American visit in February 1983. Four hundred and three years earlier, Francis Drake had claimed California as 'New Albion' on behalf of Elizabeth I. The royal visit, undertaken in part to restore good relations after the Falklands war, was afflicted by torrential rain, but the Queen was able to meet President Reagan at his ranch.

and Balmoral were sold off and a wholly different style of monarchy adopted. There was little indication that this was what the country wanted.

The pressure of public business, the expectations of a democracy, and the insatiable curiosity of the press and television have led to most members of the royal family taking an unprecedentedly active role, and certainly receiving unprecedented publicity. The Queen Mother, during her long widowhood, has sustained a remarkable programme of public engagements without the least diminution in the warmth and zest she brings to them. The duke of Edinburgh, in that most difficult of roles as royal consort, has succeeded in creating an image and function for himself. His interest in youth opportunities and environmental problems is well known. Unlike the Prince Consort, he does not aspire to be a minister or political adviser, but has set himself to convey occasional home truths to the nation: it hardly needs saying that such exhortations are not always uncontentious. In addition, he has clearly been concerned at the image which the royal family projects and in the debate on the civil list in December 1971 Norman St John Stevas described him as 'the driving-force behind the necessary modernization of the monarchy'. Prince Charles was pressed into service early on and his education at Gordonstoun was interrupted to enable him to spend several months at school in Australia. Princess Anne's equestrian ability and Prince Andrew's active service in the Falklands as a helicopter pilot brought them greatly into the public eye. But perhaps the most remarkable publicity has been reserved for the most recent recruits into the royal family, Lady Diana Spencer and Sarah Ferguson, who have brought a spirit and vivacity not always seen in princesses imported from abroad.

This, in itself, highlights a problem which exercises royal advisers—where to draw a line between the public and private spheres. It has been a continuous source of difficulty over recent decades and the uncouth intrusiveness of press photographers and gossip columnists has, at times, driven the royal family to distraction. 'If photographers poke a long lens through a keyhole into my private life,' observed the duke of Edinburgh briskly, 'then I'm bloody nasty,' and twenty years later his son Prince Charles, goaded beyond endurance at Sandringham, wished the news corps 'a particularly nasty New Year'. It has frequently been remarked that twentieth-century Britons seem to want conflicting things of the royal family—that they should be affable yet aloof, ordinary yet distinguished, warmly human yet models of rectitude. In the 1960s there were complaints that the queen could sometimes appear stolid and in the 1980s other complaints that the younger members of the family should behave with more decorum. There has certainly been a marked diminution in royal exclusiveness. Princess Anne, Princess Margaret, Princess Alexandra, and Prince Andrew have all married commoners. In 1967 the queen's cousin, Lord Harewood, having been divorced by his first wife, was permitted, on the advice of the cabinet, to remarry—which

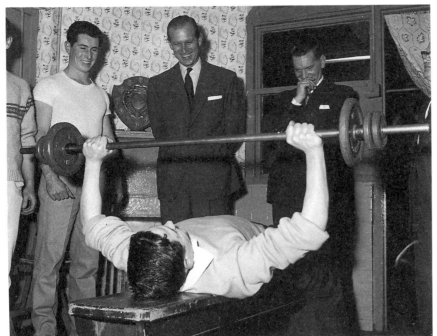

THE DUKE OF EDINBURGH'S interest in youth activities led to the setting up of his Award Scheme in 1956, in which well over two million young people have participated. Here he is seen visiting a boys' club at Wapping in December 1959. We can only speculate on the joke, which appears to have been a good one.

PRINCESS ANNE was created Princess Royal in 1987, partly in recognition of her work on behalf of charity. Here she is seen on a visit to The Gambia and Burkina Faso in 1984 on behalf of the Save the Children Fund, of which she is President.

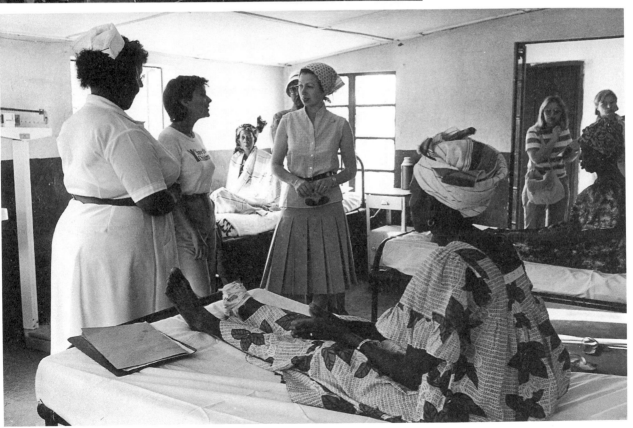

ELIZABETH II
(1952)

At 5 o'clock in the morning I was woken up by the band of the Royal Marines striking up just outside my window. I leapt out of bed and so did Bobo. We put on dressing-gowns and shoes and Bobo made me put on an eiderdown as it was so cold and we crouched in the window looking on to a cold, misty morning. There were already some people in the stands and all the time people were coming to them in a stream with occasional pauses in between. Every now and then we were hopping in and out of bed looking at the bands and the soldiers. At six o'clock Bobo got up and instead of getting up at my usual time I jumped out of bed at half-past seven. When I was going to the bathroom I passed the lift as usual, and who should walk out but Miss Daly! I was very pleased to see her. When I dressed I went into the nursery.

(12 May 1937)

THIS description of the morning of the coronation of her parents by the eleven-year-old Princess Elizabeth reminds one strongly of Queen Victoria's account of her own coronation in June 1838: there is the same zest, the same directness of gaze, the same ability to communicate atmosphere. 'Bobo' (Margaret Macdonald, the nursemaid) and Miss Daly, the swimming teacher, emerge as major figures in the drama. But the resemblance to Queen Victoria, Elizabeth's great-great-grandmother, goes deeper. Victoria was married just before she was twenty-one, Elizabeth just after: Victoria succeeded to the throne at the age of eighteen, Elizabeth at twenty-five. In each was a powerful sense of duty. Lady Airlie, meeting Princess Elizabeth at Badminton during the war, wrote of 'a grave little face under a small white net veil and a slender figure in a plain white woollen frock. The carriage of her head was unequalled, and there was about her that indescribable something which Queen Victoria had.'

In July 1939, at the age of thirteen, the princess visited Dartmouth and there met her third cousin Philip, starting his naval training. He was the son of Prince Andrew of Greece and the great-great-grandson of Victoria by her second daughter Alice, whose daughter Victoria had married Louis of Battenberg. According to Miss Crawford, the governess, Philip showed off a little, demonstrating his prowess at jumping tennis-nets. But if the governess disapproved, the cousin did not. The princess and Philip maintained a correspondence throughout the war and were married in November 1947.

The pattern of life Elizabeth II inherited had been handed down from Edwardian days—Christmas at Sandringham, Easter at Windsor, and departure in the summer for Balmoral and the grouse-season. The Duke of Windsor, in his memoirs, remarked that the sequence seemed as regular as the revolution of a planet in its orbit. It remained unchanged until the 1960s,

would certainly have not been allowed in earlier reigns. In 1969 the queen agreed to the making of a television film about the private life of the royal family, which took seventy-five days filming. The Queen Mother was seen in a later television film talking to Huw Weldon about her wartime experiences, and most of the younger members of the family have given television interviews when their engagements have been announced. On the whole, royal advisers seem to have gauged the pace of change with some skill. It is doubtful whether there is, in when the growing family became too large for Christmas at Sandringham and there was a move to Windsor. The queen's working year is a cycle of receptions and audiences, investitures and garden parties, opening ceremonies, and state visits, with the relentless stream of official boxes demanding constant attention. The weekly audience with the prime minister is usually on Tuesdays and may last an hour. Commonwealth and foreign visits take up a considerable part of most years. Since her accession, the queen has visited Canada sixteen times, Australia nine times, and New Zealand eight times. The careful preparations and meticulous etiquette that smooth public appearances are counteracted by the knowledge that every eye is on the queen and every word or gesture a subject for comment: the sheer effort of engaging dozens of people in conversation and shaking hundreds of hands calls for experience and stamina. Few foreign or Commonwealth visits are without their delicate political or constitutional side, and the advent of television has brought a particular hazard since all protest groups know that a demonstration tied to a royal visit will command disproportionate publicity. Nor can even the most exacting security eliminate real danger. In June 1981 the queen was shot at by a young man while riding to the ceremony of Trooping the Colours and though the shots were blank, no one could know that at the time. The queen patted her horse and rode on. The following year saw a more protracted ordeal when another man succeeded in climbing into Buckingham Palace early one morning, entered the queen's bedchamber, and had to be held in conversation for ten minutes before help arrived. It is not surprising that, like most monarchs, Elizabeth values the time she can spend with her family and the off-duty moments when, with dogs and horses, she can enjoy the countryside, as her father and grandfather did.

In the 1860s Walter Bagehot wrote that 'a *family* on the throne is an interesting idea. It brings down the pride of sovereignty to the level of petty life. No feeling could seem more childish than the enthusiasm of the English at the marriage of the Prince of Wales. They treated as a great political event what, looked at as a matter of pure business, was very small indeed. But no feeling could be more like common human nature as it is ... a princely marriage is the brilliant edition of a universal fact and, as such, it rivets mankind.' At the time Bagehot was writing, the concept of a royal family was comparatively new. In George III's reign, the spotlight on the sovereign himself was dim and his appearances to his subjects limited to strolls on the terrace at Windsor or occasional visits to the theatre. The life of his six daughters was said to have been 'like that of novices in a well-regulated convent'. The circumstances of George IV's married life made publicity unwise, and though William IV had a large family, they were his illegitimate offspring by Mrs Jordan, the actress. But the propriety of Victoria's domestic life, the spread of middle-class values, the establishment of a cheap press, and the invention of photography made for rapid progress in the nineteenth century. Even Bagehot, however, might have been amazed at the extent to which, in the twentieth century, the activities of the royal family seem to rivet people—the stock-in-trade of the colour supplements, stand-by of women's magazines and gossip columns, and the salvation of fashion editors. In part this is because, with the royal family, the way in which all families shape and reshape themselves each generation can be seen so clearly. Most of us are too close to our own family to be able to monitor it with much sense of detachment. But the royal family plays out its dramas on a public stage and a strong sense of continuity and development comes across—the infants cutting teeth, the toddlers brandishing Nativity-play spears, the adolescents fined for speeding, the adults 'dwindling into matrimony'. This aspect has been deliberately emphasized by royal advisers in recent years, starting with the film 'Royal Family' in 1969, which showed the queen feeding animals and going on picnics, and continuing through to the 'new look' Christmas broadcast in 1986, when she was seen chatting to her grandchildren, and remarked to her subjects that bringing up children was hard 'whether you are famous or quite unknown'.

Britain, any desire for a Scandinavian-style 'bicycle monarchy', stripped of most of its ceremony and glitter, yet the monarchy has certainly moved a considerable distance from being the preserve of the aristocracy and upper classes.

It is too soon to get into full perspective a reign which could well stretch into the twenty-first century, yet perhaps the outlines of an assessment may be attempted. That it has been a period of profound post-war and post-imperial adjustment cannot be disputed. It would be easy to write a jeremiad on the

'ARE YOU ALL RIGHT?' (*Above*) A
private moment during the wedding
of the Prince of Wales to Lady
Diana Spencer in 1981.

BOREDOM UNSPEAKABLE, OR THE
YOUNG PERSONS' GUIDE TO
PUBLIC OCCASIONS. (*Right*)
Ceremonies are terrible for the very
young. At the wedding of the Prince
of Wales in 1863, the four-year-old
future emperor of Germany,
Wilhelm II, whiled away the time
by biting his uncles' legs. At Prince
Andrew's wedding in 1986, Laura
Fellowes is gloomily resigned to her
fate, but the future William V is
desperate.

problems caused by mass immigration, the damage to the Commonwealth as a result of Britain's entry into the EEC, and the subsequent strain on Commonwealth harmony through disagreements over the treatment of South Africa. There were those who argued that to join the EEC must mean a loss of national identity and a challenge to the crown's constitutional position: it would mean, declared Hugh Gaitskell, 'the end of a thousand years of British history'. If one adds the nationalist pressures within the British Isles which appeared to be unravelling the work of the monarchy over centuries, one could see Elizabeth II's reign as the great retreat. But caution is necessary in estimating the force of nationalism, which ebbs and flows in a bewildering fashion. The Scottish National Party, which at times appeared in the 1970s an almost irresistible force bearing Scotland into independence, is itself in retreat. The strength of Quebec nationalism, which made the queen's visit to Canada in 1964 so tense, has waned. In the wake of the Kerr affair in 1976, Donald Horne predicted that Australia would be a republic 'within ten years'. It has not yet happened, though it still might. But the history of the monarchy is littered with prophets of doom being counted out. Monarchy could not last seven years, declared Tom Paine in 1792. 'The Republic must come,' wrote Joseph Chamberlain in 1871, and it will be 'in our generation.' The Abdication crisis, insisted William Gallagher in 1936, would be fatal to the monarchy. Assertions, however confident, must not be taken for profundities. In fact, the challenges and difficulties of our own time have reinforced the role of the monarchy as the keel of the ship of state, which prevents it rocking too violently in the winds of change. If that is to accept what is basically a traditional and balancing role for the monarchy, it is one which no other institution could hope to play.

OFF DUTY. The beach near Sandringham, 1984, with corgis.

Conclusion: The institution of monarchy

Elizabeth II can trace her descent from and beyond Edgar, king of the English in the later tenth century. The ritual used at her coronation in 1953 was, in essence, that used at his at Bath in 973. The text of 'Zadok the Priest and Nathan the Prophet' from the Old Testament was chanted at Edgar's crowning. It was set to music in 1727 by George Frederick Handel for the coronation of George II, and a bust of the composer was set in a place of honour by George III in the Queen's Presence Chamber at Windsor. Handel's version was sung in 1953. Her ancestor ruled over a kingdom of, at most, one million and a half subjects: Elizabeth is queen to more than one hundred million people and head of a Commonwealth which, with a population of well over one thousand million, embraces a quarter of the human race. In Edgar's kingdom, London may have had 12,000 inhabitants, York 8,000, Norwich, Lincoln, and

CORONATIONS, 1399, 1685, 1953. During these six centuries the place of crowning has remained Westminster Abbey and the ceremony is little altered. Yet the powers of the monarch in 1399 and 1953 were markedly different, and the apparent continuity of ceremony masked important changes. Henry IV's coronation in October 1399, conducted by Archbishop Arundel, was particularly lavish; for the first time, the holy oil, said to have been given by the virgin to St Thomas, was used for the annointing. James II's coronation took place in April 1685, very soon after the death of his brother Charles: the French ambassador reported that the coronation was regarded as a ceremony 'absolutely necessary for the establishment of the royal authority'. At Elizabeth II's coronation in 1953, she wore the crown of St Edward, made for Charles II at the Restoration, and the duke of Edinburgh is seen doing homage. The queen rejected the advice of her cabinet and insisted that the ceremony should, for the first time, be televised, establishing an even closer link between sovereign and people.

Winchester 5,000: in the Commonwealth, there are nine million people in Calcutta, eight million in Bombay, six million in London and in Delhi, more than three million in Sydney, two million in Toronto. The pace of travel in 973 was that of the fleetest horse—fifteen miles an hour: the rocket taking Armstrong, Aldrin, and Collins to the moon in 1969 accelerated from earth at nearly 30,000 miles an hour. In 973 a king could make himself heard at most to a few hundred subjects and could be recognized by not many hundreds more: the wedding of the Prince of Wales in 1981 was heard by a radio and television audience of one thousand million. A world of carts and buckets and shields and fishing-nets and spears has given way to a world of computers and heart-transplants, of lasers and solar heating, and of Exocet missiles.

Among these bewildering changes are threads of continuity, particularly in speech and in place-names. A *scip* is still a ship, a *hüs* is still a house, *bread* is still bread, and old Scandinavian *iarll* is still earl: north of the border, a *burgh* remains a burgh and a *laird* a laird. Place-names survive the passing of dynasties. *Londinium* is still London, old Scandinavian *Sveinn saér* is still Swansea, and the Viking city of *Jorvik* is still York. The new castle at the crossing of the Tyne is no longer very new, but it is still there, and so is the city.

Another thread of continuity is kingship. The pattern of Saxon monarchy may be discerned today just as the remains of long-deserted villages can be traced beneath the turf: the north is not harried, as it was by Edgar's men, but it complains that it is neglected by a southern-based government. Of course, within the concept of kingship, there have been vast changes and in the descent of Edgar's crown great discontinuities. The world of monarchy in which kings ruled has given way to a world of democracy in all its strange and varied twentieth-century forms. At the Conquest, the old Saxon line was finally dispossessed and it was not for several generations that men who spoke English as their first tongue sat once more upon the throne. In 1399 Richard II was pushed aside by his cousin Henry Bolingbroke and in 1485 the Yorkist line was ousted by Henry Tudor. Elizabeth's refusal to marry brought in the Scots in 1603, with a thin connection to the Tudors through James I's great-grandmother, the sister of Henry VIII. The abruptness of the change in 1688 when James II was expelled was disguised by retaining his two daughters in the succession, but in 1714 more than fifty heirs who were Catholics were nimbly passed over to bring in George I, great-grandson to James I. The Scottish royal line ending in James VI and I had, by contrast, far fewer interruptions.

These dynastic vicissitudes were accompanied by a continuous process of adaptation. First came the extension of Wessex rule over most of England and the long subsequent struggle, never wholly completed, for the political mastery of the British Isles. The Norman and Angevin monarchies consolidated their position by the further development of effective organs of royal government, national and local, and by the introduction of new processes of law and order. They, and later the Plantagenets, grappled, down to 1453, with immense French territories that, at times, were as large as England itself. The sixteenth century saw the achievement of ecclesiastical supremacy after the breach with the papacy and the successful establishment of the Protestant Church of England. A further success was the constitutional union of first Wales, then Scotland and Ireland, with England to form the United Kingdom of Great Britain and Ireland. In the decades after the Restoration a great overseas empire came into existence, though the crown was perhaps slow to perceive the vast potential of colonies. Most difficult of all, in many respects, was the process of reconciliation to a diminished political influence as, in the nineteenth and twentieth centuries, the foundations were laid for a liberal and then a democratic regime. From the time of Edward VII onwards the monarchy has taken on a more prominent public role as the embodiment of a democratic nation, replacing its previous position as the focus of an exclusive and aristocratic society, and, after the Second World War, it has adapted to a new function as head of the Commonwealth.

Politically and militarily, the monarchy has experienced heady triumphs and mortifying defeats. Against Edington, Brunanburh, Crécy, Poitiers, Agincourt, the defeat of the Armada, Blenheim, Trafalgar, and Waterloo must be set Hastings, Castillon, the loss of Calais, the humiliation in 1667 in the Medway by the Dutch, the surrenders of Saratoga and Yorktown, and the reverses of the Crimean and Boer Wars. Politically, it failed time after time to conciliate the whole of Ireland—indeed, it scarcely tried. Between Richard II's visit in 1399 and that of George IV in 1821, no monarch set foot in Ireland save James II and William III in 1689 to fight each other—four hundred years of comparative royal neglect. Though Victoria followed the example of her uncle and made state visits to Ireland, successive ministers failed to persuade her to establish a royal residence there, and perhaps it was already too late.

At times, the institution of monarchy itself seemed in peril. After the 'Maid of Norway' drowned in 1290, Scotland had two interregna and its monarchy was, in effect, suspended. In mid-fifteenth-century England, a sick and hapless Henry VI presided over dynastic and baronial strife and the loss of the great empire in France. Two hundred years later, the monarchy went down for eleven years while the Commonwealth held sway—the king beheaded, the crown jewels sold or pawned, the palaces empty and neglected, while the royal family eked out a desperate existence in foreign courts. Outside the Royal Exchange, the statue of Charles I was pulled down and replaced by an inscription which read 'Exit Tyrannus—Regum Ultimus'. The loss of the American colonies in 1783 seemed to herald a period of irreversible national decline, while thirty years later the madness of George III and the unpopularity of his son coincided dangerously with bitter wartime and post-war distress. In the 1860s and 1870s Gladstone and others despaired of the future as the queen, stricken by the death of her husband, refused to undertake public appearances. There were more grim days for George V during the Great War, with the newspapers filled by lists of casualties and the thrones of his cousins Nicholas II and Wilhelm II tottering. Even as late as the 1930s, people wondered whether the monarchy could survive the Abdication crisis.

When one ponders how such disasters and misfortunes in the past have been overcome, there seems little reason to doubt the future of the monarchy today. Of course it retains reserve or prerogative powers, the use of which must occasionally lead to controversy, but its regular political powers have been so reduced that a crisis likely to jeopardize its existence seems distinctly unlikely. For royal advisers, the most awkward task is to strike some sort of balance between under- and over-exposure of the royal family. Criticisms that the palace is too remote have to be set against warnings that the institution should not be exposed to the full glare of day. But this is scarcely a recent problem. Most monarchs have felt some tension between private fulfilment and public duty and for one, Edward VIII, the tension became unbearable. Monarchs have differed greatly in their capacity and willingness to play a public role and advisers have had to work with the materials available. When there have been flamboyant and extrovert monarchs, such as Edward III, Edward IV, James IV (of Scotland), Elizabeth I, and Edward VII, the public profile of the monarchy has been high: but monarchs such as George V and George VI, to whom florid gestures did not come easily, managed to create for themselves a quite different role and won great affection. The present policy of the palace appears to be to allow the younger members of the family to appease the demands of the popular press and television, while maintaining a certain reserve around the queen herself.

On a tour of Canada in 1969 Prince Philip remarked that if the monarchy was not wanted, 'for goodness sake, let's end the thing on amicable terms without having a row about it'. It is not easy, however, to see that any alternative offers, particularly in Britain, many advantages. There is much to be said for having a head of state who is not a party politician, and republican regimes themselves have not been free from difficulties. In the United States, it is hard for the two roles of the president to be kept scrupulously apart, especially in election years. In France, the party character of the presidency has produced tension with prime ministers of other party persuasions. The experience of many other countries suggests that there may well be considerable advantages in focusing national loyalty upon a person who cannot, by definition, entertain political ambitions, and it is one of the reasons why the spectre of army intervention in politics, which haunts so many countries, has been banished in Britain since the days of Cromwell and the Major-generals.

A further consideration is the rent that would be made in the fabric of national life in parting with an institution which has, over the centuries, been so deeply woven into the pattern of the nation's history. We have divisions enough without adding to them those of royalist and anti-royalist. It would be strange if the powers of adaptation, which have served the monarchy so well in the past, should desert it in the future.

ROYAL RESIDENCES
AND TOMBS

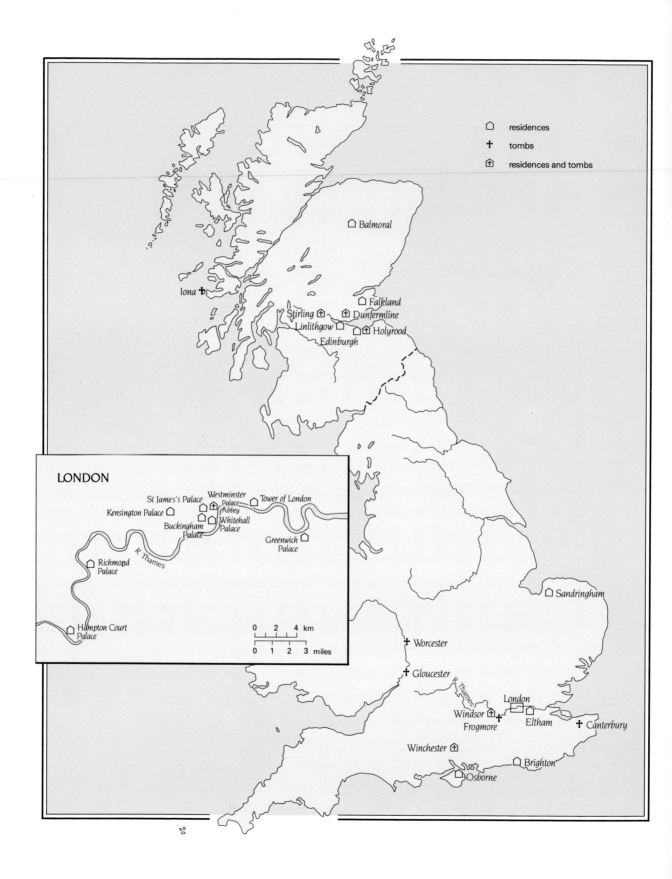

residences

tombs

residences and tombs

Balmoral

Iona

Falkland
Stirling Dunfermline
Linlithgow Holyrood
Edinburgh

LONDON

St James's Palace   Westminster   Tower of London
Kensington Palace   Palace
                         Abbey
Buckingham   Whitehall
Palace   Palace
                              Greenwich
                              Palace
R. Thames
Richmond
Palace

0   2   4   km

0   1   2   3 miles

Hampton Court
Palace

Sandringham

Worcester

Gloucester

R. Thames

Windsor   London
Frogmore   Eltham   Canterbury

Winchester

Brighton

Osborne

BUCKINGHAM PALACE, LONDON

The palace was built in 1703 for John Sheffield, duke of Buckingham. George III purchased it in 1762 and assigned it to his new queen, Charlotte. It was known first as the Queen's House, then, during the early years of George IV's reign, as the King's House, Pimlico. George employed Nash as the architect of a massive rebuilding. Marble Arch, intended as the main entrance, was later moved to its present position at the west end of Oxford Street. Victoria was the first monarch to be able to live in the new palace. The whole complex was finished in the early twentieth century, with Admiralty Arch giving entrance to the Mall and the statue of Queen Victoria placed outside the rebuilt east front.

BALMORAL, GRAMPIAN

Balmoral was the outcome of three highly successful visits to Scotland in the early years of Victoria's married life. She began renting the estate in 1848, purchased it in 1852, and commenced building on a grand scale. By 1855 Albert's castle was ready, swathed in specially designed tartan. Something of the queen's life there was conveyed in Victoria's *Leaves from the Journal of our Life in the Highlands*. Edward VII and George V were less fond of it, but George VI, whose wife was Scottish, delighted in Balmoral. It remains the private property of the queen.

BRIGHTON PAVILION, SUSSEX

Brighton Pavilion was the creation of George IV. He first visited the town in 1783 and employed Henry Holland to begin building. The grand reconstruction in Oriental style was undertaken by John Nash, the most celebrated features being the Music Room and the Great Kitchen. William IV and Victoria continued to use the Pavilion until the latter built Osborne House for seaside holidays. It was purchased by the Town Commissioners in 1850 and houses a permanent Regency exhibition, open to the public. On display is the wedding ring given by George IV to Mrs Fitzherbert in 1785: it opens to reveal his christian names on the inside.

The abbey and palace owe their popularity with Scottish kings to Margaret of England's marriage there to Malcolm III (*c*.1069). Margaret's son, David I, founded the Benedictine abbey (1150) on the site of his mother's church. Not only were Margaret and Malcolm buried there, but so were their sons and, to stress continuity of succession, Robert I. The abbey nave is the finest example of Scottish Romanesque. Remains of monastic buildings, overlooking a deep ravine, date from the early fourteenth century, after Edward I burned the abbey (1303); more rebuilding took place after Richard II's devastation (1385). Dunfermline was a royal residence in the later Middle Ages: David II (1324) and James I (1394) were born there. Though the precincts were neglected after the Reformation, the abbey guest house was converted into a palatial residence by James VI; his daughter Elizabeth (1596) and son, Charles I (1600), were born there.

EDINBURGH CASTLE, LOTHIAN

Once an important royal residence and seat of government, Edinburgh symbolizes the Scottish monarchy: the honours (or regalia) of Scotland are kept there and in 1929 statues of Robert Bruce and William Wallace were unveiled. There is no trace of early fortifications on the Rock, and St Margaret's Chapel is all that remains of the castle used by Malcolm Canmore and his English-born queen. But it was a frequent royal residence and centre of government during the twelfth and thirteenth centuries, until Edward I and the English occupied it (1296–1313). Bruce demolished the fortifications (1314) and when David II reconstructed them—especially his great tower (1367), of which foundations can still be seen—he used Edward III's new works at Windsor as his model. During the next 400 years, the castle was besieged many times, by Scottish dissidents as well as by English; it was sometimes taken and stories of great escapes abound. By the end of the fifteenth century it had ceased to be a regular royal home, although subsequently a great hall was built: Mary of Guise died there (1560) and James VI was born there (1566). It became instead an armoury and barracks, a prison, an administrative office, and a site for tournaments. The defences were periodically refurbished, and a great parade ground was constructed at the entrance early in the nineteenth century. After Charles II (1650), no monarch visited Edinburgh Castle until George IV.

ELTHAM PALACE, LONDON

The manor-house was acquired by Edward II's queen (*c*.1311), but it was Edward III who developed its apartments and gardens (1350s). It was a favourite royal residence throughout the fourteenth and fifteenth centuries: Richard II added new bathrooms and a dancing chamber, while Henry IV constructed a new study and overhauled the palace (costing £1,100 during 1399–1407). Little of this early work survives; today its most magnificent feature is Edward IV's great hall, begun in 1475 after two earlier halls had been demolished. Henry VIII met Erasmus at Eltham, and built a new chapel there in the 1520s, but thereafter the palace was neglected.

FALKLAND PALACE, FIFE

Falkland was the first Renaissance building in Scotland. Although its origins as a castle and royal hunting-lodge are obscure, in the fifteenth century it became a favourite royal residence. James II began to rebuild it in the 1450s, and his widow, Mary of Gueldres, continued his work in the 1460s. But it was James V who transformed it in the 1530s into a palace in French Renaissance style whose ornamented gatehouse, courtyard range of apartments decorated with Renaissance medallions and fluted columns, and Royal Tennis Court (1539, the oldest in Britain) were built by French craftsmen for his queens, Madeleine of France and Mary of Guise. The style is similar to that favoured by James's contemporary, Henry VIII, at Nonsuch. Still a royal possession, Falkland has long been occupied by the Crichton Stuarts, who heavily restored it: the Chapel Royal and the King's Bedchamber are especially impressive.

GREENWICH PALACE, LONDON

Greenwich was the residence of Humphrey, duke of Gloucester, uncle of Henry VI and benefactor of the Bodleian Library at Oxford. It passed to Henry VII, whose second son was born there. Elizabeth I spent much of her reign at Greenwich. After James I had given it to Anne of Denmark, she commissioned Inigo Jones to build the delightful Queen's House, though it was not completed until the following reign. Charles II established the royal observatory on the hill. William and Mary built elsewhere and offered Greenwich as a seamen's hospital, with extensions by Wren and interior decoration by Thornhill. In the nineteenth century it became a naval college, and the Maritime Museum was established there in the twentieth century.

HAMPTON COURT PALACE, LONDON

Created by Cardinal Wolsey, Hampton Court was surrendered by him to Henry VIII in a desperate bid to retain royal favour. From 1530 onwards, Henry was busy extending his new possession. Anne Boleyn and his four subsequent queens lived there. Charles I and Charles II also brought their brides to Hampton Court.

William III found the air better than that of London and built on a large scale: it was at Hampton Court that he broke his collar-bone while riding in 1702 and subsequently died. George II was the last monarch to reside there, his successor disliking the place. It is used occasionally for receptions and much of it is given over to grace and favour residences. One wing was badly damaged by fire in 1986.

PALACE OF HOLYROODHOUSE, EDINBURGH, LOTHIAN

Holyroodhouse in Edinburgh was originally an abbey founded in 1128 by David I, whose mother Margaret (d. 1073) had presented him with what she believed to be a fragment of the True Cross (or Rood). James IV decided to convert it into a royal residence, and Margaret Tudor was married there in 1503. Burned by the earl of Surrey in 1543, it was rebuilt by James V, whose remains were laid in a vault with those of David II and James II (the first Scottish king to be crowned there). In 1566 it was the scene of the murder of Rizzio, the favourite of Mary, queen of Scots. Though Charles II had the palace completely renovated, he did not visit it after the Restoration. Prince Charles Edward stayed there during the '45 and gave a celebrated ball after his victory at Prestonpans. It was used as a residence during the Napoleonic Wars by the Comte d'Artois and he returned there in 1830 after he had been overthrown as Charles X. George IV's visit in 1822 was master-minded by Sir Walter Scott.

KENSINGTON PALACE, LONDON

The palace began life as the family house of the Finches, earls of Nottingham. When William III found London air disagreeable, he purchased the property in 1689. The palace was enlarged by Wren and later adorned by William Kent. William and Mary both died there. Anne added an elegant Orangery and her celebrated quarrel with 'Mrs. Freeman' took place in a small room on the east side. George II and Caroline liked the palace and it contains handsome busts by Rysbrack. The Round Pond was constructed in that reign and the Serpentine begun. George III was not fond of Kensington Palace and allowed his brother, the duke of Kent, to live there. Princess Victoria grew up there in the 1820s and held her first royal council there in June 1837. Later royal residents include Princess May, who married George V, and Princess Margaret. The state apartments are open to the public and there is a permanent exhibition of court dress.

LINLITHGOW PALACE, LOTHIAN

A timber manor-house and stone church were built beside the loch by David I; the defences were strengthened by Edward I (1301–2), and from Robert I's day Linlithgow was rebuilt and used as a royal residence. James I built the present palace after a fire (1424); it included royal apartments and a great hall, and his successors added to it in the fifteenth century. James V's French queen, Mary of Guise, said that nothing impressed her more than its late Gothic and early Renaissance features. The palace was a refuge for Henry VI and Margaret of Anjou (1461), and the birthplace of James V (1513) and Mary, queen of Scots (1542). The ruinous north side was rebuilt in 1618–20, though Charles I was the last king to sleep there (1633). It was accidentally burned in 1746.

Osborne House was purchased in 1845 by Queen Victoria as a private retreat for her growing family. One of its charms was its privacy: 'we can walk about anywhere by ourselves,' wrote the queen, 'without being followed and mobbed.' By 1851 a new house had been erected in the Italian style, designed by the Prince Consort and built by Thomas Cubitt. It had access to a good private beach. Victoria spent much of her time there after her husband's death and died there in January 1901. Edward VII was not fond of the place and gave it for public use. The state apartments and Victoria's suite are open to the public: much of it is unchanged since the Prince Consort's time.

RICHMOND PALACE, SURREY

The history of the royal residences at Richmond, Surrey, is complex. Originally, there was no more than a manor-house at Sheen, used occasionally by Edward II. Edward III extended it and died there in 1377, watched over by his mistress, Alice Perrers. But in 1394, after Richard II's first wife, Anne of Bohemia, had died there, the king gave orders for its destruction. Something survived, for Henry V restored it and made frequent use of it. In 1497 it was completely gutted by fire. Henry VII rebuilt it on the grand scale and gave to the new palace his former title of Richmond. It was one of the most important Tudor palaces. Mary, in her brief reign, restored Sheen priory as part of her personal counter-reformation, and it was at Richmond that Elizabeth gave her last public audience, to the Venetian ambassador, in February 1603. In the Stuart period, it declined. Prince Henry, James I's eldest son, made use of it, but during the Commonwealth it fell into decay, only Richmond Lodge surviving. George II,

as Prince of Wales, lived at the Lodge with Princess Caroline in the 1720s, and George III and Queen Charlotte began their married life there. They subsequently moved to Kew House, which had belonged to George's father, Frederick, Prince of Wales. Sir William Chambers's pagoda, which survives, was erected in the early 1760s and the grounds embellished by Capability Brown. In the 1780s the royal family preferred Windsor, but George III returned to Kew in 1788 at the start of his protracted illness. He even began a new palace, to the design of James Wyatt, which would have rivalled the old Richmond, but progress was slow and it was demolished eight years after George's death. Kew Palace is open to the public as part of the Botanical Gardens, which owe their existence to the keen interest in horticulture which George's mother, Princess Augusta, shared with his tutor, the earl of Bute.

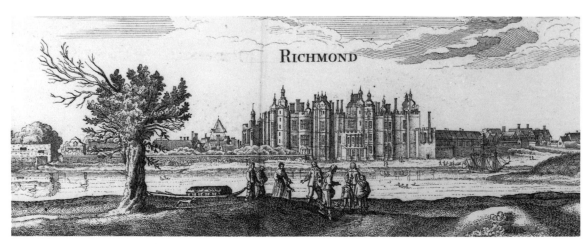

Built by Henry VIII on the site of the Hospital of St James, it consisted originally of four courtyards. Mary used the palace a great deal and died there in 1558. It was a favourite residence of Charles II and James II, and the Prince of Wales was born there in 1688—the so-called warming-pan baby. After Whitehall had been burned down, Anne divided most of her time between St James's and Kensington Palace. It was to St James's that Frederick, Prince of Wales, brought his wife in labour in 1737 so that his child should not be born under his parents' roof at Hampton Court. George III's move to Buckingham Palace meant that St James's was used mainly for official receptions. Victoria and Albert were married in the Chapel Royal in 1840. Foreign ambassadors are still accredited to the court of St James.

SANDRINGHAM HOUSE, NORFOLK

Sandringham is a private royal residence and was purchased in 1861 by the Prince Consort for the Prince of Wales, largely for its grounds. The Prince and Princess Alexandra soon began enlarging it, and for forty years entertained weekend parties and shoots there. George V, as duke of York, was devoted to it, and lived at York Cottage in the grounds for the first thirty-three years of his married life. He died there in 1936 and his second son, George VI, died there in 1952. It is the present royal family's favourite Christmas residence.

Atop an impregnable volcanic outcrop, dominating a crossing of the Forth and a mountain pass to the north, its site is easily defended. A royal castle-residence was built in the early twelfth century, and David I founded the Augustinian abbey of Cambuskenneth nearby (c.1140). Between 1174, when Henry II acquired Stirling in return for releasing William the Lion (who died there, 1214), and Bannockburn in 1314, the castle was fought over by English invaders and royal claimants. There was major rebuilding in the later Middle Ages and sixteenth century. James IV developed the castle's inner courtyard and defences (c.1500); and James V built the royal apartments in French Renaissance style (c.1540). Mary, queen of Scots, and James VI spent time at Stirling (James's son Henry was born there, 1594), and formal gardens were laid in the seventeenth century. In 1651 it fell to a parliamentary siege, but Prince Charles Edward failed to storm it (1746). Stirling was a military barracks until 1964.

THE TOWER OF LONDON

This great castle was a royal palace from the outset. Founded probably 'to overawe the Londoners' by William the Conqueror in 1066, its site was in the south-east angle of London's Roman walls. The donjon (or White Tower which gives the fortress its name) was begun a decade later and when finished (c.1100) was the castle's military and residential centre-piece. A complex scheme of defences and domestic quarters was devised for what was the most strategically placed castle in the kingdom. William Rufus created a de-

fended bailey by building stone walls on the west to complement the Roman fortifications on the east and along the river. Richard I added an outer bailey of new walls and towers further to the west. Henry III enlarged the royal apartments (including a great hall and the king's and queen's great chambers) in the inner bailey, whose defences were strengthened. He also extended the castle to east and north beyond the Roman and Norman defences, encroaching on the city and creating a perimeter wall and ditch. All told, the Tower cost him about £10,000; yet his works were surpassed by those of Edward I, who completed Henry's walls and then (1275–85) placed an outer wall and moat round the whole, creating (for about £21,000) a concentric fortress in the latest fashion. There was spacious royal accommodation at the centre of the castle, and the new entrance from the city was

elaborate and strong. Later additions were more minor, though Edward III enlarged the royal apartments and built Tower wharf. At one time or another, the Tower housed the armoury, mint, royal Treasury, and wardrobe (the crown jewels are still there), a record office, library (for Henry VII) and council chamber, and the king's menagerie (including an elephant given to Henry III by Louis IX of France). Henry VIII was the last king to use the Tower as a chief residence, and Charles II the last to spend the eve of coronation there. From c.1540 it was an armoury and a prison (though it had always held state prisoners such as John II of France)—hence 'Traitors' Gate' and 'the Bloody Tower'. Parts of the Tower were neglected and the palace was largely demolished in Charles II's time to make way for the ordnance; the Waterloo block was built in the mid-nineteenth century.

PALACE OF WESTMINSTER, LONDON

The main residence of English kings from Edward the Confessor to Henry VIII, Westminster owes its origins to Edward's abbey, built on Thorney Island in the Thames (1065). The palace was east of the abbey, beside the river, and as the king's residence it became the centre of government, despite disastrous fires in 1263, 1298, 1512, and 1834. Nothing of Edward's palace survives, but William Rufus built (1090s) a great hall to the north which was heightened by Richard II three hundred years later to form one of the largest and grandest medieval buildings in Europe. By the mid-twelfth century, Westminster was the governmental headquarters and included the Treasury and the Exchequer. The private palace was rebuilt and extended around 'old' palace yard, with a new (or White) hall, St Stephen's Chapel, and a great chamber raised by Henry II. Henry III added apartments

(1230s) and rebuilt the great chamber as the painted chamber, with fine biblical murals inside. Edward I built the great gateway, north-west of Westminster Hall, and began to rebuild St Stephen's, whose early fourteenth-century crypt chapel of St Mary Undercroft survives (restored after 1834). Rebuilding continued, especially in the private (or 'privy') palace: St Stephen's was completed by 1363 and there was a clock tower (1365–1698) in 'new' palace yard north of Westminster Hall; the Jewel Tower (1365–6), the king's private treasury, still stands at the south-west corner of the palace. After 1512, Henry VIII ceased to reside at Westminster and moved to Whitehall. The north part had long since become government offices, St Stephen's became the Commons' meeting-place after 1547, and even the Jewel Tower was taken over as the Lords' record office (1621–1864).

WHITEHALL PALACE, LONDON

Like Hampton Court, Whitehall belonged at one time to Cardinal Wolsey, in his capacity as archbishop of York. It was known as York Place. Henry VIII seized it and began a major extension to the west, building a tilt-yard, cockpit, bowling alley, and tennis court. Elizabeth I received the duke d'Alençon as suitor there. James I added a Banqueting Hall for receptions: it was destroyed by fire almost immediately. Inigo Jones's replacement is the only part of the palace to survive today: from a window on the first floor, Charles I stepped to the scaffold in 1649. Charles II spent much of his reign at Whitehall, parking out his mistresses in nearby suites. After a disastrous fire in 1698, the site was developed in the course of time for government offices.

WINCHESTER PALACE, HAMPSHIRE

Winchester is unique as a principal royal residence and seat of government in both Anglo-Saxon and Norman times. It was the seat of a bishopric from the 660s, and its minsters became the mausoleum of Anglo-Saxon kings. By the tenth century a royal palace lay west of the Old Minster, rather as Charlemagne's palace stood close to the chapel at Aachen. Winchester remained an administrative capital and crown-wearing centre after 1066, and the royal Treasury was there. In Henry II's reign it was superseded by Westminster, to which both Treasury and Exchequer were transferred. The old palace proved inadequate and William I built a 'new hall and palace' on a different site, north-west of the cathedral; they were damaged by fire when Matilda was besieged there (1141). William's castle was rebuilt in stone by Henry II and extensively altered to become a residence. Henry III, who was born there, extended the defences with towers, ditch, and gatehouses, and built the great hall (1222–35) that still stands; he spent *c*. £10,000 on the castle-palace. While Edward I and Queen Margaret were asleep in the castle in 1302 a fire gutted the royal chambers, which were never fully restored. Thereafter, kings usually stayed at the bishop's palace when visiting the city. Winchester's Arthurian associations are most spectacularly captured by the great Round Table, made probably in Edward I's reign and still hanging in the great hall. The castle was dismantled in 1651; a new palace was designed for Charles II by Wren (1683), but it was never finished and became a barracks.

WINDSOR CASTLE, BERKSHIRE

The oldest royal residence still in use, Windsor was a Norman fortress. William the Conqueror built his elongated motte and two baileys (or wards) along an escarpment above the Thames. By 1100 it had a royal lodge for hunting in the nearby forest. Its earth and wood defences were replaced by stone *c*.1180, when the round tower was built on the motte; the upper ward was ringed with walls and square towers, and a beginning made on walling the middle and lower wards. These defences withstood two sieges (1194, 1216). Henry III repaired the walls, adding round towers in the lower ward. Thereafter, the accent was on extending the domestic quarters in the upper ward and the chapels in the lower. There are remains of Henry's extensive work, and Edward III left his indelible mark when he founded the Order of the Garter (1348) and used Henry III's chapel (*c*.1240) as its headquarters and rebuilt its collegiate buildings (1350–61). Edward demolished Henry's royal apartments in the lower ward and created (1357–65) more spacious ones, including St George's hall, in the upper;

he spent over £51,000 on Windsor (1350–77). Edward IV began a new Garter chapel of St George (1475) in Perpendicular style, while the old chapel was converted by Henry VII into a lady chapel and mausoleum (though it was not used as such until George III's time). In his turn, Charles II replaced Edward III's apartments with a new palace and terrace in Baroque style, and these are the core of the present state apartments; he also laid the three-mile processional avenue to the castle from the south. The greatest reconstruction took place under George IV, whose vision was matched by the neo-Gothic architecture he favoured: the round tower was raised by one storey; new towers and a gateway were built in the upper ward, with new private apartments on its south and east sides. Victoria made some museum-like alterations in the state apartments and remodelled St George's lady chapel as a memorial to her beloved Albert. Windsor has always been a royal residence and was especially popular in the seventeenth and nineteenth centuries.

ROYAL TOMBS

Sixteen monarchs are buried in Westminster Abbey, which remained the traditional burial-place from its rebuilding by Henry III to the funeral of George II in 1760. Originally the Church of St Peter and founded years before Edward the Confessor's reign, the rivalry with the Church of St Paul, three miles to the east, produced the name of Westminster. The Confessor began enlarging the church on a grand scale but was too ill in December 1065 to attend its consecration and

was buried there a month later. The Conqueror's coronation at the end of 1066 took place there and only two subsequent monarchs have not been crowned there—Edward V, who was deposed by his uncle Richard, and Edward VIII, who abdicated within a year of his succession. The early Norman kings were buried elsewhere, but Henry III began a massive rebuilding programme in the mid-thirteenth century. He was responsible for the great new shrine of Edward

the Confessor and was buried there himself in 1272. Richard II was responsible for more building at the end of the fourteenth century: though, after his deposition, he was at first buried at King's Langley in Hertfordshire, Henry V arranged for his body to be reinterred at Westminster. Henry VII lavished attention upon the abbey and built the chapel which, for more than two centuries, was the burial-place for English kings. His own shrine (*above*) has been called 'the finest Renaissance tomb north of the Alps'. Mary and her half-sister Elizabeth were buried there. James I was responsible for the superb tomb of Elizabeth, which includes a lifelike effigy, and, as an act of filial piety, erected a tomb for his mother, Mary, queen of Scots, executed at Fotheringhay in 1587. Charles I ordered a majestic tomb in the chapel for his murdered friend Buckingham, and James I, Charles II, Mary, William, Anne, and George II were all buried there. A remarkable feature of many of the funerals were the effigies of the monarchs which accompanied the coffin: a number are still on show in the crypt and are among the best representations we have of the sovereigns concerned.

FONTEVRAULT ABBEY, FRANCE

Henry I and his son Richard I (*above, near*) are both buried in Fontevrault Abbey in Anjou, which had been founded in about 1130 as a nunnery. The stone effigies of the kings were commissioned by Henry's widow, Eleanor Aquitaine (*above, rear*), who was patroness of the abbey and is also buried there. In addition, the abbey contains the tomb of Eleanor's daughter-in-law, Isabella of Angoulême, wife of King John.

CANTERBURY CATHEDRAL, KENT

Despite the fact that Canterbury Cathedral is England's mother church, it has only one royal tomb. Henry IV was buried there with his second wife, Joan, possibly because Westminster Abbey was too strongly associated with the Plantagenet line, which he had brought to an end. In 1376, thirty-seven years earlier, the Black Prince, Edward III's eldest son, had been buried there: his effigy (*above*) is one of the most splendid in England and helped to attract funds for the new nave, which was completed *c*.1400.

There was some difficulty in deciding what to do with the body of Edward II, murdered at Berkeley Castle in Gloucestershire in 1327. The monks of St Augustine's, Bristol, are said to have refused to accept it, probably because of the king's reputation. If so, they were mistaken. It went instead to Gloucester, formerly an Anglo-Saxon monastery dedicated to St Peter and refounded in 1070 by the Normans as a Benedictine abbey. Edward's great shrine became so popular as a place of pilgrimage that the proceeds supported the large-scale rebuilding of the choir, one of the glories of the church, in the mid-fourteenth century.

FROGMORE, WINDSOR, BERKSHIRE

When Albert died in December 1861, Victoria resolved to build a special mausoleum for them both at Frogmore. This was a small estate which Queen Charlotte had used in her later years and which had passed into the hands of Victoria's mother, the duchess of Kent, who had just died and been buried there. Victoria supervised every detail of Albert's effigy, including the length of the straps that held down his trousers, and she had her own statue made at the same time for the moment when they could be reunited. A

long forty years later, it was her turn. There was trouble with the gun-carriage on the way up the hill from the station at Windsor. An eighty-one-gun salute marked each year of her life and, wearing her bridal veil from 1840, she joined her beloved Albert for ever. Edward VIII, then duke of Windsor, was, at his own request, buried at Frogmore in 1972, in death as in life slightly apart from his family, and fourteen years later the duchess, born Wallis Warfield, was laid beside him. Frogmore today remains a private mausoleum.

Eleven monarchs are buried at Windsor, which has been a castle and royal residence since the reign of William the Conqueror. When Edward III founded the order of the Garter about 1348, Windsor became its headquarters. The Knights made use of the chapel built by Henry III in 1240, but it was renovated by Edward III and totally rebuilt by Edward IV, who was buried there in 1483. Henry VIII's funeral took place there amid great pomp in 1547. The carriage was drawn by eight black-draped horses, on each of which a page carried a royal banner: the cortège was said to be four miles long and roads had been specially widened. Henry's body was laid alongside that of Jane Seymour, his third wife and the mother of his young successor, Edward VI. Windsor was not used again for royal burial until Charles I's body was taken there after his execution in January 1649. Parliament obviously considered it more private than Westminster, where there might be public disorder. Instructions were given that the expenses were not to exceed £500 and that the Anglican form of service was not to be used. As the coffin was borne to the chapel, where Henry VIII's vault had been opened up, it began to snow, and by the time it reached the door the pall was covered with white flakes. In 1820 George III's long seclusion from the world and his fondness for Windsor made St George's Chapel more appropriate than Westminster Abbey. But the ceremony was by no means unimposing and Mrs Arbuthnot found it 'a most solemn and impressive scene'. The same could hardly be said of the next royal burial, that of George IV in 1830, which was marred when the lead coffin began to bulge ominously and had to be punctured, and also by the obvious relish that the new king, William IV, took in his role. By this time, Westminster Abbey had become so crowded that a dignified resting place would not have been easy to find. Victoria was buried nearby at Frogmore, but Edward VII, George V, and George VI were all buried in St George's Chapel, Windsor.

WINCHESTER CATHEDRAL, HAMPSHIRE

Anglo-Saxon kings were buried at Winchester from the seventh century onwards—Æthelwulf, Alfred, Edward the Elder, Eadred, and Eadwig, together with the eleventh-century Danish kings Cnut and Harthacnut. After William Rufus had been shot while hunting in the New Forest in 1100, his body was taken to Winchester Cathedral and buried with little ceremony. The bones of all these monarchs were placed in mortuary chests in 1525 and are still in the choir. Four of the six chests were destroyed in the Civil War, and the bones scattered around the cathedral; these were replaced in new chests (such as the one *left*) in 1661.

WORCESTER CATHEDRAL, WORCESTERSHIRE

King John had a special reverence for Worcester, which had been founded as a monastery by St Oswald in 983, and which also contained the shrine of Wulfstan, canonized in 1203. In a codicil to his will, John asked to be buried there between the shrines of the two saints. The tomb effigy of Purbeck marble, made in 1232, was originally the lid of John's stone coffin; it shows the king lying with his head on a pillow which Oswald and Wulfstan support. This is the oldest royal effigy in England and may bear some likeness to the king; the present tomb was made in the fifteenth century. Royal tombs held great fascination for those in the late eighteenth and nineteenth centuries who were interested in the Middle Ages, and when John's tomb was opened in 1797 the king's skeleton was found to be intact.

ROYAL BURIAL-PLACES IN SCOTLAND

The burial-place of the early Scottish kings was the island of Iona, off the coast of Mull, and no subsequent site achieved the same pre-eminence. No fewer than forty-eight monarchs are said to have been buried there, in addition to Irish and Norse kings, though some had brief reigns and obscure claims to the throne. The last king to be buried at Iona was Donald Bane, son of Duncan I, who was first interred at Dunkeld in 1097, and then moved to the island. When his elder brother Malcolm III had been killed near Tynemouth in 1093, his wife Margaret, who was English and un-sympathetic to the Celtic tradition of kingship, arranged for his burial in the abbey of the royal residence at Dunfermline (q.v.). Edgar (1107), Alexander I (1124), David I (1153), Alexander III (1286), and Robert the Bruce were all buried at Dunfermline. William the Lion (1214) was buried at Arbroath and Alexander II at Melrose Abbey in 1249. David II (1371) was buried at Holyrood (q.v.), as were James II (1460) and James V (1542). Other burial-places include Scone (Robert II, 1390) and Cambuskenneth, near Stirling (q.v.), where James III was buried in 1488. His tomb, and that of his wife Margaret of Denmark, was rediscovered in 1864, when Victoria arranged for a new memorial. The burial-place of James IV, killed at Flodden, is un-certain: the coffin was reported to have been kept at the Carthusian house at Sheen in Surrey and to have been moved to St Michael's Church during the reign of Elizabeth I.

OTHER ROYAL BURIAL-PLACES

Apart from Henry II and Richard, buried at Fontev-rault, three monarchs died abroad. William the Con-queror was buried in St Stephen's Church at Caen, in Normandy, but his remains were twice disturbed, once during the French wars of religion in 1562 and again at the Revolution in 1793. James II died in exile, after the Glorious Revolution, at Saint-Germain-en-Laye in 1701: his body was buried in the church of the English Benedictines in Paris but, unlucky in death as in life, his grave was desecrated during the French Revolution and the monuments destroyed. George I died at Osnabrück in 1727 on his way to Hanover and was buried in the Leineschlosskirche. After this had been badly damaged by bombing during the Second World War, the coffin was reinterred at the family estate at Herrenhausen, near the grave of his mother, the Electress Sophia, who so narrowly missed becoming queen of England.

Other monarchs were buried in churches of which they were fond. Harold's body was brought back from Hastings and buried near the high altar of Waltham Abbey, some twelve miles north of London. Henry I was buried at Reading, and Stephen at Faversham in Kent, with his wife and son, in the choir of the Cluniac abbey which he had founded.

The exact burial-place of two monarchs who suf-fered violent deaths is not known. Edward V, the boy who succeeded in 1483, was murdered in the Tower of London with his younger brother and was almost certainly buried there. In 1674 the bones of two young boys were found at the foot of a staircase in the Tower and, by order of Charles II, were given burial at Westminster. The most ignominious funeral was re-served for Richard III, the uncle who usurped Edward's throne, and was killed in battle at Bosworth in 1485. His body was disfigured, slung over a horse, and given an obscure burial at Greyfriars in Leicester. Henry VII eventually provided a coffin but no monu-ment. At the Reformation, the bones were scattered and the coffin used for decades as a horse-trough outside a tavern.

GENEALOGIES OF
ROYAL LINES

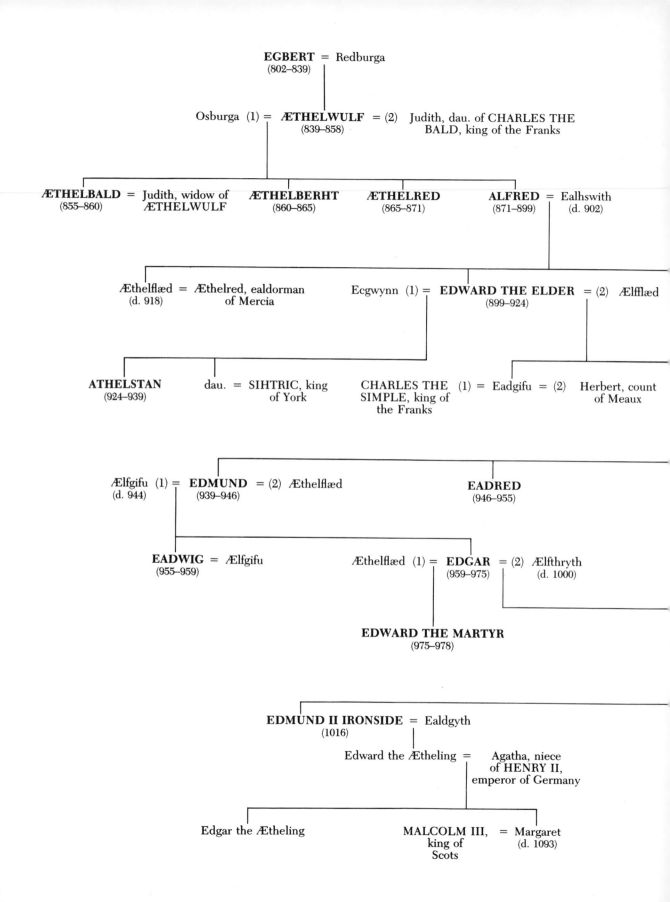

I. KINGS OF WESSEX AND ENGLAND
802–1066

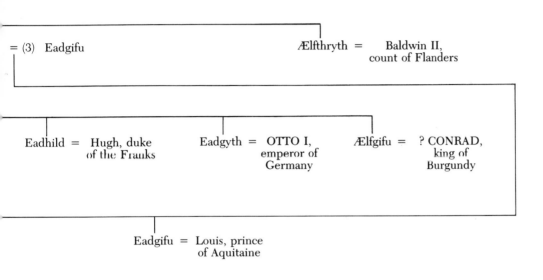

= (3) Eadgifu   Ælfthryth = Baldwin II, count of Flanders

Eadhild = Hugh, duke of the Franks   Eadgyth = OTTO I, emperor of Germany   Ælfgifu = ? CONRAD, king of Burgundy

Eadgifu = Louis, prince of Aquitaine

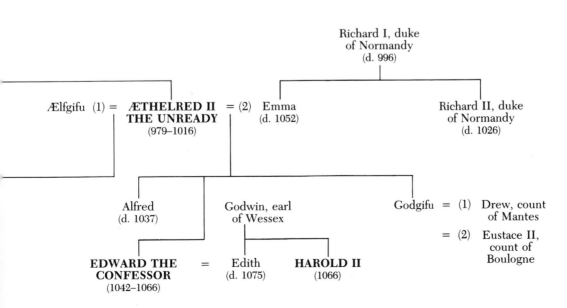

Richard I, duke of Normandy (d. 996)

Ælfgifu (1) = **ÆTHELRED II THE UNREADY** (979–1016) = (2) Emma (d. 1052)   Richard II, duke of Normandy (d. 1026)

Alfred (d. 1037)   Godwin, earl of Wessex   Godgifu = (1) Drew, count of Mantes

= (2) Eustace II, count of Boulogne

EDWARD THE CONFESSOR (1042–1066) = Edith (d. 1075)   **HAROLD II** (1066)

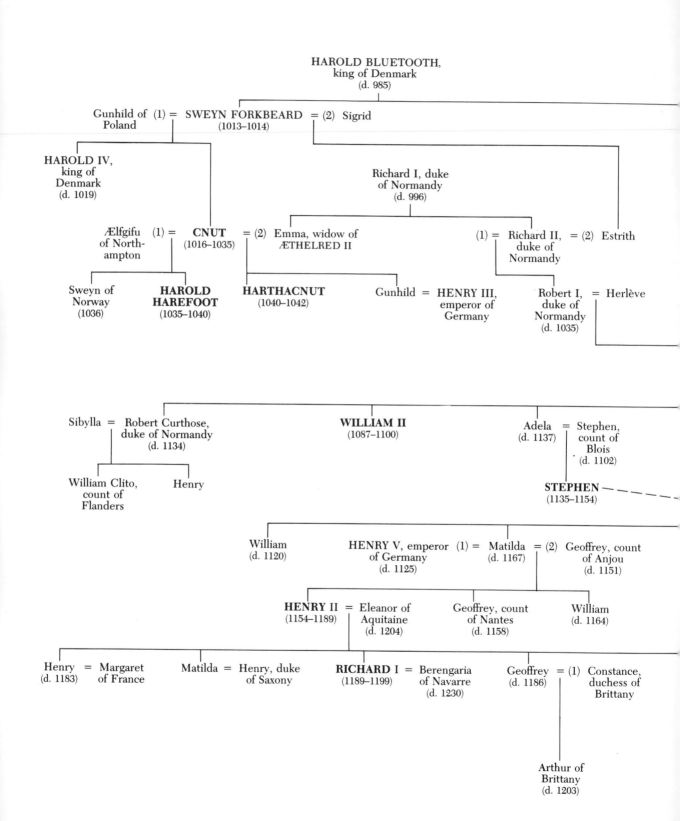

HAROLD BLUETOOTH,
king of Denmark
(d. 985)

Gunhild of (1) = SWEYN FORKBEARD = (2) Sigrid
Poland (1013–1014)

HAROLD IV,
king of
Denmark
(d. 1019)

Richard I, duke
of Normandy
(d. 996)

Ælfgifu (1) = CNUT = (2) Emma, widow of
of North- (1016–1035) ÆTHELRED II
ampton

(1) = Richard II, = (2) Estrith
duke of
Normandy

Sweyn of
Norway
(1036)

HAROLD
HAREFOOT
(1035–1040)

HARTHACNUT
(1040–1042)

Gunhild = HENRY III,
emperor of
Germany

Robert I, = Herlève
duke of
Normandy
(d. 1035)

Sibylla = Robert Curthose,
duke of Normandy
(d. 1134)

WILLIAM II
(1087–1100)

Adela = Stephen,
(d. 1137) count of
Blois
(d. 1102)

William Clito,
count of
Flanders

Henry

STEPHEN
(1135–1154)

William
(d. 1120)

HENRY V, emperor (1) = Matilda = (2) Geoffrey, count
of Germany (d. 1167) of Anjou
(d. 1125) (d. 1151)

HENRY II = Eleanor of
(1154–1189) Aquitaine
(d. 1204)

Geoffrey, count
of Nantes
(d. 1158)

William
(d. 1164)

Henry = Margaret
(d. 1183) of France

Matilda = Henry, duke
of Saxony

RICHARD I = Berengaria
(1189–1199) of Navarre
(d. 1230)

Geoffrey = (1) Constance,
(d. 1186) duchess of
Brittany

Arthur of
Brittany
(d. 1203)

II. THE CONTINENTAL DYNASTIES
1066–1216

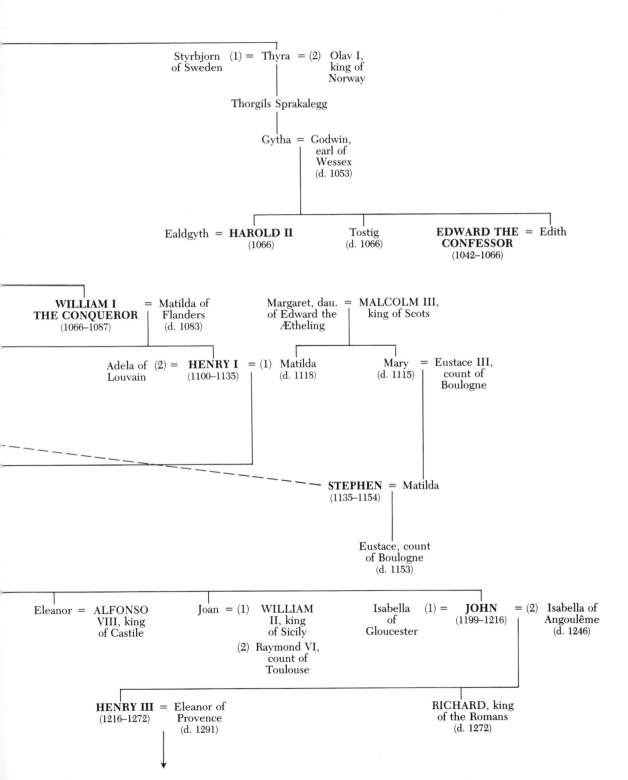

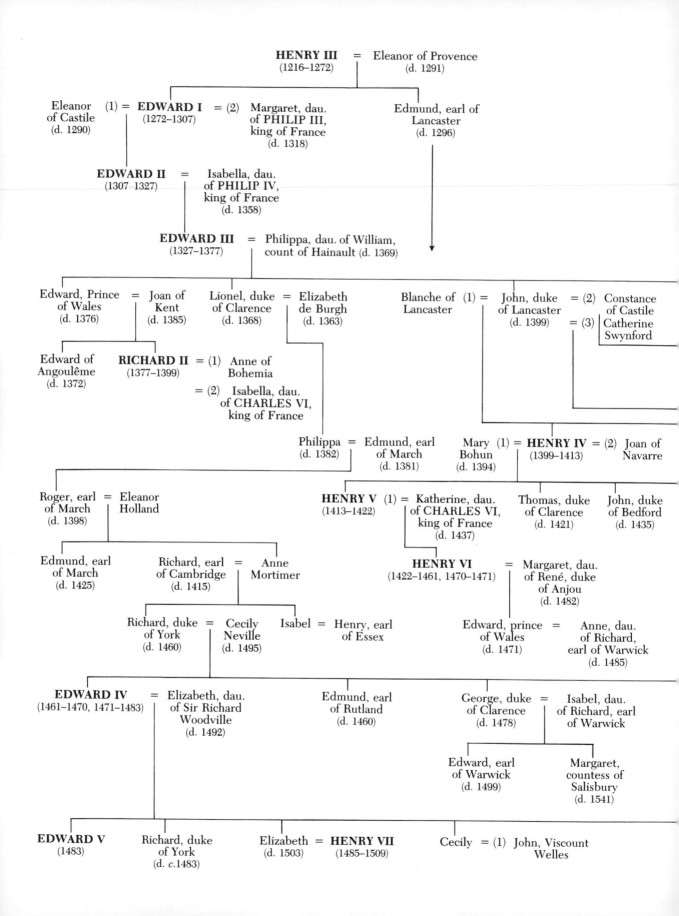

III. THE PLANTAGENET DYNASTIES
1216–1485

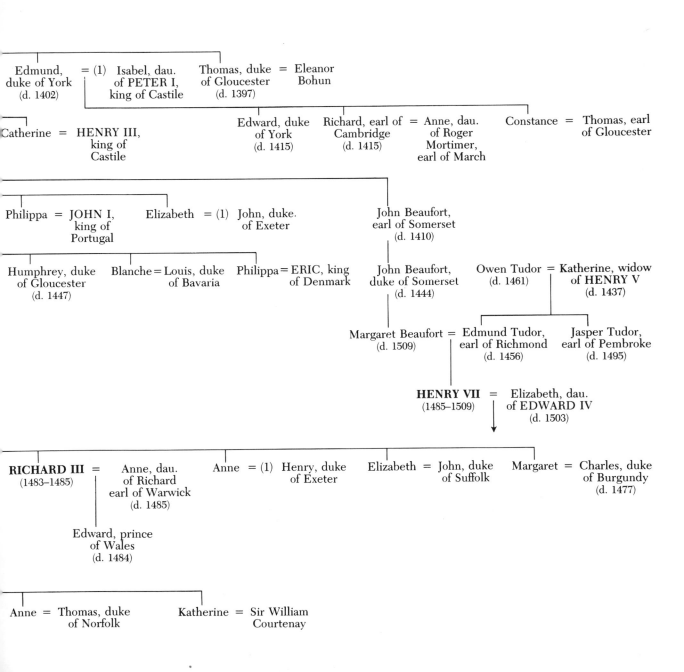

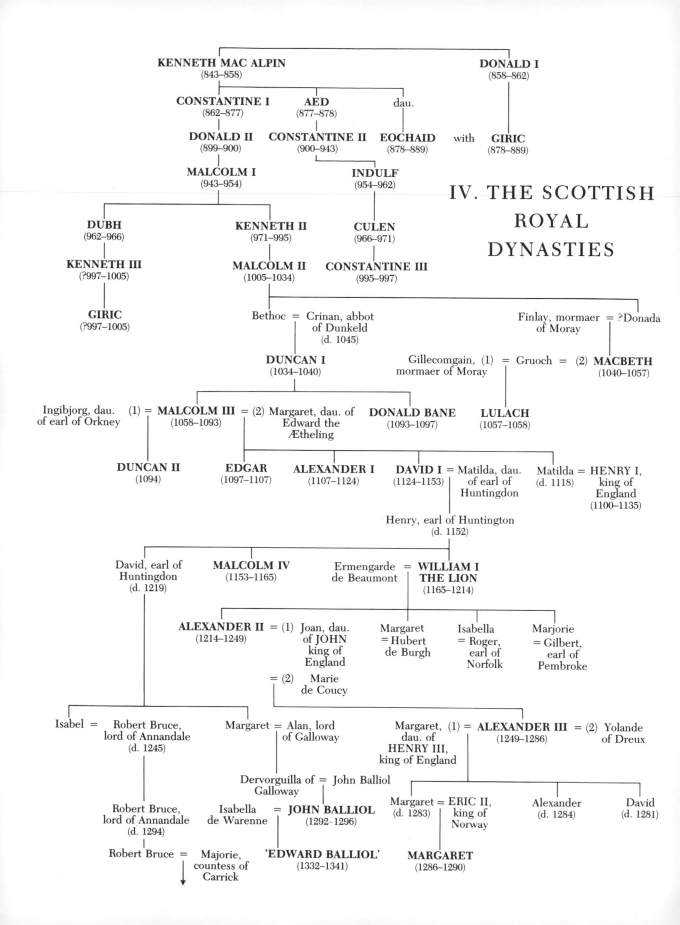

IV. THE SCOTTISH ROYAL DYNASTIES

KENNETH MAC ALPIN (843–858) **DONALD I** (858–862)

CONSTANTINE I (862–877) **AED** (877–878) dau.

DONALD II (899–900) **CONSTANTINE II** (900–943) **EOCHAID** (878–889) with **GIRIC** (878–889)

MALCOLM I (943–954) **INDULF** (954–962)

DUBH (962–966) **KENNETH II** (971–995) **CULEN** (966–971)

KENNETH III (?997–1005) **MALCOLM II** (1005–1034) **CONSTANTINE III** (995–997)

GIRIC (?997–1005)

Bethoc = Crinan, abbot of Dunkeld (d. 1045) Finlay, mormaer of Moray = ?Donada

DUNCAN I (1034–1040) Gillecomgain, (1) = Gruoch = (2) **MACBETH** mormaer of Moray (1040–1057)

Ingibjorg, dau. of earl of Orkney (1) = **MALCOLM III** (1058–1093) = (2) Margaret, dau. of Edward the Ætheling **DONALD BANE** (1093–1097) **LULACH** (1057–1058)

DUNCAN II (1094) **EDGAR** (1097–1107) **ALEXANDER I** (1107–1124) **DAVID I** (1124–1153) = Matilda, dau. of earl of Huntingdon Matilda (d. 1118) = **HENRY I**, king of England (1100–1135)

Henry, earl of Huntington (d. 1152)

David, earl of Huntingdon (d. 1219) **MALCOLM IV** (1153–1165) Ermengarde de Beaumont = **WILLIAM I THE LION** (1165–1214)

ALEXANDER II (1214–1249) = (1) Joan, dau. of **JOHN** king of England Margaret = Hubert de Burgh Isabella = Roger, earl of Norfolk Marjorie = Gilbert, earl of Pembroke

= (2) Marie de Coucy

Isabel = Robert Bruce, lord of Annandale (d. 1245) Margaret = Alan, lord of Galloway Margaret, (1) = **ALEXANDER III** (1249–1286) = (2) Yolande of Dreux dau. of **HENRY III**, king of England

Dervorguilla of = John Balliol Galloway

Robert Bruce, lord of Annandale (d. 1294) Isabella de Warenne = **JOHN BALLIOL** (1292–1296) Margaret (d. 1283) = **ERIC II**, king of Norway Alexander (d. 1284) David (d. 1281)

Robert Bruce = Majorie, countess of Carrick **'EDWARD BALLIOL'** (1332–1341) **MARGARET** (1286–1290)

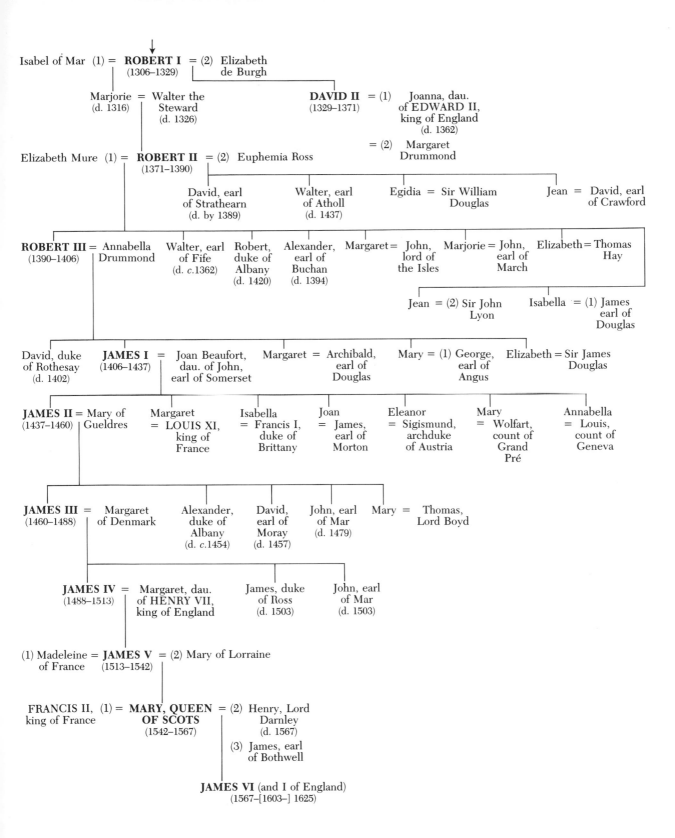

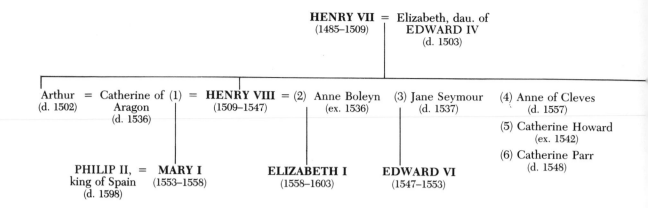

HENRY VII = Elizabeth, dau. of
(1485–1509)   EDWARD IV
                    (d. 1503)

Arthur = Catherine of (1) = HENRY VIII = (2) Anne Boleyn   (3) Jane Seymour   (4) Anne of Cleves
(d. 1502)   Aragon   (1509–1547)   (ex. 1536)   (d. 1537)   (d. 1557)
            (d. 1536)
                                                                                       (5) Catherine Howard
                                                                                            (ex. 1542)

                                                                                       (6) Catherine Parr
                                                                                            (d. 1548)

PHILIP II, = MARY I   ELIZABETH I   EDWARD VI
king of Spain   (1553–1558)   (1558–1603)   (1547–1553)
(d. 1598)

VI. THE STUARTS   1603–1714

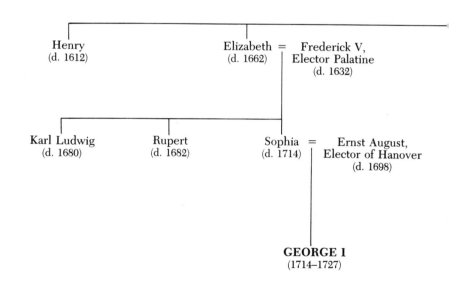

Henry   Elizabeth = Frederick V,
(d. 1612)   (d. 1662)   Elector Palatine
                                          (d. 1632)

Karl Ludwig   Rupert   Sophia = Ernst August,
(d. 1680)   (d. 1682)   (d. 1714)   Elector of Hanover
                                                   (d. 1698)

GEORGE I
(1714–1727)

V. THE TUDORS   1485–1603

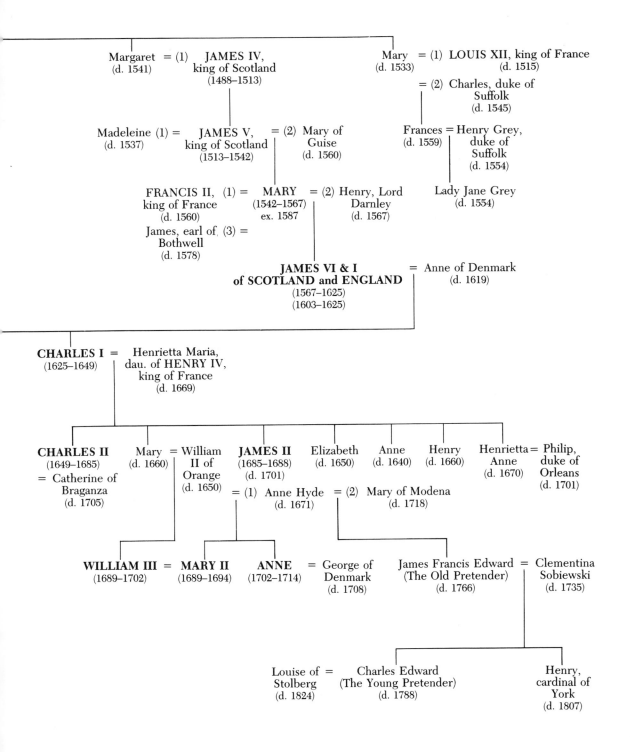

Margaret = (1)   JAMES IV,
(d. 1541)   king of Scotland
                (1488–1513)

Mary   = (1) LOUIS XII, king of France
(d. 1533)   (d. 1515)

= (2) Charles, duke of
       Suffolk
       (d. 1545)

Madeleine (1) =   JAMES V,   = (2) Mary of
(d. 1537)   king of Scotland   Guise
               (1513–1542)   (d. 1560)

Frances = Henry Grey,
(d. 1559)   duke of
            Suffolk
            (d. 1554)

FRANCIS II, (1) =   MARY   = (2) Henry, Lord
king of France   (1542–1567)   Darnley
(d. 1560)   ex. 1587   (d. 1567)
James, earl of (3) =
Bothwell
(d. 1578)

Lady Jane Grey
(d. 1554)

JAMES VI & I   = Anne of Denmark
of SCOTLAND and ENGLAND   (d. 1619)
(1567–1625)
(1603–1625)

CHARLES I =   Henrietta Maria,
(1625–1649)   dau. of HENRY IV,
              king of France
              (d. 1669)

CHARLES II   Mary = William   JAMES II   Elizabeth   Anne   Henry   Henrietta = Philip,
(1649–1685)   (d. 1660) II of   (1685–1688)   (d. 1650) (d. 1640) (d. 1660)   Anne   duke of
= Catherine of   Orange   (d. 1701)   (d. 1670)   Orleans
Braganza   (d. 1650)   (d. 1701)
(d. 1705)   = (1) Anne Hyde = (2) Mary of Modena
                                       (d. 1671)   (d. 1718)

WILLIAM III = MARY II   ANNE   = George of   James Francis Edward = Clementina
(1689–1702)   (1689–1694)   (1702–1714)   Denmark   (The Old Pretender)   Sobiewski
                                          (d. 1708)   (d. 1766)   (d. 1735)

Louise of =   Charles Edward   Henry,
Stolberg   (The Young Pretender)   cardinal of
(d. 1824)   (d. 1788)   York
                                                  (d. 1807)

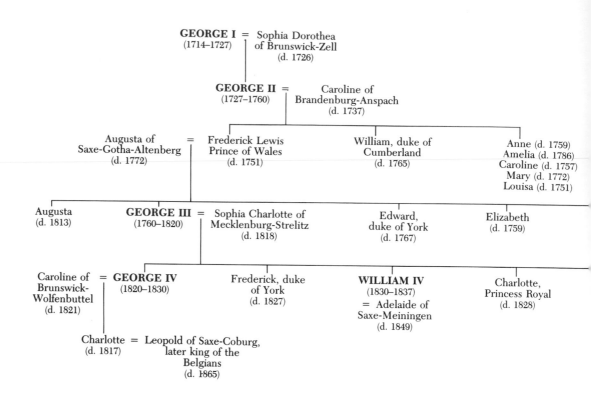

GEORGE I = Sophia Dorothea
(1714–1727)   of Brunswick-Zell
(d. 1726)

GEORGE II = Caroline of
(1727–1760)   Brandenburg-Anspach
(d. 1737)

Augusta of = Frederick Lewis   William, duke of   Anne (d. 1759)
Saxe-Gotha-Altenberg   Prince of Wales   Cumberland   Amelia (d. 1786)
(d. 1772)   (d. 1751)   (d. 1765)   Caroline (d. 1757)
                                                        Mary (d. 1772)
                                                        Louisa (d. 1751)

Augusta   GEORGE III = Sophia Charlotte of   Edward,   Elizabeth
(d. 1813)   (1760–1820)   Mecklenburg-Strelitz   duke of York   (d. 1759)
(d. 1818)   (d. 1767)

Caroline of = GEORGE IV   Frederick, duke   WILLIAM IV   Charlotte,
Brunswick-   (1820–1830)   of York   (1830–1837)   Princess Royal
Wolfenbuttel   (d. 1827)   = Adelaide of   (d. 1828)
(d. 1821)   Saxe-Meiningen
                                        (d. 1849)

Charlotte = Leopold of Saxe-Coburg,
(d. 1817)   later king of the
Belgians
(d. 1865)

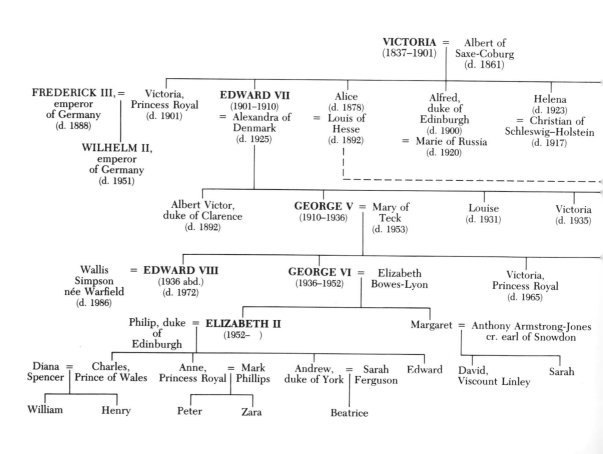

VICTORIA = Albert of
(1837–1901)   Saxe-Coburg
(d. 1861)

FREDERICK III, =   Victoria,   EDWARD VII   Alice   Alfred,   Helena
emperor   Princess Royal   (1901–1910)   (d. 1878)   duke of   (d. 1923)
of Germany   (d. 1901)   = Alexandra of   = Louis of   Edinburgh   = Christian of
(d. 1888)   Denmark   Hesse   (d. 1900)   Schleswig–Holstein
                (d. 1925)   (d. 1892)   = Marie of Russia   (d. 1917)
WILHELM II,   (d. 1920)
emperor
of Germany
(d. 1951)

Albert Victor,   GEORGE V = Mary of   Louise   Victoria
duke of Clarence   (1910–1936)   Teck   (d. 1931)   (d. 1935)
(d. 1892)   (d. 1953)

Wallis   = EDWARD VIII   GEORGE VI = Elizabeth   Victoria,
Simpson   (1936 abd.)   (1936–1952)   Bowes-Lyon   Princess Royal
née Warfield   (d. 1972)   (d. 1965)
(d. 1986)

Philip, duke = ELIZABETH II   Margaret = Anthony Armstrong-Jones
of   (1952–)   cr. earl of Snowdon
Edinburgh

Diana =   Charles,   Anne, = Mark   Andrew, = Sarah   Edward   David,   Sarah
Spencer   Prince of Wales   Princess Royal   Phillips   duke of York   Ferguson   Viscount Linley

William   Henry   Peter   Zara   Beatrice

VII. THE HANOVERIANS
1714–1837

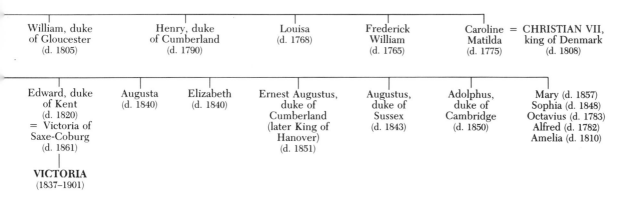

| William, duke of Gloucester (d. 1805) | Henry, duke of Cumberland (d. 1790) | Louisa (d. 1768) | Frederick William (d. 1765) | Caroline Matilda (d. 1775) = CHRISTIAN VII, king of Denmark (d. 1808) |

Edward, duke of Kent (d. 1820) = Victoria of Saxe-Coburg (d. 1861)

Augusta (d. 1840)

Elizabeth (d. 1840)

Ernest Augustus, duke of Cumberland (later King of Hanover) (d. 1851)

Augustus, duke of Sussex (d. 1843)

Adolphus, duke of Cambridge (d. 1850)

Mary (d. 1857)
Sophia (d. 1848)
Octavius (d. 1783)
Alfred (d. 1782)
Amelia (d. 1810)

VICTORIA
(1837–1901)

VIII. VICTORIA AND HER DESCENDANTS
1837–1988

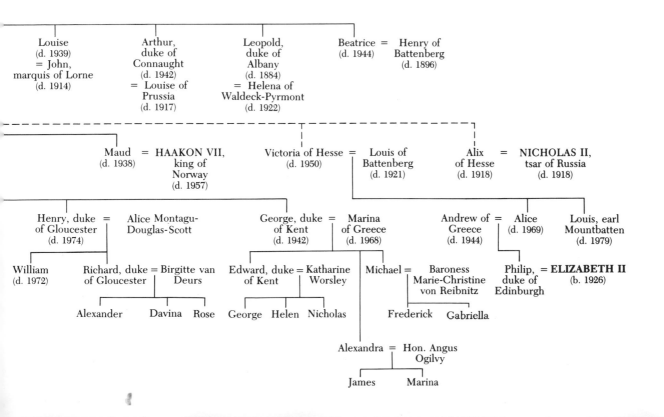

Louise (d. 1939) = John, marquis of Lorne (d. 1914)

Arthur, duke of Connaught (d. 1942) = Louise of Prussia (d. 1917)

Leopold, duke of Albany (d. 1884) = Helena of Waldeck-Pyrmont (d. 1922)

Beatrice (d. 1944) = Henry of Battenberg (d. 1896)

Maud (d. 1938) = HAAKON VII, king of Norway (d. 1957)

Victoria of Hesse (d. 1950) = Louis of Battenberg (d. 1921)

Alix of Hesse (d. 1918) = NICHOLAS II, tsar of Russia (d. 1918)

Henry, duke of Gloucester (d. 1974) = Alice Montagu-Douglas-Scott

George, duke of Kent (d. 1942) = Marina of Greece (d. 1968)

Andrew of Greece (d. 1944) = Alice (d. 1969)

Louis, earl Mountbatten (d. 1979)

William (d. 1972)

Richard, duke of Gloucester = Birgitte van Deurs

Edward, duke of Kent = Katharine Worsley

Michael = Baroness Marie-Christine von Reibnitz

Philip, duke of Edinburgh = **ELIZABETH II** (b. 1926)

Alexander   Davina   Rose

George   Helen   Nicholas

Frederick   Gabriella

Alexandra = Hon. Angus Ogilvy

James   Marina

LIST OF MONARCHS

ENGLAND

	Monarch	born	acceded	died
	ALFRED	849	April 871	26 Oct. 899
900	EDWARD THE ELDER	870	Oct. 899	17 July 924
	ATHELSTAN	895	Summer 924	27 Oct. 939
	EDMUND	921	Oct. 939	26 May 946
	EADRED		May 946	23 Nov. 955
	EADWIG	before 943	Nov. 955	1 Oct. 959
	EDGAR	943	Oct. 959	8 July 975
	EDWARD THE MARTYR	c.962	July 975	18 Mar. 978
1000	ÆTHELRED 'THE UNREADY'	c.968–9	Mar. 978	23 Apr. 1016
	EDMUND IRONSIDE	before 993	Apr. 1016	30 Nov. 1016
	CNUT	c.995	30 Nov. 1016	12 Nov. 1035
	HAROLD HAREFOOT	c.1016–17	c.1035–6	17 Mar. 1040
	HARTHACNUT	c.1018	June 1040	8 June 1042
	EDWARD THE CONFESSOR	c.1002–5	June 1042	5 Jan. 1066
	HAROLD GODWINSON	c.1020	6 Jan. 1066	14 Oct. 1066
	WILLIAM THE CONQUEROR	c.1027–8	25 Dec. 1066	9 Sept. 1087
1100	WILLIAM II	c.1056–60	26 Sept. 1087	2 Aug. 1100
	HENRY I	1068	5 Aug. 1100	1 Dec. 1135
	STEPHEN	by 1100	22 Dec. 1135	25 Oct. 1154
	HENRY II	5 Mar. 1133	19 Dec. 1154	6 July 1189
	RICHARD I	8 Sept. 1157	3 Sept. 1189	6 Apr. 1199
1200	JOHN	24 Dec. 1167	27 May 1199	18–19 Oct. 1216
	HENRY III	1 Oct. 1207	28 Oct. 1216	16 Nov. 1272
1300	EDWARD I	17–18 June 1239	20 Nov. 1272	7 July 1307
	EDWARD II	25 Apr. 1284	8 July 1307	deposed 20 Jan. 1327; died 21 Sept. 1327
	EDWARD III	13 Nov. 1312	25 Jan. 1327	21 June 1377
	RICHARD II	6 Jan. 1367	22 June 1377	deposed 29 Sept. 1399; died c.14 Feb. 1400
1400	HENRY IV	c.Apr. 1366	30 Sept. 1399	20 Mar. 1413
	HENRY V	c.16 Sept. 1387	21 Mar. 1413	31 Aug. 1422
	HENRY VI	6 Dec. 1421	1 Sept. 1422; restored 3 Oct. 1470	deposed 4 Mar. 1461; deposed 11 Apr. 1471; died 21 May 1471

WESSEX

Danish English

NORMAN

PLANTAGENET

LANCASTER

SCOTLAND

	Monarch	born	acceded	died	
1000	MALCOLM II	c.954	25 Mar. 1005	25 Nov. 1034	MAC ALPIN
	DUNCAN I		25 Nov. 1034	14 Aug. 1040	
	MACBETH	c.1005	14 Aug. 1040	15 Aug. 1057	
	LULACH	c.1032	15 Aug. 1057	17 Mar. 1058	
	MALCOLM III	c.1031	17 Mar. 1058	13 Nov. 1093	
	DONALD BANE	c.1033	13 Nov. 1093; restored 12 Nov. 1094	deposed May 1094; died Oct. 1097	
	DUNCAN II	c.1060	May 1094	12 Nov. 1094	
1100	EDGAR	c.1074	1097	c.8 Jan. 1107	CANMORE
	ALEXANDER I	c.1077	c.8 Jan. 1107	c.25 Apr. 1124	
	DAVID I	c.1085	c.25 Apr. 1124	24 May 1153	
	MALCOLM IV	c.1041	24 May 1153	9 Dec. 1165	
	WILLIAM I	c.1142	9 Dec. 1165	4 Dec. 1214	
	ALEXANDER II	24 Aug. 1198	4 Dec. 1214	8 July 1249	
1200	ALEXANDER III	4 Sept. 1241	8 July 1249	19 Mar. 1286	
	MARGARET	c.Apr. 1283	19 Mar. 1286	c.26 Sept. 1290	
	JOHN BALLIOL	c.1250	17 Nov. 1292	abdicated 10 July 1296; died Apr. 1313	BALLIOL
1300	ROBERT I	11 July 1274	25 Mar. 1306	7 June 1329	BRUCE
	DAVID II	5 Mar. 1324	7 June 1329	22 Feb. 1371	
	ROBERT II	2 Mar. 1316	22 Feb. 1371	19 Apr. 1390	STUART
1400	ROBERT III	c.1337	19 Apr. 1390	4 Apr. 1406	
	JAMES I	July 1394	4 Apr. 1406	21 Feb. 1437	
	JAMES II	16 Oct. 1430	21 Feb. 1437	3 Aug. 1460	

ENGLAND

Monarch		born	acceded	died	
EDWARD IV		28 Apr. 1442	4 Mar. 1461; restored 11 Apr. 1471	deposed 3 Oct. 1470; died 9 Apr. 1483	YORK
EDWARD V		2 Nov. 1470	9 Apr. 1483	deposed 25 June 1483; died c. summer 1483	
RICHARD III		2 Oct. 1452	26 June 1483	22 Aug. 1485	
HENRY VII		28 Jan. 1457	22 Aug. 1485	21 Apr. 1509	TUDOR
HENRY VIII		28 June 1491	22 Apr. 1509	28 Jan. 1547	
EDWARD VI		12 Oct. 1537	28 Jan. 1547	6 July 1553	
MARY I		18 Feb. 1516	19 July 1553	17 Nov. 1558	
ELIZABETH I		7 Sept. 1533	17 Nov. 1558	24 Mar. 1603	
JAMES I		19 June 1566	24 Mar. 1603	27 Mar. 1625	
CHARLES I		19 Nov. 1600	27 Mar. 1625	beheaded 30 Jan. 1649	
CHARLES II		29 May 1630	30 Jan. 1649; restored 29 May 1660	6 Feb. 1685	STUART
JAMES II		14 Oct. 1633	6 Feb. 1685	declared to have abdicated 11 Dec. 1688; died 6 Sept. 1701	
MARY II	joint sovereigns	30 Apr. 1662	13 Feb. 1689	28 Dec. 1694	
WILLIAM III		4 Nov. 1650	13 Feb. 1689	8 Mar. 1702	
ANNE		6 Feb. 1665	8 Mar. 1702	1 Aug. 1714	
GEORGE I		28 May 1660	1 Aug. 1714	11 June 1727	
GEORGE II		30 Oct. 1683	11 June 1727	25 Oct. 1760	
GEORGE III		24 May 1738	25 Oct. 1760	Regency declared 5 Feb. 1811; died 29 Jan. 1820	HANOVERIAN
GEORGE IV		12 Aug. 1762	Regent from 5 Feb. 1811; acceded 29 Jan. 1820	26 June 1830	
WILLIAM IV		21 Aug. 1765	26 June 1830	20 June 1837	
VICTORIA		24 May 1819	20 June 1837	22 Jan. 1901	
EDWARD VII		9 Nov. 1841	22 Jan. 1901	6 May 1910	DESCENDANTS OF VICTORIA
GEORGE V		3 June 1865	6 May 1910	20 Jan. 1936	
EDWARD VIII		23 June 1894	20 Jan. 1936	abdicated 11 Dec. 1936; died 28 May 1972	
GEORGE VI		14 Dec. 1895	11 Dec. 1936	6 Feb. 1952	
ELIZABETH II		21 Apr. 1926	6 Feb. 1952		

Decade markers in left margin: **1500**, **1600**, **1700**, **1800**, **1900**

SCOTLAND

	Monarch	born	acceded	died
	JAMES III	May 1452	3 Aug. 1460	11 June 1488
1500	JAMES IV	17 Mar. 1473	11 June 1488	9 Sept. 1513
	JAMES V	10 Apr. 1512	9 Sept. 1513	14 Dec. 1542
	MARY	8 Dec. 1542	14 Dec. 1542	abdicated 24 July 1567; beheaded 8 Feb. 1587
1600	JAMES VI	19 June 1566	24 July 1567; king of England 24 Mar. 1603	27 Mar. 1625

STUART

FURTHER READING

1. DIVERSE ORIGINS

THE ENGLISH KINGDOMS

L. M. Smith (ed.), *The Making of Britain: The Dark Ages* (London, 1984), an attractive synthesis of life and institutions as they developed over the entire period.

J. N. L. Myres, *The English Settlements* (Oxford, 1986), a recent review by a master.

F. M. Stenton, *Anglo-Saxon England* (3rd edn., Oxford, 1971), still a magisterial authority (first published 1943).

J. Campbell, *The Anglo-Saxons* (London, 1982), an absorbing and beautifully illustrated volume.

Michael Wood, *Domesday: A Search for the Roots of England* (London, 1986), contains much that is thought-provoking.

J. M. Wallace-Hadrill, *Early Germanic Kingship in England and on the Continent* (Oxford, 1971), and P. Wormald, *Ideal and Reality in Frankish and Anglo-Saxon Society* (Oxford, 1983), stress links with the Continent.

H. R. Loyn, *The Governance of Anglo-Saxon England, 500–1087* (London, 1984), describes the development of institutions, including monarchy.

W. A. Chaney, *The Cult of Kingship in Anglo-Saxon England: The Transition from Paganism to Christianity* (Manchester, 1970), an interesting if somewhat narrow treatment of Christian kingship.

A. C. Evans, *The Sutton Hoo Ship-burial: A Handbook* (2nd edn., London, 1986), a useful guide to the relationship between these famous finds and East Anglian kingship.

Cyril Fox, *Offa's Dyke: A Field Survey of the Western Frontier-works in Mercia in the Seventh and Eighth Centuries A.D.* (London, 1955), a classic study now undergoing reassessment.

BIOGRAPHICAL STUDIES

C. N. L. Brooke, *The Saxon and Norman Kings* (London, 1963), attempts some delightful sketches of elusive early monarchs.

Michael Wood, *In Search of the Dark Ages* (2nd edn., London, 1982), brings to life, with informed enthusiasm, Offa, Alfred, Athelstan, Eric Bloodaxe, and Æthelred the Unready.

E. Duckett, *Alfred the Great and his England* (London, 1957), and D. Woodruff, *The Life and Times of Alfred the Great* (London, 1974), are both popular biographies.

S. Keynes and M. Lapidge (trans. and eds.), *Alfred the Great* (London, 1983), an admirable translation of Asser's Life and other contemporary sources.

D. Whitelock, *History, Law and Literature in Tenth and Eleventh-Century England* (London, 1981), the collected essays of an author whose unfinished study of Alfred may yet be published.

D. Hill (ed.), *Ethelred the Unready* (Oxford, 1978), opened up new approaches to this king's reign.

S. Keynes, *The Diplomas of King Æthelred 'The Unready', 978–1016: A Study in their Use as Historical Evidence* (Cambridge, 1980), has also stimulated a reconsideration of the king.

P. Stafford, *Queens, Concubines and Dowagers: The King's Wife in the Early Middle Ages* (London, 1983), draws on material from British royalty.

WALES, SCOTLAND, AND IRELAND

Charles Thomas, *Celtic Britain* (London, 1986), a useful bird's-eye view.

W. Davies, *Wales in the Early Middle Ages* (Leicester, 1982), expertly charts the reaction of Welsh kings and kingdoms to the changes taking place in England.

I. Henderson, *The Picts* (London, 1967), assembles the known and fragmentary materials relating to their obscure kingdoms.

M. O. Anderson, *Kings and Kingship in Early Scotland* (Edinburgh, 1973), not an easy read.

A. P. Smyth, *Warlords and Holy Men in Scotland, A.D. 80–1000* (London, 1984), offers challenging interpretations.

A. A. M. Duncan, *Scotland: The Making of the Kingdom* (Edinburgh, 1975), a masterly and detailed synthesis.

T. W. Moody and F. X. Martin, *The Course of Irish History* (rev. edn., Cork, 1984), an introduction, based on a fine series of radio talks.

B. de Breffny (ed.), *The Irish World: The History and Cultural Achievements of the Irish People* (London, 1977), another good starting-point.

M. and L. de Paor, *Early Christian Ireland* (2nd edn., London, 1960).

K. Hughes, *Early Christian Ireland: Introduction to the Sources* (London, 1972).

D. O Corráin, *Ireland before the Normans* (Dublin and London, 1972), and G. Mac Niocaill, *Ireland before the Vikings* (Dublin and London, 1972), provide narratives in the Gill History of Ireland series.

F. J. Byrne, *Irish Kings and High-Kings* (London, 1973), lays valuable groundwork, but is not always easy to digest.

R. C. Newman, *Brian Boru, King of Ireland* (Dublin, 1983), a valiant attempt at biography which makes a little go a long way.

THE VIKINGS

J. Graham-Campbell, *The Viking World* (London, 1981), lavishly illustrated.

H. R. Loyn, *The Vikings in England* (London, 1977), a general view.

The Vikings in England and in their Danish Homeland (London, 1981), the exhibition catalogue of the Anglo-Danish Viking Project.

A. P. Smyth, *Scandinavian Kings in the British Isles, 850–880* (Oxford, 1977), a thought-provoking, detailed discussion of Viking kingship in Britain.

H. P. R. Finberg (ed.), *Scandinavian England: The Collected Papers of F. T. Wainwright* (Chichester, 1975), still valuable.

REFERENCE BOOKS

E. B. Fryde, D. E. Greenway, S. Porter, and I. Roy (eds.), *Handbook of British Chronology* (3rd edn., London, 1986), a clear guide to the dynasties of England, Wales, and Scotland, including the bewildering early ones.

Ordnance Survey Map of Britain before the Norman Conquest (London, 1973), a great boon.

D. Hill, *An Atlas of Anglo-Saxon England* (Oxford, 1981), more than a collection of fascinating maps.

P. Mac Neill and R. Nicholson (eds.), *The Historical Atlas of Scotland, c.400–c.1600* (St Andrews, 1975), a remarkable co-operative achievement.

T. W. Moody, F. X. Martin, and F. J. Byrne (eds.), *A New History of Ireland*, vol. viii: *A Chronology of Irish History to 1976: A Companion to Irish History* (Oxford, 1982), gives a skeleton of events, mostly deaths and battles.

D. Whitelock (ed.), *English Historical Documents*, vol. i: *c*.500–1042 (2nd edn., London, 1979), indispensable for the more expert; it includes the Anglo-Saxon Chronicle, and translations of charters, laws, letters, and diplomas.

2. THE AGE OF 'EMPIRES'

GENERAL SURVEYS

The Danish 'interlude' (1016–42) is usually treated—to its loss—as part of 'Anglo-Saxon England', for which see above.

L. M. Smith (ed.), *The Making of Britain: The Middle Ages* (London, 1985), and K. O. Morgan (ed.), *The Oxford Illustrated History of Britain* (Oxford, 1984), both take a wide perspective.

F. Barlow, *The Feudal Kingdom of England, 1042–1216* (4th edn., London, 1988) and G. W. S. Barrow, *Feudal Britain: The Completion of the Medieval Kingdoms, 1066–1314* (London, 1956), are particularly valuable.

M. T. Clanchy, *England and its Rulers, 1066–1272: Foreign Lordship and National Identity* (London, 1983), stresses the foreignness of English kingship.

S. Reynolds, *Kingdoms and Communities in Western Europe, 900–1300* (Oxford, 1984), places English and Scottish developments in a European context.

J. Le Patourel, *The Norman Empire* (Oxford, 1976), and *Feudal Empires, Norman and Plantagenet* (London, 1984), deal with concepts of 'empire' and the problems of ruling such diversified dominions.

R. A. Brown, *The Normans and the Norman Conquest* (London, 1969), and *The Normans* (London, 1984), are vigorous representatives of the 'Normanist' school.

D. J. A. Matthew, *The Norman Conquest* (London, 1966), important and more measured.

D. Bates, *Normandy before 1066* (London, 1982), gives a solid perspective to the question of the Norman debt to English history.

M. Chibnall, *Anglo-Norman England, 1066–1166* (Oxford, 1986), a new reconsideration.

R. A. Brown (ed.), *Proceedings of the Battle Conference on Anglo-Norman Studies* (Ipswich, 1979–   ), published annually and keeps the dedicated abreast of modern scholarship.

D. M. Wilson, *The Bayeux Tapestry* (London, 1985), sumptuously illustrated, capturing the drama of 1066.

J. Gillingham, *The Angevin Empire* (London, 1984), a splendid introduction.

E. M. Hallam (ed.), *The Plantagenet Chronicles* (London, 1986), a combination of vignettes by many scholars, translations of chronicles of the period 1128–1216, and superb illustration.

D. C. Douglas and G. W. Greenaway (eds.), *English Historical Documents*, vol. ii, 1042–1189 (2nd edn., London, 1981), contains authoritative texts of a wide range of sources.

A. Gransden, *Historical Writing in England, c.550–c.1307* (London, 1974), a sure guide to the value and limitations of particular chronicles.

WALES, SCOTLAND, AND IRELAND

R. R. Davies, *Conquest, Coexistence, and Change: Wales, 1063–1415* (Oxford, 1987), a richly authoritative volume.

L. H. Nelson, *The Normans in South Wales, 1070–1171* (London and Austin, Texas, 1966), and D. Walker, *The Norman Conquerors* (Swansea, 1977), analyse the Norman advance into Wales.

A. A. M. Duncan, *Scotland: The Making of the Kingdom* (Edinburgh, 1975), and G. W. S. Barrow, *Kingship and Unity: Scotland, 1000–1306* (London, 1981), are first-rate surveys.

G. W. S. Barrow, *The Kingdom of the Scots: Government, Church and Society from the Eleventh to the Fourteenth Century* (London, 1973), a collection of fundamental detailed studies.

A. J. Otway-Ruthven, *A History of Medieval Ireland* (London, 1968), a distinguished study mainly of the English impact on the country.

M. Dolley, *Anglo-Norman Ireland* (Dublin and London, 1972), a brief survey.

ROYAL GOVERNMENT

W. L. Warren, *The Governance of Norman and Angevin England, 1086–1272* (London, 1987), a stimulating appraisal.

M. R. Powicke, *Military Obligation in Medieval England* (Oxford, 1962).

V. H. Galbraith, *Domesday Book: Its Place in Administrative History* (Oxford, 1974).

E. M. Hallam, *Domesday Book through Nine Centuries* (London, 1986), a fascinating historiographical survey.

J. A. Green, *The Government of England under Henry I* (Oxford, 1986).

J. E. A. Jolliffe, *Angevin Kingship* (2nd edn., London, 1963).

J. C. Holt, *Magna Carta* (Cambridge, 1965).

——*Magna Carta and Medieval Government* (London, 1985), a collection of important essays.

ROYAL BIOGRAPHIES

L. M. Larson, *Canute the Great* (New York, 1912), still valuable, but the king needs reassessment.

F. Barlow, *Edward the Confessor* (London, 1970).

D. C. Douglas, *William the Conqueror* (London, 1964).

F. Barlow, *William Rufus* (London, 1983).

R. H. C. Davis, *King Stephen* (London, 1967).

H. A. Cronne, *The Reign of Stephen, 1135–54: Anarchy in England* (London, 1970), much more than a biography.

W. L. Warren, *Henry II* (London, 1973), large in importance and size.

F. Barlow, *Thomas Becket* (London, 1986), supplements our understanding of the greatest crisis and the most dynamic personal relationship of Henry II's reign.

J. Gillingham, *Richard the Lionheart* (London, 1978).

W. L. Warren, *King John* (London, 1961), a pioneer of the modern biographical genre.

J. C. Holt, *The Northerners: A Study in the Reign of King John* (Oxford, 1961), a revealing study in depth.

C. W. Hollister, *Monarchy, Magnates and Institutions in the Anglo-Norman World* (London, 1986), substituting at present for his long-heralded biography of Henry I.

G. W. S. Barrow (ed.), *The Acts of Malcolm IV, King of Scots, 1153–1165* (London, 1960), and with W. W. Scott (eds.), *The Acts of William I, King of Scots, 1165–1214* (London, 1971); the first vols. of the *Regesta Regum Scotorum*, containing analyses of the kings as well as their surviving archives.

G. W. S. Barrow, *David I of Scotland (1124–1153)* (Reading, 1985), a little gem.

R. Pernoud, *Eleanor of Aquitaine* (London, 1967), one of the more reliable of many indifferent biographies of the queen.

COURT LIFE

P. E. Schramm, *A History of the English Coronation*, trans. L. G. Wickham Legg (Oxford, 1937), still the standard work.

R. W. Eyton, *Court, Household and Itinerary of King Henry II* (London, 1878, repr. 1974), and H. Hall, *Court Life under the Plantagenets* (London, 1890), show how open this field remains.

C. Given-Wilson and A. Curteis, *The Royal Bastards of Medieval England* (London, 1984), titillating side-lights.

D. Jenkins, *The Law of Hywel Dda* (Llandysul, Dyfed, 1986), tells us more about this period than about Hywel Dda.

3. MONARCH AND NATION

GENERAL SURVEYS

B. Guenée, *States and Rulers in Later Medieval Europe* (Oxford, 1985), the European context.

M. H. Keen, *England in the Later Middle Ages: A Political History* (London, 1973), outstanding.

A. J. Tuck, *Crown and Nobility, 1272–1461: Political Conflict in Later Medieval England* (London, 1985), a clear and effortless narrative.

S. B. Chrimes, *Lancastrians, Yorkists and Henry VII* (2nd edn., London, 1966), C. D. Ross, *The Wars of the Roses* (London, 1976), and A. E. Goodman, *The Wars of the Roses* (London, 1981), are instructive introductions to the dynastic struggles.

ENGLISH GOVERNMENT AND THE CONSTITUTION

J. E. A. Jolliffe, *The Constitutional History of Medieval England* (4th edn., Oxford, 1961);

B. Wilkinson, *Constitutional History of Medieval England*, 3 vols. (London, 1948–58), and *Constitutional History of England in the 15th Century (1399–1485)* (London, 1964), place the monarchy in its institutional context, the latter two containing illustrative documents.

S. B. Chrimes, *English Constitutional Ideas in the XV Century* (Cambridge, 1936), a fundamental, specialized text.

A. R. Myers, *Crown, Household and Parliament in 15th Century England* (London, 1985).

T. F. Tout, *Chapters in the Administrative History of Medieval England*, 6 vols. (Manchester, 1920–33), a masterly undertaking dealing with the institutionalization of the king's wardrobe, chamber, and smaller seals down to 1399.

J. Otway-Ruthven, *The King's Secretary and the Signet Office in the XV Century* (Cambridge, 1939).

J. F. Baldwin, *The King's Council during the Middle Ages* (Oxford, 1913); still not replaced.

B. Wilkinson, *The Chancery under Edward III* (Manchester, 1929).

J. F. Willard, W. A. Morris, and W. H. Dunham (eds.), *The English Government at Work, 1327–1336*, 3 vols. (Cambridge, Mass., 1940–50); a snapshot taken at the beginning of Edward III's reign.

R. G. Davies and J. H. Denton (eds.), *The English Parliament in the Middle Ages* (Manchester, 1981), describes the growth of Parliament and its relationship with the crown.

E. B. Fryde and E. Miller (eds.), *Historical Studies of the English Parliament*, 2 vols. (Cambridge, 1970), highlights episodes of strain and conflict.

T. F. T. Plucknett, *The Legislation of Edward I* (Oxford, 1949), and *Edward I and the Criminal Law* (Cambridge, 1960); succinct and perceptive studies.

J. G. Bellamy, *The Law of Treason in England in the Later Middle Ages* (Cambridge, 1970), deals with an aspect of law peculiarly related to the monarchy.

THE NOBILITY AND FRANCE

K. B. McFarlane, *The Nobility of Later Medieval England* (Oxford, 1973); posthumously published lectures which inspired much of the writing on this subject.

C. Given-Wilson, *The English Nobility in the Late Middle Ages* (London, 1987).

J. E. Powell and K. Wallis, *The House of Lords in the Middle Ages: A History of the English House of Lords to 1540* (London, 1968).

J. R. Lander, *Crown and Nobility, 1450–1509* (London, 1976).

A. E. Goodman, *The Loyal Conspiracy: The Lords Appellant under Richard II* (London, 1971).

A. J. Tuck, *Richard II and the English Nobility* (London, 1973).

R. A. Griffiths and J. Sherborne (eds.), *Kings and Nobles in the Later Middle Ages* (Gloucester, 1986); a collection of essays.

K. A. Fowler, *The Age of Plantagenet and Valois* (London, 1967); a well-illustrated survey.

C. T. Allmand, *Lancastrian Normandy: The History of a Medieval Occupation* (Oxford, 1983).

M. G. A. Vale, *English Gascony, 1399–1453* (Oxford, 1970).

WALES, SCOTLAND AND IRELAND

R. A. Griffiths, *The Principality of Wales in the Later Middle Ages*, vol. i, *South Wales, 1277–1536* (Cardiff, 1972).

R. R. Davies, *Lordship and Society in the March of Wales, 1282–1400* (Oxford, 1978).

W. Ferguson, *Scotland's Relations with England: A Survey to 1707* (Edinburgh, 1977).

R. Nicholson, *Scotland: The Later Middle Ages* (Edinburgh, 1974); comprehensive.

A. Grant, *Independence and Nationhood: Scotland, 1306–1469* (London, 1984); a stimulating study.

J. Lydon, *The Lordship of Ireland in the Middle Ages* (Dublin, 1972); *Ireland in the Later Middle Ages* (Dublin and London, 1973); and R. Frame, *English Lordship in Ireland, 1318–1361* (Oxford, 1982), lay emphasis on English Ireland.

J. Lydon (ed.), *England and Ireland in the Later Middle Ages* (Blackrock, Dublin, 1981); a collection of essays.

K. Simms, *From Kings to Warlords: the Changing Political Structure of Gaelic Ireland in the Later Middle Ages* (Woodbridge, Suffolk, 1987); a pioneering study of monarchy in native Ireland.

S. G. Ellis, *Reform and Revival: English Government in Ireland, 1470–1534* (London, 1986).

A. Cosgrove (ed.), *A New History of Ireland*, vol. ii, *Medieval Ireland, 1169–1534* (Oxford, 1987); detailed, if traditional in design.

ROYAL BIOGRAPHIES

F. M. Powicke, *Henry III and the Lord Edward: The Community of the Realm in the Thirteenth Century*, 2 vols. (Oxford, 1947); an influential book.

M. Prestwich, *The Three Edwards: War and State in England, 1272–1377* (London, 1980), and *War, Politics and Finance under Edward I* (London, 1972), provide studies of the three Edwards in relation to their wars. His *Edward I* (London, 1988), is authoritative.

T. F. Tout, *The Place of the Reign of Edward II in English History* (Manchester 1914); still worth reading.

H. Johnstone, *Edward of Caernarvon* (Manchester, 1946), deals with Edward II's early life.

N. Fryde, *The Tyranny and Fall of Edward II, 1321–1326* (Cambridge, 1979).

P. Johnson, *The Life and Times of Edward III* (London, 1973), a light but nicely illustrated book.

A. Steel, *Richard II* (Cambridge, 1941), a valuable study of Richard on the psychologist's couch.

R. H. Jones, *The Royal Policy of Richard II: Absolutism in the Later Middle Ages* (Oxford, 1968), and F. R. H. DuBoulay and C. Barron (eds.), *The Reign of Richard II* (London, 1977), concentrate on Richard's authoritarianism.

S. B. Chrimes, C. D. Ross, and R. A. Griffiths (eds.), *Fifteenth-century England, 1399–1509* (Manchester, 1972), a foretaste of several biographies since published.

J. L. Kirby, *Henry IV of England* (London, 1970).

K. B. McFarlane, *Lancastrian Kings and Lollard Knights* (Oxford, 1972), posthumously published lectures on Henry IV and Henry V.

G. L. Harriss (ed.), *Henry V: The Practice of Kingship* (Oxford, 1985), the only authoritative modern study.

B. P. Wolffe, *Henry VI* (London, 1981).

R. A. Griffiths, *The Reign of King Henry VI* (London, 1981), more than a biography of the king.

C. D. Ross, *Edward IV* (London, 1974), and *Richard III* (London, 1981); dispassionate studies of kings who arouse degrees of passion.

A. Hanham, *Richard III and his Early Historians* (Oxford, 1975), an exposé of the Ricardian tradition.

R. A. Griffiths and R. S. Thomas, *The Making of the Tudor Dynasty* (Gloucester, 1985), includes a discussion of Henry VII's early life.

G. Williams, *Henry Tudor and Wales* (Cardiff, 1985).

R. L. Storey, *Henry VII* (London, 1968), and S. B. Chrimes, *Henry VII* (London, 1972), carry general authority.

A. Grant, *Henry VII* (London, 1986), brief and up to date.

G. W. S. Barrow, *Robert Bruce and the Community of the Realm of Scotland* (3rd edn., Edinburgh, 1988).

E. W. M. Balfour-Melville, *James I, King of Scots, 1406–1437* (London, 1936).

N. Macdougall, *James III: A Political Study* (Edinburgh, 1982).

R. L. Mackie, *King James IV of Scotland: A Brief Survey of his Life and Times* (Edinburgh, 1958).

D. Stephenson, *The Governance of Gwynedd in the Thirteenth Century* (Cardiff, 1984), discusses state-building by the princes of Gwynedd.

——*The Last Prince of Wales* (Buckingham, 1983), and A. D. Carr, *Llywelyn ap Gruffudd* (Cardiff, 1982); brief commemorative studies.

J. B. Smith, *Llywelyn ap Gruffudd: Tywysog Cymru* (Cardiff, 1986); an English translation is in preparation.

J. E. Lloyd, *Owen Glendower* (Oxford, 1931).

G. Williams, *Owen Glendower* (London, 1966).

R. Barber, *Edward, Prince of Wales and Aquitaine: A Biography of the Black Prince* (London, 1978); the best among a number of studies.

S. Armitage-Smith, *John of Gaunt* (London, 1904).

K. H. Vickers, *Humphrey, Duke of Gloucester: a Biography* (London, 1907).

M. A. Hicks, *False, Fleeting, Perjur'd Clarence: George, Duke of Clarence, 1449–78* (Gloucester, 1980).

J. J. Bagley, *Margaret of Anjou* (London, 1948), suffers from the constraints on research in wartime.

A. Crawford, 'The King's Burden?: the Consequences of Royal Marriage in Fifteenth-century England', in R. A. Griffiths (ed.), *Patronage, the Crown and the Provinces in Later Medieval England* (Gloucester, 1981), offers an agendum for queenly study.

P. H. Buchanan, *Margaret Tudor, Queen of Scots* (Edinburgh, 1985).

COURT LIFE

N. Orme, *From Childhood to Chivalry: The Education of English Kings and Aristocracy, 1066–1530* (London, 1984).

J. Vale, *Edward III and Chivalry: Chivalric Society and its Context, 1270–1350* (Woodbridge, Suffolk, 1982).

G. Mathew, *The Court of Richard II* (London, 1968).

C. Given-Wilson, *The Royal Household and the King's Affinity: Service, Politics and Finance in England, 1360–1413* (New Haven, Conn., and London, 1986).

V. J. Scattergood and J. W. Sherborne (eds.), *English Court Culture in the Later Middle Ages* (London, 1983).

A. R. Myers (ed.), *The Household of Edward IV* (Manchester, 1959).

S. Anglo, *Spectacle, Pageantry and Early Tudor Policy* (London, 1969).

D. M. Loades, *The Tudor Court* (London, 1986), begins *c.*1450.

D. Starkey *et al.*, *The English Court from the Wars of the Roses to the Civil War* (London, 1987); a series of suggestive essays.

REFERENCE BOOKS

L. Stephen and S. Lee (eds.), *The Dictionary of National Biography*, 63 vols. (London, 1885–1900; repr. Oxford, 1921–2), includes biographies of all kings and queens.

J. E. Lloyd and R. T. Jenkins (eds.), *The Dictionary of Welsh Biography down to 1940* (London, 1959), includes biographies of Welsh kings and princes.

G. Donaldson and R. S. Morpeth, *Who's Who in Scottish History* (Oxford, 1973), includes biographies of Scottish kings, in chronological order.

M. Falkus and J. Gillingham (eds.), *Historical Atlas of Britain* (London, 1981), including maps of some regal matters.

N. Denholm-Young (ed.), *The Life of Edward the Second* (London, 1957); an example of contemporary royal biography.

F. Taylor and J. S. Roskell (eds.), *Gesta Henrici Quinti: The Deeds of Henry the Fifth* (Oxford, 1975), composed by a contemporary in praise of the king.

A. F. Sutton and P. W. Hammond (eds.), *The Coronation of Richard III: The Extant Documents* (Gloucester, 1983).

H. Rothwell (ed.), *English Historical Documents*, vol. iii, 1189–1327 (London, 1975); and A. R. Myers (ed.), *English Historical Documents*, vol. iv, 1327–1485 (London, 1969), the essential compendia of sources.

4. GOVERNING MONARCHY

GENERAL SURVEYS

J. Wormald, *Court, Kirk and Community: Scotland, 1470–1625* (London, 1981), brief but good.

G. Donaldson, *Scotland: James V to James VII* (Edinburgh, 1965), a volume in the Edinburgh History of Scotland.

T. W. Moody, F. X. Martin, and F. J. Byrne (eds.), *A New History of Ireland*, vol. iii, 1534–1691 (Oxford, 1976).

D. Loades, *Politics and the Nation, 1450–1660* (Brighton, 1974), particularly concerned with the rise and fall of the Tudor monarchy.

P. Williams, *The Tudor Regime* (Oxford, 1979), good on the mechanics of government.

G. R. Elton, *Reform and Reformation, 1509–1558* (London, 1977), very critical of Henry VIII and Mary as rulers.

D. Hirst, *Authority and Conflict, 1603–1658* (London, 1986).

C. Russell, *The Crisis of Parliaments, 1509–1660* (London, 1971), despite its title a broad political account.

D. M. Palliser, *The Age of Elizabeth: England under the Later Tudors, 1547–1603* (London, 1983), strong on economic and social developments.

J. P. Kenyon, *Stuart England* (London, 1978), a fine general survey.

B. Coward, *The Stuart Age* (London, 1980), introductory political and constitutional history with a good bibliography.

ROYAL BIOGRAPHIES

J. J. Scarisbrick, *Henry VIII* (London, 1968), a fine authoritative assessment, by no means uncritical.

E. W. Ives, *Anne Boleyn* (Oxford, 1986), one of the few lives of queens which is impressive and informative.

W. K. Jordan, *Edward VI: The Young King* (London, 1968), the frail young monarch is almost overwhelmed by these two massive volumes.

——*Edward VI: The Threshhold of Power* (London, 1970).

H. F. M. Prescott, *Spanish Tudor: The Life of Bloody Mary* (London, 1940), dated but useful.

D. Loades, *The Reign of Mary Tudor: Politics, Government and Religion in England, 1553–1558* (New York, 1979), in the absence of an up-to-date biography, this general work is very helpful.

A. Fraser, *Mary Queen of Scots* (London, 1969), a full and sympathetic treatment.

J. E. Neale, *Queen Elizabeth* (London, 1934), a respectful biography by an expert in the field.

B. W. Beckingsale, *Elizabeth I* (London, 1963), brief but still very readable.

P. Johnson, *Elizabeth I: A Study in Power and Intellect* (London, 1974), an admiring assessment.

D. H. Willson, *James VI & I* (London, 1956), a hostile portrait.

D. Mathew, *James I* (London, 1967), a balanced and sympathetic treatment.

J. Bowle, *Charles I* (London, 1975), readable portrait of an obstinate, isolated man.

C. Carlton, *Charles I* (London, 1983), a psychological study attaching much importance to Charles's boyhood and upbringing.

P. Gregg, *King Charles I* (London, 1981), a study of a man ill-suited to his calling.

A. Bryant, *King Charles II* (London, 1931), immensely popular study but distinctly sentimental towards an unsentimental monarch.

J. R. Jones, *Charles II: Royal Politician* (London, 1987), an admirable study of the king's influence on policy.

A. Fraser, *King Charles II* (London, 1979), readable and well illustrated.

F. Turner, *James II* (London, 1948), the author not one of James's admirers.

J. Miller, *James II: A Study in Kingship* (Hove, 1978), gives James the benefit of the doubt over toleration.

PARTICULAR TOPICS

G. R. Elton, *The Tudor Revolution in Government* (Cambridge, 1953), an immensely influential work tracing the reforms of Thomas Cromwell.

A. G. Dickens, *The English Reformation* (London, 1964), a powerful and original study of the religious changes.

C. Cross, *Church and People, 1450–1660* (London, 1976), excellent survey of religious developments.

G. Mattingly, *The Defeat of the Spanish Armada* (London, 1959), a classic account of the struggle, reissued with good illustrations.

R. Ashton, *The English Civil War: Conservatism and Revolution, 1603–1649* (London, 1978), dissents from Marxist and Whig interpretations, stressing the conservatism of Stuart society.

I. Roots, *The Great Rebellion, 1642–1660* (London, 1966), an excellent survey.

P. Young and R. Holmes, *The English Civil War* (London, 1974), a good military description of the conflict.

C. H. Firth, *Oliver Cromwell and the Rule of the Puritans* (London, 1900), still a fine account by an outstanding historian.

C. Hill, *God's Englishman* (London, 1970), not a biography of Cromwell but interesting comments.

A. Fraser, *Cromwell: Our Chief of Men* (London, 1973), a good popular biography.

J. R. Jones, *The First Whigs* (Oxford, 1961), the great exclusion crisis at the end of Charles II's reign.

LETTERS AND MEMOIRS

The Lisle Letters, ed. M. St. C. Byrne, 6 vols. (Chicago, 1981), a remarkable sequence, largely in the 1530s, of correspondence of Lord Lisle, governor of Calais.

The Chronicle and Political Papers of Edward VI, ed. W. K. Jordan (London, 1966), the young king's terse diary.

The Letters of King James VI & I, ed. G. P. V. Akrigg (California, 1984).

The Writings and Speeches of Oliver Cromwell, ed. W. C. Abbott, 4 vols. (Harvard, 1929).

The Letters of King Charles II, ed. A. Bryant (London, 1935), a selection.

Samuel Pepys, *Diary*, ed. R. C. Latham and W. Matthews, 11 vols. (London, 1970–83), an incomparable portrait of London during the Restoration years.

John Evelyn, *Diary*, ed. E. S. de Beer, 6 vols. (Oxford, 1955), from before the Civil War to the reign of Anne.

DOCUMENTS AND BIBLIOGRAPHIES

Scottish Historical Documents, ed. G. Donaldson (Edinburgh, 1970).
G. R. Elton, *The Tudor Constitution: Documents and Commentary* (Cambridge, 1960).
J. P. Kenyon, *The Stuart Constitution, 1603–1688* (Cambridge, 1966).
English Historical Documents: 1485–1558, ed. C. H. Williams (London, 1971).
Bibliography of British History, 1485–1603, ed. C. Read (Oxford, 1959).
Bibliography of British History, 1603–1714, ed. M. F. Keeler (Oxford, 1970).
M. Levine, *Bibliographical Handbooks: Tudor England, 1485–1603* (Cambridge, 1968).
J. S. Morrill, *Seventeenth Century Britain, 1603–1714* (Folkestone, 1980).

5. MIXED MONARCHY

GENERAL SURVEYS

W. Ferguson, *Scotland: 1689 to the Present* (Edinburgh, 1968).
E. M. Johnston, *Ireland in the Eighteenth Century* (Dublin, 1974).
J. R. Jones, *Country and Court: England, 1658–1714* (London, 1978); W. A. Speck, *Stability and Strife: England, 1714–1760* (London, 1977); I. R. Christie, *Wars and Revolutions: Britain, 1760–1815* (Cambridge, Mass., 1982): these three volumes, in the Arnold *New History of England*, from the best general guide to the period.
J. B. Owen, *The Eighteenth Century, 1714–1815* (London, 1974), an excellent outline, strong on political and constitutional questions.
B. Kemp, *King and Commons, 1660–1832* (London, 1957), a valuable brief sketch.
J. C. D. Clark, *English Society, 1688–1832* (Cambridge, 1985), insists on the continuing strength of the crown after 1688.

ROYAL BIOGRAPHIES

S. Baxter, *William III* (London, 1966), probably the best biography.
N. C. Robb, *William of Orange* (London, 1966).
H. and B. van der Zee, *William and Mary* (London, 1973), good on family life.
D. Green, *Queen Anne* (London, 1970), very sympathetic to the political and medical problems she faced.
E. Gregg, *Queen Anne* (London, 1980), argues for a more prominent role for the queen.
R. Hatton, *George I* (London, 1978), an outstanding piece of scholarship, strong on diplomacy and making use of the Hanoverian archives.
C. Chenevix Trench, *George II* (London, 1973), until a better work is available.
J. Brooke, *King George the Third* (London, 1972), a very sympathetic and informed study, strong on personality.
S. Ayling, *George the Third* (London, 1973), a good, balanced biography.
C. Hibbert, *George IV*, 2 vols. (London, 1972, 1973), very readable and makes good use of the Windsor archives.

PARTICULAR TOPICS

J. R. Jones, *The Revolution of 1688 in England* (London, 1972), a detailed study, good on electoral matters.
J. H. Plumb, *The Growth of Political Stability in England, 1675–1725* (London, 1967), justly influential Ford lectures, tracing a theme that many subsequent historians have explored.

H. T. Dickinson, *Liberty and Property: Political Ideology in Eighteenth-Century Britain* (London, 1977), assesses much pamphlet material and discusses constitutional theory.

J. M. Beattie, *The English Court in the Reign of George I* (London, 1967), one of the few specialist studies of the subject.

G. Holmes, *British Politics in the Age of Anne* (London, 1967), standard guide to a turbulent period.

W. A. Speck, *Tory and Whig: The Struggle in the Constituencies* (London, 1970), party and electoral analysis for Anne's reign.

G. Holmes, *Augustan England: Professions, State and Society, 1680–1730* (London, 1982), suggests that the growth of professions helped political stability.

L. Colley, *In Defiance of Oligarchy* (Cambridge, 1982), shows how popular Toryism died hard despite fifty years of royal disfavour.

D. Daiches, *Charles Edward Stuart* (London, 1973), biography of the Young Pretender with good illustrations.

W. A. Speck, *The Butcher* (Oxford, 1981), studies Cumberland and the campaign of '45.

B. Lenman, *The Jacobite Risings in Britain, 1689–1746* (London, 1980), an unsentimental assessment of Jacobite military chances.

E. Cruickshanks (ed.), *Ideology and Conspiracy: Aspects of Jacobitism, 1689–1759* (Edinburgh, 1982), essays reiterating the importance of Jacobitism.

L. B. Namier, *The Structure of Politics at the Accession of George III* (London, 1929), a classic destroying many myths and marking the new study of Hanoverian England.

—— *England in the Age of the American Revolution* (London, 1930), a companion volume.

H. Butterfield, *George III and the Historians* (London, 1957), a sharp attack on Namier's methodology and discussion of the role of George III.

R. Pares, *George III and the Politicians* (Oxford, 1953), admirable constitutional commentary.

J. Brewer, *Party Ideology and Popular Politics at the Accession of George III* (Cambridge, 1976), important criticism of the limitations of the Namier approach.

I. R. Christie, *The End of North's Ministry, 1780–1782* (London, 1958), detailed study of the final years of the American war.

P. D. G. Thomas, *British Politics and the Stamp Act crisis* (Oxford, 1975), the preliminaries to the loss of the American colonies.

R. Middlekauff, *The Glorious Cause: The American Revolution 1763–1789* (Oxford, 1982), American treatment of the War of Independence.

P. Mackesy, *The War for America, 1775–1783* (London, 1964), a very readable account of the armed struggle.

J. A. Cannon, *The Fox–North Coalition: Crisis of the Constitution, 1782–4* (Cambridge, 1969), detailed study of the king's struggle against the Whigs.

J. W. Derry, *The Regency Crisis and the Whigs, 1788–9* (Cambridge, 1963), discusses the political effects of George III's first major illness.

LETTERS AND MEMOIRS

B. C. Brown (ed.), *The Letters of Queen Anne* (London, 1935), a convenient selection.

R. R. Sedgwick (ed.), *The Letters from George III to Lord Bute, 1756–66* (London, 1939), important for the development of the king's character.

J. W. Fortescue (ed.), *The Correspondence of King George the Third*, 6 vols. (London, 1927–8), poorly edited but indispensable.

A. Aspinall (ed.), *The Later Correspondence of George III* (London, 1962–70), carefully edited and annotated.

L. B. Namier, *Addition and Corrections to Sir John Fortescue's edition* (London, 1937), a slim but savage volume which had a marked effect upon editorial standards.

A. Aspinall (ed.), *The Correspondence of George, Prince of Wales, 1770–1812* (London, 1963–71), of great political importance.

——(ed.), *The Letters of King George IV* (London, 1938), vital for the 1820s.

Memoirs of the Reign of George II by John, Lord Hervey, ed. R. R. Sedgwick, 3 vols. (London, 1931), a brilliant, malicious, and colourful account of court life in the 1730s.

The Political Journal of George Bubb Dodington, ed. J. Carswell and L. A. Dralle (Oxford, 1965), the aspirations of a famous time-server.

Memoirs of the Reign of George II by Horace Walpole, ed. J. Brooke, 3 vols. (Yale, 1985), entertaining and well edited.

Memoirs of the Reign of George III by Horace Walpole, ed. G. F. R. Barker, 4 vols. (London, 1894), source of many of the myths about the king but needs a new edition.

Letters of Horace Walpole, ed. W. S. Lewis, 48 vols. (Yale, 1937–83), witty and intelligent comments over more than fifty years.

The Journals and Letters of Fanny Burney, ed. J. Hemlow, 12 vols. (Oxford, 1972–84), some excellent descriptions of the pleasures and miseries of court life in the 1790s.

DOCUMENTS AND BIBLIOGRAPHIES

English Historical Documents: 1660–1714, ed. A. Browning (London, 1953).

English Historical Documents: American Colonial Documents to 1776, ed. M. Jensen (London, 1955).

English Historical Documents: 1714–1783, ed. D. B. Horn and M. Ransome (London, 1957).

English Historical Documents: 1783–1832, ed. A. Aspinall and E. A. Smith (London, 1959).

E. N. Williams, *The Eighteenth-Century Constitution, 1688–1815* (Cambridge, 1960).

J. S. Morrill, *Seventeenth-Century Britain, 1603–1714* (Folkestone, 1980).

M. F. Keeler, *Bibliography of British History, 1603–1714* (Oxford, 1970).

S. Pargellis and D. J. Medley, *Bibliography of British History, 1714–1789* (Oxford, 1951).

L. M. Brown and I. R. Christie, *Bibliography of British History, 1789–1851* (Oxford, 1977).

6. POPULAR MONARCHY

GENERAL SURVEYS

G. O'Tuathaigh, *Ireland before the Famine* (London, 1972).

F. S. L. Lyons, *Ireland since the Famine* (London, 1971).

W. Ferguson, *Scotland: 1689 to the Present* (Edinburgh, 1968).

A. Briggs, *The Age of Improvement: 1783–1867* (London, 1959), an outstandingly good survey.

N. Gash, *Aristocracy and People: Britain, 1815–1865* (London, 1979), a volume in an excellent series.

M. D. Pugh, *The Making of Modern British Politics, 1867–1939* (Oxford, 1982), strong on decline of Liberalism.

K. Robbins, *The Eclipse of a Great Power, 1870–1975* (New York, 1982), explores the internal relationships of the United Kingdom.

A. J. P. Taylor, *English History, 1914–1945* (Oxford, 1965), lively and readable.

M. Beloff, *Wars and Welfare: Britain, 1914–1945* (London, 1984).

C. J. Bartlett, *A History of Post-War Britain, 1945–74* (London, 1977).

ROYAL BIOGRAPHIES

P. Ziegler, *King William IV* (London, 1971), a lively account of one of the strangest of modern monarchs.

C. B. Woodham-Smith, *Queen Victoria, her Life and Times* (London, 1972), up to the death of Albert.

E. Longford, *Victoria, R.I.* (London, 1966), particularly good on family life.

P. Magnus, *King Edward the Seventh* (New York, 1964), a very friendly biography of a 'thoroughly conscientious monarch' who 'enhanced the prestige of the monarchy'.

G. Brook-Shepherd, *Uncle of Europe* (London, 1975), arguing for considerable diplomatic influence.

C. Hibbert, *Edward VII: A Portrait* (London, 1976), another friendly personal study.

H. Nicolson, *King George the Fifth* (London, 1952), political study based on Windsor Archives.

K. Rose, *King George V* (London, 1983), an excellent, readable, and well-illustrated study.

F. Donaldson, *Edward VIII* (London, 1974), candid but not unsympathetic appraisal.

J. W. Wheeler-Bennett, *King George VI* (London, 1958), an official biography.

D. Judd, *King George VI* (London, 1982), a good popular biography.

R. Lacey, *Majesty: Elizabeth II and the House of Windsor* (London, 1977), a useful interim account.

PARTICULAR TOPICS

M. Brock, *The Great Reform Act* (London, 1973), the great crisis of William IV's reign.

R. R. James, *Albert, Prince Consort* (London, 1983), portrait of Albert as an 'astute and ambitious politician'.

R. Fulford, *The Prince Consort* (London, 1949), stresses his important role in the evolution of the British monarchy.

F. Eyck, *The Prince Consort* (London, 1959), concentrates on his political and constitutional significance.

A. Palmer, *The Banner of Battle: The Story of the Crimean War* (London, 1987).

F. Hardie, *The Political Influence of Queen Victoria* (London, 1953), a pioneer study which overstates the case.

——*The Political Influence of the British Monarchy, 1868–1952* (London, 1970).

T. Pakenham, *The Boer War* (London, 1979), the first obvious faltering of British power.

K. Robbins, *The First World War* (Oxford, 1984), excellent study of a crucial period.

B. H. Liddell Hart, *History of the First World War* (London, 1970).

——*History of the Second World War* (London, 1970).

LETTERS AND MEMOIRS

The Correspondence of the late Earl Grey and King William IV, ed. Henry, Earl Grey, 2 vols. (London, 1867), the very important exchanges, dealing with the Reform Bill, mediated by Sir Herbert Taylor.

The Girlhood of Queen Victoria, ed. Viscount Esher, 2 vols. (London, 1912), enchanting extracts from the diary of the young queen, with an unforgettable portrait of Melbourne.

Letters of the Prince Consort, 1831–1861, ed. K. Jagow (London, 1938), important for assessment of political influence.

Letters of Queen Victoria, 1837–1861, ed. A. C. Benson and Lord Esher, 3 vols. (London, 1907), revealing something of Victoria's vivacity as a writer.

Letters of Queen Victoria, 1862–1885, ed. G. E. Buckle, 3 vols. (London, 1926).

Letters of Queen Victoria, 1886–1901, ed. G. E. Buckle, 3 vols. (London, 1930–2).

Queen Victoria, *Leaves from the Journal of our Life in the Highlands* (New York, 1868), the Queen's tribute to Scotland.

——*More Leaves from the Journal of a Life in the Highlands* (London, 1884).

Sir Frederick Ponsonby, *Side Lights on Queen Victoria* (New York, 1930), an inside view of the later years of Victoria's reign.

Lord Ponsonby, *Henry Ponsonby: Queen Victoria's Private Secretary: His Life from his Letters* (London, 1942).

Dearest Mama, ed. R. Fulford (London, 1968), Victoria's correspondence with her elder daughter the Crown Princess of Prussia, 1861–4.

Your dear letter, ed. R. Fulford (London, 1971), continued from 1865 to 1871.

Darling Child, ed. R. Fulford (London, 1976), from 1871 to 1878.

Beloved Mama, ed. R. Fulford (London, 1981), from 1878 to 1885.

Advice to a Grand-daughter, ed. R. Hough (London, 1975), Queen Victoria's correspondence with Princess Victoria of Hesse.

A King's Story: Memoirs of HRH the Duke of Windsor (London, 1951), Edward VIII's reminiscences.

The Duke of Windsor, *The Crown and the People, 1902–53* (London, 1953).

—— *A Family Album* (London, 1960).

Wallis and Edward: Letters 1931–37, ed. M. Bloch (London, 1986), very revealing and intimate correspondence of Edward VIII and Mrs Simpson.

DOCUMENTS AND BIBLIOGRAPHIES

English Historical Documents, 1783–1832, ed. A. Aspinall and E. A. Smith (London, 1959).

English Historical Documents, 1833–1874, ed. G. M. Young and W. D. Handcock (London, 1956).

English Historical Documents, 1874–1914, ed. W. D. Handcock (London, 1973).

G. H. L. le May, *The Victorian Constitution: Conventions, Usages and Contingencies* (New York, 1979).

H. J. Hanham, *The Nineteenth Century Constitution, 1815–1914* (Cambridge, 1969).

Bibliography of British History, 1789–1851, ed. L. M. Brown and I. R. Christie (Oxford, 1977).

Bibliography of British History, 1851–1914, ed. H. J. Hanham (Oxford, 1976).

ILLUSTRATION SOURCES

Chronicle of Matthew Paris. Thirteenth century. British Library, MS Cott. Claud. D. VI (photo Weidenfeld and Nicolson Archives).

92 Château Gaillard, near Rouen. E. M. Janet le Caisne.

95 Harold Godwinson, later Harold II, swearing an oath to William, duke of Normandy. From the Bayeux Tapestry, before 1082. Michael Holford.

98 Brough Castle, Cumbria. A. F. Kersting. Brougham Castle, Cumbria. A. F. Kersting.

100 Cormac's Chapel, Rock of Cashel, co. Tipperary. Bord Fáilte.
Dromore Castle, co. Down. Aerofilms.

103 King Edward the Confessor on his deathbed. From the Bayeux Tapestry, before 1082. Michael Holford.

104 A medieval king and his counsellors. An illustration from the 'Romance of Alexander'. Thirteenth century. The Master and Fellows of Trinity College, Cambridge, MS 0.9.34.

107 Thomas Becket arguing with Henry II. From a fifteenth-century pedigree-chronicle, British Library, MS Cott. Claud. D. II.
Casket which contained relics of St Thomas Becket, c.1190. From the British Rail Pension Fund's Works of Art Collection.

108 David I and Malcolm IV of Scotland. From a charter to Kelso Abbey in 1159. By permission of the Duke of Roxburghe (photo The National Library of Scotland).

110 Tiles depicting Richard I and Saladin, c.1260. British Museum.

111 A Welsh king, from a Latin version of the *Laws of Hywel Dda*. Thirteenth century. The National Library of Wales, Peniarth MS 28B.

112 The Great Seal of King John, 1203. Reproduced by permission of the Provost and Fellows of Eton College.

114 The coronation of King Edward the Confessor. From *La estoire de Seint Aedward le rei*, mid-thirteenth century. By permission of the Syndics of Cambridge University Library, MS Ee.3.59.

115 Harold II, enthroned. From the Bayeux Tapestry, before 1082. Michael Holford.

116 English royal regalia: anointing spoon, late twelfth century; and ampulla, late fourteenth century. Reproduced by gracious permission of Her Majesty the Queen (photo Department of the Environment).

117 William I. From Orderic Vitalis's copy of *The Deeds of the Norman Dukes* by William of Jumièges, early twelfth century. Bibliothèque Municipale, Rouen, MS Y 14.

119 Coronation of an English king. From an Order of Service, c.1330–9. The Master and Fellows of Corpus Christi College, Cambridge, MS 20.

120 King William Rufus, from a stone capital, now lost. Engraving of the 1830s. By courtesy of the Dean and Chapter of Westminster.

122 The writ and seal of King Edward the Confessor, 1062–6. By courtesy of the Dean and Chapter of Westminster.

124 The marriage of an Irish king to his country. From a copy of *Topography of Ireland* by Gerald of Wales. Mid-thirteenth century. Bodleian Library, Oxford, MS Laud. Misc. 720.

126 Henry I's nightmares. From John of Worcester's *Chronicle*, c.1140. President and Fellows of Corpus Christi College, Oxford and Bodleian Library, Oxford, MS C.C.C. 157

127 Silver penny of William I, c.1077–80. British Museum.

128 Magna Carta, an authorized copy of the 1225 version. British Library, Add. MS 46144.

131 Henry I lamenting the wreck of the White Ship. From a fifteenth-century pedigree-chronicle. British Library, MS Cott. Claud. D. II.

132 Coronation of Henry, the 'Young King'. From a Life of St Thomas of Canterbury, c.1230–40 (photo The Mansell Collection).

134 King Edward the Confessor accuses Earl Godwin of murdering his brother. From the Domesday *Abbreviato*, c.1240. Public Record Office, London, MS E 36/284.

136 Emma receiving an account of her life, *Emmae Anglorum Reginae*, by a monk of St Omer, c.1040. British Library, Add. MS 33241.

138 King Stephen as a huntsman. From a fifteenth-century pedigree-chronicle. British Library, MS Cott. Claud. D. II.

139 Eleanor of Aquitaine. Tomb-effigy, c.1205, in Fontevrault Abbey, Maine-et-Loire. The Ancient Art and Architecture Collection.

143 Stone coffin of Joan, Wife of Llywelyn the Great. Probably fourteenth century. National Monuments Record for Wales.

144 Silver penny of David I of Scotland, 1124–53. British Museum.

146 Effigy of Geoffrey, Count of Anjou, c.1150–60. Lauros-Giraudon.

148 Henry, the 'Young King'. Tomb effigy in Rouen Cathedral. Roger-Viollet.

149 William I's charter to London. c.1067. Corporation of London Record Office, Ch. 1a.

151 Henry II. Tomb-effigy, c.1200–5, in Fontevrault Abbey, Maine-et-Loire. The Ancient Art and Architecture Collection.

153 Silver penny of William II, c.1087. British Museum.

155 King John hunting. From a fifteenth-century pedigree-chronicle. British Library, MS Cott. Claud. D. II.

157 A page from the Great Domesday Book, 1086–7. Public Record Office, London, MS E 31/2.

158 Great Seal of King Stephen, 1139. British Library.

159 Richard I. Tomb-effigy, c.1200–5, in Fontevrault Abbey, Maine-et-Loire. The Ancient Art and Architecture Collection.

160 Silver penny of Henry II, c.1180–9. British Museum.

161 Rock-crystal vase once belonging to Eleanor of Aquitaine, c.1137. Louvre, Musées Nationaux, Paris.

163 King Edmund of East Anglia depicted as a martyr. From a Life of St Edmund, c.1125–30. Pierpont Morgan, MS 736. © The Pierpont Morgan Library, 1987.

166 The shrine of King Edward the Confessor, Westminster Abbey. By courtesy of the Dean and Chapter of Westminster (photo Angelo Hornak).

169 Eilean Donan Castle, Ross and Cromarty. Royal Commission on Ancient Monuments, Scotland.

170 The Great Seal of King William the Lion (d. 1214). British Library.

171 Dunfermline Abbey, Fife. A. F. Kersting.

172 Lord Rhys ap Gruffydd. Alleged tomb-effigy in St David's Cathedral. Probably early fourteenth century. By kind permission of Dr Roger S. Thomas.

174 King John. Tomb-effigy in Worcester Cathedral, 1232. A. F. Kersting.

CHAPTER 3

177 The descent of Henry VII and his children. From an early sixteenth-century pedigree-chronicle. British Library, MS Kings 395.

179 Edward I creating his son Edward Prince of Wales. From a Rochester Chronicle of the early fourteenth century. British Library, MS Cott. Nero D. II (photo Weidenfeld and Nicolson Archives).

182 Edward I facing Philip IV of France. From Exchequer, Lord Treasurer's Remembrancer, Memoranda Roll, 1297–8. Public Record Office, London E 368/69.

184 Charles VII chasing Henry VI out of France. From a copy of *The Chronicles of the Kings of France*, c.1483. National Library of Wales, MS 21247E.

185 Death of Llywelyn ab Iorwerth, Prince of Wales. From *The Greater Chronicle* of Matthew Paris, c.1240–59. Master and Fellows of Corpus Christi College, Cambridge, MS 16 (photo Courtauld Institute of Art and Weidenfeld and Nicolson Archives).

187 The Great Seal of Alexander II of Scotland, 1229. British Library.

188 Princess Scota landing on the shores of Scotland. From *Scotichronicon*, c.1425. Master and Fellows of Corpus Christi College, Cambridge, MS 171.

189 Henry III. Tomb-effigy in Westminster Abbey, 1291. By courtesy of the Dean and Chapter of Westminster (photo Angelo Hornak).

191 'Wild Irishmen' from a mid-thirteenth-century copy of the *Topography of Ireland* by Gerald of Wales. Bodleian Library, Oxford, MS Laud Misc. 720.

193 English Parliament in session presided over by Edward I. From the Garter Book, c.1524, Windsor Castle, Royal Library, MS 1113. © 1987 Her Majesty the Queen.

195 Silver groat of James III of Scotland, c.1485. British Museum.

199 The battle of Poitiers, 1356. From a copy of *The Greater Chronicles of France*. Late fourteenth century. British Library, MS Cott. Nero E. II (2).

200 Henry VI at the abbey of Bury St Edmunds, 1434. From John Lydgate's presentation copy of his *Lives of Sts Edmund and Fremund*. British Library, MS Harl. 2278.

201 Coronation of a king and queen. From *Liber Regalis*. Late fourteenth century. By courtesy of the Dean and Chapter of Westminster.

204 Groat of Henry VII, early sixteenth century. British Museum.

207 Edward I and Margaret of France, c.1310. From St Thomas's Church, Winchelsea, Sussex. Weidenfeld and Nicolson Ltd. (photo A. Vaughan Kimber).

209 The Wilton Diptych, c.1394–6 (or ? early fifteenth century). Reproduced by courtesy of the Trustees of the National Gallery, London.

210 Edward II surrendering his crown to his son, Edward, 1327. From Peter Langtoft's *Chronicle*, written in the time of Edward II. British Library, MS Roy. 20 A II.

212 Henry VI and his Parliament kneeling before the Virgin Mary. From the foundation charter of King's College, Cambridge, 1441. King's College Library, Cambridge, MS Mun. KC/18/NI (photo Christopher Hurst).

214 Richard, duke of York. From a stained-glass window in Trinity College, Cambridge. Mid-fifteenth century. National Monuments Record.

(detail). Louvre (photo Giraudon).
Catherine Parr, c.1545 (detail). Artist unknown. National Portrait Gallery, London.

327 Henry VIII and his wives and children. From a later addition to the early sixteenth-century pedigree-chronicle reproduced on p. 177, British Library, MS Kings 395.

329 Edward VI, c.1546. Artist unknown. Reproduced by gracious permission of Her Majesty the Queen (photo Weidenfeld and Nicolson Archives).

331 Mary I, 1544, by Master John. National Portrait Gallery, London.

333 Mary I and Philip of Spain, 1557, attributed to Hans Eworth. By kind permission of the Marquess of Tavistock and the Trustees of the Bedford Estates.

336 Mary Queen of Scots, 1559, by François Clouet. Bibliothèque Nationale, Paris (photo Giraudon).

337 Henry, Lord Darnley, and his younger brother, 1563, by Hans Eworth. Reproduced by gracious permission of Her Majesty the Queen.

338 Elizabeth I at a picnic. From *The Noble Art of Venerie or Hunting* by George Turberville, 1575 (photo BBC Hulton Picture Library).

339 Elizabeth I at prayer. From *Christian Prayers and Meditations in English, French, Italian, Spanish, Greeke and Latine*, 1569. By kind permission of the Archbishop of Canterbury and the Trustees of Lambeth Palace Library.

342 Elizabeth I, 1572, by Nicholas Hilliard. National Portrait Gallery, London.

345 Mary, Queen of Scots, c.1575–80. The Trustees of Blair's College, Aberdeen.

346 Elizabeth I, 1592, by Marcus Gheeraerts the Younger. By courtesy of the National Portrait Gallery, London.

347 Robert Devereux, earl of Essex, 1590, by William Segar. National Gallery of Ireland.

348–9 The Garter Procession of 1576 by Marcus Gheeraerts (photo John Freeman and Company).

350 Elizabeth I and the three goddesses, 1569, by Hans Eworth. Reproduced by gracious permission of Her Majesty the Queen.

351 'A Strange bird taken at Crowley.' From William Woodwall's autograph of *The Actes of Queen Elizabeth Allegorized*, 1599–1603. Bodleian Library, Oxford, MS Eng. Hist. e 198.
Elizabeth and the Virtues. From *Sphaera civitatis* by John Case, 1588.

355 Henry, Prince of Wales, c.1611, by Robert Peake. The collection at Parham Park, West Sussex.

357 Union of the crowns of England and Scotland. A panel, designed by Rubens, c.1635, from the ceiling of the Banqueting Hall, Whitehall. National Monuments Record.

358 James VI and I, 1595. Artist unknown. National Galleries of Scotland.
James VI and I, c.1606 by Jan de Critz (detail). National Maritime Museum, London.
James VI and I, 1622. Ashmolean Museum, Oxford.

359 Design for the flags of St Andrew and St George, c.1604. The Trustees of the National Library of Scotland, MS 2517.

362 James I rides to Parliament, 1625. From Michael Van Meer's *Album Amicorum*, 1614–30. Edinburgh University Library, MS La. III 283.

364 The Somerset House Conference, 1604.

Artist unknown. National Portrait Gallery, London.

366 George Villiers, duke of Buckingham, c.1626. The Mansell Collection.
George Villiers, duke of Buckingham, c.1616 (detail). Attributed to William Larkin. National Portrait Gallery, London.

367 Charles I and his Court in Greenwich Park, 1632, by Adriaen van Stalbent and Jan van Belcamp. Reproduced by gracious permission of Her Majesty the Queen.

370–1 Charles I and Henrietta Maria as Apollo and Diana, with the duke of Buckingham as Mercury. Details from the painting, 1628, by Gerrit van Honthorst for the Queen's Staircase at Hampton Court. By gracious permission of Her Majesty the Queen.

373 Charles I (photo John Freeman and Company).

374 Charles I dining at Whitehall Palace, 1635, by Gervit Houckgeest. Reproduced by gracious permission of Her Majesty the Queen.

375 Charles I, 1628, by Daniel Mytens (detail). Reproduced by gracious permission of Her Majesty the Queen.
Charles I, c.1636, by Peter Lely after Anthony van Dyke. Staatliche Kunstammlungen, Dresden (photo the Courtauld Institute).

377 Massacre of Protestants in Ulster, 1641. The Mansell Collection.

379 Charles I with Sir Edward Walker. Artist and date unknown. National Portrait Gallery, London.

382 Prince Rupert's poodle 'Boye', c.1640, by Louise, Princess Palatine, Prince Rupert's sister. By kind permission of Mrs Evadne Nicholas.

383 Prince Rupert hiding in a beanfield. From a satirical pamphlet, 1644.
Three of Charles I's children, 1647, by John Hoskins. Fitzwilliam Museum, Cambridge.

385 Death warrant of Charles I, January 1649. Now in the House of Lords Record Office, and reproduced by permission of the Clerk of the Records.

386 Execution of Charles I, January 1649. From a contemporary German engraving. National Portrait Gallery, London.

387 Charles I as martyr. From an embroidery of the third quarter of the seventeenth century. The Trustees of the Victoria and Albert Museum.

390 'The Royall Oake of Brittayne', a satirical print of 1649. The Trustees of the British Museum.

392 'The Scots holding their Young Kings nose to ye Grinstone', a satirical print of 1651. The Trustees of the British Museum.

394 Cromwell dismissing the Rump Parliament. From a Dutch engraving in the British Museum, 1653 (photo John Freeman and Company).

396 Bust of Oliver Cromwell made by Edward Pierce after Cromwell's death. Ashmolean Museum, Oxford.

398 The ball given to Charles II at The Hague on his departure for England, 1660, by Cornelius Janssens. Reproduced by gracious permission of Her Majesty the Queen.

399 Richard Cromwell. From a miniature by an unknown artist. National Portrait Gallery, London.

401 George Monck, duke of Albermarle, 1660–4. An unfinished sketch by Samuel Cooper. Reproduced by gracious permission of Her Majesty the Queen.

403 Coronation of Charles II, April 1661.

British Museum (photo John Freeman and Company).

404 Statue of Charles II in Parliament Square, Edinburgh. Scottish Tourist Board.

405 Charles II, 1662. Chalk drawing by Samuel Cooper. Windsor Castle, Royal Library. © Her Majesty the Queen.

407 Nell Gwyn, c.1670, possibly by Simon Verelst. Private collection (photo National Portrait Gallery, London).
Louise de Kéroualle, 1682, by Pierre Mignard. National Portrait Gallery, London.

412 Charles II. From initial letter of the *Coram Rege* roll of the Court of Kings' Bench, Michaelmas Term, 1661. Public Record Office, KB 27/1837. Crown copyright.

413 Titus Oates being flogged through the streets of London, May 1685. From a Dutch engraving. The Mansell Collection.

415 'The Royal Gift of Healing', engraved by Robert White. From *Adenochoiradelogin* by John Browne, 1684. The Mansell Collection.

416 *Last Race on Datchet Mead, Windsor*, 1684, Francis Barlow. Reproduced by gracious permission of Her Majesty the Queen.

418 'A History of the New Plot', a broadsheet on the Rye House Plot, 1683. British Museum (photo John Freeman and Company).

419 The Monument in remembrance of the Great Fire, engraved by Thomas Bowles in 1752. British Museum (photo John Freeman and Company).

421 Banquet in Westminster Hall for the coronation of James II, 1685. From Sandford's *Coronation of James II*, 1687 (photo John Freeman and Company).

422 Monmouth's entry into Lyme Regis, 1685. Three scenes represented on playing cards in the British Museum (photos Weidenfeld and Nicholson Archives).

424 Archbishop Sancroft and six bishops released from the Tower, 1688. From a Dutch engraving of 1689 (photo John Freeman and Company).

426 James II, 1685, by Nicolas de Largillière. National Maritime Museum, London.

428 William and Mary, from a contemporary engraving. British Museum (photo John Freeman and Company).

429 William of Orange landing at Torbay, 1688. Artist unknown. Reproduced by gracious permission of Her Majesty the Queen.

430 Siege of Londonderry, July 1689. From a Dutch engraving of 1690 (photo BBC Hulton Picture Library).

431 Engraved goblet in remembrance of William III's victory at the battle of the Boyne, 1690, made x.1745. Ulster Museum, Belfast.

CHAPTER 5

435 Mary II; 1685, by William Wissing. Reproduced by gracious permission of Her Majesty the Queen.

439 Mary II lying in state. From a Dutch engraving. The Mansell Collection.

440 William Henry, duke of Gloucester, c.1699. Studio of Godfrey Kneller. National Portrait Gallery, London.

443 William III, 1685, by William Wissing. Reproduced by gracious permission of Her Majesty the Queen.

446 Queen Anne by Charles Boit. National Museum, Stockholm (photo Statens Konstmuseer).

449 Letter from the duke of Marlborough to

his wife, Sarah, 13 August 1704. By kind permission of His Grace the duke of Marlborough (photo Jeremy Whitaker).

450 'The Fall of Lille', one of a series of tapestries commemorating Marlborough's victories, completed for Blenheim Palace by Judocus de Vos in 1715. By kind permission of His Grace the duke of Marlborough (photo Bridgeman Art Library).

451 John, first duke of Marlborough, *c.*1685–90, possibly by J. Closterman after John Riley. National Portrait Gallery, London.
Sarah, duchess of Marlborough, *c.*1703, by Godfrey Kneller (detail). By kind permission of His Grace the duke of Marlborough (photo Jeremy Whitaker).

452 Blenheim Palace. From an engraving published in 1745. British Museum (photo John Freeman and Company).

454 'Sacheverell's Triumph'. Design for a playing-card, 1710. British Museum (photo John Freeman and Company).

455 *Queen Anne's Procession to the Houses of Parliament*, attributed to Alexander van Gaelen. Reproduced by gracious permission of Her Majesty the Queen.

458 Queen Anne, by Michael Rysbrack, 1734. By kind permission of His Grace the duke of Marlborough (photo Jeremy Whitaker).

460 Coronation medal of George I, 1715. British Museum.
Jacobite medal, 1721. British Museum.

463 James Francis Edward Stuart, *c.*1712. From the studio of Alexis Belle. National Portrait Gallery, London.

466 George I, *c.*1714. From the studio of Godfrey Kneller. National Portrait Gallery, London.

468 'The Bubblers bubbl'd or the Devil take the Hindmost', a satirical print on the South Sea Company's Scheme, 1720. The Mansell Collection.

471 Celebration of the Peace of Aix-la-Chapelle on 15 May 1749. Coloured print. Heritage of Music.

472 Robert Walpole and Arthur Onslow in the House of Commons. From an engraving by A. Fogg of a painting by William Hogarth and James Thornhill, published in 1803. British Museum (photo John Freeman and Company).

473 Frederick, Prince of Wales, and his sisters, 1733, by Philippe Mercier. By courtesy of the National Portrait Gallery, London.

474 George II at Dettingen, 1743, by John Wootton. National Army Museum, London.

475 George II, 1738, and Queen Caroline, 1739. Terracotta busts by Michael Rysbrack, now in Kensington Palace. Reproduced by gracious permission of Her Majesty the Queen.

477 William, duke of Cumberland (detail), *c.*1750, by John Morier. Reproduced by gracious permission of Her Majesty the Queen.

478 Prince Charles Edward Stuart, the Young Pretender, *c.*1729. Studio of Antonio David. National Portrait Gallery, London.

479 Engraved Jacobite wine-glass, 1747–52. The Trustees of the Victoria and Albert Museum.
Medal to commemorate the duke of Cumberland's successes against the Jacobites, struck in 1745.

482 *Vauxhall Gardens: the Grand Walk*, *c.*1751, by Canaletto. Reproduced by kind permission of Lord and Lady Trevor (photo Barbican Art Gallery).

483 George II mug. Dyson Perrins Museum Trust, Worcester.
George II, in the 1750s. Sketch by George Townshend. National Portrait Gallery, London.

485 George III as a boy with his brother, Edward, duke of York, *c.*1749, by Richard Wilson. National Portrait Gallery, London.

487 Lord Bute, 1773, by Joshua Reynolds. National Portrait Gallery, London.

490 George Prince of Wales, with his brother Frederick, duke of York, 1765, by Johann Zoffany. Reproduced by gracious permission of Her Majesty the Queen.

491 Queen Charlotte with the Princess Royal, 1767, by Francis Cotes. Reproduced by gracious permission of Her Majesty the Queen.

492 John Wilkes, an engraving of 1763 by William Hogarth (photo John Freeman and Company).

494 'View of Syon House', by George III when Prince of Wales. Windsor Castle, Royal Library. © Her Majesty the Queen.

497 Lord North, 1775, by Nathaniel Dance. National Portrait Gallery, London.

502 The attack upon Quebec, September 1759. From an engraving published in 1797. British Museum (photo John Freeman and Company).

508 The Boston massacre, March 1770. From a contemporary print. The Mansell Collection.

509 'The able Doctor or America Swallowing the Bitter Draught.' From a satirical drawing published in 1774. British Museum (photo John Freeman and Company).
'News from America or the Patriots in the Dumps.' From the *London Magazine*, November 1776. The Trustees of the British Museum.

510 Siege of Gibraltar, September 1782. From an Austrian Imperial print.

512 The ball at St James's on George III's birthday, 4 June 1782, engraved for the *Lady's Magazine*. Museum of London.

513 George III at the Royal Academy, 1789. Engraved by P. Martini after a painting by P. Kamberg. Museum of London.

515 'Carlo Khan's triumphal Entry into Leadenhall Street.' Cartoon by James Sayers, published in December 1783. The Trustees of the British Museum.

517 George III, 1771, by Johann Zoffany. Reproduced by gracious permission of Her Majesty the Queen.

519 'Affability' by James Gillray, published in February 1795. The Mansell Collection.
George III with his family on the terrace at Windsor. BBC Hulton Picture Library.

520 Queen's House, 1800, by Auguste-Charles Pugin and Thomas Rowlandson. The Trustees of the Victoria and Albert Museum (photo Bridgeman Art Library).

521 Prince of Wales, 1805, by Henry Bone. Ashmolean Museum, Oxford.

522 Library at Windsor Castle. Reproduced by gracious permission of Her Majesty the Queen.

523 'Filial Piety' by Thomas Rowlandson, published in November 1788. British Museum (photo John Freeman and Company).

524 Queen Charlotte, 1807, by Peter Edward Stroehling. Reproduced by gracious permission of Her Majesty the Queen.

525 George III, 1807, by Peter Edward Stroehling. Reproduced by gracious permission of Her Majesty the Queen.

527 Duke of Wellington, *c.*1813, by Thomas

Heaphy (detail). National Portrait Gallery, London.
Lord Nelson, by John Hoppner, 1806 (detail). Reproduced by gracious permission of Her Majesty the Queen.

529 George III, *c.*1820, by Joseph Lee, Windsor Castle, Royal Library. © Her Majesty the Queen.

CHAPTER 6

532 'Cyfarthfa Ironworks, Merthyr Tydfil', *c.*1795, by Julius Caesar Ibbetson. Cyfarthfa Castle Museum (photo Tait's Gallery).

536 Edmund Kean as Richard III, 1814. By kind permission of the Royal Victoria Hall Foundation and the University of Bristol Theatre Collection.

537 Sketch of Caroline of Brunswick by George Hayter. The Trustees of the British Museum.

539 'Reflection', a cartoon of 1820 by Robert Cruikshank. British Museum (photo John Freeman and Company).

540 *The Banquet at the Coronation of George IV, 1821*, by George Jones. Reproduced by gracious permission of Her Majesty the Queen.

541 'A correct representation of the company going to and returning from His Majesty's drawing room at Buckingham Palace, St James's Park', 1822. Museum of London.

542 The Corridor, Windsor Castle, 1828, by Joseph Nash. Windsor Castle, Royal Library © Her Majesty the Queen.

543 The Music Room and the Great Kitchen from *Views of the Royal Pavilion*, 1826, by Joseph Nash. By permission of The Royal Pavilion, Museums and Art Gallery, Brighton.

544 George IV, 1821, by Thomas Lawrence. Reproduced by gracious permission of Her Majesty the Queen.

547 'A Great Actor Rehearsing his Part', by John Doyle, published in 1834. The Mansell Collection.

548 William IV, *c.*1800, by Martin Archer Shee. National Portrait Gallery, London.

552 *Queen Victoria's First Council at Kensington Palace, 20 June 1837*, by David Wilkie. Reproduced by gracious permission of Her Majesty the Queen.

554 Lord Melbourne, 1844, by John Partridge. National Portrait Gallery, London.

556 Victoria, *c.*1840, by A. E. Penley. National Portrait Gallery, London.
Victoria, 1887. Royal Archives, Windsor Castle. Copyright reserved. Reproduced by gracious permission of Her Majesty the Queen.

557 Victoria's confinement in November 1840. From an anonymous drawing in the British Museum (photo John Freeman and Company).
Christening of the Princess Royal at Buckingham Palace, February 1841, by C. R. Leslie. Reproduced by gracious permission of Her Majesty the Queen.

558 Victoria's drawings of herself, 1845, and Albert, *c.*1840. Windsor Castle, Royal Library. © Her Majesty the Queen.

559 Victoria with her children, *c.*1851. Royal Archives, Windsor Castle. Copyright reserved. Reproduced by gracious permission of Her Majesty the Queen.

561 *Opening of the Great Exhibition*, 1851, by David Roberts. Reproduced by gracious permission of Her Majesty the Queen.

562 Albert, 1844, by Robert Thorburn. Reproduced by gracious permission of Her

Majesty the Queen.

Albert, 1861. Royal Archives, Windsor Castle. Copyright reserved. Reproduced by gracious permission of Her Majesty the Queen.

564 Victoria and Princess Alice with a bust of the Prince Consort, Windsor, 1862. Royal Archives, Windsor Castle. Copyright reserved. Reproduced by gracious permission of Her Majesty the Queen.

567 Part of the Diamond Jubilee procession in June 1897. BBC Hulton Picture Library.

569 *Ely Cathedral: Luncheon in Dean's Pasture on the occasion of the marriage of Princess Alexandra to Prince Albert Edward, 1863,* by J. W. H. Southby. By courtesy of the Dean and Chapter of Ely Cathedral (copyright Walter Scott (Bradford) Ltd.).

570 'The rare, the rather awful visits of Albert Edward, Prince of Wales, to Windsor Castle', *c.*1895, by Max Beerbohm. By permission of Mrs Eva Reichmann.

571 Victoria, the Princess of Wales, the duchess of York, and Prince Edward of York in 1894. BBC Hulton Picture Library.

572 *The Shah of Persia arriving at Windsor Castle, June 20th, 1874,* by N. Chevalier. Windsor Castle, Royal Library. © Her Majesty the Queen.

573 *Ghillies' Ball at Balmoral,* 1859, attributed to Egron Lundgren. Windsor Castle, Royal Library. © Her Majesty the Queen.

580 Edward VII and a shooting party at Sandringham. Popperfoto.

581 Queen Alexandra in her coronation robes, 1902. The Museum of London.

583 Albert Edward, Prince of Wales, in 1862, 1871, and *c.*1890. Royal Archives, Windsor Castle. Copyright reserved. Reproduced by gracious permission of Her Majesty the Queen.

585 Edward VII at Drury Lane, October 1909, by S. Begg. From the *Illustrated London News.* The Museum of London.

586 Prince George as a naval cadet, December 1877. Royal Archives, Windsor Castle. Copyright reserved. Reproduced by gracious permission of Her Majesty the Queen.

588 George V on a tiger shoot in India, 1912. BBC Hulton Picture Library.

589 George V and Lord Stamfordham in the gardens of Buckingham Palace, June 1918. Royal Archives, Windsor Castle. Copyright reserved. Reproduced by gracious permission of Her Majesty the Queen.

592 George V on a visit to Sunderland, 1918. Popperfoto.

593 George V and Queen Mary on a visit to Shadwell, Essex, 1922. Popperfoto.

594 George V and Queen Mary, when they were duke and duchess of York, at York House, 1895. Royal Archives, Windsor Castle. Copyright reserved. Reproduced by gracious permission of Her Majesty the Queen.

596 George V at Cowes in 1924. BBC Hulton Picture Library.

597 George V and Queen Mary at Bognor Regis, 1928. Popperfoto.

598–9 *Reception at the West Door of St Paul's Cathedral before the Jubilee Service, 1935, for King George V and Queen Mary,* by Frank Salisbury. Guildhall Art Gallery. By kind permission of Mrs M. Norris (photo Bridgeman Art Library).

599 George V broadcasting. From *King's*

Grace 1910–1935: George V by John Buchan.

601 Edward VIII at a reception at Buckingham Palace, 1936. Popperfoto.

604 Edward VIII and Mrs Simpson, 1936. Popperfoto.

606 Lady Elizabeth Bowes-Lyon in 1907. Syndication International.

607 Prince Albert, duke of York, 1914. Popperfoto.

609 Duke and duchess of Windsor with Hitler, 1937. Popperfoto.

612 George VI and Queen Elizabeth inspecting bomb damage, 1940. Popperfoto.

Princess Elizabeth and Princess Margaret buying War Savings Certificates, 1943. Syndication International.

614 *Conversation Piece at Royal Lodge, Windsor,* 1950, by James Gunn. National Portrait Gallery, London.

615 Elizabeth II with her mother and grandmother at George VI's funeral, 1952. The Keystone Collection.

617 Commonwealth prime ministers' conference, 1962. Syndication International.

618 Cartoon by Cummings for the *Daily Express,* 5 June 1974. By kind permission of Michael Cummings and the London Express News and Features Services.

619 The Queen and the duke of Edinburgh in Australia in 1963. Syndication International.

622 Elizabeth I at a Maundy ceremony, *c.*1560. Enlarged from a miniature attributed to Nicholas Hilliard. By kind permission of the Countess of Beauchamp.

Elizabeth II presenting the Maundy money in Worcester Cathedral, April 1980. Tim Graham.

623 The Queen inspecting a guard of honour in San Diego, California, 1983. Tim Graham.

625 The duke of Edinburgh at a boys' club in Wapping, 1959. Syndication International.

The Princess Royal on a 'Save the Children' tour to Gambia and Upper Volta, 1984. Tim Graham.

626 Queen Elizabeth II, 1985–6, by Michael Leonard, commissioned by Reader's Digest for Her Majesty's sixtieth birthday. Copyright *Reader's Digest.*

628 The Prince of Wales and Lady Diana Spencer at their wedding in July 1981. The Keystone Collection.

Prince William with Laura Fellowes at the wedding of Prince Andrew and Miss Sarah Ferguson in 1986. Syndication International.

629 The Queen on the beach near Sandringham, 1984. Syndication International.

630 Coronation of Henry IV, 1399. From Jean Froissart's *Chronicles,* fifteenth century British Library, MS Harl. 4380 (photo Bridgeman Art Library).

631 Coronation of James II, 1685. From *History of the Coronation of James II* by Francis Sandford, 1687. Museum of London.

Coronation of Elizabeth II: the duke of Edinburgh kneels in homage, June 1953. Paul Popper.

ROYAL RESIDENCES

639 'Buckingham Palace', London, by E. Walker, published in 1852. Bridgeman Art Library.

Balmoral Castle, Grampian, in the 1870s. Royal Commission on Ancient Monuments, Scotland.

Brighton Pavilion, Sussex. A. F. Kersting.

640 Dunfermline Palace, Fife. Royal Commission on Ancient Monuments, Scotland.

Edinburgh Castle, Lothian. Royal Commission on Ancient Monuments, Scotland.

641 Eltham Palace, London: Edward IV's great hall. By courtesy of Lt.-Col. J. Birkbeck.

Falkland Palace, Fife. Scottish Tourist Board.

Greenwich Palace, London: Queen's House. A. F. Kersting.

642 *Hampton Court Palace in the Reign of George I,* 1703, by Leonard Knyff. Reproduced by gracious permission of Her Majesty the Queen.

Palace of Holyroodhouse, Edinburgh, Lothian. A. F. Kersting.

643 Kensington Palace, London: the King's Grand Staircase, with paintings by William Kent. Department of the Environment. Crown copyright reserved.

Linlithgow Palace, Lothian, *c.*1890. Royal Commission on Ancient Monuments, Scotland.

644 Osborne House, Isle of Wight. National Monuments Record.

Richmond Palace, Surrey, from a seventeenth-century engraving. Guildhall Library (photo Godfrey New).

645 St James's Palace, London. Aerofilms.

Sandringham House, Norfolk, in 1902. *Country Life.*

646 Stirling Castle, Central Scotland. A. F. Kersting.

The Tower of London. Aerofilms.

647 'Westminster Abbey, London and its precincts, *c.*1537', reconstructed by Drake Brookshaw. Woodmansterne.

648 Whitehall Palace, London, 1749, by Inigo Jones. The Trustees of the Victoria and Albert Museum.

Winchester Palace, Hampshire: the great hall. A. F. Kersting.

649 Windsor Castle, Berkshire. Aerofilms.

ROYAL TOMBS

650 Westminster Abbey, London: Henry VII's chapel. By courtesy of the Dean and Chapter of Westminster (photo Angelo Hornak).

651 Westminster Abbey, London: tomb of Henry VII and Elizabeth of York. By courtesy of the Dean and Chapter of Westminster (photo Angelo Hornak).

652 Fontevrault Abbey, Maine-et-Loire: Richard I and Eleanor of Aquitaine. Cap-Viollet.

Canterbury Cathedral, Klut: the Black Prince. Entwistle Photographic Services.

653 Gloucester Cathedral, Gloucestershire: Edward II. A. F. Kersting.

654 Frogmore, Windsor, Berkshire: the Royal Mausoleum, 1869, by H. W. Brewer. Windsor Castle, Royal Library. © Her Majesty the Queen.

655 St George's Chapel, Windsor, Berkshire. A. F. Kersting.

656 Winchester Cathedral, Hampshire: mortuary chest. By courtesy of the Dean and Chapter of Winchester.

Worcester Cathedral, Worcestershire: King John. A. F. Kersting.

INDEX

INDIVIDUALS are entered under the names by which they are most commonly known, e.g. Disraeli, Benjamin, rather than Beaconsfield, earl of. Cross-references are provided where necessary. Peers are normally entered under their titles, e.g. Melbourne, William Lamb, Viscount. Entries in *italics* refer to the captions of illustrations. A complete list of illustrations can be found on pp. 693–8.